PROFESSIONAL

CUDA® C Programming

John Cheng
Max Grossman
Ty McKercher

wrox™
A Wiley Brand

Professional CUDA® C Programming

Published by
John Wiley & Sons, Inc.
10475 Crosspoint Boulevard
Indianapolis, IN 46256
www.wiley.com

Published simultaneously in Canada

ISBN: 978-1-118-73932-7

ISBN: 978-1-118-73927-3 (ebk)

ISBN: 978-1-118-73931-0 (ebk)

Manufactured in the United States of America

10 9 8 7 6 5 4 3 2 1

For general information on our other products and services please contact our Customer Care Department within the United States at (877) 762-2974, outside the United States at (317) 572-3993 or fax (317) 572-4002.

Wiley publishes in a variety of print and electronic formats and by print-on-demand. Some material included with standard print versions of this book may not be included in e-books or in print-on-demand. If this book refers to media such as a CD or DVD that is not included in the version you purchased, you may download this material at http://booksupport.wiley.com. For more information about Wiley products, visit www.wiley.com.

Library of Congress Control Number: 2014937184

CREDITS

ACQUISITIONS EDITOR
Mary James

PROJECT EDITOR
...

TECHNICAL EDITORS
...
Chris Zhao

PRODUCTION MANAGER
Kathleen Wisor

COPY EDITOR
Katherine Burt

MANAGER OF CONTENT DEVELOPMENT AND ASSEMBLY
Mary Beth Wakefield

DIRECTOR OF COMMUNITY MARKETING
David Mayhew

MARKETING MANAGER
Carrie Sherrill

BUSINESS MANAGER
Amy Knies

VICE PRESIDENT AND EXECUTIVE GROUP PUBLISHER
Richard Swadley

ASSOCIATE PUBLISHER
Jim Minatel

PROJECT COORDINATOR, COVER
Patrick Redmond

PROOFREADER
Nancy Carrasco

INDEXER
Jacqhe vanHoose Dinse

COVER DESIGNER
Wiley

COVER IMAGE
© Sholk comhando

ABOUT THE AUTHORS

 JOHN (RUNWEI) CHENG is a research scientist with extensive industry experience in high-performance computing on heterogeneous computing platforms. Before joining the oil and gas industry, John worked in the finance industry for more than ten years as an expert in computational intelligence, providing advanced solutions based on genetic algorithms hybridized with data mining and statistical learning to solve real world business challenges. As an internationally recognized researcher in the field of genetic algorithms and their application to industrial engineering, John has co-authored three books. John's first book, *Genetic Algorithms and Engineering Design*, published by John Wiley and Sons in 1997, is still used as a textbook in universities worldwide. John has a wide range of experience in both academic research and industry development, and is gifted in making complex subjects accessible to readers with a concise, illustrative, and edifying approach. John earned his doctoral degree in computational intelligence from the Tokyo Institute of Technology.

 MAX GROSSMAN has been working as a developer with various GPU programming models for nearly a decade. His experience is focused in developing novel GPU programming models and implementing scientific algorithms on GPU hardware. Max has applied GPUs to a wide range of domains, including geoscience, plasma physics, medical imaging, and machine learning, and enjoys understanding the computational patterns of new domains and finding new and unusual ways to apply GPUs to them. Lessons learned from these domains help to guide Max's work in programming models and frameworks. Max earned his degree in computer science from Rice University with a focus in parallel computing.

 TY MCKERCHER is a Principal Solution Architect with NVIDIA, leading a team that specializes in visual computing systems architecture across multiple industries. He often serves as a liaison between customer and product engineering teams during emerging technology evaluations. He has been engaged in CUDA-based projects since he participated in the first CUDA kitchen training session held at NVIDIA headquarters in 2006. Since then, Ty has helped architect GPU-based supercomputing environments at some of the largest and most demanding production datacenters in the world. Ty earned his mathematics degree with emphasis in geophysics and computer science from the Colorado School of Mines.

ABOUT THE TECHNICAL EDITORS

WEI ZHANG is a scientific programmer and has been working in the high-performance computing area for 15 years. He has developed or co-developed many scientific software packages for molecular simulation, computer-aided drug design, EM structure reconstruction, and seismic depth imaging. He is now focusing his effort on improving the performance of seismic data processing using new technologies such as CUDA.

CHAO ZHAO joined Chevron in 2008 and currently serves as Geophysical Application Software Development Specialist. In this role, Chao is responsible for designing and developing software products for geoscientists. Prior to joining Chevron, Chao was a software developer for Knowledge Systems Inc. and Seismic Micro Technology Inc. With more than 13 years of software developing experience in the exploration and production industry, Chao has gained rich knowledge in the fields of geology and geophysics. Having a broad education in science, Chao likes to see CUDA programming used widely in scientific research and enjoys contributing to it as much as he can. He holds a Bachelor of Science degree in chemistry from Peking University and a Master of Science in computer science from the University of Rhode Island.

ACKNOWLEDGMENTS

IT WOULD BE HARD TO IMAGINE this project making it to the finish line without the suggestions, constructive criticisms, help, and resources of our colleagues and friends.

We would like to express our thanks to NVIDIA for granting access to many GTC conference presentations and CUDA technical documents that add both great value and authority to this book.

In particular, we owe much gratitude to Dr. Paulius Micikevicius and Dr. Peng Wang, Developer Technology Engineers at NVIDIA, for their kind advice and help during the writing of this book. Special thanks to Mark Ebersole, NVIDIA Chief CUDA Educator, for his guidance and feedback during the review process.

We would like to thank Mr. Will Ramey, Sr. Product Manager at NVIDIA, and Mr. Nadeem Mohammad, Product Marketing at NVIDIA, for their support and encouragement during the entire project.

We would like to thank Mr. Paul Holzhauer, Director of Oil & Gas at NVIDIA, for his support during the initial phase of this project.

Especially, we owe an enormous debt of gratitude to many presenters and speakers in past GTC conferences for their inspiring and creative work on GPU computing technologies. We have recorded all your credits in our suggested reading lists.

After years of work using GPUs in real production projects, John is very grateful to the people who helped him become a GPU computing enthusiast. Especially, John would like to thank Dr. Nanxun Dai and Dr. Bao Zhao for their encouragement, support, and guidance on seismic imaging projects at BGP. John also would like to thank his colleagues Dr. Zhengzhen Zhou, Dr. Wei Zhang, Mrs. Grace Zhang, and Mr. Kai Yang. They are truly brilliant and very pleasant to work with. John loves the team and feels very privileged to be one of them. John would like to extend a special thanks to Dr. Mitsuo Gen, an internationally well-known professor, the supervisor of John's doctoral program, for giving John the opportunity to teach at universities in Japan and co-author academic books, especially for his fully supporting John during the years when John was running a startup based on evolutionary computation technologies in Tokyo. John is very happy working on this project with Ty and Max as a team and learned a lot from them during the process of book writing. John owes a debt of gratitude to his wife, Joly, and his son, Rick, for their love, support, and considerable patience during evenings and weekends over the past year while Dad was yet again "doing his own book work."

For over 25 years, Ty has been helping software developers solve HPC grand challenges. Ty is delighted to work at NVIDIA to help clients extend their current knowledge to unlock the potential from massively parallel GPUs. There are so many NVIDIANs to thank, but Ty would like to specifically recognize Dr. Paulius Micikevicius for his gifted insights and strong desire to always improve while doing the heavy lifting for numerous projects. When John asked Ty to help share

CUDA knowledge in a book project, he welcomed the challenge. Dave Jones, NVIDIA, senior director approved Ty's participation in this project, and sadly last year Dave lost his courageous battle against cancer. Our hearts go out to Dave and his family — his memory serves to inspire, to press on, and to pursue your passions. The encouragements from Shanker Trivedi and Marc Hamilton have been especially helpful. Yearning to maintain his life/work balance, Ty recruited Max to join this project. It was truly a pleasure to learn from John and Max as they developed the book content that Ty helped review. Finally, Ty's wife, Judy, and his four children deserve recognition for their unconditional support and love — it is a blessing to receive encouragement and motivation while pursuing those things that bring joy to your life.

Max has been fortunate to collaborate with and be guided by a number of brilliant and talented engineers, researchers, and mentors. First, thanks have to go to Professor Vivek Sarkar and the whole Habanero Research Group at Rice University. There, Max got his first taste of HPC and CUDA. The mentorship of Vivek and others in the group was invaluable in enabling him to explore the exciting world of research. Max would also like to thank Mauricio Araya-Polo and Gladys Gonzalez at Repsol. The experience gained under their mentorship was incredibly valuable in writing a book that would be truly useful to real-world work in science and engineering. Finally, Max would like to thank John and Ty for inviting him along on this writing adventure in CUDA and for the lessons this experience has provided in CUDA, writing, and life.

It would not be possible to make a quality professional book without input from technical editors, development editors, and reviewers. We would like to extend our sincere appreciation to Mary E. James, our acquisitions editor; Martin V. Minner, our project editor; Katherine Burt, our copy editor; and Wei Zhang and Chao Zhao, our technical editors. You are an insightful and professional editorial team and this book would not be what it is without you. It was a great pleasure to work with you on this project.

CONTENTS

FOREWORD

GPUs have come a long way. From their origins as specialized graphics processors that could rapidly produce images for output to a display unit, they have become a go-to technology when ultrafast processing is needed. In the past few years, GPUs have increasingly been attached to CPUs to accelerate a broad array of computations in so-called *heterogeneous computing*. Today, GPUs are configured on many desktop systems, on compute clusters, and even on many of the largest supercomputers in the world. In their extended role as a provider of large amounts of compute power for technical computing, GPUs have enabled advances in science and engineering in a broad variety of disciplines. They have done so by making it possible for huge numbers of compute cores to work in parallel while keeping the power budgets very reasonable.

Fortunately, the interfaces for programming GPUs have kept up with this rapid change. In the past, a major effort was required to use them for anything outside the narrow range of applications they were intended for, and the GPU programmer needed to be familiar with many concepts that made good sense only to the graphics programmer. Today's systems provide a much more convenient means to create application software that will run on them. In short, we have CUDA.

CUDA is one of the most popular application programming interfaces for accelerating a range of compute kernels on the GPU. It can enable code written in C or C++ to run efficiently on a GPU with very reasonable programming effort. It strikes a balance between the need to know about the architecture in order to exploit it well, and the need to have a programming interface that is easy to use and results in readable programs.

This book will be a valuable resource for anyone who wants to use GPUs for scientific and technical programming. It provides a comprehensive introduction to the CUDA programming interface and its usage. For a start, it describes the basics of parallel computing on heterogeneous architectures and introduces the features of CUDA. It then explains how CUDA programs are executed. CUDA exposes the execution and memory model to the programmer; as a result, the CUDA programmer has direct control of the massively parallel environment. In addition to giving details of the CUDA memory model, the text provides a wealth of information on how it can be utilized. The following chapter discusses streams, as well as how to execute concurrent and overlapping kernels. Next comes information on tuning, on using CUDA libraries, and on using OpenACC directives to program GPUs. After a chapter on multi-GPU programming, the book concludes by discussing some implementation considerations. Moreover, a variety of examples are given to help the reader get started, many of which can be downloaded and executed.

CUDA provides a nice balance between expressivity and programmability that has proven itself in practice. However, those of us who have made it their mission to simplify application development know that this is an on-going story. For the past few years, CUDA researchers have worked to improve heterogeneous programming tools. CUDA 6 introduces many new features, including unified memory and plug-in libraries, to make GPU programming even easier. They have also provided a set of directives called OpenACC, which is introduced in this book. OpenACC promises to complement CUDA by offering an even simpler means to exploit GPU programming power when less direct control over the execution is needed. Results so far are very promising. OpenACC, CUDA 6, and other topics covered in this book will allow CUDA developers to accelerate their applications for more performance than ever. This book will need to have a permanent place on your bookshelf.

Happy programming!

BARBARA CHAPMAN
CACDS and Department of Computer Science
University of Houston

PREFACE

Years ago when we were porting our production code from legacy C programs to CUDA C, we encountered many troubles as any beginner does, problems with solutions that were far beyond what you could dig out of a simple web search. At that time, we thought that it would be great if there were a book written *by* programmers, *for* programmers, that focused on what programmers need for production CUDA development. Fulfilling that need with lessons from our own experiences in CUDA is the motivation for this book. This book is specially designed to address the needs of the high-performance and scientific computing communities.

When learning a new framework or programming language, most programmers drag out a piece of code from anywhere, test it, and then build up their own code based on that trial. Learning by example with a trial-and-error approach is a quintessential learning technique for many software developers. This book is designed to fit these habits. Each chapter focuses on one topic, using concise explanations to provide foundational knowledge, and illustrating concepts with simple and fully workable code samples. Learning concepts and code side-by-side empowers you to quickly start experimenting with these topics. This book uses a profile-driven approach to guide you deeper and deeper into each topic.

The major difference between parallel programming in C and parallel programming in CUDA C is that CUDA architectural features, such as memory and execution models, are exposed directly to programmers. This enables you to have more control over the massively parallel GPU environment. Even though some still consider CUDA concepts to be low-level, having some knowledge of the underlying architecture is a necessity for harnessing the power of GPUs. Actually, the CUDA platform can perform well even if you have limited knowledge of the architecture.

Parallel programming is always motivated by performance and driven by profiling. CUDA programming is unique in that the exposed architectural features enable you, the programmer, to extract every iota of performance from this powerful hardware platform, if you so choose. After you have mastered the skills taught through the exercises provided in this book, you will find that programming in CUDA C is easy, enjoyable, and rewarding.

INTRODUCTION

WELCOME TO THE WONDERFUL WORLD of heterogeneous parallel programming with CUDA C!

Modern heterogeneous systems are evolving toward a future of intriguing computational possibilities. Heterogeneous computing is constantly being applied to new fields of computation — everything from science to databases to machine learning. The future of programming is heterogeneous parallel programming!

This book gets you started quickly with GPU (Graphical Processing Unit) computing using the CUDA platform, CUDA Toolkit, and CUDA C language. The examples and exercises in this book are designed to jump-start your CUDA expertise to a professional level!

WHO THIS BOOK IS FOR

This book is for anyone who wants to leverage the power of GPU computing to accelerate applications. It covers the most up-to-date technologies in CUDA C programming, with a focus on:

- ➤ Concise style
- ➤ Straightforward approach
- ➤ Illustrative description
- ➤ Extensive examples
- ➤ Deliberately designed exercises
- ➤ Comprehensive coverage
- ➤ Content well-focused for the needs of high-performance computing

If you are an experienced C programmer who wants to add high-performance computing to your repertoire by learning CUDA C, the examples and exercises in the book will build on your existing knowledge so as to simplify mastering CUDA C programming. Using just a handful of CUDA extensions to C, you can benefit from the power of massively parallel hardware. The CUDA platform, programming models, tools, and libraries make programming heterogeneous architectures straightforward and immediately rewarding.

If you are a professional with domain expertise outside of computer science who wants to quickly get up to speed with parallel programming on GPUs, maximize your productivity, and enhance the performance of your applications, you have picked the right book. The clear and concise explanations in this book, supported by well-designed examples and guided by a profile-driven approach, will help you gain insight into GPU programming and quickly become proficient with CUDA.

If you are a professor or a researcher in any discipline and wish to accelerate discovery and innovation through GPU computing, this book will improve your time-to-solution. With minimal past programming experience, parallel computing concepts, and knowledge of computer science, you can quickly dive into the exciting world of parallel programming with heterogeneous architectures.

If you are new to C but are interested in exploring heterogeneous programming, this book does not assume copious amounts of experience in C programming. While the CUDA C and C programming languages obviously share some syntax, the abstractions and underlying hardware for each are different enough that experience with one does not make the other significantly easier to learn. As long as you have an interest in heterogeneous programming, are excited about new topics and new ways of thinking, and have a passion for deep understanding of technical topics, this book is a great fit for you.

Even if you have experience with CUDA C, this book can still be a useful tool to refresh your knowledge, discover new tools, and gain insight into the latest CUDA features. While this book is designed to create CUDA professionals from scratch, it also provides a comprehensive overview of many advanced CUDA concepts, tools, and frameworks that will benefit existing CUDA developers.

WHAT THIS BOOK COVERS

This book provides foundational concepts and techniques of CUDA C programming for people that need to drastically accelerate the performance of their applications. This book covers the newest features released with CUDA Toolkit 6.0 and NVIDIA Kepler GPUs. After briefly introducing the paradigm shift in parallel programming from homogeneous architectures to heterogeneous architectures, this book guides you through essential programming skills and best practices in CUDA, including but not limited to the CUDA programming model, GPU execution model, GPU memory model, CUDA streams and events, techniques for programming multiple GPUs, CUDA-aware MPI programming, and NVIDIA development tools.

This book takes a unique approach to teaching CUDA by mingling foundational descriptions of concepts with illustrative examples that use a profile-driven approach to guide you toward optimal performance. Each topic is thoroughly covered in a step-by-step process based heavily on code examples. This book will help you quickly master the CUDA development process by teaching you not only how to use CUDA-based tools, but also how to interpret results in each step of the development process based on insights and intuitions from the abstract programming model.

Each chapter handles one main topic with workable code examples to demonstrate the basic features and techniques of GPU programming, followed by well-designed exercises that facilitate your exploration of each topic to deepen your understanding.

All examples are developed using a Linux system with CUDA 5.0 or higher and a Kepler or Fermi GPU. Since CUDA C is a cross-platform language, examples in the book are also applicable to other platforms, such as embedded systems, tablets, notebooks, PCs, workstations, and high-performance computing servers. Many OEM suppliers support NVIDIA GPUs in a variety of form-factors.

HOW THIS BOOK IS STRUCTURED

This book consists of ten chapters, and covers the following topics:

Chapter 1: Heterogeneous Parallel Computing with CUDA begins with a brief introduction to the heterogeneous architecture that complements CPUs with GPUs, as well as the paradigm shift towards heterogeneous parallel programming.

Chapter 2: CUDA Programming Model introduces the CUDA programming model and the general structure of a CUDA program. It explains the logical view for massively parallel computing in CUDA: two levels of thread hierarchy exposed intuitively through the programming model. It also discusses thread configuration heuristics and their impact on performance.

Chapter 3: CUDA Execution Model inspects kernel execution from the hardware point of view by studying how thousands of threads are scheduled on a GPU. It explains how compute resources are partitioned among threads at multiple granularities. It also shows how the hardware view can be used to guide kernel design, and guides you in developing and optimizing a kernel using a profile-driven approach. Then, CUDA dynamic parallelism and nested execution are illustrated with examples.

Chapter 4: Global Memory introduces the CUDA memory model, probes the global memory data layout, and analyzes access patterns to global memory. This chapter explains the performance implications of various memory access patterns and demonstrates how a new feature in CUDA 6, Unified Memory, can simplify CUDA programming and improve your productivity.

Chapter 5: Shared Memory and Constant Memory explains how shared memory, a program-managed low-latency cache, can be used to improve kernel performance. It describes the optimal data layout for shared memory and illustrates how to avoid poor performance. Last, it illustrates how to perform low-latency communication between neighboring threads.

Chapter 6: Streams and Concurrency describes how multi-kernel concurrency can be implemented with CUDA streams, how to overlap communication and computation, and how different job dispatching strategies affect inter-kernel concurrency.

Chapter 7: Tuning Instruction-Level Primitives explains the nature of floating-point operations, standard and intrinsic mathematical functions, and CUDA atomic operations. It shows how to use relatively low-level CUDA primitives and compiler flags to tune the performance, accuracy, and correctness of an application.

Chapter 8: GPU-Accelerated CUDA Libraries and OpenACC introduces a new level of parallelism with CUDA domain-specific libraries, including specific examples in linear algebra, Fourier transforms, and random number generation. It explains how OpenACC, a compiler-directive-based GPU programming model, complements CUDA by offering a simpler means to exploit GPU computational power.

Chapter 9: Multi-GPU Programming introduces GPUDirect technology for peer-to-peer GPU memory access. It explains how to manage and execute computation across multiple GPUs. It also illustrates how to scale applications across a GPU-accelerated compute cluster by using CUDA-aware MPI with GPUDirect RDMA to realize near linear performance scalability.

Chapter 10: Implementation Considerations discusses the CUDA development process and a variety of profile-driven optimization strategies. It demonstrates how to use CUDA debugging tools to debug kernel and memory errors. It also provides a case study in porting a legacy C application to CUDA C using step-by-step instructions to help solidify your understanding of the methodology, visualize the process, and demonstrate the tools.

WHAT YOU NEED TO USE THIS BOOK

This book does not require either GPU or parallel programming experience. Before you jump in, it would be best if you have basic experience working with Linux. To run all examples in the book, the ideal environment is:

- ➤ A Linux system
- ➤ A C/C++ compiler
- ➤ CUDA 6.0 Toolkit installed
- ➤ NVIDIA Kepler GPU

However, most examples will run on Fermi devices, though some examples using CUDA 6 features might require Kepler GPUs. Most of these examples can be compiled with CUDA 5.5.

CUDA TOOLKIT DOWNLOAD

You can download the CUDA 6.0 Toolkit from `https://developer.nvidia.com/cuda-toolkit`.

The CUDA Toolkit includes a compiler for NVIDIA GPUs, CUDA math libraries, and tools for debugging and optimizing the performance of your applications. You will also find programming guides, user manuals, an API reference, and other documentation to help you start accelerating your application with GPUs.

CONVENTIONS

To help you get the most from the text, we have used a number of conventions throughout the book.

We *highlight new terms* and important words when we they are introduced.

We show file names, URLs, and code within the text like so: `this_is_a_kernel_file.cu`.

We present code in following way:

```
// distributing jobs among devices
for (int i = 0; i < ngpus; i++)
{
    cudaSetDevice(i);
    cudaMemcpyAsync(d_A[i], h_A[i], iBytes, cudaMemcpyDefault,stream[i]);
    cudaMemcpyAsync(d_B[i], h_B[i], iBytes, cudaMemcpyDefault,stream[i]);
    iKernel<<<grid, block,0,stream[i]>>> (d_A[i], d_B[i], d_C[i],iSize);
    cudaMemcpyAsync(gpuRef[i], d_C[i], iBytes, cudaMemcpyDefault,stream[i]);
}
```

We introduce CUDA runtime functions in the following way:

```
cudaError_t cudaDeviceSynchronize (void);
```

We present the output of programs as follows:

```
./reduce starting reduction at device 0: Tesla M2070
    with array size 16777216  grid 32768 block 512
cpu reduce        elapsed 0.029138 sec cpu_sum: 2139353471
gpu Warmup        elapsed 0.011745 sec gpu_sum: 2139353471 <<<grid 32768 block 512>>>
gpu Neighbored    elapsed 0.011722 sec gpu_sum: 2139353471 <<<grid 32768 block 512>>>
```

We give command-line instructions as follows:

```
$ nvprof --devices 0 --metrics branch_efficiency ./reduce
```

SOURCE CODE

As you work through the examples in this book, you might choose either to type in all the code manually or to use the source code files that accompany the book. All of the source code used in this book is available for download at www.wrox.com/go/procudac. Once at the site, simply locate the book's title (either by using the Search box or by using one of the title lists) and click the Download Code link on the book's detail page to obtain all the source code for the book.

When you work on the exercises at the end of each chapter, we highly encourage you to try to write them yourself by referencing the example codes. All the exercise code files are also downloadable from the Wrox website.

ERRATA

We make every effort to ensure that there are no errors in the text or in the code. However, no one is perfect, and mistakes do occur. If you find an error in one of our books, like a spelling mistake or faulty piece of code, we would be very grateful for your feedback. By sending in errata, you might save another reader hours of frustration and at the same time you will be helping us provide even higher quality information.

To find the errata page for this book, go to www.wrox.com/go/procudac. Then, on the book's details page, click the Book Errata link. On this page you can view all errata that has been submitted for this book and posted by Wrox editors.

P2P.WROX.COM

For author and peer discussion, join the P2P forums at p2p.wrox.com. The forums are a web-based system for you to post messages relating to Wrox books and related technologies and interact with other readers and technology users. The forums offer a subscription feature where topics of interest of your choosing when new posts are made to the forums can be sent to you via e-mail. Wrox authors, editors, other industry experts, and your fellow readers are present on these forums.

At http://p2p.wrox.com you will find a number of different forums that will help you not only as you read this book, but also as you develop your own applications. To join the forums, just follow these steps:

1. Go to p2p.wrox.com and click the Register link.

2. Read the terms of use and click Agree.

3. Complete the required information to join as well as any optional information you wish to provide and click Submit.

4. You will receive an e-mail with information describing how to verify your account and complete the joining process.

You can read messages in the forums without joining P2P, but in order to post your own messages, you must join. Once you join, you can post new messages and respond to messages other users post. You can read messages at any time on the web. If you would like to have new messages from a particular forum sent to your e-mail address, click the "Subscribe to this Forum" icon by the forum name in the forum listing.

For more information about how to use the Wrox P2P, be sure to read the P2P FAQs for answers to questions about how the forum software works as well as many common questions specific to P2P and Wrox books. To read the FAQs, click the FAQ link on any P2P page.

USEFUL LINKS

GTC On-Demand: http://on-demand-gtc.gputechconf.com/gtcnew/on-demand-gtc.php

GTC Express Webinar Program: https://developer.nvidia.com/gpu-computing-webinars

Developer Zone: www.gputechconf.com/resources/developer-zone

NVIDIA Parallel Programming Blog: http://devblogs.nvidia.com/parallelforall

NVIDIA Developer Zone Forums: devtalk.nvidia.com

NVIDIA support e-mail: devtools-support@nvidia.com

1

Heterogeneous Parallel Computing with CUDA

WHAT'S IN THIS CHAPTER?

➤ Understanding heterogeneous computing architectures

➤ Recognizing the paradigm shift of parallel programming

➤ Grasping the basic elements of GPU programming

➤ Knowing the differences between CPU and GPU programming

> **CODE DOWNLOAD** *The wrox.com code downloads for this chapter are found at* www.wrox.com/go/procudac *on the Download Code tab. The code is in the Chapter 1 download and individually named according to the names throughout the chapter.*

The *high-performance computing* (HPC) landscape is always changing as new technologies and processes become commonplace, and the definition of HPC changes accordingly. In general, it pertains to the use of multiple processors or computers to accomplish a complex task concurrently with high throughput and efficiency. It is common to consider HPC as not only a computing architecture but also as a set of elements, including hardware systems, software tools, programming platforms, and parallel programming paradigms.

Over the last decade, high-performance computing has evolved significantly, particularly because of the emergence of GPU-CPU heterogeneous architectures, which have led to a fundamental paradigm shift in parallel programming. This chapter begins your understanding of heterogeneous parallel programming.

PARALLEL COMPUTING

During the past several decades, there has been ever-increasing interest in parallel computation. The primary goal of parallel computing is to improve the speed of computation.

From a pure calculation perspective, *parallel computing* can be defined as a form of computation in which many calculations are carried out simultaneously, operating on the principle that large problems can often be divided into smaller ones, which are then solved concurrently.

From the programmer's perspective, a natural question is how to map the concurrent calculations onto computers. Suppose you have multiple computing resources. Parallel computing can then be defined as the simultaneous use of multiple computing resources (cores or computers) to perform the concurrent calculations. A large problem is broken down into smaller ones, and each smaller one is then solved concurrently on different computing resources. The software and hardware aspects of parallel computing are closely intertwined together. In fact, parallel computing usually involves two distinct areas of computing technologies:

➤ Computer architecture (hardware aspect)

➤ Parallel programming (software aspect)

Computer architecture focuses on supporting parallelism at an architectural level, while *parallel programming* focuses on solving a problem concurrently by fully using the computational power of the computer architecture. In order to achieve parallel execution in software, the hardware must provide a platform that supports concurrent execution of multiple processes or multiple threads.

Most modern processors implement the *Harvard architecture,* as shown in Figure 1-1, which is comprised of three main components:

➤ Memory (instruction memory and data memory)

➤ Central processing unit (control unit and arithmetic logic unit)

➤ Input/Output interfaces

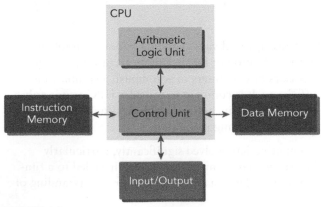

FIGURE 1-1

The key component in high-performance computing is the *central processing unit* (CPU), usually called the *core*. In the early days of the computer, there was only one core on a chip. This architecture is referred to as a *uniprocessor*. Nowadays, the trend in chip design is to integrate multiple cores onto a single processor, usually termed *multicore*, to support parallelism at the architecture level. Therefore, programming can be viewed as the process of mapping the computation of a problem to available cores such that parallel execution is obtained.

When implementing a sequential algorithm, you may not need to understand the details of the computer architecture to write a correct program. However, when implementing algorithms for multicore machines, it is much more important for programmers to be aware of the characteristics of the underlying computer architecture. Writing both correct and efficient parallel programs requires a fundamental knowledge of multicore architectures.

The following sections cover some basic concepts of parallel computing and how these concepts relate to CUDA programming.

Sequential and Parallel Programming

When solving a problem with a computer program, it is natural to divide the problem into a discrete series of calculations; each calculation performs a specified task, as shown in Figure 1-2. Such a program is called a *sequential program*.

The problem is divided into small pieces of calculations.

execution order

FIGURE 1-2

There are two ways to classify the relationship between two pieces of computation: Some are related by a precedence restraint and therefore must be calculated sequentially; others have no such restraints and can be calculated concurrently. Any program containing tasks that are performed concurrently is a *parallel program*. As shown in Figure 1-3, a parallel program may, and most likely will, have some sequential parts.

From the eye of a programmer, a program consists of two basic ingredients: instruction and data. When a computational problem is broken down into many small pieces of computation, each piece is called a *task*. In a task, individual instructions consume inputs, apply a function, and produce outputs. A *data dependency* occurs when an instruction consumes data produced by a preceding instruction. Therefore, you can classify the relationship between any two tasks as either dependent, if one consumes the output of another, or independent.

Analyzing data dependencies is a fundamental skill in implementing parallel algorithms because dependencies are one of the primary inhibitors to parallelism, and understanding them is necessary to obtain application speedup in the modern programming world. In most cases, multiple independent chains of dependent tasks offer the best opportunity for parallelization.

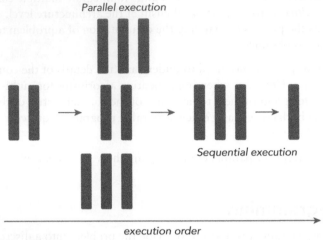

FIGURE 1-3

Parallelism

Nowadays, parallelism is becoming ubiquitous, and parallel programming is becoming mainstream in the programming world. Parallelism at multiple levels is the driving force of architecture design. There are two fundamental types of parallelism in applications:

➤ Task parallelism

➤ Data parallelism

Task parallelism arises when there are many tasks or functions that can be operated independently and largely in parallel. Task parallelism focuses on distributing functions across multiple cores.

Data parallelism arises when there are many data items that can be operated on at the same time. Data parallelism focuses on distributing the data across multiple cores.

CUDA programming is especially well-suited to address problems that can be expressed as data-parallel computations. The major focus of this book is how to solve a data-parallel problem with CUDA programming. Many applications that process large data sets can use a data-parallel model to speed up the computations. Data-parallel processing maps data elements to parallel threads.

The first step in designing a data parallel program is to partition data across threads, with each thread working on a portion of the data. In general, there are two approaches to partitioning data: block partitioning and cyclic partitioning. In block partitioning, many consecutive elements of data are chunked together. Each chunk is assigned to a single thread in any order, and threads generally process only one chunk at a time. In cyclic partitioning, fewer data elements are chunked together. Neighboring threads receive neighboring chunks, and each thread can handle more than one chunk. Selecting a new chunk for a thread to process implies jumping ahead as many chunks as there are threads.

Figure 1-4 shows two simple examples of 1D data partitioning. In the block partition, each thread takes only one portion of the data to process, and in the cyclic partition, each thread takes more than one portion of the data to process. Figure 1-5 shows three simple examples of 2D data partitioning: block partitioning along the y dimension, block partitioning on both dimensions, and cyclic partitioning along the x dimension. The remaining patterns — block partitioning along the x dimension, cyclic partitioning on both dimensions, and cyclic partitioning along the y dimension — are left as an exercise.

Usually, data is stored one-dimensionally. Even when a logical multi-dimensional view of data is used, it still maps to one-dimensional physical storage. Determining how to distribute data among threads is closely related to both how that data is stored physically, as well as how the execution of each thread is ordered. The way you organize threads has a significant effect on the program's performance.

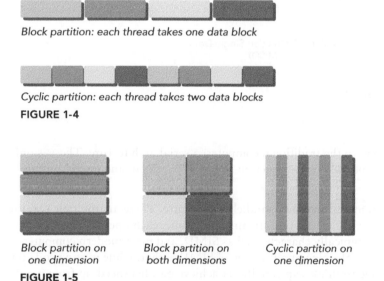

Block partition: each thread takes one data block

Cyclic partition: each thread takes two data blocks

FIGURE 1-4

Block partition on
one dimension

Block partition on
both dimensions

Cyclic partition on
one dimension

FIGURE 1-5

DATA PARTITIONS

There are two basic approaches to partitioning data:

➤ **Block:** Each thread takes one portion of the data, usually an equal portion of the data.

➤ **Cyclic:** Each thread takes more than one portion of the data.

The performance of a program is usually sensitive to the block size. Determining an optimal partition for both block and cyclic partitioning is closely related to the computer architecture. You will learn more about this through the examples in this book.

Computer Architecture

There are several different ways to classify computer architectures. One widely used classification scheme is *Flynn's Taxonomy*, which classifies architectures into four different types according to how instructions and data flow through cores (see Figure 1-6), including:

➤ Single Instruction Single Data (SISD)

➤ Single Instruction Multiple Data (SIMD)

➤ Multiple Instruction Single Data (MISD)

➤ Multiple Instruction Multiple Data (MIMD)

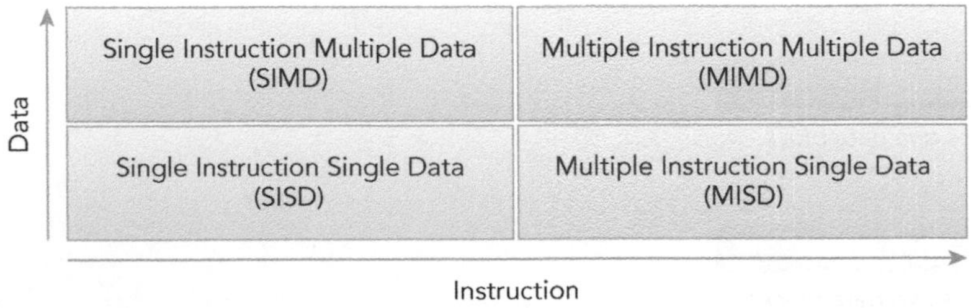

FIGURE 1-6

Single Instruction Single Data refers to the traditional computer: a serial architecture. There is only one core in the computer. At any time only one instruction stream is executed, and operations are performed on one data stream.

Single Instruction Multiple Data refers to a type of parallel architecture. There are multiple cores in the computer. All cores execute the same instruction stream at any time, each operating on different data streams. Vector computers are typically characterized as SIMD, and most modern computers employ a SIMD architecture. Perhaps the biggest advantage of SIMD is that, while writing code on the CPU, programmers can continue to think sequentially yet achieve parallel speed-up from parallel data operations because the compiler takes care of the details.

Multiple Instruction Single Data refers to an uncommon architecture, where each core operates on the same data stream via separate instruction streams.

Multiple Instruction Multiple Data refers to a type of parallel architecture in which multiple cores operate on multiple data streams, each executing independent instructions. Many MIMD architectures also include SIMD execution sub-components.

At the architectural level, many advances have been made to achieve the following objectives:

➤ Decrease latency

➤ Increase bandwidth

➤ Increase throughput

Latency is the time it takes for an operation to start and complete, and is commonly expressed in microseconds. *Bandwidth* is the amount of data that can be processed per unit of time, commonly expressed as megabytes/sec or gigabytes/sec. *Throughput* is the amount of operations that can be processed per unit of time, commonly expressed as *gflops* (which stands for billion floating-point operations per second), especially in fields of scientific computation that make heavy use of floating-point calculations. Latency measures the time to complete an operation, while throughput measures the number of operations processed in a given time unit.

Computer architectures can also be subdivided by their memory organization, which is generally classified into the following two types:

➤ Multi-node with distributed memory

➤ Multiprocessor with shared memory

In a multi-node system, large scale computational engines are constructed from many processors connected by a network. Each processor has its own local memory, and processors can communicate the contents of their local memory over the network. Figure 1-7 shows a typical multi-node system with distributed memory. These systems are often referred to as *clusters*.

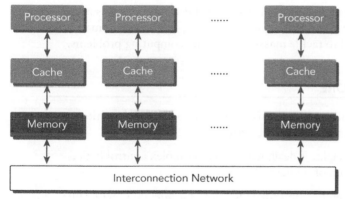

FIGURE 1-7

Multiprocessor architectures typically range in size from dual-processor to dozens or hundreds of processors. These processors are either physically connected to the same memory (as shown in Figure 1-8), or share a low-latency link (such as PCI-Express or PCIe). Although sharing memory implies a shared address space, it does not necessarily mean there is a single physical memory. Such multiprocessors include both single-chip systems with multiple cores, known as *multicore*, and computers consisting of multiple chips, each of which might have a multicore design. Multicore architectures have displaced single-core architectures permanently.

The term *many-core* is usually used to describe multicore architectures with an especially high number of cores (tens or hundreds). Recently, computer architectures have been transitioning from multi-core to many-core.

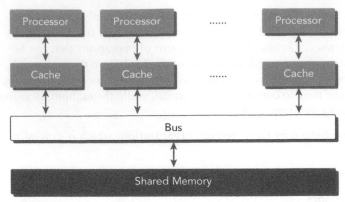

FIGURE 1-8

GPUs represent a many-core architecture, and have virtually every type of parallelism described previously: multithreading, MIMD, SIMD, and instruction-level parallelism. NVIDIA coined the phrase *Single Instruction, Multiple Thread* (SIMT) for this type of architecture.

GPUs and CPUs do not share a common ancestor. Historically, GPUs are graphics accelerators. Only recently have GPUs evolved to be powerful, general-purpose, fully programmable, task and data parallel processors, ideally suited to tackle massively parallel computing problems.

GPU CORE VERSUS CPU CORE

Even though many-core and multicore are used to label GPU and CPU architectures, a GPU core is quite different than a CPU core.

A CPU core, relatively heavy-weight, is designed for very complex control logic, seeking to optimize the execution of sequential programs.

A GPU core, relatively light-weight, is optimized for data-parallel tasks with simpler control logic, focusing on the throughput of parallel programs.

HETEROGENEOUS COMPUTING

In the earliest days, computers contained only central processing units (CPUs) designed to run general programming tasks. Since the last decade, mainstream computers in the high-performance computing community have been switching to include other processing elements. The most prevalent is the GPU, originally designed to perform specialized graphics computations in parallel. Over time, GPUs have become more powerful and more generalized, enabling them to be applied to general-purpose parallel computing tasks with excellent performance and high power efficiency.

Typically, CPUs and GPUs are discrete processing components connected by the PCI-Express bus within a single compute node. In this type of architecture, GPUs are referred to as discrete devices.

The switch from homogeneous systems to heterogeneous systems is a milestone in the history of high-performance computing. *Homogeneous computing* uses one or more processor of the same architecture to execute an application. *Heterogeneous computing* instead uses a suite of processor architectures to execute an application, applying tasks to architectures to which they are well-suited, yielding performance improvement as a result.

Although heterogeneous systems provide significant advantages compared to traditional high-performance computing systems, effective use of such systems is currently limited by the increased application design complexity. While parallel programming has received much recent attention, the inclusion of heterogeneous resources adds complexity.

If you are new to parallel programming, then you can benefit from the performance improvements and advanced software tools now available on heterogeneous architectures. If you are already a good parallel programmer, adapting to parallel programming on heterogeneous architectures is straightforward.

Heterogeneous Architecture

A typical heterogeneous compute node nowadays consists of two multicore CPU sockets and two or more many-core GPUs. A GPU is currently not a standalone platform but a co-processor to a CPU. Therefore, GPUs must operate in conjunction with a CPU-based host through a PCI-Express bus, as shown in Figure 1-9. That is why, in GPU computing terms, the CPU is called the *host* and the GPU is called the *device*.

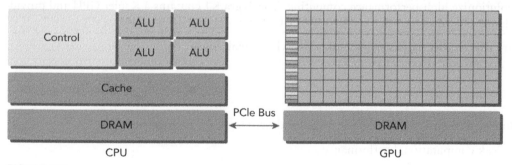

FIGURE 1-9

A heterogeneous application consists of two parts:

➤   Host code

➤   Device code

Host code runs on CPUs and *device code* runs on GPUs. An application executing on a heterogeneous platform is typically initialized by the CPU. The CPU code is responsible for managing the environment, code, and data for the device before loading compute-intensive tasks on the device.

With computational intensive applications, program sections often exhibit a rich amount of data parallelism. GPUs are used to accelerate the execution of this portion of data parallelism. When a hardware component that is physically separate from the CPU is used to accelerate computationally intensive sections of an application, it is referred to as a *hardware accelerator*. GPUs are arguably the most common example of a hardware accelerator.

NVIDIA's GPU computing platform is enabled on the following product families:

➤ Tegra

➤ GeForce

➤ Quadro

➤ Tesla

The Tegra product family is designed for mobile and embedded devices such as tablets and phones, GeForce for consumer graphics, Quadro for professional visualization, and Tesla for datacenter parallel computing. Fermi, the GPU accelerator in the Tesla product family, has recently gained widespread use as a computing accelerator for high-performance computing applications. Fermi, released by NVIDIA in 2010, is the world's first complete GPU computing architecture. Fermi GPU accelerators have already redefined and accelerated high-performance computing capabilities in many areas, such as seismic processing, biochemistry simulations, weather and climate modeling, signal processing, computational finance, computer-aided engineering, computational fluid dynamics, and data analysis. Kepler, the current generation of GPU computing architecture after Fermi, released in the fall of 2012, offers much higher processing power than the prior GPU generation and provides new methods to optimize and increase parallel workload execution on the GPU, expecting to further revolutionize high-performance computing. The Tegra K1 contains a Kepler GPU and provides everything you need to unlock the power of the GPU for embedded applications.

There are two important features that describe GPU capability:

➤ Number of CUDA cores

➤ Memory size

Accordingly, there are two different metrics for describing GPU performance:

➤ Peak computational performance

➤ Memory bandwidth

Peak computational performance is a measure of computational capability, usually defined as how many single-precision or double-precision floating point calculations can be processed per second. Peak performance is usually expressed in `gflops` (billion floating-point operations per second) or `tflops` (trillion floating-point calculations per second). *Memory bandwidth* is a measure of the ratio at which data can be read from or stored to memory. Memory bandwidth is usually expressed in gigabytes per second, GB/s. Table 1-1 provides a brief summary of Fermi and Kepler architectural and performance features.

TABLE 1-1: Fermi and Kepler

	FERMI (TESLA C2050)	KEPLER (TESLA K10)
CUDA Cores	448	2 x 1536
Memory	6 GB	8 GB
Peak Performance*	1.03 Tflops	4.58 Tflops
Memory Bandwidth	144 GB/s	320 GB/s

* Peak single-precision floating point performance

Most examples in this book can be run on both Fermi and Kepler GPUs. Some examples require special architectural features only included with Kepler GPUs.

COMPUTE CAPABILITIES

NVIDIA uses a special term, *compute capability*, to describe hardware versions of GPU accelerators that belong to the entire Tesla product family. The version of Tesla products is given in Table 1-2.

Devices with the same major revision number are of the same core architecture.

➤ Kepler class architecture is major version number 3.

➤ Fermi class architecture is major version number 2.

➤ Tesla class architecture is major version number 1.

The first class of GPUs delivered by NVIDIA contains the same Tesla name as the entire family of Tesla GPU accelerators.

All examples in this book require compute capability above 2.

TABLE 1-2: Compute Capabilities of Tesla GPU Computing Products

GPU	COMPUTE CAPABILITY
Tesla K40	3.5
Tesla K20	3.5
Tesla K10	3.0
Tesla C2070	2.0
Tesla C1060	1.3

Paradigm of Heterogeneous Computing

GPU computing is not meant to replace CPU computing. Each approach has advantages for certain kinds of programs. CPU computing is good for control-intensive tasks, and GPU computing is good for data-parallel computation-intensive tasks. When CPUs are complemented by GPUs, it makes for a powerful combination. The CPU is optimized for dynamic workloads marked by short sequences of computational operations and unpredictable control flow; and GPUs aim at the other end of the spectrum: workloads that are dominated by computational tasks with simple control flow. As shown in Figure 1-10, there are two dimensions that differentiate the scope of applications for CPU and GPU:

➤ Parallelism level

➤ Data size

If a problem has a small data size, sophisticated control logic, and/or low-level parallelism, the CPU is a good choice because of its ability to handle complex logic and instruction-level parallelism. If the problem at hand instead processes a huge amount of data and exhibits massive data parallelism, the GPU is the right choice because it has a large number of programmable cores, can support massive multi-threading, and has a larger peak bandwidth compared to the CPU.

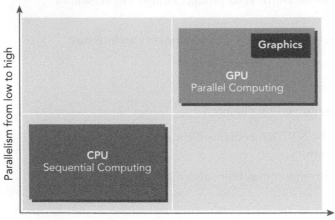

FIGURE 1-10

CPU + GPU heterogeneous parallel computing architectures evolved because the CPU and GPU have complementary attributes that enable applications to perform best using both types of processors. Therefore, for optimal performance you may need to use both CPU and GPU for your application, executing the sequential parts or task parallel parts on the CPU and intensive data parallel parts on the GPU, as shown in Figure 1-11.

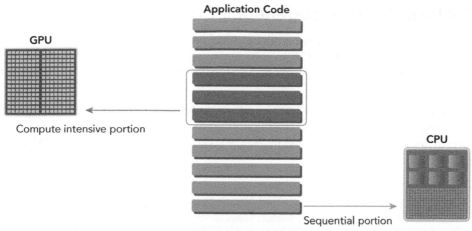

FIGURE 1-11

Writing code this way ensures that the characteristics of the GPU and CPU complement each other, leading to full utilization of the computational power of the combined CPU + GPU system. To support joint CPU + GPU execution of an application, NVIDIA designed a programming model called CUDA. This new programming model is the focus for the rest of this book.

CPU THREAD VERSUS GPU THREAD

Threads on a CPU are generally heavyweight entities. The operating system must swap threads on and off CPU execution channels to provide multithreading capability. Context switches are slow and expensive.

Threads on GPUs are extremely lightweight. In a typical system, thousands of threads are queued up for work. If the GPU must wait on one group of threads, it simply begins executing work on another.

CPU cores are designed to minimize latency for one or two threads at a time, whereas GPU cores are designed to handle a large number of concurrent, lightweight threads in order to maximize throughput.

Today, a CPU with four quad core processors can run only 16 threads concurrently, or 32 if the CPUs support hyper-threading.

Modern NVIDIA GPUs can support up to 1,536 active threads concurrently per multiprocessor. On GPUs with 16 multiprocessors, this leads to more than 24,000 concurrently active threads.

CUDA: A Platform for Heterogeneous Computing

CUDA is a general-purpose parallel computing platform and programming model that leverages the parallel compute engine in NVIDIA GPUs to solve many complex computational problems in a more efficient way. Using CUDA, you can access the GPU for computation, as has been traditionally done on the CPU.

The CUDA platform is accessible through CUDA-accelerated libraries, compiler directives, application programming interfaces, and extensions to industry-standard programming languages, including C, C++, Fortran, and Python (as illustrated by Figure 1-12). This book focuses on CUDA C programming.

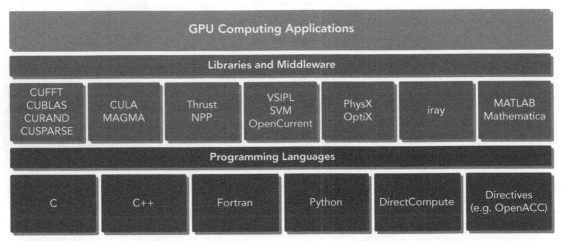

FIGURE 1-12

CUDA C is an extension of standard ANSI C with a handful of language extensions to enable heterogeneous programming, and also straightforward APIs to manage devices, memory, and other tasks. CUDA is also a scalable programming model that enables programs to transparently scale their parallelism to GPUs with varying numbers of cores, while maintaining a shallow learning curve for programmers familiar with the C programming language.

CUDA provides two API levels for managing the GPU device and organizing threads, as shown in Figure 1-13.

➤ CUDA Driver API

➤ CUDA Runtime API

The *driver API* is a low-level API and is relatively hard to program, but it provides more control over how the GPU device is used. The *runtime API* is a higher-level API implemented on top of the driver API. Each function of the runtime API is broken down into more basic operations issued to the driver API.

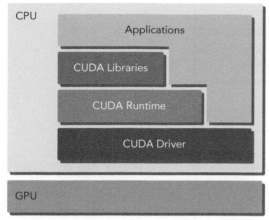

FIGURE 1-13

RUNTIME API VERSUS DRIVER API

There is no noticeable performance difference between the runtime and driver APIs. How your kernels use memory and how you organize your threads on the device have a much more pronounced effect.

These two APIs are mutually exclusive. You must use one or the other, but it is not possible to mix function calls from both. All examples throughout this book use the runtime API.

A CUDA program consists of a mixture of the following two parts:

➤ The host code runs on CPU.

➤ The device code runs on GPU.

NVIDIA's CUDA nvcc compiler separates the device code from the host code during the compilation process. As shown in Figure 1-14, the host code is standard C code and is further compiled with C compilers. The device code is written using CUDA C extended with keywords for labeling data-parallel functions, called *kernels*. The device code is further compiled by nvcc. During the link stage, CUDA runtime libraries are added for kernel procedure calls and explicit GPU device manipulation.

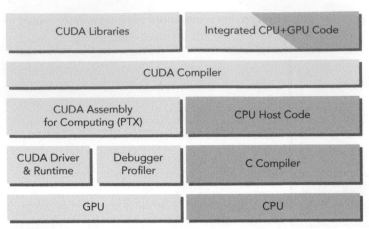

FIGURE 1-14

The CUDA `nvcc` compiler is based on the widely used *LLVM* open source compiler infrastructure. You can create or extend programming languages with support for GPU acceleration using the CUDA Compiler SDK, as shown in Figure 1-15.

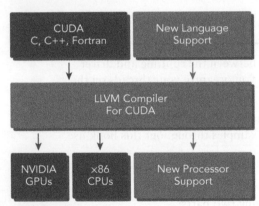

FIGURE 1-15

The CUDA platform is also a foundation that supports a diverse parallel computing ecosystem, as shown in Figure 1-16. Today, the CUDA ecosystem is growing rapidly as more and more companies provide world-class tools, services, and solutions. If you want to build your applications on GPUs, the easiest way to harness the performance of GPUs is with the CUDA Toolkit (`https://developer.nvidia.com/cuda-toolkit`), which provides a comprehensive development environment for C and C++ developers. The CUDA Toolkit includes a compiler, math libraries, and tools for debugging and optimizing the performance of your applications. You will also find code samples, programming guides, user manuals, API references, and other documentation to help you get started.

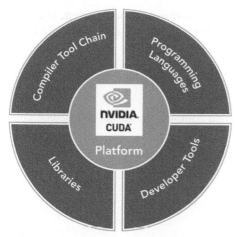

FIGURE 1-16

HELLO WORLD FROM GPU

The best way to learn a new programming language is by writing programs using the new language. In this section, you are going to write your first kernel code running on the GPU. The first program is the same for all languages: Print the string "Hello World."

If this is your first time working with CUDA, you may want to check that the CUDA compiler is installed properly with the following command on a Linux system.

```
$ which nvcc
```

A typical response would be:

```
/usr/local/cuda/bin/nvcc
```

You also need to check if a GPU accelerator card is attached in your machine. You can do so with the following command on a Linux system:

```
$ ls -l /dev/nv*
```

A typical response would be:

```
crw-rw-rw- 1 root root 195,   0 Jul  3 13:44 /dev/nvidia0
crw-rw-rw- 1 root root 195,   1 Jul  3 13:44 /dev/nvidia1
crw-rw-rw- 1 root root 195, 255 Jul  3 13:44 /dev/nvidiactl
crw-rw---- 1 root root  10, 144 Jul  3 13:39 /dev/nvram
```

In this example, you have two GPU cards installed (your configuration may be different, and may show more or fewer devices). Now you are ready to write your first CUDA C code. To write a CUDA C program, you need to:

1. Create a source code file with the special file name extension of .cu.

2. Compile the program using the CUDA nvcc compiler.

3. Run the executable file from the command line, which contains the kernel code executable on the GPU.

As a starting point, write a C program to print out "Hello World" as follows:

```
#include <stdio.h>
int main(void)
{
    printf("Hello World from CPU!\n");
}
```

Save the code into the file hello.cu and then compile it with nvcc. The CUDA nvcc compiler has similar semantics to gcc and other compilers.

```
$ nvcc hello.cu -o hello
```

If you run the executable file hello, it will print:

```
Hello World from CPU!
```

Next, write a kernel function, named helloFromGPU, to print the string of "Hello World from GPU!" as follows:

```
__global__ void helloFromGPU(void)
{
    printf("Hello World from GPU!\n");
}
```

The qualifier __global__ tells the compiler that the function will be called from the CPU and executed on the GPU. Launch the kernel function with the following code:

```
helloFromGPU <<<1,10>>>();
```

Triple angle brackets mark a call from the host thread to the code on the device side. A kernel is executed by an array of threads and all threads run the same code. The parameters within the triple angle brackets are the execution configuration, which specifies how many threads will execute the kernel. In this example, you will run 10 GPU threads. Putting all of these things together, you have the program shown in Listing 1-1:

LISTING 1-1: Hello World from GPU (hello.cu)

```
#include <stdio.h>

__global__ void helloFromGPU (void)
{
    printf("Hello World from GPU!\n");
```

```
}

int main(void)
{
    // hello from cpu
    printf("Hello World from CPU!\n");

    helloFromGPU <<<1, 10>>>();
    cudaDeviceReset();
    return 0;
}
```

The function `cudaDeviceReset()` will explicitly destroy and clean up all resources associated with the current device in the current process. Compile the code with the switch `-arch sm_20` on the nvcc command line as follows:

```
$ nvcc  -arch sm_20 hello.cu -o hello
```

The switch `-arch sm_20` causes the compiler to generate device code for the Fermi architecture. Run the executable file and it will print 10 strings of "Hello World from GPU!" as follows, from each thread.

```
$ ./hello
Hello World from CPU!
Hello World from GPU!
Hello World from GPU!
Hello World from GPU!
Hello World from GPU!
Hello World from CPU!
Hello World from GPU!
Hello World from GPU!
Hello World from GPU!
Hello World from GPU!
Hello World from GPU!
```

CUDA PROGRAM STRUCTURE

A typical CUDA program structure consists of five main steps:

1. Allocate GPU memories.

2. Copy data from CPU memory to GPU memory.

3. Invoke the CUDA kernel to perform program-specific computation.

4. Copy data back from GPU memory to CPU memory.

5. Destroy GPU memories.

In the simple program `hello.cu`, you only see the third step: Invoke the kernel. For the remainder of this book, examples will demonstrate each step in the CUDA program structure.

IS CUDA C PROGRAMMING DIFFICULT?

The main difference between CPU programming and GPU programming is the level of programmer exposure to GPU architectural features. Thinking in parallel and having a basic understanding of GPU architecture enables you to write parallel programs that scale to hundreds of cores as easily as you write a sequential program.

If you want to write efficient code as a parallel programmer, you need a basic knowledge of CPU architectures. For example, *locality* is a very important concept in parallel programming. Locality refers to the reuse of data so as to reduce memory access latency. There are two basic types of reference locality. *Temporal locality* refers to the reuse of data and/or resources within relatively small time durations. *Spatial locality* refers to the use of data elements within relatively close storage locations. Modern CPU architectures use large caches to optimize for applications with good spatial and temporal locality. It is the programmer's responsibility to design their algorithm to efficiently use CPU cache. Programmers must handle low-level cache optimizations, but have no introspection into how threads are being scheduled on the underlying architecture because the CPU does not expose that information.

CUDA exposes you to the concepts of both memory hierarchy and thread hierarchy, extending your ability to control thread execution and scheduling to a greater degree, using:

➤ Memory hierarchy structure

➤ Thread hierarchy structure

For example, a special memory, called *shared memory*, is exposed by the CUDA programming model. Shared memory can be thought of as a software-managed cache, which provides great speedup by conserving bandwidth to main memory. With shared memory, you can control the locality of your code directly.

When writing a parallel program in ANSI C, you need to explicitly organize your threads with either *pthreads* or *OpenMP*, two well-known techniques to support parallel programing on most processor architectures and operating systems. When writing a program in CUDA C, you actually just write a piece of serial code to be called by only one thread. The GPU takes this kernel and makes it parallel by launching thousands of threads, all performing that same computation. The CUDA programming model provides you with a way to organize your threads hierarchically. Manipulating this organization directly affects the order in which threads are executed on the GPU. Because CUDA C is an extension of C, it is often straightforward to port C programs to CUDA C. Conceptually, peeling off the loops of your code yields the kernel code for a CUDA C implementation.

CUDA abstracts away the hardware details and does not require applications to be mapped to traditional graphics APIs. At its core are three key abstractions: a hierarchy of thread groups, a hierarchy of memory groups, and barrier synchronization, which are exposed to you as a minimal set of language extensions. With each release of CUDA, NVIDIA is simplifying parallel programming. Though some still consider CUDA concepts to be low-level, raising the abstraction level any higher would damage your ability to control the interaction between your application and the platform. Without that ability, the performance of your application is beyond your control no matter what knowledge you have of the underlying architecture.

Therefore, the challenge to you is to learn the basics of GPU architecture and master the CUDA development tools and environment.

CUDA DEVELOPMENT ENVIRONMENT

NVIDIA provides a comprehensive development environment for C and C++ developers to build GPU-accelerated applications, including:

➤ NVIDIA Nsight™ integrated development environment

➤ CUDA-GDB command line debugger

➤ Visual and command line profiler for performance analysis

➤ CUDA-MEMCHECK memory analyzer

➤ GPU device management tools

After you become familiar with these tools, programming with CUDA C is straightforward and rewarding.

SUMMARY

As both computer architectures and parallel programming models have evolved, the design of each has intertwined to produce modern heterogeneous systems. The CUDA platform helps improve performance and programmer productivity on heterogeneous architectures.

CPU + GPU systems have become mainstream in the high-performance computing world. This change has led to a fundamental shift in the parallel programming paradigm: The data-parallel workload is executed on the GPU, while the serial and task-parallel workload is executed on the CPU.

Fermi and Kepler GPU accelerators, as complete GPU computing architectures, have already redefined the high-performance computing capabilities in many areas. After reading and understanding the concepts in this book, you will discover that writing CUDA programs that scale to hundreds or thousands of cores in a heterogeneous system is as easy as writing sequential programs.

1. Refer to Figure 1-5 and illustrate the following patterns of data partition:
   - Block partition along the x dimension for 2D data
   - Cyclic partition along the y dimension for 2D data
   - Cyclic partition along the z dimension for 3D data

2. Remove the `cudaDeviceReset` function from `hello.cu`, then compile and run it to see what would happen.

3. Replace the function `cudaDeviceReset` in `hello.cu` with `cudaDeviceSynchronize`, then compile and run it to see what happens.

4. Refer to the section "Hello World from GPU." Remove the device architecture flag from the compiler command line and compile it as follows to see what happens.

   ```
   $ nvcc  hello.cu -o hello
   ```

5. Refer to the CUDA online document (`http://docs.nvidia.com/cuda/index.html`). Based on the section "CUDA Compiler Driver NVCC," what file suffixes does nvcc support compilation on?

6. Each thread that executes the kernel is given a unique thread ID that is accessible within the kernel through the built-in *threadIdx.x* variable. Modify the kernel function in `hello.cu` with the thread index to let the output be:

   ```
   $ ./hello
   Hello World from CPU!
   Hello World from GPU thread 5!
   ```

CUDA Programming Model

WHAT'S IN THIS CHAPTER?

➤ Writing a CUDA program

➤ Executing a kernel function

➤ Organizing threads with grids and blocks

➤ Measuring GPU performance

> **CODE DOWNLOAD** *The wrox.com code downloads for this chapter are found at www.wrox.com/go/procudac on the Download Code tab. The code is in the Chapter 2 download and individually named according to the names throughout the chapter.*

CUDA is a parallel computing platform and programming model with a small set of extensions to the C language. With CUDA, you can implement a parallel algorithm as easily as you write C programs. You can build applications for a myriad of systems with CUDA on NVIDIA GPUs, ranging from embedded devices, tablet devices, laptops, desktops, and workstations to HPC clustered systems. Familiar C programming software tools have been extended to help you edit, debug, and analyze your CUDA program during the lifetime of your project. In this chapter, you are going to learn how to write a CUDA program through two simple examples: vector addition and matrix addition.

INTRODUCING THE CUDA PROGRAMMING MODEL

Programming models present an abstraction of computer architectures that act as a bridge between an application and its implementation on available hardware. Figure 2-1 illustrates the important layers of abstraction that lie between the program and the programming model implementation. The communication abstraction is the boundary between the program and the programming model implementation, which is realized through a compiler or libraries using privileged hardware primitives and the operating system. The program, written for a programming model, dictates how components of the program share information and coordinate their activities. The programming model provides a logical view of specific computing architectures. Typically, it is embodied in a programming language or programming environment.

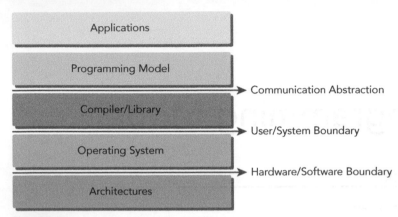

FIGURE 2-1

In addition to sharing many abstractions with other parallel programming models, the CUDA programming model provides the following special features to harness the computing power of GPU architectures.

➤   A way to organize threads on the GPU through a hierarchy structure

➤   A way to access memory on the GPU through a hierarchy structure

You will focus on the first topic in this and the next chapter, and learn the second topic in Chapters 4 and 5.

From the perspective of a programmer, you can view parallel computation from different levels, such as:

➤   Domain level

➤   Logic level

➤   Hardware level

As you work through your program and algorithm design, your main concern is at the domain level: how to decompose data and functions so as to solve the problem correctly and efficiently while running in a parallel environment. When you enter the programming phase, your concern turns to how to organize your concurrent threads. During this phase you are thinking at the logic level to ensure your threads and calculations solve the problem correctly. In C parallel programming, you must manage your threads explicitly using either *pthreads* or *OpenMP* techniques. CUDA exposes a thread hierarchy abstraction to allow you to control thread behavior. As you walk through examples in this book, you will see that this abstraction delivers superior scalability for parallel programming. At the hardware level, being able to understand how threads are mapped to cores may help improve performance.

The CUDA threading model exposes sufficient information to you without forcing too many low-level details. You will learn more about this in Chapter 3.

CUDA Programming Structure

The CUDA programming model enables you to execute applications on heterogeneous computing systems by simply annotating code with a small set of extensions to the C programming language. A heterogeneous environment consists of CPUs complemented by GPUs, each with its own memory separated by a PCI-Express bus. Therefore, you should note the following distinction:

➤ **Host:** the CPU and its memory (host memory)

➤ **Device:** the GPU and its memory (device memory)

To help clearly designate the different memory spaces, example code in this book uses variable names that start with h_ for host memory, and d_ for device memory.

Starting with CUDA 6, NVIDIA introduced a programming model improvement called *Unified Memory*, which bridges the divide between host and device memory spaces. This improvement allows you to access both the CPU and GPU memory using a single pointer, while the system automatically migrates the data between the host and device. More details about the unified memory will be covered in Chapter 4. For now, it is important that you learn how to allocate both the host and device memory, and explicitly copy data that is shared between the CPU and GPU. This programmer-managed control of memory and data gives you the power to optimize your application and maximize hardware utilization.

A key component of the CUDA programming model is the kernel — the code that runs on the GPU device. As the developer, you can express a kernel as a sequential program. Behind the scenes, CUDA manages scheduling programmer-written kernels on GPU threads. From the host, you define how your algorithm is mapped to the device based on application data and GPU device capability. The intent is to enable you to focus on the logic of your algorithm in a straightforward fashion (by writing sequential code) and not get bogged down with details of creating and managing thousands of GPU threads.

The host can operate independently of the device for most operations. When a kernel has been launched, control is returned immediately to the host, freeing the CPU to perform additional tasks complemented by data parallel code running on the device. The CUDA programming model is primarily asynchronous so that GPU computation performed on the GPU can be overlapped with host-device communication. A typical CUDA program consists of serial code complemented by parallel code. As shown in Figure 2-2, the serial code (as well as task parallel code) is executed on the host, while the parallel code is executed on the GPU device. The host code is written in ANSI C, and the device code is written using CUDA C. You can put all the code in a single source file, or you can use multiple source files to build your application or libraries. The NVIDIA C Compiler (nvcc) generates the executable code for both the host and device.

A typical processing flow of a CUDA program follows this pattern:

1. Copy data from CPU memory to GPU memory.

2. Invoke kernels to operate on the data stored in GPU memory.

3. Copy data back from GPU memory to CPU memory.

You will start by learning about memory management and data movement between the host and device. Later, this chapter will cover more details on GPU kernel execution.

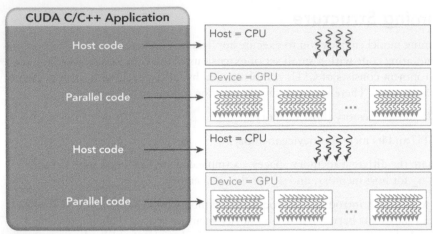

FIGURE 2-2

Managing Memory

The CUDA programming model assumes a system composed of a host and a device, each with its own separate memory. Kernels operate out of device memory. To allow you to have full control and achieve the best performance, the CUDA runtime provides functions to allocate device memory, release device memory, and transfer data between the host memory and device memory. Table 2-1 lists the standard C functions and their corresponding CUDA C functions for memory operations.

TABLE 2-1: Host and Device Memory Functions

STANDARD C FUNCTIONS	CUDA C FUNCTIONS
malloc	cudaMalloc
memcpy	cudaMemcpy
memset	cudaMemset
free	cudaFree

The function used to perform GPU memory allocation is cudaMalloc, and its function signature is:

```
cudaError_t cudaMalloc ( void** devPtr, size_t size )
```

This function allocates a linear range of device memory with the specified size in bytes. The allocated memory is returned through devPtr. You may notice the striking similarity between cudaMalloc and the standard C runtime library malloc. This is intentional. By keeping the interface as close to the standard C runtime libraries as possible, CUDA eases application porting.

The function used to transfer data between the host and device is: cudaMemcpy, and its function signature is:

```
cudaError_t cudaMemcpy ( void* dst, const void* src, size_t count,
    cudaMemcpyKind kind )
```

This function copies the specified bytes from the source memory area, pointed to by src, to the destination memory area, pointed to by dst, with the direction specified by kind, where kind takes one of the following types:

➤ cudaMemcpyHostToHost

➤ cudaMemcpyHostToDevice

➤ cudaMemcpyDeviceToHost

➤ cudaMemcpyDeviceToDevice

This function exhibits synchronous behavior because the host application blocks until cudaMemcpy returns and the transfer is complete. Every CUDA call, except kernel launches, returns an error code of an enumerated type cudaError_t. For example, if GPU memory is successfully allocated, it returns:

```
cudaSuccess
```

Otherwise, it returns:

```
cudaErrorMemoryAllocation
```

You can convert an error code to a human-readable error message with the following CUDA runtime function:

```
char*  cudaGetErrorString(cudaError_t error)
```

The cudaGetErrorString function is analogous to the Standard C strerror function.

The CUDA programming model exposes an abstraction of memory hierarchy from the GPU architecture. Figure 2-3 illustrates a simplified GPU memory structure, containing two major ingredients: global memory and shared memory. You will learn more about the GPU memory hierarchy in Chapters 4 and 5.

MEMORY HIERARCHY

One of the more notable characteristics of the CUDA programming model is the exposed memory hierarchy. Each GPU device has a set of different memory types used for different purposes. You will learn much more detail about this hierarchy in Chapters 4 and 5.

In the GPU memory hierarchy, the two most important types of memory are global memory and shared memory. Global memory is analogous to CPU system memory, while shared memory is similar to the CPU cache. However, GPU shared memory can be directly controlled from a CUDA C kernel.

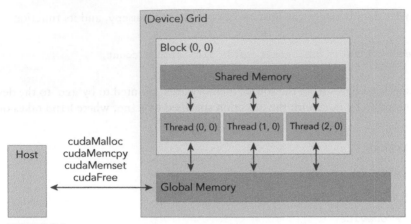

FIGURE 2-3

For now, you are going to learn how to manage data movement between the host and device, and how to program with CUDA C through a simple example of summing two arrays. As illustrated in Figure 2-4, the first element of array a is added to the first element of array b, and the result is assigned to the first element of array c. This calculation is repeated for all successive array elements.

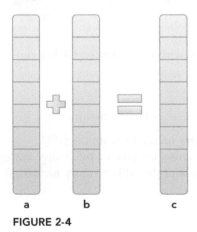

FIGURE 2-4

First, you start with the host code to add two arrays together (see Listing 2-1).

LISTING 2-1: Host-based array summation (sumArraysOnHost.c)

```c
#include <stdlib.h>
#include <string.h>
#include <time.h>

void sumArraysOnHost(float *A, float *B, float *C, const int N) {
    for (int idx=0; idx<N; idx++) {
```

```
        C[idx] = A[idx] + B[idx];
    }
}

void initialData(float *ip,int size) {
    // generate different seed for random number
    time_t t;
    srand((unsigned int) time(&t));

    for (int i=0; i<size; i++) {
        ip[i] = (float)( rand() & 0xFF )/10.0f;
    }
}

int main(int argc, char **argv) {
    int nElem = 1024;
    size_t nBytes = nElem * sizeof(float);

    float *h_A, *h_B, *h_C;
    h_A = (float *)malloc(nBytes);
    h_B = (float *)malloc(nBytes);
    h_C = (float *)malloc(nBytes);

    initialData(h_A, nElem);
    initialData(h_B, nElem);

    sumArraysOnHost(h_A, h_B, h_C, nElem);

    free(h_A);
    free(h_B);
    free(h_C);

    return(0);
}
```

Because this is a pure C program, you can compile it with your C compiler. You also can compile and run this example with nvcc as follows. It will finish silently.

```
$ nvcc -Xcompiler -std=c99 sumArraysOnHost.c -o sum
$ ./sum
```

The CUDA compiler allows you to pass many options directly to the internal compilation tools that nvcc encapsulates. The flag -Xcompiler specifies options directly to the C compiler or preprocessor. In the preceding example, -std=c99 is passed to the compiler because the C code here is written with the code style according to the C99 standard. You can find compiler options in the CUDA compiler document (http://docs.nvidia.com/cuda/cuda-compiler-driver-nvcc/index.html).

Now, you can modify the code to perform array summation on the GPU. Use cudaMalloc to allocate the memory on the GPU.

```
float *d_A, *d_B, *d_C;
cudaMalloc((float**)&d_A, nBytes);
cudaMalloc((float**)&d_B, nBytes);
cudaMalloc((float**)&d_C, nBytes);
```

Use `cudaMemcpy` to transfer the data from the host memory to the GPU global memory with the parameter `cudaMemcpyHostToDevice` specifying the transfer direction.

```
cudaMemcpy(d_A, h_A, nBytes, cudaMemcpyHostToDevice);
cudaMemcpy(d_B, h_B, nBytes, cudaMemcpyHostToDevice);
```

When the data has been transferred to the GPU global memory, the kernel function can be invoked from the host side to perform the array summation on the GPU. As soon as the kernel is called, the control is immediately returned back to the host. At this point, the host may be able to perform other functions while the kernel is running on the GPU. Thus, the kernel is asynchronous with respect to the host.

When the kernel has finished processing all array elements on the GPU, the result is stored on the GPU global memory in array `d_C`. Copy the result from the GPU memory back to the host array `gpuRef` using `cudaMemcpy`.

```
cudaMemcpy(gpuRef, d_C, nBytes, cudaMemcpyDeviceToHost);
```

The `cudaMemcpy` call causes the host to block. The results stored in the array `d_C` on the GPU are copied to `gpuRef` as specified with `cudaMemcpyDeviceToHost`. Finally, use `cudaFree` to release the memory used on the GPU.

```
cudaFree(d_A);
cudaFree(d_B);
cudaFree(d_C);
```

DIFFERENT MEMORY SPACES

One of the most common mistakes made by those learning to program in CUDA C is to improperly dereference the different memory spaces. For the memory allocated on the GPU, the device pointers may not be dereferenced in the host code. If you improperly use an assignment, for example:

```
gpuRef = d_C
```

instead of using

```
cudaMemcpy(gpuRef, d_C, nBytes, cudaMemcpyDeviceToHost)
```

the application will crash at runtime.

To help avoid these types of mistakes, Unified Memory was introduced with CUDA 6, which lets you access both CPU and GPU memory by using a single pointer. You will learn more about unified memory in Chapter 4.

Organizing Threads

When a kernel function is launched from the host side, execution is moved to a device where a large number of threads are generated and each thread executes the statements specified by the kernel function. Knowing how to organize threads is a critical part of CUDA programming. CUDA exposes a thread hierarchy abstraction to enable you to organize your threads. This is a two-level thread hierarchy decomposed into blocks of threads and grids of blocks, as shown in Figure 2-5.

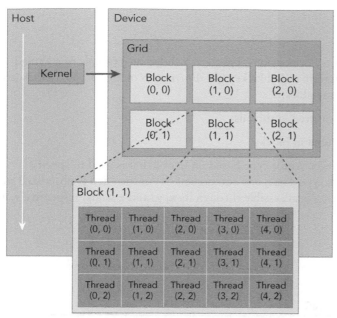

FIGURE 2-5

All threads spawned by a single kernel launch are collectively called a *grid*. All threads in a grid share the same global memory space. A grid is made up of many thread blocks. A thread block is a group of threads that can cooperate with each other using:

➤ Block-local synchronization

➤ Block-local shared memory

Threads from different blocks cannot cooperate.

Threads rely on the following two unique coordinates to distinguish themselves from each other:

➤ blockIdx (block index within a grid)

➤ threadIdx (thread index within a block)

These variables appear as built-in, pre-initialized variables that can be accessed within kernel functions. When a kernel function is executed, the coordinate variables blockIdx and threadIdx are assigned to each thread by the CUDA runtime. Based on the coordinates, you can assign portions of data to different threads.

The coordinate variable is of type uint3, a CUDA built-in vector type, derived from the basic integer type. It is a structure containing three unsigned integers, and the 1st, 2nd, and 3rd components are accessible through the fields x, y, and z respectively.

```
blockIdx.x
blockIdx.y
blockIdx.z
```

```
threadIdx.x
threadIdx.y
threadIdx.z
```

CUDA organizes grids and blocks in three dimensions. Figure 2-5 shows an example of a thread hierarchy structure with a 2D grid containing 2D blocks. The dimensions of a grid and a block are specified by the following two built-in variables:

➤ blockDim (block dimension, measured in threads)

➤ gridDim (grid dimension, measured in blocks)

These variables are of type dim3, an integer vector type based on uint3 that is used to specify dimensions. When defining a variable of type dim3, any component left unspecified is initialized to 1. Each component in a variable of type dim3 is accessible through its x, y, and z fields, respectively, as shown in the following example:

```
blockDim.x
blockDim.y
blockDim.z
```

GRID AND BLOCK DIMENSIONS

Usually, a grid is organized as a 2D array of blocks, and a block is organized as a 3D array of threads.

Both grids and blocks use the dim3 type with three unsigned integer fields. The unused fields will be initialized to 1 and ignored.

There are two distinct sets of grid and block variables in a CUDA program: manually-defined dim3 data type and pre-defined uint3 data type. On the host side, you define the dimensions of a grid and block using a dim3 data type as part of a kernel invocation. When the kernel is executing, the CUDA runtime generates the corresponding built-in, pre-initialized grid, block, and thread variables, which are accessible within the kernel function and have type uint3. The manually-defined grid and block variables for the dim3 data type are only visible on the host side, and the built-in, pre-initialized grid and block variables of the uint3 data type are only visible on the device side.

In Listing 2-2, you are going to examine how these variables work. First, define the data size to be used in the program. For the purposes of illustration, a small data size is used.

```
int nElem = 6;
```

Next, define the block size and calculate the grid size based on the block and data size. In the following example, a 1D block is defined containing 3 threads and a 1D grid with the number of blocks defined based on the data and block sizes.

```
dim3 block(3);
dim3 grid((nElem+block.x-1)/block.x);
```

You may have noticed that the grid size is rounded up to the multiple of the block size. You will learn the reason why you must calculate the grid size in this way in the next chapter. The following code segment on the host side checks the grid and block dimensions:

```
printf("grid.x %d grid.y %d grid.z %d\n",grid.x, grid.y, grid.z);
printf("block.x %d block.y %d block.z %d\n",block.x, block.y, block.z);
```

In the kernel function, each thread prints out its own thread index, block index, block dimension, and grid dimension as follows:

```
printf("threadIdx:(%d, %d, %d)  blockIdx:(%d, %d, %d)  blockDim:(%d, %d, %d) "
    "gridDim:(%d, %d, %d)\n", threadIdx.x, threadIdx.y, threadIdx.z,
    blockIdx.x, blockIdx.y, blockIdx.z, blockDim.x, blockDim.y, blockDim.z,
    gridDim.x,gridDim.y,gridDim.z);
```

You combine the code together into a file named checkDimension.cu, as shown in Listing 2-2.

LISTING 2-2: Check grid and block indices and dimensions (checkDimension.cu)

```
#include <cuda_runtime.h>
#include <stdio.h>

__global__ void checkIndex(void) {
    printf("threadIdx:(%d, %d, %d)  blockIdx:(%d, %d, %d)  blockDim:(%d, %d, %d) "
        "gridDim:(%d, %d, %d)\n", threadIdx.x, threadIdx.y, threadIdx.z,
        blockIdx.x, blockIdx.y, blockIdx.z, blockDim.x, blockDim.y, blockDim.z,
        gridDim.x,gridDim.y,gridDim.z);
}

int main(int argc, char **argv) {
    // define total data element
    int nElem = 6;

    // define grid and block structure
    dim3 block (3);
    dim3 grid  ((nElem+block.x-1)/block.x);

    // check grid and block dimension from host side
    printf("grid.x %d grid.y %d grid.z %d\n",grid.x, grid.y, grid.z);
    printf("block.x %d block.y %d block.z %d\n",block.x, block.y, block.z);

    // check grid and block dimension from device side
    checkIndex <<<grid, block>>> ();

    // reset device before you leave
    cudaDeviceReset();

    return(0);
}
```

Now you are ready to compile and run this example using:

```
$ nvcc -arch=sm_20 checkDimension.cu -o check
$ ./check
```

Because the `printf` function is only supported on architectures starting with Fermi GPUs, the `-arch=sm_20` compiler option must be added. By default, `nvcc` will generate code for the lowest GPU architecture. The result of this application is shown below. You can see that each thread has its own coordinate, and all threads have the same block dimension and grid dimension.

```
grid.x 2 grid.y 1 grid.z 1
block.x 3 block.y 1 block.z 1
threadIdx:(0, 0, 0)  blockIdx:(1, 0, 0) blockDim:(3, 1, 1) gridDim:(2, 1, 1)
threadIdx:(1, 0, 0)  blockIdx:(1, 0, 0) blockDim:(3, 1, 1) gridDim:(2, 1, 1)
threadIdx:(2, 0, 0)  blockIdx:(1, 0, 0) blockDim:(3, 1, 1) gridDim:(2, 1, 1)
threadIdx:(0, 0, 0)  blockIdx:(0, 0, 0) blockDim:(3, 1, 1) gridDim:(2, 1, 1)
threadIdx:(1, 0, 0)  blockIdx:(0, 0, 0) blockDim:(3, 1, 1) gridDim:(2, 1, 1)
threadIdx:(2, 0, 0)  blockIdx:(0, 0, 0) blockDim:(3, 1, 1) gridDim:(2, 1, 1)
```

ACCESS GRID/BLOCK VARIABLES FROM THE HOST AND DEVICE SIDE

It is important to distinguish between the host and device access of grid and block variables. For example, using a variable declared as block from the host, you define the coordinates and access them as follows:

`block.x`, `block.y`, and `block.z`

On the device side, you have pre-initialized, built-in block size variable available as:

`blockDim.x`, `blockDim.y`, and `blockDim.z`

In summary, you define variables for grid and block on the host before launching a kernel, and access them there with the x, y and z fields of the vector structure from the host side. When the kernel is launched, you can use the pre-initialized, built-in variables within the kernel.

For a given data size, the general steps to determine the grid and block dimensions are:

➤ Decide the block size.

➤ Calculate the grid dimension based on the application data size and the block size.

To determine the block dimension, you usually need to consider:

➤ Performance characteristics of the kernel

➤ Limitations on GPU resources

You will learn more details about these factors from examples in subsequent chapters in this book. Listing 2-3 uses a 1D grid and 1D blocks to illustrate that when the block size is altered, the grid size will be changed accordingly.

LISTING 2-3: Define grid and block dimensions on the host (defineGridBlock.cu)

```
#include <cuda_runtime.h>
#include <stdio.h>

int main(int argc, char **argv) {
    // define total data elements
    int nElem = 1024;

    // define grid and block structure
    dim3 block (1024);
    dim3 grid  ((nElem+block.x-1)/block.x);
    printf("grid.x %d block.x %d \n",grid.x, block.x);

    // reset block
    block.x = 512;
    grid.x  = (nElem+block.x-1)/block.x;
    printf("grid.x %d block.x %d \n",grid.x, block.x);

    // reset block
    block.x = 256;
    grid.x  = (nElem+block.x-1)/block.x;
    printf("grid.x %d block.x %d \n",grid.x, block.x);

    // reset block
    block.x = 128;
    grid.x  = (nElem+block.x-1)/block.x;
    printf("grid.x %d block.x %d \n",grid.x, block.x);

    // reset device before you leave
    cudaDeviceReset();
    return(0);
}
```

Compile and run this example with the following command:

```
$ nvcc defineGridBlock.cu -o block
$ ./block
```

Below is a sample output. Because the application data size is fixed, when the block size changes, the grid size changes accordingly.

```
grid.x 1 block.x 1024
grid.x 2 block.x 512
grid.x 4 block.x 256
grid.x 8 block.x 128
```

THREAD HIERARCHY

One of CUDA's distinguishing features is that it exposes a two-level thread hierarchy through the programming model. Because the grid and block dimensionality of a kernel launch affect performance, exposing this simple abstraction provides the programmer with an additional avenue for optimization.

There are several restrictions on the dimensions of grids and blocks. One of the major limiting factors on block size is available compute resources, such as registers, shared memory, and so on. Some limits can be retrieved by querying the GPU device.

Grids and blocks represent a logical view of the thread hierarchy of a kernel function. In Chapter 3, you will see that this type of thread organization gives you the ability to efficiently execute the same application code on different devices, each with varying amounts of compute and memory resources.

Launching a CUDA Kernel

You are familiar with the following C function call syntax:

```
function_name (argument list);
```

A CUDA kernel call is a direct extension to the C function syntax that adds a kernel's *execution configuration* inside triple-angle-brackets:

```
kernel_name <<<grid, block>>>(argument list);
```

As explained in the previous section, the CUDA programming model exposes the thread hierarchy. With the execution configuration, you can specify how the threads will be scheduled to run on the GPU. The first value in the execution configuration is the grid dimension, the number of blocks to launch. The second value is the block dimension, the number of threads within each block. By specifying the grid and block dimensions, you configure:

➤   The total number of threads for a kernel

➤   The layout of the threads you want to employ for a kernel

The threads within the same block can easily communicate with each other, and threads that belong to different blocks cannot cooperate. For a given problem, you can use a different grid and block layout to organize your threads. For example, suppose you have 32 data elements for a calculation. You can group 8 elements into each block, and launch four blocks as follows:

```
kernel_name<<<4, 8>>>(argument list);
```

Figure 2-6 illustrates the layout of threads in the above configuration.

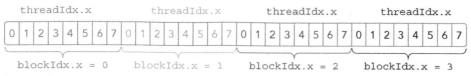

FIGURE 2-6

Because the data is stored linearly in global memory, you can use the built-in variables `blockIdx.x` and `threadIdx.x` to:

➤ Identify a unique thread in the grid.

➤ Establish a mapping between threads and data elements.

If you group all 32 elements into one block, then you just have one block as follows:

```
kernel_name<<<1, 32>>>(argument list);
```

If you let each block just have one element, you have 32 blocks as follows:

```
kernel_name<<<32, 1>>>(argument list);
```

A kernel call is asynchronous with respect to the host thread. After a kernel is invoked, control returns to the host side immediately. You can call the following function to force the host application to wait for all kernels to complete.

```
cudaError_t cudaDeviceSynchronize(void);
```

Some CUDA runtime APIs perform an implicit synchronization between the host and the device. When you use cudaMemcpy to copy data between the host and device, implicit synchronization at the host side is performed and the host application must wait for the data copy to complete.

```
cudaError_t cudaMemcpy(void* dst, const void* src, size_t count, cudaMemcpyKind kind);
```

It starts to copy after all previous kernel calls have completed. When the copy is finished, control returns to the host side immediately.

ASYNCHRONOUS BEHAVIORS

Unlike a C function call, all CUDA kernel launches are asynchronous. Control returns to the CPU immediately after the CUDA kernel is invoked.

Writing Your Kernel

A kernel function is the code to be executed on the device side. In a kernel function, you define the computation for a single thread, and the data access for that thread. When the kernel is called, many different CUDA threads perform the same computation in parallel. A kernel is defined using the `__global__` declaration specification as shown:

```
__global__ void kernel_name(argument list);
```

A kernel function must have a `void` return type.

Table 2-2 provides a summary of function type qualifiers used in CUDA C programming. Function type qualifiers specify whether a function executes on the host or on the device and whether it is callable from the host or from the device.

TABLE 2-2: Function Type Qualifiers

QUALIFIERS	EXECUTION	CALLABLE	NOTES
`__global__`	Executed on the device	Callable from the host Callable from the device for devices of compute capability 3	Must have a `void` return type
`__device__`	Executed on the device	Callable from the device only	
`__host__`	Executed on the host	Callable from the host only	Can be omitted

The `__device__` and `__host__` qualifiers can be used together, in which case the function is compiled for both the host and the device.

CUDA KERNELS ARE FUNCTIONS WITH RESTRICTIONS

The following restrictions apply for all kernels:

➤ Access to device memory only

➤ Must have `void` return type

➤ No support for a variable number of arguments

➤ No support for static variables

➤ No support for function pointers

➤ Exhibit an asynchronous behavior

As an illustration, consider a simple example of adding two vectors A and B of size N. The C code for vector addition on the host is given below:

```
void sumArraysOnHost(float *A, float *B, float *C, const int N) {
    for (int i = 0; i < N; i++)
        C[i] = A[i] + B[i];
}
```

This is a sequential code that iterates N times. Peeling off the loop would produce the following kernel function:

```
__global__ void sumArraysOnGPU(float *A, float *B, float *C) {
    int i = threadIdx.x;
    C[i] = A[i] + B[i];
}
```

What is different between the C function and the kernel function? You'll notice that the loop is missing, the built-in thread coordinate variables are used to replace the array index, and there is no reference to N as it is implicitly defined by only launching N threads.

Supposing a vector with the length of 32 elements, you can invoke the kernel with 32 threads as follows:

```
sumArraysOnGPU<<<1,32>>>(float *A, float *B, float *C);
```

Verifying Your Kernel

Now that you have written your kernel, how do you know if it will operate properly? You need a host function to verify the result from the kernel.

```
void checkResult(float *hostRef, float *gpuRef, const int N) {
    double epsilon = 1.0E-8;
    int match = 1;
    for (int i = 0; i < N; i++) {
        if (abs(hostRef[i] - gpuRef[i]) > epsilon) {
            match = 0;
            printf("Arrays do not match!\n");
            printf("host %5.2f gpu %5.2f at current %d\n",
                hostRef[i], gpuRef[i], i);
            break;
        }
    }
    if (match) printf("Arrays match.\n\n");
    return;
}
```

VERIFYING KERNEL CODE

Besides many useful debugging tools, there are two very basic but useful means by which you can verify your kernel code.

First, you can use `printf` in your kernel for Fermi and later generation devices.

Second, you can set the execution configuration to `<<<1,1>>>`, so you force the kernel to run with only one block and one thread. This emulates a sequential implementation. This is useful for debugging and verifying correct results. Also, this helps you verify that numeric results are bitwise exact from run-to-run if you encounter order of operations issues.

Handling Errors

Since many CUDA calls are asynchronous, it may be difficult to identify which routine caused an error. Defining an error-handling macro to wrap all CUDA API calls simplifies the error checking process:

```
#define CHECK(call)                                                          \
{                                                                            \
    const cudaError_t error = call;                                          \
    if (error != cudaSuccess)                                                \
    {                                                                        \
        printf("Error: %s:%d, ", __FILE__, __LINE__);                        \
        printf("code:%d, reason: %s\n", error, cudaGetErrorString(error));   \
        exit(1);                                                             \
    }                                                                        \
}
```

For example, you can use the macro on the following code:

```
CHECK(cudaMemcpy(d_C, gpuRef, nBytes, cudaMemcpyHostToDevice));
```

If the memory copy or a previous asynchronous operation caused an error, the macro reports the error code, prints a human readable message, and then stops the program. It also can be used after a kernel invocation in the following way to check for kernel errors:

```
kernel_function<<<grid, block>>>(argument list);
CHECK(cudaDeviceSynchronize());
```

CHECK(cudaDeviceSynchronize()) blocks the host thread until the device has completed all preceding requested tasks, and ensures that no errors occurred as part of the last kernel launch. This technique should be used just for debugging purposes, because adding this check point after kernel launches will block the host thread and make that point a global barrier.

Compiling and Executing

Now combine all the code together into a file named sumArraysOnGPU-small-case.cu, as shown in Listing 2-4.

LISTING 2-4: GPU-based vector summation (sumArraysOnGPU-small-case.cu)

```
#include <cuda_runtime.h>
#include <stdio.h>

#define CHECK(call)                                                          \
{                                                                            \
    const cudaError_t error = call;                                          \
    if (error != cudaSuccess)                                                \
    {                                                                        \
        printf("Error: %s:%d, ", __FILE__, __LINE__);                        \
        printf("code:%d, reason: %s\n", error, cudaGetErrorString(error));   \
        exit(1);                                                             \
    }                                                                        \
}
```

```
void checkResult(float *hostRef, float *gpuRef, const int N) {
    double epsilon = 1.0E-8;
    bool match = 1;
    for (int i=0; i<N; i++) {
        if (abs(hostRef[i] - gpuRef[i]) > epsilon) {
            match = 0;
            printf("Arrays do not match!\n");
            printf("host %5.2f gpu %5.2f at current %d\n",hostRef[i],gpuRef[i],i);
            break;
        }
    }

    if (match) printf("Arrays match.\n\n");
}

void initialData(float *ip,int size) {
    // generate different seed for random number
    time_t t;
    srand((unsigned) time(&t));

    for (int i=0; i<size; i++) {
        ip[i] = (float)( rand() & 0xFF )/10.0f;
    }
}

void sumArraysOnHost(float *A, float *B, float *C, const int N) {
    for (int idx=0; idx<N; idx++)
        C[idx] = A[idx] + B[idx];
}

__global__ void sumArraysOnGPU(float *A, float *B, float *C) {
    int i = threadIdx.x;
    C[i] = A[i] + B[i];
}

int main(int argc, char **argv) {
    printf("%s Starting...\n", argv[0]);

    // set up device
    int dev = 0;
    cudaSetDevice(dev);

    // set up data size of vectors
    int nElem = 32;
    printf("Vector size %d\n", nElem);

    // malloc host memory
    size_t nBytes = nElem * sizeof(float);

    float *h_A, *h_B, *hostRef, *gpuRef;
    h_A     = (float *)malloc(nBytes);
    h_B     = (float *)malloc(nBytes);
    hostRef = (float *)malloc(nBytes);
    gpuRef  = (float *)malloc(nBytes);
```

continues

LISTING 2-4 *(continued)*

```
// initialize data at host side
initialData(h_A, nElem);
initialData(h_B, nElem);

memset(hostRef, 0, nBytes);
memset(gpuRef,  0, nBytes);

// malloc device global memory
float *d_A, *d_B, *d_C;
cudaMalloc((float**)&d_A, nBytes);
cudaMalloc((float**)&d_B, nBytes);
cudaMalloc((float**)&d_C, nBytes);

// transfer data from host to device
cudaMemcpy(d_A, h_A, nBytes, cudaMemcpyHostToDevice);
cudaMemcpy(d_B, h_B, nBytes, cudaMemcpyHostToDevice);

// invoke kernel at host side
dim3 block (nElem);
dim3 grid  (nElem/block.x);

sumArraysOnGPU<<< grid, block  >>>(d_A, d_B, d_C);
printf("Execution configuration <<<%d, %d>>>\n",grid.x,block.x);

// copy kernel result back to host side
cudaMemcpy(gpuRef, d_C, nBytes, cudaMemcpyDeviceToHost);

// add vector at host side for result checks
sumArraysOnHost(h_A, h_B, hostRef, nElem);

// check device results
checkResult(hostRef, gpuRef, nElem);

// free device global memory
cudaFree(d_A);
cudaFree(d_B);
cudaFree(d_C);

// free host memory
free(h_A);
free(h_B);
free(hostRef);
free(gpuRef);

return(0);
}
```

In this code, the vector size was set to 32 as follows:

```
int nElem = 32;
```

The execution configuration was set to one block, containing 32 elements as follows:

```
dim3 block (nElem);
dim3 grid  (nElem/block.x);
```

Compile and execute this code with the following command:

```
$ nvcc sumArraysOnGPU-small-case.cu -o addvector
$ ./addvector
```

The system reports the result as follows:

```
./addvector Starting...
Vector size 32
Execution configuration <<<1, 32>>>
Arrays match.
```

If you redefine the execution configuration to 32 blocks, and each block has only one element as follows:

```
dim3 block (1);
dim3 grid  (nElem);
```

then you will need to modify the kernel function sumArraysOnGPU in Listing 2-4 to replace

```
int i - threadIdx.x;
```

with

```
int i = blockIdx.x;
```

For the general case, you can calculate the unique index of global data access for a given thread based on the 1D grid and block information as follows:

```
__global__ void sumArraysOnGPU(float *A, float *B, float *C) {
        int i = blockIdx.x * blockDim.x + threadIdx.x;
        C[i] = A[i] + B[i];
}
```

You should make these changes for the general case to guarantee correct results are reported.

TIMING YOUR KERNEL

Knowing how long a kernel takes to execute is helpful and critical during the performance turning of kernels. There are several ways to measure kernel performance. The simplest method is to use either a CPU timer or a GPU timer to measure kernel executions from the host side. In this section you will build a CPU timer, as well as learn to measure execution time using the NVIDIA profiler. Chapter 6 will teach you how to use CUDA-specific timing routines.

Timing with CPU Timer

A CPU timer can be created by using the `gettimeofday` system call to get the system's wall-clock time, which returns the number of seconds since the epoch. You need to include the `sys/time.h` header file, as shown in Listing 2-5.

```
double cpuSecond() {
    struct timeval tp;
    gettimeofday(&tp,NULL);
    return ((double)tp.tv_sec + (double)tp.tv_usec*1.e-6);
}
```

You can measure your kernel with `cpuSecond` in the following way:

```
double iStart = cpuSecond();
kernel_name<<<grid, block>>>(argument list);
cudaDeviceSynchronize();
double iElaps = cpuSecond() - iStart;
```

Because a kernel call is asynchronous with respect to the host, you need to use `cudaDeviceSynchronize` to wait for all GPU threads to complete. The variable `iElaps` reports the time spent as if you had measured kernel execution with your wristwatch (in seconds).

Now test a big vector with 16M elements by setting the size of the data set as follows:

```
int nElem = 1<<24;
```

You need to modify the kernel for GPU scalability by calculating a row-major array index `i` using the block and thread indices, and by adding a test (`i < N`) that checks for those indices that may exceed array bounds, as follows:

```
__global__ void sumArraysOnGPU(float *A, float *B, float *C, const int N) {
    int i = blockIdx.x * blockDim.x + threadIdx.x;
    if (i < N) C[i] = A[i] + B[i];
}
```

With these changes, you are ready to measure the kernel using different execution configurations. To handle the case where the total number of threads created is larger than the total number of vector elements, you need to restrict your kernel from illegal global memory access, as shown in Figure 2-7.

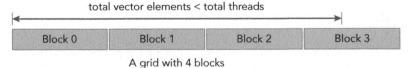

A grid with 4 blocks

FIGURE 2-7

Listing 2-5 shows you how to measure the vector addition kernel with the CPU timer in the `main` function.

LISTING 2-5: Measuring the vector summation kernel (sumArraysOnGPU-timer.cu)

```
#include <cuda_runtime.h>
#include <stdio.h>
#include <sys/time.h>

int main(int argc, char **argv) {
    printf("%s Starting...\n", argv[0]);

    // set up device
    int dev = 0;
    cudaDeviceProp deviceProp;
    CHECK(cudaGetDeviceProperties(&deviceProp, dev));
    printf("Using Device %d: %s\n", dev, deviceProp.name);
    CHECK(cudaSetDevice(dev));

    // set up date size of vectors
    int nElem = 1<<24;
    printf("Vector size %d\n", nElem);

    // malloc host memory
    size_t nBytes = nElem * sizeof(float);

    float *h_A, *h_B, *hostRef, *gpuRef;
    h_A     = (float *)malloc(nBytes);
    h_B     = (float *)malloc(nBytes);
    hostRef = (float *)malloc(nBytes);
    gpuRef  = (float *)malloc(nBytes);

    double iStart, iElaps;

    // initialize data at host side
    iStart = cpuSecond();
    initialData (h_A, nElem);
    initialData (h_B, nElem);
    iElaps = cpuSecond() - iStart;

    memset(hostRef, 0, nBytes);
    memset(gpuRef,  0, nBytes);

    // add vector at host side for result checks
    iStart = cpuSecond();
    sumArraysOnHost (h_A, h_B, hostRef, nElem);
    iElaps = cpuSecond() - iStart;

    // malloc device global memory
    float *d_A, *d_B, *d_C;
    cudaMalloc((float**)&d_A, nBytes);
    cudaMalloc((float**)&d_B, nBytes);
    cudaMalloc((float**)&d_C, nBytes);
```

continues

LISTING 2-5 *(continued)*

```
    // transfer data from host to device
    cudaMemcpy(d_A, h_A, nBytes, cudaMemcpyHostToDevice);
    cudaMemcpy(d_B, h_B, nBytes, cudaMemcpyHostToDevice);

    // invoke kernel at host side
    int iLen = 1024;
    dim3 block (iLen);
    dim3 grid  ((nElem+block.x-1)/block.x);

    iStart = cpuSecond();
    sumArraysOnGPU <<<grid, block>>>(d_A, d_B, d_C,nElem);
    cudaDeviceSynchronize();
    iElaps = cpuSecond() - iStart;
    printf("sumArraysOnGPU <<<%d,%d>>> Time elapsed %f" \
      "sec\n", grid.x, block.x, iElaps);

    // copy kernel result back to host side
    cudaMemcpy(gpuRef, d_C, nBytes, cudaMemcpyDeviceToHost);

    // check device results
    checkResult(hostRef, gpuRef, nElem);

    // free device global memory
    cudaFree(d_A);
    cudaFree(d_B);
    cudaFree(d_C);

    // free host memory
    free(h_A);
    free(h_B);
    free(hostRef);
    free(gpuRef);

    return(0);
}
```

The default execution configuration is set as a 1D grid that contains 16,384 blocks, and each block has 1,024 threads. Compile and run it with the following command:

```
$ nvcc sumArraysOnGPU-timer.cu -o sumArraysOnGPU-timer
$ ./sumArraysOnGPU-timer
```

Testing on an Intel Sandy Bridge-based system, the example from Listing 2-5 reports that GPU vector addition is 3.86 times faster than CPU vector addition.

```
./sumArraysOnGPU-timer Starting...
Using Device 0: Tesla M2070
Vector size 16777216
sumArraysOnGPU <<<16384, 1024>>>  Time elapsed 0.002456 sec
Arrays match.
```

Reducing the block dimension to 512 leads to 32,768 blocks being created. With this new configuration, the performance of this kernel improves 1.19 times.

```
sumArraysOnGPU <<<32768, 512>>>   Time elapsed 0.002058 sec
```

If you further reduce the block dimension to 256, the system reports the following error message, indicating that the total number of blocks exceeds the limit of the 1D grid.

```
./sumArraysOnGPU-timer Starting...
Using Device 0: Tesla M2070
Vector size 16777216
sumArraysOnGPU <<<65536, 256>>>   Time elapsed 0.000183 sec
Error: sumArraysOnGPU-timer.cu:153, code:9, reason: invalid configuration argument
```

KNOW YOUR LIMITATIONS

A key concept to understand while tweaking the execution configuration is the limitations on grid and block dimensions. The maximum size at each level of the thread hierarchy is device dependent.

CUDA provides the ability to query the GPU for these limits. More information about this topic is covered in the "Managing Devices" section of this chapter.

For Fermi devices, the maximum number of threads per block is 1,024, and the maximum grid dimension for each x, y, and z dimension is 65,535.

Timing with nvprof

Since CUDA 5.0, a command-line profiling tool, called nvprof, is available to help you to collect timeline information from your application's CPU and GPU activity, including kernel execution, memory transfers, and CUDA API calls. Its usage is shown here.

```
$ nvprof [nvprof_args] <application> [application_args]
```

More information about nvprof options can be found by using the following command:

```
$ nvprof --help
```

You can use nvprof to measure your kernel as follows:

```
$ nvprof ./sumArraysOnGPU-timer
```

The output reported by nvprof varies based on the type of GPU you are using. The following report was collected on a Tesla GPU:

```
./sumArraysOnGPU-timer Starting...
Using Device 0: Tesla M2070
==17770== NVPROF is profiling process 17770, command: ./sumArraysOnGPU-timer
Vector size 16777216
sumArraysOnGPU <<<16384, 1024>>>   Time elapsed 0.003266 sec
Arrays match.
```

```
==17770== Profiling application: ./sumArraysOnGPU-timer
==17770== Profiling result:
Time(%)      Time  Calls       Avg       Min       Max  Name
 70.35%  52.667ms      3  17.556ms  17.415ms  17.800ms  [CUDA memcpy HtoD]
 25.77%  19.291ms      1  19.291ms  19.291ms  19.291ms  [CUDA memcpy DtoH]
  3.88%  2.9024ms      1  2.9024ms  2.9024ms  2.9024ms  sumArraysOnGPU
(float*, float*, int)
```

The first half of the message contains output from the program, and the second half contains output from nvprof. Note that the CPU timer reported the elapsed kernel time as 3.26 milliseconds, and nvprof reported the elapsed kernel time as 2.90 milliseconds. For this case, the nvprof result is more accurate than the host-side timing result, because the time measured with the CPU timer included overhead from nvprof.

nvprof is a powerful tool to help you understand where time is being spent in your application. Notice that in this example, data transfer between the host and device takes more time than the kernel execution. A timeline view, as depicted in Figure 2-8 (not drawn to scale), shows time spent in CPU, time spent in data transfer, and time spent computing on the GPU.

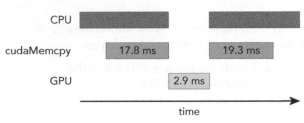

FIGURE 2-8

For HPC workloads, it is important to understand the compute to communication ratio in a program. If your application spends more time computing than transferring data, then it may be possible to overlap these operations and completely hide the latency associated with transferring data. If your application spends less time computing than transferring data, it is important to minimize the transfer between the host and device. In Chapter 6, you will learn how to overlap computation with communication using CUDA streams and events.

COMPARING APP PERFORMANCE TO MAXIMIZE THEORETICAL LIMITS

While performing application optimization, it is important to determine how your application compares to theoretical limits. Counters collected from nvprof can help you derive instruction and memory throughput for your application. If you compare application measured values to theoretical peak values, you can determine if your application is limited by arithmetic or by memory bandwidth. Theoretical ratios can be derived as follows using Tesla K10 as an example:

➤ **Tesla K10 Peak Single Precision FLOPS:**

745 MHz core clock * 2 GPUs/board * (8 multiprocessors * 192 fp32 cores/multiprocessor) * 2 ops/cycle = 4.58 TFLOPS

➤ **Tesla K10 Peak Memory Bandwidth:**

2 GPUs/board * 256 bit * 2500 MHz mem-clock * 2 DDR / 8 bits/byte = 320 GB/s

➤ **Ratio of instruction:bytes:**

4.58 TFLOPS / 320 GB/s yields 13.6 instructions:1 byte

For Tesla K10, if your application issues more than 13.6 instructions for every byte accessed, then your application is bound by arithmetic performance. Most HPC workloads are bound by memory bandwidth.

ORGANIZING PARALLEL THREADS

You have seen from the preceding examples that if you properly organize threads using the right grid and block size, it can make a big impact on kernel performance. In the example of vector addition, you adjusted the block size for optimal performance, and the grid size was calculated based on the block size and the vector data size.

You are now going to examine this issue in more depth through a matrix addition example. For matrix operations, a natural approach is to use a layout that contains a 2D grid with 2D blocks to organize the threads in your kernel. You will see that a naive approach will not yield the best performance. You are going to learn more about grid and block heuristics using the following layouts for matrix addition:

➤ 2D grid with 2D blocks

➤ 1D grid with 1D blocks

➤ 2D grid with 1D blocks

Indexing Matrices with Blocks and Threads

Typically, a matrix is stored linearly in global memory with a row-major approach. Figure 2-9 illustrates a small case for an 8 x 6 matrix.

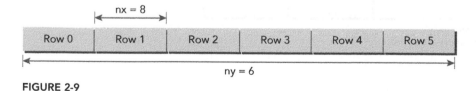

FIGURE 2-9

In a matrix addition kernel, a thread is usually assigned one data element to process. Accessing the assigned data from global memory using block and thread index is the first issue you need to solve. Typically, there are three kinds of indices for a 2D case you need to manage:

➤ Thread and block index

➤ Coordinate of a given point in the matrix

➤ Offset in linear global memory

For a given thread, you can obtain the offset in global memory from the block and thread index by first mapping the thread and block index to coordinates in the matrix, then mapping those matrix coordinates to a global memory location.

In the first step, you can map the thread and block index to the coordinate of a matrix with the following formula:

```
ix = threadIdx.x + blockIdx.x * blockDim.x
iy = threadIdx.y + blockIdx.y * blockDim.y
```

In the second step, you can map a matrix coordinate to a global memory location/index with the following formula:

```
idx = iy * nx + ix
```

Figure 2-10 illustrates the corresponding relationship among block and thread indices, matrix coordinates, and linear global memory indices.

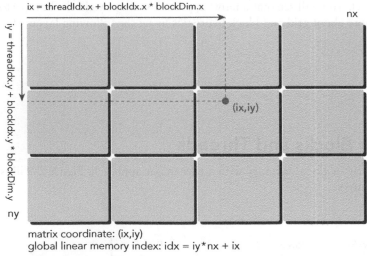

matrix coordinate: (ix,iy)
global linear memory index: idx = iy*nx + ix

FIGURE 2-10

The function `printThreadInfo` is used to print out the following information about each thread:

➤ Thread index

➤ Block index

➤ Matrix coordinate

➤ Global linear memory offset

➤ Value of corresponding elements

Compile and run the program with the following command:

```
$ nvcc -arch=sm_20 checkThreadIndex.cu -o checkIndex
$ ./checkIndex
```

You have the following information reported for each thread:

```
thread_id (2,1) block_id (1,0) coordinate (6,1) global index 14 ival 14
```

Figure 2-11 illustrates the relationship among these three indices.

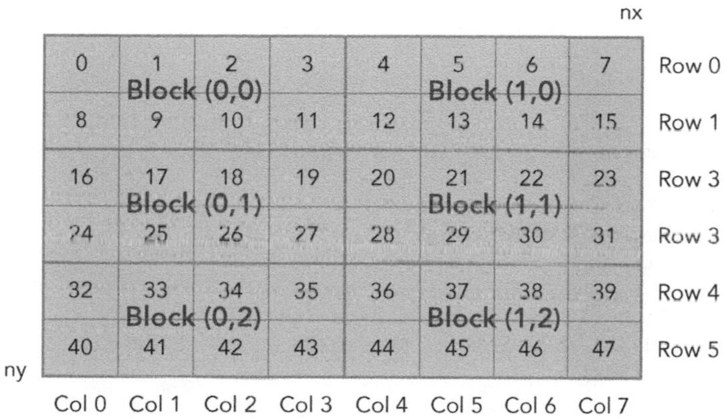

nx

0	1	2	3	4	5	6	7	Row 0
	Block (0,0)				Block (1,0)			
8	9	10	11	12	13	14	15	Row 1
16	17	18	19	20	21	22	23	Row 3
	Block (0,1)				Block (1,1)			
24	25	26	27	28	29	30	31	Row 3
32	33	34	35	36	37	38	39	Row 4
	Block (0,2)				Block (1,2)			
40	41	42	43	44	45	46	47	Row 5

ny

Col 0   Col 1   Col 2   Col 3   Col 4   Col 5   Col 6   Col 7

FIGURE 2-11

LISTING 2-6: Check block and thread index (checkThreadIndex.cu)

```c
#include <cuda_runtime.h>
#include <stdio.h>

#define CHECK(call)                                                          \
{                                                                            \
   const cudaError_t error = call;                                           \
   if (error != cudaSuccess)                                                 \
   {                                                                         \
      printf("Error: %s:%d, ", __FILE__, __LINE__);                          \
      printf("code:%d, reason: %s\n", error, cudaGetErrorString(error));  \
      exit(-10*error);                                                       \
```

continues

LISTING 2-6 *(continued)*

```
        }                                                                \
    }

    void initialInt(int *ip, int size) {
        for (int i=0; i<size; i++) {
            ip[i] = i;
        }
    }

    void printMatrix(int *C, const int nx, const int ny) {
        int *ic = C;
        printf("\nMatrix: (%d.%d)\n",nx,ny);
        for (int iy=0; iy<ny; iy++) {
            for (int ix=0; ix<nx; ix++) {
                printf("%3d",ic[ix]);

            }
            ic += nx;
            printf("\n");
        }
        printf("\n");
    }

    __global__ void printThreadIndex(int *A, const int nx, const int ny) {

        int ix = threadIdx.x + blockIdx.x * blockDim.x;
        int iy = threadIdx.y + blockIdx.y * blockDim.y;
        unsigned int idx = iy*nx + ix;

        printf("thread_id (%d,%d) block_id (%d,%d) coordinate (%d,%d) "
            "global index %2d ival %2d\n", threadIdx.x, threadIdx.y, blockIdx.x,
            blockIdx.y, ix, iy, idx, A[idx]);
    }

    int main(int argc, char **argv) {
        printf("%s Starting...\n", argv[0]);

        // get device information
        int dev = 0;
        cudaDeviceProp deviceProp;
        CHECK(cudaGetDeviceProperties(&deviceProp, dev));
        printf("Using Device %d: %s\n", dev, deviceProp.name);
        CHECK(cudaSetDevice(dev));

        // set matrix dimension
        int nx = 8;
        int ny = 6;
        int nxy = nx*ny;
        int nBytes = nxy * sizeof(float);
```

```
    // malloc host memory
    int *h_A;
    h_A = (int *)malloc(nBytes);

    // iniitialize host matrix with integer
    initialInt(h_A, nxy);
    printMatrix(h_A, nx, ny);

    // malloc device memory
    int *d_MatA;
    cudaMalloc((void **)&d_MatA, nBytes);

    // transfer data from host to device
    cudaMemcpy(d_MatA, h_A, nBytes, cudaMemcpyHostToDevice);

    // set up execution configuration
    dim3 block(4, 2);
    dim3 grid((nx+block.x-1)/block.x, (ny+block.y-1)/block.y);

    // invoke the kernel
    printThreadIndex <<< grid, block >>>(d_MatA, nx, ny);
    cudaDeviceSynchronize();

    // free host and devide memory
    cudaFree(d_MatA);
    tree(h_A);

    // reset device
    cudaDeviceReset();

    return (0);
}
```

Summing Matrices with a 2D Grid and 2D Blocks

In this section, you will write a matrix addition kernel that uses a 2D grid with 2D blocks. First, a validation host function should be written to verify that the matrix addition kernel produces the correct results:

```
void sumMatrixOnHost (float *A, float *B, float *C, const int nx, const int ny) {
    float *ia = A;
    float *ib = B;
    float *ic = C;

    for (int iy=0; iy<ny; iy++) {
        for (int ix=0; ix<nx; ix++) {
            ic[ix] = ia[ix] + ib[ix];
        }
        ia += nx; ib += nx; ic += nx;
    }
```

```
    }
```

Then, you create a new kernel to sum the matrix with a 2D thread block:

```
__global__ void sumMatrixOnGPU2D(float *MatA, float *MatB, float *MatC,
        int nx, int ny) {
    unsigned int ix = threadIdx.x + blockIdx.x * blockDim.x;
    unsigned int iy = threadIdx.y + blockIdx.y * blockDim.y;
    unsigned int idx = iy*nx + ix;

    if (ix < nx && iy < ny)
        MatC[idx] = MatA[idx] + MatB[idx];
}
```

The key to this kernel is the step mapping each thread from its thread index to the global linear memory index, as illustrated in Figure 2-12.

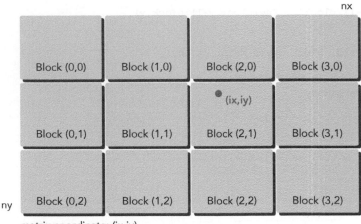

matrix coordinate: (ix,iy)
global linear memory index: idx = iy*nx + ix

FIGURE 2-12

Next, the matrix size can be set to 16,384 elements in each dimension as follows:

```
    int nx = 1<<14;
    int ny = 1<<14;
```

Then, the kernel execution configuration can be set to use a 2D grid and 2D blocks as follows:

```
    int dimx = 32;
    int dimy = 32;
    dim3 block(dimx, dimy);
    dim3 grid((nx + block.x - 1) / block.x, (ny + block.y - 1) / block.y);
```

Combine all the code together into the file sumMatrixOnGPU-2D-grid-2D-block.cu. The main function is shown in Listing 2-7.

LISTING 2-7: Matrix summation with a 2D grid and 2D blocks
(sumMatrixOnGPU-2D-grid-2D-block.cu)

```
int main(int argc, char **argv) {
    printf("%s Starting...\n", argv[0]);

    // set up device
    int dev = 0;
    cudaDeviceProp deviceProp;
    CHECK(cudaGetDeviceProperties(&deviceProp, dev));
    printf("Using Device %d: %s\n", dev, deviceProp.name);
    CHECK(cudaSetDevice(dev));

    // set up date size of matrix
    int nx = 1<<14;
    int ny = 1<<14;

    int nxy = nx*ny;
    int nBytes = nxy * sizeof(float);
    printf("Matrix size: nx %d ny %d\n",nx, ny);

    // malloc host memory
    float *h_A, *h_B, *hostRef, *gpuRef;
    h_A = (float *)malloc(nBytes);
    h_B = (float *)malloc(nBytes);
    hostRef = (float *)malloc(nBytes);
    gpuRef = (float *)malloc(nBytes);

    // initialize data at host side
    double iStart = cpuSecond();
    initialData (h_A, nxy);
    initialData (h_B, nxy);
    double iElaps = cpuSecond() - iStart;

    memset(hostRef, 0, nBytes);
    memset(gpuRef, 0, nBytes);

    // add matrix at host side for result checks
    iStart = cpuSecond();
    sumMatrixOnHost (h_A, h_B, hostRef, nx,ny);
    iElaps = cpuSecond() - iStart;

    // malloc device global memory
    float *d_MatA, *d_MatB, *d_MatC;
    cudaMalloc((void **)&d_MatA, nBytes);
    cudaMalloc((void **)&d_MatB, nBytes);
    cudaMalloc((void **)&d_MatC, nBytes);

    // transfer data from host to device
    cudaMemcpy(d_MatA, h_A, nBytes, cudaMemcpyHostToDevice);
    cudaMemcpy(d_MatB, h_B, nBytes, cudaMemcpyHostToDevice);
```

continues

LISTING 2-7 *(continued)*

```
        // invoke kernel at host side
        int dimx = 32;
        int dimy = 32;
        dim3 block(dimx, dimy);
        dim3 grid((nx+block.x-1)/block.x, (ny+block.y-1)/block.y);

        iStart = cpuSecond();
        sumMatrixOnGPU2D <<< grid, block >>>(d_MatA, d_MatB, d_MatC, nx, ny);
        cudaDeviceSynchronize();
        iElaps = cpuSecond() - iStart;
        printf("sumMatrixOnGPU2D <<<(%d,%d), (%d,%d)>>> elapsed %f sec\n", grid.x,
         grid.y, block.x, block.y, iElaps);

        // copy kernel result back to host side
        cudaMemcpy(gpuRef, d_MatC, nBytes, cudaMemcpyDeviceToHost);

        // check device results
        checkResult(hostRef, gpuRef, nxy);

        // free device global memory
        cudaFree(d_MatA);
        cudaFree(d_MatB);
        cudaFree(d_MatC);

        // free host memory
        free(h_A);
        free(h_B);
        free(hostRef);
        free(gpuRef);

        // reset device
        cudaDeviceReset();

        return (0);
    }
```

Compile and run this code with the following command:

```
$ nvcc -arch=sm_20 sumMatrixOnGPU-2D-grid-2D-block.cu -o matrix2D
$ ./matrix2D
```

The result on a Tesla M2070 is:

```
./a.out Starting...
Using Device 0: Tesla M2070
Matrix size: nx 16384 ny 16384
sumMatrixOnGPU2D <<<(512,512), (32,32)>>> elapsed 0.060323 sec
Arrays match.
```

Next, alter the block dimensions to 32 x 16 and recompile and rerun. The kernel becomes nearly two times faster:

```
sumMatrixOnGPU2D <<<(512,1024), (32,16)>>> elapsed 0.038041 sec
```

You may wonder why the kernel performance nearly doubled just by altering the execution configuration. Intuitively, you may reason that the second configuration has twice as many blocks as the first configuration, so there is twice as much parallelism. The intuition is right. However, if you further reduce the block size to 16 x 16, you have quadrupled the number of blocks compared to the first configuration. The result of this configuration, as shown below, is better than the first but worse than the second.

```
sumMatrixOnGPU2D <<<  (1024,1024), (16,16)  >>> elapsed 0.045535 sec
```

Table 2-3 summarizes the performance for different execution configurations. From the results, you can see that increasing the number of blocks does not necessarily always increase the performance of the kernel. In Chapter 3, you will learn why different execution configurations impact kernel performance.

TABLE 2-3: Matrix Summation with Different Execution Configuration

KERNEL CONFIGURATION	KERNEL ELAPSED TIME	BLOCK NUMBER
(32,32)	0.060323 sec	512 x 512
(32,16)	0.038041 sec	512 x 1024
(16,16)	0.045535 sec	1024 x 1024

Summing Matrices with a 1D Grid and 1D Blocks

To use a 1D grid with 1D blocks, you need to write a new kernel in which each thread processes ny data elements, as shown in Figure 2-13.

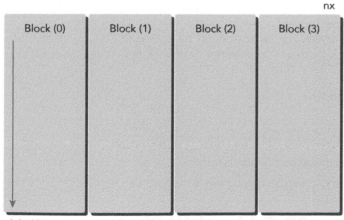

global linear memory index: idx = iy*nx + ix

FIGURE 2-13

Because each thread in the new kernel handles ny elements, the mapping from thread and block index to the global linear memory index will be different compared to the matrix sum kernel that used a 2D grid and 2D blocks. Because a 1D block layout is used for this kernel launch, only threadIdx.x is useful and a loop inside the kernel is used to handle ny elements in each thread.

```
__global__ void sumMatrixOnGPU1D(float *MatA, float *MatB, float *MatC,
        int nx, int ny) {
    unsigned int ix = threadIdx.x + blockIdx.x * blockDim.x;
    if (ix < nx ) {
        for (int iy=0; iy<ny; iy++) {
            int idx = iy*nx + ix;
            MatC[idx] = MatA[idx] + MatB[idx];
        }
    }
}
```

Next, set the 1D grid and block configuration as follows:

```
dim3 block(32,1);
dim3 grid((nx+block.x-1)/block.x,1);
```

Invoke the kernel with the 1D configuration as follows:

```
sumMatrixOnGPU1D <<< grid, block >>>(d_MatA, d_MatB, d_MatC, nx, ny);
```

Replace sections from Listing 2-7 with these changes using a 1D grid and 1D blocks, save it into the file sumMatrixOnGPU-1D-grid-1D-block.cu, and compile and run it with the following command:

```
$ nvcc -arch=sm_20 sumMatrixOnGPU-1D-grid-1D-block.cu -o matrix1D
$ ./matrix1D
```

The result shows that performance is basically the same compared to the result using a 2D grid and block (32 x 32) configuration.

```
Starting...
Using Device 0: Tesla M2070
Matrix size: nx 16384 ny 16384
sumMatrixOnGPU1D <<<(512,1), (32,1)>>> elapsed 0.061352 sec
Arrays match.
```

Next, increase the block size as follows:

```
dim3 block(128,1);
dim3 grid((nx+block.x-1)/block.x,1);
```

Recompile and run it. You will see the kernel becomes faster.

```
sumMatrixOnGPU1D <<<(128,1),(128,1)>>> elapsed 0.044701 sec
```

Summing Matrices with a 2D Grid and 1D Blocks

When using a 2D grid that contains 1D blocks, each thread takes care of only one data element and the second dimension of grid equals ny, as shown in Figure 2-14.

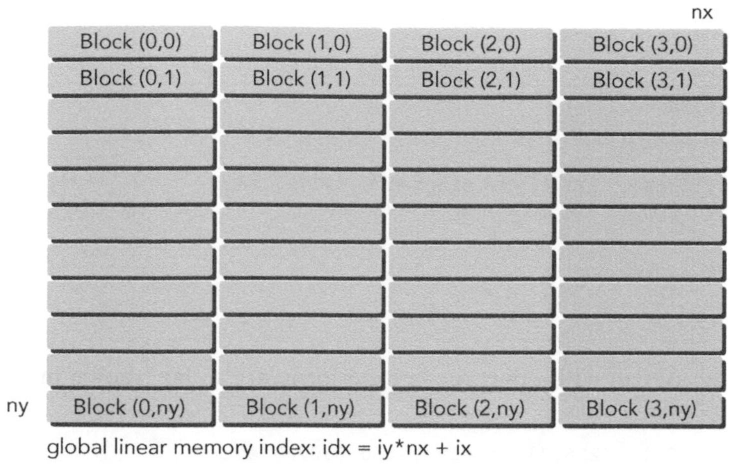

global linear memory index: idx = iy*nx + ix

FIGURE 2-14

This can be viewed as a special case of a 2D grid with 2D blocks, where the second dimension of the block is 1. Therefore, the mapping from block and thread index to the matrix coordinate becomes:

```
ix = threadIdx.x + blockIdx.x * blockDim.x;
iy = blockIdx.y;
```

The mapping from matrix coordinates to global linear memory offsets stays the same. The new kernel is shown here:

```
__global__ void sumMatrixOnGPUMix(float *MatA, float *MatB, float *MatC,
    int nx, int ny) {
  unsigned int ix = threadIdx.x + blockIdx.x * blockDim.x;
  unsigned int iy = blockIdx.y;
  unsigned int idx = iy*nx + ix;

  if (ix < nx && iy < ny)
    MatC[idx] = MatA[idx] + MatB[idx];
}
```

Note that the 2D kernel sumMatrixOnGPU2D works for this execution configuration also. The only merit to writing the new kernel is that you save one integer multiplication and one integer addition operation for each thread.

Set the block dimension to 32 and calculate the grid size based on it:

```
dim3 block(32);
dim3 grid((nx + block.x - 1) / block.x,ny);
```

Invoke the kernel as follows:

```
sumMatrixOnGPUMix <<< grid, block >>>(d_MatA, d_MatB, d_MatC, nx, ny);
```

Substitute these changes from Listing 2-7, and save it into sumMatrixOnGPU-2D-grid-1D-block.cu. Compile and run it with the following command:

```
$ nvcc -arch=sm_20 sumMatrixOnGPU-2D-grid-1D-block.cu -o mat2D1D
$ ./mat2D1D
```

The result is:

```
./a.out Starting...
Using Device 0: Tesla M2070
Matrix size nx 16384 ny 16384
Matrix initialization
elapsed 0.397689 sec
sumMatrixOnGPUMix <<<(512,16384), (32,1)>>> elapsed 0.073727 sec
Arrays match.
```

Now, increase the block size to 256 as follows:

```
dim3 block(256);
```

Then recompile and run it, and the system will report the best performance so far (shown in Table 2-4):

```
sumMatrixOnGPUMix <<<(64,16384), (256,1)>>> elapsed 0.030765 sec
```

TABLE 2-4: Results Comparison of Different Kernel Implementations

KERNEL	EXECUTION CONFIGURE	TIME ELAPSED
sumMatrixOnGPU2D	(512,1024), (32,16)	0.038041
sumMatrixOnGPU1D	(128,1), (128,1)	0.044701
sumMatrixOnGPUMix	(64,16384), (256,1)	0.030765

From the matrix addition examples, you can see several things:

➤ Changing execution configurations affects performance.

➤ A naive kernel implementation does not generally yield the best performance.

➤ For a given kernel, trying different grid and block dimensions may yield better performance.

In Chapter 3, you will learn more about what causes these issues from a hardware perspective.

MANAGING DEVICES

NVIDIA provides several means by which you can query and manage GPU devices. It is important to learn how to query this information, because you can use it to help set the kernel execution configuration at runtime.

You will learn the following two basic and powerful means to query and manage GPU devices in this section:

➤ The CUDA runtime API functions

➤ The NVIDIA Systems Management Interface (nvidia-smi) command-line utility

Using the Runtime API to Query GPU Information

Many functions are available in the CUDA runtime API to help you manage devices. You can use the following function to query all information about GPU devices:

```
cudaError_t cudaGetDeviceProperties(cudaDeviceProp* prop, int device);
```

The properties of the GPU device are returned in the cudaDeviceProp structure, whose contents can be found online at: http://docs.nvidia.com/cuda/cuda-runtime-api/index.html#structcudaDeviceProp.

Listing 2-8 provides an example that queries generally useful properties of general interest. Compile and run it with the following command:

```
$ nvcc checkDeviceInfor.cu -o checkDeviceInfor
$ ./checkDeviceInfor
```

Depending on your configuration, checkDeviceInfor will report different information on the installed devices. A sample output is below:

```
./checkDeviceInfor Starting...
Detected 2 CUDA Capable device(s)
Device 0: "Tesla M2070"
  CUDA Driver Version / Runtime Version          5.5 / 5.5
  CUDA Capability Major/Minor version number:    2.0
  Total amount of global memory:                 5.25 MBytes (5636554752 bytes)
  GPU Clock rate:                                1147 MHz (1.15 GHz)
  Memory Clock rate:                             1566 Mhz
  Memory Bus Width:                              384-bit
  L2 Cache Size:                                 786432 bytes
  Max Texture Dimension Size (x,y,z) 1D=(65536), 2D=(65536,65535), 3D=(2048,2048,2048)
  Max Layered Texture Size (dim) x layers 1D=(16384) x 2048, 2D=(16384,16384) x 2048
  Total amount of constant memory:               65536 bytes
  Total amount of shared memory per block:       49152 bytes
  Total number of registers available per block: 32768
  Warp size:                                     32
  Maximum number of threads per multiprocessor:  1536
  Maximum number of threads per block:           1024
  Maximum sizes of each dimension of a block:    1024 x 1024 x 64
  Maximum sizes of each dimension of a grid:     65535 x 65535 x 65535
  Maximum memory pitch:                          2147483647 bytes
```

LISTING 2-8: Query device information with the runtime API (checkDeviceInfor.cu)

```
#include <cuda_runtime.h>
#include <stdio.h>

int main(int argc, char **argv) {
    printf("%s Starting...\n", argv[0]);

    int deviceCount = 0;
    cudaError_t error_id = cudaGetDeviceCount(&deviceCount);
```

continues

LISTING 2-8 *(continued)*

```
if (error_id != cudaSuccess) {
    printf("cudaGetDeviceCount returned %d\n-> %s\n",
        (int)error_id, cudaGetErrorString(error_id));
    printf("Result = FAIL\n");
    exit(EXIT_FAILURE);
}

if (deviceCount == 0) {
    printf("There are no available device(s) that support CUDA\n");
} else {
    printf("Detected %d CUDA Capable device(s)\n", deviceCount);
}

int dev, driverVersion = 0, runtimeVersion = 0;

dev =0;
cudaSetDevice(dev);
cudaDeviceProp deviceProp;
cudaGetDeviceProperties(&deviceProp, dev);
printf("Device %d: \"%s\"\n", dev, deviceProp.name);

cudaDriverGetVersion(&driverVersion);
cudaRuntimeGetVersion(&runtimeVersion);
printf("  CUDA Driver Version / Runtime Version          %d.%d / %d.%d\n",
    driverVersion/1000, (driverVersion%100)/10,
    runtimeVersion/1000, (runtimeVersion%100)/10);
printf("  CUDA Capability Major/Minor version number:    %d.%d\n",
    deviceProp.major, deviceProp.minor);
printf("  Total amount of global memory:                 %.2f MBytes (%llu bytes)\n",
    (float)deviceProp.totalGlobalMem/(pow(1024.0,3)),
    (unsigned long long) deviceProp.totalGlobalMem);
printf("  GPU Clock rate:                                %.0f MHz (%0.2f GHz)\n",
    deviceProp.clockRate * 1e-3f, deviceProp.clockRate * 1e-6f);
printf("  Memory Clock rate:                             %.0f Mhz\n",
    deviceProp.memoryClockRate * 1e-3f);
printf("  Memory Bus Width:                              %d-bit\n",
    deviceProp.memoryBusWidth);
if (deviceProp.l2CacheSize) {
    printf("  L2 Cache Size:                             %d bytes\n",
        deviceProp.l2CacheSize);
}
printf("  Max Texture Dimension Size (x,y,z)             "
    "  1D=(%d), 2D=(%d,%d), 3D=(%d,%d,%d)\n",
    deviceProp.maxTexture1D    , deviceProp.maxTexture2D[0],
    deviceProp.maxTexture2D[1],
    deviceProp.maxTexture3D[0], deviceProp.maxTexture3D[1],
    deviceProp.maxTexture3D[2]);
printf("  Max Layered Texture Size (dim) x layers
1D=(%d) x %d, 2D=(%d,%d) x %d\n",
    deviceProp.maxTexture1DLayered[0], deviceProp.maxTexture1DLayered[1],
    deviceProp.maxTexture2DLayered[0], deviceProp.maxTexture2DLayered[1],
    deviceProp.maxTexture2DLayered[2]);
```

```
    printf("  Total amount of constant memory:              %lu bytes\n",
        deviceProp.totalConstMem);
    printf("  Total amount of shared memory per block:      %lu bytes\n",
        deviceProp.sharedMemPerBlock);
    printf("  Total number of registers available per block: %d\n",
        deviceProp.regsPerBlock);
    printf("  Warp size:                                    %d\n", deviceProp.warpSize);
    printf("  Maximum number of threads per multiprocessor: %d\n",
        deviceProp.maxThreadsPerMultiProcessor);
    printf("  Maximum number of threads per block:          %d\n",
        deviceProp.maxThreadsPerBlock);
    printf("  Maximum sizes of each dimension of a block:   %d x %d x %d\n",
        deviceProp.maxThreadsDim[0],
        deviceProp.maxThreadsDim[1],
        deviceProp.maxThreadsDim[2]);
    printf("  Maximum sizes of each dimension of a grid:    %d x %d x %d\n",
        deviceProp.maxGridSize[0],
        deviceProp.maxGridSize[1],
        deviceProp.maxGridSize[2]);
    printf("  Maximum memory pitch:                         %lu bytes\n", deviceProp.
memPitch);

    exit(EXIT_SUCCESS);
}
```

Determining the Best GPU

Some systems support multiple GPUs. In the case where each GPU is different, it may be important to select the best GPU to run your kernel. One way to identify the most computationally capable GPU is by the number of multiprocessors it contains. If you have a multi-GPU system, you can use the following code to select the most computationally capable device:

```
int numDevices = 0;
cudaGetDeviceCount(&numDevices);
if (numDevices > 1) {
    int maxMultiprocessors = 0, maxDevice = 0;
    for (int device=0; device<numDevices; device++) {
        cudaDeviceProp props;
        cudaGetDeviceProperties(&props, device);
        if (maxMultiprocessors < props.multiProcessorCount) {
            maxMultiprocessors = props.multiProcessorCount;
            maxDevice = device;
        }
    }
    cudaSetDevice(maxDevice);
}
```

Using nvidia-smi to Query GPU Information

The command-line tool nvidia-smi assists you with managing and monitoring GPU devices, and allows you to query and modify device state.

You can invoke `nvidia-smi` from the command line. For example, to determine how many GPUs are installed on a system and the device ID for each GPU, use the following command:

```
$ nvidia-smi -L
GPU 0: Tesla M2070 (UUID: GPU-68df8aec-e85c-9934-2b81-0c9e689a43a7)
GPU 1: Tesla M2070 (UUID: GPU-382f23c1-5160-01e2-3291-ff9628930b70)
```

You can use the following command to report details about GPU 0:

```
$ nvidia-smi -q -i 0
```

You can also reduce the amount of information `nvidia-smi` reports using one of following display options:

➤ MEMORY

➤ UTILIZATION

➤ ECC

➤ TEMPERATURE

➤ POWER

➤ CLOCK

➤ COMPUTE

➤ PIDS

➤ PERFORMANCE

➤ SUPPORTED_CLOCKS

➤ PAGE_RETIREMENT

➤ ACCOUNTING

For example, to display device memory information only, use the following command:

```
$ nvidia-smi -q -i 0 -d MEMORY | tail -n 5
    Memory Usage
        Total              : 5375 MB
        Used               : 9 MB
        Free               : 5366 MB
```

To display device utilization information only, use the following command:

```
$ nvidia-smi -q -i 0 -d UTILIZATION | tail -n 4
    Utilization
        Gpu                : 0 %
        Memory             : 0 %
```

Setting Devices at Runtime

Systems that support multiple GPUs are common. For a system that has N GPUs installed, the device IDs reported by `nvidia-smi` are labeled 0 through N-1. Using the environment variable

CUDA_VISIBLE_DEVICES, it is possible for you to specify which GPUs to use at runtime without having to change your application.

You can set the environment variable CUDA_VISIBLE_DEVICES=2 at runtime. The nvidia driver masks off the other GPUs so that device 2 appears to your application as device 0.

You can also use CUDA_VISIBLE_DEVICES to specify multiple devices. For example, if you want to test GPUs 2 and 3, then set CUDA_VISIBLE_DEVICES=2,3. Then, at runtime, the nvidia driver will only use device IDs 2 and 3 and will map their device IDs to 0 and 1, respectively.

SUMMARY

Compared with parallel programming in C, the thread hierarchy in CUDA programming is a distinguishing feature. By exposing an abstract two-level thread hierarchy, CUDA gives you the ability to control a massively parallel environment. Through the examples in this chapter, you also have seen that grid and block dimensions have a big impact on kernel performance.

For a given problem, you have several options to implement the kernel and different configurations to execute the kernel. Usually, the naive implementation does not yield the best performance. Therefore, learning how to organize threads is one of the central practices of CUDA programming. The best way to understand grid and block heuristics is to write programs that extend your skills and knowledge through trial-and-error.

Grids and blocks represent a logical view of the thread layout for kernel execution. In Chapter 3, you will study the same issues from a different perspective: the hardware view.

CHAPTER 2 EXERCISES

1. Using the program sumArraysOnGPU-timer.cu, set the block.x = 1023. Recompile and run it. Compare the result with the execution configuration of block.x = 1024. Try to explain the difference and the reason.

2. Refer to sumArraysOnGPU-timer.cu, and let block.x = 256. Make a new kernel to let each thread handle two elements. Compare the results with other execution configurations.

3. Refer to sumMatrixOnGPU-2D-grid-2D-block.cu. Adapt it to integer matrix addition. Find the best execution configuration.

4. Refer to sumMatrixOnGPU-2D-grid-1D-block.cu. Make a new kernel to let each thread handle two elements. Find the best execution configuration.

5. Using checkDeviceInfor.cu, find the maximum size supported by your system for each grid and block dimension.

3

CUDA Execution Model

WHAT'S IN THIS CHAPTER?

➤ Developing kernels with a profile-driven approach

➤ Understanding the nature of warp execution

➤ Exposing more parallelism to the GPU

➤ Mastering grid and block configuration heuristics

➤ Learning various CUDA performance metrics and events

➤ Probing dynamic parallelism and nested execution

> **CODE DOWNLOAD** *The wrox.com code downloads for this chapter are found at* www.wrox.com/go/procudac *on the Download Code tab. The code is in the Chapter 3 download and individually named according to the names throughout the chapter.*

Through the exercises in the last chapter, you learned how to organize threads into grids and blocks to deliver the best performance. While you can find the best execution configuration through trial-and-error, you might be left wondering why the selected execution configuration outperforms others. You might want to know if there are some guidelines for selecting grid and block configurations. This chapter will answer those questions and provide you with deeper insight into kernel launch configurations and performance profile information, but from a different angle: the hardware perspective.

INTRODUCING THE CUDA EXECUTION MODEL

In general, an execution model provides an operational view of how instructions are executed on a specific computing architecture. The CUDA execution model exposes an abstract view of the GPU parallel architecture, allowing you to reason about thread concurrency. In Chapter 2, you learned that the CUDA programming model exposes two primary abstractions: a memory hierarchy and a thread hierarchy that allow you to control the massively parallel GPU. Accordingly, the CUDA execution model provides insights that are useful for writing efficient code in terms of both instruction throughput and memory accesses.

You will focus on instruction throughput in this chapter and learn more about efficient memory accesses in Chapters 4 and 5.

GPU Architecture Overview

The GPU architecture is built around a scalable array of *Streaming Multiprocessors* (SM). GPU hardware parallelism is achieved through the replication of this architectural building block. Figure 3-1 illustrates the key components of a Fermi SM:

➤ CUDA Cores

➤ Shared Memory/L1 Cache

➤ Register File

➤ Load/Store Units

➤ Special Function Units

➤ Warp Scheduler

Each SM in a GPU is designed to support concurrent execution of hundreds of threads, and there are generally multiple SMs per GPU, so it is possible to have thousands of threads executing concurrently on a single GPU. When a kernel grid is launched, the thread blocks of that kernel grid are distributed among available SMs for execution. Once scheduled on an SM, the threads of a thread block execute concurrently only on that assigned SM. Multiple thread blocks may be assigned to the same SM at once and are scheduled based on the availability of SM resources. Instructions within a single thread are pipelined to leverage instruction-level parallelism, in addition to the thread-level parallelism you are already familiar with in CUDA.

CUDA employs a *Single Instruction Multiple Thread* (SIMT) architecture to manage and execute threads in groups of 32 called *warps*. All threads in a warp execute the same instruction at the same time. Each thread has its own instruction address counter and register state, and carries out the current instruction on its own data. Each SM partitions the thread blocks assigned to it into 32-thread warps that it then schedules for execution on available hardware resources.

The SIMT architecture is similar to the SIMD (*Single Instruction, Multiple Data*) architecture. Both SIMD and SIMT implement parallelism by broadcasting the same instruction to multiple execution units. A key difference is that SIMD requires that all vector elements in a vector execute together in a unified synchronous group, whereas SIMT allows multiple threads in the same warp to execute independently. Even though all threads in a warp start together at the same program address, it is possible for individual threads to have different behavior. SIMT enables you to write thread-level parallel code for independent, scalar threads, as well as data-parallel code for coordinated threads. The SIMT model includes three key features that SIMD does not:

➤ Each thread has its own instruction address counter.

➤ Each thread has its own register state.

➤ Each thread can have an independent execution path.

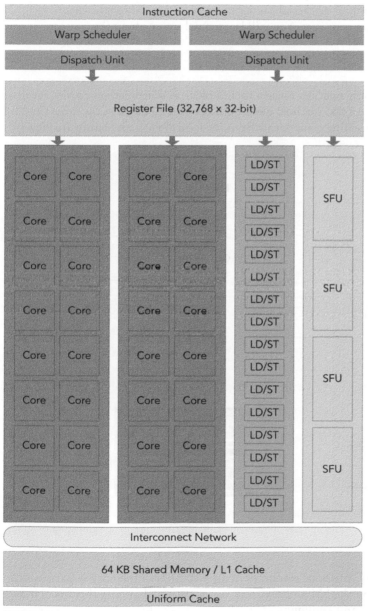

FIGURE 3-1

> **A MAGIC NUMBER: 32**
>
> The number 32 is a magic number in CUDA programming. It comes from hardware, and has a significant impact on the performance of software.
>
> Conceptually, you can think of it as the granularity of work processed simultaneously in SIMD fashion by an SM. Optimizing your workloads to fit within the boundaries of a warp (group of 32 threads) will generally lead to more efficient utilization of GPU compute resources. You will learn much more about this issue in subsequent chapters.

A thread block is scheduled on only one SM. Once a thread block is scheduled on an SM, it remains there until execution completes. An SM can hold more than one thread block at the same time. Figure 3-2 illustrates the corresponding components from the logical view and hardware view of CUDA programming.

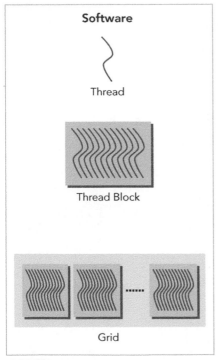
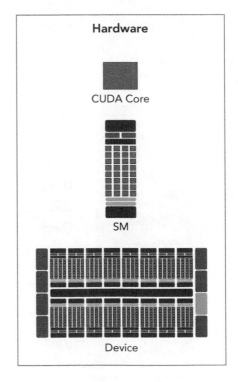

FIGURE 3-2

Shared memory and registers are precious resources in an SM. Shared memory is partitioned among thread blocks resident on the SM and registers are partitioned among threads. Threads in a thread block can cooperate and communicate with each other through these resources. While all threads in a thread block run logically in parallel, not all threads can execute physically at the same time. As a result, different threads in a thread block may make progress at a different pace.

Sharing data among parallel threads may cause a race condition: Multiple threads accessing the same data with an undefined ordering, which results in unpredictable program behavior. CUDA provides a means to synchronize threads within a thread block to ensure that all threads reach certain points in execution before making further progress. However, no primitives are provided for inter-block synchronization.

While warps within a thread block may be scheduled in any order, the number of active warps is limited by SM resources. When a warp idles for any reason (for example, waiting for values to be read from device memory), the SM is free to schedule another available warp from any thread block that is resident on the same SM. Switching between concurrent warps has no overhead because hardware resources are partitioned among all threads and blocks on an SM, so the state of the newly scheduled warp is already stored on the SM.

SM: THE HEART OF THE GPU ARCHITECTURE

The Streaming Multiprocessor (SM) is the heart of the GPU architecture. Registers and shared memory are scarce resources in the SM. CUDA partitions these resources among all threads resident on an SM. Therefore, these limited resources impose a strict restriction on the number of active warps in an SM, which corresponds to the amount of parallelism possible in an SM. Knowing some basic facts about the hardware components of an SM will help you organize threads and configure kernel execution to get the best performance.

In the next section, you will receive a brief tour of two different versions of NVIDIA GPU architecture: the Fermi and Kepler architectures. Special attention will be given to their hardware resources. You will learn about their hardware features through examples and exercises, and this will help you gain insights into improving kernel performance.

The Fermi Architecture

The Fermi architecture was the first complete GPU computing architecture to deliver the features required for the most demanding HPC applications. Fermi has been widely adopted for accelerating production workloads.

Figure 3-3 illustrates a logical block diagram of the Fermi architecture focused on GPU computing with graphics-specific components largely omitted. Fermi features up to 512 accelerator cores, called *CUDA cores*. Each CUDA core has a fully pipelined integer arithmetic logic unit (*ALU*) and a floating-point unit (*FPU*) that executes one integer or floating-point instruction per clock cycle. The CUDA cores are organized into 16 *streaming multiprocessors* (SM), each with 32 CUDA cores. Fermi has six 384-bit GDDR5 DRAM memory interfaces supporting up to a total of 6 GB of global on-board memory, a key compute resource for many applications. A host interface connects the GPU to the CPU via the PCI Express bus. The *GigaThread* engine (shown in orange on the left side of the diagram) is a global scheduler that distributes thread blocks to the SM warp schedulers.

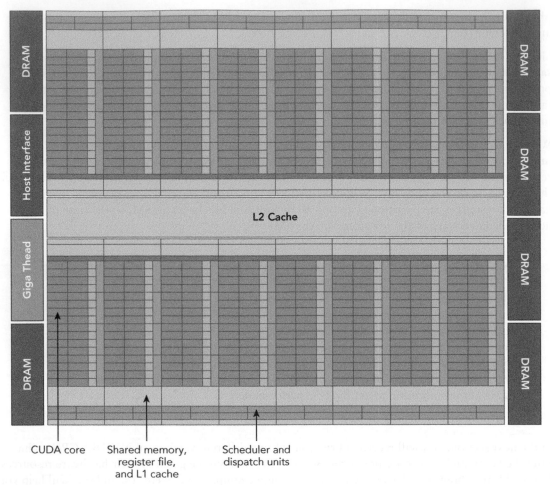

CUDA core   Shared memory,   Scheduler and
               register file,   dispatch units
               and L1 cache

FIGURE 3-3

Fermi includes a coherent 768 KB L2 cache, shared by all 16 SMs. Each SM in Figure 3-3 is represented by a vertical rectangular strip containing:

➤ Execution units (CUDA cores)

➤ Scheduler and dispatcher units that schedule warps

➤ Shared memory, the register file, and L1 cache

Each multiprocessor has 16 load/store units (shown in Figure 3-1), allowing source and destination addresses to be calculated for 16 threads (a half-warp) per clock cycle. Special function units (*SFUs*) execute intrinsic instructions such as sine, cosine, square root, and interpolation. Each SFU can execute one intrinsic instruction per thread per clock cycle.

Each SM features two *warp schedulers* and two *instruction dispatch units*. When a thread block is assigned to an SM, all threads in a thread block are divided into warps. The two warp schedulers select two warps and issue one instruction from each warp to a group of 16 CUDA cores, 16 load/store units, or 4 special function units (illustrated in Figure 3-4). The Fermi architecture, compute capability 2.x, can simultaneously handle 48 warps per SM for a total of 1,536 threads resident in a single SM at a time.

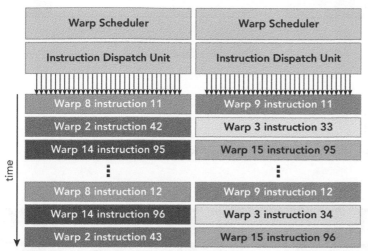

FIGURE 3-4

One key feature of Fermi is the 64 KB on-chip configurable memory, which is partitioned between shared memory and L1 cache. For many high-performance applications, shared memory is a key enabler for performance. Shared memory allows threads within a block to cooperate, facilitates extensive reuse of on-chip data, and greatly reduces off-chip traffic. CUDA provides a runtime API that can be used to adjust the amount of shared memory and L1 cache. Modifying the on-chip memory configuration can lead to performance improvements depending on the usage of shared memory or cache in a given kernel. This topic will be covered in more detail in Chapters 4 and 5.

Fermi also supports concurrent kernel execution: multiple kernels launched from the same application context executing on the same GPU at the same time. Concurrent kernel execution allows programs that execute a number of small kernels to fully utilize the GPU, as illustrated in Figure 3-5. Fermi allows up to 16 kernels to be run on the device at the same time. Concurrent kernel execution makes the GPU appear more like a MIMD architecture from the programmer's perspective.

The Kepler Architecture

The Kepler GPU architecture, released in the fall of 2012, is a fast and highly efficient, high-performance computing architecture. Kepler features make hybrid computing even more accessible to you. Figure 3-6 illustrates the Kepler K20X chip block diagram, containing 15 streaming multiprocessors (SMs) and six 64-bit memory controllers. Three important innovations in the Kepler architecture are:

➤ Enhanced SMs

➤ Dynamic Parallelism

➤ Hyper-Q

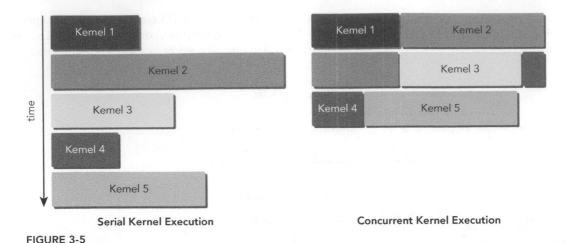

FIGURE 3-5

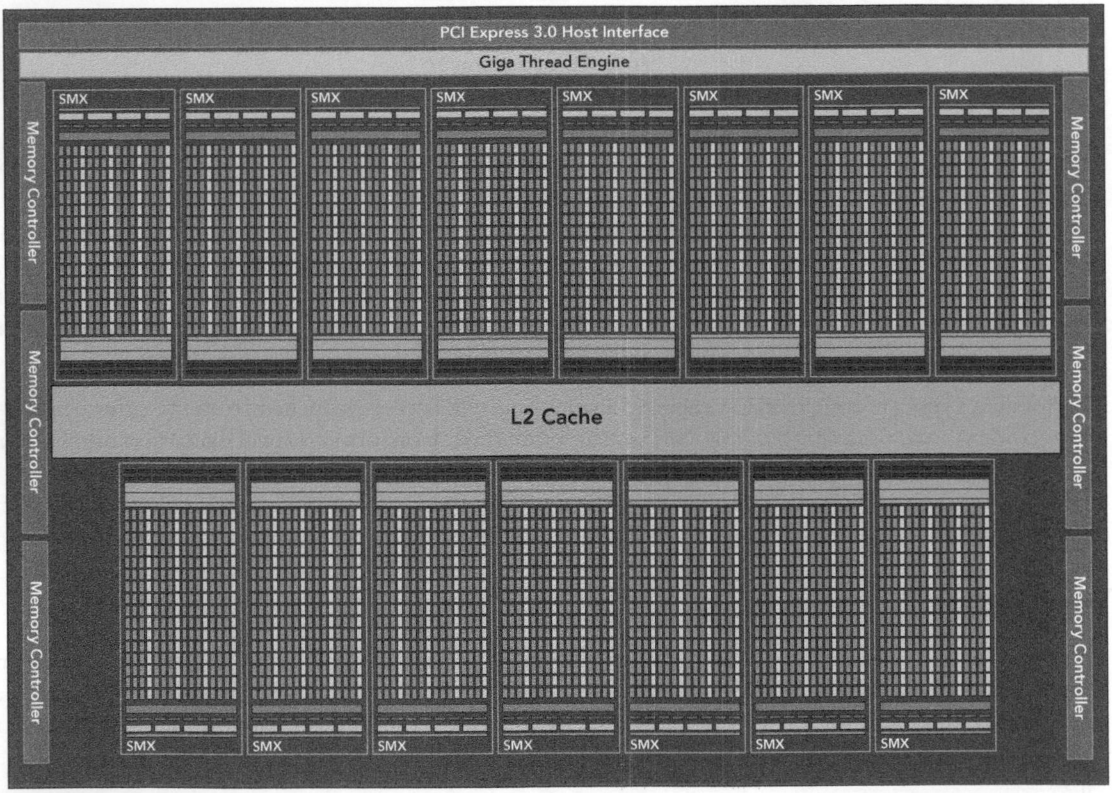

FIGURE 3-6

At the heart of the Kepler K20X is a new SM unit, which comprises several architectural innovations that improve programmability and power efficiency. Each Kepler SM unit consists of 192 single-precision CUDA cores, 64 double-precision units, 32 special function units (SFU), and 32 load/store units (LD/ST) (shown in Figure 3-7).

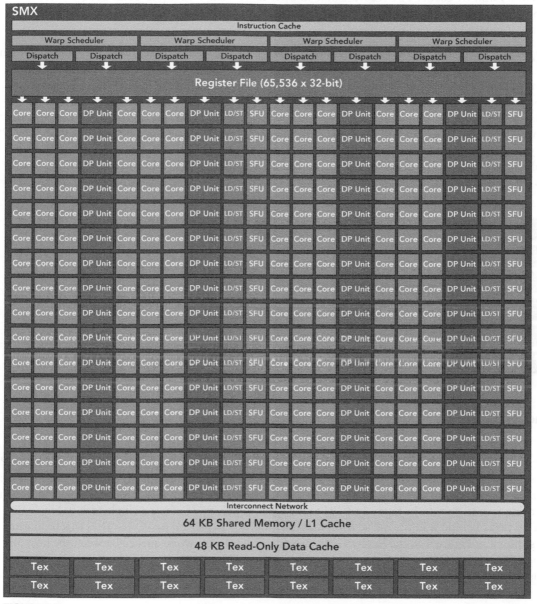

FIGURE 3-7

Each Kepler SM includes four warp schedulers and eight instruction dispatchers, enabling four warps to be issued and executed concurrently on a single SM. The Kepler K20X architecture (compute capability 3.5) can schedule 64 warps per SM for a total of 2,048 threads resident in a single SM at a time. The K20X architecture increases the register file size to 64K, compared to 32K on Fermi. The K20X also allows for more partitions of on-chip memory between shared memory and L1 cache. The K20X is able to offer more than 1 TFlop of peak double-precision computing power with 80 percent power efficiency improvements and 3 times the performance per watt compared to Fermi designs.

Dynamic Parallelism is a new feature introduced with Kepler GPUs that allows the GPU to dynamically launch new grids. With this feature, any kernel can launch another kernel and manage any inter-kernel dependencies needed to correctly perform additional work. This feature makes it easier for you to create and optimize recursive and data-dependent execution patterns. As illustrated in Figure 3-8, without dynamic parallelism the host launches every kernel on the GPU; with dynamic parallelism, the GPU can launch nested kernels, eliminating the need to communicate with the CPU. Dynamic parallelism broadens GPU applicability in various disciplines. You can launch small and medium-sized parallel workloads dynamically in cases where it was previously too expensive to do so.

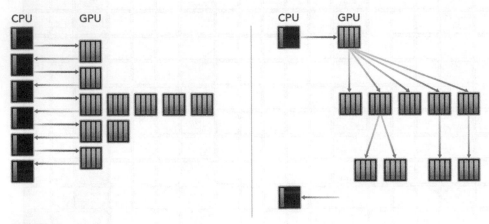

FIGURE 3-8

Hyper-Q adds more simultaneous hardware connections between the CPU and GPU, enabling CPU cores to simultaneously run more tasks on the GPU. As a result, you can expect increased GPU utilization and reduced CPU idle time when using Kepler GPUs. Fermi GPUs rely on a single hardware work queue to pass tasks from the CPU to the GPU, which could cause a single task to block all other tasks behind it in the queue from making progress. Kepler Hyper-Q removes this limitation. As shown in Figure 3-9, the Kepler GPUs provide 32 hardware work queues between the host and the GPU. Hyper-Q enables more concurrency on the GPU, maximizing GPU utilization and increasing overall performance.

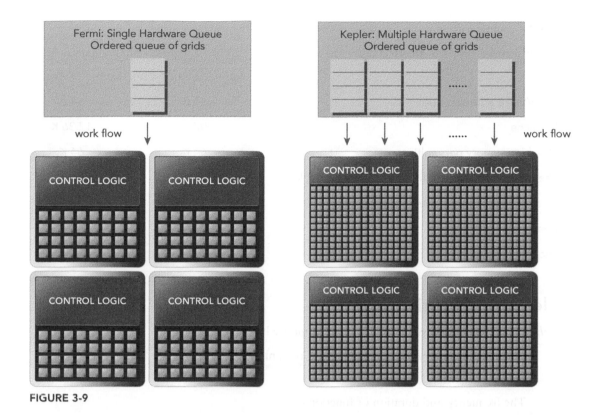

FIGURE 3-9

The major architectural features for different compute capabilities are briefly summarized in Table 3-1.

TABLE 3-1: Important Facts Pertaining to Compute Capability

ARCHITECTURE SPECIFICATIONS	COMPUTE CAPABILITY			
	2.0	2.1	3.0	3.5
Number of cores for integer and floating-point arithmetic function operations per multiprocessor	32	48	192	
Number of special function units for single-precision floating-point transcendental functions per multiprocessor	4	8	32	
Number of warp schedulers per multiprocessor	2		4	
Number of instructions issued at once by scheduler	1	2	2	
Number of load/store units per multiprocessor	16		32	

continues

TABLE 3-1 *(continued)*

ARCHITECTURE SPECIFICATIONS	COMPUTE CAPABILITY			
	2.0	2.1	3.0	3.5
Load/Store address width	64 B		64 B	
L2 cache	768 K		1,536 K	
On-chip memory per multiprocessor	64 K		64 K	
Shared memory per multiprocessor (configurable)	48 K or 16 K		48 K/32 K/16 K	
L1 cache per multiprocessor (configurable)	16 K or 48 K		48 K/32 K/16 K	
Read-only data cache	N/A		48 K	
Global memory	Up to 6 GB		Up to 12 GB	

Profile-Driven Optimization

Profiling is the act of analyzing program performance by measuring:

➤ The space (memory) or time complexity of application code

➤ The use of particular instructions

➤ The frequency and duration of function calls

Profiling is a critical step in program development, especially for optimizing HPC application code. Profiling often requires a basic understanding of the execution model of a platform to help make application optimization decisions. Developing an HPC application usually involves two major steps:

1. Developing the code for correctness

2. Improving the code for performance

It is natural to use a profile-driven approach for the second step. Profile-driven development is particularly important in CUDA programming for the following reasons:

➤ A naive kernel implementation generally does not yield the best performance. Profiling tools can help you find the critical regions of your code that are performance bottlenecks.

➤ CUDA partitions the compute resources in an SM among multiple resident thread blocks. This partitioning causes some resources to become performance limiters. Profiling tools can help you gain insight into how compute resources are being utilized.

➤ CUDA provides an abstraction of the hardware architecture enabling you to control thread concurrency. Profiling tools can help you measure, visualize, and guide your optimizations.

Profiling tools provide deep insight into kernel performance and help you identify bottlenecks in kernels. CUDA provides two primary profiling tools: nvvp, a standalone visual profiler; and nvprof, a command-line profiler.

nvvp is a *Visual Profiler,* which helps you to visualize and optimize the performance of your CUDA program. This tool displays a timeline of program activity on both the CPU and GPU, helping you to identify opportunities for performance improvement. In addition, nvvp analyzes your application for potential performance bottlenecks and suggests actions to take to eliminate or reduce those bottlenecks. The tool is available as both a standalone application and as part of the *Nsight Eclipse Edition (nsight).*

nvprof collects and displays profiling data on the command line. nvprof was introduced with CUDA 5 and evolved from an older command-line CUDA profiling tool. Like nvvp, it enables the collection of a timeline of CUDA-related activities on both the CPU and GPU, including kernel execution, memory transfers, and CUDA API calls. It also enables you to collect hardware counters and performance metrics for CUDA kernels.

In addition to predefined metrics, you can also define your own metrics based on hardware counters gathered by the profiler.

EVENTS AND METRICS

In CUDA profiling, an event is a countable activity that corresponds to a hardware counter collected during kernel execution. A metric is a characteristic of a kernel calculated from one or more events. Keep in mind the following concepts about events and metrics:

➤ Most counters are reported per streaming multiprocessor but not the entire GPU.

➤ A single run can only collect a few counters. The collection of some counters is mutually exclusive. Multiple profiling runs are often needed to gather all relevant counters.

➤ Counter values may not be exactly the same across repeated runs due to variations in GPU execution (such as thread block and warp scheduling order).

To identify the performance bottleneck of a kernel, it is important to choose appropriate performance metrics and compare measured performance to theoretical peak performance. Throughout the examples and exercises in this book, you will learn about the proper metrics for analyzing kernels with the command-line profiler and master the skill of writing an efficient kernel using the profile-driven approach.

In this book, you will mainly use nvprof to dissect your kernel with the goal of improving performance. You will learn how to select appropriate counters and metrics, and use nvprof from the command line to collect profiling data, which can then be used to plan an optimization strategy. You will learn how to analyze your kernel from multiple angles using different counters and metrics.

There are three common limiters to performance for a kernel that you may encounter:

➤ Memory bandwidth

➤ Compute resources

➤ Instruction and memory latency

This chapter focuses on the issue of instruction latency and partially on compute resource limitations. Subsequent chapters will cover the remaining performance limiters.

KNOWING HARDWARE RESOURCE DETAILS

As a C programmer, when writing code just for correctness you can safely ignore the cache line size; however, when tuning code for peak performance, you must consider cache characteristics in your code structure.

This is true for CUDA C programming as well. As a CUDA C programmer, you must have some understanding of hardware resources if you are to improve kernel performance.

If you do not understand the hardware architecture, the CUDA compiler will still do a good job of optimizing your kernel, but it can only do so much. Even basic knowledge of the GPU architecture will enable you to write much better code and fully exploit the capability of your device.

In the subsequent sections of this chapter, you will see how hardware concepts are connected to performance metrics, and how metrics can be used to guide optimization.

UNDERSTANDING THE NATURE OF WARP EXECUTION

When launching a kernel, what do you see from the software point of view? To you, it seems that all threads in the kernel run in parallel. From a logical point-of-view this is true, but from the hardware point of view not all threads can physically execute in parallel at the same time. This chapter has already covered the concept of grouping 32 threads into a single execution unit: a warp. Now you will take a closer look at warp execution from the hardware perspective, and gain insights that will help guide kernel design.

Warps and Thread Blocks

Warps are the basic unit of execution in an SM. When you launch a grid of thread blocks, the thread blocks in the grid are distributed among SMs. Once a thread block is scheduled to an SM, threads in the thread block are further partitioned into warps. A warp consists of 32 consecutive threads and all threads in a warp are executed in Single Instruction Multiple Thread (SIMT) fashion; that is, all threads execute the same instruction, and each thread carries out that operation on its own private data. Figure 3-10 illustrates the relationship between the logical view and hardware view of a thread block.

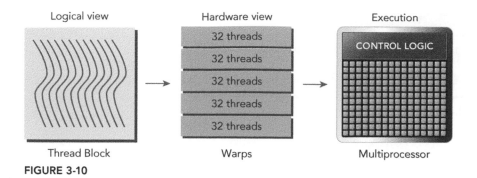

FIGURE 3-10

Thread blocks can be configured to be one-, two-, or three-dimensional. However, from the hardware perspective, all threads are arranged one-dimensionally. Each thread has a unique ID in a block. For a one-dimensional thread block, the unique thread ID is stored in the CUDA built-in variable `threadIdx.x`, and threads with consecutive values for `threadIdx.x` are grouped into warps. For example, a one-dimensional thread block with 128 threads will be organized into 4 warps as follows:

```
Warp 0: thread  0, thread  1, thread  2, ... thread 31
Warp 1: thread 32, thread 33, thread 34, ... thread 63
Warp 3: thread 64, thread 65, thread 66, ... thread 95
Warp 4: thread 96, thread 97, thread 98, ... thread 127
```

The logical layout of a two or three-dimensional thread block can be converted into its one-dimensional physical layout by using the x dimension as the innermost dimension, the y dimension as the second dimension, and the z dimension as the outermost. For example, given a 2D thread block, a unique identifier for each thread in a block can be calculated using the built-in `threadIdx` and `blockDim` variables:

```
threadIdx.y * blockDim.x + threadIdx.x.
```

The same calculation for a 3D thread block is as follows:

```
threadIdx.z * blockDim.y * blockDim.x + threadIdx.y * blockDim.x + threadIdx.x
```

The number of warps for a thread block can be determined as follows:

$$WarpsPerBlock = ceil\left(\frac{ThreadsPerBlock}{warpSize}\right)$$

Thus, the hardware always allocates a discrete number of warps for a thread block. A warp is never split between different thread blocks. If thread block size is not an even multiple of warp size, some threads in the last warp are left inactive. Figure 3-11 illustrates a two-dimensional thread block with 40 threads in the x dimension and 2 threads in the y dimension. From the application perspective, there are 80 threads laid out in a two-dimensional grid.

The hardware will allocate 3 warps for this thread block, resulting in a total of 96 hardware threads to support 80 software threads. Note that the last half-warp is inactive. Even though these threads are unused they still consume SM resources, such as registers.

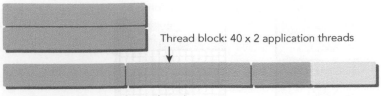

Thread block: 40 x 2 application threads

3 warps: 32 x 3 hardware threads

FIGURE 3-11

> **THREAD BLOCK: LOGICAL VIEW VERSUS HARDWARE VIEW**
>
> From the logical perspective, a thread block is a collection of threads organized in a 1D, 2D, or 3D layout.
>
> From the hardware perspective, a thread block is a 1D collection of warps. Threads in a thread block are organized in a 1D layout, and each set of 32 consecutive threads forms a warp.

Warp Divergence

Control flow is one of the fundamental constructs in any high-level programming language. GPUs support traditional, C-style, explicit flow-control constructs, such as if...then...else, for, and while.

CPUs include complex hardware to perform branch prediction, that is, to predict at each conditional check which branch an application's control flow will take. If the prediction is correct, branching on CPUs incurs only a small performance penalty. If the prediction is not correct, the CPU may stall for a number of cycles as the instruction pipeline is flushed. It is not necessary for you to fully understand why CPUs are good at handling complex control flow; this explanation just serves as a backdrop for contrast.

GPUs are comparatively simple devices without complex branch prediction mechanisms. Because all threads in a warp must execute identical instructions on the same cycle, if one thread executes an instruction, all threads in the warp must execute that instruction. This could become a problem if threads in the same warp take different paths through an application. For example, consider the following statement:

```
if (cond) {
    ...
} else {
    ...
}
```

Suppose for 16 threads in a warp executing this code, cond is true, but for the other 16 cond is false. Then half of the warp will need to execute the instructions in the if block, and the other half will need to execute the instructions in the `else` block. Threads in the same warp executing different instructions is referred to as *warp divergence*. Warp divergence would seem to cause a paradox, as you already know that all threads in a warp must execute the same instruction on each cycle.

If threads of a warp diverge, the warp serially executes each branch path, disabling threads that do not take that path. Warp divergence can cause significantly degraded performance. In the preceding example, the amount of parallelism in the warp was cut by half: only 16 threads were actively executing at a time while the other 16 were disabled. With more conditional branches, the loss of parallelism would be even greater.

Take note that branch divergence occurs only within a warp. Different conditional values in different warps do not cause warp divergence.

Figure 3-12 illustrates warp divergence. All threads within a warp must take both branches of the `if...then` statement. If the condition is `true` for a thread, it executes the `if` clause; otherwise, the thread stalls while waiting for that execution to complete.

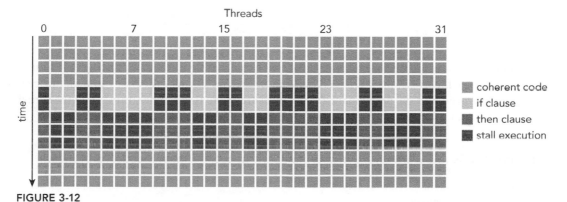

FIGURE 3-12

To obtain the best performance, you should avoid different execution paths within the same warp. Keep in mind that the warp assignment of threads in a thread block is deterministic. Therefore, it may be possible (though not trivial, depending on the algorithm) to partition data in such a way as to ensure all threads in the same warp take the same control path in an application.

For example, suppose you have two branches, as shown in the following simple arithmetic kernel. You can simulate a poor partitioning of data with an even and odd threads approach, causing warp divergence. The condition (`tid%2==0`) makes even numbered threads take the `if` clause and odd numbered threads take the `else` clause.

```
__global__ void mathKernel1(float *c) {
    int tid = blockIdx.x * blockDim.x + threadIdx.x;
    float a, b;
    a = b = 0.0f;

    if (tid % 2 == 0) {
        a = 100.0f;
```

```
    } else {
        b = 200.0f;
    }
    c[tid] = a + b;
}
```

If you interleave data using a warp approach (instead of a thread approach), you can avoid warp divergence and achieve 100 percent utilization of the device. The condition (tid/warpSize)%2==0 forces the branch granularity to be a multiple of warp size; the even warps take the if clause, and the odd warps take the else clause. This kernel produces the same output, but in a different order.

```
__global__ void mathKernel2(void) {
    int tid = blockIdx.x * blockDim.x + threadIdx.x;
    float a, b;
    a = b = 0.0f;

    if ((tid / warpSize) % 2 == 0) {
        a = 100.0f;
    } else {
        b = 200.0f;
    }
    c[tid] = a + b;
}
```

Now, you can measure the performance of these two kernels using the code in Listing 3-1. You can also download the file simpleDivergence.cu from Wrox.com. Because the first run on a device may have added overhead and the performance being measured here is very fine-grain, an extra kernel launch (warmingup, which is the same as mathKernel2) is added to remove this overhead.

LISTING 3-1: Simple warp divergence (simpleDivergence.cu) (main function only listed)

```
int main(int argc, char **argv) {
    // set up device
    int dev = 0;
    cudaDeviceProp deviceProp;
    cudaGetDeviceProperties(&deviceProp, dev);
    printf("%s using Device %d: %s\n", argv[0],dev, deviceProp.name);

    // set up data size
    int size = 64;
    int blocksize = 64;
    if(argc > 1) blocksize = atoi(argv[1]);
    if(argc > 2) size      = atoi(argv[2]);
    printf("Data size %d ", size);

    // set up execution configuration
    dim3 block (blocksize,1);
    dim3 grid ((size+block.x-1)/block.x,1);
    printf("Execution Configure (block %d grid %d)\n",block.x, grid.x);

    // allocate gpu memory
    float *d_C;
    size_t nBytes = size * sizeof(float);
```

```
        cudaMalloc((float**)&d_C, nBytes);

        // run a warmup kernel to remove overhead
        size_t iStart,iElaps;
        cudaDeviceSynchronize();
        iStart = seconds();
        warmingup<<<grid, block>>> (d_C);
        cudaDeviceSynchronize();
        iElaps = seconds() - iStart;
        printf("warmup      <<< %4d %4d >>> elapsed %d sec \n",grid.x,block.x, iElaps );

        // run kernel 1
        iStart = seconds();
        mathKernel1<<<grid, block>>>(d_C);
        cudaDeviceSynchronize();
        iElaps = seconds() - iStart;
        printf("mathKernel1 <<< %4d %4d >>> elapsed %d sec \n",grid.x,block.x,iElaps );

        // run kernel 3
        iStart = seconds();
        mathKernel2<<<grid, block>>>(d_C);
        cudaDeviceSynchronize();
        iElaps = seconds () - iStart;
        printf("mathKernel2 <<< %4d %4d >>> elapsed %d sec \n",grid.x,block.x,iElaps );

        // run kernel 3
        iStart = seconds ();
        mathKernel3<<<grid, block>>>(d_C);
        cudaDeviceSynchronize(),
        iElaps = seconds () - iStart;
        printf("mathKernel3 <<< %4d %4d >>> elapsed %d sec \n",grid.x,block.x,iElaps);

        // run kernel 4
        iStart = seconds ();
        mathKernel4<<<grid, block>>>(d_C);
        cudaDeviceSynchronize();
        iElaps = seconds () - iStart;
        printf("mathKernel4 <<< %4d %4d >>> elapsed %d sec \n",grid.x,block.x,iElaps);
        // free gpu memory and reset divece
        cudaFree(d_C);
        cudaDeviceReset();
        return EXIT_SUCCESS;
}
```

Compile this source with the following command:

```
$ nvcc -O3 -arch=sm_20 simpleDivergence.cu -o simpleDivergence
```

The output from simpleDivergence run on a Fermi M2070 GPU is reported here. The elapsed times for the two kernels are quite similar.

```
$ ./simpleDivergence using Device 0: Tesla M2070
Data size 64 Execution Configuration (block 64 grid 1)
Warmingup    elapsed 0.000040 sec
mathKernel1 elapsed 0.000016 sec
mathKernel2 elapsed 0.000014 sec
```

You can also directly observe warp divergence by using the `nvprof` profiler to collect metrics from the GPU. Here, `nvprof`'s `branch_efficiency` metric is calculated for a sample execution of `simpleDivergence`:

```
$ nvprof --metrics branch_efficiency ./simpleDivergence
```

The following results are reported by `nvprof`.

```
Kernel: mathKernel1(void)
1   branch_efficiency   Branch Efficiency      100.00%     100.00%     100.00%
Kernel: mathKernel2(void)
1   branch_efficiency   Branch Efficiency      100.00%     100.00%     100.00%
```

Branch Efficiency is defined as the ratio of non-divergent branches to total branches, and can be calculated using the following formula:

$$Branch\ Efficiency = 100 \times \left(\frac{\#\,Branches - \#\,Divergent\,Branches}{\#\,Branches} \right)$$

It is odd that no branch divergence is reported (that is, branch efficiency is at 100%). This oddity is caused by a CUDA compiler optimization that replaces branch instructions (which cause actual control flow to diverge) with predicated instructions for short, conditional code segments.

In branch predication, a predicate variable for each thread is set to 1 or 0 according to a conditional. Both conditional flow paths are fully executed, but only instructions with a predicate of 1 are executed. Instructions with a predicate of 0 do not, but the corresponding thread does not stall either. The difference between this and actual branch instructions is subtle, but important to understand. The compiler replaces a branch instruction with predicated instructions only if the number of instructions in the body of a conditional statement is less than a certain threshold. Therefore, a long code path will certainly result in warp divergence.

You can re-write the `mathKernel1` kernel to directly expose branch predication in the kernel code as follows:

```
__global__ void mathKernel3(float *c) {
    int tid = blockIdx.x * blockDim.x + threadIdx.x;
    float ia, ib;
    ia = ib = 0.0f;

    bool ipred = (tid % 2 == 0);
    if (ipred) {
        ia = 100.0f;
    }
    if (!ipred) {
        ib = 200.0f;
    }
    c[tid] = ia + ib;
}
```

Compile and run the file `simpleDivergence.cu` again with `mathKernel3` added, and the following performance is reported:

```
Warmingup   elapsed 0.105021 sec
mathKernel1 elapsed 0.000017 sec
```

```
mathKernel2 elapsed 0.000014 sec
mathKernel3 elapsed 0.000014 sec
```

You can force the CUDA compiler to not optimize your kernel using branch predication with the following command:

```
$ nvcc -g -G -arch=sm_20 simpleDivergence.cu -o simpleDivergence
```

Check the divergence again of the unoptimized kernels with nvprof as follows:

```
$ nvprof --metrics branch_efficiency ./simpleDivergence
```

The results are summarized as follows:

```
mathKernel1: Branch Efficiency        83.33%
mathKernel2: Branch Efficiency       100.00%
mathKernel3: Branch Efficiency        71.43%
```

You can also obtain the event counters for branch and divergent branch using nvprof as follows:

```
$ nvprof --events branch,divergent_branch ./simpleDivergence
```

The results are summarized as follows:

```
mathKernel1: branch    12    divergent_branch    2
mathKernel2: branch    12    divergent_branch    0
mathKernel3: branch    14    divergent_branch    4
```

The CUDA nvcc compiler still performed limited optimizations on mathKernel1 and mathKernel3 to keep their branch efficiencies above 50 percent. Note that the only reason mathKernel2 does not report branch divergence is that its branch granularity is a multiple of warp size. Also, separating a single if. . .else statement in mathKernel1 into multiple if statements in mathKernel3 doubled the number of divergent branches.

KEY REMINDERS

➤   Warp divergence occurs when threads within a warp take different code paths.

➤   Different if-then-else branches are executed serially.

➤   Try to adjust branch granularity to be a multiple of warp size to avoid warp divergence.

➤   Different warps can execute different code with no penalty on performance.

Resource Partitioning

The local execution context of a warp mainly consists of the following resources:

➤   Program counters

➤   Registers

➤   Shared memory

The execution context of each warp processed by an SM is maintained on-chip during the entire lifetime of the warp. Therefore, switching from one execution context to another has no cost.

Each SM has a set of 32-bit registers stored in a register file that are partitioned among threads, and a fixed amount of shared memory that is partitioned among thread blocks. The number of thread blocks and warps that can simultaneously reside on an SM for a given kernel depends on the number of registers and amount of shared memory available on the SM and required by the kernel.

Figure 3-13 illustrates that when each thread consumes more registers, fewer warps can be placed on an SM. If you can reduce the number of registers a kernel consumes, more warps will be processed simultaneously. Figure 3-14 illustrates that when a thread block consumes more shared memory, fewer thread blocks are processed simultaneously by an SM. If you can reduce the amount of shared memory used by each thread block, then more thread blocks can be processed simultaneously.

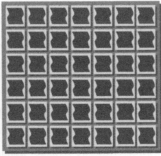

More threads with fewer registers per thread

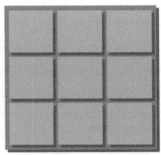

Fewer threads with more registers per thread

FIGURE 3-13

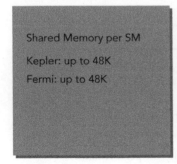

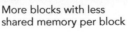

More blocks with less shared memory per block

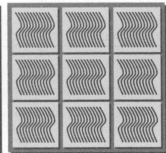

Fewer blocks with more shared memory per block

FIGURE 3-14

Resource availability generally limits the number of resident thread blocks per SM. The number of registers and the amount of shared memory per SM vary for devices of different compute capability. If there are insufficient registers or shared memory on each SM to process at least one block, the kernel launch will fail. Some of the key limits are shown in Table 3-2.

TABLE 3-2: Resource Limits Pertaining to Compute Capability

TECHNICAL SPECIFICATIONS	COMPUTE CAPABILITY			
	2.0	2.1	3.0	3.5
Maximum number of threads per block	1,024			
Maximum number of concurrent blocks per multiprocessor	8		16	
Maximum number of concurrent warps per multiprocessor	48		64	
Maximum number of concurrent threads per multiprocessor	1,536		2,048	
Number of 32-bit registers per multiprocessor	32 K		64 K	
Maximum number of 32-bit registers per thread	63		255	
Maximum amount of shared memory per multiprocessor	48 K			

A thread block is called an *active block* when compute resources, such as registers and shared memory, have been allocated to it. The warps it contains are called *active warps*. Active warps can be further classified into the following three types:

➤   Selected warp

➤   Stalled warp

➤   Eligible warp

The warp schedulers on an SM select active warps on every cycle and dispatch them to execution units. A warp that is actively executing is called a *selected warp*. If an active warp is ready for execution but not currently executing, it is an *eligible warp*. If a warp is not ready for execution, it is a *stalled warp*. A warp is eligible for execution if both of the following two conditions is met:

➤   Thirty-two CUDA cores are available for execution.

➤   All arguments to the current instruction are ready.

For example, the number of active warps on a Kepler SM at any time from launch to completion must be less than or equal to the architecture limit of 64 concurrent warps. The number of selected warps at any cycle is less than or equal to 4. If a warp stalls, the warp scheduler picks up an eligible warp to execute in its place. Because compute resources are partitioned among warps and kept on-chip during the entire lifetime of the warp, switching warp contexts is very fast. In the following sections, you will learn that you need to keep a large number of warps active in order to hide the latency caused by warps stalling.

Compute resource partitioning requires special attention in CUDA programming: The compute resources limit the number of active warps. Therefore, you must be aware of the restrictions imposed by the hardware, and the resources used by your kernel. In order to maximize GPU utilization, you need to maximize the number of active warps.

Latency Hiding

An SM relies on thread-level parallelism to maximize utilization of its functional units. Utilization is therefore directly linked to the number of resident warps. The number of clock cycles between an instruction being issued and being completed is defined as instruction *latency*. Full compute resource utilization is achieved when all warp schedulers have an eligible warp at every clock cycle. This ensures that the latency of each instruction can be hidden by issuing other instructions in other resident warps.

Compared with C programming on the CPU, *latency hiding* is particularly important in CUDA programming. CPU cores are designed to *minimize latency* for one or two threads at a time, whereas GPUs are designed to handle a large number of concurrent and lightweight threads in order to *maximize throughput*. GPU instruction latency is hidden by computation from other warps.

When considering instruction latency, instructions can be classified into two basic types:

➤ Arithmetic instructions

➤ Memory instructions

Arithmetic instruction latency is the time between an arithmetic operation starting and its output being produced. Memory instruction latency is the time between a load or store operation being issued and the data arriving at its destination. The corresponding latencies for each case are approximately:

➤ 10-20 cycles for arithmetic operations

➤ 400-800 cycles for global memory accesses

Figure 3-15 illustrates a simple case for an execution pipeline in which warp 0 stalls. The warp scheduler picks up other warps to execute and then executes warp 0 when it is eligible again.

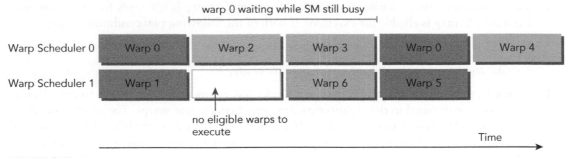

FIGURE 3-15

You may wonder how to estimate the number of active warps required to hide latency. *Little's Law* can provide a reasonable approximation. Originally a theorem in queue theory, it can also be applied to GPUs:

$$Number\ of\ Required\ Warps = Latency \times Throughput$$

Figure 3-16 illustrates Little's Law visually. Suppose the average latency for an instruction in your kernel is 5 cycles. To keep a throughput of 6 warps executed per cycle, you will need at least 30 warps in-flight.

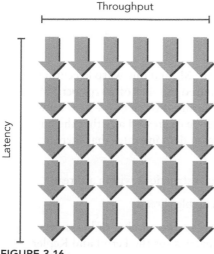

FIGURE 3-16

> ## THROUGHPUT AND BANDWIDTH
>
> Bandwidth and throughput are often confused, but may be used interchangeably depending on the situation. Both throughput and bandwidth are rate metrics used to measure performance.
>
> Bandwidth is usually used to refer to a theoretical peak value, while throughput is used to refer to an achieved value.
>
> Bandwidth is usually used to describe the highest possible amount of data transfer per time unit, while throughput can be used to describe the rate of any kind of information or operations carried out per time unit, such as, how many instructions are completed per cycle.

For arithmetic operations, the required parallelism can be expressed as the number of operations required to hide arithmetic latency. Table 3-3 lists the number of required operations for Fermi and Kepler devices. The arithmetic operation used as an example here is a 32-bit floating-point multiply-add ($a + b \times c$), expressed as the number of operations per clock cycle per SM. The throughput varies for different arithmetic instructions.

TABLE 3-3: SM Parallelism Required to Maintain Full Arithmetic Utilization

GPU MODEL	INSTRUCTION LATENCY (CYCLES)	THROUGHPUT (OPERATIONS/CYCLE)	PARALLELISM (OPERATIONS)
Fermi	20	32	640
Kepler	20	192	3,840

Throughput is specified in number of operations per cycle per SM, and one warp executing one instruction corresponds to 32 operations. Therefore, the required number of warps per SM to maintain full compute resource utilization can be calculated for Fermi GPUs as 640 ÷ 32 = 20 warps. Hence, the required parallelism for arithmetic operations can be expressed as either the number of operations or the number of warps. This simple unit conversion demonstrates that there are two ways to increase parallelism:

➤ **Instruction-level parallelism (ILP):** More independent instructions within a thread

➤ **Thread-level parallelism (TLP):** More concurrently eligible threads

For memory operations, the required parallelism is expressed as the number of bytes per cycle required to hide memory latency. Table 3-4 lists the metrics for the Fermi and Kepler architectures.

TABLE 3-4: Device Parallelism Required to Maintain Full Memory Utilization

GPU MODEL	INSTRUCTION LATENCY (CYCLES)	BANDWIDTH (GB/SEC)	BANDWIDTH (B/CYCLE)	PARALLELISM (KB)
Fermi	800	144	92	74
Kepler	800	250	96	77

Because memory throughput is usually expressed as gigabytes per second, you need to first convert the throughput into gigabytes per cycle using the corresponding memory frequency. You can check your device's memory frequency with the following command:

```
$ nvidia-smi -a -q -d CLOCK | fgrep -A 3 "Max Clocks" | fgrep "Memory"
```

An example Fermi memory frequency (measured on a Tesla C2070) is 1.566 GHz. An example Kepler memory frequency (measured on a Tesla K20) is 2.6 GHz. Because 1 Hz is defined as one cycle per second, you then can convert the bandwidth from gigabytes per second to gigabytes per cycle as follows:

$$144 \text{ GB/Sec} \div 1.566 \text{ GHz} \cong 92 \text{ Bytes/Cycle}$$

Multiplying bytes per cycle by memory latency, you derive the required parallelism for Fermi memory operations at nearly 74 KB of memory I/O in-flight to achieve full utilization. This value is for the entire device, not per SM, because memory bandwidth is given for the entire device.

Connecting these values to warp or thread counts depends on the application. Suppose each thread moves one `float` of data (4 bytes) from global memory to the SM for computation, you would require 18,500 threads or 579 warps to hide all memory latency on Fermi GPUs:

$$74 \text{ KB} \div 4 \text{ bytes/thread} \cong 18,500 \text{ threads}$$

$$18,500 \text{ threads} \div 32 \text{ threads/warp} \cong 579 \text{ warps}$$

The Fermi architecture has 16 SMs. Therefore, you require 579 warps ÷ 16 SMs = 36 warps per SM to hide all memory latency. If each thread performed more than one independent 4-byte load, fewer threads would be required to hide the memory latency.

Much like instruction latency, you can increase the available parallelism by either creating more independent memory operations within each thread/warp, or creating more concurrently active threads/warps.

Latency hiding depends on the number of active warps per SM, which is implicitly determined by the execution configuration and resource constraints (registers and shared memory usage in a kernel). Choosing an optimal execution configuration is a matter of striking a balance between latency hiding and resource utilization. You will examine this issue in more detail in the next section.

> ### EXPOSING SUFFICIENT PARALLELISM
>
> Because the GPU partitions compute resources among threads, switching between concurrent warps has very little overhead (on the order of one or two cycles) as the required state is already available on-chip. If there are sufficient concurrently active threads, you can keep the GPU busy in every pipeline stage on every cycle. In this situation, the latency of one warp is hidden by the execution of other warps. Therefore, exposing sufficient parallelism to SMs is beneficial to performance.
>
> A simple formula for calculating the required parallelism is to multiply the number of cores per SM by the latency of one arithmetic instruction on that SM. For example, Fermi has 32 single-precision floating-point pipeline lanes and the latency of one arithmetic instruction is 20 cycles, so at minimum 32 x 20 = 640 threads per SM are required to keep your device busy. However, this is a lower bound.

Occupancy

Instructions are executed sequentially within each CUDA core. When one warp stalls, the SM switches to executing other eligible warps. Ideally, you want to have enough warps to keep the cores of the device occupied. *Occupancy* is the ratio of active warps to maximum number of warps, per SM.

$$occupancy = \frac{active \ warps}{maximum \ warps}$$

You can check the maximum warps per SM for your device using the following function:

```
cudaError_t cudaGetDeviceProperties(struct cudaDeviceProp *prop, int device);
```

Various statistics from your device are returned in the cudaDeviceProp struct. The maximum number of threads per SM is returned in the following variable:

```
maxThreadsPerMultiProcessor
```

You can derive the maximum warps by dividing *maxThreadsPerMultiProcessor* by 32. Listing 3-2 shows you how to use cudaGetDeviceProperties to obtain GPU configuration information.

LISTING 3-2: Simple device property query (simpleDeviceQuery.cu)

```
#include <stdio.h>
#include <cuda_runtime.h>

int main(int argc, char *argv[]) {
    int iDev = 0;
    cudaDeviceProp iProp;
    cudaGetDeviceProperties(&iProp, iDev);

    printf("Device %d: %s\n", iDev, iProp.name);
    printf("Number of multiprocessors: %d\n", iProp.multiProcessorCount);
    printf("Total amount of constant memory: %4.2f KB\n",
        iProp.totalConstMem/1024.0);
    printf("Total amount of shared memory per block: %4.2f KB\n",
            iProp.sharedMemPerBlock/1024.0);
    printf("Total number of registers available per block: %d\n",
        iProp.regsPerBlock);
    printf("Warp size%d\n", deviceProp.warpSize);
    printf("Maximum number of threads per block: %d\n", iProp.maxThreadsPerBlock);
    printf(Maximum number of threads per multiprocessor: %d\n",
            iProp.maxThreadsPerMultiProcessor);
    printf("Maximum number of warps per multiprocessor: %d\n",
            iProp.maxThreadsPerMultiProcessor/32);
    return EXIT_SUCCESS;
}
```

You can download simpleDeviceQuery.cu from Wrox.com. Compile and run this example using the following command:

```
$ nvcc simpleDeviceQuery.cu -o simpleDeviceQuery
$ ./simpleDeviceQuery
```

The output on a Tesla M2070 is reported here. The maximum number of threads per SM is 1,536. Therefore, the maximum number of warps per SM is 48.

```
Device 0: Tesla M2070
Number of multiprocessors: 14
Total amount of constant memory: 64.00 KB
Total amount of shared memory per block: 48.00 KB
```

```
Total number of registers available per block: 32768
Warp size: 32
Maximum number of threads per block: 1024
Maximum number of threads per multiprocessor: 1536
Maximum number of warps per multiprocessor: 48
```

The CUDA Toolkit includes a spreadsheet, called the *CUDA Occupancy Calculator,* which assists you in selecting grid and block dimensions to maximize occupancy for a kernel. Figure 3-17 shows a screenshot of the Occupancy Calculator.

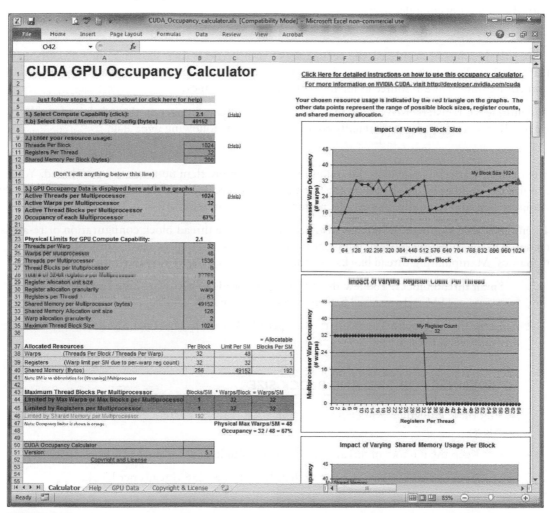

FIGURE 3-17

There are several sections in the Occupancy Calculator. First, you must provide information about your GPU's compute capability and your kernel's resource usage.

After you have specified the compute capability, the data in the physical limits section is automatically filled in. Next, you need to enter the following kernel resource information:

➤ Threads per block (execution configuration)

➤ Registers per thread (resource usage)

➤ Shared memory per block (resource usage)

The registers per thread and shared memory per block resource usage can be obtained from nvcc with the following compiler flag:

```
--ptxas-options=-v
```

Once this data has been entered, the occupancy of your kernel is then shown in the GPU Occupancy Data section. The other sections provide you with the necessary information to adjust your execution configuration and resource usage for better device occupancy.

The number of registers used by a kernel can have a significant impact on the number of resident warps. Register usage can be manually controlled using the following nvcc flag.

```
-maxrregcount=NUM
```

The option -maxrregcount tells the compiler to not use more than NUM registers per thread. You can use the number of registers recommended by the Occupancy Calculator in conjunction with this compiler flag to potentially improve the performance of your application.

To enhance your occupancy, you may also need to resize the thread block configuration or re-adjust resource usage to permit more simultaneously active warps and improve utilization of compute resources. Manipulating thread blocks to either extreme can restrict resource utilization:

➤ **Small thread blocks:** Too few threads per block leads to hardware limits on the number of warps per SM to be reached before all resources are fully utilized.

➤ **Large thread blocks:** Too many threads per block leads to fewer per-SM hardware resources available to each thread.

GUIDELINES FOR GRID AND BLOCK SIZE

Using these guidelines will help your application scale on current and future devices:

➤ Keep the number of threads per block a multiple of warp size (32).

➤ Avoid small block sizes: Start with at least 128 or 256 threads per block.

➤ Adjust block size up or down according to kernel resource requirements.

➤ Keep the number of blocks much greater than the number of SMs to expose sufficient parallelism to your device.

➤ Conduct experiments to discover the best execution configuration and resource usage.

Although each case will hit different hardware limits, both cause compute resources to be under-utilized and hinder the creation of sufficient parallelism to hide instruction and memory latency. Occupancy focuses exclusively on the number of concurrent threads or warps per SM. However, full occupancy is not the only goal for performance optimization. Once a certain level of occupancy is achieved for a kernel, further increases may not lead to performance improvement. There are also many other factors you need to examine for performance tuning. You will learn all these issues in detail in subsequent chapters.

Synchronization

Barrier synchronization is a primitive that is common in many parallel programming languages. In CUDA, synchronization can be performed at two levels:

➤ **System-level:** Wait for all work on both the host and the device to complete.

➤ **Block-level:** Wait for all threads in a thread block to reach the same point in execution on the device.

Since many CUDA API calls and all kernel launches are asynchronous with respect to the host, cudaDeviceSynchronize can be used to block the host application until all CUDA operations (copies, kernels, and so on) have completed:

```
cudaError_t cudaDeviceSynchronize(void);
```

This function may return errors from previous asynchronous CUDA operations.

Because warps in a thread block are executed in an undefined order, CUDA provides the ability to synchronize their execution with a block-local barrier. You can mark synchronization points in the kernel using:

```
__device__ void __syncthreads(void);
```

When __syncthreads is called, each thread in the same thread block must wait until all other threads in that thread block have reached this synchronization point. All global and shared memory accesses made by all threads prior to this barrier will be visible to all other threads in the thread block after the barrier. The function is used to coordinate communication between threads in the same block, but it can negatively affect performance by forcing warps to become idle.

Threads within a thread block can share data through shared memory and registers. When sharing data between threads you need to be careful to avoid race conditions. *Race conditions*, or hazards, are unordered accesses by multiple threads to the same memory location. For example, a read-after-write hazard occurs when an unordered read of a location occurs following a write. Because there is no ordering between the read and the write, it is undefined if the read should have loaded the value of that location before the write or after the write. Other examples of hazards are write-after-read or write-after-write. While threads in a thread block run logically in parallel, not all threads can execute physically at the same time. If thread A tries to read data that is written by thread B in a different warp, you can only be sure that thread B has finished writing if proper synchronization is used. Otherwise, a race condition occurs. You will examine these synchronization issues in more depth in Chapter 4.

There is no thread synchronization among different blocks. The only safe way to synchronize across blocks is to use the global synchronization point at the end of every kernel execution; that is, terminate the current kernel and start a new kernel for the work to be performed after global synchronization.

By not allowing threads in different blocks to synchronize with each other, GPUs can execute blocks in any order. This enables CUDA programs to be scalable across massively parallel GPUs.

Scalability

Scalability is a desirable feature for any parallel application. Scalability implies that providing additional hardware resources to a parallel application yields speedup relative to the amount of added resources. For example, a CUDA application is scalable to two SMs if running on two SMs halves the execution time, relative to running on one SM. A scalable parallel program uses all compute resources efficiently to improve performance. Scalability implies that performance can be improved with added compute cores. Serial code is inherently not scalable as running a sequential single threaded application on thousands of cores has no effect on performance. Parallel code has the potential to be scalable, but real scalability depends on algorithm design and hardware features.

The ability to execute the same application code on a varying number of compute cores is referred to as *transparent scalability*. A transparently scalable platform broadens the use-cases for existing applications, and reduces the burden on developers because they can avoid making changes for new or different hardware. Scalability can be more important than efficiency. A scalable but inefficient system can handle larger workloads by simply adding hardware cores. An efficient but un-scalable system may quickly reach an upper limit on achievable performance.

When a CUDA kernel is launched, thread blocks are distributed among multiple SMs. Thread blocks in a grid can be executed in any order, in parallel or in series. This independence makes CUDA programs scalable across an arbitrary number of compute cores.

Figure 3-18 illustrates an example of the CUDA architecture's scalability. On the left side, you have a GPU with two SMs that executes two blocks at the same time; on the right side, you have a GPU with four SMs that executes four blocks at the same time. Without any code changes, an application can run on different GPU configurations and the required execution time will scale according to the available resources.

EXPOSING PARALLELISM

For a better understanding of the nature of warp execution, you will examine the sumMatrixOnGPU2D kernel below using different execution configurations. You will check nvprof profile metrics to help you understand why some combinations of grid/block dimensions are better than others. These exercises will provide hands-on experience with *grid and block heuristics* — a must-have skill for CUDA programmers.

The 2D matrix summation kernel is as follows:

```
__global__ void sumMatrixOnGPU2D(float *A, float *B, float *C, int NX, int NY) {
    unsigned int ix = blockIdx.x * blockDim.x + threadIdx.x;
```

```
    unsigned int iy = blockIdx.y * blockDim.y + threadIdx.y;
    unsigned int idx = iy * NX + ix;

    if (ix < NX && iy < NY) {
        C[idx] = A[idx] + B[idx];
    }
}
```

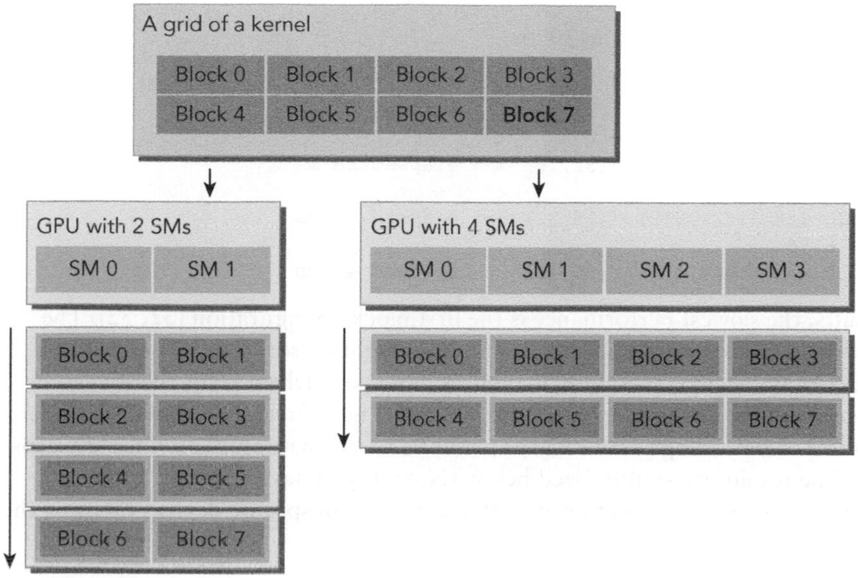

FIGURE 3-18

Specify a large matrix with 16,384 elements in each dimension:

```
int nx = 1<<14;
int ny = 1<<14;
```

The following code snippet allows block dimensions to be configurable from the command line:

```
if (argc > 2) {
    dimx = atoi(argv[1]);
    dimy = atoi(argv[2]);
}
dim3 block(dimx, dimy);
dim3 grid((nx + block.x - 1) / block.x, (ny + block.y - 1) / block.y);
```

You can find the full code for this example in sumMatrix.cu, downloadable from Wrox.com. Compile the code with the following command.

```
$ nvcc -O3 -arch=sm_20 sumMatrix.cu -o sumMatrix
```

You will use the generated sumMatrix executable to experiment with block and grid configurations in upcoming sections.

Checking Active Warps with nvprof

First, you need to create a reference result as a baseline for performance. To do so, start by testing a set of basic thread block configurations, in particular, thread blocks of size (32,32), (32,16), (16,32), and (16,16). Recall that sumMatrix accepts the x-dimension of the thread block configuration as its first argument, and the y-dimension of the thread block configuration as its second argument. You can test various thread block configurations by invoking sumMatrix with the appropriate command line arguments.

The following results are output on a Tesla M2070:

```
$ ./sumMatrix 32 32
sumMatrixOnGPU2D <<< (512,512),  (32,32) >>> elapsed 60 ms
$ ./sumMatrix 32 16
sumMatrixOnGPU2D <<< (512,1024), (32,16) >>> elapsed 38 ms
$ ./sumMatrix 16 32
sumMatrixOnGPU2D <<< (1024,512), (16,32) >>> elapsed 51 ms
$ ./sumMatrix 16 16
sumMatrixOnGPU2D <<< (1024,1024),(16,16) >>> elapsed 46 ms
```

Comparing these results, the slowest performance is the first block configuration (32, 32). The fastest is the second thread block configuration (32, 16). You might reason that the second case has more thread blocks than the first, therefore, it exposes more parallelism. This theory can be confirmed using nvprof and the achieved_occupancy metric. The *achieved occupancy* of a kernel is defined as the ratio of the average active warps per cycle to the maximum number of warps supported on an SM. The results are summarized below (Note: if you have a system with multiple GPUs, you can direct nvprof to collect profile information from specific devices by using the --devices command line option):

```
$ nvprof --metrics achieved_occupancy ./sumMatrix 32 32
sumMatrixOnGPU2D <<<(512,512),  (32,32)>>> Achieved Occupancy    0.501071
$ nvprof --metrics achieved_occupancy ./sumMatrix 32 16
sumMatrixOnGPU2D <<<(512,1024), (32,16)>>> Achieved Occupancy    0.736900
$ nvprof --metrics achieved_occupancy ./sumMatrix 16 32
sumMatrixOnGPU2D <<<(1024,512), (16,32)>>> Achieved Occupancy    0.766037
$ nvprof --metrics achieved_occupancy ./sumMatrix 16 16
sumMatrixOnGPU2D <<<(1024,1024),(16,16)>>> Achieved Occupancy    0.810691
```

From the results you can observe two things:

➤ Because the second case has more blocks than the first case, it exposed more active warps to the device. This is likely the reason why the second case has a higher achieved occupancy and better performance than the first case.

➤ The fourth case has the highest achieved occupancy, but it is not the fastest; therefore, a higher occupancy does not always equate to higher performance. There must be other factors that restrict performance.

Checking Memory Operations with nvprof

There are three memory operations in the sumMatrix kernel (C[idx] = A[idx] + B[idx]): two memory loads and one memory store. The efficiency of these memory operations can be checked using nvprof. First, check the memory read efficiency of the kernel using the gld_throughput metric to observe the differences for each execution configuration:

```
$ nvprof --metrics gld_throughput./sumMatrix 32 32
sumMatrixOnGPU2D <<<(512,512),  (32,32)>>> Global Load Throughput  35.908GB/s
$ nvprof --metrics gld_throughput./sumMatrix 32 16
sumMatrixOnGPU2D <<<(512,1024), (32,16)>>> Global Load Throughput  56.478GB/s
$ nvprof --metrics gld_throughput./sumMatrix 16 32
sumMatrixOnGPU2D <<<(1024,512), (16,32)>>> Global Load Throughput  85.195GB/s
$ nvprof --metrics gld_throughput./sumMatrix 16 16
sumMatrixOnGPU2D <<<(1024,1024),(16,16)>>> Global Load Throughput  94.708GB/s
```

While the fourth case has the highest load throughput, it is slower than the second case (which only demonstrates around half the load throughput). From this, you can see that a higher load throughput does not always equate to higher performance. The reason will be clear when you learn how memory transactions work inside the GPU device in Chapter 4.

Next, check the global load efficiency using the gld_efficiency metric, which is the ratio of requested global load throughput to required global load throughput. It measures how well the application's load operations use device memory bandwidth. The results are summarized below:

```
$ nvprof --metrics gld_efficiency ./sumMatrix 32 32
sumMatrixOnGPU2D <<<(512,512),  (32,32)>>> Global Memory Load Efficiency 100.00%
$ nvprof --metrics gld_efficiency ./sumMatrix 32 16
sumMatrixOnGPU2D <<<(512,1024), (32,16)>>> Global Memory Load Efficiency 100.00%
$ nvprof --metrics gld_efficiency ./sumMatrix 16 32
sumMatrixOnGPU2D <<<(1024,512), (16,32)>>> Global Memory Load Efficiency 49.96%
$ nvprof --metrics gld_efficiency ./sumMatrix 16 16
sumMatrixOnGPU2D <<<(1024,1024),(16,16)>>> Global Memory Load Efficiency 49.80%
```

From these results, you can see that the load efficiency for the last two cases was half that of the first two cases. This would explain why the higher load throughput and achieved occupancy of the last two cases did not yield improved performance. Even though the number of loads being performed (that is, throughput) is greater for the last two cases, the effectiveness of those loads (that is, efficiency) is lower.

Note that the common feature for the last two cases is that their block size in the innermost dimension is half of a warp. As stated earlier, for grid and block heuristics the innermost dimension should always be a multiple of the warp size. Chapter 4 will discuss how half-warp thread blocks impact performance.

Exposing More Parallelism

One conclusion you can draw from the previous section is that the innermost dimension of a block (block.x) should be a multiple of warp size. Doing so drastically improved load efficiency. You might still be curious:

➤   Is it possible to increase the load throughput further by adjusting block.x?

➤   Is it possible to expose more parallelism?

Now that a performance baseline has been established, these questions can be answered by testing summatrix with a wider range of thread configurations:

```
$ ./sumMatrix 64 2
sumMatrixOnGPU2D <<<(256,8192), (64,2) >>> elapsed 0.033567 sec
$ ./sumMatrix 64 4
sumMatrixOnGPU2D <<<(256,4096), (64,4) >>> elapsed 0.034908 sec
$ ./sumMatrix 64 8
sumMatrixOnGPU2D <<<(256,2048), (64,8) >>> elapsed 0.036651 sec
$ ./sumMatrix 128 2
sumMatrixOnGPU2D <<<(128,8192), (128,2)>>> elapsed 0.032688 sec
$ ./sumMatrix 128 4
sumMatrixOnGPU2D <<<(128,4096), (128,4)>>> elapsed 0.034786 sec
$ ./sumMatrix 128 8
sumMatrixOnGPU2D <<<(128,2048), (128,8)>>> elapsed 0.046157 sec
$ ./sumMatrix 256 2
sumMatrixOnGPU2D <<<(64,8192),  (256,2)>>> elapsed 0.032793 sec
$ ./sumMatrix 256 4
sumMatrixOnGPU2D <<<(64,4096),  (256,4)>>> elapsed 0.038092 sec
$ ./sumMatrix 256 8
sumMatrixOnGPU2D <<<(64,2048),  (256,8)>>> elapsed 0.000173 sec
Error: sumMatrix.cu:163, code:9, reason: invalid configuration argument
```

Here are some observations and conclusions from these results:

➤ The last execution configuration with block size (256, 8) is invalid. The total threads in a block exceeds 1,024, the hardware limit for this GPU.

➤ The best results are achieved with the fourth case using block dimensions of (128, 2).

➤ While the first case with block dimension (64, 2) launches the most thread blocks, it is not the fastest configuration.

➤ Because the second case with block configuration (64, 4) has the same number of thread blocks as the best case, the two cases should expose the same parallelism on the device. Because this case still underperforms relative to (128, 2) you can conclude that the size of the innermost dimension of a thread block plays a key role in performance. This repeats the conclusion drawn in the previous section.

➤ All remaining cases have fewer thread blocks than the best case. Therefore, exposing more parallelism is still an important factor in performance optimization.

You might guess that examples with the least thread blocks should report lower achieved occupancy, and examples with the most thread blocks should report higher achieved occupancy. This theory can be examined by measuring the achieved_occupancy metric with nvprof:

```
$ nvprof --metrics achieved_occupancy ./sumMatrix 64 2
sumMatrixOnGPU2D <<<(256,8192), (64,2) >>>  Achieved Occupancy    0.554556
$ nvprof --metrics achieved_occupancy ./sumMatrix 64 4
sumMatrixOnGPU2D <<<(256,4096), (64,4) >>>  Achieved Occupancy    0.798622
$ nvprof --metrics achieved_occupancy ./sumMatrix 64 8
sumMatrixOnGPU2D <<<(256,2048), (64,8) >>>  Achieved Occupancy    0.753532
$ nvprof --metrics achieved_occupancy ./sumMatrix 128 2
sumMatrixOnGPU2D <<<(128,8192), (128,2)>>>  Achieved Occupancy    0.802598
$ nvprof --metrics achieved_occupancy ./sumMatrix 128 4
sumMatrixOnGPU2D <<<(128,4096), (128,4)>>>  Achieved Occupancy    0.746367
```

```
$ nvprof --metrics achieved_occupancy ./sumMatrix 128 8
sumMatrixOnGPU2D <<<(128,2048), (128,8)>>>  Achieved Occupancy    0.573449
$ nvprof --metrics achieved_occupancy ./sumMatrix 256 2
sumMatrixOnGPU2D <<<(64,8192), (256,2) >>>  Achieved Occupancy    0.760901
$ nvprof --metrics achieved_occupancy ./sumMatrix 256 4
sumMatrixOnGPU2D <<<(64,4096), (256,4) >>>  Achieved Occupancy    0.595197
```

You might be surprised that the first case (64, 2) has the lowest achieved occupancy among all cases, yet it has the most thread blocks. This case is encountering hardware limits on the maximum number of thread blocks.

The fourth (128, 2) and seventh (256, 2) cases, the two highest performing configurations, have nearly identical achieved occupancy. It might be interesting to observe how performance is affected if you expose more inter-block parallelism by setting block.y to 1 for both cases. This reduces the size of each thread block, causing more thread blocks to be launched to process the same amount of data. Doing so produces the following results:

```
$ ./sumMatrix 128 1
sumMatrixOnGPU2D <<<(128,16384),(128,1)>>> elapsed 0.032602 sec
$ ./sumMatrix 256 1
sumMatrixOnGPU2D <<<(64,16384), (256,1)>>> elapsed 0.030959 sec
```

These configurations produce the best performance so far. In particular, a block configuration of (256, 1) outperforms (128, 1). You can check achieved occupancy, load throughput, and load efficiency with the following commands:

```
$ nvprof --metrics achieved_occupancy ./sumMatrix 256 1
$ nvprof --metrics gld_throughput ./sumMatrix 256 1
$ nvprof --metrics gld_efficiency ./sumMatrix 256 1
```

The following results are reported:

```
Achieved Occupancy           0.808622
Global Load Throughput       69.762GB/s
Global Memory Load Efficiency 100.00%
```

Note that the best execution configuration you found has neither the highest achieved occupancy nor the highest load throughput recorded. From these tests, you can conclude that no single metric is directly equivalent to improved performance. You need to look for a good balance of several related metrics to reach the best overall performance.

METRICS AND PERFORMANCE

➤ In most cases, no single metric can prescribe optimal performance.

➤ Which metric or event most directly relates to overall performance depends on the nature of the kernel code.

➤ Seek a good balance among related metrics and events.

➤ Check the kernel from different angles to find a balance among the related metrics.

➤ Grid/block heuristics provide a good starting point for performance tuning.

AVOIDING BRANCH DIVERGENCE

Sometimes, control flow depends on thread indices. Conditional execution within a warp may cause warp divergence that can lead to poor kernel performance. By rearranging data access patterns, you can reduce or avoid warp divergence. In this section, you will study basic techniques in avoiding branch divergence using a parallel reduction example.

The Parallel Reduction Problem

Suppose you want to calculate the sum of an array of integers with N elements. It would be quite easy for you to implement the algorithm using sequential code as follows:

```
int sum = 0;
for (int i = 0; i < N; i++)
    sum += array[i];
```

What if there is a huge number of data elements? How can you accelerate this sum by executing it in parallel? Due to the associative and commutative properties of addition, the elements of this array can be summed in any order. So you can perform parallel addition in the following way:

1. Partition the input vector into smaller chunks.

2. Have a thread calculate the partial sum for each chunk.

3. Add the partial results from each chunk into a final sum.

A common way to accomplish parallel addition is using an iterative pairwise implementation: A chunk contains only a pair of elements, and a thread sums those two elements to produce one partial result. These partial results are then stored *in-place* in the original input vector. These new values are used as the input to be summed in the next iteration. Because the number of input values halves on every iteration, a final sum has been calculated when the length of the output vector reaches one.

Depending on where output elements are stored in-place for each iteration, pairwise parallel sum implementations can be further classified into the following two types:

➤ **Neighbored pair:** Elements are paired with their immediate neighbor.

➤ **Interleaved pair:** Paired elements are separated by a given stride.

Figure 3-19 illustrates the neighbored pair implementation. In this implementation, a thread takes two adjacent elements to produce one partial sum at each step. For an array with N elements, this implementation requires $N - 1$ sums and $\log_2 N$ steps.

Figure 3-20 illustrates the interleaved pair implementation. Note that in this implementation the inputs to a thread are strided by half the length of the input on each step.

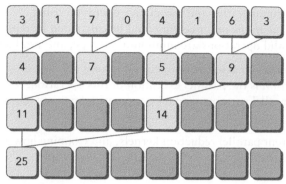

FIGURE 3-19

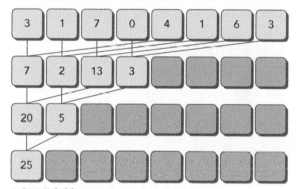

FIGURE 3-20

The following C function is a recursive implementation of the interleaved pair approach:

```
int recursiveReduce(int *data, int const size) {
    // terminate check
    if (size == 1) return data[0];

    // renew the stride
    int const stride = size / 2;

    // in-place reduction
    for (int i = 0; i < stride; i++) {
        data[i] += data[i + stride];
    }

    // call recursively
    return recursiveReduce(data, stride);
}
```

While the code above implements addition, any commutative and associative operation could replace addition. For example, the maximum value in the input vector could be calculated by replacing the sum with a call to max. Other example valid operations are minimum, average, and product.

This general problem of performing a commutative and associative operation across a vector is known as the *reduction* problem. *Parallel reduction* is the parallel execution of this operation. Parallel reduction is one of the most common parallel patterns, and a key operation in many parallel algorithms.

In this section, you will implement several different parallel reduction kernels, and examine how the different implementations affect kernel performance.

Divergence in Parallel Reduction

As a starting point, you will experiment with a kernel implementing the neighbored pair approach illustrated in Figure 3-21. Each thread adds two adjacent elements to produce a partial sum.

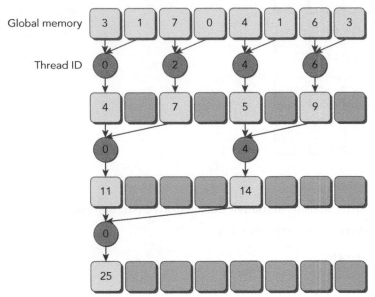

FIGURE 3-21

In this kernel, there are two global memory arrays: one large array for storing the entire array to reduce, and one smaller array for holding the partial sums of each thread block. Each thread block operates independently on a portion of the array. One iteration of a loop performs a single reduction step. The reduction is done in-place, which means that the values in global memory are replaced by partial sums at each step. The __syncthreads statement ensures that all partial sums for every thread in the current iteration have been saved to global memory before any threads in the same thread block enter the next iteration. All threads that enter the next iteration consume the values produced in the previous step. After the final round, the sum for the entire thread block is saved into global memory.

```
__global__ void reduceNeighbored(int *g_idata, int *g_odata, unsigned int n) {
    // set thread ID
    unsigned int tid = threadIdx.x;

    // convert global data pointer to the local pointer of this block
    int *idata = g_idata + blockIdx.x * blockDim.x;

    // boundary check
    if (idx >= n) return;

    // in-place reduction in global memory
    for (int stride = 1; stride < blockDim.x; stride *= 2) {
        if ((tid % (2 * stride)) == 0) {
            idata[tid] += idata[tid + stride];
        }

        // synchronize within block
        __syncthreads();
    }

    // write result for this block to global mem
    if (tid == 0) g_odata[blockIdx.x] = idata[0];
}
```

The distance between two neighbor elements, `stride`, is initialized to 1 at first. After each reduction round, this distance is multiplied by 2. After the first round, the even elements of `idata` will be replaced by partial sums. After the second round, every fourth element of `idata` will be replaced with further partial sums. Because there is no synchronization between thread blocks, the partial sum produced by each thread block is copied back to the host and summed sequentially there, as illustrated in Figure 3-22.

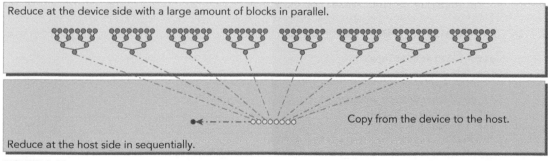

FIGURE 3-22

You can find the full source code in `reduceInteger.cu` available from `Wrox.com`. Listing 3-3 shows only the `main` function.

LISTING 3-3: Reduce integer (reduceInteger.cu) (main function only listed)

```
int main(int argc, char **argv) {
   // set up device
   int dev = 0;
   cudaDeviceProp deviceProp;
   cudaGetDeviceProperties(&deviceProp, dev);
   printf("%s starting reduction at ", argv[0]);
   printf("device %d: %s ", dev, deviceProp.name);
   cudaSetDevice(dev);

   bool bResult = false;

   // initialization
   int size = 1<<24; // total number of elements to reduce
   printf("    with array size %d  ", size);

   // execution configuration
   int blocksize = 512;    // initial block size
   if(argc > 1) {
      blocksize = atoi(argv[1]);    // block size from command line argument
   }
   dim3 block (blocksize,1);
   dim3 grid  ((size+block.x-1)/block.x,1);
   printf("grid %d block %d\n",grid.x, block.x);

   // allocate host memory
   size_t bytes = size * sizeof(int);
   int *h_idata = (int *) malloc(bytes);
   int *h_odata = (int *) malloc(grid.x*sizeof(int));
   int *tmp     = (int *) malloc(bytes);

   // initialize the array
   for (int i = 0; i < size; i++) {
      // mask off high 2 bytes to force max number to 255
      h_idata[i] = (int)(rand() & 0xFF);
   }
   memcpy (tmp, h_idata, bytes);

   size_t iStart,iElaps;
   int gpu_sum = 0;

   // allocate device memory
   int *d_idata = NULL;
   int *d_odata = NULL;
   cudaMalloc((void **) &d_idata, bytes);
   cudaMalloc((void **) &d_odata, grid.x*sizeof(int));

   // cpu reduction
   iStart = seconds ();
   int cpu_sum = recursiveReduce(tmp, size);
   iElaps = seconds () - iStart;
   printf("cpu reduce      elapsed %d ms cpu_sum: %d\n",iElaps,cpu_sum);

   // kernel 1: reduceNeighbored
   cudaMemcpy(d_idata, h_idata, bytes, cudaMemcpyHostToDevice);
```

```
        cudaDeviceSynchronize();
        iStart = seconds ();
        warmup<<<grid, block>>>(d_idata, d_odata, size);
        cudaDeviceSynchronize();
        iElaps = seconds () - iStart;
        cudaMemcpy(h_odata, d_odata, grid.x*sizeof(int), cudaMemcpyDeviceToHost);
        gpu_sum = 0;
        for (int i=0; i<grid.x; i++) gpu_sum += h_odata[i];
        printf("gpu Warmup     elapsed %d ms gpu_sum: %d <<<grid %d block %d>>>\n",
               iElaps,gpu_sum,grid.x,block.x);

        // kernel 1: reduceNeighbored
        cudaMemcpy(d_idata, h_idata, bytes, cudaMemcpyHostToDevice);
        cudaDeviceSynchronize();
        iStart = seconds ();
        reduceNeighbored<<<grid, block>>>(d_idata, d_odata, size);
        cudaDeviceSynchronize();
        iElaps = seconds () - iStart;
        cudaMemcpy(h_odata, d_odata, grid.x*sizeof(int), cudaMemcpyDeviceToHost);
        gpu_sum = 0;
        for (int i=0; i<grid.x; i++) gpu_sum += h_odata[i];
        printf("gpu Neighbored  elapsed %d ms gpu_sum: %d <<<grid %d block %d>>>\n",
               iElaps,gpu_sum,grid.x,block.x);

        cudaDeviceSynchronize();
        iElaps - seconds() - iStart;
        cudaMemcpy(h_odata, d_odata, grid.x/8*sizeof(int), cudaMemcpyDeviceToHost);

        gpu_sum = 0;
        for (int i = 0; i < grid.x / 8; i++) gpu_sum += h_odata[i];
        printf("gpu Cmptnroll   elapsed %d ms gpu_sum: %d <<<grid %d block %d>>>\n",
               iElaps,gpu_sum,grid.x/8,block.x);


        /// free host memory
        free(h_idata);
        free(h_odata);

        // free device memory
        cudaFree(d_idata);
        cudaFree(d_odata);

        // reset device
        cudaDeviceReset();

        // check the results
        bResult = (gpu_sum == cpu_sum);
        if(!bResult) printf("Test failed!\n");
        return EXIT_SUCCESS;
}
```

The input array is initialized to contain 16M elements:

```
        int size = 1<<24;
```

Then, the kernel is configured with a 1D grid and 1D blocks:

```
dim3 block (blocksize, 1);
dim3 grid  ((size + block.x - 1) / block.x, 1);
```

You can compile the file with the following command:

```
$ nvcc -O3 -arch=sm_20 reduceInteger.cu -o reduceInteger
```

Run the executable. Sample results are reported below.

```
$ ./reduceInteger starting reduction at device 0: Tesla M2070
        with array size 16777216  grid 32768 block 512
cpu reduce      elapsed 29 ms cpu_sum: 2139353471
gpu Neighbored  elapsed 11 ms gpu_sum: 2139353471 <<<grid 32768 block 512>>>
```

These results will be used as a baseline for performance tuning in the upcoming sections.

Improving Divergence in Parallel Reduction

Examine the kernel `reduceNeighbored` and note the following conditional statement:

```
if ((tid % (2 * stride)) == 0)
```

Because this statement is only true for even numbered threads, it causes highly divergent warps. In the first iteration of parallel reduction, only even threads execute the body of this conditional statement but all threads must be scheduled. On the second iteration, only one fourth of all threads are active but still all threads must be scheduled. Warp divergence can be reduced by rearranging the array index of each thread to force neighboring threads to perform the addition. Figure 3-23 illustrates this implementation. Comparing with Figure 3-21, the store location of partial sums has not changed, but the working threads have been updated.

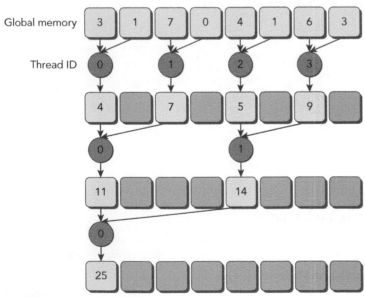

FIGURE 3-23

The kernel code for this change is listed here:

```
__global__ void reduceNeighboredLess (int *g_idata, int *g_odata, unsigned int n) {
    // set thread ID
    unsigned int tid = threadIdx.x;
    unsigned int idx = blockIdx.x * blockDim.x + threadIdx.x;

    // convert global data pointer to the local pointer of this block
    int *idata = g_idata + blockIdx.x*blockDim.x;

    // boundary check
    if(idx >= n) return;

    // in-place reduction in global memory
    for (int stride = 1; stride < blockDim.x; stride *= 2) {
        // convert tid into local array index
        int index = 2 * stride * tid;
        if (index < blockDim.x) {
            idata[index] += idata[index + stride];
        }

        // synchronize within threadblock
        __syncthreads();
    }

    // write result for this block to global mem
    if (tid == 0) g_odata[blockIdx.x] = idata[0];
}
```

Notice the following statement in the kernel, which sets the array access index for each thread.

```
int index = 2 * stride * tid;
```

Because stride is multiplied by 2, the following statement uses the first half of a thread block to execute the addition:

```
if (index < blockDim.x)
```

With a thread block size of 512 threads, the first 8 warps execute the first round of reduction, and the remaining 8 warps do nothing. In the second round, the first 4 warps execute the reduction, and the remaining 12 warps do nothing. Therefore, there is no divergence at all. Divergence only occurs in the last 5 rounds when the total number of threads at each round is less than the warp size. You will learn how to handle this issue in the next section.

This new kernel is called in the following code segment in the main function after the call to the baseline kernel.

```
// kernel 2: reduceNeighbored with less divergence
cudaMemcpy(d_idata, h_idata, bytes, cudaMemcpyHostToDevice);
cudaDeviceSynchronize();
iStart = seconds();
reduceNeighboredLess<<<grid, block>>>(d_idata, d_odata, size);
cudaDeviceSynchronize();
iElaps = seconds() - iStart;
cudaMemcpy(h_odata, d_odata, grid.x*sizeof(int), cudaMemcpyDeviceToHost);
gpu_sum = 0;
```

```
      for (int i=0; i<grid.x; i++) gpu_sum += h_odata[i];
      printf("gpu Neighbored2 elapsed %d ms gpu_sum: %d <<<grid %d block %d>>>\n",
          iElaps,gpu_sum,grid.x,block.x);
```

Testing with `reduceNeighboredLess` and the earlier kernels produces the following report:

```
$ ./reduceInteger Starting reduction at device 0: Tesla M2070
      vector size 16777216 grid 32768 block 512
cpu reduce        elapsed 0.029138 sec cpu_sum: 2139353471
gpu Neighbored  elapsed 0.011722 sec gpu_sum: 2139353471 <<<grid 32768 block 512>>>
gpu NeighboredL elapsed 0.009321 sec gpu_sum: 2139353471 <<<grid 32768 block 512>>>
```

The new implementation is 1.26 times faster than the original implementation.

You can test different metrics to explain the different behaviors between these two kernels. Use the `inst_per_warp` metric to check the average number of instructions executed by each warp:

```
$ nvprof --metrics inst_per_warp ./reduceInteger
```

The results are summarized below. The original kernel executed more than twice as many instructions per warp as the new kernel, an indicator of high divergence in the original implementation.

```
Neighbored    Instructions per warp  295.562500
NeighboredLess Instructions per warp  115.312500
```

Use the `gld_throughput` metric to check memory load throughput:

```
$ nvprof --metrics gld_throughput ./reduceInteger
```

The results are summarized below. The new implementation also has a much higher load throughput as it is performing the same amount of I/O but over a much shorter period of time.

```
Neighbored  Global Load Throughput  67.663GB/s
NeighboredL Global Load Throughput  80.144GB/s
```

Reducing with Interleaved Pairs

The interleaved pair approach reverses the striding of elements compared to the neighbored approach: The stride is started at half of the thread block size and then reduced by half on each iteration (illustrated in Figure 3-24). Each thread adds two elements separated by the current stride to produce a partial sum at each round. Compared with Figure 3-23, the working threads in interleaved reduction are not changed. However, the load/store locations in global memory for each thread are different.

The kernel code for interleaved reduction is as follows:

```
/// Interleaved Pair Implementation with less divergence
__global__ void reduceInterleaved (int *g_idata, int *g_odata, unsigned int n) {
    // set thread ID
    unsigned int tid = threadIdx.x;
    unsigned int idx = blockIdx.x * blockDim.x + threadIdx.x;

    // convert global data pointer to the local pointer of this block
    int *idata = g_idata + blockIdx.x * blockDim.x;
```

```
// boundary check
if(idx >= n) return;

// in-place reduction in global memory
for (int stride = blockDim.x / 2; stride > 0; stride >>= 1) {
    if (tid < stride) {
        idata[tid] += idata[tid + stride];
    }

    __syncthreads();
}

// write result for this block to global mem
if (tid == 0) g_odata[blockIdx.x] = idata[0];
}
```

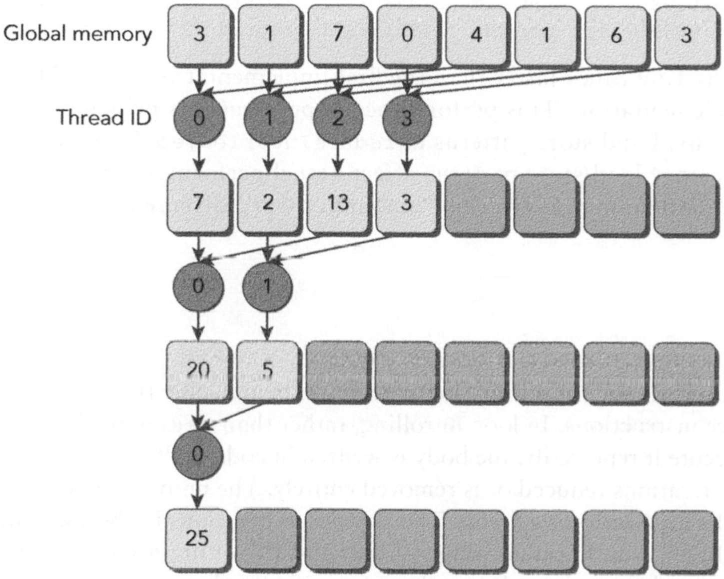

FIGURE 3-24

Notice the following statement in the kernel. The stride between two elements is initialized to half of the thread block size, and then is reduced by half in each round.

```
for (int stride = blockDim.x / 2; stride > 0; stride >>= 1) {
```

The following statement forces the first half of the thread block to execute the addition on the first iteration, the first quarter of a thread block on the second iteration, and so on.

```
if (tid < stride)
```

The following code is added to the main function to execute interleaved reduction:

```
cudaMemcpy(d_idata, h_idata, bytes, cudaMemcpyHostToDevice);
cudaDeviceSynchronize();
iStart = seconds();
```

```
reduceInterleaved  <<< grid, block >>> (d_idata, d_odata, size);
cudaDeviceSynchronize();
iElaps = seconds() - iStart;
cudaMemcpy(h_odata, d_odata, grid.x*sizeof(int), cudaMemcpyDeviceToHost);
gpu_sum = 0;
for (int i = 0; i < grid.x; i++) gpu_sum += h_odata[i];
printf("gpu Interleaved elapsed %f sec gpu_sum: %d <<<grid %d block %d>>>\n",
        iElaps,gpu_sum,grid.x,block.x);
```

Testing with `reduceInterleaved` and the earlier kernels produces the following output:

```
$ ./reduce starting reduction at device 0: Tesla M2070
        with array size 16777216  grid 32768 block 512
cpu reduce       elapsed 0.029138 sec cpu_sum: 2139353471
gpu Warmup       elapsed 0.011745 sec gpu_sum: 2139353471 <<<grid 32768 block 512>>>
gpu Neighbored   elapsed 0.011722 sec gpu_sum: 2139353471 <<<grid 32768 block 512>>>
gpu NeighboredL  elapsed 0.009321 sec gpu_sum: 2139353471 <<<grid 32768 block 512>>>
gpu Interleaved  elapsed 0.006967 sec gpu_sum: 2139353471 <<<grid 32768 block 512>>>
```

The interleaved implementation is 1.69 times faster than the first implementation and 1.34 times faster than the second implementation. This performance improvement is primarily a result of the global memory load and store patterns in `reduceInterleaved`. You will learn more about how global memory load/store patterns affect kernel performance in Chapter 4. `reduceInterleaved` also maintains the same amount of warp divergence as `reduceNeighboredLess`.

UNROLLING LOOPS

Loop unrolling is a technique that attempts to optimize loop execution by reducing the frequency of branches and loop maintenance instructions. In loop unrolling, rather than writing the body of a loop once and using a loop to execute it repeatedly, the body is written in code multiple times. Any enclosing loop then either has its iterations reduced or is removed entirely. The number of copies made of the loop body is called the *loop unrolling factor*. The number of iterations in the enclosing loop is divided by the loop unrolling factor. Loop unrolling is most effective at improving performance for sequential array processing loops where the number of iterations is known prior to execution of the loop. Consider the code fragment below:

```
for (int i = 0; i < 100; i++) {
    a[i] = b[i] + c[i];
}
```

If you replicate the body of the loop once, the number of iterations can be reduced to half of the original loop:

```
for (int i = 0; i < 100; i += 2) {
    a[i]   = b[i]   + c[i];
    a[i+1] = b[i+1] + c[i+1];

}
```

The reason for performance gains from loop unrolling may not be readily apparent by looking at the high-level code. The improvement comes from low-level instruction improvements and optimizations that the compiler performs to the unrolled loop. For example, in the unrolled loop example above, the condition i<100 is only checked fifty times, compared to one hundred times in the original loop. Additionally, because the reads and writes performed in each statement of each loop are independent, the memory operations can be issued simultaneously by the CPU.

Unrolling in CUDA can mean a variety of things. However, the goal is still the same: Improving performance by reducing instruction overheads and creating more independent instructions to schedule. As a result, more concurrent operations are added to the pipeline leading to higher saturation of instruction and memory bandwidth. This provides the warp scheduler with more eligible warps that can help hide instruction or memory latency.

Reducing with Unrolling

You may notice that each thread block in the reduceInterleaved kernel handles just one portion of the data, which you can consider a data block. What if you manually unrolled the processing of two data blocks by a single thread block? The following kernel is a revision to the reduceInterleaved kernel: For each thread block, data from two data blocks is summed. This is an example of cyclic partitioning (introduced in Chapter 1): Each thread works on more than one data block and processes a single element from each data block.

```
__global__ void reduceUnrolling2 (int *g_idata, int *g_odata, unsigned int n) {
    // set thread ID
    unsigned int tid = threadIdx.x;
    unsigned int idx = blockIdx.x * blockDim.x * 2 + threadIdx.x;

    // convert global data pointer to the local pointer of this block
    int *idata = g_idata + blockIdx.x * blockDim.x * 2;

    // unrolling 2 data blocks
    if (idx + blockDim.x < n) g_idata[idx] += g_idata[idx + blockDim.x];
    __syncthreads();

    // in-place reduction in global memory
    for (int stride = blockDim.x / 2; stride > 0; stride >>= 1) {
        if (tid < stride) {
            idata[tid] += idata[tid + stride];
        }


        // synchronize within threadblock
        __syncthreads();
    }

    // write result for this block to global mem
    if (tid == 0) g_odata[blockIdx.x] = idata[0];
}
```

Note the following statement added at the start of the kernel. Here, each thread is adding an element from the neighboring data block. Conceptually, you can think of this as an iteration of the reduction loop that reduces across data blocks.

```
if (idx + blockDim.x < n) g_idata[idx] += g_idata[idx+blockDim.x];
```

The global array index is adjusted accordingly, as shown below, because you only need half as many thread blocks to process the same data set. Note that this also implies less warp- and block-level parallelism is exposed to the device for the same data set size. Figure 3-25 illustrates the data access for each thread.

```
unsigned int idx = blockIdx.x * blockDim.x * 2 + threadIdx.x;
int *idata = g_idata + blockIdx.x * blockDim.x * 2;
```

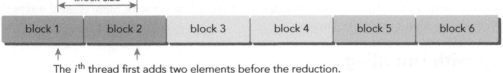

The ith thread first adds two elements before the reduction.

FIGURE 3-25

Adding the following code segment to `main` calls the new kernel.

```
cudaMemcpy(d_idata, h_idata, bytes, cudaMemcpyHostToDevice);
cudaDeviceSynchronize();
iStart = seconds();
reduceUnrolling2  <<< grid.x/2, block >>> (d_idata, d_odata, size);
cudaDeviceSynchronize();
iElaps = seconds() - iStart;
cudaMemcpy(h_odata, d_odata, grid.x/2*sizeof(int), cudaMemcpyDeviceToHost);
gpu_sum = 0;
for (int i = 0; i < grid.x / 2; i++) gpu_sum += h_odata[i];
printf("gpu Unrolling2  elapsed %f sec gpu_sum: %d <<<grid %d block %d>>>\n",
        iElaps,gpu_sum,grid.x/2,block.x);
```

Because each thread block now handles two data blocks, you need to adjust the execution configuration of the kernel by reducing its grid size by half:

```
reduceUnrolling2<<<grid.x / 2, block>>>(d_idata, d_odata, size);
```

Now compile and run the code. The following result is reported:

```
gpu Unrolling2  elapsed 0.003430 sec gpu_sum: 2139353471 <<<grid 16384 block 512>>>
```

Even with that simple change, the kernel is now executing 3.42 times faster than the original implementation. Can further unrolling produce better performance? The file `reduceInteger.cu` includes two other implementations of unrolled kernels as follows:

```
reduceUnrolling4  : each threadblock handles 4 data blocks
reduceUnrolling8  : each threadblock handles 8 data blocks
```

The corresponding results are summarized below:

```
gpu Unrolling2 elapsed 0.003430 sec gpu_sum: 2139353471 <<<grid 16384 block 512>>>
gpu Unrolling4 elapsed 0.001829 sec gpu_sum: 2139353471 <<<grid 8192 block 512>>>
gpu Unrolling8 elapsed 0.001422 sec gpu_sum: 2139353471 <<<grid 4096 block 512>>>
```

Just as you might expect, more independent memory load/store operations in a single thread yield better performance as memory latency can be better hidden. You can confirm this is the cause for the performance gains using the device memory read throughput metric.

```
$ nvprof --metrics dram_read_throughput ./reduceInteger
```

The results are summarized below. There is a definite positive relationship between unrolling for the reduction test case and device read throughput.

```
Unrolling2 Device Memory Read Throughput  26.295GB/s
Unrolling4 Device Memory Read Throughput  49.546GB/s
Unrolling8 Device Memory Read Throughput  62.764GB/s
```

Reducing with Unrolled Warps

__syncthreads is used for intra-block synchronization. In the reduction kernels, it is used in each round to ensure that all threads writing partial results to global memory have completed before any thread continues to the next round.

However, consider the case when there are 32 or fewer threads left (that is, a single warp). Because warp execution is SIMT, there is implicit intra-warp synchronization after each instruction. The last 6 iterations of the reduction loop can therefore be unrolled as follows:

```
if (tid < 32) {
    volatile int *vmem = idata;
    vmem[tid] += vmem[tid + 32];
    vmem[tid] += vmem[tid + 16];
    vmem[tid] += vmem[tid +  8];
    vmem[tid] += vmem[tid +  4];
    vmem[tid] += vmem[tid +  2];
    vmem[tid] += vmem[tid +  1];
}
```

This warp unrolling avoids executing loop control and thread synchronization logic.

Note that the variable vmem is declared with the volatile qualifier, which tells the compiler that it must store vmem[tid] back to global memory with every assignment. If the volatile qualifier is omitted, this code will not work correctly because the compiler or cache may optimize out some reads or writes to global or shared memory. If a variable located in global or shared memory is declared volatile, the compiler assumes that its value can be changed or used at any time by other threads. Therefore, any reference to volatile variables forces a read or write directly to memory, and not simply to cache or a register.

Based on reduceUnrolling8, warp unrolling can be added to the reduction kernel as follows:

```
__global__ void reduceUnrollWarps8 (int *g_idata, int *g_odata, unsigned int n) {
    // set thread ID
    unsigned int tid = threadIdx.x;
    unsigned int idx = blockIdx.x*blockDim.x*8 + threadIdx.x;

    // convert global data pointer to the local pointer of this block
    int *idata = g_idata + blockIdx.x*blockDim.x*8;

    // unrolling 8
    if (idx + 7*blockDim.x < n) {
        int a1 = g_idata[idx];
        int a2 = g_idata[idx+blockDim.x];
        int a3 = g_idata[idx+2*blockDim.x];
        int a4 = g_idata[idx+3*blockDim.x];
        int b1 = g_idata[idx+4*blockDim.x];
```

```
        int b2 = g_idata[idx+5*blockDim.x];
        int b3 = g_idata[idx+6*blockDim.x];
        int b4 = g_idata[idx+7*blockDim.x];
        g_idata[idx] = a1+a2+a3+a4+b1+b2+b3+b4;
    }
    __syncthreads();

    // in-place reduction in global memory
    for (int stride = blockDim.x / 2; stride > 32; stride >>= 1) {
        if (tid < stride) {
            idata[tid] += idata[tid + stride];
        }

      // synchronize within threadblock
      __syncthreads();
    }

    // unrolling warp
    if (tid < 32) {
        volatile int *vmem = idata;
        vmem[tid] += vmem[tid + 32];
        vmem[tid] += vmem[tid + 16];
        vmem[tid] += vmem[tid +  8];
        vmem[tid] += vmem[tid +  4];
        vmem[tid] += vmem[tid +  2];
        vmem[tid] += vmem[tid +  1];
    }

    // write result for this block to global mem
    if (tid == 0) g_odata[blockIdx.x] = idata[0];
}
```

Because each thread handles eight data blocks in this implementation, you invoke this kernel with its grid size reduced by a factor of eight:

```
reduceUnrollWarps8<<<grid.x / 8, block>>> (d_idata, d_odata, size);
```

The execution time for this kernel is 1.05 times faster than `reduceUnrolling8` and 8.65 times faster than the original kernel `reduceNeighbored`:

```
gpu UnrollWarp8 elapsed 0.001355 sec gpu_sum: 2139353471 <<<grid 4096 block 512>>>
```

The `stall_sync` metric can be used to verify that fewer warps are stalling due to `__syncthreads` synchronization, using the command below:

```
$ nvprof --metrics stall_sync ./reduce
```

The results are summarized here. By unrolling the last warp, the percentage nearly halves, indicating that `__syncthreads` is causing fewer of the stalls in the new kernel.

```
Unrolling8     Issue Stall Reasons 58.37%
UnrollWarps8   Issue Stall Reasons 30.60%
```

Reducing with Complete Unrolling

If you know the number of iterations in a loop at compile-time, you can completely unroll it. Because the maximum number of threads per block on either Fermi or Kepler is limited to 1024 (refer to Table 3-2), and the loop iteration count in these reduction kernels is based on a thread block dimension, it is possible to completely unroll the reduction loop:

```
__global__ void reduceCompleteUnrollWarps8 (int *g_idata, int *g_odata,
    unsigned int n) {
// set thread ID
unsigned int tid = threadIdx.x;
unsigned int idx = blockIdx.x * blockDim.x * 8 + threadIdx.x;

// convert global data pointer to the local pointer of this block
int *idata = g_idata + blockIdx.x * blockDim.x * 8;

// unrolling 8
if (idx + 7*blockDim.x < n) {
    int a1 = g_idata[idx];
    int a2 = g_idata[idx + blockDim.x];
    int a3 = g_idata[idx + 2 * blockDim.x];
    int a4 = g_idata[idx + 3 * blockDim.x];
    int b1 = g_idata[idx + 4 * blockDim.x];
    int b2 = g_idata[idx + 5 * blockDim.x];
    int b3 = g_idata[idx + 6 * blockDim.x];
    int b4 = g_idata[idx + 7 * blockDim.x];
    g_idata[idx] = a1 + a2 + a3 + a4 + b1 + b2 + b3 + b4;
}
__syncthreads();

// in-place reduction and complete unroll
if (blockDim.x>=1024 && tid < 512) idata[tid] += idata[tid + 512];
__syncthreads();

if (blockDim.x>=512 && tid < 256) idata[tid] += idata[tid + 256];
__syncthreads();

if (blockDim.x>=256 && tid < 128) idata[tid] += idata[tid + 128];
__syncthreads();

if (blockDim.x>=128 && tid < 64) idata[tid] += idata[tid + 64];
__syncthreads();
// unrolling warp
if (tid < 32) {
    volatile int *vsmem = idata;
    vsmem[tid] += vsmem[tid + 32];
    vsmem[tid] += vsmem[tid + 16];
    vsmem[tid] += vsmem[tid +  8];
    vsmem[tid] += vsmem[tid +  4];
    vsmem[tid] += vsmem[tid +  2];
    vsmem[tid] += vsmem[tid +  1];
}
```

```
    // write result for this block to global mem
    if (tid == 0) g_odata[blockIdx.x] = idata[0];
}
```

Invoke this kernel with the following execution configuration:

```
reduceCompleteUnrollWarps8<<<grid.x / 8, block>>>(d_idata, d_odata, size);
```

Kernel time again shows marginal improvement, executing 1.06 times faster than reduceUnrollWarps8, and 9.16 times faster than the original implementation.

```
gpu CmptUnroll8 elapsed 0.001280 sec gpu_sum: 2139353471 <<<grid 4096 block 512>>>
```

Reducing with Template Functions

While it is possible to manually unroll loops, using template functions can help to further reduce branch overhead. CUDA supports template parameters on device functions. You can specify the block size as a parameter of the template function as follows:

```
template <unsigned int iBlockSize>
__global__ void reduceCompleteUnroll(int *g_idata, int *g_odata, unsigned int n) {
    // set thread ID
    unsigned int tid = threadIdx.x;
    unsigned int idx = blockIdx.x * blockDim.x * 8 + threadIdx.x;

    // convert global data pointer to the local pointer of this block
    int *idata = g_idata + blockIdx.x * blockDim.x * 8;

    // unrolling 8
    if (idx + 7*blockDim.x < n) {
        int a1 = g_idata[idx];
        int a2 = g_idata[idx + blockDim.x];
        int a3 = g_idata[idx + 2 * blockDim.x];
        int a4 = g_idata[idx + 3 * blockDim.x];
        int b1 = g_idata[idx + 4 * blockDim.x];
        int b2 = g_idata[idx + 5 * blockDim.x];
        int b3 = g_idata[idx + 6 * blockDim.x];
        int b4 = g_idata[idx + 7 * blockDim.x];
        g_idata[idx] = a1+a2+a3+a4+b1+b2+b3+b4;
    }
    __syncthreads();

    // in-place reduction and complete unroll
    if (iBlockSize>=1024 && tid < 512) idata[tid] += idata[tid + 512];
    __syncthreads();

    if (iBlockSize>=512 && tid < 256)  idata[tid] += idata[tid + 256];
    __syncthreads();
```

```
        if (iBlockSize>=256 && tid < 128)   idata[tid] += idata[tid + 128];
        __syncthreads();

        if (iBlockSize>=128 && tid < 64)    idata[tid] += idata[tid + 64];
        __syncthreads();
        // unrolling warp
        if (tid < 32) {
            volatile int *vsmem = idata;
            vsmem[tid] += vsmem[tid + 32];
            vsmem[tid] += vsmem[tid + 16];
            vsmem[tid] += vsmem[tid +  8];
            vsmem[tid] += vsmem[tid +  4];
            vsmem[tid] += vsmem[tid +  2];
            vsmem[tid] += vsmem[tid +  1];
        }

        // write result for this block to global mem
        if (tid == 0) g_odata[blockIdx.x] = idata[0];
    }
```

The only difference compared to reduceCompleteUnrollWarps8 is that you replaced block size with a template parameter. The if statements that check the block size will be evaluated at compile time and removed if the condition is not true, resulting in a very efficient inner loop. For example, if this kernel were invoked with a thread block size of 256 the statement:

```
    iBlockSize>=1024 && tid < 512
```

would always be false. The compiler would automatically remove it from the executed kernel.

The kernel must be called with the switch-case structure as shown here. This allows the compiler to automatically optimize code for particular block sizes, but means it is only valid to launch reduceCompleteUnroll with certain block sizes.

```
        switch (blocksize) {
            case 1024:
                reduceCompleteUnroll<1024><<<grid.x/8, block>>>(d_idata, d_odata, size);
                break;
            case 512:
                reduceCompleteUnroll<512><<<grid.x/8, block>>>(d_idata, d_odata, size);
                break;
            case 256:
                reduceCompleteUnroll<256><<<grid.x/8, block>>>(d_idata, d_odata, size);
                break;
            case 128:
                reduceCompleteUnroll<128><<<grid.x/8, block>>>(d_idata, d_odata, size);
                break;
            case 64:
                reduceCompleteUnroll<64><<<grid.x/8, block>>>(d_idata, d_odata, size);
                break;
        }
```

Table 3-5 summarizes the results of all parallel reduction implementations covered in this section.

TABLE 3-5: Reduction Kernel Performance

KERNEL	TIME (S)	STEP SPEEDUP	CUMULATIVE SPEEDUP
Neighbored (divergence)	0.011722		
Neighbored (no divergence)	0.009321	1.26	1.26
Interleaved	0.006967	1.34	1.68
Unroll 8 blocks	0.001422	4.90	8.24
Unroll 8 blocks + last warp	0.001355	1.05	8.65
Unroll 8 blocks + loop + last warp	0.001280	1.06	9.16
Templatized kernel	0.001253	1.02	9.35

Note that the largest relative performance gain is achieved by the `reduceUnrolling8` kernel, in which each thread handles 8 data blocks before starting the reduce. With 8 independent memory accesses, you will better saturate memory bandwidth and hide load/store latency. You can check memory load/store efficiency metrics using the following command:

```
$nvprof --metrics gld_efficiency,gst_efficiency ./reduceInteger
```

The results are summarized in Table 3-6 for all kernels. In Chapter 4, you will examine global memory access in more detail and gain additional insight into how memory accesses affect kernel performance.

TABLE 3-6: Load/Store Efficiency

KERNEL	TIME (S)	LOAD EFFICIENCY	STORE EFFICIENCY
Neighbored (divergence)	0.011722	16.73%	25.00%
Neighbored (no divergence)	0.009321	16.75%	25.00%
Interleaved	0.006967	77.94%	95.52%
Unroll 8 blocks	0.001422	94.68%	97.71%
Unroll 8 blocks + last warp	0.001355	98.99%	99.40%
Unroll 8 blocks + loop + last warp	0.001280	98.99%	99.40%
Templatized the last kernel	0.001253	98.99%	99.40%

DYNAMIC PARALLELISM

So far in this book, all kernels have been invoked from the host thread. The GPU workload is completely under the control of the CPU. CUDA *Dynamic Parallelism* allows new GPU kernels to be created and synchronized directly on the GPU. The ability to dynamically add parallelism to a GPU application at arbitrary points in a kernel offers exciting new capabilities.

Up until now, you had to express your algorithms as individual, massively data parallel kernel launches. Dynamic parallelism enables a more hierarchical approach where concurrency can be expressed in multiple levels in a GPU kernel. Using dynamic parallelism can make your recursive algorithm more transparent and easier to understand.

With dynamic parallelism, you can postpone the decision of exactly how many blocks and grids to create on a GPU until runtime, taking advantage of the GPU hardware schedulers and load balancers dynamically and adapting in response to data-driven decisions or workloads.

The ability to create work directly from the GPU can also reduce the need to transfer execution control and data between the host and device, as launch configuration decisions can be made at runtime by threads executing on the device.

In this section, you will gain a basic understanding of how to use dynamic parallelism by implementing the recursive reduction kernel example using dynamic parallelism.

Nested Execution

With dynamic parallelism, the kernel execution concepts (grids, blocks, launch configuration, and so on) that you are already familiar with can also be applied to kernel invocation directly on the GPU. The same kernel invocation syntax is used to launch a new kernel within a kernel.

In dynamic parallelism, kernel executions are classified into two types: parent and child. A *parent thread*, *parent thread block*, or *parent grid* has launched a new grid, the *child grid*. A *child thread*, *child thread block*, or *child grid* has been launched by a parent. A child grid must complete before the parent thread, parent thread block, or parent grids are considered complete. A parent is not considered complete until all of its child grids have completed.

Figure 3-26 illustrates the scope of a parent grid and child grid. The parent grid is configured and launched by the host thread, and the child grid is configured and launched by the parent grid. The invocation and completion of the child grid must be properly nested, meaning that the parent grid is not considered complete until all child grids created by its threads have completed. If the invoking threads do not explicitly synchronize on the launched child grids, the runtime guarantees an implicit synchronization between the parent and child. In this figure, a barrier is set in the parent thread to explicitly synchronize with its child grid.

Grid launches in a device thread are visible across a thread block. This means that a thread may synchronize on the child grids launched by that thread or by other threads in the same thread block. Execution of a thread block is not considered complete until all child grids created by all threads in the block have completed. If all threads in a block exit before all child grids have completed, implicit synchronization on those child grids is triggered.

When a parent launches a child grid, the child is not guaranteed to begin execution until the parent thread block explicitly synchronizes on the child.

Parent and child grids share the same global and constant memory storage, but have distinct local and shared memory. Parent and child grids have concurrent access to global memory, with weak consistency guarantees between child and parent. There are two points in the execution of a child grid when its view of memory is fully consistent with the parent thread: at the start of a child grid, and when the child grid completes. All global memory operations in the parent thread prior to a child grid invocation are guaranteed to be visible to the child grid. All memory operations of the child grid are guaranteed to be visible to the parent after the parent has synchronized on the child grid's completion.

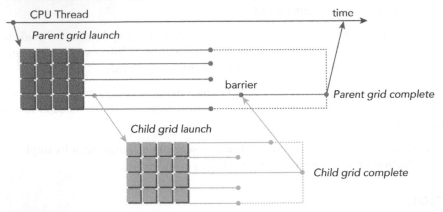

FIGURE 3-26

Shared and local memory are private to a thread block or thread, respectively, and are not visible or coherent between parent and child. Local memory is private storage for a thread, and is not visible outside of that thread. It is invalid to pass a pointer to local memory as an argument when launching a child grid.

Nested Hello World on the GPU

For an initial understanding of dynamic parallelism, you will create a kernel that uses dynamic parallelism to print "Hello World". Figure 3-27 illustrates the nested, recursive execution constructed by this kernel using dynamic parallelism. The host application invokes the parent grid with 8 threads in a single thread block. Then, thread 0 in that grid invokes a child grid with half as many threads. Next, thread 0 in the first child grid invokes a new child grid with half as many threads again, and so on until only one thread is left in the final nesting.

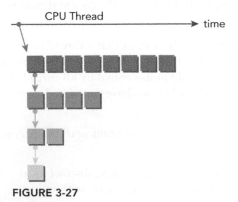

FIGURE 3-27

The kernel code implementing this logic is listed here. Execution of the kernel by every thread starts with printing `"Hello World"`. Then, each thread checks if it should terminate. If the thread count at this nested layer is greater than one, thread 0 recursively invokes a child grid with half as many threads.

```
__global__ void nestedHelloWorld(int const iSize,int iDepth) {
    int tid = threadIdx.x;
    printf("Recursion=%d: Hello World from thread %d"
        "block %d\n",iDepth,tid,blockIdx.x);

    // condition to stop recursive execution
    if (iSize == 1) return;

    // reduce block size to half
    int nthreads = iSize>>1;

    // thread 0 launches child grid recursively
    if(tid == 0 && nthreads > 0) {
        nestedHelloWorld<<<1, nthreads>>>(nthreads,++iDepth);
        printf("-------> nested execution depth: %d\n",iDepth);
    }
}
```

You can find the full code for this example in `nestedHelloWorld.cu`, downloadable from `Wrox.com`. Compile the code with the following command:

```
$ nvcc -arch=sm_35 -rdc=true nestedHelloWorld.cu -o nestedHelloWorld -lcudadevrt
```

As dynamic parallelism is supported by the device runtime library, `nestedHelloWorld` must be explicitly linked with `-lcudadevrt` on the command line.

The flag `-rdc=true` forces the generation of relocatable device code, a requirement for dynamic parallelism. You will learn more about relocatable device code in Chapter 10 of this book.

The output of the nested kernel is shown here:

```
./nestedHelloWorld Execution Configuration: grid 1 block 8
Recursion=0: Hello World from thread 0 block 0
Recursion=0: Hello World from thread 1 block 0
Recursion=0: Hello World from thread 2 block 0
Recursion=0: Hello World from thread 3 block 0
Recursion=0: Hello World from thread 4 block 0
Recursion=0: Hello World from thread 5 block 0
Recursion=0: Hello World from thread 6 block 0
Recursion=0: Hello World from thread 7 block 0
-------> nested execution depth: 1
Recursion=1: Hello World from thread 0 block 0
Recursion=1: Hello World from thread 1 block 0
Recursion=1: Hello World from thread 2 block 0
Recursion=1: Hello World from thread 3 block 0
-------> nested execution depth: 2
Recursion=2: Hello World from thread 0 block 0
Recursion=2: Hello World from thread 1 block 0
-------> nested execution depth: 3
Recursion=3: Hello World from thread 0 block 0
```

From the output messages, you can see that the parent grid invoked by the host has 1 block and 8 threads. The nestedHelloWorld kernel was recursively invoked three times, and at each invocation the number of threads halved. You can confirm this using nvvp with the following command.

```
$ nvvp ./nestedHelloWorld
```

Figure 3-28 illustrates the nested execution exposed by nvvp. The child grids are properly nested and each parent grid waits until its child grid is completed. White space is used to indicate a kernel spending time waiting for a child to complete.

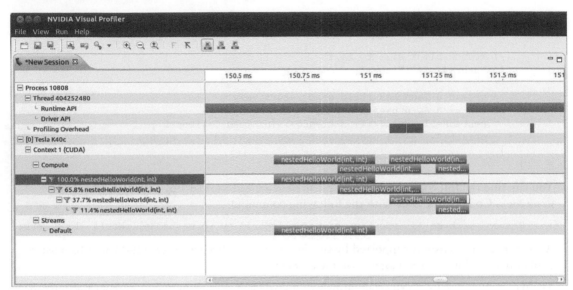

FIGURE 3-28

Now, try invoking the parent grid with two blocks instead of only one:

```
$ ./nestedHelloWorld 2
```

The output of the nested kernel program is now:

```
./nestedHelloWorld 2Execution Configuration: grid 2 block 8
Recursion=0: Hello World from thread 0 block 1
Recursion=0: Hello World from thread 1 block 1
Recursion=0: Hello World from thread 2 block 1
Recursion=0: Hello World from thread 3 block 1
Recursion=0: Hello World from thread 4 block 1
Recursion=0: Hello World from thread 5 block 1
Recursion=0: Hello World from thread 6 block 1
Recursion=0: Hello World from thread 7 block 1
Recursion=0: Hello World from thread 0 block 0
Recursion=0: Hello World from thread 1 block 0
```

```
Recursion=0: Hello World from thread 2 block 0
Recursion=0: Hello World from thread 3 block 0
Recursion=0: Hello World from thread 4 block 0
Recursion=0: Hello World from thread 5 block 0
Recursion=0: Hello World from thread 6 block 0
Recursion=0: Hello World from thread 7 block 0
-------> nested execution depth: 1
-------> nested execution depth: 1
Recursion=1: Hello World from thread 0 block 0
Recursion=1: Hello World from thread 1 block 0
Recursion=1: Hello World from thread 2 block 0
Recursion=1: Hello World from thread 3 block 0
Recursion=1: Hello World from thread 0 block 0
Recursion=1: Hello World from thread 1 block 0
Recursion=1: Hello World from thread 2 block 0
Recursion=1: Hello World from thread 3 block 0
-------> nested execution depth: 2
-------> nested execution depth: 2
Recursion=2: Hello World from thread 0 block 0
Recursion=2: Hello World from thread 1 block 0
Recursion=2: Hello World from thread 0 block 0
Recursion=2: Hello World from thread 1 block 0
-------> nested execution depth: 3
-------> nested execution depth: 3
Recursion=3: Hello World from thread 0 block 0
Recursion=3: Hello World from thread 0 block 0
```

Why are the block ID for the child grids all 0 in the output messages? Figure 3-29 illustrates how child grids are invoked recursively with two initial thread blocks. While the parent grid contains two blocks, all nested child grids still contain only one because of the thread configuration of the kernel launch inside nestedHelloWorld:

```
nestedHelloWorld<<<1, nthreads>>>(nthreads, ++iDepth);
```

You can try different launching strategies. Figure 3-30 illustrates another way to generate an identical amount of parallelism, which is left as an exercise for the reader.

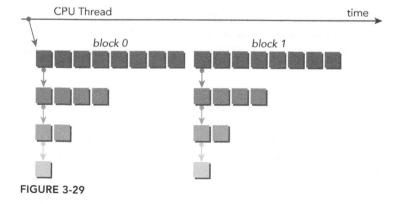

FIGURE 3-29

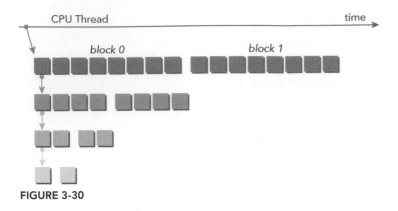

FIGURE 3-30

RESTRICTIONS ON DYNAMIC PARALLELISM

Dynamic Parallelism is only supported by devices of compute capability 3.5 and higher.

Kernels invoked through dynamic parallelism cannot be launched on physically separate devices. It is permitted, however, to query properties for any CUDA capable device in the system.

The maximum nesting depth of dynamic parallelism is limited to 24, but in reality most kernels will be limited by the amount of memory required by the device runtime system at each new level, as the device runtime reserves additional memory for synchronization management between every parent and child grid at each nested level.

Nested Reduction

Reduction can naturally be expressed as a recursive function. The section in this chapter titled "Avoiding Branch Divergence" already demonstrated recursive reduction in C. Using dynamic parallelism in CUDA enables a recursive reduction kernel in CUDA to be just as straightforward as the C implementation.

The kernel code for recursive reduction with dynamic parallelism is listed next. This kernel takes the approach as illustrated in Figure 3-29, with the original grid containing many blocks, but all nested child grids holding only one block which is invoked by thread 0 of its parent. The first step in this kernel is to convert the global memory address g_idata into the address local to each thread block. Then, if the stop condition is met (that is, if this is a leaf in the nested execution tree), results are copied back to global memory, and control is immediately returned back to the parent kernel. If this is not a leaf kernel, the size of the local reduction is calculated and half of the threads perform an in-place reduction. After the in-place reduction is complete, the block is synchronized to ensure all partial sums are computed. Then, thread 0 generates a child grid with one thread block and half as many threads as the current block. After the child grid is invoked, a barrier point is set for all child grids. Because only one child grid is generated by one thread in each block, this barrier point only synchronizes with the one child grid.

```
__global__ void gpuRecursiveReduce (int *g_idata, int *g_odata,
    unsigned int isize) {
  // set thread ID
  unsigned int tid = threadIdx.x;

  // convert global data pointer to the local pointer of this block
  int *idata = g_idata + blockIdx.x*blockDim.x;
  int *odata = &g_odata[blockIdx.x];

  // stop condition
  if (isize == 2 && tid == 0) {
    g_odata[blockIdx.x] = idata[0]+idata[1];
    return;
  }

  // nested invocation
  int istride = isize>>1;
  if(istride > 1 && tid < istride) {
    // in place reduction
    idata[tid] += idata[tid + istride];
  }

  // sync at block level
  __syncthreads();

  // nested invocation to generate child grids
  if(tid==0) {
    gpuRecursiveReduce <<<1, istride>>>(idata,odata,istride);

    // sync all child grids launched in this block
    cudaDeviceSynchronize();
  }

  // sync at block level again
  __syncthreads();
}
```

You can download the full code for this example in `nestedReduce.cu` from `Wrox.com`. Compile the code with the following command:

```
$ nvcc -arch=sm_35 -rdc=true nestedReduce.cu -o nestedReduce -lcudadevrt
```

The output using a Kepler K40 device is shown here. Compared with the flat kernel implemented using the neighbor-paired approach, the nested kernel is unacceptably slow.

```
./nestedReduce starting reduction at device 0: Tesla K40c
  array 1048576 grid 2048 block 512
cpu reduce        elapsed 0.000689 sec cpu_sum: 1048576
gpu Neighbored    elapsed 0.000532 sec gpu_sum: 1048576<<<grid 2048 block 512>>>
gpu nested        elapsed 0.172036 sec gpu_sum: 1048576<<<grid 2048 block 512>>>
```

As shown in the output, there are 2,048 blocks initially. Because each block performs 8 recursions, 16,384 child blocks were created, and intra-block synchronization with __syncthreads was also invoked 16,384 times. Such a large amount of kernel invocation and synchronization is likely the main cause for such poor kernel performance.

When a child grid is invoked, its view of memory is fully consistent with the parent thread. Because each child thread only needs its parent's values to conduct the partial reduction, the in-block synchronization performed before the child grids are launched is unnecessary. Removing all synchronization operations produces the following kernel:

```
__global__ void gpuRecursiveReduceNosync (int *g_idata, int *g_odata,
        unsigned int isize) {
    // set thread ID
    unsigned int tid = threadIdx.x;

    // convert global data pointer to the local pointer of this block
    int *idata = g_idata + blockIdx.x * blockDim.x;
    int *odata = &g_odata[blockIdx.x];

    // stop condition
    if (isize == 2 && tid == 0) {
        g_odata[blockIdx.x] = idata[0] + idata[1];
        return;
    }

    // nested invoke
    int istride = isize>>1;
    if(istride > 1 && tid < istride) {
        idata[tid] += idata[tid + istride];
        if(tid==0) {
            gpuRecursiveReduceNosync<<<1, istride>>>(idata,odata,istride);
        }
    }
}
```

You can download the full code for this example in nestedReduceNosync.cu from Wrox.com. Compile and run it. The output on a Kepler K40 device is listed below. The elapsed time is reduced to one third of the time for the first dynamic parallelism implementation.

```
./nestedReduceNoSync starting reduction at device 0: Tesla K40c
array 1048576 grid 2048 block 512
cpu reduce      elapsed 0.000689 sec cpu_sum: 1048576
gpu Neighbored  elapsed 0.000532 sec gpu_sum: 1048576<<<grid 2048 block 512>>>
gpu nested      elapsed 0.172036 sec gpu_sum: 1048576<<<grid 2048 block 512>>>
gpu nestedNosyn elapsed 0.059125 sec gpu_sum: 1048576<<<grid 2048 block 512>>>
```

However, performance is still poor compared to the neighbor-paired kernel. Next, consider how to reduce the overhead caused by the large number of child grid launches. In the current implementation, each block generates a child grid, resulting in a huge number of invocations. If instead the approach shown in Figure 3-30 was used, the number of thread blocks per child grid would increase while the number of child grids created would decrease, maintaining the same amount of parallelism.

The following kernel implements this approach: The first thread in the first block of a grid invokes the child grids for each nested step. Comparing the two kernel signatures, you will find that a new argument has been added. Because at each nested invocation the child block size is reduced to half of its parent block size, the parent block dimension must be passed to the nested child grid. This allows each thread to calculate the correct global memory offset for its portion of the workload. Note that in this implementation all idle threads are removed from each kernel launch, compared to the first implementation where half of all threads are idling during kernel execution at each nested level. This change will free half of the compute resources consumed by the first kernel so as to allow more thread blocks to become active.

```
__global__ void gpuRecursiveReduce2(int *g_idata, int *g_odata, int iStride,
    int const iDim) {
  // convert global data pointer to the local pointer of this block
  int *idata = g_idata + blockIdx.x*iDim;

  // stop condition
  if (iStride == 1 && threadIdx.x == 0) {
    g_odata[blockIdx.x] = idata[0]+idata[1];
    return;
  }

  // in place reduction
  idata[threadIdx.x] += idata[threadIdx.x + iStride];

  // nested invocation to generate child grids
  if(threadIdx.x == 0 && blockIdx.x == 0) {
    gpuRecursiveReduce2 <<<gridDim.x,iStride/2>>>(
        g_idata,g_odata,iStride/2,iDim);
  }
}
```

You can download the full code for this example in nestedReduce2.cu from Wrox.com. The output on a K40 GPU is shown here:

```
./nestedReduce2 starting reduction at device 0: Tesla K40c
array 1048576 grid 2048 block 512
cpu reduce       elapsed 0.000689 sec cpu_sum: 1048576
gpu Neighbored   elapsed 0.000532 sec gpu_sum: 1048576<<<grid 2048 block 512>>>
gpu nested       elapsed 0.172036 sec gpu_sum: 1048576<<<grid 2048 block 512>>>
gpu nestedNosyn  elapsed 0.059125 sec gpu_sum: 1048576<<<grid 2048 block 512>>>
gpu nested2      elapsed 0.000797 sec gpu_sum: 1048576<<<grid 2048 block 512>>>
```

From the results you can see that the third implementation of the recursive reduction kernel is again much faster than the first two implementations, likely due to decreased overhead from fewer child grid invocations. You can verify the reason for this performance gain using nvprof:

```
$ nvprof ./nestedReduce2
```

Part of the output is summarized below. Consider the second column, which shows the number of device kernel invocations. The first and second kernels created 16,384 child grids on the device. The gpuRecursiveReduce2 kernel only created 8 child grids for 8 levels of nested parallelism.

Calls (host)	Calls (device)	Avg	Min	Max	Name
1	16384	441.48us	2.3360us	171.34ms	gpuRecursiveReduce
1	16384	51.140us	2.2080us	57.906ms	gpuRecursiveReduceNosync
1	8	56.195us	22.048us	100.74us	gpuRecursiveReduce2
1	0	352.67us	352.67us	352.67us	reduceNeighbored

This recursive reduction example demonstrates dynamic parallelism. For a given algorithm, you may have several possible implementations using different dynamic parallelism techniques. Avoiding a large number of nested invocations helps reduce overhead and improve performance. Synchronization is very important for both performance and correctness, but reducing the number of in-block synchronizations will likely lead to more efficient nested kernels. Because the device runtime system reserves extra memory at each nesting level, the maximum number of kernel nestings will likely be limited. The extent of that limit is kernel-dependent and may restrict the scale, performance, and other properties of any application that uses dynamic parallelism.

SUMMARY

In this chapter, you examined kernel execution from the hardware point-of-view. The two most distinguished features of the CUDA execution model on GPU devices are:

➤ Threads are executed in warps in SIMT fashion.

➤ Hardware resources are partitioned among blocks and threads.

These features of the execution model are exposed to you, allowing you to control how your application saturates instruction and memory bandwidth as you increase parallelism and performance. GPU devices with different compute capabilities have different hardware limits; therefore, grid and block heuristics play a very important role in optimizing kernel performance for different platforms.

Dynamic parallelism gives you the ability to create new work directly from the device. It enables you to express recursive or data-dependent parallel algorithms in a more natural and easy-to-understand way. To implement an efficient nested kernel, attention must be given to how the device runtime is used, including the child grid launch strategy, parent-child synchronization, and the depth of nested levels.

In this chapter, you also learned how to dissect kernel performance using the command-line profiling tool, nvprof. The profile-driven approach is particularly important in CUDA programming because a naive kernel implementation may not yield very good performance. Profiling provides insights on kernel behavior and helps you focus on the major factors that will deliver the best performance.

In Chapters 4 and 5, you will learn about kernel execution from a different perspective: the CUDA memory model.

CHAPTER 3 EXERCISES

1. What are the two primary causes of performance improvement when unrolling loops, data blocks, or warps in CUDA? Explain how each type of unrolling improves instruction throughput.

2. Refer to the kernel reduceUnrolling8 and implement the kernel reduceUnrolling16, in which each thread handles 16 data blocks. Compare kernel performance with reduceUnrolling8 and use the proper metrics and events with nvprof to explain any difference in performance.

3. Refer to the kernel `reduceUnrolling8` and replace the following code segment:

```
int a1 = g_idata[idx];
int a2 = g_idata[idx+blockDim.x];
int a3 = g_idata[idx+2*blockDim.x];
int a4 = g_idata[idx+3*blockDim.x];
int b1 = g_idata[idx+4*blockDim.x];
int b2 = g_idata[idx+5*blockDim.x];
int b3 = g_idata[idx+6*blockDim.x];
int b4 = g_idata[idx+7*blockDim.x];
g_idata[idx] = a1+a2+a3+a4+b1+b2+b3+b4;
```

with the functionally equivalent code below:

```
int *ptr = g_idata + idx;
int tmp = 0;

// Increment tmp 8 times with values strided by blockDim.x
for (int i = 0; i < 8; i++) {
    tmp += *ptr; ptr += blockDim.x;
}

g_idata[idx] = tmp;
```

Compare the performance of each and explain the difference using nvprof metrics.

4. Refer to the kernel `reduceCompleteUnrollWarps8`. Instead of declaring vmem as `volatile`, use `__syncthreads`. Note that `__syncthreads` must be called by all threads in a block. Compare the performance of the two kernels. Use nvprof to explain any differences.

5. Implement sum reduction of `floats` in C.

6 Refer to the kernel `reduceInterleaved` and the kernel `reduceCompleteUnrollWarps8` and implement a version of each for `floats`. Compare their performance and choose proper metrics and/or events to explain any differences. Are there any differences compared to operating on integer data types?

7. When are the changes to global data made by a dynamically spawned child guaranteed to be visible to its parent?

8. Refer to the file `nestedHelloWorld.cu` and implement a new kernel using the methods illustrated in Figure 3-30.

9. Refer to the file `nestedHelloWorld.cu` and implement a new kernel that can limit nesting levels to a given depth.

Global Memory

> **CODE DOWNLOAD** *The wrox.com code downloads for this chapter are found at www.wrox.com/go/procudac on the Download Code tab. The code is in the Chapter 4 download and individually named according to the names throughout the chapter.*

In the last chapter, you studied how threads are executed on GPUs and learned how to optimize kernel performance by manipulating warp execution. However, kernel performance cannot be explained purely through an understanding of warp execution. Recall in Chapter 3, from the section titled "Checking Memory Options with nvprof," that setting the inner-most dimension of a thread block to half the warp size caused memory load efficiency to drop substantially. This performance loss could not be explained by the scheduling of warps or the amount of exposed parallelism. The real cause of the performance loss was poor access patterns to global memory.

In this chapter, you are going to dissect kernel interaction with global memory to help understand how those interactions affect performance. This chapter will explain the CUDA memory model and, by analyzing different global memory access patterns, teach you how to use global memory efficiently from your kernel.

INTRODUCING THE CUDA MEMORY MODEL

Memory access and management are important parts of any programming language. Memory management has a particularly large impact on high performance computing in modern accelerators.

Because many workloads are limited by how rapidly they can load and store data, having a large amount of low-latency, high-bandwidth memory can be very beneficial to performance. However, procuring large capacity, high-performance memory is not always possible or economical. Instead, you must rely on the memory model to achieve optimal latency and bandwidth, given the hardware memory subsystem. The CUDA memory model unifies separate host and device memory systems and exposes the full memory hierarchy so that you can explicitly control data placement for optimal performance.

Benefits of a Memory Hierarchy

In general, applications do not access arbitrary data or run arbitrary code at any point-in-time. Instead, applications often follow the *principle of locality*, which suggests that they access a relatively small and localized portion of their address space at any point-in-time. There are two different types of locality:

➤   Temporal locality (locality in time)

➤   Spatial locality (locality in space)

Temporal locality assumes that if a data location is referenced, then it is more likely to be referenced again within a short time period and less likely to be referenced as more and more time passes. Spatial locality assumes that if a memory location is referenced, nearby locations are likely to be referenced as well.

Modern computers use a *memory hierarchy* of progressively lower-latency but lower-capacity memories to optimize performance. This memory hierarchy is only useful because of the principle of locality. A memory hierarchy consists of multiple levels of memory with different latencies, bandwidths, and capacities. In general, as processor-to-memory latency increases, the capacity of that memory increases. A typical hierarchy is illustrated in Figure 4-1. The types of storage at the bottom of Figure 4-1 are generally characterized by:

➤   Lower cost per bit

➤   Higher capacity

➤   Higher latency

➤   Less frequently accessed by the processor

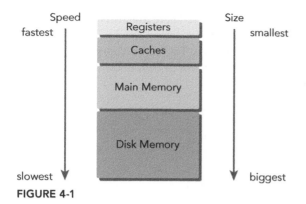

FIGURE 4-1

Main memory for both CPUs and GPUs is implemented using *DRAM* (Dynamic Random Access Memory), while lower-latency memory (such as CPU L1 cache) is implemented using *SRAM* (Static Random Access Memory). The largest and slowest level in the memory hierarchy is generally implemented using a magnetic disk or flash drive. In this memory hierarchy, data is either kept in low-latency, low-capacity memory when it is actively being used by the processor, or in high-latency, high-capacity memory when it is being stored for later use. This memory hierarchy can provide the illusion of large but low-latency memory.

Both GPUs and CPUs use similar principles and models in memory hierarchy design. The key difference between GPU and CPU memory models is that the CUDA programming model exposes more of the memory hierarchy and gives you more explicit control over its behavior.

CUDA Memory Model

To programmers, there are generally two classifications of memory:

➤ Programmable: You explicitly control what data is placed in programmable memory.

➤ Non-programmable: You have no control over data placement, and rely on automatic techniques to achieve good performance.

In the CPU memory hierarchy, L1 cache and L2 cache are examples of non-programmable memory. On the other hand, the CUDA memory model exposes many types of programmable memory to you:

➤ Registers

➤ Shared memory

➤ Local memory

➤ Constant memory

➤ Texture memory

➤ Global memory

Figure 4-2 illustrates the hierarchy of these memory spaces. Each has a different scope, lifetime, and caching behavior. A thread in a kernel has its own private local memory. A thread block has its own shared memory, visible to all threads in the same thread block, and whose contents persist for the lifetime of the thread block. All threads can access global memory. There are also two read-only memory spaces accessible by all threads: the constant and texture memory spaces. The global, constant, and texture memory spaces are optimized for different uses. Texture memory offers different address modes and filtering for various data layouts. The contents of global, constant, and texture memory have the same lifetime as an application.

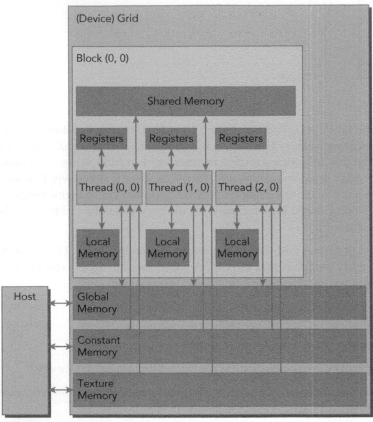

FIGURE 4-2

Registers

Registers are the fastest memory space on a GPU. An automatic variable declared in a kernel without any other type qualifiers is generally stored in a register. Arrays declared in a kernel may also be stored in registers, but only if the indices used to reference the array are constant and can be determined at compile time.

Register variables are private to each thread. A kernel typically uses registers to hold frequently accessed thread-private variables. Register variables share their lifetime with the kernel. Once a kernel completes execution, a register variable cannot be accessed again.

Registers are scarce resources that are partitioned among active warps in an SM. On Fermi GPUs, there is a hardware limit of 63 registers per thread. Kepler expands this limit to 255 registers per thread. Using fewer registers in your kernels may allow more thread blocks to reside on an SM. More concurrent thread blocks per-SM can increase occupancy and improve performance.

You can check the hardware resources used by a kernel with the nvcc compiler option below. For example, this will print the number of registers, bytes of shared memory, and bytes of constant memory used by each thread.

```
-Xptxas -v,-abi=no
```

If a kernel uses more registers than the hardware limit, the excess registers will spill over to local memory. This *register spilling* can have adverse performance consequences. The nvcc compiler uses heuristics to minimize register usage and avoid register spilling. You can optionally aid these heuristics by providing additional information for each kernel to the compiler in the form of launch bounds:

```
__global__ void
__launch_bounds__(maxThreadsPerBlock, minBlocksPerMultiprocessor)
kernel(...) {
    // your kernel body
}
```

maxThreadsPerBlock specifies the maximum number of threads per block that a kernel will launch. minBlocksPerMultiprocessor is optional, and specifies the desired minimum number of resident blocks per SM. Optimal launch bounds for a given kernel will usually differ across major architectural revisions.

You can also control the maximum number of registers used by all kernels in a compilation unit using the maxrregcount compiler option. In this example:

```
-maxrregcount=32
```

the value specified (32) is ignored for any kernels that have launch bounds specified.

Local Memory

Variables in a kernel that are eligible for registers but cannot fit into the register space allocated for that kernel will spill into local memory. Variables that the compiler is likely to place in local memory are:

➤   Local arrays referenced with indices whose values cannot be determined at compile-time.

➤   Large local structures or arrays that would consume too much register space.

➤   Any variable that does not fit within the kernel register limit.

The name "local memory" is misleading: Values spilled to local memory reside in the same physical location as global memory, so local memory accesses are characterized by high latency and low bandwidth and are subject to the requirements for efficient memory access that are described in the section "Memory Access Patterns" found later in this chapter. For GPUs with compute capability 2.0 and higher, local memory data is also cached in a per-SM L1 and per-device L2 cache.

Shared Memory

Variables decorated with the following attribute in a kernel are stored in shared memory:

```
__shared__
```

Because shared memory is on-chip, it has a much higher bandwidth and much lower latency than local or global memory. It is used similarly to CPU L1 cache, but is also programmable.

Each SM has a limited amount of shared memory that is partitioned among thread blocks. Therefore, you must be careful to not over-utilize shared memory or you will inadvertently limit the number of active warps.

Shared memory is declared in the scope of a kernel function but shares its lifetime with a thread block. When a thread block is finished executing, its allocation of shared memory will be released and assigned to other thread blocks.

Shared memory serves as a basic means for inter-thread communication. Threads within a block can cooperate by sharing data stored in shared memory. Access to shared memory must be synchronized using the following CUDA runtime call introduced in earlier chapters:

```
void __syncthreads();
```

This function creates a barrier which all threads in the same thread block must reach before any other thread is allowed to proceed. By creating a barrier for all threads within a thread block, you can prevent a potential data hazard. Data hazards were covered in more depth in Chapter 3. They occur when there is an undefined ordering of multiple accesses to the same memory location from different threads, where at least one of those accesses is a write. __syncthreads may also affect performance by forcing the SM to idle frequently.

The L1 cache and shared memory for an SM use the same 64 KB of on-chip memory, which is statically partitioned but can be dynamically configured at runtime using:

```
cudaError_t cudaFuncSetCacheConfig(const void* func, enum cudaFuncCache
    cacheConfig);
```

This function configures the partitioning of on-chip memory on a per-kernel basis, setting the configuration for the kernel function specified by func. The supported cache configurations are:

```
cudaFuncCachePreferNone:   no preference (default)
cudaFuncCachePreferShared: prefer 48KB shared memory and 16KB L1 cache
cudaFuncCachePreferL1:     prefer 48KB L1 cache and 16KB shared memory
cudaFuncCachePreferEqual:  Prefer equal size of L1 cache and shared memory,
    both 32KB
```

Fermi devices support the first three configurations, and Kepler devices support all of them.

Constant Memory

Constant memory resides in device memory and is cached in a dedicated, per-SM constant cache. A constant variable is decorated with the following attribute:

```
__constant__
```

Constant variables must be declared with global scope, outside of any kernels. A limited amount of constant memory can be declared — 64 KB for all compute capabilities. Constant memory is statically declared and visible to all kernels in the same compilation unit.

Kernels can only read from constant memory. Constant memory must therefore be initialized by the host using:

```
cudaError_t cudaMemcpyToSymbol(const void* symbol, const void* src,
    size_t count);
```

This function copies count bytes from the memory pointed to by src to the memory pointed to by symbol, which is a variable that resides on the device in global or constant memory. This function is synchronous in most cases.

Constant memory performs best when all threads in a warp read from the same memory address. For example, a coefficient for a mathematical formula is a good use case for constant memory because all threads in a warp will use the same coefficient to conduct the same calculation on different data. If each thread in a warp reads from a different address, and only reads once, then constant memory is not the best choice because a single read from constant memory broadcasts to all threads in a warp.

Texture Memory

Texture memory resides in device memory and is cached in a per-SM, read-only cache. Texture memory is a type of global memory that is accessed through a dedicated read-only cache. The read-only cache includes support for hardware filtering, which can perform floating-point interpolation as part of the read process. Texture memory is optimized for 2D spatial locality, so threads in a warp that use texture memory to access 2D data will achieve the best performance. For some applications, this is ideal and provides a performance advantage due to the cache and the filtering hardware. However, for other applications using texture memory can be slower than global memory.

Global Memory

Global memory is the largest, highest-latency, and most commonly used memory on a GPU. The name *global* refers to its scope and lifetime. Its state can be accessed on the device from any SM throughout the lifetime of the application.

A variable in global memory can either be declared statically or dynamically. You can declare a global variable statically in device code using the following qualifier:

```
__device__
```

In the "CUDA Programming Model" section of Chapter 2, you learned how to dynamically allocate global memory. Global memory is allocated by the host using cudaMalloc and freed by the host using cudaFree. Pointers to global memory are then passed to kernel functions as parameters. Global memory allocations exist for the lifetime of an application and are accessible to all threads of all kernels. You must take care when accessing global memory from multiple threads. Because thread execution cannot be synchronized across thread blocks, there is a potential hazard of multiple threads in different thread blocks concurrently modifying the same location in global memory, which will lead to an undefined program behavior.

Global memory resides in device memory and is accessible via 32-byte, 64-byte, or 128-byte memory transactions. These memory transactions must be naturally aligned; that is, the first address must be a multiple of 32 bytes, 64 bytes, or 128 bytes. Optimizing memory transactions are vital to obtaining optimal performance. When a warp performs a memory load/store, the number of transactions required to satisfy that request typically depends on the following two factors:

➤ Distribution of memory addresses across the threads of that warp.

➤ Alignment of memory addresses per transaction.

In general, the more transactions necessary to satisfy a memory request, the higher the potential for unused bytes to be transferred, causing a reduction in throughput efficiency.

For a given warp memory request, the number of transactions and the throughput efficiency are determined by the compute capability of the device. For devices of compute capability 1.0 and 1.1, the requirements on global memory access are very strict. For devices with compute capabilities beyond 1.1, the requirements are more relaxed because memory transactions are cached. Cached memory transactions exploit data locality to improve throughput efficiency.

The following sections will examine how to optimize global memory accesses and how to maximize global memory throughput efficiency.

GPU Caches

Like CPU caches, GPU caches are non-programmable memory. There are four types of cache in GPU devices:

➤ L1

➤ L2

➤ Read-only constant

➤ Read-only texture

There is one L1 cache per-SM and one L2 cache shared by all SMs. Both L1 and L2 caches are used to store data in local and global memory, including register spills. On Fermi GPus and Kepler K40 or later GPUs, CUDA allows you to configure whether reads are cached in both L1 and L2, or only in L2.

On the CPU, both memory loads and stores can be cached. However, on the GPU only memory load operations can be cached; memory store operations cannot be cached.

Each SM also has a read-only constant cache and read-only texture cache that are used to improve read performance from their respective memory spaces in device memory.

CUDA Variable Declaration Summary

Table 4-1 summarizes CUDA variable declarations and their corresponding memory location, scope, lifespan, and qualifier.

TABLE 4-1: CUDA Variable and Type Qualifier

QUALIFIER	VARIABLE NAME	MEMORY	SCOPE	LIFESPAN
	`float var`	Register	Thread	Thread
	`float var[100]`	Local	Thread	Thread

QUALIFIER	VARIABLE NAME	MEMORY	SCOPE	LIFESPAN
__shared__	float var †	Shared	Block	Block
__device__	float var †	Global	Global	Application
__constant__	float var †	Constant	Global	Application

† Can be either scalar variable or array variable

The principal traits of the various memory types are summarized in Table 4-2.

TABLE 4-2: Salient Features of Device Memory

MEMORY	ON/OFF CHIP	CACHED	ACCESS	SCOPE	LIFETIME
Register	On	n/a	R/W	1 thread	Thread
Local	Off	†	R/W	1 thread	Thread
Shared	On	n/a	R/W	All threads in block	Block
Global	Off	†	R/W	All threads + host	Host allocation
Constant	Off	Yes	R	All threads + host	Host allocation
Texture	Off	Yes	R	All threads + host	Host allocation

† Cached only on devices of compute capability 2.x

Static Global Memory

The following code illustrates how to statically declare a global variable. As shown in Listing 4-1, a global variable of type `float` is declared with file scope. In the kernel function `checkGlobalVariable`, the value of that global variable is printed and then its value is changed. In function `main`, the value of that global variable is initialized using the function `cudaMemcpyToSymbol`. After `checkGlobalVariable` is executed, the value of the global variable is altered. Its new value is then copied back to the host using `cudaMemcpyFromSymbol`.

LISTING 4-1: Static declared global variable (globalVariable.cu)

```
#include <cuda_runtime.h>
#include <stdio.h>

__device__ float devData;

__global__ void checkGlobalVariable() {
    // display the original value
    printf("Device: the value of the global variable is %f\n",devData);
```

continues

LISTING 4-1 *(continued)*

```
        // alter the value
        devData +=2.0f;
    }

    int main(void) {
        // initialize the global variable
        float value = 3.14f;
        cudaMemcpyToSymbol(devData, &value, sizeof(float));
        printf("Host:   copied %f to the global variable\n", value);

        // invoke the kernel
        checkGlobalVariable <<<1, 1>>>();

        // copy the global variable back to the host
        cudaMemcpyFromSymbol(&value, devData, sizeof(float));
        printf("Host:   the value changed by the kernel to %f\n", value);

        cudaDeviceReset();
        return EXIT_SUCCESS;
    }
```

Compile and run this example with the following command:

```
$ nvcc -arch=sm_20 globalVariable.cu -o globalVariable
$ ./globalVariable
```

The following is a sample output:

```
Host:   copied 3.140000 to the global variable
Device: the value of the global variable is 3.140000
Host:   the value changed by the kernel to 5.140000
```

Even though the host and device code are stored in the same file, they exist in completely different worlds. The host code cannot directly access a device variable even if it is visible in the same file scope. Similarly, device code cannot directly access a host variable either.

You might argue that the host code in fact can access the device global variable using the following code:

```
cudaMemcpyToSymbol(devD6ata, &value, sizeof(float));
```

Yes, but notice that:

➤   cudaMemcpyToSymbol is in the CUDA runtime API and uses GPU hardware behind the scenes to perform the access.

➤   The variable devData is passed here as a symbol, not as the address of the variable in device global memory.

➤   In the kernel, devData is used as a variable in global memory.

cudaMemcpy cannot be used to transfer data into devData using the address of the variable:

```
cudaMemcpy(&devData, &value, sizeof(float),cudaMemcpyHostToDevice);
```

You cannot use the reference operator & on a device variable from the host, because it is simply a symbol representing the physical location on the GPU. However, you can acquire the address of a global variable by explicitly making a call using the following CUDA API:

```
cudaError_t cudaGetSymbolAddress(void** devPtr, const void* symbol);
```

This function fetches the physical address of the global memory associated with the provided device symbol. After acquiring the address of the variable devData, you then can use the cudaMemcpy function as follows:

```
float *dptr = NULL;
cudaGetSymbolAddress((void**)&dptr, devData);
cudaMemcpy(dptr, &value, sizeof(float), cudaMemcpyHostToDevice);
```

There is a single exception to being able to directly reference GPU memory from the host: CUDA pinned memory. Both host code and device code can access pinned memory directly by simply dereferencing a pointer. You will learn about pinned memory in the next section.

> ### VARIABLES IN FILE SCOPE: VISIBLE VERSUS ACCESSIBLE
>
> In CUDA programming, you work in two distinct worlds: the host and the device. In general, device kernels cannot access host variables and host functions cannot access device variables, even though these variables are declared in the same file scope.
>
> The CUDA runtime API can access both host and device variables, but it is up to you to provide the correct arguments to the correct functions so that they operate properly on the correct variables. Because the runtime API makes assumptions about the memory space of certain parameters, passing a host variable where it expects a device variable or vice versa will result in undefined behavior (likely crashing your application).

MEMORY MANAGEMENT

Memory management in CUDA programming is similar to C programming, with the added programmer responsibility of explicitly managing data movement between the host and device. While NVIDIA is methodically moving closer to unifying the host and device memory space with each CUDA release, for most applications manual data movement is still a requirement. The latest advancements in this area will be covered in this chapter under "Unified Memory." For now, you will focus on how you can explicitly manage memory and data movement using CUDA functions to:

➤ Allocate and deallocate device memory

➤ Transfer data between the host and device

In order to achieve maximum performance, CUDA provides functions that prepare device memory on the host and explicitly transfer data to and from the device.

Memory Allocation and Deallocation

The CUDA programming model assumes a heterogeneous system that consists of a host and a device, each with its own separate memory space. Kernel functions operate in the device memory space, and the CUDA runtime provides functions to allocate and deallocate device memory. You can allocate global memory on the host using the following function:

```
cudaError_t cudaMalloc(void **devPtr, size_t count);
```

This function allocates count bytes of global memory on the device and returns the location of that memory in pointer devPtr. The allocated memory is suitably aligned for any variable type, including integers, floating-point values, booleans, and so on. The cudaMalloc function returns cudaErrorMemoryAllocation in the case of failure. The values contained in the allocated global memory are not cleared. It is your responsibility to either fill the allocated global memory with data transferred from the host, or initialize it with the following function:

```
cudaError_t cudaMemset(void *devPtr, int value, size_t count);
```

This function fills each of the count bytes starting at the device memory address devPtr with the value stored in the variable value.

Once an application is no longer using a piece of allocated global memory, it can be deallocated using:

```
cudaError_t cudaFree(void *devPtr);
```

This function frees the global memory pointed to by devPtr, which must have been previously allocated using a device allocation function (such as cudaMalloc). Otherwise, it returns an error cudaErrorInvalidDevicePointer. cudaFree also returns an error if the address has already been freed.

Device memory allocation and deallocation are expensive operations, so device memory should be reused by applications whenever possible to minimize the impact on overall performance.

Memory Transfer

Once global memory is allocated, you can transfer data to the device from the host using the following function:

```
cudaError_t cudaMemcpy(void *dst, const void *src, size_t count,
                       enum cudaMemcpyKind kind);
```

This function copies count bytes from the memory location src to the memory location dst. The variable kind specifies the direction of the copy and can have the following values:

```
cudaMemcpyHostToHost
cudaMemcpyHostToDevice
cudaMemcpyDeviceToHost
cudaMemcpyDeviceToDevice
```

If the pointers dst and src do not match the direction of the copy specified by kind, the behavior of cudaMemcpy is undefined. This function exhibits synchronous behavior in most cases.

An example that uses cudaMemcpy is shown in Listing 4-2. This example transfers data back and forth between the host and the device. Global memory is allocated using cudaMalloc and data is transferred to the device using cudaMemcpy with the direction specified as cudaMemcpyHostToDevice. Data is then transferred back to the host with cudaMemcpy and a direction of cudaMemcpyDeviceToHost.

LISTING 4-2: Simple memory transfer (memTransfer.cu)

```
#include <cuda_runtime.h>
#include <stdio.h>

int main(int argc, char **argv) {
    // set up device
    int dev = 0;
    cudaSetDevice(dev);

    // memory size
    unsigned int isize = 1<<22;
    unsigned int nbytes = isize * sizeof(float);

    // get device information
    cudaDeviceProp deviceProp;
    cudaGetDeviceProperties(&deviceProp, dev);
    printf("%s starting at ", argv[0]);
    printf("device %d: %s memory size %d nbyte %5.2fMB\n", dev,
            deviceProp.name,isize,nbytes/(1024.0f*1024.0f));

    // allocate the host memory
    float *h_a = (float *)malloc(nbytes);

    // allocate the device memory
    float *d_a;
    cudaMalloc((float **)&d_a, nbytes);

    // initialize the host memory
    for(unsigned int i=0;i<isize;i++) h_a[i] = 0.5f;

    // transfer data from the host to the device
    cudaMemcpy(d_a, h_a, nbytes, cudaMemcpyHostToDevice);

    // transfer data from the device to the host
    cudaMemcpy(h_a, d_a, nbytes, cudaMemcpyDeviceToHost);

    // free memory
    cudaFree(d_a);
    free(h_a);

    // reset device
    cudaDeviceReset();
    return EXIT_SUCCESS;
}
```

Compile the code using nvcc and run it with nvprof as follows:

```
$ nvcc -O3 memTransfer.cu -o memTransfer
$ nvprof ./memTransfer
```

The output running on a Fermi M2090 is shown below:

```
==3369== NVPROF is profiling process 3369, command: ./memTransfer
./ memTransfer starting at device 0: Tesla M2090 memory size 4194304 nbyte 16.00MB
==3369== Profiling application: ./memTransfer
==3369== Profiling result:
Time(%)      Time     Calls      Avg       Min       Max   Name
 53.50%   3.7102ms        1   3.7102ms   3.7102ms   3.7102ms   [CUDA memcpy DtoH]
 46.50%   3.2249ms        1   3.2249ms   3.2249ms   3.2249ms   [CUDA memcpy HtoD]
```

The data transfer from the host to the device is labeled HtoD, and from the device to the host DtoH.

Figure 4-3 highlights the connectivity of CPU and GPU memory. From the diagram you can see that the theoretical peak bandwidth between the GPU chip and the on-board GDDR5 GPU memory is very high, 144 GB/sec for a Fermi C2050 GPU. The link between CPU and GPU through the PCI Express (PCIe) Gen2 bus shows a much lower theoretical peak bandwidth of 8 GB/sec (the PCIe-Gen3 maximum theoretical limit is 16 GB/sec). This disparity means that data transfers between the host and device can throttle overall application performance if not managed properly. Therefore, as a basic principle of CUDA programming, you should always be thinking of ways to minimize host-device transfers.

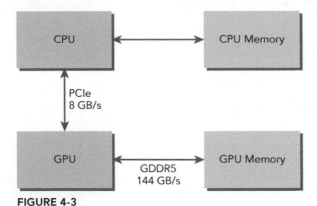

FIGURE 4-3

Pinned Memory

Allocated host memory is by default *pageable*, that is, subject to page fault operations that move data in host *virtual memory* to different physical locations as directed by the operating system. Virtual memory offers the illusion of much more main memory than is physically available, just as the L1 cache offers the illusion of much more on-chip memory than is physically available.

The GPU cannot safely access data in pageable host memory because it has no control over when the host operating system may choose to physically move that data. When transferring data from pageable host memory to device memory, the CUDA driver first allocates temporary *page-locked* or *pinned* host memory, copies the source host data to pinned memory, and then transfers the data from pinned memory to device memory, as illustrated on the left side of Figure 4-4.

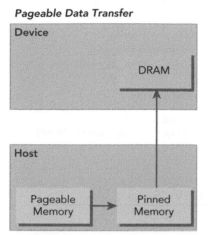 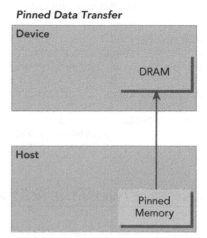

FIGURE 4-4

The CUDA runtime allows you to directly allocate pinned host memory using:

```
cudaError_t cudaMallocHost(void **devPtr, size_t count);
```

This function allocates count bytes of host memory that is page-locked and accessible to the device. Since the pinned memory can be accessed directly by the device, it can be read and written with much higher bandwidth than pageable memory. However, allocating excessive amounts of pinned memory might degrade host system performance, since it reduces the amount of pageable memory available to the host system for storing virtual memory data.

The following code snippet demonstrates allocating pinned host memory with error checking and elementary error handling:

```
cudaError_t status = cudaMallocHost((void**)&h_aPinned, bytes);
if (status != cudaSuccess) {
    fprintf(stderr, "Error returned from pinned host memory allocation\n");
    exit(1);
}
```

Pinned host memory must be freed with:

```
cudaError_t cudaFreeHost(void *ptr);
```

You can try replacing pageable host memory with pinned host memory in the file memTransfer.cu, or you can download the file pinMemTransfer.cu from Wrox.com.

Compile the code using nvcc and then run it with nvprof as follows:

```
$ nvcc -O3 pinMemTransfer.cu -o pinMemTransfer
$ nvprof ./pinMemTransfer
```

The output below clearly shows that performance is improved when using pinned memory, compared to the output generated by memTransfer. On this platform the transfers originally took a total of 6.94 ms with pageable host memory, but now only take 5.3485 ms with pinned host memory.

```
$ nvprof ./pinMemTransfer
==3425== NVPROF is profiling process 3425, command: ./ pinMemTransfer
./ pinMemTransfer starting at device 0: Tesla M2090 memory size 4194304
    nbyte 16.00MB
==3425== Profiling application: ./ pinMemTransfer
==3425== Profiling result:
Time(%)      Time    Calls       Avg       Min       Max  Name
 52.34%   2.7996ms       1   2.7996ms   2.7996ms   2.7996ms  [CUDA memcpy HtoD]
 47.66%   2.5489ms       1   2.5489ms   2.5489ms   2.5489ms  [CUDA memcpy DtoH]
```

> ### MEMORY TRANSFER BETWEEN THE HOST AND DEVICE
>
> Pinned memory is more expensive to allocate and deallocate than pageable memory, but it provides higher transfer throughput for large data transfers.
>
> The speedup achieved when using pinned memory relative to pageable memory depends on device compute capability. For example, on Fermi devices it is generally beneficial to use pinned memory when transferring more than 10 MB of data.
>
> Batching many small transfers into one larger transfer improves performance because it reduces per-transfer overhead.
>
> Data transfers between the host and device can sometimes be overlapped with kernel execution. You will learn more about this topic in Chapter 6, "Streams and Concurrency." You should either minimize or overlap data transfers between the host and device whenever possible.

Zero-Copy Memory

In general, the host cannot directly access device variables, and the device cannot directly access host variables. There is one exception to this rule: *zero-copy* memory. Both the host and device can access zero-copy memory.

GPU threads can directly access zero-copy memory. There are several advantages to using zero-copy memory in CUDA kernels, such as:

- ➤ Leveraging host memory when there is insufficient device memory
- ➤ Avoiding explicit data transfer between the host and device
- ➤ Improving PCIe transfer rates

When using zero-copy memory to share data between the host and device, you must synchronize memory accesses across the host and device. Modifying data in zero-copy memory from both the host and device at the same time will result in undefined behavior.

Zero-copy memory is pinned (non-pageable) memory that is mapped into the device address space. You can create a mapped, pinned memory region with the following function:

```
cudaError_t cudaHostAlloc(void **pHost, size_t count, unsigned int flags);
```

This function allocates `count` bytes of host memory that is page-locked and accessible to the device. Memory allocated by this function must be freed with `cudaFreeHost`. The `flags` parameter enables further configuration of special properties of the allocated memory:

➤   `cudaHostAllocDefault`

➤   `cudaHostAllocPortable`

➤   `cudaHostAllocWriteCombined`

➤   `cudaHostAllocMapped`

`cudaHostAllocDefault` makes the behavior of `cudaHostAlloc` identical to `cudaMallocHost`. Setting `cudaHostAllocPortable` returns pinned memory that can be used by all CUDA contexts, not just the one that performed the allocation. The flag `cudaHostAllocWriteCombined` returns write-combined memory, which can be transferred across the PCI Express bus more quickly on some system configurations but cannot be read efficiently by most hosts. Therefore, write-combined memory is a good option for buffers that will be written by the host and read by the device using either mapped pinned memory or host-to-device transfers. The most relevant flag to zero-copy memory is `cudaHostAllocMapped`, which returns host memory that is mapped into the device address space.

You can obtain the device pointer for mapped pinned memory using the following function:

```
cudaError_t cudaHostGetDevicePointer(void **pDevice, void *pHost, unsigned int flags);
```

This function returns a device pointer in `pDevice` that can be referenced on the device to access mapped, pinned host memory. This function will fail if the device does not support mapped, pinned memory. `flag` is reserved for future use. For now, it must be set to zero.

Using zero-copy memory as a supplement to device memory with frequent read/write operations will significantly slow performance. Because every memory transaction to mapped memory must pass over the PCIe bus, a significant amount of latency is added even when compared to global memory. You can confirm the performance of zero-copy memory using the same `sumArrays` kernel that you used in Chapter 2:

```
__global__ void sumArraysZeroCopy(float *A, float *B, float *C, const int N) {
    int i = blockIdx.x * blockDim.x + threadIdx.x;
    if (i < N) C[i] = A[i] + B[i];
}
```

To test the performance of zero-copy read operations, you allocate arrays `A` and `B` as zero-copy memory, and allocate array `C` in device memory. The `main` function for this is provided in Listing 4-3. You can download the source code in `sumArrayZerocopy.cu` from `Wrox.com`.

The `main` function contains two parts: In the first part, you load from and store to device memory; and in the second part, you load data from zero-copy memory, and store data to device memory. At the beginning, you also need to check if the device supports mapped pinned memory.

To allow the kernel to read from zero-copy memory, you need to allocate arrays A and B as mapped pinned memory. You then can directly initialize arrays A and B on the host, and do not need to transfer them to device memory. Next, you obtain the device pointer of the mapped pinned memory for kernel use. Once the memory is allocated and initialized, you can invoke the kernel.

LISTING 4-3: Sum arrays with zero-copy memory (sumArrayZerocopy.cu) (main function only listed)

```
int main(int argc, char **argv) {
    // part 0: set up device and array
    // set up device
    int dev = 0;
    cudaSetDevice(dev);

    // get device properties
    cudaDeviceProp deviceProp;
    cudaGetDeviceProperties(&deviceProp, dev);

    // check if support mapped memory
    if (!deviceProp.canMapHostMemory) {
        printf("Device %d does not support mapping CPU host memory!\n", dev);
        cudaDeviceReset();
        exit(EXIT_SUCCESS);
    }
    printf("Using Device %d: %s ", dev, deviceProp.name);

    // set up date size of vectors
    int ipower = 10;
    if (argc>1) ipower = atoi(argv[1]);
    int nElem = 1<<ipower;
    size_t nBytes = nElem * sizeof(float);
    if (ipower < 18) {
        printf("Vector size %d power %d  nbytes  %3.0f KB\n", nElem,\
                ipower,(float)nBytes/(1024.0f));
    } else {
        printf("Vector size %d power %d  nbytes  %3.0f MB\n", nElem,\
                ipower,(float)nBytes/(1024.0f*1024.0f));
    }

    // part 1: using device memory
    // malloc host memory
    float *h_A, *h_B, *hostRef, *gpuRef;
    h_A     = (float *)malloc(nBytes);
    h_B     = (float *)malloc(nBytes);
    hostRef = (float *)malloc(nBytes);
    gpuRef  = (float *)malloc(nBytes);

    // initialize data at host side
    initialData(h_A, nElem);
    initialData(h_B, nElem);
    memset(hostRef, 0, nBytes);
    memset(gpuRef,  0, nBytes);
```

```
// add vector at host side for result checks
sumArraysOnHost(h_A, h_B, hostRef, nElem);

// malloc device global memory
float *d_A, *d_B, *d_C;
cudaMalloc((float**)&d_A, nBytes);
cudaMalloc((float**)&d_B, nBytes);
cudaMalloc((float**)&d_C, nBytes);

// transfer data from host to device
cudaMemcpy(d_A, h_A, nBytes, cudaMemcpyHostToDevice);
cudaMemcpy(d_B, h_B, nBytes, cudaMemcpyHostToDevice);

// set up execution configuration
int iLen = 512;
dim3 block (iLen);
dim3 grid  ((nElem+block.x-1)/block.x);

// invoke kernel at host side
sumArrays <<<grid, block>>>(d_A, d_B, d_C, nElem);

// copy kernel result back to host side
cudaMemcpy(gpuRef, d_C, nBytes, cudaMemcpyDeviceToHost);

// check device results
checkResult(hostRef, gpuRef, nElem);

// free device global memory
cudaFree(d_A);
cudaFree(d_B);
free(h_A);
free(h_B);

// part 2: using zerocopy memory for array A and B
// allocate zerocpy memory
unsigned int flags = cudaHostAllocMapped;
cudaHostAlloc((void **)&h_A, nBytes, flags);
cudaHostAlloc((void **)&h_B, nBytes, flags);

// initialize data at host side
initialData(h_A, nElem);
initialData(h_B, nElem);
memset(hostRef, 0, nBytes);
memset(gpuRef,  0, nBytes);

// pass the pointer to device
cudaHostGetDevicePointer((void **)&d_A, (void *)h_A, 0);
cudaHostGetDevicePointer((void **)&d_B, (void *)h_B, 0);

// add at host side for result checks
sumArraysOnHost(h_A, h_B, hostRef, nElem);
```

continues

LISTING 4-3 *(continued)*

```
        // execute kernel with zero copy memory
        sumArraysZeroCopy <<<grid, block>>>(d_A, d_B, d_C, nElem);

        // copy kernel result back to host side
        cudaMemcpy(gpuRef, d_C, nBytes, cudaMemcpyDeviceToHost);

        // check device results
        checkResult(hostRef, gpuRef, nElem);

        // free  memory
        cudaFree(d_C);
        cudaFreeHost(h_A);
        cudaFreeHost(h_B);

        free(hostRef);
        free(gpuRef);

        // reset device
        cudaDeviceReset();
        return EXIT_SUCCESS;
    }
```

Compile the source with the following command:

```
$ nvcc -O3 -arch=sm_20 sumArrayZerocpy.cu -o sumZerocpy
```

Collect profile information using `nvprof`. A sample output from a Fermi M2090 is summarized below:

```
$ nvprof ./sumZerocpy
Using Device 0: Tesla M2090 Vector size 1024 power 10  nbytes    4 KB
Time(%)      Time    Calls      Avg       Min       Max  Name
 27.18%   3.7760us        1   3.7760us   3.7760us   3.7760us  sumArraysZeroCopy
 11.80%   1.6390us        1   1.6390us   1.6390us   1.6390us  sumArrays
 25.56%   3.5520us        3   1.1840us   1.0240us   1.5040us  [CUDA memcpy HtoD]
 35.47%   4.9280us        2   2.4640us   2.4640us   2.4640us  [CUDA memcpy DtoH]
```

Compare the elapsed time for the `sumArraysZeroCopy` kernel to the `sumArrays` kernel. When processing 1,024 elements, the elapsed time of the kernel reading from zero-copy memory is 2.31 times slower than the kernel using only device memory. Also notice the time reported to transfer data from device to host (DtoH) reports time from both kernels because they both use `cudaMemcpy` to update the host with the results from the calculation performed on the device.

Next, you can check performance for different array sizes by running the following command. Samples results are summarized in Table 4-3.

```
$ ./sumZerocopy <size-log-2>
```

TABLE 4-3: Comparison of Zero-copy Memory vs Device Memory

SIZE	DEVICE MEMORY (ELAPSED TIME)	ZERO-COPY MEMORY (ELAPSED TIME)	SLOWDOWN
1 K	1.5820 us	2.9150 us	1.84
4 K	1.6640 us	3.7900 us	2.28
16 K	1.6740 us	7.4570 us	4.45
64 K	2.3910 us	22.586 us	9.45
256 K	7.2890 us	82.733 us	11.35
1 M	28.267 us	321.57 us	11.38
4 M	104.17 us	1.2741 ms	12.23
16 M	408.03 us	5.0903 ms	12.47
64 M	1.6276 ms	20.347 ms	12.50

Tesla M2090 ECC on and L1 cache enabled
Slowdown = Elapsed Time of Zero-copy Reads / Elapsed Time of Device Memory Reads

From the results, you can see that if you share a small amount of data between the host and device, zero-copy memory may be a good choice because it simplifies programming and offers reasonable performance. For larger datasets with discrete GPUs connected via the PCIe bus, zero-copy memory is a poor choice and causes significant performance degradation.

ZERO-COPY MEMORY

There are two common categories of heterogeneous computing system architectures: Integrated and discrete.

In integrated architectures, CPUs and GPUs are fused onto a single die and physically share main memory. In this architecture, zero-copy memory is more likely to benefit both performance and programmability because no copies over the PCIe bus are necessary.

For discrete systems with devices connected to the host via PCIe bus, zero-copy memory is advantageous only in special cases.

Because the mapped pinned memory is shared between the host and device, you must synchronize memory accesses to avoid any potential data hazards caused by multiple threads accessing the same memory location without synchronization.

Be careful to not overuse zero-copy memory. Device kernels that read from zero-copy memory can be very slow due to its high-latency.

Unified Virtual Addressing

Devices with compute capability 2.0 and later support a special addressing mode called *Unified Virtual Addressing* (UVA). UVA, introduced in CUDA 4.0, is supported on 64-bit Linux systems. With UVA, host memory and device memory share a single virtual address space, as illustrated in Figure 4-5.

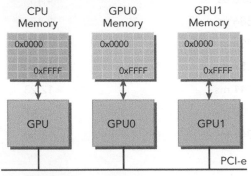

No UVA: multiple memory spaces   UVA: single memory space

FIGURE 4-5

Prior to UVA, you needed to manage which pointers referred to host memory and which referred to device memory. Using UVA, the memory space referenced by a pointer becomes transparent to application code.

Under UVA, pinned host memory allocated with `cudaHostAlloc` has identical host and device pointers. You can therefore pass the returned pointer directly to a kernel function. Recall the zero-copy example from the previous section where you:

➤ Allocated mapped, pinned host memory.

➤ Acquired the device pointer to the mapped, pinned memory using a CUDA runtime function.

➤ Passed the device pointer to your kernel.

With UVA, there is no need to acquire the device pointer or manage two pointers to what is physically the same data. UVA would further simplify the `sumArrayZerocpy.cu` example from the previous section:

```
// allocate zero-copy memory at the host side
cudaHostAlloc((void **)&h_A, nBytes, cudaHostAllocMapped);
cudaHostAlloc((void **)&h_B, nBytes, cudaHostAllocMapped);

// initialize data at the host side
initialData(h_A, nElem);
initialData(h_B, nElem);

// invoke the kernel with zero-copy memory
sumArraysZeroCopy<<<grid, block>>>(h_A, h_B, d_C, nElem);
```

Note that the pointers returned by `cudaHostAlloc` are passed directly to the kernel. The updated code using UVA can be found in `sumArrayZerocpyUVA.cu`, available from `Wrox.com`. It can be compiled with the following command:

```
$ nvcc -O3 -arch=sm_20 sumArrayZerocpyUVA.cu -o sumArrayZerocpyUVA
```

Running the same tests as the previous section will produce identical performance results. Generating the same results using less code improves both the readability and maintainability of your application.

Unified Memory

With CUDA 6.0, a new feature called *Unified Memory* was introduced to simplify memory management in the CUDA programming model. Unified Memory creates a pool of managed memory, where each allocation from this memory pool is accessible on both the CPU and GPU with the same memory address (that is, pointer). The underlying system automatically migrates data in the unified memory space between the host and device. This data movement is transparent to the application, greatly simplifying the application code.

Unified Memory depends on Unified Virtual Addressing (UVA) support, but they are entirely different technologies. UVA provides a single virtual memory address space for all processors in the system. However, UVA does not automatically migrate data from one physical location to another; that is a capability unique to Unified Memory.

Unified Memory offers a "single-pointer-to-data" model that is conceptually similar to zero-copy memory. However, zero-copy memory is allocated in host memory, and as a result kernel performance generally suffers from high-latency accesses to zero-copy memory over the PCIe bus. Unified Memory, on the other hand, decouples memory and execution spaces so that data can be transparently migrated on demand to the host or device to improve locality and performance.

Managed memory refers to Unified Memory allocations that are automatically managed by the underlying system and is interoperable with device-specific allocations, such as those created using the `cudaMalloc` routine. Therefore, you can use both types of memory in a kernel: managed memory that is controlled by the system, and un-managed memory that must be explicitly allocated and transferred by the application. All CUDA operations that are valid on device memory are also valid on managed memory. The primary difference is that the host is also able to reference and access managed memory.

Managed memory can be allocated statically or dynamically. You can statically declare a device variable as a managed variable by adding a `__managed__` annotation to its declaration. This can only be done in file-scope and global-scope. The variable can be referenced directly from either host or device code:

```
__device__ __managed__ int y;
```

You can also allocate managed memory dynamically using the following CUDA runtime function:

```
cudaError_t cudaMallocManaged(void **devPtr, size_t size, unsigned int flags=0);
```

This function allocates `size` bytes of managed memory and returns a pointer in `devPtr`. The pointer is valid on all devices and the host. The behavior of a program with managed memory is functionally unchanged to its counterpart with un-managed memory. However, a program that uses managed memory can take advantage of automatic data migration and duplicate pointer elimination.

In CUDA 6.0, device code cannot call `cudaMallocManaged`. All managed memory must be dynamically allocated from the host or statically declared in global scope.

The upcoming section in this chapter titled, "Matrix Addition with Unified Memory" will give you an opportunity to gain hands-on experience with CUDA Unified Memory.

MEMORY ACCESS PATTERNS

Most device data access begins in global memory, and most GPU applications tend to be limited by memory bandwidth. Therefore, maximizing your application's use of global memory bandwidth is a fundamental step in kernel performance tuning. If you do not tune global memory usage properly, other optimizations will likely have a negligible effect.

To achieve the best performance when reading and writing data, memory access operations must meet certain conditions. One of the distinguishing features of the CUDA execution model is that instructions are issued and executed per warp. Memory operations are also issued per warp. When executing a memory instruction, each thread in a warp provides a memory address it is loading or storing. Cooperatively, the 32 threads in a warp present a single memory access request comprised of the requested addresses, which is serviced by one or more device memory transactions. Depending on the distribution of memory addresses within a warp, memory accesses can be classified into different patterns. In this section, you are going to examine different memory access patterns and learn how to achieve optimal global memory access.

Aligned and Coalesced Access

Global memory loads/stores are staged through caches, as shown in Figure 4-6. Global memory is a logical memory space that you can access from your kernel. All application data initially resides in DRAM, the physical device memory. Kernel memory requests are typically served between the device DRAM and SM on-chip memory using either 128-byte or 32-byte memory transactions.

All accesses to global memory go through the L2 cache. Many accesses also pass through the L1 cache, depending on the type of access and your GPU's architecture. If both L1 and L2 caches are used, a memory access is serviced by a 128-byte memory transaction. If only the L2 cache is used, a memory access is serviced by a 32-byte memory transaction. On architectures that allow the L1 cache to be used for global memory caching, the L1 cache can be explicitly enabled or disabled at compile time.

An L1 cache line is 128 bytes, and it maps to a 128-byte aligned segment in device memory. If each thread in a warp requests one 4-byte value, that results in 128 bytes of data per request, which maps perfectly to the cache line size and device memory segment size.

There are two characteristics of device memory accesses that you should strive for when optimizing your application:

- ➤ Aligned memory accesses
- ➤ Coalesced memory accesses

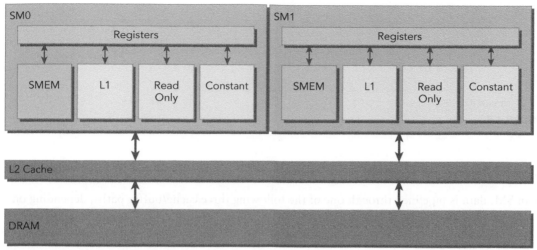

FIGURE 4-6

Aligned memory accesses occur when the first address of a device memory transaction is an even multiple of the cache granularity being used to service the transaction (either 32 bytes for L2 cache or 128 bytes for L1 cache). Performing a misaligned load will cause wasted bandwidth.

Coalesced memory accesses occur when all 32 threads in a warp access a contiguous chunk of memory.

Aligned coalesced memory accesses are ideal: A wrap accessing a contiguous chunk of memory starting at an aligned memory address. To maximize global memory throughput, it is important to organize memory operations to be both aligned and coalesced. Figure 4-7 illustrates an aligned and coalesced memory load operation. In this case, only a single 128-byte memory transaction is required to read the data from device memory. Figure 4-8 illustrates a misaligned and uncoalesced memory access. In this case, there may be as many as three 128-byte memory transactions to read the data from device memory: one starting at offset 0 to include the data being read below the contiguous region, one at offset 256 to read the data being read above the contiguous region, and one at offset 128 that fetches the bulk of the data. Note that most of the bytes fetched by the lower and upper memory transactions will not be used, leading to wasted bandwidth.

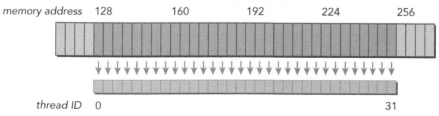

FIGURE 4-7

In general, you should optimize for memory transaction efficiency: Use the least number of transactions to service the maximum number of memory requests. How many transactions are needed, and how much throughput is delivered, varies with device compute capability.

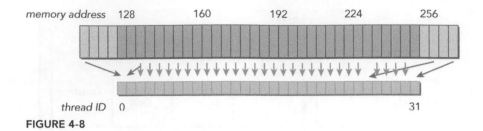

FIGURE 4-8

Global Memory Reads

In an SM, data is pipelined through one of the following three cache/buffer paths, depending on what type of device memory is being referenced:

➤   L1/L2 cache

➤   Constant cache

➤   Read-only cache

L1/L2 cache is the default path. To pass data through the other two paths requires explicit management by the application, but can lead to performance improvement depending on the access patterns used. Whether global memory load operations pass through the L1 cache depends on two factors:

➤   Device compute capability

➤   Compiler options

On Fermi GPUs (compute capability 2.x) and Kepler K40 or later GPUs (compute capability 3.5 and up), L1 caching of global memory loads can be either enabled or disabled with compiler flags. By default, the L1 cache is enabled for global memory loads on Fermi devices and disabled on K40 and later GPUs. The following flags inform the compiler to disable the L1 cache:

```
-Xptxas -dlcm=cg
```

With the L1 cache disabled, all load requests to global memory go directly to the L2 cache; when an L2 miss occurs, the requests are serviced by DRAM. Each memory transaction may be conducted by one, two, or four segments, where one segment is 32 bytes.

The L1 cache can also be explicitly enabled with the following flag:

```
-Xptxas -dlcm=ca
```

With this flag set, global memory load requests first attempt to hit in L1 cache. On an L1 miss, the requests go to L2. On an L2 miss, the requests are serviced by DRAM. In this mode, a load memory request is serviced by a 128-byte device memory transaction.

On Kepler K10, K20, and K20x GPUs, the L1 cache is not used to cache global memory loads. The L1 cache is exclusively used to cache register spills to local memory.

MEMORY LOAD ACCESS PATTERNS

There are two types of memory loads:

➤ Cached load (L1 cache enabled)

➤ Uncached load (L1 cache disabled)

The access pattern for memory loads can be characterized by the following combinations:

➤ Cached versus uncached: The load is cached if L1 cache is enabled

➤ Aligned versus misaligned: The load is aligned if the first address of a memory access is a multiple of 32 bytes

➤ Coalesced versus uncoalesced: The load is coalesced if a warp accesses a contiguous chunk of data

---

You will examine the impact that these memory access patterns have on kernel performance in the next sections.

Cached Loads

Cached load operations pass through L1 cache and are serviced by device memory transactions at the granularity of an L1 cache line, 128 bytes. Cached loads can be classified as aligned/misaligned and coalesced/uncoalesced.

Figure 4-9 illustrates the ideal case: aligned and coalesced memory accesses. The addresses requested by all threads in a warp fall within one cache line of 128 bytes. Only a single 128-byte transaction is required to complete the memory load operation. Bus utilization is 100 percent, and there is no unused data in this transaction.

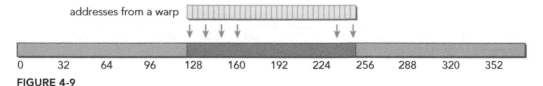

FIGURE 4-9

Figure 4-10 illustrates another case in which the access is aligned and the referenced addresses are not consecutive by thread ID, but rather randomized within a 128-byte range. Because the addresses requested by the threads in a warp still fall within one cache line, only one 128-byte transaction is needed to fulfill this memory load operation. Bus utilization is still 100 percent, and as long as each thread requests a separate 4-bytes in the 128-byte range, there is no unused data in this transaction.

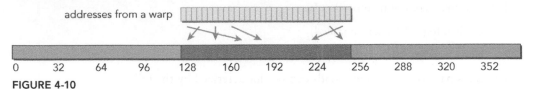

FIGURE 4-10

Figure 4-11 illustrates a case in which a warp requests 32 consecutive four-byte data elements that are not aligned. The addresses requested by the threads in the warp fall across two 128-byte segments in global memory. Because the physical load operations performed by an SM must be aligned at 128-byte boundaries when the L1 cache is enabled, two 128-byte transactions are required to fulfill this memory load operation. Bus utilization is 50 percent, and half the bytes loaded in these two transactions are unused.

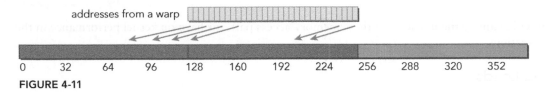

FIGURE 4-11

Figure 4-12 illustrates a case in which all threads in the warp request the same address. Because the bytes referenced fall on a single cache line only one memory transaction is required, but bus utilization is very low. If the value loaded is 4-bytes, the bus utilization is 4 bytes requested / 128 bytes loaded = 3.125%.

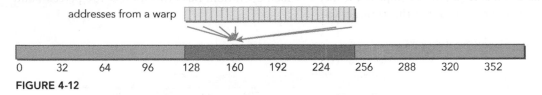

FIGURE 4-12

Figure 4-13 illustrates a worst-case scenario in which the threads in a warp request 32 four-byte addresses scattered across global memory. Even though the total number of bytes requested by the warp is only 128 bytes, the addresses can fall across N cache lines, where $0 < N \le 32$. N memory transactions are required to complete a single memory load operation.

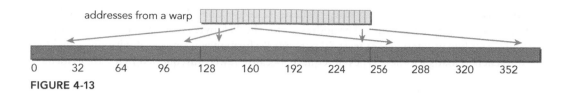

FIGURE 4-13

DIFFERENCE BETWEEN CPU L1 CACHE AND GPU L1 CACHE

The CPU L1 cache is optimized for both spatial and temporal locality. The GPU L1 cache is designed for spatial but not temporal locality. Frequent access to a cached L1 memory location does not increase the probability that the data will stay in cache.

Uncached Loads

Uncached loads do not pass through the L1 cache and are performed at the granularity of memory segments (32-bytes) and not cache lines (128-bytes). These are more fine-grained loads, and can lead to better bus utilization for misaligned or uncoalesced memory accesses.

Figure 4-14 illustrates the ideal case, an aligned and coalesced memory access. The addresses for the 128 bytes requested fall within four segments, and bus utilization is 100 percent.

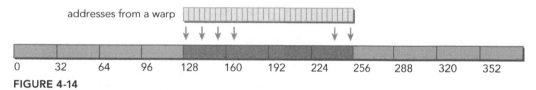

FIGURE 4-14

Figure 4-15 illustrates the case in which the memory access is aligned and thread accesses are not sequential, but randomized within a 128-byte range. As long as each thread requests a unique address, the addresses will fall within four segments and no loads are wasted. Such randomized accesses will not inhibit kernel performance.

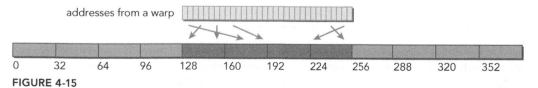

FIGURE 4-15

Figure 4-16 illustrates a case in which a warp requests 32 consecutive 4-byte elements but the load is not aligned to a 128-byte boundary. The addresses for the 128 bytes requested fall within at most five segments, and bus utilization is at least 80 percent. Performance is improved with uncached loads compared to cached loads for these types of requests because fewer unrequested bytes are loaded.

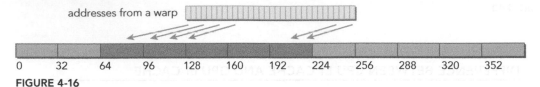

FIGURE 4-16

Figure 4-17 illustrates a case in which all threads in the warp request the same data. The addresses fall within one segment and bus utilization is 4 bytes requested / 32 bytes loaded = 12.5%, again better than cached load performance in this scenario.

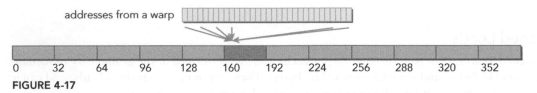

FIGURE 4-17

Figure 4-18 illustrates the worst-case scenario in which a warp requests 32 4-byte words scattered across global memory. Because the requested 128 bytes fall within at most N 32-byte segments instead of N 128-byte cache lines, worst-case is improved relative to a cached load.

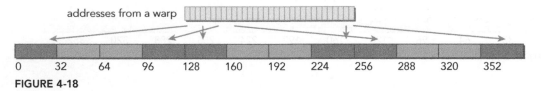

FIGURE 4-18

Example of Misaligned Reads

Because access patterns are often determined by the algorithm an application implements, it can be challenging to coalesce memory loads for some applications. However, there are techniques that can help to align application memory accesses in most cases.

To illustrate the effect of misaligned accesses on kernel performance, you will modify the vector addition code used in Chapter 3 to specify an offset by which all memory load operations are shifted. Note there are two indices used in the following kernel. The new index k is shifted up by a given offset, which might cause misaligned loads depending on the value of offset. Only the load operations for arrays A and B will use index k. The write operation to array C will still use the original index i, ensuring that write accesses remain well-aligned.

```
__global__ void readOffset(float *A, float *B, float *C, const int n,
    int offset) {
    unsigned int i = blockIdx.x * blockDim.x + threadIdx.x;
    unsigned int k = i + offset;
    if (k < n) C[i] = A[k] + B[k];
}
```

To be able to verify the correctness of the transformed kernel the host code should also be modified accordingly:

```
void sumArraysOnHost(float *A, float *B, float *C, const int n,
    int offset) {
    for (int idx = offset, k = 0; idx < n; idx++, k++) {
        C[k] = A[idx] + B[idx];
    }
}
```

The main function is provided in Listing 4-4. You should already be familiar with most of this code. You can download the full source in readSegment.cu from Wrox.com. The default value for offset is zero, but it can be overwritten by a command-line argument.

LISTING 4-4: Read memory with offset (readSegment.cu) (only the main function listed)

```
int main(int argc, char **argv) {
    // set up device
    int dev = 0;
    cudaDeviceProp deviceProp;
    cudaGetDeviceProperties(&deviceProp, dev);
    printf("%s starting reduction at ", argv[0]);
    printf("device %d: %s ", dev, deviceProp.name);
    cudaSetDevice(dev);

    // set up array size
    int nElem = 1<<20; // total number of elements to reduce
    printf(" with array size %d\n", nElem);
    size_t nBytes = nElem * sizeof(float);

    // set up offset for summary
    int blocksize = 512;
    int offset = 0;
    if (argc>1) offset    = atoi(argv[1]);
    if (argc>2) blocksize = atoi(argv[2]);

    // execution configuration
    dim3 block (blocksize,1);
    dim3 grid  ((nElem+block.x-1)/block.x,1);

    // allocate host memory
    float *h_A = (float *)malloc(nBytes);
    float *h_B = (float *)malloc(nBytes);
    float *hostRef = (float *)malloc(nBytes);
    float *gpuRef  = (float *)malloc(nBytes);
```

continues

LISTING 4-4 *(continued)*

```
// initialize host array
initialData(h_A, nElem);
memcpy(h_B,h_A,nBytes);

// summary at host side
sumArraysOnHost(h_A, h_B, hostRef,nElem,offset);

// allocate device memory
float *d_A,*d_B,*d_C;
cudaMalloc((float**)&d_A, nBytes);
cudaMalloc((float**)&d_B, nBytes);
cudaMalloc((float**)&d_C, nBytes);

// copy data from host to device
cudaMemcpy(d_A, h_A, nBytes, cudaMemcpyHostToDevice);
cudaMemcpy(d_B, h_A, nBytes, cudaMemcpyHostToDevice);

// kernel 1:
double iStart = seconds();
warmup <<< grid, block >>> (d_A, d_B, d_C, nElem, offset);
cudaDeviceSynchronize();
double iElaps = seconds() - iStart;
printf("warmup    <<< %4d, %4d >>> offset %4d elapsed %f sec\n",
    grid.x, block.x,
    offset, iElaps);

iStart = seconds();
readOffset <<< grid, block >>> (d_A, d_B, d_C, nElem, offset);
cudaDeviceSynchronize();
iElaps = seconds() - iStart;
printf("readOffset <<< %4d, %4d >>> offset %4d elapsed %f sec\n",
    grid.x, block.x,
    offset, iElaps);

// copy kernel result back to host side and check device results
cudaMemcpy(gpuRef, d_C, nBytes, cudaMemcpyDeviceToHost);
checkResult(hostRef, gpuRef, nElem-offset);

// copy kernel result back to host side and check device results
cudaMemcpy(gpuRef, d_C, nBytes, cudaMemcpyDeviceToHost);
checkResult(hostRef, gpuRef, nElem-offset);

// copy kernel result back to host side and check device results
cudaMemcpy(gpuRef, d_C, nBytes, cudaMemcpyDeviceToHost);
checkResult(hostRef, gpuRef, nElem-offset);

// free host and device memory
cudaFree(d_A);
cudaFree(d_B);
cudaFree(d_C);
free(h_A);
free(h_B);
```

```
    // reset device
    cudaDeviceReset();
    return EXIT_SUCCESS;
}
```

Compile the code with the following command:

```
$ nvcc -O3 -arch=sm_20 readSegment.cu  -o readSegment
```

You can experiment with different offsets. Sample outputs from a Fermi M2050 are included below:

```
$ ./readSegment 0
readOffset <<< 32768,   512 >>> offset     0 elapsed 0.001820 sec
$ ./readSegment 11
readOffset <<< 32768,   512 >>> offset    11 elapsed 0.001949 sec
$ ./readSegment 128
readOffset <<< 32768,   512 >>> offset   128 elapsed 0.001821 sec
```

Using `offset=11` causes memory loads from arrays A and B to be misaligned. The elapsed time for this case is also the slowest. You can verify these misaligned accesses are the cause for lost performance by collecting information on the global load efficiency metric:

$$\text{gld\_efficiency} = \frac{\text{Requested Global Memory Load Throughput}}{\text{Required Global Memory Load Throughput}}$$

Required Global Memory Load Throughput includes replayed memory load instructions that required more than one memory transaction, whereas Requested Global Memory Load Throughput does not.

You can collect the `gld_efficiency` metric using nvprof with the readSegment test case and different offset values:

```
$ nvprof --devices 0 --metrics gld_transactions ./readSegment 0
$ nvprof --devices 0 --metrics gld_transactions ./readSegment 11
$ nvprof --devices 0 --metrics gld_transactions ./readSegment 128
```

Sample results are included below:

```
Offset    0:  gld_efficiency  100.00%
Offset   11:  gld_efficiency   49.81%
Offset  128:  gld_efficiency  100.00%
```

For the misaligned case (`offset=11`), global load efficiency is halved, implying that the required global memory load throughput doubled. You can verify this directly with the global load transactions metric:

```
$ nvprof --devices 0 --metrics gld_transactions ./readSegment $OFFSET
```

Sample results are included below:

```
Offset    0: gld_transactions 65184
Offset   11: gld_transactions 131039
Offset  128: gld_transactions 65744
```

As predicted, the number of global load transactions doubled for the case `offset=11`.

You can also observe how disabling the L1 cache for global memory loads affects performance. To force uncached loads, recompile the code and add the following nvcc option:

```
-Xptxas -dlcm=cg
```

Note that this compiler flag will only change the behavior of Fermi and Kepler K40 or later GPUs. Sample outputs are included below:

```
$ ./readSegment 0
readOffset <<< 32768,  512 >>> offset    0 elapsed 0.001825 sec
$ ./readSegment 11
readOffset <<< 32768,  512 >>> offset   11 elapsed 0.002309 sec
$ ./  128
readOffset <<< 32768,  512 >>> offset  128 elapsed 0.001823 sec
```

The results show that overall performance with uncached loads is slightly slower than the cached accesses. The case with misaligned accesses is particularly affected by a lack of caching. With the cache enabled, a misaligned access might bring data into the L1 cache that would be used to satisfy part of a later, misaligned memory request. However, without the L1 cache, each of the misaligned requests requires multiple memory transactions and provide no benefit for future requests.

You can also check global load efficiency with uncached loads. Sample results are included below:

```
Offset   0:  gld_efficiency  100.00%
Offset  11:  gld_efficiency   80.00%
Offset 128:  gld_efficiency  100.00%
```

For the misaligned case, load efficiency improved with L1 cache disabled, from 49.8 percent efficiency to 80 percent efficiency. Since the L1 cache is disabled, each load request is serviced at a 32-byte granularity instead of 128-byte; therefore the number of loaded (but unused) bytes is reduced.

You might notice that overall time was not reduced with uncached loads, even though global load efficiency improved. This is true, but just for this simple test case. With higher device occupancy, uncached loads might help improve overall bus utilization. The amount of unused data transferred might be significantly reduced for uncached, misaligned load patterns.

Read-Only Cache

The read-only cache was originally reserved for use by texture memory loads. For GPUs of compute capability 3.5 and higher, the read-only cache can also support global memory loads as an alternative to the L1 cache.

The granularity of loads through the read-only cache is 32 bytes. In general, these finer granularity loads are better for scattered reads than the L1 cache.

There are two ways to direct memory reads through the read-only cache:

➤ Using the function __ldg

➤ Using a declaration qualifier on the pointer being dereferenced

For example, consider the following copy kernel:

```
__global__ void copyKernel(int *out, int *in) {
    int idx = blockIdx.x * blockDim.x + threadIdx.x;
    out[idx] = in[idx];
}
```

You can use the intrinsic function __ldg to direct the read accesses for array in through the read-only cache:

```
__global__ void copyKernel(int *out, int *in) {
    int idx  = blockIdx.x * blockDim.x + threadIdx.x;
    out[idx] = __ldg(&in[idx]);
}
```

You can also apply const __restrict__ qualifiers to pointers. These qualifiers help the nvcc compiler recognize non-aliased pointers (that is, pointers which are used exclusively to access a particular array). nvcc will automatically direct loads from non-aliased pointers through the read-only cache.

```
__global__ void copyKernel(int * __restrict__ out,
    const    int * __restrict__ in) {
    int idx  = blockIdx.x * blockDim.x + threadIdx.x;
    out[idx] = in[idx];
}
```

Global Memory Writes

Memory store operations are relatively simple. The L1 cache is not used for store operations on either Fermi or Kepler GPUs, store operations are only cached in the L2 cache before being sent to device memory. Stores are performed at a 32-byte segment granularity. Memory transactions can be one, two, or four segments at a time. For example, if two addresses fall within the same 128-byte region but not within an aligned 64-byte region, one four-segment transaction will be issued (that is, issuing a single four-segment transaction performs better than issuing two one-segment transactions).

Figure 4-19 illustrates the ideal case in which the memory access is aligned and all threads in a warp access a consecutive 128-byte range. The store request is serviced by one four-segment transaction.

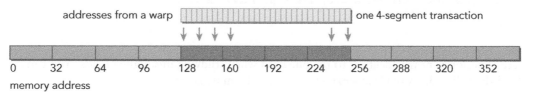

FIGURE 4-19

Figure 4-20 illustrates the case in which the memory access is aligned, but the addresses are scattered along a 192-byte range. This store request is serviced by three one-segment transactions.

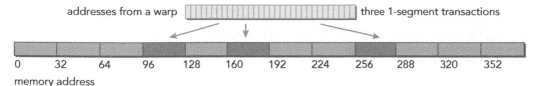

FIGURE 4-20

Figure 4-21 illustrates the case in which the memory access is aligned and the addresses accessed are in a consecutive 64-byte range. This store request is serviced with one two-segment transaction.

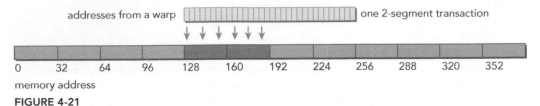

FIGURE 4-21

Example of Misaligned Writes

To verify the effect of misalignment on memory store efficiency, modify the vector addition kernel as follows. Two different indices are still used: Index k is shifted by a given offset, but index i is not (and therefore should result in aligned accesses). Loading from arrays A and B uses the aligned index i, causing good memory load efficiency. Writing to array C uses the offset index k, likely causing misaligned writes depending on the value of the offset.

```
__global__ void writeOffset(float *A, float *B, float *C,
        const int n, int offset) {
    unsigned int i = blockIdx.x * blockDim.x + threadIdx.x;
    unsigned int k = i + offset;
    if (k < n) C[k] = A[i] + B[i];
}
```

The host vector addition code must be revised to match these changes:

```
void sumArraysOnHost(float *A, float *B, float *C, const int n,
        int offset) {
    for (int idx = offset, k = 0; idx < n; idx++, k++) {
        C[idx] = A[k] + B[k];
    }
}
```

The main function is nearly identical to the one used when studying misaligned loads. You can download the full code example in writeSegment.cu from Wrox.com.

Compile the code with the following command, and run it.

```
$ nvcc -O3 -arch=sm_20 writeSegment.cu -o writeSegment
```

Sample outputs with offsets of 0, 11, and 128 are included below:

```
$ ./writeSegment 0
writeOffset <<< 2048,  512 >>> offset    0 elapsed 0.000134 sec
$ ./writeSegment 11
writeOffset <<< 2048,  512 >>> offset   11 elapsed 0.000184 sec
$ ./writeSegment 128
writeOffset <<< 2048,  512 >>> offset  128 elapsed 0.000134 sec
```

Clearly, the misaligned case (offset=11) reports the worst performance. You can verify the cause for this misalignment by collecting global load and store efficiency metrics using nvprof:

```
$ nvprof --devices 0 --metrics gld_efficiency --metrics gst_efficiency \
     ./writeSegment $OFFSET
```

Sample outputs of nvprof are included below:

```
writeOffset Offset    0:  gld_efficiency  100.00%
writeOffset Offset    0:  gst_efficiency  100.00%

writeOffset Offset  11:  gld_efficiency  100.00%
writeOffset Offset  11:  gst_efficiency   80.00%

writeOffset Offset 128:  gld_efficiency  100.00%
writeOffset Offset 128:  gst_efficiency  100.00%
```

All load and store efficiencies are 100 percent except stores in the misaligned case (offset=11). The store efficiency for misaligned writes is 80 percent. With offset=11, when a 128-byte write request is issued from a warp, the request will be serviced by one four-segment transaction and one one-segment transaction. Therefore, 128 bytes were requested and 160 bytes were loaded, resulting in 80 percent efficiency.

Array of Structures versus Structure of Arrays

As a C programmer, you should be familiar with two ways of organizing data: an *array of structures* (AoS), and a *structure of arrays* (SoA). This is always an interesting topic, because each represents a different way to take advantage of two powerful data types (struct and array) when storing sets of structured data.

Consider the following illustrative example that stores a set of paired float data elements. First, consider how a set of these paired data elements would be stored using the AoS approach. Define a structure named innerStruct as follows:

```
struct innerStruct {
    float x;
    float y;
};
```

Then, define an array of these structs as shown below. This is the AoS way of organizing data. It stores related data (for example, *x* and *y*) spatially close together, which results in good cache locality on the CPU.

```
struct innerStruct myAoS[N];
```

Next, consider the data stored using an SoA approach:

```
struct innerArray {
    float x[N];
    float y[N];
};
```

Here, all values for each field in the original struct are separated into their own array. This stores data for neighboring data points together, but stores the data for a single data point across multiple arrays. You can define a variable using this structure as follows:

```
struct innerArray moa;
```

Figure 4-22 illustrates the memory layout of both AoS and SoA approaches. Storing the example data in AoS format on the GPU and performing an operation that only requires the *x* field would result in a 50 percent loss of bandwidth as *y* values are implicitly loaded in each 32-byte segment or 128-byte cache line. An AoS format would also waste L2 cache space on unneeded *y* values.

Storing the data in SoA fashion makes full use of GPU memory bandwidth. Because there is no interleaving of elements of the same field, the SoA layout on the GPU provides coalesced memory accesses and can achieve more efficient global memory utilization.

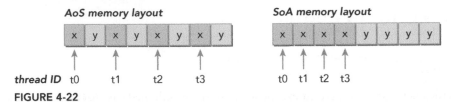

FIGURE 4-22

AOS VERSUS SOA

Many parallel programming paradigms, in particular SIMD-style paradigms, prefer SoA. In CUDA C programming, SoA is also typically preferred because data elements are pre-arranged for efficient coalesced access to global memory, since data elements of the same field that would be referenced by the same memory operation are stored adjacent to each other.

To help understand the performance implications of accessing data in each data layout, you will compare two kernels with the same simple math operation: one implemented to process an AoS data layout, and the other for the SoA data layout.

Example: Simple Math with the AoS Data Layout

The following kernel is implemented using an AoS layout. The global memory array of structs is stored linearly with the variables *x* and *y* interleaved. The inputs and outputs of each thread are the same: a single `innerStruct` structure.

```
__global__ void testInnerStruct(innerStruct *data,
    innerStruct *result, const int n) {
    unsigned int i = blockIdx.x * blockDim.x + threadIdx.x;

    if (i < n) {
        innerStruct tmp = data[i];
        tmp.x += 10.f;
        tmp.y += 20.f;
        result[i] = tmp;
    }
}
```

The input length is defined as 1M:

```
#define LEN 1<<20
```

Global memory is allocated with the following statements:

```
int nElem = LEN;
size_t nBytes = nElem * sizeof(innerStruct);

innerStruct *d_A,*d_C;
cudaMalloc((innerStruct**)&d_A, nBytes);
cudaMalloc((innerStruct**)&d_C, nBytes);
```

The input array is initialized with the following host function:

```
void initialInnerStruct(innerStruct *ip, int size) {
    for (int i = 0; i < size; i++) {
        ip[i].x = (float)(rand() & 0xFF) / 100.0f;
        ip[i].y = (float)(rand() & 0xFF) / 100.0f;
    }
    return;
}
```

The `main` function is shown in Listing 4-5. You can download the full code for this example in `simpleMathAoS.cu` from `Wrox.com`. In the following code, a warm-up kernel is run to limit the impact of CUDA startup overhead and make it possible to obtain a more accurate time measurement of the `testInnerStruct` kernel.

LISTING 4-5: Simple math with AoS data layout (simpleMethAoS.cu)
(main function only listed)

```
int main(int argc, char **argv) {
    // set up device
    int dev = 0;
    cudaDeviceProp deviceProp;
    cudaGetDeviceProperties(&deviceProp, dev);
    printf("%s test struct of array at ", argv[0]);
    printf("device %d: %s \n", dev, deviceProp.name);
    cudaSetDevice(dev);

    // allocate host memory
    int nElem = LEN;
    size_t nBytes = nElem * sizeof(innerStruct);
    innerStruct     *h_A = (innerStruct *)malloc(nBytes);
    innerStruct *hostRef = (innerStruct *)malloc(nBytes);
    innerStruct *gpuRef  = (innerStruct *)malloc(nBytes);


    //  initialize host array
    initialInnerStruct(h_A, nElem);
    testInnerStructHost(h_A, hostRef,nElem);

    // allocate device memory
    innerStruct *d_A,*d_C;
```

continues

LISTING 4-5 *(continued)*

```
        cudaMalloc((innerStruct**)&d_A, nBytes);
        cudaMalloc((innerStruct**)&d_C, nBytes);

        // copy data from host to device
        cudaMemcpy(d_A, h_A, nBytes, cudaMemcpyHostToDevice);

        // set up offset for summary
        int blocksize = 128;
        if (argc>1) blocksize = atoi(argv[1]);

        // execution configuration
        dim3 block (blocksize,1);
        dim3 grid  ((nElem+block.x-1)/block.x,1);

        //  kernel 1: warmup
        double iStart = seconds();
        warmup <<< grid, block >>> (d_A, d_C, nElem);
        cudaDeviceSynchronize();
        double iElaps = seconds() - iStart;
        printf("warmup      <<< %3d, %3d >>> elapsed %f sec\n",grid.x,
            block.x,iElaps);
        cudaMemcpy(gpuRef, d_C, nBytes, cudaMemcpyDeviceToHost);
        checkInnerStruct(hostRef, gpuRef, nElem);

        // kernel 2: testInnerStruct
        iStart = seconds();
        testInnerStruct <<< grid, block >>> (d_A, d_C, nElem);
        cudaDeviceSynchronize();
        iElaps = seconds() - iStart;
        printf("innerstruct <<< %3d, %3d >>> elapsed %f sec\n",grid.x,
            block.x,iElaps);
        cudaMemcpy(gpuRef, d_C, nBytes, cudaMemcpyDeviceToHost);
        checkInnerStruct(hostRef, gpuRef, nElem);

        // free memories both host and device
        cudaFree(d_A);
        cudaFree(d_C);
        free(h_A);
        free(hostRef);
        free(gpuRef);

        // reset device
        cudaDeviceReset();
        return EXIT_SUCCESS;
}
```

Compile the example with the following command, and run it.

```
$ nvcc -O3 -arch=sm_20 simpleMathAoS.cu -o simpleMathAoS
$ ./simpleMathAoS
```

A sample output from a Fermi M2070 is included below.

```
innerStruct <<< 8192, 128 >>> elapsed 0.000286 sec
```

Run the following `nvprof` command to gather global load efficiency and global store efficiency metrics:

```
$ nvprof --devices 0 --metrics gld_efficiency,gst_efficiency ./simpleMathAoS
```

The results are summarized below. An efficiency of 50 percent indicates that both load and store memory requests are replayed for the AoS data layout. Because the fields *x* and *y* are stored adjacent in memory and have the same size, every time a memory transaction is performed to load the values of a particular field, exactly half of the bytes loaded must also belong to the other field. Thus, 50 percent of all required load and store bandwidth is unused.

```
gld_efficiency    50.00%
gst_efficiency    50.00%
```

Example: Simple Math with the SoA Data Layout

The following kernel is implemented using an SoA layout. Two 1D global memory arrays of primitives are allocated to store all values for the two fields, *x* and *y*. The kernel below fetches the appropriate values by indexing into each primitive array.

```
__global__ void testInnerArray(InnerArray *data,
    InnerArray *result, const int n) {
  unsigned int i = blockIdx.x * blockDim.x + threadIdx.x;

  if (i<n) {
      float tmpx = data->x[i];
      float tmpy = data->y[i];

      tmpx += 10.f;
      tmpy += 20.f;
      result->x[i] = tmpx;
      result->y[i] = tmpy;
  }
}
```

The input length used is the same as the AoS test case, 1M:

```
#define LEN 1<<20
```

Allocate global memory with the following statements. Note that `sizeof(InnerArray)` includes the size of its statically declared fields, *x* and *y*.

```
int nElem = LEN;
size_t nBytes = sizeof(InnerArray);

InnerArray *d_A,*d_C;
cudaMalloc((InnerArray **)&d_A, nBytes);
cudaMalloc((InnerArray **)&d_C, nBytes);
```

The `main` function for the SoA test is very similar to the `main` function in the previous `simpleMathAoS.cu` example. You can download the full example code in `simpleMathSoA.cu` from `Wrox.com`. Compile the file with the following command and launch a test.

```
$ nvcc -O3 -arch=sm_20 simpleMathSoA.cu  -o simpleSoA
$ ./simpleSoA
```

A sample output of `simpleMathSoA` running on a Fermi M2070 is included below. Note that performance improves marginally relative to `simpleAoS`. The performance improvement is more noticeable at large input sizes.

```
innerArray   <<< 8192, 128 >>> elapsed 0.000200 sec
```

Run the following `nvprof` command to gather global load efficiency and global store efficiency metrics:

```
$ nvprof --devices 0 --metrics gld_efficiency,gst_efficiency ./simpleMathSoA
```

The results are summarized below. An efficiency of 100 percent indicates that neither load nor store memory requests are replayed when processing the SoA data layout. Each access is handled by a single memory transaction.

```
gld_efficiency  100.00%
gst_efficiency  100.00%
```

Performance Tuning

There are two goals to strive for when optimizing device memory bandwidth utilization:

➤ Aligned and coalesced memory accesses that reduce wasted bandwidth

➤ Sufficient concurrent memory operations to hide memory latency

In the preceding section, you learned how to organize memory access patterns so they are aligned and coalesced. Doing so will ensure efficient use of bytes moving between device DRAM and SM on-chip memory or registers.

Chapter 3 discussed optimizing kernels for instruction throughput. Recall that maximizing concurrent memory accesses is achieved by:

➤ Increasing the number of independent memory operations performed within each thread.

➤ Experimenting with the execution configuration of a kernel launch to expose sufficient parallelism to each SM.

Unrolling Techniques

Unrolling loops that contain memory operations adds more independent, memory operations to the pipeline. You are already familiar with unrolling from the reduction example in Chapter 3.

Consider the earlier `readSegment` example. Revise the `readOffset` kernel such that each thread performs four independent memory operations, as follows. Because each of these loads is independent, you can expect more concurrent memory accesses.

```
__global__ void readOffsetUnroll4(float *A, float *B, float *C,
    const int n, int offset) {
  unsigned int i = blockIdx.x * blockDim.x * 4 + threadIdx.x;
  unsigned int k = i + offset;
  if (k + 3 * blockDim.x < n) {
    C[i]                = A[k]
```

```
    C[i + blockDim.x]     = A[k + blockDim.x]     + B[k + blockDim.x];
    C[i + 2 * blockDim.x] = A[k + 2 * blockDim.x] + B[k + 2 * blockDim.x];
    C[i + 3 * blockDim.x] = A[k + 3 * blockDim.x] + B[k + 3 * blockDim.x];
  }
}
```

You can download the full source in readSegmentUnroll.cu from Wrox.com. Compile the file with L1 cache enabled (-Xptxas -dlcm=ca) and run the following tests:

```
$ ./readSegmentUnroll 0
warmup    <<< 32768,  512 >>> offset    0 elapsed 0.001990 sec
unroll4   <<< 8192,   512 >>> offset    0 elapsed 0.000599 sec
$ ./readSegmentUnroll 11
warmup    <<< 32768,  512 >>> offset   11 elapsed 0.002114 sec
unroll4   <<< 8192,   512 >>> offset   11 elapsed 0.000615 sec
$ ./readSegmentUnroll 128
warmup    <<< 32768,  512 >>> offset  128 elapsed 0.001989 sec
unroll4   <<< 8192,   512 >>> offset  128 elapsed 0.000598 sec
```

Surprised? This unrolling technique has a tremendous impact on performance, even more than address alignment. Relative to the original readSegment example with no loop unrolling, these test runs demonstrate between 3.04 times and 3.17 times speedup. For such an I/O-bound kernel, it makes sense that exposing sufficient memory access parallelism is a high priority. Note that, as expected, the two aligned test cases still outperform the case where accesses are misaligned.

However, unrolling does not affect the number of memory operations performed (only the number concurrently in-flight). You can confirm this by measuring load and store efficiency metrics of both the original and unrolled kernels using the following command to test the misaligned case (offset=11).

```
$ nvprof --devices 0 --metrics gld_efficiency,gst_efficiency ./readSegmentUnroll 11
```

Sample results are summarized below. The load and store efficiency is the same for the two kernels.

```
readOffset           gld_efficiency   49.69%
readOffset           gst_efficiency  100.00%
readOffsetUnroll4    gld_efficiency   50.79%
readOffsetUnroll4    gst_efficiency  100.00%
```

Now, try measuring the number of load and store transactions in the misaligned case (offset=11).

```
$ nvprof --devices 0 --metrics gld_transactions,gst_transactions
  ./readSegmentUnroll 11
```

Sample results are summarized below. The number of read/write transactions performed in the unrolled kernel is significantly reduced.

```
readOffset           gld_transactions 132384
readOffset           gst_transactions 32928
readOffsetUnroll4    gld_transactions 33152
readOffsetUnroll4    gst_transactions 8064
```

Exposing More Parallelism

To expose sufficient parallelism, you should experiment with the grid and block size of a kernel launch to find the best execution configuration for that kernel. Run the following tests to experiment with block size for properly aligned memory accesses (offset=0). Note that you likely will need to use a third command-line argument to specify the data size, otherwise you will hit the limit on thread blocks in a grid.

```
$ ./readSegmentUnroll 0 1024 22
unroll4    <<< 1024, 1024 >>> offset      0 elapsed 0.000169 sec
$ ./readSegmentUnroll 0 512 22
unroll4    <<< 2048,  512 >>> offset      0 elapsed 0.000159 sec
$ ./readSegmentUnroll 0 256 22
unroll4    <<< 4096,  256 >>> offset      0 elapsed 0.000157 sec
$ ./readSegmentUnroll 0 128 22
unroll4    <<< 8192,  128 >>> offset      0 elapsed 0.000158 sec
```

The best block size for the unrolled kernel is 256 threads per block, doubling the number of blocks created compared to the default 512 threads per block used in the earlier tests.

Even though 128 threads per block exposes more parallelism to the GPU, it performed marginally worse than 256 threads per block. To understand why, refer to Table 3-2, "Resource Limits per Compute Capability," in Chapter 3. There are two hardware limits in particular that require attention. Because the test system in this case has a Fermi GPU, the maximum number of concurrent blocks per SM is 8, and the maximum number of concurrent warps per SM is 48. When using 128 threads per block there are 4 warps per block. Because only 8 blocks can be simultaneously placed on a Fermi SM, this kernel is limited to 32 warps per SM. This potentially leads to underutilization of the SM computational resources as the upper bound of 48 warps is not hit. You could also use the CUDA Occupancy tool introduced in
Chapter 3 to reach this same conclusion.

Now, test the effect of thread block size on performance when misaligned accesses are being performed. The results below show similar behavior to the aligned test cases, with 128, 256, and 512 threads per block performing very similarly. This suggests that the same per-SM hardware resource limitations are still playing a role in kernel performance, regardless of access alignment.

```
$ ./readSegmentUnroll 11 1024 22
unroll4    <<< 1024, 1024 >>> offset     11 elapsed 0.000184 sec
$ ./readSegmentUnroll 11 512 22
unroll4    <<< 2048,  512 >>> offset     11 elapsed 0.000162 sec
$ ./readSegmentUnroll 11 256 22
unroll4    <<< 4096,  256 >>> offset     11 elapsed 0.000162 sec
$ ./readSegmentUnroll 11 128 22
unroll4    <<< 8192,  128 >>> offset     11 elapsed 0.000162 sec
```

MAXIMIZING BANDWIDTH UTILIZATION

There are two major factors that influence the performance of device memory operations:

➤ Efficient use of bytes moving between device DRAM and SM on-chip memory: To avoid wasting device memory bandwidth, memory access patterns should be aligned and coalesced.

➤ Number of memory operations concurrently in-flight: Maximizing the number of in-flight memory operations is possible through either 1) unrolling, yielding more independent memory accesses per thread, or 2) modifying the execution configuration of a kernel launch to expose more parallelism to each SM.

WHAT BANDWIDTH CAN A KERNEL ACHIEVE?

When analyzing kernel performance, it is important to focus on *memory latency*, the time to satisfy an individual memory request, and *memory bandwidth*, the rate at which device memory can be accessed by an SM, measured in bytes per time unit.

In the last section, you experimented with two methods for improving kernel performance:

➤ Hiding memory latency by maximizing the number of concurrently executing warps, leading to better saturation of the bus by keeping more memory accesses in-flight.

➤ Maximizing memory bandwidth efficiency by properly aligning and coalescing memory accesses.

However, sometimes a bad access pattern is inherent to the nature of the problem at hand. How good is good enough for such a kernel? What is the best achievable performance in suboptimal situations? In this section, you will use a matrix transpose example to learn how kernel bandwidth can be adjusted using various tuning techniques. You will see that even with an inherently imperfect access pattern, there are still several options in redesigning your kernel to achieve good performance.

Memory Bandwidth

Most kernels are very sensitive to memory bandwidth, that is, they are memory bandwidth-bound. As a result, it is often important to focus on memory bandwidth metrics while tuning kernels. Bandwidth can be dramatically affected by how data in global memory is arranged, and how that data is accessed by a warp. There are two types of bandwidth:

➤ Theoretical bandwidth

➤ Effective bandwidth

Theoretical bandwidth is the absolute maximum bandwidth achievable with the hardware at hand. For a Fermi M2090 with ECC disabled, the peak theoretical device memory bandwidth is 177.6 GB/s. *Effective bandwidth* is the measured bandwidth that a kernel actually achieves, and is calculated using the following equation:

$$\text{effective bandwidth (GB/s)} = \frac{(\text{bytes read} + \text{bytes written}) \times 10^{-9}}{\text{time elapsed}}$$

For example, for a copy of a 2048 × 2048 matrix containing 4-byte integers to and from the device, the effective bandwidth can be computed with the following formula:

$$\text{effective bandwidth (GB/s)} = \frac{2048 \times 048 \times 4 \times 2 \times 10^{-9}}{\text{time elapsed}}$$

You will measure and tune the effective bandwidth of the matrix transpose kernel in the following section.

Matrix Transpose Problem

Matrix transpose is a basic problem in linear algebra. While basic, it is used in many applications. Taking the transpose of a matrix implies exchanging each row with the corresponding column. Figure 4-23 illustrates a simple matrix and its transpose.

matrix

transposed

FIGURE 4-23

The following is a host-based implementation of an out-of-place transpose algorithm using single-precision floating-point values. Suppose the matrix is stored in a 1D array. The transpose can be easily calculated by transforming array index values to reverse row and column coordinates.

```
void transposeHost(float *out, float *in, const int nx, const int ny) {
    for (int iy = 0; iy < ny; ++iy) {
        for (int ix = 0; ix < nx; ++ix) {
            out[ix*ny+iy] = in[iy*nx+ix];
        }
    }
}
```

There are two 1D arrays storing matrices in this function: The input matrix `in` and the transposed matrix `out`. The matrix dimensionality is defined as nx rows by ny columns. The result of the transpose operation when implemented on a 1D array is illustrated in Figure 4-24.

data layout of original matrix

data layout of transposed matrix

FIGURE 4-24

Observing the input and output layouts, you will notice:

➤ **Reads:** accessed by rows in the original matrix; results in coalesced access.

➤ **Writes:** accessed by columns in the transposed matrix; results in strided access.

Strided access is the worst memory access pattern for performance on GPUs. However, it is unavoidable in matrix transpose operations. For the remainder of this section, you will focus on improving bandwidth utilization using two versions of the transpose kernel: one that reads by rows and stores by columns, and one that reads by columns and stores by rows.

Figure 4-25 illustrates the first approach, and Figure 4-26 illustrates the second approach. Can you predict the relative performance of these two implementations? If the L1 cache is disabled for loads these two implementations are theoretically identical. However, if L1 cache is enabled, the second implementation should demonstrate better performance. While the reads performed by column will be uncoalesced (hence bandwidth will be wasted on bytes that were not requested), bringing those extra bytes into the L1 cache means that the next read may be serviced out of cache rather than global memory. Because writes are not cached in L1, the example that writes by column does not benefit from any caching. On Kepler K10, K20, and K20x devices, there should be no difference in performance between these two approaches because the L1 cache is not used for global memory accesses.

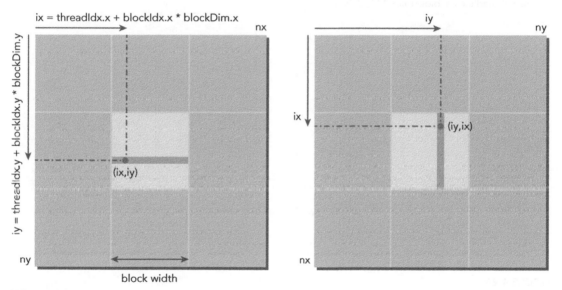

FIGURE 4-25

Setting An Upper and Lower Performance Bound for Transpose Kernels

Before implementing the matrix transpose kernel, you can first create two copy kernels to calculate rough upper and lower bounds for all transpose kernels:

➤   Copy the matrix by loading and storing rows (upper bound). This simulates performing the same amount of memory operations as the transpose but with only coalesced accesses.

➤   Copy the matrix by loading and storing columns (lower bound). This simulates performing the same amount of memory operations as the transpose but with only strided accesses.

The kernel implementations are below:

```
__global__ void copyRow(float *out, float *in, const int nx, const int ny) {
    unsigned int ix = blockDim.x * blockIdx.x + threadIdx.x;
    unsigned int iy = blockDim.y * blockIdx.y + threadIdx.y;
```

```
    if (ix < nx && iy < ny) {
        out[iy*nx + ix] = in[iy*nx + ix];
    }
}

__global__ void copyCol(float *out, float *in, const int nx,
    const int ny) {
    unsigned int ix = blockDim.x * blockIdx.x + threadIdx.x;
    unsigned int iy = blockDim.y * blockIdx.y + threadIdx.y;

    if (ix < nx && iy < ny) {
        out[ix*ny + iy] = in[ix*ny + iy];
    }
}
```

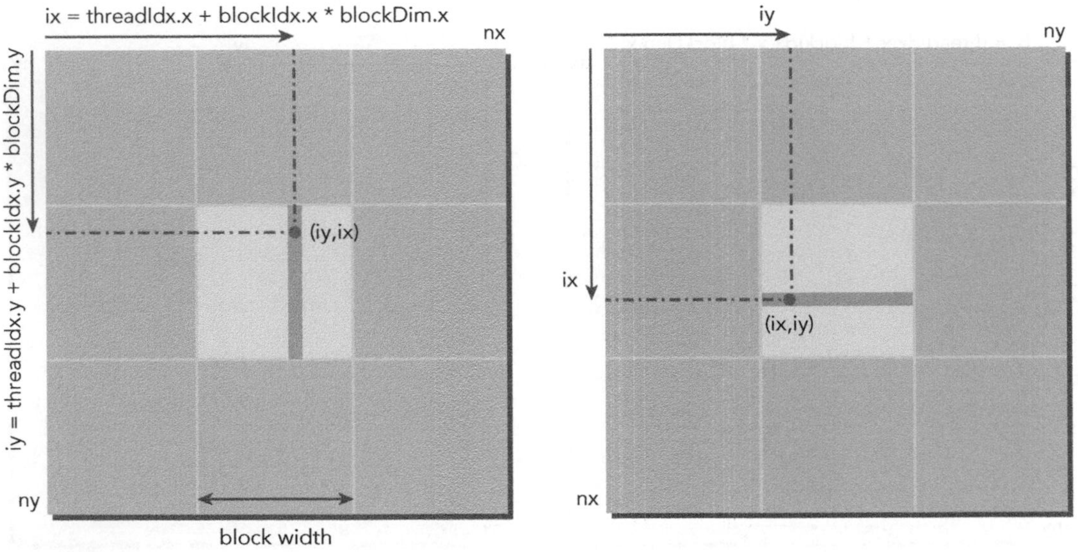

FIGURE 4-26

The main program for calling these upper and lower bound kernels is provided in Listing 4-6. You can also download the full source in transpose.cu from Wrox.com. Note that a kernel identifier iKernel is used to select which kernel to run in this example using a switch statement at the bottom of main.

LISTING 4-6: Matrix transpose (transpose.cu) (main function only listed)

```
int main(int argc, char **argv) {
    // set up device
    int dev = 0;
    cudaDeviceProp deviceProp;
    cudaGetDeviceProperties(&deviceProp, dev);
    printf("%s starting transpose at ", argv[0]);
```

```
printf("device %d: %s ", dev, deviceProp.name);
cudaSetDevice(dev);

// set up array size 2048
int nx = 1<<11;
int ny = 1<<11;

// select a kernel and block size
int iKernel = 0;
int blockx = 16;
int blocky = 16;
if (argc>1) iKernel = atoi(argv[1]);
if (argc>2) blockx  = atoi(argv[2]);
if (argc>3) blocky  = atoi(argv[3]);
if (argc>4) nx   = atoi(argv[4]);
if (argc>5) ny   = atoi(argv[5]);

printf(" with matrix nx %d ny %d with kernel %d\n", nx,ny,iKernel);
size_t nBytes = nx*ny * sizeof(float);

// execution configuration
dim3 block (blockx,blocky);
dim3 grid  ((nx+block.x-1)/block.x,(ny+block.y-1)/block.y);

// allocate host memory
float *h_A = (float *)malloc(nBytes);
float *hostRef = (float *)malloc(nBytes);
float *gpuRef  = (float *)malloc(nBytes);

// initialize host array
initialData(h_A, nx*ny);

// transpose at host side
transposeHost(hostRef,h_A, nx,ny);

// allocate device memory
float *d_A,*d_C;
cudaMalloc((float**)&d_A, nBytes);
cudaMalloc((float**)&d_C, nBytes);

// copy data from host to device
cudaMemcpy(d_A, h_A, nBytes, cudaMemcpyHostToDevice);

// warmup to avoide startup overhead
double iStart = seconds();
warmup <<< grid, block >>> (d_C, d_A, nx, ny);
cudaDeviceSynchronize();
double iElaps = seconds() - iStart;
printf("warmup         elapsed %f sec\n",iElaps);

// kernel pointer and descriptor
void (*kernel)(float *, float *, int, int);
char *kernelName;
```

continues

LISTING 4-6 *(continued)*

```
    // set up kernel
    switch (iKernel) {
        case 0:
            kernel = &copyRow;
            kernelName = "CopyRow         ";
            break;

        case 1:
            kernel = &copyCol;
            kernelName = "CopyCol         ";
            break;
    }

    // run kernel
    iStart = seconds();
    kernel <<< grid, block >>> (d_C, d_A, nx, ny);
    cudaDeviceSynchronize();
    iElaps = seconds() - iStart;

    // calculate effective_bandwidth
    float ibnd = 2*nx*ny*sizeof(float)/1e9/iElaps;
    printf("%s elapsed %f sec <<< grid (%d,%d) block (%d,%d)>>> "
        "effective bandwidth %f GB\n", kernelName, iElaps, grid.x, grid.y,
        block.x, block.y, ibnd);

    // check kernel results
    if (iKernel>1) {
        cudaMemcpy(gpuRef, d_C, nBytes, cudaMemcpyDeviceToHost);
        checkResult(hostRef, gpuRef, nx*ny, 1);
    }

    // free host and device memory
    cudaFree(d_A);
    cudaFree(d_C);
    free(h_A);
    free(hostRef);
    free(gpuRef);

    // reset device
    cudaDeviceReset();
    return EXIT_SUCCESS;
}
```

Compile the code with L1 load caching enabled:

```
$ nvcc -arch=sm_20 -Xptxas -dlcm=ca transpose.cu -o transpose
```

Run the following commands to check the performance of the two copy kernels:

```
$ ./transpose 0
$ ./transpose 1
```

The performance of the two copy kernels on a Fermi M2090 with ECC disabled is given in Table 4-4. These measurements provide an upper bound, which is about 70 percent of theoretical peak bandwidth, and a lower bound, which is about 33 percent of theoretical peak bandwidth.

TABLE 4-4: Effective Bandwidth of Kernels (L1 Cache Enabled)

KERNEL	BANDWIDTH	RATIO TO PEAK BANDWIDTH
Theoretical peak bandwidth	177.6 GB/s	
CopyRow : Load/store using rows	125.67 GB/s	Upper bound: 70.76%
CopyCol : Load/store using columns	58.76 GB/s	Lower bound: 33.09%

Block size: 16 x 16; Matrix size: 2,048 x 2,048; Unit of Effective Bandwidth: GB/sec

Naive Transpose: Reading Rows versus Reading Columns

The naïve row-based transpose kernel is straightforward to implement based on the host implementation. This version of transpose loads by row and stores by column:

```
__global__ void transposeNaiveRow(float *out, float *in, const int nx,
    const int ny) {
  unsigned int ix = blockDim.x * blockIdx.x + threadIdx.x;
  unsigned int iy = blockDim.y * blockIdx.y + threadIdx.y;

  if (ix < nx && iy < ny) {
    out[ix * ny + iy] = in[iy * nx + ix];
  }
}
```

By exchanging the read and write indices, you produce the naïve column-based version of the transpose kernel. This version loads by column and stores by row:

```
__global__ void transposeNaiveCol(float *out, float *in, const int nx,
    const int ny) {
  unsigned int ix = blockDim.x * blockIdx.x + threadIdx.x;
  unsigned int iy = blockDim.y * blockIdx.y + threadIdx.y;

  if (ix < nx && iy < ny) {
    out[iy*nx + ix] = in[ix*ny + iy];
  }
}
```

The following cases are added to the kernel switch statement for these kernels:

```
case 2:
    kernel = &transposeNaiveRow;
    kernelName = "NaiveRow      ";
    break;

case 3:
    kernel = &transposeNaiveCol;
    kernelName = "NaiveCol      ";
    break;
```

Recompile the code with L1 cache enabled and run the following commands to measure the performance of these two transpose kernels. The results are summarized in Table 4-5.

```
$ ./transpose 2
$ ./transpose 3
```

TABLE 4-5: Effective Bandwidth of Kernels (L1 Cache Enabled)

KERNEL	BANDWIDTH	RATIO TO PEAK BANDWIDTH
NaiveRow : Load rows/store columns	64.16 GB/s	36.13%
NaiveCol : Load columns/store rows	81.64 GB/s	45.97%

Block size: 16 x 16; Matrix size: 2,048 x 2,048; Unit of Effective Bandwidth: GB/sec

The NaiveCol approach performs better than the NaiveRow approach. As explained earlier, one likely cause of this improvement in performance is that the strided reads are cached. Even if the bytes read into L1 cache by a certain access are not all used by that access, they remain in cache and may cause a cache hit for a future access. To verify this is the case, try recompiling with L1 cache disabled (using -Xptxas -dlcm=cg).

Run the following commands to obtain the performance of all kernels without L1 load caching enabled. The results in Table 4-6 clearly show that disabling load caching has a dramatic impact on strided read access patterns.

```
$ ./transpose 0
$ ./transpose 1
$ ./transpose 2
$ ./transpose 3
```

TABLE 4-6: Effective Bandwidth of Kernels (L1 Cache Disabled)

KERNEL	BANDWIDTH	NOTES
CopyRow : Load/store using rows	128.07 GB/s	Upper bound
CopyCol : Load/store using columns	40.42 GB/s	Lower bound
NaiveRow : Load rows/store columns	63.79 GB/s	Strided write/coalesced read
NaiveCol : Load columns/store rows	47.13 GB/s	Strided read/coalesced write

Block size: 16 x 16; Matrix size: 2,048 x 2,048; Unit of Effective Bandwidth: GB/sec L1 disabled

You can also directly examine cached loads using nvprof with the command below. The results are summarized in Table 4-7.

```
$ nvprof --devices 0 --metrics gld_throughput,gst_throughput ./transpose \
    $KERNEL 16 16 2048 2048
```

TABLE 4-7: Load/Store Throughput of Kernels (L1 Cache Enabled)

KERNEL	LOAD THROUGHPUT	STORE THROUGHPUT
CopyRow : Load/store using rows	131.46 GB/s	65.32 GB/s
CopyCol : Load/store using columns	475.67 GB/s	118.52 GB/s
NaiveRow : Load rows/store columns	129.05 GB/s	64.31 GB/s
NaiveCol : Load columns/store rows	642.33 GB/s	40.02 GB/s

Block size: 16 x 16; Matrix size: 2,048 x 2,048

The results show that the highest load throughput is obtained with cached, strided reads. In the case of cached reads, each memory request is serviced with a 128-byte cache line. Reading data by columns causes each memory request in a warp to replay 32 times (because the stride is 2048 data elements), resulting in good latency hiding from many in-flight global memory reads and then excellent L1 cache hit ratios once bytes are pre-fetched into L1 cache.

Next, you can examine the load/store efficiency using the following metrics.

```
--metrics gld_efficiency,gst_efficiency
```

Results across all kernels are summarized in Table 4-8.

TABLE 4-8: Load/Store Efficiency of Kernels (L1 Cache Enabled)

KERNEL	LOAD EFFICIENCY	STORE EFFICIENCY
CopyRow : Load/store using rows	49.81%	100.00%
CopyCol : Load/store using columns	6.23%	25.00%
NaiveRow : Load rows/store columns	50.00%	25.00%
NaiveCol : Load columns/store rows	6.21%	100.00%

Block size: 16 x 16; Matrix size: 2,048 x 2,048

The results show that for the NaiveCol implementation, store requests are never replayed due to coalesced writes, but load requests are replayed many times due to strided reads. This demonstrates that even with poor load efficiency, caching of loads in L1 cache can limit the negative performance impact of strided loads.

Unrolling Transpose: Reading Rows versus Reading Columns

Next, you will use unrolling techniques to improve the transpose memory bandwidth utilization. The goal of unrolling in this example is to assign more independent work to each thread in order to maximize in-flight memory requests.

The following is a row-based implementation with an unrolling factor of four. Two new array indices are introduced: one for row access, and the other for column access.

```
__global__ void transposeUnroll4Row(float *out, float *in, const int nx,
    const int ny) {
  unsigned int ix = blockDim.x * blockIdx.x*4 + threadIdx.x;
  unsigned int iy = blockDim.y * blockIdx.y + threadIdx.y;

  unsigned int ti = iy*nx + ix;    // access in rows
  unsigned int to = ix*ny + iy;    // access in columns

  if (ix+3*blockDim.x < nx && iy < ny) {
    out[to]                = in[ti];
    out[to + ny*blockDim.x]   = in[ti+blockDim.x];
    out[to + ny*2*blockDim.x] = in[ti+2*blockDim.x];
    out[to + ny*3*blockDim.x] = in[ti+3*blockDim.x];
  }
}
```

Exchanging the read and write indices produce a column-based implementation with similar unrolling:

```
__global__ void transposeUnroll4Col(float *out, float *in, const int nx,
    const int ny) {
  unsigned int ix = blockDim.x * blockIdx.x*4 + threadIdx.x;
  unsigned int iy = blockDim.y * blockIdx.y + threadIdx.y;

  unsigned int ti = iy*nx + ix;    // access in rows
  unsigned int to = ix*ny + iy;    // access in columns

  if (ix+3*blockDim.x < nx && iy < ny) {
    out[ti]              = in[to];
    out[ti +   blockDim.x] = in[to+   blockDim.x*ny];
    out[ti + 2*blockDim.x] = in[to+ 2*blockDim.x*ny];
    out[ti + 3*blockDim.x] = in[to+ 3*blockDim.x*ny];
  }
}
```

Add the following code segment to the kernel switch statement. Note, because unrolling was added, the grid size for these kernels must be adjusted accordingly.

```
case 4:
  kernel = & transposeUnroll4Row;
  kernelName = " Unroll4Row    ";
  grid.x = (nx+block.x*4-1)/(block.x*4);
  break;

case 5:
  kernel = & transposeUnroll4Col;
  kernelName = " Unroll4Col    ";
  grid.x = (nx+block.x*4-1)/(block.x*4);
  break;
```

Recompile the code with L1 cache enabled, and run the following commands to compare performance between the two new transpose kernels. The results measured on a Fermi M2090 are summarized in Table 4-9.

```
$ ./transpose 4
$ ./transpose 5
```

TABLE 4-9: Effective Bandwidth of Kernels (L1 Cache Enabled)

KERNEL	BANDWIDTH	RATIO TO PEAK BANDWIDTH
Unroll4Row : Load rows/store columns	44.15 GB/s	24.85%
Unroll4Col : Load columns/store rows	90.20 GB/s	50.76%

Block size: 16 x 16; Matrix size: 2,048 x 2,048; Unit of Effective Bandwidth: GB/sec

Again, with L1 cache enabled loading columns and storing rows yields better effective bandwidth and overall execution time.

Diagonal Transpose: Reading Rows versus Reading Columns

When you launch a grid of thread blocks, the thread blocks are distributed among SMs. While programming model abstractions may present that grid to you in a 1D or 2D layout, from the hardware perspective all blocks are arranged one-dimensionally. Each block has its own unique identifier, bid, which is calculated using a row-major ordering of thread blocks in a grid:

```
int bid = blockIdx.y * gridDim.x + blockIdx.x;
```

Figure 4-27 illustrates a simple example of a 4 x 4 grid of thread blocks and the corresponding block ID of each thread block.

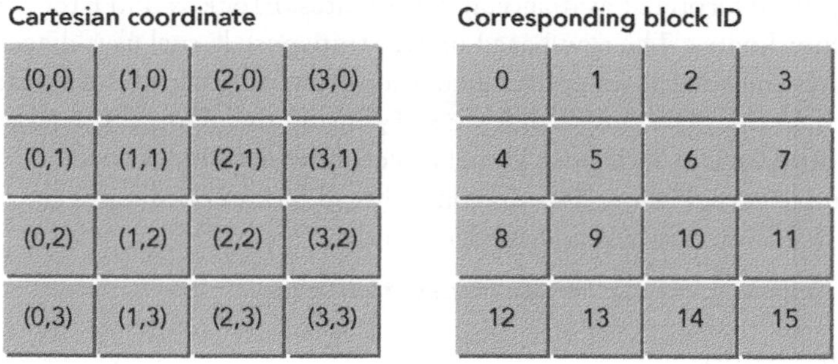

Cartesian coordinate

(0,0)	(1,0)	(2,0)	(3,0)
(0,1)	(1,1)	(2,1)	(3,1)
(0,2)	(1,2)	(2,2)	(3,2)
(0,3)	(1,3)	(2,3)	(3,3)

Corresponding block ID

0	1	2	3
4	5	6	7
8	9	10	11
12	13	14	15

FIGURE 4-27

When a kernel is launched, the order in which thread blocks are assigned to SMs is determined by the block ID. Once all SMs are at full occupancy any remaining thread blocks are held until currently executing ones complete. Once a thread block completes, another thread block is assigned to that SM. Because the speed and order in which thread blocks complete is not deterministic, active thread blocks that are initially contiguous by bid become less contiguous over time as execution of the kernel progresses.

Although you do not have direct control over the order in which thread blocks are scheduled, you can be flexible in how you interpret the block coordinates blockIdx.x and blockIdx.y. Figure 4-27 illustrated block coordinates corresponding to the Cartesian coordinate system. Figure 4-28 illustrates a different way of interpreting blockIdx.x and blockIdx.y: using a diagonal block coordinate system.

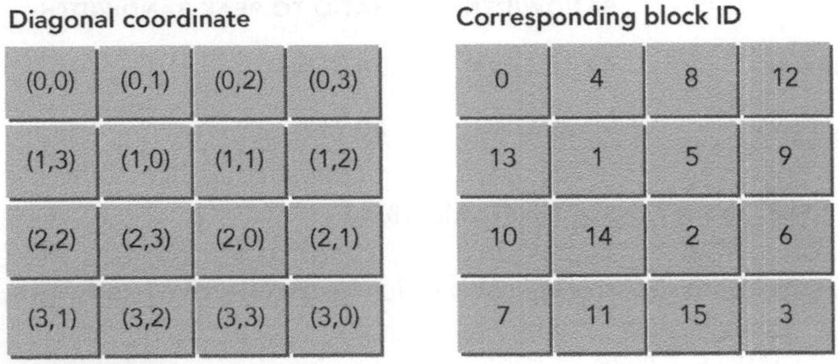

Diagonal coordinate

(0,0)	(0,1)	(0,2)	(0,3)
(1,3)	(1,0)	(1,1)	(1,2)
(2,2)	(2,3)	(2,0)	(2,1)
(3,1)	(3,2)	(3,3)	(3,0)

Corresponding block ID

0	4	8	12
13	1	5	9
10	14	2	6
7	11	15	3

FIGURE 4-28

The diagonal coordinate system is used to determine 1D thread block ID. However, for data access, you still need to use the Cartesian coordinate system. Therefore, when interpreting block IDs as diagonal coordinates, you need to map from diagonal coordinates to Cartesian coordinates so that you can access the correct data block. For a square matrix, this mapping can be calculated with the following equation:

```
block_x = (blockIdx.x + blockIdx.y) % gridDim.x;
block_y = blockIdx.x;
```

Here, blockIdx.x and blockIdx.y are interpreted as diagonal coordinates. block_x and block_y are their corresponding Cartesian coordinates. The row-based matrix transpose kernel uses diagonal coordinates as follows. You simply include the mapping calculation from diagonal to Cartesian at the beginning of the kernel, and then calculate thread index (ix, iy) using the mapped Cartesian coordinates (block_x, block_y). This diagonal transpose kernel affects how data blocks are assigned to thread blocks. The example kernel below uses diagonal thread block coordinates to implement the matrix transpose with coalesced reads and strided writes:

```
__global__ void transposeDiagonalRow(float *out, float *in, const
    int nx, const int ny) {
  unsigned int blk_y = blockIdx.x;
  unsigned int blk_x = (blockIdx.x+blockIdx.y)%gridDim.x;

  unsigned int ix = blockDim.x * blk_x + threadIdx.x;
  unsigned int iy = blockDim.y * blk_y + threadIdx.y;

  if (ix < nx && iy < ny) {
    out[ix*ny + iy] = in[iy*nx + ix];
  }
}
```

The column-based version that uses diagonal coordinates is below:

```
__global__ void transposeDiagonalCol(float *out, float *in, const
    int nx, const int ny) {
unsigned int blk_y = blockIdx.x;
unsigned int blk_x = (blockIdx.x+blockIdx.y)%gridDim.x;

unsigned int ix = blockDim.x * blk_x + threadIdx.x;
unsigned int iy = blockDim.y * blk_y + threadIdx.y;

if (ix < nx && iy < ny) {
    out[iy*nx + ix] = in[ix*ny + iy];
}
}
```

Add the following code into the kernel `switch` statement to call these kernels:

```
case 6:
    kernel = &transposeDiagonalRow;
    kernelName = "DiagonalRow    ";
    break;

case 7:
    kernel = &transposeDiagonalCol;
    kernelName = "DiagonalCol    ";
    break;
```

Recompile the code with L1 cache enabled and run the following commands to compare performance between the two new transpose kernels. The results are summarized in Table 4-10.

```
$ ./transpose 6
$ ./transpose 7
```

TABLE 4-10: Effective Bandwidth of Kernels (L1 Cache Enabled)

KERNEL	BANDWIDTH	RATIO TO PEAK BANDWIDTH
DiagonalRow : Load rows/store columns	73.42 GB/s	41.32%
DiagonalCol : Load columns/store rows	75.92 GB/s	42.72%

Block size: 16 x 16; Matrix size: 2,048 x 2,048; Unit of Effective Bandwidth: GB/sec

By altering the thread block execution order using diagonal coordinates, the performance achieved
by the row-based kernel improves considerably. However, the column-based kernel still performs
better with Cartesian block coordinates than diagonal block coordinates. The diagonal kernel
implementation could be further improved by unrolling blocks, but that implementation is not as
straightforward as it was with the Cartesian-based kernel.

The reason for this performance improvement is related to the parallel access of DRAM. Requests
to global memory are serviced by DRAM partitions. Successive 256-byte regions of device memory
are assigned to successive partitions. When using Cartesian coordinates to map thread blocks to
data blocks, global memory accesses may not be evenly distributed among DRAM partitions, and

a phenomenon called *partition camping* may occur. In partition camping, memory requests are queued at some partitions while other partitions remain unused. Because the diagonal coordinate mapping causes non-linear mappings from thread blocks to the data blocks they process, strided accesses are unlikely to fall into a single partition, and performance improves as a result.

For best performance, concurrent access to global memory by all active warps should be divided evenly among partitions. Figure 4-29 illustrates a simplified model to help you visualize partition camping when Cartesian coordinates are used to interpret the block IDs. In this figure, suppose you only have two partitions through which to access global memory, each with a partition width of 256 bytes, and that your kernel is launched with a block size of 32 x 32 threads. If each data block is 128 bytes wide, you will load data for thread blocks 0, 1, 2, and 3 using two partitions. However, you will store data for thread blocks 0, 1, 2, and 3 using only one partition and thus causing partition camping.

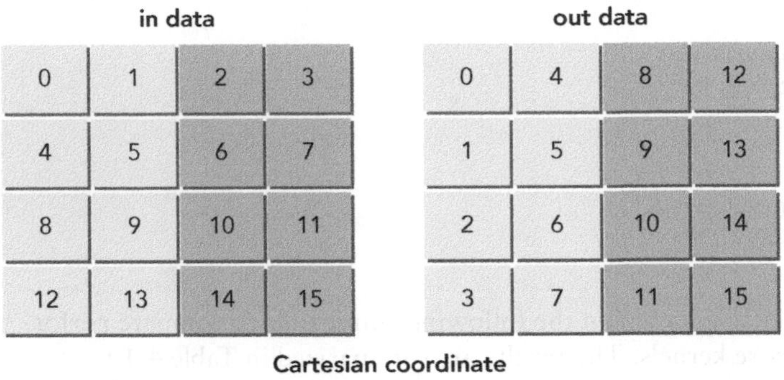

in data					out data			
0	1	2	3		0	4	8	12
4	5	6	7		1	5	9	13
8	9	10	11		2	6	10	14
12	13	14	15		3	7	11	15

Cartesian coordinate

FIGURE 4-29

Figure 4-30 borrows from the simplified model illustrated in Figure 4-29, but this time uses diagonal coordinates to interpret block IDs. In this case, you will load and store data for thread blocks 0, 1, 2, and 3 using two partitions. Both load and store requests are evenly distributed between the two partitions. This explains why the diagonal kernel achieves better performance.

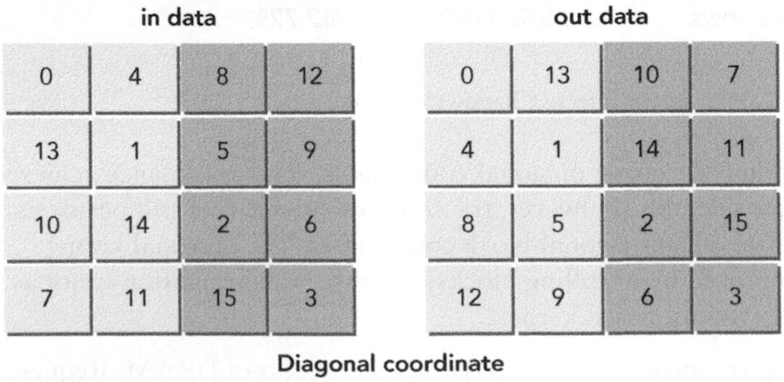

in data					out data			
0	4	8	12		0	13	10	7
13	1	5	9		4	1	14	11
10	14	2	6		8	5	2	15
7	11	15	3		12	9	6	3

Diagonal coordinate

FIGURE 4-30

Expose More Parallelism with Thin Blocks

The simplest way to expose more parallelism is to adjust block size. Previous sections have already demonstrated the effectiveness of this simple technique for improving performance. Try experimenting further with the block size used for the `NaiveCol` column-based kernel (accessed via case 3 in the kernel `switch` statement). Sample results of exhaustive block size testing are summarized in Table 4-11.

TABLE 4-11: Effective Bandwidth of Kernels (L1 Cache Disabled)

KERNEL	BLOCK SIZE	BANDWIDTH
NaiveCol	(32, 32)	38.13 GB/s
NaiveCol	(32, 16)	51.46 GB/s
NaiveCol	(32, 8)	54.82 GB/s
NaiveCol	(16, 32)	73.42 GB/s
NaiveCol	(16, 16)	80.27 GB/s
NaiveCol	(16, 8)	70.34 GB/s
NaiveCol	(8, 32)	102.76 GB/s
NaiveCol	(8, 16)	82.64 GB/s
NaiveCol	(8, 8)	59.59 GB/s

Matrix size: 2,048 x 2,048; Unit of Effective Bandwidth: GB/sec: Kernel: the naive implementation that loads columns and stores rows

The optimal block size by far was (8, 32), even though it exposes the same amount of parallelism as (16, 16). This performance improvement is caused by the "thin" block dimensions of (8, 32), as shown in Figure 4-31.

A "thin" block improves the effectiveness of store operations (shown in Table 4-12) by increasing the number of consecutive elements stored by a thread block as a result of a larger value in the innermost dimension of the thread block. You can confirm this by using `nvprof` to measure the load and store throughput metrics.

```
$ nvprof --devices 0 --metrics gld_throughput,gst_throughput\
    ./transpose 3 16
$ nvprof --devices 0 --metrics gld_throughput,gst_throughput\
    ./transpose 3 8 32
```

TABLE 4-12: Effective Bandwidth of Kernels (L1 Cache Enabled)

EXECUTION CONFIGURATION	LOAD THROUGHPUT	STORE THROUGHPUT
(16, 16)	660.89 GB/s	41.11 GB/s
(8, 32)	406.43 GB/s	50.80 GB/s

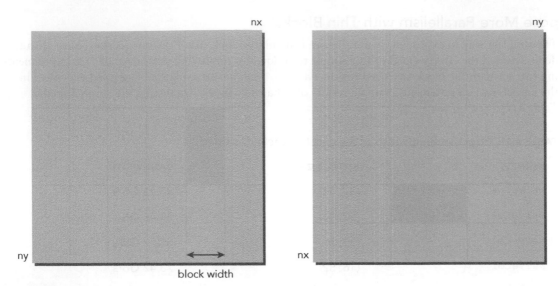

FIGURE 4-31

Next, try the following commands using a block size of (8, 32) to compare bandwidth between the different kernel implementations.

```
$ ./transpose 0 8 32
$ ./transpose 1 8 32
$ ./transpose 2 8 32
$ ./transpose 3 8 32
$ ./transpose 4 8 32
```

Sample results are summarized in Table 4-13. So far, the kernel `Unroll4Col` demonstrates the best performance and even outperforms the upper-bound copy kernel. Achieving an effective bandwidth that is 60 to 80 percent of peak bandwidth is quite an accomplishment.

TABLE 4-13: Effective Bandwidth of Kernels (L1 Cache Enabled)

KERNEL	BANDWIDTH	RATIO TO PEAK BANDWIDTH
Theoretical peak bandwidth	177.6	
`CopyRow` : Load/store using rows	102.30	57.57%
`NaiveRow` : Load rows/store columns	95.33	53.65%
`NaiveCol` : Load columns/store rows	101.99	57.39%
`Unroll4Row` : Load rows/store columns	82.04	46.17%
`Unroll4Col` : Load columns/store rows	113.36	63.83%

Block size: 8 x 32; Matrix size: 2,048 x 2,048; Unit of Effective Bandwidth: GB/sec

MATRIX ADDITION WITH UNIFIED MEMORY

You learned how to add two matrices on the GPU in Chapter 2. To simplify managing separate host and device memory spaces and to help make this CUDA program more readable and easier to maintain, you could apply the following revisions to the `main` function of matrix addition using Unified Memory:

➤ Replace the host and device memory allocations with managed memory allocations to eliminate duplicate pointers.

➤ Remove all explicit memory copies.

You can start by declaring and allocating three managed arrays: A and B are used for input and gpuRef is used for output:

```
float *A, *B, *gpuRef;
cudaMallocManaged((void **)&A, nBytes);
cudaMallocManaged((void **)&B, nBytes);
cudaMallocManaged((void **)&gpuRef,  nBytes);
```

Then, you should initialize the two input matrices on the host using the pointers to managed memory:

```
initialData(A, nxy);
initialData(B, nxy);
```

Finally, invoke the matrix addition kernel with the pointers to managed memory:

```
sumMatrixGPU<<<grid, block>>>(A, B, gpuRef, nx, ny);
cudaDeviceSynchronize();
```

Because the kernel launch is asynchronous with respect to the host and a blocking call to cudaMemcpy is no longer necessary with managed memory, you need to explicitly synchronize on the host side before directly accessing the output of the kernel. Compared to the un-managed memory version of matrix addition program from the earlier section in this chapter, the code here is greatly simplified thanks to Unified Memory.

You can download the full code example in `sumMatrixGPUManaged.cu` from `Wrox.com`. You can also find its counterpart `sumMatrixGPUManual.cu`, which uses the exact same matrix addition kernel but does not use managed memory. Instead it performs explicit memory copies to and from the device. Both versions run a warm-up kernel beforehand to avoid kernel startup overhead and obtain more accurate timing results. Using CUDA 6.0 and a Kepler or later GPU, compile both versions, naming one `managed` and the other `manual`.

```
$ nvcc -arch=sm_30 sumMatrixGPUManaged.cu -o managed
$ nvcc -arch=sm_30 sumMatrixGPUManual.cu -o manual
```

If you are testing on a system with more than one GPU device, an extra step is required for the managed app. Because managed memory allocations are visible to all devices in a system, you will want to constrain which device is visible to your application so that managed memory is allocated on just one device. To do this, set the CUDA_VISIBLE_DEVICES environment variable to expose a single GPU to CUDA applications:

```
$ export CUDA_VISIBLE_DEVICES=0
```

First, run the managed program.

```
$ ./managed 14
```

The results measured on a Kepler K40 are as follows:

```
$ ./managed
Starting using Device 0: Tesla K40m
Matrix size: nx 16384 ny 16384
initialization:          5.930170 sec
sumMatrix on host:       0.504631 sec
sumMatrix on gpu :       0.025203 sec <<<(512,512), (32,32)>>>
```

Next, run the manual program that does not use managed memory:

```
$ ./manual 14
```

The result measured on a Kepler K40 is as follows:

```
$ ./manual
Starting using Device 0: Tesla K40m
Matrix size: nx 16384 ny 16384
initialization:          1.835069 sec
sumMatrix on host:       0.474370 sec
sumMatrix on gpu :       0.020226 sec <<<(512,512), (32,32)>>>
```

These results show that kernel performance with managed memory is nearly as fast as explicitly copying data between host and device, and requires significantly less programming effort.

Trace both programs with nvprof as follows:

```
$ nvprof --profile-api-trace runtime ./managed
$ nvprof --profile-api-trace runtime ./manual
```

The results on a Kepler K40 are summarized in Table 4-14. The largest difference in performance is in CPU data initialization time — it takes much longer using managed memory. While the matrix is initially allocated on the GPU, it is first referenced on the CPU as it is populated with initial values. This requires that the underlying system transfer the matrix contents from the device to the host before initialization, a transfer that is not performed in the manual version.

When the host matrix sum function is executed, the full matrix is already resident on the CPU and so execution time is comparable to non-managed memory. Next, the warm-up kernel causes the full matrix to be migrated back to the device so that when the actual matrix addition kernel is launched, the data is already on the GPU. If the warm-up kernel was not executed, the kernel using managed memory would run significantly slower.

TABLE 4-14: Performance Comparison on Programs With Versus Without Managed Memory

KERNEL OR RUNTIME FUNCTIONS	WITH MANAGED MEMORY	WITHOUT MANAGED MEMORY
Matrix Kernel	1.6114	1.6024
CUDA Kernel Launch	49.259	70.717
CUDA memcpy HtoD		37.987
CUDA memcpy DtoH		20.252

KERNEL OR RUNTIME FUNCTIONS	WITH MANAGED MEMORY	WITHOUT MANAGED MEMORY
CPU data initialization	5930.17	1835.07
CPU matrix Addition	504.63	474.37
CPU timer on Matrix Kernel	25.203	20.226

Matrix Size: 4096 x 4096; Unit: milliseconds

Inspecting Unified Memory performance is fully supported by both nvvp and nvprof. Both profilers allow you to measure unified memory traffic for each GPU in your system. This feature is turned off by default. Passing the following flag to nvprof enables unified memory-related metrics.

```
$ nvprof --unified-memory-profiling per-process-device  ./managed
```

--print-gpu-trace will also provide information on Unified Memory behavior. The following report is extracted from the results on a Kepler K40.

```
==28893== Unified Memory profiling result:
Device "Tesla K40m (0)"
                           Count       Avg      Min       Max
    Host To Device (bytes)     8  1.3422e+08      0  2.68e+08
    Device To Host (bytes)   507  5490570.86      0  4.03e+08
           CPU Page faults   507    48909.01      0     98304
```

Note that CPU page faults are reported alongside device-to-host data transfer. A page fault occurs when a host application references an address in CPU virtual memory that is not in physical memory. Unified Memory uses CPU page faults to trigger device-to-host data transfers when the CPU requires access to managed memory that is currently resident on the GPU. The number of page faults measured is closely related to data size. Try running the program again with a small matrix of 256 × 256 elements:

```
$ nvprof --unified-memory-profiling per-process-device ./managed 8
```

The results are as follows. Note that the number of page faults is reduced greatly.

```
==29464== Unified Memory profiling result:
Device "Tesla K40m (0)"
                           Count       Avg      Min       Max
    Host To Device (bytes)     2   524288.00      0   1048576
    Device To Host (bytes)     9   505628.44      0   1572864
           CPU Page faults     9      123.44      0       384
```

You can also check unified memory behavior visually using nvvp. Launch nvvp on the managed memory implementation as follows:

```
$ nvvp ./managed
```

In the Executable Properties tab labeled "Create New Session," enter 14 in the "Arguments" field to test a large matrix, and select "Next." Then select the "Enable unified memory profiling" check box, as shown in Figure 4-32.

Figure 4-33 illustrates the timeline for the managed program. You can see from the figure that host page faults are closely correlated with DtoH Data Migration. Unified Memory optimizes performance by migrating data toward the GPU. The underlying system maintains coherency between host and device, and tries to place data where it can be most efficiently accessed.

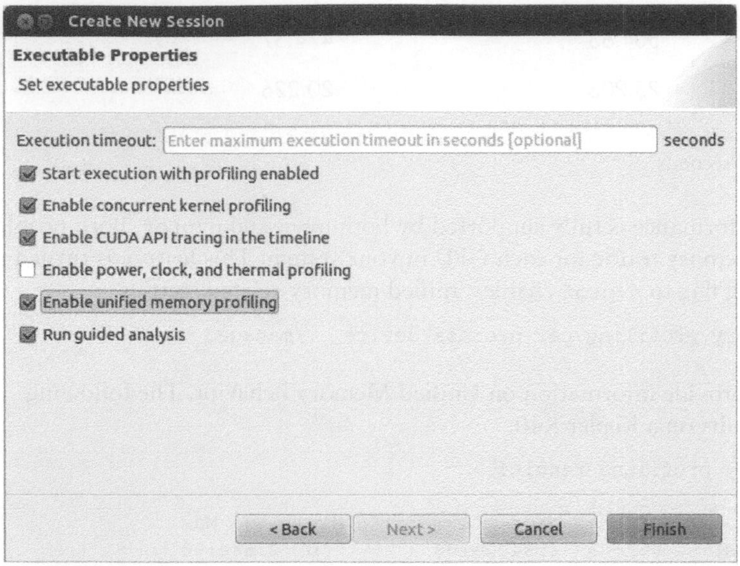

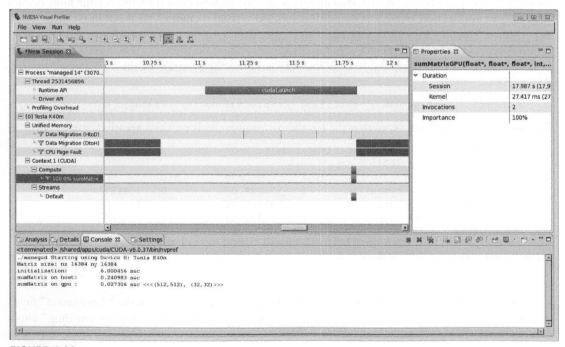

FIGURE 4-32

FIGURE 4-33

Figure 4-34 illustrates the timeline for the program without using unified memory. Comparing the two figures, you can see that explicitly managing data movement only uses one device-to-host transfer whereas using Unified Memory causes two.

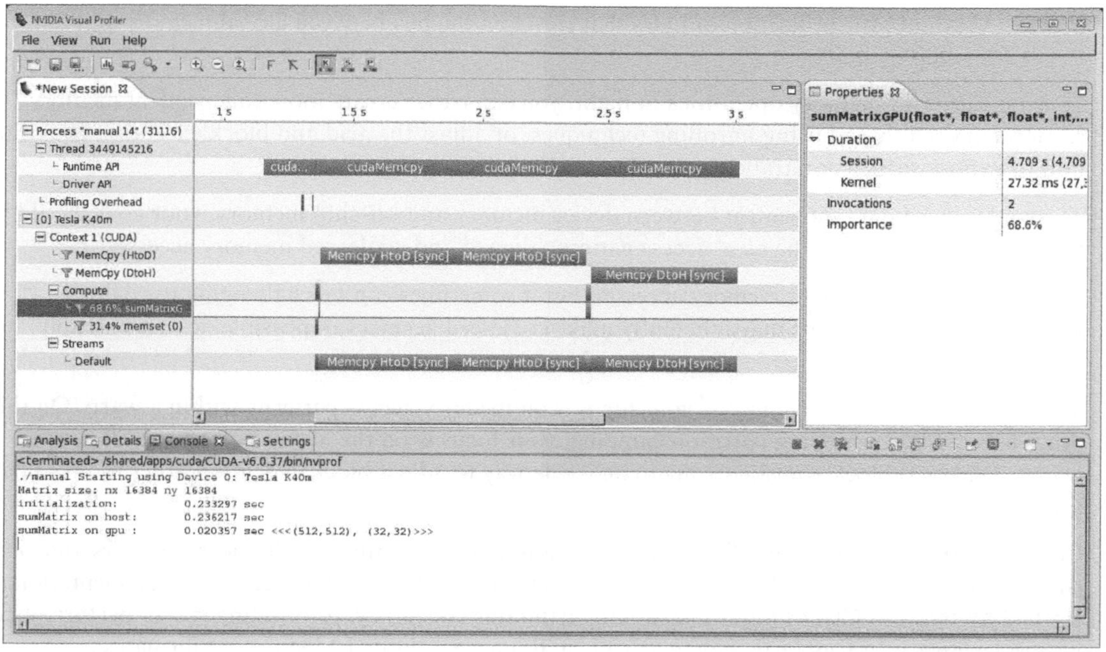

FIGURE 4-34

The version of Unified Memory released with CUDA 6.0 is designed to enhance programmer productivity. The underlying system emphasizes coherence and correctness over performance. While the results shown here demonstrate that manually optimizing data movement in your CUDA application has performance benefits over Unified Memory, you can be certain that NVIDIA plans to introduce future hardware and software releases that bolster Uniform Memory performance and programmability.

SUMMARY

One of the distinguishing features of the CUDA programming model is that it directly exposes the programmer to the GPU memory hierarchy. Providing you with more control over data movement and placement enables more aggressive optimizations and higher peak performance.

Global memory is the largest, highest-latency, and most commonly used memory. Requests to global memory can be serviced by either 32-byte or 128-byte transactions. Keeping these characteristics and granularities in mind can be important for tuning global memory usage in your applications.

Through examples in this chapter, you learned the following two guidelines for improving bandwidth utilization:

➤ Maximize the number of concurrent memory accesses in-flight.

➤ Maximize the utilization of bytes that travel on the bus between global memory and SM on-chip memory.

To keep sufficient memory operations in flight, you can either create more independent memory requests in each thread using unrolling techniques, or adjust the grid and block execution configuration to expose sufficient parallelism to SMs.

To avoid unused data movement between device memory and on-chip memory, your goal should be to strive for and achieve the ideal access pattern: aligned and coalesced memory accesses.

It is relatively easy to align memory accesses, but it sometimes can be challenging to coalesce accesses. Some algorithms may inherently make coalesced accesses impossible or unreasonably difficult.

When improving coalesced access, your focus is on memory access patterns within a warp. On the other hand, when removing partition camping, your focus is on the access patterns of all active warps. Diagonal block coordinate mapping is one way to adjust block execution order to avoid partition camping.

Unified Memory greatly simplifies CUDA programming by eliminating duplicate pointers and eliminating the need to explicitly transfer data between the host and device. The implementation of Unified Memory in CUDA 6.0 transparently maintains coherency, prioritizing it over performance. Future hardware and software enhancements will improve Unified Memory performance.

The next chapter will cover details of two topics touched on briefly in this chapter: constant memory and shared memory.

CHAPTER 4 EXERCISES

1. Refer to the file `globalVariable.cu`. Declare statically a global float array with a size of five elements. Initialize the global array with the same value of 3.14. Modify the kernel to let each thread change the value of the array element with the same index as the thread index. Let the value be multiplied with the thread index. Invoke the kernel with five threads.

2. Refer to the file `globalVariable.cu`. Replace the following symbol copy functions:

   ```
   cudaMemcpyToSymbol()
   cudaMemcpyFromSymbol()
   ```

   with the data transfer function

   ```
   cudaMemcpy()
   ```

   You will need to acquire the address of the global variable using

   ```
   cudaGetSymbolAddress()
   ```

3. Compare performance of the pinned and pageable memory copies in `memTransfer` and `pinMemTransfer` using `nvprof` and different sizes: 2M, 4M, 8M, 16M, 32M, 64M, 128M.

4. Using the same examples, compare the performance of pinned and pageable memory allocation and deallocations using CPU timers and different sizes: 2M, 4M, 8M, 16M, 32M, 64M, 128M.

5. Modify `sumArrayZerocopy.cu` to access A, B, and C at an offset. Compare performance with and without L1 cache enabled. If your GPU does not support configuring the L1 cache, reason about the expected results.

6. Modify `sumArrayZerocopyUVA.cu` to access A, B, and C at an offset. Compare performance with and without the L1 cache enabled. If your GPU does not support configuring the L1 cache, explain the results you would expect to see with and without L1 cache enabled.

7. Compile the file `readSegment.cu` and run the following command on offsets 0, 4, 8, 16, 32, 64, 96, 128, 160, 192, 224, and 256:

    ```
    ./iread $OFFSET
    ```

    Confirm what byte the aligned address must be a multiple of.

8. Refer to the file `Makefile` for `readSegment.cu`. Disable L1 cache in the `Makefile` and generate the executable `iread_l2`. Test it with the following command on offset 0, 11, and 128:

    ```
    ./iread_l2 $OFFSET
    ```

    Compare the result with L1 cache enabled to see what is different.

9. Run the following command for offsets 0, 11, and 128:

    ```
    nvprof --devices 0 \
            --metrics gld_efficiency \
            --metrics gld_throughput \
            ./iread_l2 $OFFSET;
    ```

    Compare the results with L1 enabled and explain the difference.

10. Refer to the file `simpleMathAoS.cu`. Define `innerStruct` as struct `__align__(8) innerStruct`, aligning it to eight bytes. Use `nvprof` to compare performance, and explain any difference using `nvprof` metrics.

11. Based on the revision in Exercise 10, modify the kernel to read/write variable x only. Compare the result with the file `simpleMathSoA.cu`. Use proper `nvprof` metrics to explain the difference.

12. Refer to the file `writeSegment.cu`. Make a new kernel, `readWriteOffset`, that offsets reads and writes and run with offsets 32, 33, 64, 65, 128, and 129. Compare performance with `readOffset` and `writeOffset`, and explain any difference.

13. Apply an unrolling factor of four to `readWriteOffset` and compare performance with the original, using proper metrics with `nvprof` to explain the difference.

14. Adjust the execution configuration for kernels `readWriteOffset` and `readWriteOffsetUnroll4` and find the best one, using proper metrics to explain why one is better.

15. Refer to the kernel `tranposeUnroll4Row`. Implement a new kernel, `tranposeRow`, to let each thread handle all elements in a row. Compare the performance with existing kernels and use proper metrics to explain the difference.

16. Refer to the kernel `tranposeUnroll4Row`. Implement a new kernel, `tranposeUnroll8Row`, to let each thread handle eight elements. Compare the performance with existing kernels and use proper metrics to explain the difference.

17. Refer to the kernels `transposeDiagonalCol` and `tranposeUnroll4Row`. Implement a new kernel, `transposeDiagonalColUnroll4`, to let each thread handle four elements. Compare the performance with existing kernels and use proper metrics to explain the difference.

18. Refer to the program `sumArrayZerocpy.cu` and implement array addition using unified memory. Compare performance with `sumArrays` and `sumArraysZeroCopy` using `nvprof`.

19. Refer to the program `sumMatrixGPUManaged.cu`. If the warm-up kernel were removed, how would performance change? If you can, measure performance with `nvprof` and `nvvp`.

20. Refer to the program `sumMatrixGPUManaged.cu`. Would removing the `memset`s below affect performance? If you can, check performance with `nvprof` or `nvvp`.

    ```
    memset(hostRef, 0, nBytes);
    memset(gpuRef, 0, nBytes);
    ```

5

Shared Memory and Constant Memory

WHAT'S IN THIS CHAPTER?

- ➤ Learning how data is arranged in shared memory

- ➤ Mastering index conversion from 2D shared memory to linear global memory

- ➤ Resolving bank conflicts for different access modes

- ➤ Caching data in shared memory to reduce global memory accesses

- ➤ Avoiding non-coalesced global memory access using shared memory

- ➤ Understanding the difference between the constant cache and the read-only cache

- ➤ Programming with the warp shuffle instruction

> **CODE DOWNLOAD** *The wrox.com code downloads for this chapter are found at www.wrox.com/go/procudac on the Download Code tab. The code is in the Chapter 5 download and individually named according to the names throughout the chapter.*

In the preceding chapter, you examined various global memory access patterns. You learned how to realize good performance and avoid wasting transactions by arranging global memory access patterns so they are and coalesced. Misaligned memory accesses are not as problematic since modern GPU hardware includes an L1 cache, but non-coalesced memory accesses that stride through global memory still cause suboptimal bandwidth utilization. Depending on the nature of your algorithms and the corresponding access patterns, non-coalesced accesses may be unavoidable. However, it is possible to improve global memory coalesced access using shared memory in many cases. Shared memory is a key enabler for many high-performance computing applications.

In this chapter, you will learn how to program with shared memory, how data is stored in shared memory, and how data elements are mapped to memory banks using different access modes. You will master the skill of using shared memory to improve kernel performance.

INTRODUCING CUDA SHARED MEMORY

You have already learned that GPUs are equipped with two types of memory:

➤   On-board memory

➤   On-chip memory

Global memory is large, on-board memory and is characterized by relatively high latencies. Shared memory is smaller, low-latency on-chip memory that offers much higher bandwidth than global memory. You can think of it as a program-managed cache. Shared memory is generally useful as:

➤   An intra-block thread communication channel

➤   A program-managed cache for global memory data

➤   Scratch pad memory for transforming data to improve global memory access patterns

In this chapter, you will gain experience programming with shared memory through two examples: a reduction kernel, and a matrix transpose kernel.

Shared Memory

Shared memory (SMEM) is one of the key components of the GPU. Physically, each SM contains a small low-latency memory pool shared by all threads in the thread block currently executing on that SM. Shared memory enables threads within the same thread block to cooperate, facilitates reuse of on-chip data, and can greatly reduce the global memory bandwidth needed by kernels. Because the contents of shared memory are explicitly managed by the application, it is often described as a program-managed cache.

Fermi and Kepler GPUs have similar memory hierarchies, except Kepler includes an additional compiler-directed cache for read-only data. As illustrated in Figure 5-1, all load and store requests to global memory go through the L2 cache, which is the primary point of data unification between SM units. Note that shared memory and L1 cache are physically closer to the SM than both the L2 cache and global memory. As a result, shared memory latency is roughly 20 to 30 times lower than global memory, and bandwidth is nearly 10 times higher.

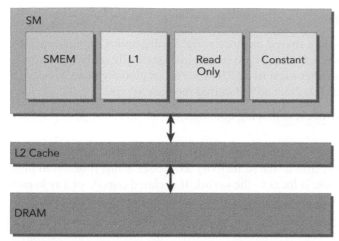

FIGURE 5-1

A fixed amount of shared memory is allocated to each thread block when it starts executing. This shared memory address space is shared by all threads in a thread block. Its contents have the same lifetime as the thread block in which it was created. Shared memory accesses are issued per warp. Ideally, each request to access shared memory by a warp is serviced in one transaction. In the worst case, each request to shared memory is executed sequentially in 32 unique transactions. If multiple threads access the same word in shared memory, one thread fetches the word, and sends it to the other threads via multicast. More details on avoiding multi-transaction shared memory requests are provided in the following sections.

Shared memory is partitioned among all resident thread blocks on an SM; therefore, shared memory is a critical resource that limits device parallelism. The more shared memory used by a kernel, the fewer possible concurrently active thread blocks.

PROGRAM-MANAGED CACHE

In C programming, loop transformations are a common cache optimization. Loop transformations can improve cache locality during loop traversal by re-arranging the order of iterations. At the algorithm level, you need to manually adjust loops to achieve better spatial locality while considering cache size. The cache is transparent to your program, and the compiler handles all data movement. You have no ability to control cache eviction.

Shared memory is a program-managed cache. You have full control over when data is moved into shared memory, and when data is evicted. By allowing you to manually manage shared memory, CUDA makes it easier for you to optimize your application code by providing more fine-grained control over data placement and improving on-chip data movement.

Shared Memory Allocation

There are several ways to allocate or declare shared memory variables depending on your application requirements. You can allocate shared memory variables either statically or dynamically. Shared memory can also be declared as either local to a CUDA kernel or globally in a CUDA source code file. CUDA supports declaration of 1D, 2D, and 3D shared memory arrays.

A shared memory variable is declared with the following qualifier:

```
__shared__
```

The following code segment statically declares a shared memory 2D `float` array. If declared inside a kernel function, the scope of this variable is local to the kernel. If declared outside of any kernels in a file, the scope of this variable is global to all kernels.

```
__shared__ float tile[size_y][size_x];
```

If the size of shared memory is unknown at compile time, you can declare an un-sized array with the `extern` keyword. For example, the following code segment declares a shared memory 1D un-sized `int` array. This declaration can be made either inside a kernel or outside of all kernels.

```
extern __shared__ int tile[];
```

Because the size of this array is unknown at compile-time, you need to dynamically allocate shared memory at each kernel invocation by specifying the desired size in bytes as a third argument inside the triple angled brackets, as follows:

```
kernel<<<grid, block, isize * sizeof(int)>>>(...)
```

Note that you can only declare 1D arrays dynamically.

Shared Memory Banks and Access Mode

There are two key properties to measure when optimizing memory performance: latency and bandwidth. Chapter 4 explained the impact on kernel performance of latency and bandwidth caused by different global memory access patterns. Shared memory can be used to hide the performance impact of global memory latency and bandwidth. To fully exploit these resources, it is helpful to understand how shared memory is arranged.

Memory Banks

To achieve high memory bandwidth, shared memory is divided into 32 equally-sized memory modules, called *banks*, which can be accessed simultaneously. There are 32 banks because there are 32 threads in a warp. Shared memory is a 1D address space. Depending on the compute capability of a GPU, the addresses of shared memory are mapped to different banks in different patterns (more on this later). If a shared memory load or store operation issued by a warp does not access more than one memory location per bank, the operation can be serviced by one memory transaction. Otherwise, the operation is serviced by multiple memory transactions, thereby decreasing memory bandwidth utilization.

Bank Conflict

When multiple addresses in a shared memory request fall into the same memory bank, a *bank conflict* occurs, causing the request to be replayed. The hardware splits a request with a bank conflict into as many separate conflict-free transactions as necessary, decreasing the effective bandwidth by a factor equal to the number of separate memory transactions required.

Three typical situations occur when a request to shared memory is issued by a warp:

➤ **Parallel access:** multiple addresses accessed across multiple banks

➤ **Serial access:** multiple addresses accessed within the same bank

➤ **Broadcast access:** a single address read in a single bank

Parallel access is the most common pattern: multiple addresses accessed by a warp that fall into multiple banks. This pattern implies that some, if not all, of the addresses can be serviced in a single memory transaction. Optimally, a conflict-free shared memory access is performed when every address is in a separate bank.

Serial access is the worst pattern: When multiple addresses fall into the same bank, the request must be serialized. If all 32 threads in a warp access different memory locations in a single bank, 32 memory transactions will be required and satisfying those accesses will take 32 times as long as a single request.

In the case of broadcast access, all threads in a warp read the same address within a single bank. One memory transaction is executed, and the accessed word is broadcast to all requesting threads. While only a single memory transaction is required for a broadcast access, bandwidth utilization is poor because only a small number of bytes are read.

Figure 5-2 illustrates the optimal parallel access pattern. Each thread accesses one 32-bit word. There is no bank conflict because each thread accesses an address in a different bank. Figure 5-3 illustrates an irregular, random access pattern. There is still no bank conflict, because each thread accesses a different bank. Figure 5-4 illustrates another irregular access pattern where several threads access the same bank. There are two possible behaviors for such a request:

➤ Conflict-free broadcast access if threads access the same address within a bank

➤ Bank conflict access if threads access different addresses within a bank

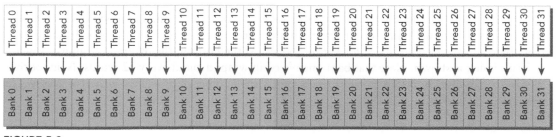

FIGURE 5-2

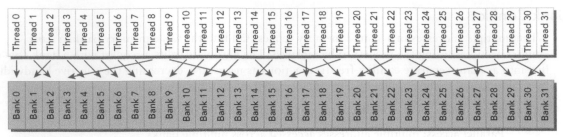

FIGURE 5-3

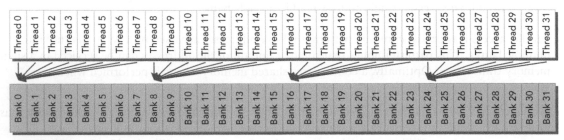

FIGURE 5-4

Access Mode

Shared memory bank width defines which shared memory addresses are in which shared memory banks. Memory bank width varies for devices depending on compute capability. There are two different bank widths:

➤ 4 bytes (32-bits) for devices of compute capability 2.x

➤ 8 bytes (64-bits) for devices of compute capability 3.x

For a Fermi device, the bank width is 32-bits and there are 32 banks. Each bank has a bandwidth of 32 bits per two clock cycles. Successive 32-bit words map to successive banks. Hence, the mapping from shared memory address to bank index can be calculated as follows:

$$bank\ index = (byte\ address \div 4\ bytes/bank)\ \%\ 32\ banks$$

The byte address is divided by 4 to convert to a 4-byte word index, and the modulo 32 operation converts the 4-byte word index into a bank index. The top of Figure 5-5 illustrates the mapping from byte address to word index for Fermi devices. At the bottom, the mapping from word index to bank index is shown. Note that bank membership wraps around every 32 words. Neighboring words are classified in different banks to maximize the number of possible concurrent accesses for a warp.

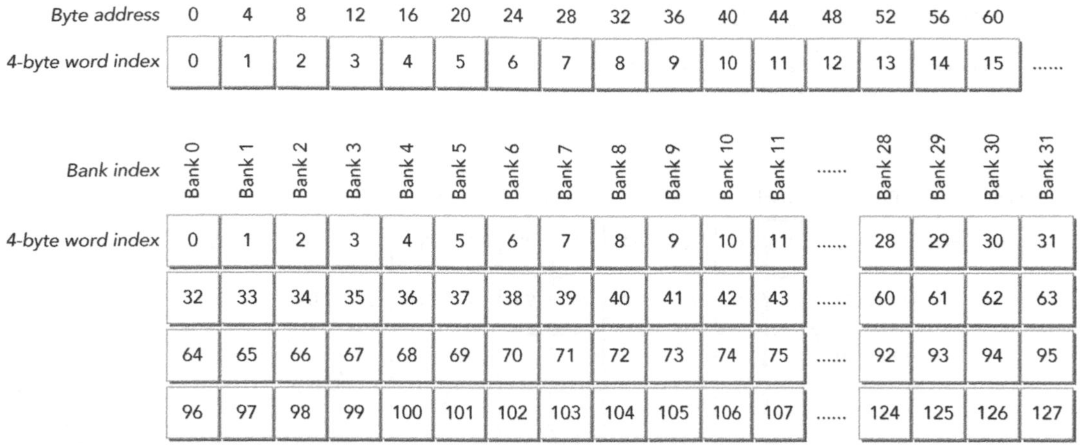

Byte address	0	4	8	12	16	20	24	28	32	36	40	44	48	52	56	60	
4-byte word index	0	1	2	3	4	5	6	7	8	9	10	11	12	13	14	15	......

Bank index	Bank 0	Bank 1	Bank 2	Bank 3	Bank 4	Bank 5	Bank 6	Bank 7	Bank 8	Bank 9	Bank 10	Bank 11		Bank 28	Bank 29	Bank 30	Bank 31
4-byte word index	0	1	2	3	4	5	6	7	8	9	10	11	......	28	29	30	31
	32	33	34	35	36	37	38	39	40	41	42	43	......	60	61	62	63
	64	65	66	67	68	69	70	71	72	73	74	75	......	92	93	94	95
	96	97	98	99	100	101	102	103	104	105	106	107	......	124	125	126	127

FIGURE 5-5

A bank conflict does not occur when two threads from the same warp access the same address. In that case, for read accesses, the word is broadcast to the requesting threads, and for write accesses, the word is written by only one of the threads — which thread performs the write is undefined.

For Kepler devices, shared memory has 32 banks with the following two address modes:

➤ 64-bit mode

➤ 32-bit mode

In 64-bit mode, successive 64-bit words map to successive banks. Each bank has a bandwidth of 64 bits per clock cycle. The mapping from shared memory address to bank index can be calculated as follows:

$$bank\ index = (byte\ address \div 8\ bytes/bank)\ \%\ 32\ banks$$

A shared memory request from a warp does not generate a bank conflict if two threads access any sub-word within the same 64-bit word because only a single 64-bit read is necessary to satisfy both requests. As a result, 64-bit mode always causes the same or fewer bank conflicts for the same access pattern on Kepler devices relative to Fermi.

In 32-bit mode, successive 32-bit words map to successive banks. However, because Kepler has a bandwidth of 64 bits per clock cycle, accessing two 32-bit words in the same bank does not always imply a retry. It may be possible to read 64-bits in a single clock cycle and pass only the 32 bits requested to each thread. Figure 5-6 illustrates the mapping from byte address to bank index for 32-bit mode. The top figure is shared memory labeled with byte addresses and 4-byte word indices. The bottom figure shows the mapping from 4-byte word indices to bank indices. Though word 0 and word 32 are both in bank 0, reading both in the same memory request would not imply a bank conflict.

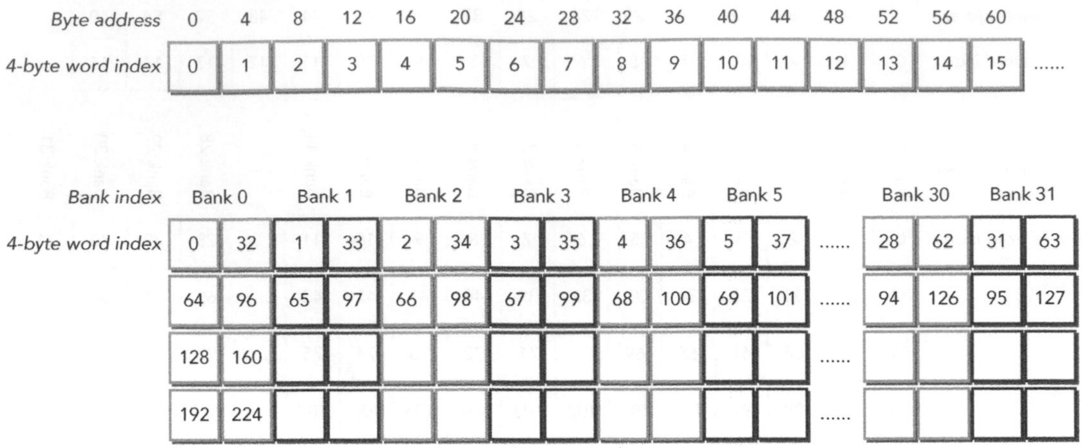

Byte address
0 4 8 12 16 20 24 28 32 36 40 44 48 52 56 60
4-byte word index
0 1 2 3 4 5 6 7 8 9 10 11 12 13 14 15 ......
Bank index
Bank 0 Bank 1 Bank 2 Bank 3 Bank 4 Bank 5 Bank 30 Bank 31
4-byte word index
0 32 1 33 2 34 3 35 4 36 5 37 ...... 28 62 31 63
64 96 65 97 66 98 67 99 68 100 69 101 ...... 94 126 95 127
128 160
192 224

FIGURE 5-6

Figure 5-7 illustrates one case of conflict-free access in 64-bit mode, where each thread accesses different banks. Figure 5-8 illustrates another case of conflict-free access in 64-bit mode, where two threads access words in the same bank and within the same 8-byte word. Figure 5-9 illustrates a two-way bank conflict where two threads access the same bank, but the addresses fall in two different 8-byte words. Figure 5-10 illustrates a three-way bank conflict, where three threads access the same bank and the addresses fall in three different 8-byte words.

threads access
Bank 0
Bank 1
Bank 2
Bank 30
Bank 31

FIGURE 5-7

threads access
Bank 0
Bank 1
Bank 2
Bank 30
Bank 31

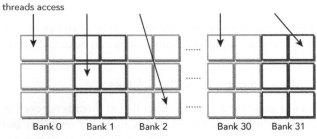

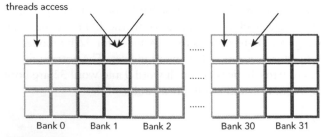

FIGURE 5-8

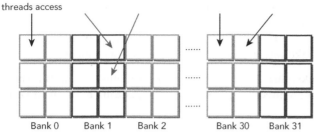

FIGURE 5-9

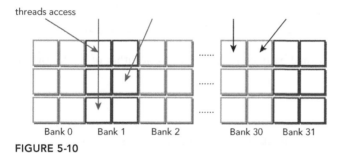

FIGURE 5-10

Memory Padding

Memory padding is one way to avoid bank conflicts. Figure 5-11 illustrates memory padding with a simple case. Suppose you have only five shared memory banks. If all threads access different locations in bank 0, a five-way bank conflict occurs. One way to resolve this type of bank conflict is to add a word of padding after every N elements, where N is the number of banks. This changes the mapping from words to banks, as illustrated on the right side of Figure 5-11. The words that used to all belong to bank 0 are now spread across different banks because of the padding.

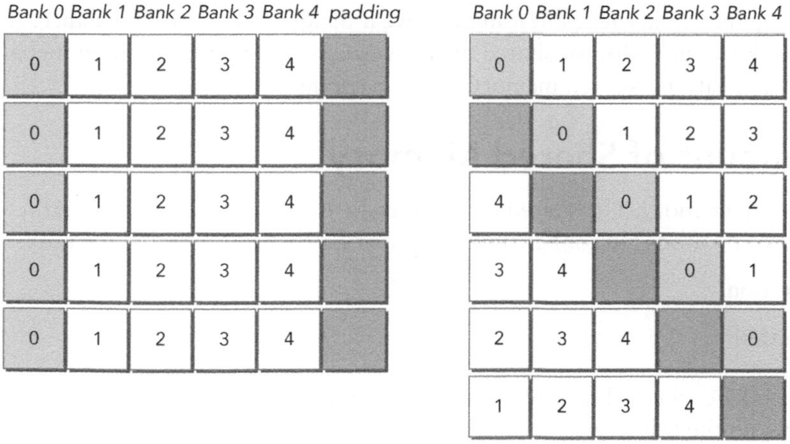

FIGURE 5-11

The padded memory is never used for data storage. Its sole function is to shift data elements so that data that originally resided in the same bank are distributed among banks. As a result, the total amount of useful shared memory available to a thread block will decrease. After padding, you will also need to recalculate array indices to make sure you access the correct data elements.

While both Fermi and Kepler have 32 banks, their bank widths differ. You must be careful when padding shared memory on these different architectures. Some memory padding patterns in Fermi might lead to bank conflicts in Kepler.

Access Mode Configuration

Recall that Kepler devices support 4-byte and 8-byte shared memory access modes. The default is 4-byte mode. The access mode can be queried using the following CUDA runtime API function:

```
cudaError_t cudaDeviceGetSharedMemConfig(cudaSharedMemConfig *pConfig);
```

The result is returned in pConfig. The returned bank configuration can be either of the following values:

```
cudaSharedMemBankSizeFourByte
cudaSharedMemBankSizeEightByte
```

You can use the following function to set a new bank size on devices with configurable shared memory banks:

```
cudaError_t cudaDeviceSetSharedMemConfig(cudaSharedMemConfig config);
```

The supported bank configurations are:

```
cudaSharedMemBankSizeDefault
cudaSharedMemBankSizeFourByte
cudaSharedMemBankSizeEightByte
```

Changing the shared memory configuration between kernel launches might require an implicit device synchronization point. Changing the shared memory bank size will not increase shared memory usage or affect occupancy of kernels, but it might have a major effect on performance. A large bank size may yield higher bandwidth for shared memory access, but may result in more bank conflicts depending on the application's shared memory access patterns.

Configuring the Amount of Shared Memory

Each SM has 64 KB of on-chip memory. The shared memory and L1 cache share this hardware resource. CUDA provides two methods for configuring the size of L1 cache and shared memory:

➤   Per-device configuration
➤   Per-kernel configuration

You can configure how much L1 cache and how much shared memory will be used by kernels launched on a given device with the following runtime function:

```
cudaError_t cudaDeviceSetCacheConfig(cudaFuncCache cacheConfig);
```

The argument `cacheConfig` specifies how on-chip memory should be partitioned between the L1 cache and shared memory on the current CUDA device. The supported cache configurations are:

```
cudaFuncCachePreferNone:    no preference(default)
cudaFuncCachePreferShared:  prefer 48KB shared memory and 16 KB L1 cache
cudaFuncCachePreferL1:      prefer 48KB L1 cache and 16 KB shared memory
cudaFuncCachePreferEqual:   prefer 32KB L1 cache and 32 KB shared memory
```

Which mode is better depends on how much you use shared memory in your kernel. The typical cases are:

➤ Prefer more shared memory when a kernel uses more shared memory.

➤ Prefer more L1 cache when a kernel uses more registers.

If your kernel uses a lot of shared memory, then you will likely find that configuring 48 KB of shared memory enables higher occupancy and hence better performance. On the other hand, if your kernel uses a small amount of shared memory, then you should configure `cacheConfig` with 48 KB for L1 cache. For Kepler devices, L1 cache is used for register spills. You can determine how many registers your kernel uses by specifying the `-Xptxas -v` option to `nvcc`. When your kernel uses more registers than the available hardware limits allow, you should configure a large L1 cache for register spilling. For Fermi devices, local memory is used for spilling registers but loads from local memory may be cached in L1. In that case, a large L1 cache may also be beneficial.

The CUDA runtime makes a best effort to use the requested device on-chip memory configuration, but it is free to choose a different configuration if required to execute a kernel function. A per-kernel configuration can also override the device-wide setting, and can be set using the following runtime function:

```
cudaError_t cudaFuncSetCacheConfig(const void* func,
    enum cudaFuncCacheca cheConfig);
```

The kernel to apply this configuration to is specified by the kernel function pointer `func`. Launching a kernel with a different preference than the most recent preference setting might result in implicit device synchronization. You only need to call this function once for each kernel. The on-chip memory configuration does not have to be re-set on every kernel launch.

Even though L1 cache and shared memory are located in the same on-chip hardware, several things are quite different between them. Shared memory is accessed through 32 banks, while L1 cache is accessed by cache line. With shared memory, you have full control over what gets stored and where, while with L1 cache, data eviction is done by the hardware.

GPU CACHE VERSUS CPU CACHE

In general, GPU cache behavior is more difficult to reason about than CPU cache behavior. The GPU uses different heuristic algorithms to evict data. On GPUs, hundreds of threads share the same L1 cache, and thousands of threads share the same L2 cache; therefore, data eviction might occur more often and unpredictably on a GPU. You can use GPU shared memory to explicitly manage data and guarantee locality to an SM.

Synchronization

Synchronization among parallel threads is a key mechanism for any parallel computing language. As its name suggests, shared memory can be simultaneously accessed by multiple threads within a thread block. Doing so will cause inter-thread conflicts when the same shared memory location is modified by multiple threads without synchronization. CUDA provides several runtime functions to perform intra-block synchronization. In general, there are two basic approaches to synchronization:

> ➤ Barriers
>
> ➤ Memory fences

At a barrier, all calling threads wait for all other calling threads to reach the barrier point. At a memory fence, all calling threads stall until all modifications to memory are visible to all other calling threads. However, before studying CUDA's intra-block barriers and memory fences, it is important to understand the weakly-ordered memory model adopted by CUDA.

Weakly-Ordered Memory Model

Modern memory architectures have a relaxed memory model. This means that the memory accesses are not necessarily executed in the order in which they appear in the program. CUDA adopts a weakly-ordered memory model to enable more aggressive compiler optimizations.

The order in which a GPU thread writes data to different memories, such as shared memory, global memory, page-locked host memory, or the memory of a peer device, is not necessarily the same order of those accesses in the source code. The order in which a thread's writes become visible to other threads may not match the actual order in which those writes were performed.

The order in which a thread reads data from different memories is not necessarily the order in which the read instructions appear in the program if instructions are independent of each other.

To explicitly force a certain ordering for program correctness, memory fences and barriers must be inserted in application code. This is the only way to guarantee the correct behavior of a kernel that shares resources with other threads.

Explicit Barrier

In CUDA, it is only possible to perform a barrier among threads in the same thread block. You can specify a barrier point in a kernel by calling the following intrinsic function:

```
void __syncthreads();
```

__syncthreads acts as a barrier point at which threads in a block must wait until all threads have reached that point. __syncthreads also ensures that all global and shared memory accesses made by these threads prior to the barrier point are visible to all threads in the same block.

__syncthreads is used to coordinate communication between the threads of the same block. When some threads within a block access the same addresses in shared or global memory, there are potential hazards (read-after-write, write-after-read, and write-after-write) which will result in undefined application behavior and undefined state at those memory locations. This undesirable behavior can be avoided by synchronizing threads between conflicting accesses.

You must be particularly careful when using __syncthreads in conditional code. It is only valid to call __syncthreads if a conditional is guaranteed to evaluate identically across the entire thread block. Otherwise execution is likely to hang or produce unintended side effects. For example, the following code segment may cause threads in a block to wait indefinitely for each other because all threads in a block never hit the same barrier point.

```
if (threadID % 2 == 0) {
    __syncthreads();
} else {
    __syncthreads();
}
```

By not allowing synchronization across blocks, thread blocks can be executed in any order, in parallel or in series, on any SM. This independent nature of block execution makes CUDA programming scalable across an arbitrary number of cores. If a CUDA kernel requires global synchronization across blocks, you can likely achieve the desired behavior by splitting the kernel apart at the synchronization point and performing multiple kernel launches. Because each successive kernel launch must wait for the preceding kernel launch to complete, this produces an implicit global barrier.

Memory Fence

Memory fence functions ensure that any memory write before the fence is visible to other threads after the fence. There are three variants of memory fences depending on the desired scope: block, grid, or system.

You can create a memory fence within a thread block using the following intrinsic function:

```
void __threadfence_block();
```

__threadfence_block ensures that all writes to shared memory and global memory made by a calling thread before the fence are visible to other threads in the same block after the fence. Recall that memory fences do not perform any thread synchronization, and so it is not necessary for all threads in a block to actually execute this instruction.

You can create a memory fence at the grid level using the following intrinsic function:

```
void __threadfence();
```

__threadfence stalls the calling thread until all of its writes to global memory are visible to all threads in the same grid.

You can also set a memory fence across the system (including host and device) using the following intrinsic function:

```
void __threadfence_system();
```

__threadfence_system stalls the calling thread to ensure all its writes to global memory, page-locked host memory, and the memory of other devices are visible to all threads in all devices and host threads.

Volatile Qualifier

Declaring a variable in global or shared memory using the *volatile qualifier* prevents compiler optimization which might temporally cache data in registers or local memory. With the volatile qualifier, the compiler assumes that the variable's value can be changed or used at any time by any other thread. Therefore, any reference to this variable is compiled to a global memory read or global memory write instruction that skips the cache.

SHARED MEMORY VERSUS GLOBAL MEMORY

GPU global memory resides in device memory (DRAM), and it is much slower to access than GPU shared memory. Compared to DRAM, shared memory has:

➤   20 to 30 times lower latency than DRAM

➤   Greater than 10 times higher bandwidth than DRAM

The access granularity of shared memory is also smaller. While the access granularity of DRAM is either 32 bytes or 128 bytes, the access granularity of shared memory is as follows:

➤   **Fermi:** 4 bytes bank width

➤   **Kepler:** 8 bytes bank width

CHECKING THE DATA LAYOUT OF SHARED MEMORY

To fully understand how to use shared memory effectively, this section will examine several simple examples using shared memory, including the following topics:

➤   Square versus rectangular arrays

➤   Row-major versus column-major accesses

➤   Static versus dynamic shared memory declarations

➤   File-scope versus kernel-scope shared memory

➤   Memory padding versus no memory padding

When designing your own kernels that use shared memory, your focus should be on the following two concepts:

➤   Mapping data elements across memory banks

➤   Mapping from thread index to shared memory offset

With these concepts clear in mind, you can design an efficient kernel to avoid bank conflict and fully utilize the benefits of shared memory.

Square Shared Memory

You can use shared memory to cache global data with square dimensions in a straightforward fashion. The simple dimensionality of a square array makes it easy to calculate 1D memory offsets from 2D thread indices. Figure 5-12 illustrates a shared memory tile with 32 elements in each dimension, stored in row-major order. The top figure shows the actual arrangement of 1D data layout, and the bottom figure shows the logical 2D shared memory view with a mapping between 4-byte data elements and banks.

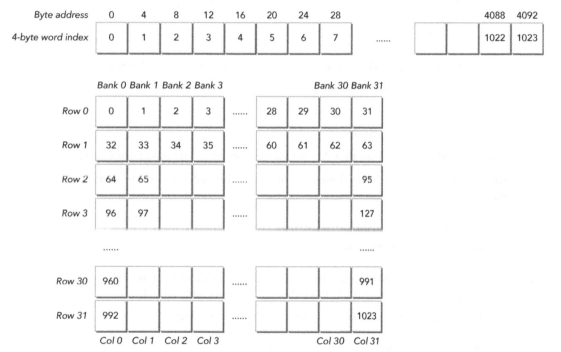

FIGURE 5-12

You can declare a 2D shared memory variable statically, as follows:

```
__shared__ int tile[N][N];
```

Because this shared memory tile is square, you can choose to access it from a 2D thread block with neighboring threads accessing neighboring elements in either the x or y dimension:

```
tile[threadIdx.y][threadIdx.x]
tile[threadIdx.x][threadIdx.y]
```

Which of these access methods is likely to perform better? You need to pay attention to how threads map to shared memory banks. Recall that it is optimal to have threads in the same warp accessing separate banks. Threads in the same warp can be identified by consecutive values of `threadIdx.x`. Elements in shared memory belonging to different banks are also stored consecutively, by word offset. Therefore, it is best to have threads with consecutive values of `threadIdx.x` accessing consecutive locations in shared memory. From this, you can conclude that the first access pattern (`tile[threadIdx.y][threadIdx.x]`) will exhibit better performance and fewer bank conflicts than the second (`tile[threadIdx.x][threadIdx.y]`), because neighboring threads are accessing neighboring array cells along the innermost array dimension.

Accessing Row-Major versus Column-Major

Consider an example in which one grid with one 2D block containing 32 threads in each dimension is used. You can define the block dimensions using the following macro:

```
#define BDIMX 32
#define BDIMY 32
```

You can also use that macro to define the execution configuration for the kernel:

```
dim3 block (BDIMX,BDIMY);
dim3 grid  (1,1);
```

The kernel has two simple operations:

➤ Write global thread indices to a 2D shared memory array in row-major order.

➤ Read those values from shared memory in row-major order and store them to global memory.

First, you can declare a 2D shared memory array statically as follows:

```
__shared__ int tile[BDIMY][BDIMX];
```

Next, you need to calculate the global thread index for each thread from its 2D thread ID. Because only one thread block will be launched, the index conversion can be simplified:

```
unsigned int idx = threadIdx.y * blockDim.x + threadIdx.x;
```

For the examples in this section, `idx` will be used to simulate a value read from an input matrix. Storing the value of `idx` to the output array allows you to visualize the access pattern of the kernel based on where threads write their global IDs.

Writing the global thread index into the shared memory tile in row-major order can be performed as follows:

```
tile[threadIdx.y][threadIdx.x] = idx;
```

Once a synchronization point is reached (using `syncthreads`), all threads must have stored data to the shared memory tile, so you can then assign values to global memory from shared memory in row-major order as follows:

```
out[idx] = tile[threadIdx.y][threadIdx.x];
```

The kernel code is as follows:

```
__global__ void setRowReadRow(int *out) {
    // static shared memory
    __shared__ int tile[BDIMY][BDIMX];

    // mapping from thread index to global memory index
    unsigned int idx = threadIdx.y * blockDim.x + threadIdx.x;

    // shared memory store operation
    tile[threadIdx.y][threadIdx.x] = idx;

    // wait for all threads to complete
    __syncthreads();

    // shared memory load operation
    out[idx] = tile[threadIdx.y][threadIdx.x] ;
}
```

So far, you have three memory operations in the kernel:

➤   One store operation on shared memory

➤   One load operation on shared memory

➤   One store operation on global memory

Because threads in the same warp have consecutive threadIdx.x values and use threadIdx.x to index the innermost dimension of the shared memory array tile, this kernel is free of bank conflicts.

On the other hand, if you swap threadIdx.y and threadIdx.x when assigning data to the shared memory tile, the memory accesses of a warp will be in column-major order. Every shared memory load and store will cause a 32-way bank conflict for a Fermi device, and a 16-way bank conflict for a Kepler device.

```
__global__ void setColReadCol(int *out) {
    // static shared memory
    __shared__ int tile[BDIMX][BDIMY];

    // mapping from thread index to global memory index
    unsigned int idx = threadIdx.y * blockDim.x + threadIdx.x;

    // shared memory store operation
    tile[threadIdx.x][threadIdx.y] = idx;

    // wait for all threads to complete
    __syncthreads();

    // shared memory load operation
    out[idx] = tile[threadIdx.x][threadIdx.y];
}
```

Before testing the performance of these kernels, you will need to prepare global memory. You are encouraged to write the main function yourself. The code for this example and all of the example kernels in this section is also available in checkSmemSquare.cu from Wrox.com. Compile it to an executable file named smemSquare using the command below:

```
$ nvcc checkSmemSquare.cu -o smemSquare
```

First, measure elapsed time using the following command:

```
$ nvprof ./smemSquare
```

The results on a Tesla K40c with 4-byte shared memory access mode are shown here. They clearly show that accessing shared memory by row improved performance, as a result of neighboring threads referencing neighboring words.

```
./smemSquare at device 0 of Tesla K40c with Bank Mode:4-byte
<<< grid (1,1) block (32,32)>>>
Time(%)     Time     Calls      Avg      Min      Max  Name
 13.25%   2.6880us       1   2.6880us  2.6880us  2.6880us  setColReadCol(int*)
 11.36%   2.3040us       1   2.3040us  2.3040us  2.3040us  setRowReadRow(int*)
```

Next, you can check for bank conflicts in the two kernel functions using the following nvprof metrics:

```
shared_load_transactions_per_request
shared_store_transactions_per_request
```

The results reported from nvprof are as follows. These results indicate that the store and load requests from a warp in kernel setRowReadRow are serviced by one transaction, while the same requests in kernel setColReadCol are serviced by 16 transactions. This confirms that the kernel has a 16-way bank conflict on a Kepler device using a shared memory bank width of 8 bytes.

```
Kernel:setColReadCol (int*)
    1   shared_load_transactions_per_request   16.000000
    1   shared_store_transactions_per_request  16.000000
Kernel:setRowReadRow(int*)
    1   shared_load_transactions_per_request   1.000000
    1   shared_store_transactions_per_request  1.000000
```

Writing Row-Major and Reading Column-Major

The following kernel implements shared memory writes in row-major order, and shared memory reads in column-major order. Writing to the shared memory tile in row-major order is implemented by putting the innermost dimension of thread index as the column index of the 2D shared memory tile (identical to the last example):

```
tile[threadIdx.y][threadIdx.x] = idx;
```

Assigning values to global memory from the shared memory tile in column-major order is implemented by swapping the two thread indices when referencing shared memory:

```
out[idx] = tile[threadIdx.x][threadIdx.y];
```

Figure 5-13 illustrates the two memory operations using a simplified five-bank shared memory implementation.

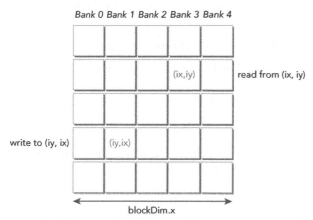

FIGURE 5-13

The kernel code is as follows:

```
__global__ void setRowReadCol(int *out) {
    // static shared memory
    __shared__ int tile[BDIMY][BDIMX];

    // mapping from thread index to global memory index
    unsigned int idx = threadIdx.y * blockDim.x + threadIdx.x;

    // shared memory store operation
    tile[threadIdx.y][threadIdx.x] = idx;

    // wait for all threads to complete
    __syncthreads();

    // shared memory load operation
    out[idx] = tile[threadIdx.x][threadIdx.y];
}
```

After checking the memory transactions for this kernel with nvprof, the following metrics will be reported:

```
Kernel:setRowReadCol (int*)
    1   shared_load_transactions_per_request   16.000000
    1   shared_store_transactions_per_request  1.000000
```

The store operation is conflict-free, but the load operation reports a 16-way conflict.

Dynamic Shared Memory

You can implement these same kernels by declaring shared memory dynamically. You can either declare dynamic shared memory outside the kernel to make it global to file scope, or inside the kernel to restrict it to kernel scope. Dynamic shared memory must be declared as an unsized 1D array; therefore, you need to calculate memory access indices based on 2D thread indices. Because you are going to write in row-major order and read in column-major order in this kernel, you need to maintain two indices as follows:

➤ row_idx: 1D row-major memory offset calculated from 2D thread indices

➤ col_idx: 1D column-major memory offset calculated from 2D thread indices

You write to shared memory in row-major order using the calculated row_idx as follows:

```
tile[row_idx] = row_idx;
```

Using proper synchronization after the shared memory tile has been filled, you then read it in column-major order and assign to global memory as follows:

```
out[row_idx] = tile[col_idx];
```

Because out is stored in global memory and threads are arranged in row-major order within a thread block, you want to write to out in row-major order by thread coordinate to ensure coalesced stores. The kernel code is as follows:

```
__global__ void setRowReadColDyn(int *out) {
    // dynamic shared memory
    extern __shared__ int tile[];

    // mapping from thread index to global memory index
    unsigned int row_idx = threadIdx.y * blockDim.x + threadIdx.x;
    unsigned int col_idx = threadIdx.x * blockDim.y + threadIdx.y;

    // shared memory store operation
    tile[row_idx] = row_idx;

    // wait for all threads to complete
    __syncthreads();

    // shared memory load operation
    out[row_idx] = tile[col_idx];
}
```

The shared memory size must be specified when launching the kernel, as follows:

```
setRowReadColDyn<<<grid, block, BDIMX * BDIMY * sizeof(int)>>>(d_C);
```

This kernel is also available in checkSmemSquare.cu. Try checking the memory transactions of the setRowReadColDyn kernel with nvprof. The following is reported:

```
Kernel: setRowReadColDyn(int*)
    1   shared_load_transactions_per_request   16.000000
    1   shared_store_transactions_per_request   1.000000
```

These results are identical to the previous setRowReadCol example, but use dynamically declared shared memory with 1D array index calculation instead. The write operation is conflict-free, while the read operation reports a 16-way conflict.

Padding Statically Declared Shared Memory

As described in the "Memory Padding" segment of this chapter, padding arrays is one way to avoid bank conflict. Padding statically declared shared memory is straightforward. Simply add a column to the 2D shared memory allocation as follows:

```
__shared__ int tile[BDIMY][BDIMX+1];
```

The following kernel is a revision of the kernel setRowReadCol, which reported a 16-way conflict when reading in column-major order. By padding one element in each row, the column elements are distributed among different banks, so both reading and writing operations are conflict-free.

```
__global__ void setRowReadColPad(int *out) {
    // static shared memory
    __shared__ int tile[BDIMY][BDIMX+IPAD];

    // mapping from thread index to global memory offset
    unsigned int idx = threadIdx.y * blockDim.x + threadIdx.x;

    // shared memory store operation
    tile[threadIdx.y][threadIdx.x] = idx;

    // wait for all threads to complete
    __syncthreads();

    // shared memory load operation
    out[idx] = tile[threadIdx.x][threadIdx.y];
}
```

Check the memory transactions of this kernel with nvprof. The following is reported:

```
Kernel: setRowReadColPad(int*)
    1   shared_load_transactions_per_request   1.000000
    1   shared_store_transactions_per_request  1.000000
```

For Fermi devices, you need to pad one column to resolve bank conflict. For Kepler devices, this is not always true. The number of data elements needed to pad each row for Kepler devices depends on the size of 2D shared memory. Therefore, you will need to perform more tests to determine the proper number of padding elements for 64-bit access mode.

Padding Dynamically Declared Shared Memory

Padding a dynamically declared shared memory array is more complex. You must skip one padded memory space for each row when performing the index conversion from 2D thread indices to 1D memory indices, as follows:

```
unsigned int row_idx = threadIdx.y * (blockDim.x + 1) + threadIdx.x;
unsigned int col_idx = threadIdx.x * (blockDim.x + 1) + threadIdx.y;
```

Figure 5-14 illustrates these memory index calculations using a simplified five-bank shared memory implementation.

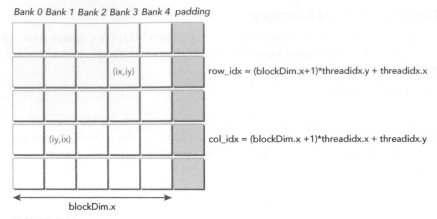

FIGURE 5-14

Because the global memory used to store data in the following kernel is smaller than the padded shared memory, you need three indices: one index for row-major writes to shared memory, one index for column-major reads from shared memory, and one index for coalesced accesses to unpadded global memory, as shown:

```
__global__ void setRowReadColDynPad(int *out) {
    // dynamic shared memory
    extern __shared__ int tile[];

    // mapping from thread index to global memory index
    unsigned int row_idx = threadIdx.y * (blockDim.x + IPAD) + threadIdx.x;
    unsigned int col_idx = threadIdx.x * (blockDim.x + IPAD) + threadIdx.y;

    unsigned int g_idx = threadIdx.y * blockDim.x + threadIdx.x;

    // shared memory store operation
    tile[row_idx] = g_idx;

    // wait for all threads to complete
    __syncthreads();

    // shared memory load operation
    out[g_idx] = tile[col_idx];
}
```

Specify the size of padded shared memory when launching the kernel, as follows:

```
setRowReadColDynPad<<<grid, block, (BDIMX + 1) * BDIMY * sizeof(int)>>>(d_C);
```

Check the memory transactions of this kernel with nvprof. The following results are reported on a K40:

```
Kernel: setRowReadColDynPad(int*)
    1   shared_load_transactions_per_request  1.000000
    1   shared_store_transactions_per_request 1.000000
```

Note that these results are identical to padding statically declared shared memory, so both types of shared memory can be effectively padded.

Comparing the Performance of the Square Shared Memory Kernels

You can see from the elapsed times below for all kernels you have implemented so far that:

➤ Kernels using padding gain performance due to reduced bank conflicts.

➤ Kernels with dynamically declared shared memory add a small amount of overhead.

```
$ nvprof ./smemSquare
./smemSquare at device 0: Tesla K40c with Bank Mode:4-Byte
<<< grid (1,1) block (32,32)>>>
Time(%)      Time  Calls      Avg       Min       Max  Name
  5.32%  3.6160us      1  3.6160us  3.6160us  3.6160us  setColReadCol(int*)
  4.57%  3.1040us      1  3.1040us  3.1040us  3.1040us  setRowReadColDyn(int*)
  4.24%  2.8800us      1  2.8800us  2.8800us  2.8800us  setColReadRow(int*)
  3.81%  2.5920us      1  2.5920us  2.5920us  2.5920us  setRowReadCol(int*)
  3.20%  2.1760us      1  2.1760us  2.1760us  2.1760us  setRowReadColDynPad(int*)
  3.15%  2.1440us      1  2.1440us  2.1440us  2.1440us  setRowReadRow(int*)
  3.15%  2.1440us      1  2.1440us  2.1440us  2.1440us  setRowReadColPad(int*)
```

To display the contents of the 2D matrix generated by each kernel, first reduce the dimension of the shared memory tile to 4 to make it simpler to visualize:

```
#define BDIMX 4
#define BDIMY 4
```

Then, compile and run the following command to list the output of all kernels. From the result, you can see that if the read and write operations use different ordering (for example, read uses row-major order while write uses column-major order), the kernel generates a transpose matrix. These simple kernels constitute the basis for more complex transpose algorithms.

```
$./smemSquare 1
./smemSquare at device 0: Tesla K40c with Bank Mode:4-Byte <<< grid (1,1) block
(4,4)>>>
set col read col          : 0  1  2  3  4  5  6  7  8  9 10 11 12 13 14 15
set row read row          : 0  1  2  3  4  5  6  7  8  9 10 11 12 13 14 15
set col read row          : 0  4  8 12  1  5  9 13  2  6 10 14  3  7 11 15
set row read col          : 0  4  8 12  1  5  9 13  2  6 10 14  3  7 11 15
set row read col  Dynamic : 0  4  8 12  1  5  9 13  2  6 10 14  3  7 11 15
set row read col  Padding : 0  4  8 12  1  5  9 13  2  6 10 14  3  7 11 15
set row read col  Dyn Pad : 0  4  8 12  1  5  9 13  2  6 10 14  3  7 11 15
```

Rectangular Shared Memory

Rectangular shared memory is a more general case of 2D shared memory, where the number of rows and columns in an array are not equal.

```
__shared__ int tile[Row][Col];
```

You cannot simply switch the thread coordinates used to reference a rectangular array when performing a transpose operation, like the square shared memory implementation. Doing so would cause a memory access violation when using rectangular shared memory. You will need to re-implement all of the kernels described in the previous section by recalculating access indices based on matrix dimensions.

Without loss of generality, you are going to examine a rectangular shared memory array with 32 elements per row and 16 elements per column. The dimensions are defined in the following macros:

```
#define BDIMX 32
#define BDIMY 16
```

The rectangular shared memory tile is allocated as follows:

```
__shared__ int tile[BDIMY][BDIMX];
```

For simplicity, the kernel will be launched with only one grid, and one 2D block using the same size as the rectangular shared memory array, as follows:

```
dim3 block (BDIMX,BDIMY);
dim3 grid  (1,1);
```

Accessing Row-Major versus Accessing Column-Major

The first two kernels you will investigate were also used in the square case:

```
__global__ void setRowReadRow(int *out);
__global__ void setColReadCol(int *out);
```

You need to pay careful attention to the declaration of the rectangular shared memory array in each kernel. In the kernel setRowReadRow, the length of the innermost dimension of the shared memory array tile is set to the same dimension as the innermost dimension of the 2D thread block:

```
__shared__ int tile[BDIMY][BDIMX];
```

In the kernel setColReadCol, the length of the innermost dimension of the shared memory array tile is set to the same dimension as the outermost dimension of the 2D thread block:

```
__shared__ int tile[BDIMX][BDIMY];
```

You can download the code for this example in the file checkSmemRectangle.cu from Wrox.com. Compile it and check the bank conflict results with the following nvprof metrics:

```
shared_load_transactions_per_request
shared_store_transactions_per_request
```

The results on a K40 are reported as follows:

```
Kernel:setRowReadRow(int*)
    1  shared_load_transactions_per_request  1.000000
    1  shared_store_transactions_per_request 1.000000
Kernel:setColReadCol(int*)
    1  shared_load_transactions_per_request  8.000000
    1  shared_store_transactions_per_request 8.000000
```

The store and load requests to shared memory are serviced by one transaction in the kernel `setRowReadRow`. The same requests are serviced by eight transactions in the kernel `setColReadCol`. The Kepler K40 bank width is eight words, and 16 4-byte data elements in a column are arranged into eight banks, as illustrated in Figure 5-6; therefore, the operation reports an eight-way conflict.

Writing Row-Major and Reading Column-Major

In this section, you will implement a kernel that writes to shared memory in row-major order and reads from shared memory in column-major order using a rectangular shared memory array. This kernel is applicable in real-world applications; it performs a matrix transpose using shared memory to improve performance by maximizing low-latency loads and stores, and coalescing global memory accesses.

The 2D shared memory tile is declared as follows:

```
__shared__ int tile[BDIMY][BDIMX];
```

The kernel has three memory operations:

➤   Write to a shared memory row with each warp to avoid bank conflicts.

➤   Read from a shared memory column with each warp to perform a matrix transpose.

➤   Write to a global memory row from each warp with coalesced access.

The procedure for calculating the proper shared and global memory accesses is as follows. First, the 2D thread index of the current thread is converted to a 1D global thread ID:

```
unsigned int idx = threadIdx.y * blockDim.x + threadIdx.x;
```

This 1D, row-major mapping ensures that global memory accesses are coalesced. Because data elements in the output global memory are transposed, you then need to calculate the new coordinate in the transpose matrix, as follows:

```
unsigned int irow = idx / blockDim.y;
unsigned int icol = idx % blockDim.y;
```

You initialize the shared memory tile by storing the global thread IDs to the 2D shared memory tile as follows:

```
tile[threadIdx.y][threadIdx.x] = idx;
```

At this point, the data in shared memory is stored linearly from 0 to BDIMX×BDIMY-1. Since each warp performs row-major writes to shared memory, there is no bank-conflict during the write operation.

Now, you can access the shared memory data to be transposed with the coordinates calculated earlier. By accessing shared memory using swapped `irow` and `icol`, you can write the transposed data to global memory using the 1D thread IDs. As shown in the following snippet, a warp reads data elements from one column in shared memory, and performs a coalesced write to global memory.

```
out[idx] = tile[icol][irow];
```

The complete kernel code is as follows:

```
__global__ void setRowReadCol(int *out) {
    // static shared memory
    __shared__ int tile[BDIMY][BDIMX];

    // mapping from 2D thread index to linear memory
    unsigned int idx = threadIdx.y * blockDim.x + threadIdx.x;

    // convert idx to transposed coordinate (row, col)
    unsigned int irow = idx / blockDim.y;
    unsigned int icol = idx % blockDim.y;

    // shared memory store operation
    tile[threadIdx.y][threadIdx.x] = idx;

    // wait for all threads to complete
    __syncthreads();

    // shared memory load operation
    out[idx] = tile[icol][irow];
}
```

When you check the memory transactions with `nvprof`, it reports the following:

```
Kernel:setRowReadCol(int*)
    1   shared_load_transactions_per_request  8.000000
    1   shared_store_transactions_per_request 1.000000
```

The store operation is conflict-free and the load operation reports an eight-way conflict. You can print out the contents of the generated matrix with the following command:

```
$ ./smemRectangle 1
```

Notice that all of the data elements in global memory are transposed.

Dynamically Declared Shared Memory

Because dynamic shared memory can only be declared a 1D array, a new index is required to convert from 2D thread coordinates to 1D shared memory indices when writing by rows and reading by columns:

```
unsigned int col_idx = icol * blockDim.x + irow;
```

Because `icol` corresponds to the innermost dimension of the thread block, this conversion yields column-major access to shared memory, which results in bank conflicts. The kernel code is as follows:

```
__global__ void setRowReadColDyn(int *out) {
    // dynamic shared memory
    extern __shared__ int tile[];

    // mapping from thread index to global memory index
    unsigned int idx = threadIdx.y * blockDim.x + threadIdx.x;
```

```
    // convert idx to transposed (row, col)
    unsigned int irow = idx / blockDim.y;
    unsigned int icol = idx % blockDim.y;

    // convert back to smem idx to access the transposed element
    unsigned int col_idx = icol * blockDim.x + irow;

    // shared memory store operation
    tile[idx] = idx;

    // wait for all threads to complete
    __syncthreads();

    // shared memory load operation
    out[idx] = tile[col_idx];
}
```

Shared memory size must be specified as part of the kernel launch:

```
setRowReadColDyn<<<grid, block, BDIMX * BDIMY * sizeof(int)>>>(d_C);
```

When you check the shared memory transactions with nvprof, the following is reported:

```
Kernel: setRowReadColDyn(int*)
    1    shared_load_transactions_per_request   8.000000
    1    shared_store_transactions_per_request  1.000000
```

The write operation is conflict-free, while the read operation reports an eight-way conflict. Dynamically allocating shared memory does not affect bank conflicts.

Padding Statically Declared Shared Memory

You can also use shared memory padding to resolve bank conflicts for rectangular shared memory. However, for Kepler devices you must calculate how many padding elements are needed. For the ease of coding, use a macro to define the number of padding columns added to each row:

```
#define NPAD   2
```

The padded static shared memory is then declared as follows:

```
__shared__ int tile[BDIMY][BDIMX + NPAD];
```

The setRowReadColPad kernel is identical to setRowReadCol, except for the added shared memory padding:

```
__global__ void setRowReadColPad(int *out) {
    // static shared memory
    __shared__ int tile[BDIMY][BDIMX+IPAD];

    // mapping from 2D thread index to linear memory
    unsigned int idx = threadIdx.y * blockDim.x + threadIdx.x;

    // convert idx to transposed (row, col)
    unsigned int irow = idx / blockDim.y;
    unsigned int icol = idx % blockDim.y;
```

```
    // shared memory store operation
    tile[threadIdx.y][threadIdx.x] = idx;

    // wait for all threads to complete
    __syncthreads();

    // shared memory load operation
    out[idx] = tile[icol][irow] ;
}
```

Checking the memory transactions with nvprof reports the following results:

```
Kernel: setRowReadColPad(int*)
    1   shared_load_transactions_per_request   1.000000
    1   shared_store_transactions_per_request  1.000000
```

Changing the number of padding data elements from two to one in the preceding macro results in nvprof reporting that the shared memory load operations are serviced by two transactions; that is, a two-way bank conflict occurs. You are encouraged to experiment with different values of NPAD, analyze the results you observe, and explain them.

Padding Dynamically Declared Shared Memory

Padding techniques can also be applied to dynamic shared memory kernels that use rectangular shared memory regions. Because the padded shared memory and global memory will have different sizes, three per-thread indices must be maintained in the kernel:

➤ row_idx: a row-major index to the padded shared memory. Using this index, a warp can access a single matrix row.

➤ col_idx: a column-major index to the padded shared memory. Using this index, a warp can access a single matrix column.

➤ g_idx: an index to linear global memory. Using this index, a warp can perform coalesced accesses to global memory.

These indices are calculated using the following code snippet:

```
    // mapping from thread index to global memory index
    unsigned int g_idx = threadIdx.y * blockDim.x + threadIdx.x;

    // convert idx to transposed (row, col)
    unsigned int irow = g_idx / blockDim.y;
    unsigned int icol = g_idx % blockDim.y;
    unsigned int row_idx = threadIdx.y * (blockDim.x + IPAD) + threadIdx.x;

    // convert back to smem idx to access the transposed element
    unsigned int col_idx = icol * (blockDim.x + IPAD) + irow;
```

The full kernel code is as follows:

```
__global__ void setRowReadColDynPad(int *out) {
    // dynamic shared memory
    extern __shared__ int tile[];

    // mapping from thread index to global memory index
    unsigned int g_idx = threadIdx.y * blockDim.x + threadIdx.x;

    // convert idx to transposed (row, col)
    unsigned int irow = g_idx / blockDim.y;
    unsigned int icol = g_idx % blockDim.y;

    unsigned int row_idx = threadIdx.y * (blockDim.x + IPAD) + threadIdx.x;

    // convert back to smem idx to access the transposed element
    unsigned int col_idx = icol * (blockDim.x + IPAD) + irow;

    // shared memory store operation
    tile[row_idx] = g_idx;

    // wait for all threads to complete
    __syncthreads();

    // shared memory load operation
    out[g_idx] = tile[col_idx];
}
```

You can check that shared memory padding works as expected by reducing transactions per request. The following is reported:

```
Kernel: setRowReadColDynPad(int*)
    1  shared_load_transactions_per_request  1.000000
    1  shared_store_transactions_per_request 1.000000
```

Comparing the Performance of the Rectangular Shared Memory Kernels

Run the following command to measure the elapsed time for all kernels implemented in this section using rectangular arrays. In general, kernels using shared memory padding gain performance by removing bank conflicts, and kernels with dynamic shared memory report a small amount of overhead.

```
$ nvprof ./smemRectangle
./smemRectangle at device 0: Tesla K40c with Bank Mode:4-Byte
<<< grid (1,1) block (32,16)>>>
Time(%)     Time   Calls      Avg       Min       Max  Name
  5.35%  2.4000us      1  2.4000us  2.4000us  2.4000us  setRowReadColDyn(int*)
  4.99%  2.2400us      1  2.2400us  2.2400us  2.2400us  setRowReadColDynPad(int*)
  4.85%  2.1760us      1  2.1760us  2.1760us  2.1760us  setRowReadCol(int*)
  4.71%  2.1120us      1  2.1120us  2.1120us  2.1120us  setRowReadColPad(int*)
  4.07%  1.8240us      1  1.8240us  1.8240us  1.8240us  setRowReadRow(int*)
```

To display the contents generated by all kernels, redefine the dimension of the rectangular shared memory array with a very small size as follows:

```
#define BDIMX 8
#define BDIMY 2
```

Then, compile and run with the following command to list the contents of the 2D matrix generated by all kernels. The first kernel generates the original matrix, and all other kernels perform a transpose operation using rectangular shared memory arrays.

```
$ ./smemRectangle 1
./smemRectangle at device 0: Tesla K40c with Bank Mode:4-Byte <<< grid (1,1) block
(8,2)>>>
setRowReadRow        :   0  1  2  3  4  5  6  7  8  9 10 11 12 13 14 15
setRowReadCol        :   0  8  1  9  2 10  3 11  4 12  5 13  6 14  7 15
setRowReadColDyn     :   0  8  1  9  2 10  3 11  4 12  5 13  6 14  7 15
setRowReadColPad     :   0  8  1  9  2 10  3 11  4 12  5 13  6 14  7 15
setRowReadColDynPad  :   0  8  1  9  2 10  3 11  4 12  5 13  6 14  7 15
```

REDUCING GLOBAL MEMORY ACCESS

One of the primary reasons to use shared memory is to cache data on-chip, thereby reducing the number of global memory accesses in your kernel. Chapter 3 introduced parallel reduction kernels using global memory, and focused on the following issues:

➤ How to avoid warp divergence by rearranging data access patterns

➤ How to unroll loops to keep sufficient operations in flight to saturate instruction and memory bandwidth

In this section, you will re-examine those parallel reduction kernels, but this time using shared memory as a program-managed cache to reduce global memory accesses.

Parallel Reduction with Shared Memory

The reduceGmem kernel below will be used as a starting point for baseline performance. It should look familiar from Chapter 3. Parallel reduction is implemented using only global memory and the inner loop over input elements is completely unrolled. The code for the following kernels can be found in reduceInteger.cu on Wrox.com.

```
__global__ void reduceGmem(int *g_idata, int *g_odata, unsigned int n) {
    // set thread ID
    unsigned int tid = threadIdx.x;
    int *idata = g_idata + blockIdx.x * blockDim.x;

    // boundary check
    unsigned int idx = blockIdx.x * blockDim.x + threadIdx.x;
    if (idx >= n) return;

    // in-place reduction in global memory
    if (blockDim.x >= 1024 && tid < 512) idata[tid] += idata[tid + 512];
```

```
        __syncthreads();

        if (blockDim.x >= 512 && tid < 256) idata[tid] += idata[tid + 256];
        __syncthreads();

        if (blockDim.x >= 256 && tid < 128) idata[tid] += idata[tid + 128];
        __syncthreads();

        if (blockDim.x >= 128 && tid < 64) idata[tid] += idata[tid + 64];
        __syncthreads();

        // unrolling warp
        if (tid < 32) {
            volatile int *vsmem = idata;
            vsmem[tid] += vsmem[tid + 32];
            vsmem[tid] += vsmem[tid + 16];
            vsmem[tid] += vsmem[tid +  8];
            vsmem[tid] += vsmem[tid +  4];
            vsmem[tid] += vsmem[tid +  2];
            vsmem[tid] += vsmem[tid +  1];
        }
        // write result for this block to global mem
        if (tid == 0) g_odata[blockIdx.x] = idata[0];
    }
```

This kernel has four major sections. First, an offset is computed for the chunk of data that belongs to this thread block, relative to the global input:

```
int *idata = g idata + blockIdx.x * blockDim.x;
```

Next, the kernel performs an in-place reduction using global memory into 32 elements:

```
    // in-place reduction in global memory
    if (blockDim.x >= 1024 && tid < 512) idata[tid] += idata[tid + 512];
    __syncthreads();

    if (blockDim.x >= 512 && tid < 256) idata[tid] += idata[tid + 256];
    __syncthreads();

    if (blockDim.x >= 256 && tid < 128) idata[tid] += idata[tid + 128];
    __syncthreads();

    if (blockDim.x >= 128 && tid < 64) idata[tid] += idata[tid + 64];
    __syncthreads();
```

Then, the kernel performs an in-place reduction using only the first warp of each thread block. Note in the loop unrolling section, the use of a `volatile` qualifier is used to ensure that as the warp executes in lock step, only the latest values are read.

```
    volatile int *vsmem = idata;
    vsmem[tid] += vsmem[tid + 32];
    vsmem[tid] += vsmem[tid + 16];
    vsmem[tid] += vsmem[tid +  8];
    vsmem[tid] += vsmem[tid +  4];
```

```
vsmem[tid] += vsmem[tid +  2];
vsmem[tid] += vsmem[tid +  1];
```

Finally, the total sum for the chunk of input data assigned to this thread block is written back to global memory:

```
if (tid == 0) g_odata[blockIdx.x] = idata[0];
```

For all tests, the array length will be set to 16M using the following statement. This corresponds to the number of integers to reduce.

```
int size = 1<<24;
```

The block size is set to a constant 128 threads with the following macro:

```
#define DIM 128
```

Now, compile the file using:

```
$ nvcc reduceInteger.cu -o reduce
```

Measure the elapsed time for this reduction kernel that uses only global memory with nvprof:

```
$ nvprof ./reduce
```

The baseline results using a Tesla K40c are summarized as follows:

```
reduce at device 0: Tesla K40c with array size 16777216  grid 131072 block 128
Time(%)      Time     Calls      Avg       Min       Max  Name
  2.01%   2.1206ms       1  2.1206ms  2.1206ms  2.1206ms  reduceGmem()
```

Next examine the following in-place reduction kernel reduceSmem, which augments global memory operations with shared memory. This kernel is nearly identical to the original reduceGmem kernel. However, rather than using a subset of the global memory input array to perform an in-place reduction, the shared memory array smem is used. smem is declared to have the same dimensions as each thread block:

```
__shared__ int smem[DIM];
```

Each thread block initializes smem with the chunk of global input data it is responsible for:

```
smem[tid] = idata[tid];
__syncthreads();
```

Then, the in-place reduction is performed using shared memory (smem), rather than global memory (idata). The code for the reduceSmem kernel is included below:

```
__global__ void reduceSmem(int *g_idata, int *g_odata, unsigned int n) {
    __shared__ int smem[DIM];

    // set thread ID
    unsigned int tid = threadIdx.x;

    // boundary check
```

```
    unsigned int idx = blockIdx.x * blockDim.x + threadIdx.x;
    if (idx >= n) return;

    // convert global data pointer to the local pointer of this block
    int *idata = g_idata + blockIdx.x * blockDim.x;

    // set to smem by each threads
    smem[tid] = idata[tid];
    __syncthreads();

    // in-place reduction in shared memory
    if (blockDim.x >= 1024 && tid < 512) smem[tid] += smem[tid + 512];
    __syncthreads();

    if (blockDim.x >= 512 && tid < 256) smem[tid] += smem[tid + 256];
    __syncthreads();

    if (blockDim.x >= 256 && tid < 128) smem[tid] += smem[tid + 128];
    __syncthreads();

    if (blockDim.x >= 128 && tid < 64)  smem[tid] += smem[tid + 64];
    __syncthreads();

    // unrolling warp
    if (tid < 32) {
        volatile int *vsmem = smem;
        vsmem[tid] += vsmem[tid + 32];
        vsmem[tid] += vsmem[tid + 16];
        vsmem[tid] += vsmem[tid +  8];
        vsmem[tid] += vsmem[tid +  4];
        vsmem[tid] += vsmem[tid +  2];
        vsmem[tid] += vsmem[tid +  1];
    }
    // write result for this block to global mem
    if (tid == 0) g_odata[blockIdx.x] = smem[0];
}
```

Measure the elapsed time for both kernels (with and without shared memory) using nvprof:

```
$ nvprof ./reduce
```

The results using a Tesla K40c are summarized as follows:

```
reduce at device 0: Tesla K40c with array size 16777216  grid 131072 block 128
Time(%)     Time    Calls      Avg       Min       Max  Name
  2.01%  2.1206ms      1   2.1206ms  2.1206ms  2.1206ms  reduceGmem()
  1.10%  1.1536ms      1   1.1536ms  1.1536ms  1.1536ms  reduceSmem()
```

The kernel using shared memory is 1.84 times faster than the kernel using only global memory. Next, you can check the global memory load and store transactions to see how well shared memory use reduced global memory accesses using the following metrics:

```
gld_transactions:  Number of global memory load transactions
gst_transactions:  Number of global memory store transactions
```

The results are summarized here:

```
Device "Tesla K40c (0)"
        Kernel: reduceSmem(int*, int*, unsigned int)
          1                Global Load Transactions      524288
          1                Global Store Transactions     131072
        Kernel: reduceGmem(int*, int*, unsigned int)
          1                Global Load Transactions     2883584
          1                Global Store Transactions    1179648
```

It is clear from the results that using shared memory reduced global memory access by a significant amount.

Parallel Reduction with Unrolling

In the preceding kernels, each thread block handles one block of data. In Chapter 3, you unrolled blocks to improve kernel performance by enabling multiple I/O operations to be in-flight at once. The following kernel unrolls four blocks; that is, each thread handles data elements from four data blocks. With unrolling, you expect the following benefits:

➤ Increased global memory throughput by exposing more parallel I/O per thread

➤ Reduction of global memory store transactions by one-fourth

➤ Overall kernel performance improvement

The kernel code is as follows:

```
__global__ void reduceSmemUnroll(int *g_idata, int *g_odata, unsigned int n) {
    // static shared memory
    __shared__ int smem[DIM];

    // set thread ID
    unsigned int tid = threadIdx.x;

    // global index, 4 blocks of input data processed at a time
    unsigned int idx = blockIdx.x * blockDim.x * 4 + threadIdx.x;

    // unrolling 4 blocks
    int tmpSum = 0;

    // boundary check
    if (idx + 3 * blockDim.x <= n) {
        int a1 = g_idata[idx];
        int a2 = g_idata[idx + blockDim.x];
        int a3 = g_idata[idx + 2 * blockDim.x];
        int a4 = g_idata[idx + 3 * blockDim.x];
        tmpSum = a1 + a2 + a3 + a4;
    }

    smem[tid] = tmpSum;
```

```
   __syncthreads();

   // in-place reduction in shared memory
   if (blockDim.x >= 1024 && tid < 512) smem[tid] += smem[tid + 512];
   __syncthreads();

   if (blockDim.x >= 512 && tid < 256)  smem[tid] += smem[tid + 256];
   __syncthreads();

   if (blockDim.x >= 256 && tid < 128)  smem[tid] += smem[tid + 128];
   __syncthreads();

   if (blockDim.x >= 128 && tid < 64)   smem[tid] += smem[tid + 64];
   __syncthreads();

   // unrolling warp
   if (tid < 32) {
      volatile int *vsmem = smem;
      vsmem[tid] += vsmem[tid + 32];
      vsmem[tid] += vsmem[tid + 16];
      vsmem[tid] += vsmem[tid +  8];
      vsmem[tid] += vsmem[tid +  4];
      vsmem[tid] += vsmem[tid +  2];
      vsmem[tid] += vsmem[tid +  1];
   }
   // write result for this block to global mem
   if (tid == 0) g_odata[blockIdx.x] = smem[0];
}
```

To enable each thread to handle four data elements, the first step is recalculating the offset in the global input data based on the block and thread index of each thread:

```
unsigned int idx = blockIdx.x * blockDim.x * 4 + threadIdx.x;
```

Because each thread reads four data elements, the starting point for each thread's processing is now offset as if there were four times as many thread blocks. From this new offset, each thread reads four data elements and then adds them to a local variable tmpSum. tmpSum is then used to initialize shared memory, rather than initializing it directly from global memory.

```
int tmpSum = 0;
if (idx + 3 * blockDim.x <= n) {
   int a1 = g_idata[idx];
   int a2 = g_idata[idx + blockDim.x];
   int a3 = g_idata[idx +2 * blockDim.x];
   int a4 = g_idata[idx +3 * blockDim.x];
   tmpSum = a1 + a2 + a3 + a4;
}
```

With this unrolling, the number of global memory load transactions in the kernel is unchanged, but the number of global memory store transactions is reduced by one-fourth. Additionally, with four global load operations in flight at once, the GPU has more flexibility in scheduling them concurrently, potentially leading to better global memory utilization.

The grid size of this kernel must be reduced to account for four times as much work being performed by each thread::

```
reduceGmemUnroll<<<grid.x / 4, block>>>(d_idata, d_odata, size);
```

With these changes, check the elapsed time with `nvprof`. The shared memory kernel with unrolling by 4 (`reduceSmemUnroll`) is 2.76 times faster than the previous shared memory kernel (`reduceSmem`) on an example system. The results are summarized below:

```
reduce at device 0: Tesla K40c with array size 16777216   grid 131072 block 128
Time(%)      Time    Calls       Avg       Min       Max  Name
  1.10%   1.1536ms       1   1.1536ms  1.1536ms  1.1536ms  reduceSmem()
  0.40%   418.27us       1   418.27us  418.27us  418.27us  reduceSmemUnroll()
```

It is also interesting to check the global memory transactions using `nvprof`. The number of store transactions in `reduceSmemUnroll` is reduced by one-fourth compared to `reduceSmem` while the number of load transactions remains the same, as shown in the following results:

```
Kernel: reduceSmem(int*, int*, unsigned int)
        1                 Global Load Transactions        524288
        1                 Global Store Transactions       131072
Kernel: reduceSmemUnroll(int*, int*, unsigned int)
        1                 Global Load Transactions        524288
        1                 Global Store Transactions        32768
```

Finally, check the global memory throughput. The load throughput has increased 2.57 times and store throughput has decreased 1.56 times. The load throughput increase is attributed to a greater number of simultaneous load requests. The store throughput decreases because there are fewer store requests in-flight to saturate the bus. The results are summarized as follows:

```
Kernel: reduceSmem(int*, int*, unsigned int)
        1         Requested Global Load Throughput     63.537GB/s
        1         Requested Global Store Throughput    496.38 MB/s
Kernel: reduceSmemUnroll(int*, int*, unsigned int)
        1         Requested Global Load Throughput     162.57 GB/s
        1         Requested Global Store Throughput    317.53 MB/s
```

Parallel Reduction with Dynamic Shared Memory

You can implement parallel reduction kernels using dynamic shared memory by replacing the static shared memory in the kernel `reduceSmemUnroll` with the following declaration:

```
extern __shared__ int smem[];
```

When launching the kernel, the amount of shared memory to dynamically allocate must be specified:

```
reduceSmemUnrollDyn<<<grid.x / 4, block, DIM * sizeof(int)>>>(d_idata, d_odata,
size);
```

If you measure the elapsed time of the kernel with nvprof, you will find there is no significant difference between the kernels implemented with dynamically allocated shared memory and statically allocated shared memory.

Effective Bandwidth

Because the reduction kernels are bound by memory bandwidth, the appropriate performance metric to use when evaluating them is their effective bandwidth. Effective bandwidth is the amount of I/O performed (in bytes) over the kernel's complete execution time. For memory-bound applications, effective bandwidth is a good metric for estimating actual bandwidth utilization. It can be expressed as:

$$effective\ bandwidth = (bytes\ read + bytes\ written) \div (time\ elapsed \times 10^9)\ GB/s$$

Table 5-1 summarizes the achieved effective bandwidth for each kernel. Clearly, you can achieve significant effective bandwidth improvements by unrolling blocks. Doing so causes each thread to expose more requests in-flight at once, leading to higher saturation of the memory bus.

TABLE 5-1: Achieved Effective Bandwidth of Reduction Kernels on Tesla K40c

KERNELS	ELAPSED TIME (MS)	READ DATA ELEMENTS	WRITE DATA ELEMENTS	TOTAL BYTES	BANDWIDTH (GB/S)
reduceGmem	2.1357	16777216	131072	67633152	31.67
reduceSmem	1.1206	16777216	131072	67633152	60.35
reduceSmemUnroll	0.4171	16777216	32768	67239936	161.21
reduceSmemUnrollDyn	0.4169	16777216	32768	67239936	161.29

COALESCING GLOBAL MEMORY ACCESSES

Using shared memory can also help avoid non-coalesced global memory access. Matrix transpose is a typical example of this: The read operation is naturally coalesced, but the write operation is accessed in stride. Chapter 4 demonstrated that strided access is the worst access pattern for global memory because it wastes bus bandwidth. With the help of shared memory, you can perform the transpose operation first in shared memory and then perform coalesced writes to global memory.

Earlier in this chapter, you tested a matrix transpose kernel that used a single thread block to write to a matrix row in shared memory and read from a column. In this section, you are going to extend that kernel to use multiple thread blocks to re-order stride-based global memory accesses into coalesced accesses.

Baseline Transpose Kernel

As a baseline, the following kernel is a naive implementation of matrix transpose that uses only global memory.

```
__global__ void naiveGmem(float *out, float *in, const int nx, const int ny) {
    // matrix coordinate (ix,iy)
    unsigned int ix = blockIdx.x * blockDim.x + threadIdx.x;
    unsigned int iy = blockIdx.y * blockDim.y + threadIdx.y;

    // transpose with boundary test
    if (ix < nx && iy < ny) {
        out[ix*ny+iy] = in[iy*nx+ix];
    }
}
```

Because ix is along the innermost dimension of this kernel's 2D thread configuration, the global memory read operation is coalesced within a warp, while the global memory write operation exhibits strided access between neighboring threads. The performance for this naiveGmem kernel is a lower bound that progressive optimizations covered in this section will be measured against.

Changing the write operation to perform coalesced accesses would result in a copy kernel. Because both the read and write operations would be coalesced but still performing the same amount of I/O, the copy kernel copyGmem serves as an approximate upper performance bound:

```
__global__ void copyGmem(float *out, float *in, const int nx, const int ny) {
    // matrix coordinate (ix,iy)
    unsigned int ix = blockIdx.x * blockDim.x + threadIdx.x;
    unsigned int iy = blockIdx.y * blockDim.y + threadIdx.y;

    // transpose with boundary test
    if (ix < nx && iy < ny) {
        out[iy * nx + ix] = in[iy * nx + ix];
    }
}
```

The kernels and host code for this section can be found in transposeRectangle.cu on Wrox.com. For these tests, the matrix size is set to 4,096 × 4,096 and a 2D thread block with dimensions 32 × 16 is used.

The results for copyGmem and naiveGmem kernels measured on a Tesla M2090 and a Tesla K40c are summarized in Table 5-2.

TABLE 5-2: Performance of Transpose Kernels

KERNELS	TESLA M2090 (ECC OFF)		TESLA K40C (ECC OFF)	
	ELAPSED TIME (MS)	BANDWIDTH (GB/S)	ELAPSED TIME (MS)	BANDWIDTH (GB/S)
copyGmem	1.048	128.07	0.758	177.15
naiveGmem	3.611	37.19	1.947	68.98

The naive kernel is nearly three times slower than the copy kernel. Because the naive kernel writes to global memory with a stride of 4,096 elements, a store memory operation from a single warp is serviced by 32 global memory transactions. You can confirm this using the following nvprof metrics:

```
gld_transactions_per_request: average number of transactions per load request
gst_transactions_per_request: average number of transactions per store request
```

These nvprof metrics measure the average number of transactions for load and store global memory requests. The following results are reported on the Tesla K40c, and show that store requests to global memory are replayed 32 times in the naiveGmem kernel.

```
Device "Tesla K40c (0)"   Metrics      Transactions
Kernel:copyGmem(float*, float*, int, int)
  1     gld_transactions_per_request   1.000000
  1     gst_transactions_per_request   1.000000
Kernel:naiveGmem(float*, float*, int, int)
  1     gld_transactions_per_request   1.000000
  1     gst_transactions_per_request  32.000000
```

Matrix Transpose with Shared Memory

To avoid strided global memory access, 2D shared memory can be used to cache data from the original matrix. A column read from 2D shared memory can be transferred to a transposed matrix row stored in global memory. While a naive implementation will result in shared memory bank conflicts, the performance will be much better than non-coalesced global memory accesses. Figure 5-15 illustrates how shared memory is used in matrix transpose.

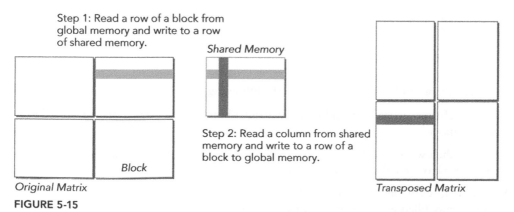

Step 1: Read a row of a block from global memory and write to a row of shared memory.

Shared Memory

Step 2: Read a column from shared memory and write to a row of a block to global memory.

Block

Original Matrix

Transposed Matrix

FIGURE 5-15

The following kernel implements a matrix transpose with shared memory. It can be viewed as an extension of the setRowReadCol kernel discussed earlier in the chapter. The difference between these two kernels is that setRowReadCol handles the transpose of a single block of the input matrix using one thread block. The kernel transposeSmem extends the transpose operations to use multiple thread blocks and multiple data blocks.

```
__global__ void transposeSmem(float *out, float *in, int nx, int ny) {
    // static shared memory
    __shared__ float tile[BDIMY][BDIMX];

    // coordinate in original matrix
    unsigned int ix,iy,ti,to;
    ix = blockIdx.x *blockDim.x + threadIdx.x;
    iy = blockIdx.y *blockDim.y + threadIdx.y;

    // linear global memory index for original matrix
    ti = iy*nx + ix;

    // thread index in transposed block
    unsigned int bidx,irow,icol;
    bidx = threadIdx.y*blockDim.x + threadIdx.x;
    irow = bidx/blockDim.y;
    icol = bidx%blockDim.y;

    // coordinate in transposed matrix
    ix = blockIdx.y * blockDim.y + icol;
    iy = blockIdx.x * blockDim.x  + irow;

    // linear global memory index for transposed matrix
    to = iy*ny + ix;

    // transpose with boundary test
    if (ix < nx && iy < ny)
    {
        // load data from global memory to shared memory
        tile[threadIdx.y][threadIdx.x] = in[ti];

        // thread synchronization
        __syncthreads();

        // store data to global memory from shared memory
        out[to] = tile[icol][irow];
    }
}
```

kerneltransposeSmem can be broken down into the following steps:

1. A warp performs a coalesced read of a row from a block of the original matrix stored in global memory.

2. The warp then writes the data into shared memory using row-major ordering. As a result, there are no bank conflicts for this write.

3. After all read/write operations in the thread block are synchronized, you have a 2D shared memory array filled with data from global memory.

4. The warp reads a column from the 2D shared memory array. Since the shared memory is not padded, bank conflicts occur.

5. The warp then performs a coalesced write of that data into a row of the transposed matrix stored in global memory.

For each thread to fetch the right data from both global and shared memory, multiple indices must be calculated for each thread. For a given thread, you first calculate its coordinate in the original matrix based on its thread index and block index as follows:

```
ix = blockIdx.x * blockDim.x  + threadIdx.x;
iy = blockIdx.y * blockDim.y  + threadIdx.y;
```

The index into global memory can then be calculated:

```
ti = iy * nx + ix;
```

Because `ix` is along the innermost dimension of the thread block, a warp of 32 threads can use `ti` to perform a coalesced read from global memory.

Similarly, the coordinates of the transpose matrix are calculated as follows:

```
ix = blockIdx.y * blockDim.y + icol;
iy = blockIdx.x * blockDim.x + irow;
```

Compared to the calculation of the coordinates for a thread in the original matrix, there are two main differences.

First, the offset of a block in the transpose matrix swaps the use of the `blockDim` and `blockIdx` built-ins: The x dimension of the thread configuration is used to calculate the column coordinate in the transposed matrix, and the y dimension is used to calculate the row coordinate.

Also, two new variables `icol` and `irow` are introduced in place of `threadIdx`. These variables are the indices to the corresponding transposed block:

```
bidx = threadIdx.y * blockDim.x + threadIdx.x;
irow = bidx / blockDim.y;
icol = bidx % blockDim.y;
```

The index into global memory used to store the transposed matrix can then be calculated as:

```
to = iy * ny + ix;
```

Using the calculated offsets, a warp of threads can then read contiguously from global memory and write to a row of the 2D shared memory array `tile` as follows:

```
tile[threadIdx.y][threadIdx.x]  = in[ti];
```

The read from global memory is coalesced and the write to shared memory banks are conflict-free. A warp of threads can then read a column from shared memory `tile` and write contiguously to global memory:

```
out[to]  = tile[icol][irow];
```

The write to global memory is coalesced, but the read from shared memory causes a bank conflict because each warp reads data along a column in `tile`. The bank conflict issue will be resolved later in this section using shared memory padding. Figure 5-16 illustrates the index calculations.

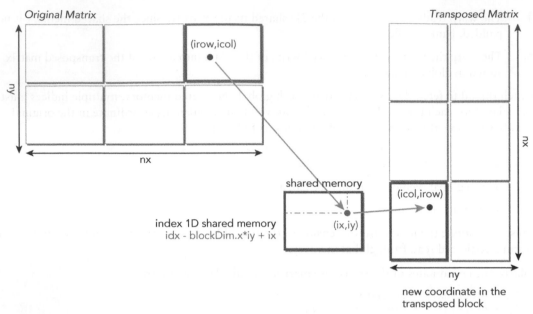

FIGURE 5-16

Using shared memory increases performance of the transpose kernel, as shown in Table 5-3.

TABLE 5-3: Performance of Transpose Kernels

KERNELS	TESLA M2090 (ECC OFF)		TESLA K40 (ECC OFF)	
	ELAPSED TIME (MS)	BANDWIDTH (GB/S)	ELAPSED TIME (MS)	BANDWIDTH (GB/S)
copyGmem	1.048	128.07	0.758	177.15
naiveGmem	3.611	37.19	1.947	68.98
transposeSmem	1.551	86.54	1.149	116.82

The number of global memory transactions performed per request reported by nvprof for the transposeSmem kernel is:

```
Device "Tesla K40c (0)"  Metrics    Transactions
Kernel: transposeSmem (float*, float*, int, int)
   1   gld_transactions_per_request  1.000000
   1   gst_transactions_per_request  2.000000
```

The replay of global memory stores is reduced from 32 to 2. Because the block width in the transposed block is 16, the writes of the first half of a warp and the second half of a warp are strided by 4,080; therefore, a warp request to write to global memory is serviced by two transactions. Changing the thread block size to 32x32 would reduce the replay count to 1. However, a thread block configuration of 32x16 exposes more parallelism than the 32x32 launch configuration. Later, you will investigate which optimization is more beneficial.

Below are results measuring shared memory transactions per shared memory load and store request on a Tesla K40:

```
Device "Tesla K40c (0)"   Metrics     Transactions
Kernel: transposeSmem (float*, float*, int, int)
   1     shared_load_transactions_per_request   8.000000
   1     shared_store_transactions_per_request  1.000000
```

Clearly, reads from a column of the 2D shared memory array create bank conflicts. Running this kernel on the Tesla M2090 would yield a replay of 16 transactions. Accessing a column on a Fermi GPU with a bank width of 4 bytes would therefore result in a 16-way conflict because one column has 16 data elements each with a length of 4 bytes. However, the Tesla K40 has a bank width of 8 bytes, leading to a reduction in bank-conflicts by half.

Matrix Transpose with Padded Shared Memory

By adding column padding to each row in the 2D shared memory array tile, the data elements in the same column of the original matrix can be evenly distributed among shared memory banks. The number of columns that must be padded depends on device compute capability and thread block size. For the tested kernel with a 32×16 thread block, two columns of padding must be added for a Tesla K40 and one column for a Tesla M2090. The following statement declares the padded shared memory for the Tesla K40:

```
__shared__ float tile[BDIMY][BDIMX + 2];
```

Additionally, stores to and loads from tile must be transformed to account for the extra two columns in each row. Padding columns gives you additional speedup, as shown in Table 5-4.

TABLE 5-4: Performance of Transpose Kernels

KERNELS	TESLA M2090 (ECC OFF)		TESLA K40 (ECC OFF)	
	ELAPSED TIME (MS)	BANDWIDTH (GB/S)	ELAPSED TIME (MS)	BANDWIDTH (GB/S)
copyGmem	1.048	128.07	0.758	177.15
naiveGmem	3.611	37.19	1.947	68.98
transposeSmem	1.551	86.54	1.149	116.82
transposeSmemPad	1.416	94.79	1.102	121.83

The following results measure the shared memory transactions per request on a Tesla K40. Adding column padding to the shared memory array eliminated all bank conflicts.

```
Device "Tesla K40c (0)"   Metrics     Transactions
Kernel: transposeSmemPad (float*, float*, int, int)
   1     shared_load_transactions_per_request   1.000000
   1     shared_store_transactions_per_request  1.000000
```

Matrix Transpose with Unrolling

The following kernel unrolls the simultaneous processing of two data blocks: Each thread now transposes two data elements strided by one data block. The goal of this transformation is to improve device memory bandwidth utilization by creating more simultaneous in-flight loads and stores.

```
__global__ void transposeSmemUnrollPad(float *out, float *in, const int nx,
    const int ny) {
    // static 1D shared memory with padding
    __shared__ float tile[BDIMY*(BDIMX*2+IPAD)];

    // coordinate in original matrix
    unsigned int ix = 2 * blockIdx.x * blockDim.x + threadIdx.x;
    unsigned int iy = blockIdx.y * blockDim.y + threadIdx.y;

    // linear global memory index for original matrix
    unsigned int ti = iy*nx + ix;

    // thread index in transposed block
    unsigned int bidx = threadIdx.y * blockDim.x + threadIdx.x;
    unsigned int irow = bidx / blockDim.y;
    unsigned int icol = bidx % blockDim.y;

    // coordinate in transposed matrix
    unsigned int ix2 = blockIdx.y * blockDim.y + icol;
    unsigned int iy2 = 2 * blockIdx.x * blockDim.x + irow;

    // linear global memory index for transposed matrix
    unsigned int to = iy2*ny + ix2;

    if (ix+blockDim.x < nx && iy < ny)
    {
        // load two rows from global memory to shared memory
        unsigned int row_idx = threadIdx.y * (blockDim.x * 2 + IPAD) + threadIdx.x;
        tile[row_idx]       = in[ti];
        tile[row_idx+BDIMX] = in[ti+BDIMX];

        // thread synchronization
        __syncthreads();

        // store two rows to global memory from two columns of shared memory
        unsigned int col_idx = icol*(blockDim.x*2+IPAD) + irow;
        out[to] = tile[col_idx];
        out[to+ny*BDIMX] = tile[col_idx+BDIMX];
    }
}
```

In this kernel, a 1D shared memory array tile with added column padding is declared statically:

```
__shared__ float tile[BDIMY * (BDIMX * 2 + IPAD)];
```

For a given thread, the input matrix coordinates and the index into the global memory array used to store the input matrix are calculated as follows:

```
ix = blockIdx.x * blockDim.x * 2 + threadIdx.x;
iy = blockIdx.y * blockDim.y + threadIdx.y;
ti = iy * nx + ix;
```

As illustrated in Figure 5-17, a thread block configuration of 32×16 is used with an unrolled data block of size $(32 + 32) \times 16$.

The new thread index in the transposed block in shared memory is calculated as follows:

```
bidx = threadIdx.y * blockDim.x + threadIdx.x;
irow = bidx / blockDim.y;
icol = bidx % blockDim.y;
```

Because the shared memory array `tile` is 1D, the 2D thread index must be converted to a 1D shared memory index in order to access the padded 1D shared memory:

```
row_idx = threadIdx.y * (blockDim.x * 2 + IPAD) + threadIdx.x;
col_idx = icol * (blockDim.x * 2 + IPAD) + irow;
```

Because the padded memory is not used to store data, padded columns must be skipped when calculating indices.

Finally, the output matrix coordinates in the transposed matrix and the corresponding index into global memory used to store the result are calculated as follows:

```
ix2 = blockIdx.y * blockDim.y * 2 + icol;
iy2 = blockIdx.x * blockDim.x * 2 + irow;
to  = iy2 * ny + ix2;
```

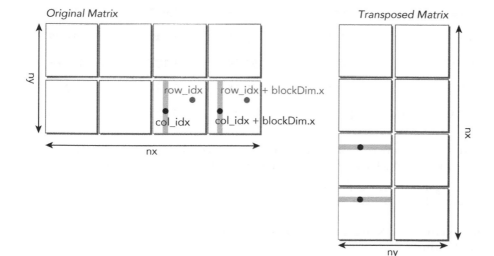

FIGURE 5-17

Using the indices into global and shared memory calculated above, each thread reads two data elements from a row of global memory and writes them to a row of shared memory, as follows:

```
tile[row_idx]        = in[ti];
tile[row_idx + BDIMX] = in[ti + BDIMX];
```

After synchronization, each thread reads two data elements from a column of shared memory and writes them to a row of global memory. Note that because the shared memory array `tile` has the added padding, these shared memory requests along the same column will not cause bank conflicts.

```
out[to] = tile[col_idx];
out[to + ny * BDIMX] = tile[col_idx + BDIMX];
```

A slight extension to this kernel could provide more flexibility. You could replace the declaration of the shared memory array `tile` with the line below to allow for dynamic shared memory allocation. As observed in previous examples, a slight performance degradation is expected.

```
extern __shared__ float tile[];
```

From the results shown in Table 5-5, you can see that unrolling by two blocks provides a significant performance improvement on both the Tesla K40 and Tesla M2090.

TABLE 5-5: Performance of Transpose Kernels

KERNELS	TESLA M2090 (ECC OFF)		TESLA K40 (ECC OFF)	
	ELAPSED TIME (MS)	BANDWIDTH (GB/S)	ELAPSED TIME (MS)	BANDWIDTH (GB/S)
copyGmem (upper bound)	1.048	128.07	0.758	177.15
naiveGmem (lower bound)	3.611	37.19	1.947	68.98
transposeSmem	1.551	86.54	1.149	116.82
transposeSmemPad	1.416	94.79	1.102	121.83
transposeSmemUnrollPad	1.036	129.55	0.732	183.34
transposeSmemUnrollPadDyn	1.039	129.18	0.732	183.33

By unrolling by two blocks, more memory requests are simultaneously in-flight and read/write throughput improves as a result. This can be checked using the following `nvprof` metrics:

```
dram_read_throughput: Device Memory Read Throughput
dram_write_throughput: Device Memory Write Throughput
```

The `nvprof` results on the Tesla K40 are summarized below. The throughput for the unrolled kernel is improved nearly 1.5 times.

```
Kernel: transposeSmemUnrollPad(float*, float*, int, int)
    1    dram_read_throughput    94.135GB/s
    1    dram_write_throughput   94.128GB/s
Kernel: transposeSmemUnrollPadDyn(float*, float*, int, int)
```

```
    1    dram_read_throughput    94.112GB/s
    1    dram_write_throughput   94.110GB/s
Kernel: transposeSmemPad(float*, float*, int, int)
    1    dram_read_throughput    62.087GB/s
    1    dram_write_throughput   62.071GB/s
Kernel: transposeSmem (float*, float*, int, int)
    1    dram_read_throughput    59.646GB/s
    1    dram_write_throughput   59.636GB/s
Kernel: naiveGmem(float*, float*, int, int)
    1    dram_read_throughput    34.791GB/s
    1    dram_write_throughput   44.497GB/s
Kernel: copyGmem(float*, float*, int, int)
    1    dram_read_throughput    94.018GB/s
    1    dram_write_throughput   94.011GB/s
```

Exposing More Parallelism

One simple but effective optimization technique is the adjustment of thread block dimensions to discover the best execution configuration. Table 5-6 summarizes test results on the Tesla K40 for a variety of thread block configurations. The block size 16×16 demonstrates the best performance because it exposes the most device parallelism with more concurrent thread blocks.

TABLE 5-6: Performance of Transpose Kernels Using Different Thread Block Configurations

KERNELS	BLOCK SIZE (32X32)		BLOCK SIZE (32X16)		BLOCK SIZE (16X16)	
	ELAPSED TIME (MS)	BANDWIDTH (GB/S)	ELAPSED TIME (MS)	BANDWIDTH (GB/S)	ELAPSED TIME (MS)	BANDWIDTH (GB/S)
SmemUnrollPad	0.779	172.21	0.732	183.34	0.723	185.66
SmemUnrollPadDyn	0.782	171.55	0.732	183.33	0.722	185.99

Table 5-7 summarizes Tesla K40 nvprof results for global memory throughput and shared memory bank conflicts collected from the transposeSmemUnrollPadDyn kernel. While a thread block configuration of 32×16 minimizes bank conflicts, global memory throughput is maximized by a thread block configuration of 16×16. From this, you can conclude that this kernel is bound more by global memory throughput than shared memory throughput.

TABLE 5-7: Performance of Transpose Kernels under Different Block Size

METRICS	BLOCK SIZE (32X32)	BLOCK SIZE (32X16)	BLOCK SIZE (16X16)
gst_throughput	87.724 GB/s	94.118 GB/s	95.010 GB/s
gld_throughput	87.724 GB/s	94.118 GB/s	95.010 GB/s
shared_load_transactions_per_request	2.000	1.000	1.000
shared_store_transactions_per_ request	1.046	1.000	1.625

CONSTANT MEMORY

Constant memory is a special-purpose memory used for data that is read-only and accessed uniformly by threads in a warp. While constant memory is read-only from kernel codes, it is both readable and writable from the host.

Constant memory resides in device DRAM (like global memory) and has a dedicated on-chip cache. Like the L1 cache and shared memory, reading from the per-SM constant cache has a much lower latency than reading directly from constant memory. There is 64 KB limit on the size of constant memory cache per SM.

Constant memory has a different optimal access pattern than any of the other types of memory studied so far in this book. It is best if all threads in a warp access the same location in constant memory. Accesses to different addresses by threads within a warp are serialized. Thus, the cost of a constant memory read scales linearly with the number of unique addresses read by threads within a warp.

Constant variables must be declared in global scope with the following qualifier:

```
__constant__
```

Constant memory variables exist for the lifespan of the application and are accessible from all threads within a grid and from the host through runtime functions. Constant memory variables can be visible across multiple source files when using the CUDA separate compilation capability (more details on separate compilation in Chapter 10). Because the device is only able to read constant memory, values in constant memory must be initialized from host code using the following runtime function:

```
cudaError_t cudaMemcpyToSymbol(const void *symbol, const void * src,
                size_t count, size_t offset, cudaMemcpyKind kind)
```

The function `cudaMemcpyToSymbol` copies the data pointed to by `src` to the constant memory location specified by `symbol` on the device. The enum variable `kind` specifies the direction of the transfer. By default, `kind` is `cudaMemcpyHostToDevice`.

Implementing a 1D Stencil with Constant Memory

In the numerical analysis domain, a stencil computation applies a function to a collection of geometric points and updates the value of a single point with the output. Stencils are the basis for many algorithms that solve partial differential equations. In one dimension, a nine-point stencil around a point at position x would apply some function to the values at these positions:

$$\{x - 4h, x - 3h, x - 2h, x - h, x, x + h, x + 2h, x + 3h, x + 4h\}$$

A nine-point stencil is illustrated in Figure 5-18.

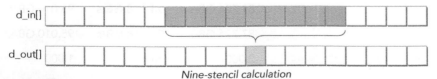

Nine-stencil calculation

FIGURE 5-18

An example of a nine-point stencil is the eighth-order centered difference formula for the first derivative of a function f of a real variable at a point x. While it is not important to understand the application of this formula, simply recognize that it takes as input the nine points described above and produces a single output. This formula will be used as an example stencil during this section.

$$f'(x) \approx c_0 \left(f(x+4h) - f(x-4h) \right) + c_1 \left(f(x+3h) - f(x-3h) \right) - c_2 \left(f(x+2h) - f(x-2h) \right) + c_3 \left(f(x+h) - f(x-h) \right)$$

Applying this formula across a 1D array is a data parallel operation that maps well to CUDA. You assign a position x to each thread and have it calculate $f'(x)$. You can follow along with code for this example by downloading constantStencil.cu from Wrox.com.

Now, where can constant memory be applied in this stencil computation? In the case of the preceding stencil formula, the coefficients c0, c1, c2, and c3 are the same across all threads and are never modified. This makes them excellent candidates for constant memory because they are read-only and will exhibit a broadcast access pattern: Every thread in a warp references the same constant memory location at the same time.

The following kernel implements a 1D stencil calculation based on the preceding formula. Because each thread takes nine points to calculate one point, you will want to use shared memory to cache data in order to reduce redundant accesses to global memory.

```
__shared__ float smem[BDIM + 2 * RADIUS];
```

RADIUS defines the number of points on either side of a point x that are used to calculate its value. For this example, RADIUS is defined as four to form a nine-point stencil: Four points on either side of x plus the value at position x. As illustrated in Figure 5-19, each block needs a halo of RADIUS elements at its left and right boundaries.

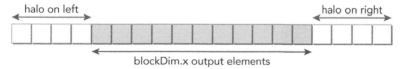

FIGURE 5-19

Calculating the index to access global memory can be done using:

```
int idx = blockIdx.x * blockDim.x + threadIdx.x;
```

Calculating the index for each thread to access shared memory is done as follows:

```
int sidx = threadIdx.x + RADIUS;
```

While reading data from global memory to shared memory, the first four threads are responsible for reading data from the halo on the left and from the halo on the right into shared memory, as follows:

```
if (threadIdx.x < RADIUS) {
    smem[sidx - RADIUS] = in[idx - RADIUS];
    smem[sidx + BDIM] = in[idx + BDIM];
}
```

The stencil calculation is straightforward. Note the `coef` array is the constant memory array that holds the coefficients discussed above. Also, `#pragma unroll` is used as a hint to the CUDA compiler that this loop should be automatically unrolled.

```
#pragma unroll
for( int i = 1; i <= RADIUS; i++) {
    tmp += coef[i] * (smem[sidx+i] - smem[sidx-i]);
}
```

Because the finite difference coefficients are stored in constant memory, which is prepared by the host thread, you simply access them in your kernel as you would access an array. The full kernel is the following:

```
__global__ void stencil_1d(float *in, float *out) {
    // shared memory
    __shared__ float smem[BDIM + 2*RADIUS];

    // index to global memory
    int idx = threadIdx.x + blockIdx.x * blockDim.x;

    // index to shared memory for stencil calculatioin
    int sidx = threadIdx.x + RADIUS;

    // Read data from global memory into shared memory
    smem[sidx] = in[idx];

    // read halo part to shared memory
    if (threadIdx.x < RADIUS) {
        smem[sidx - RADIUS] = in[idx - RADIUS];
        smem[sidx + BDIM] = in[idx + BDIM];
    }

    // Synchronize (ensure all the data is available)
    __syncthreads();

    // Apply the stencil
    float tmp = 0.0f;
    #pragma unroll
    for (int i = 1; i <= RADIUS; i++) {
        tmp += coef[i] * (smem[sidx+i] - smem[sidx-i]);
    }

    // Store the result
    out[idx] = tmp;
}
```

Declaring the `coef` array in constant memory is as simple as:

```
__constant__ float coef[RADIUS + 1];
```

Initializing constant memory from the host side is then done using the `cudaMemcpyToSymbol` CUDA API call:

```
void setup_coef_constant(void) {
    const float h_coef[] = {a0, a1, a2, a3, a4};
```

```
    cudaMemcpyToSymbol(coef, h_coef, (RADIUS + 1) * sizeof(float));
}
```

Comparing with the Read-Only Cache

Kepler GPUs add the ability to use the GPU texture pipeline as a read-only cache for data stored in global memory. Because this is a separate read-only cache with separate memory bandwidth from normal global memory reads, use of this feature can yield a performance benefit for bandwidth-limited kernels.

There is a total of 48 KB of read-only cache per Kepler SM. Generally, the read-only cache is better for scattered reads than the L1 cache, and should not be used when threads in a warp all read the same address. The granularity of the read-only cache is 32 bytes.

To access global memory through the read-only cache, you need to indicate to the compiler that data is read-only for the duration of a kernel. There are two ways to achieve this:

➤ Using an intrinsic function __ldg

➤ Qualifying pointers to global memory

The intrinsic __ldg is used in place of a normal pointer dereference to force a load to go through the read-only data cache, as shown in the following code snippet:

```
__global__ void kernel(float* output, float* input) {
    ...
    output[idx] += __ldg(&input[idx]);
    ...
}
```

You can also qualify pointers as const __restrict__ to indicate that they should be accessed through the read-only cache:

```
void kernel(float* output, const float* __restrict__ input) {
    ...
    output[idx] += input[idx];
}
```

In cases where more explicit control over the read-only cache mechanism is desired, or where the code is sufficiently complex that the compiler may be unable to detect that read-only cache use is safe, the intrinsic __ldg is a better choice.

The read-only cache is separate and distinct from the constant cache. Data loaded through the constant cache must be relatively small and must be accessed uniformly for good performance (all threads of a warp should access the same location at any given time), whereas data loaded through the read-only cache can be much larger and can be accessed in a non-uniform pattern.

The following kernel is revised from the previous stencil kernel. It uses the read-only cache to store the coefficients that were previously stored in constant memory. If you compare the two kernels, you will discover the only difference is the function declaration.

```
__global__ void stencil_1d_read_only (float* in,
        float* out, const float *__restrict__ dcoef) {
    // shared memory
```

```
    __shared__ float smem[BDIM + 2*RADIUS];

    // index to global memory
    int idx = threadIdx.x + blockIdx.x * blockDim.x;

    // index to shared memory for stencil calculatioin
    int sidx = threadIdx.x + RADIUS;

    // Read data from global memory into shared memory
    smem[sidx] = in[idx];

    // read halo part to shared memory
    if (threadIdx.x < RADIUS) {
        smem[sidx - RADIUS] = in[idx - RADIUS];
        smem[sidx + BDIM]   = in[idx + BDIM];
    }

    // Synchronize (ensure all the data is available)
    __syncthreads();

    // Apply the stencil
    float tmp = 0.0f;
    #pragma unroll
    for (int i=1; i<=RADIUS; i++) {
        tmp += dcoef[i]*(smem[sidx+i]-smem[sidx-i]);
    }

    // Store the result
    out[idx] = tmp;
}
```

Because the coefficients are stored originally in global memory and read into cache, before invoking the kernel you must allocate and initialize global memory to store the coefficients on the device, as follows:

```
const float h_coef[] = {a0, a1, a2, a3, a4};
cudaMalloc((float**)&d_coef, (RADIUS + 1) * sizeof(float));
cudaMemcpy(d_coef, h_coef, (RADIUS + 1) * sizeof(float), cudaMemcpyHostToDevice);
```

You can download the file constantReadOnly.cu containing this code from Wrox.com. The following results measured by nvprof on a Tesla K40 show that performance actually degrades while using read-only memory for this application. This is due to the broadcast access pattern used for the coef array, which is more optimized for constant memory than for the read-only cache:

```
Tesla K40c array size: 16777216 (grid, block) 524288,32
    3.4517ms  stencil_1d(float*, float*)
    3.6816ms  stencil_1d_read_only(float*, float*, float const *)
```

> ### CONSTANT CACHE VERSUS READ-ONLY CACHE
>
> ➤ Both constant cache and read-only cache are read-only from the device.
>
> ➤ Both have limited per-SM resources: The constant cache is 64 KB, and the read-only cache is 48 KB.
>
> ➤ Constant cache performs better on uniform reads (where every thread in a warp accesses the same address).
>
> ➤ Read-only cache is better for scattered reads.

THE WARP SHUFFLE INSTRUCTION

In this chapter, you have already learned how to perform low-latency exchanges of data between threads in a thread block using shared memory. Starting with the Kepler family of GPUs (compute capability 3.0 or higher), the *shuffle* instruction was introduced as a mechanism to allow threads to directly read another thread's register, as long as both threads are in the same warp.

The shuffle instruction enables threads in a warp to exchange data with each other directly, rather than going through shared or global memory. The shuffle instruction has lower latency than shared memory and does not consume extra memory to perform a data exchange. The shuffle instruction therefore offers an attractive way for applications to rapidly interchange data among threads in a warp.

Because the shuffle instruction is performed between threads within a warp, it is important to first introduce the concept of a *lane* in a warp. A lane simply refers to a single thread within a warp. Each lane in a warp is uniquely identified by a *lane index* in the range [0,31]. Each thread in a warp has a unique lane index, though multiple threads in the same thread block can have the same lane index (just as multiple threads in the same grid can have the same value for threadIdx.x). However, there is no built-in variable for lane index as there is for thread index. In a 1D thread block, the lane index and warp index for a given thread can be calculated as:

```
laneID = threadIdx.x % 32
warpID = threadIdx.x / 32
```

For example, threads 1 and 33 in a thread block would both have lane ID 1, but different warp IDs. For 2D thread blocks, you can convert a 2D thread coordinate into a 1D thread index, and apply the preceding formulas to determine the lane and warp indices.

Variants of the Warp Shuffle Instruction

There are two sets of shuffle instructions: one for integer variables and another for float variables. Each set has four variants of the shuffle instruction. To exchange integer variables within a warp, the basic function signature is as follows:

```
int __shfl(int var, int srcLane, int width=warpSize);
```

The intrinsic instruction __shfl returns the value var passed to __shfl by the thread in the same warp identified by srcLane. The meaning of srcLane changes depending on the value of width (more details below). This function makes it possible for each thread in a warp to directly fetch a value from a specific thread. This operation occurs simultaneously for all active threads within a warp, moving 4 bytes of data per thread.

Optionally, the variable width can be set to any power-of-2 between 2 and 32, inclusive. When set to the default warpSize (that is, 32) a shuffle instruction is performed across the entire warp and srcLane specifies the lane index of the source thread. However, setting width permits subdivision of a warp into segments containing width threads each, with a separate shuffle operation performed in each segment. For values of width other than 32, the lane ID of a thread and its ID in a shuffle operation are not necessarily equal. In that case, the shuffle ID of a thread in a 1D thread block can be calculated as:

```
shuffleID = threadIdx.x % width;
```

For example, if shfl were called from every thread in a warp with the following arguments:

```
int y = shfl(x, 3, 16);
```

Then threads 0 through 15 would receive the value of x from thread 3, and threads 16 through 31 would receive the value of x from thread 19 (the thread with offset 3 in the top 16 threads of the warp). For simplicity, srcLane will be referred to as a lane index for the remainder of this section.

When the lane index passed to shfl is the same value for all threads in a warp, the instruction performs a warp broadcast operation from the specified lane to all threads in the warp, as illustrated in Figure 5-20.

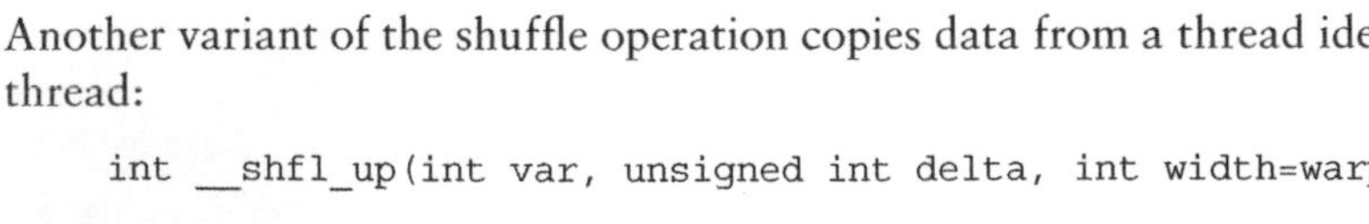

_shfl (val,2): a broadcast from lane 2 to all threads in the warp

FIGURE 5-20

Another variant of the shuffle operation copies data from a thread identified relative to the calling thread:

```
int __shfl_up(int var, unsigned int delta, int width=warpSize)
```

__shfl_up calculates the source lane index by subtracting delta from the caller's lane index. The value held by the source thread is returned. Hence, this instruction shifts var up the warp by delta lanes. There is no wrap around with __shfl_up, so the lowest delta threads in a warp will be unchanged, as illustrated in Figure 5-21.

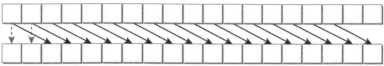

_shfl_up (val,2): Shift the value to the right two lanes.

FIGURE 5-21

The third variant of the shuffle instruction instead copies from a thread with higher index relative to the calling thread:

```
int __shfl_down(int var, unsigned int delta, int width=warpSize)
```

__shfl_down calculates a source lane index by adding delta to the caller's lane index. The value held by the source thread is returned. Hence, this instruction shifts var down the warp by delta lanes. There is no wrap around when using __shfl_down, so the upper delta lanes in a warp will remain unchanged, as illustrated in Figure 5-22.

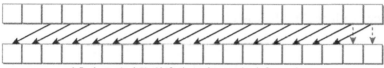

_shfl_down (val,2): Shift the value to the left two lanes.

FIGURE 5-22

The last variant of the shuffle instruction transfers data from a lane based on a bitwise XOR of the caller's own lane index:

```
int __shfl_xor(int var, int laneMask, int width=warpSize)
```

The intrinsic instruction calculates a source lane index by performing a bitwise XOR of the caller's lane index with laneMask. The value held by the source thread is returned. This instruction facilitates a butterfly addressing pattern, as illustrated in Figure 5-23.

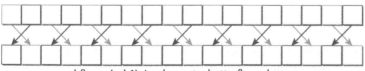

_shfl_xor (val,1): Implement a butterfly exchange.

FIGURE 5-23

All of the shuffle functions discussed in this section also support single-precision floating-point values. Floating-point shuffle functions take a float for the var argument, and return a float. Otherwise, their usage is identical to integer shuffle functions.

Sharing Data within a Warp

In this section, several examples of the warp shuffle instruction will be used to illustrate its benefits. Shuffle instructions will be applied to the following three integer variable types:

➤ Scalar variable

➤ Array

➤ Vector-typed variable

Broadcast of a Value across a Warp

The following kernel implements a warp-level broadcast operation. Each thread has one register variable value. The source lane is specified by the variable srcLane, which is equal across all threads. Each thread directly copies the value from the source thread.

```
__global__ void test_shfl_broadcast(int *d_out, int *d_in, int const srcLane) {
    int value = d_in[threadIdx.x];
    value = __shfl(value, srcLane, BDIMX);
    d_out[threadIdx.x] = value;
}
```

For simplicity, a 1D thread block with 16 threads is used:

```
#define BDIMX 16
```

The kernel is invoked as follows. The source lane is set by the third argument to test_shfl_broadcast to be the third thread in each warp. Two pieces of global memory are passed to the kernel: the input data and the output data.

```
test_shfl_broadcast<<<1, BDIMX>>>(d_outData, d_inData, 2);
```

You can download this sample code in the file simpleShfl.cu from Wrox.com. The initial value for each thread in the warp is set according to its own thread index. After the __shfl call, the third thread (which is in lane 2 with value equal to 2) broadcasts its value to all other threads. The following result is reported on a Tesla K40 under CUDA 6.0:

```
initialData:  0  1  2  3  4  5  6  7  8  9 10 11 12 13 14 15
shfl bcast :  2  2  2  2  2  2  2  2  2  2  2  2  2  2  2  2
```

Shift Up within a Warp

The following kernel implements the shuffle shift-up operation. The source lane for each thread in a warp is unique and determined by subtracting delta from its own thread index.

```
__global__ void test_shfl_up(int *d_out, int *d_in, unsigned int const delta) {
    int value = d_in[threadIdx.x];
    value = __shfl_up(value, delta, BDIMX);
    d_out[threadIdx.x] = value;
}
```

This kernel is included in the same file `simpleShfl.cu`. Invoke the kernel by specifying a `delta` of 2:

```
test_shfl_up<<<1, BDIMX>>>(d_outData, d_inData, 2);
```

As a result, the value of each thread is shifted to the right by two lanes, as shown in the following result. The values in the two leftmost lanes are unchanged.

```
initialData:  0  1  2  3  4  5  6  7  8  9 10 11 12 13 14 15
shfl up    :  0  1  0  1  2  3  4  5  6  7  8  9 10 11 12 13
```

Shift Down within a Warp

The following kernel implements the shift-down operation. The source thread for each thread in a warp is unique and determined by adding `delta` to its own thread index.

```
__global__ void test_shfl_down(int *d_out, int *d_in, unsigned int const delta) {
    int value = d_in[threadIdx.x];
    value = __shfl_down(value, delta, BDIMX);
    d_out[threadIdx.x] = value;
}
```

This kernel is included in the same file `simpleShfl.cu`. Invoke the kernel by specifying a `delta` of 2:

```
test_shfl_down<<<1, BDIMX>>>(d_outData, d_inData, 2);
```

The value of each thread is shifted to the left by two lanes, as shown in the following result. The values in the two rightmost lanes are unchanged.

```
initialData:  0  1  2  3  4  5  6  7  8  9 10 11 12 13 14 15
shfl down  :  2  3  4  5  6  7  8  9 10 11 12 13 14 15 14 15
```

Shift within a warp with Wrap Around

The following kernel implements the shift wrap-around operation across a warp. The source lane for each thread is different and determined by adding `offset` from its own lane index. The offset can be either positive or negative.

```
__global__ void test_shfl_wrap(int *d_out, int *d_in, int const offset) {
    int value = d_in[threadIdx.x];
    value = __shfl(value, threadIdx.x + offset, BDIMX);
    d_out[threadIdx.x] = value;
}
```

Invoke the kernel by specifying a positive offset as follows:

```
test_shfl_wrap<<<1,BDIMX>>>(d_outData, d_inData, 2);
```

This kernel implements a shift-to-left wrap-around operation, as shown below. Unlike the result generated by `test_shfl_down`, the values for the two rightmost lanes are changed here.

```
initialData     :  0  1  2  3  4  5  6  7  8  9 10 11 12 13 14 15
shfl wrap left  :  2  3  4  5  6  7  8  9 10 11 12 13 14 15  0  1
```

Invoke the kernel by specifying a negative offset as follows:

```
test_shfl_wrap <<< 1, block >>>(d_outData, d_inData, -2);
```

The kernel performed a shift to a right wrap-around operation as shown below. This test is similar to the test_shfl_up kernel except the two leftmost lanes are changed here.

```
initialData     :  0  1  2  3  4  5  6  7  8  9 10 11 12 13 14 15
shfl wrap right: 14 15  0  1  2  3  4  5  6  7  8  9 10 11 12 13
```

Butterfly Exchange across the Warp

The following kernel implements a butterfly addressing pattern between two threads, determined by the calling thread and the thread mask.

```
__global__ void test_shfl_xor(int *d_out, int *d_in, int const mask) {
    int value = d_in[threadIdx.x];
    value = __shfl_xor (value, mask, BDIMX);
    d_out[threadIdx.x] = value;
}
```

Invoking the kernel with mask as 1 will result in adjacent threads exchanging their values.

```
test_shfl_xor<<<1, BDIMX>>>(d_outData, d_inData, 1);
```

The output of this kernel launch is the following:

```
initialData:  0  1  2  3  4  5  6  7  8  9 10 11 12 13 14 15
shfl xor   :  1  0  3  2  5  4  7  6  9  8 11 10 13 12 15 14
```

Exchange Values of an Array across a Warp

Consider the situation where an array of registers is used in your kernel, and you want to exchange some part of the data among threads in a warp. You can use the shuffle instruction to exchange elements of an array among threads in a warp.

In the following kernel, each thread has an array of registers value with size SEGM. Each thread reads a chunk of data from global memory d_in into value, exchanges that chunk with a neighbor thread determined by mask, and then writes the received data back to the global memory array d_out.

```
__global__ void test_shfl_xor_array(int *d_out, int *d_in, int const mask) {
    int idx = threadIdx.x * SEGM;
    int value[SEGM];

    for (int i = 0; i < SEGM; i++) value[i] = d_in[idx + i];

    value[0] = __shfl_xor (value[0], mask, BDIMX);
    value[1] = __shfl_xor (value[1], mask, BDIMX);
    value[2] = __shfl_xor (value[2], mask, BDIMX);
    value[3] = __shfl_xor (value[3], mask, BDIMX);
```

```
        for (int i = 0;i < SEGM; i++) d_out[idx + i] = value[i];
    }
```

The array size is set to 4 by the following macro.

```
    #define SEGM   4
```

Because each thread holds 4 elements, the block size then is reduced to one fourth of the original size. Invoke the kernel as follows:

```
    test_shfl_xor_int4<<<1, BDIMX / SEGM>>>(d_outData, d_inData, 1);
```

Because the mask is set to 1, adjacent threads exchange their array values, as shown below:

```
    initialData:  0  1  2  3  4  5  6  7  8  9 10 11 12 13 14 15
    shfl array :  4  5  6  7  0  1  2  3 12 13 14 15  8  9 10 11
```

Exchange Values Using Array Indices Across a Warp

In the preceding kernel, the array elements being exchanged by each shuffle operation are from the same offset in each thread's local array. If you want to swap elements between two threads at different offsets in their respective arrays, you require a swap function based on the shuffle instruction.

The following function swaps a pair of values between two threads. The boolean variable pred is used to identify the first calling thread in a pair of threads that are exchanging data. The data elements to be swapped are identified by offset firstIdx in the first thread, and secondIdx in the second thread. The first calling thread starts by swapping the elements at firstIdx and secondIdx, but only in its local array. A butterfly exchange is then performed on the location secondIdx between two threads. Lastly, the first thread swaps the element received in secondIdx back to firstIdx.

```
    __inline__ __device__
void swap(int *value, int laneIdx, int mask, int firstIdx, int secondIdx) {
    bool pred = ((laneIdx / mask + 1) == 1);
    if (pred) {
        int tmp = value[firstIdx];
        value[firstIdx] = value[secondIdx];
        value[secondIdx]= tmp;
    }

    value[secondIdx] = __shfl_xor(value[secondIdx], mask, BDIMX);

    if (pred) {
        int tmp = value[firstIdx];
        value[firstIdx] = value[secondIdx];
        value[secondIdx]= tmp;
    }
}
```

The following kernel swaps two elements at different offsets between two threads based on the preceding swap function.

```
__global__
void test_shfl_swap(int *d_out, int *d_in, int const mask, int firstIdx,
                    int secondIdx) {
    int idx = threadIdx.x * SEGM;
    int value[SEGM];

    for (int i = 0; i < SEGM; i++) value[i] = d_in[idx + i];

    swap(value, threadIdx.x, mask, firstIdx, secondIdx);

    for (int i = 0; i < SEGM; i++) d_out[idx + i] = value[i];
}
```

Invoke the kernel by specifying the mask as 1, the first index as 0, and the second index as 3:

```
test_shfl_swap<<<1, block / SEGM >>>(d_outData, d_inData, 1, 0, 3);
```

These two functions are included in the same file simpleShfl.cu. As shown in the following results, for each pair of threads the first element in the array of the first calling thread is swapped with the fourth element in the array of the second calling thread.

```
initial   : 0  1  2  3  4  5  6  7  8  9 10 11 12 13 14 15
shfl swap : 7  1  2  3  4  5  6  0 15  9 10 11 12 13 14  8
```

Parallel Reduction Using the Warp Shuffle Instruction

In an earlier section, "Parallel Reduction with Shared Memory," you learned how to use shared memory to optimize parallel reduction algorithms. In this section, you will learn how to solve the same problem using warp shuffle instructions.

The basic idea is fairly simple. It consists of three levels of reduction:

➤   Warp-level reduction

➤   Block-level reduction

➤   Grid-level reduction

A thread block may have several warps. For warp-level reduction, each warp performs its own reduction. Instead of using shared memory, each thread uses a register to store one data element, reading from global memory:

```
int mySum = g_idata[idx];
```

Warp-level reduction is implemented as an inline function, as follows:

```
__inline__ __device__ int warpReduce(int mySum) {
  mySum += __shfl_xor(mySum, 16);
  mySum += __shfl_xor(mySum, 8);
  mySum += __shfl_xor(mySum, 4);
  mySum += __shfl_xor(mySum, 2);
  mySum += __shfl_xor(mySum, 1);
  return mySum;
}
```

Upon return from this function, each warp sum is saved to shared memory based on thread index and warp size, as shown:

```
int laneIdx = threadIdx.x % warpSize;
int warpIdx = threadIdx.x / warpSize;
mySum = warpReduce(mySum);
if (laneIdx == 0) smem[warpIdx] = mySum;
```

For block-level reduction, the block is synchronized and then the same warp reduction function is used to add together each warp's sum. The final output produced by the block is then saved to global memory by the first thread in the block, as shown:

```
__syncthreads();
mySum = (threadIdx.x < SMEMDIM) ? smem[laneIdx] : 0;
if (warpIdx == 0) mySum = warpReduce(mySum);
if (threadIdx.x == 0) g_odata[blockIdx.x] = mySum;
```

For the grid-level reduction, g_odata is copied back to the host where the final reduction is performed. Here is the complete reduceShfl kernel:

```
__global__ void reduceShfl(int *g_idata, int *g_odata, unsigned int n) {
    // shared memory for each warp sum
    __shared__ int smem[SMEMDIM];

    // boundary check
    unsigned int idx = blockIdx.x*blockDim.x + threadIdx.x;
    if (idx >= n) return;

    // read from global memory
    int mySum = g_idata[idx];

    // calculate lane index and warp index
    int laneIdx = threadIdx.x % warpSize;
    int warpIdx = threadIdx.x / warpSize;

    // block-wide warp reduce
    mySum = warpReduce(mySum);

    // save warp sum to shared memory
    if (laneIdx==0) smem[warpIdx] = mySum;

    // block synchronization
    __syncthreads();

    // last warp reduce
    mySum = (threadIdx.x < SMEMDIM) ? smem[laneIdx]:0;
    if (warpIdx==0) mySum = warpReduce(mySum);

    // write result for this block to global mem
    if (threadIdx.x == 0) g_odata[blockIdx.x] = mySum;
}
```

You can download the file `reduceIntegerShfl.cu` from `Wrox.com`. The result on Tesla K40 with CUDA 6.0 follows. You gain 1.42 times speedup from using the shuffle instruction to implement warp-level parallel reduction.

Time(%)	Time	Calls	Avg	Min	Max	Name
24.95%	4.0000us	1	4.0000us	4.0000us	4.0000us	reduceSmem()
17.76%	2.8480us	1	2.8480us	2.8480us	2.8480us	reduceShfl()

SUMMARY

To obtain maximum application performance, you need a memory hierarchy that can be explicitly managed. In C programming, there are no means to directly control data movement. In this chapter, you learned about different CUDA memory hierarchy types, such as shared memory, constant memory, and read-only cache. You learned how to explicitly control when data is brought in or evicted from shared memory to significantly improve performance. You also learned about the behavior of constant memory and the read-only cache and how to use them most effectively.

Shared memory can be declared as a 1D or 2D array, providing a simple logical view to ease programming. Physically, shared memory is one-dimensional, and is accessed through 32 banks. Avoiding bank conflicts is an important factor during application optimization of shared memory. Shared memory is partitioned among all resident thread blocks; therefore, it is a critical resource and might limit kernel occupancy.

There are two main reasons to use shared memory in a kernel. One is to cache data on-chip and reduce the amount of global memory traffic. The other is to transform how data is arranged in shared memory to avoid non-coalesced global memory accesses.

Constant memory is optimized for read-only data that is broadcast to many threads at a time. Constant memory also uses its own per-SM cache, preventing reads from constant memory from interfering with global memory accesses passing through the L1 cache. As a result, using constant memory for appropriate data will not only optimize the accesses to that particular item but also likely improve overall global memory throughput.

The read-only texture cache offers an alternative to constant memory that is more optimized for scattered reads of data. This read-only cache accesses data in global memory, but uses a separate memory access pipeline and separate cache to make that data accessible to the SM. As a result, the read-only cache shares many of its benefits with constant memory, but is optimized for a different access pattern.

The shuffle instruction is a warp-level intrinsic function that enables threads in a warp to share data with each other quickly and directly. The shuffle instruction has lower latency than shared memory and does not require allocating additional resources. Using the shuffle instruction can reduce the number of warp-synchronous optimizations for a kernel. However, in many cases the shuffle instruction is not a replacement for shared memory as shared memory is visible to an entire thread block.

This chapter went into depth on a number of special-purpose types of memory. Although the use of each of these memory types is less general than global memory, using them appropriately can improve bandwidth utilization and decrease overall memory latency. Keeping shared memory, constant memory, the read-only cache, and shuffle instructions in mind is important when you are investigating optimization opportunities.

CHAPTER 5 EXERCISES

1. Suppose you have a shared memory tile with dimensions [32][32]. Pad a column to it and then draw an illustration showing the mapping between data elements and banks for a Kepler device in 4-byte access mode.

2. Refer to the kernel `setRowReadCol` in the file `checkSmemSquare.cu`. Make a new kernel named `setColReadRow` to perform the operations of writing to columns and reading from rows. Check the memory transactions with `nvprof` and observe the output.

3. Refer to the kernel `setRowReadColDyn` in the file `checkSmemSquare.cu`. Make a new kernel named `setColReadRowDyn` that declares shared memory dynamically, and then perform the operations of writing to columns and reading from rows. Check the memory transactions with `nvprof` and observe the output.

4. Refer to the kernel `setRowReadColPad` in the file `checkSmemSquare.cu`. Make a new kernel named `setColReadRowPad` that pads by one column. Then, implement the operation of writing by columns and reading from rows. Check the memory transactions with `nvprof` and observe the output.

5. Suppose the size of the square shared memory array in `checkSmemSquare.cu` was 16×16 instead of 32×32. How would the number of shared memory transactions change on both Fermi and Kepler devices? Try to draw a picture of the shared memory arrangement in each case.

6. Refer to kernel `setRowReadCol` in the file `checkSmemRectangle.cu`. Make a new kernel named `setColReadRow` that writes by columns and reads by rows. Check the memory transactions with `nvprof` and observe the output.

7. Refer to the kernel `setRowReadColPad` in the file `checkSmemRectangle.cu`. Make a new kernel named `setColReadRowPad` that writes by columns and reads by rows. Check the memory transactions with `nvprof` and observe the output.

8. Refer to the file `reduceInteger.cu`. Test block sizes of 64, 128, 512, and 1024. Measure elapsed times for the kernels with `nvprof`. Determine the best execution configuration.

9. Refer to the kernel `stencil_1d_read_only`. Write a kernel using global memory to store the finite difference coefficients. Compare three kernels with `nvprof`: the kernel using constant cache, the one using read-only cache, and the one using global memory with L1 cache enabled.

10. Refer to kernel `test_shfl_up` in the file `simpleShfl.cu`, invoke it with a negative delta as follows:

    ```
    test_shfl_up<<<1, BDIMX>>>(d_outData, d_inData, -2);
    ```

    Check the results and reason about the output.

11. Refer to kernel `test_shfl_wrap` in the file `simpleShfl.cu`, make a new kernel that can generate the following result:

    ```
    Initial: 0  1  2  3  4  5  6  7  8  9 10 11 12 13 14 15
    Result : 2  4  6  8 10 12 14 16 18 20 22 24 26 28 14 16
    ```

12. Refer to the kernel `test_shfl_xor` in the file `simpleShfl.cu`, make a new kernel that can generate the following result:

    ```
    Initial: 0  1  2  3  4  5  6  7  8  9 10 11 12 13 14 15
    Result : 1  1  5  5  9  9 13 13 17 17 21 21 25 25 29 29
    ```

13. Refer to the kernel `test_shfl_xor_array` in the file `simpleShfl.cu`, make a new kernel that just performs one operation as follows:

    ```
    value[3] = __shfl_xor (value[0], mask, BDIMX);
    ```

    Check the result and reason about its cause.

14. Refer to the kernel `test_shfl_wrap` in the file `simpleShfl.cu`. Make a new kernel that can shift double-precision variables in a wrap-around warp approach.

15. Refer to the inline function `warpReduce` in the file `reduceIntegerShfl.cu`. Write an equivalent function that uses the `__shfl_down` instruction instead.

Streams and Concurrency

> **CODE DOWNLOAD** *The wrox.com code downloads for this chapter are found at* www.wrox.com/go/procudac *on the Download Code tab. The code is in the Chapter 6 download and individually named according to the names throughout the chapter.*

Generally speaking, there are two levels of concurrency in CUDA C programming:

➤ Kernel level concurrency

➤ Grid level concurrency

Up to this point, your focus has been solely on *kernel level concurrency*, in which a single task, or kernel, is executed in parallel by many threads on the GPU. Several ways to improve kernel performance have been covered from the programming model, execution model, and memory model points-of-view. You have developed your ability to dissect and analyze your kernel's behavior using the command-line profiler.

This chapter will examine *grid level concurrency*. In grid level concurrency, multiple kernel launches are executed simultaneously on a single device, often leading to better device utilization. In this chapter, you will learn how to use CUDA streams to implement grid level concurrency. You will also use the CUDA Visual Profiler nvvp to visualize concurrent kernel execution.

INTRODUCING STREAMS AND EVENTS

A CUDA *stream* refers to a sequence of asynchronous CUDA operations that execute on a device in the order issued by the host code. A stream encapsulates these operations, maintains their ordering, permits operations to be queued in the stream to be executed after all preceding operations, and allows for querying the status of queued operations. These operations can include host-device data transfer, kernel launches, and most other commands that are issued by the host but handled by the device. The execution of an operation in a stream is always asynchronous with respect to the host. The CUDA runtime will determine when that operation is eligible for execution on the device. It is your responsibility to use CUDA APIs to ensure an asynchronous operation has completed before using the result. While operations within the same CUDA stream have a strict ordering, operations in different streams have no restriction on execution order. By using multiple streams to launch multiple simultaneous kernels, you can implement *grid level concurrency*.

Because all operations queued in a CUDA stream are asynchronous, it is possible to overlap their execution with other operations in the host-device system. Doing so allows you to hide the cost of performing those operations by performing other useful work at the same time.

Throughout this book, a typical pattern in CUDA programming has been:

1. Move input data from the host to the device.

2. Execute a kernel on the device.

3. Move the result from the device back to the host.

In many cases, more time is spent executing the kernel than transferring data. In these situations, you may be able to completely hide CPU-GPU communication latency. By dispatching kernel execution and data transfer into separate streams, these operations can be overlapped, and the total elapsed time of the program can be shortened. Streams can be used to implement pipelining or double buffering at the granularity of CUDA API calls.

The functions in the CUDA API can generally be classified as either synchronous or asynchronous. Functions with *synchronous behavior* block the host thread until they complete. Functions with *asynchronous behavior* return control to the host immediately after being called. Asynchronous functions and streams are the two basic pillars on which you build grid-level concurrency in CUDA.

While from a software point of view CUDA operations in different streams run concurrently; that may not always be the case on physical hardware. Depending on PCIe bus contention or the availability of per-SM resources, different CUDA streams may still need to wait for each other in order to complete.

In this chapter, you will take a close look at how streams behave on devices with various compute capabilities.

CUDA Streams

All CUDA operations (both kernels and data transfers) either explicitly or implicitly run in a stream. There are two types of streams:

➤   Implicitly declared stream (NULL stream)

➤   Explicitly declared stream (non-NULL stream)

The *NULL stream* is the default stream that kernel launches and data transfers use if you do not explicitly specify a stream. All examples in the previous chapters of this book used the NULL or *default stream*.

On the other hand, *non-null streams* are explicitly created and managed. If you want to overlap different CUDA operations, you must use non-null streams. Asynchronous, stream-based kernel launches and data transfers enable the following types of *coarse-grain concurrency*:

➤   Overlapped host computation and device computation

➤   Overlapped host computation and host-device data transfer

➤   Overlapped host-device data transfer and device computation

➤   Concurrent device computation

Consider the following code snippet using the default stream:

```
cudaMemcpy(..., cudaMemcpyHostToDevice);
kernel<<<grid, block>>>(...);
cudaMemcpy(..., cudaMemcpyDeviceToHost);
```

To understand the behavior of a CUDA program, you should always consider it from the viewpoint of both the device and the host. From the device perspective, all three operations in the previous code segment are issued to the default stream, and are executed in the order that they were issued. The device has no awareness of any other host operations being performed. From the host perspective, each data transfer is synchronous and forces idle host time while waiting for them to complete. The kernel launch is asynchronous, and so the host application almost immediately resumes execution afterwards, regardless of whether the kernel completed or not. This default asynchronous behavior for kernel launches makes it straightforward to overlap device and host computation.

Data transfers can also be issued asynchronously; however, you must explicitly set the CUDA stream to place them in. The CUDA runtime provides the following asynchronous version of cudaMemcpy:

```
cudaError_t cudaMemcpyAsync(void* dst, const void* src, size_t count,
    cudaMemcpyKind kind, cudaStream_t stream = 0);
```

Note the added stream identifier as the fifth argument. By default, the stream identifier is set to the default stream. This function is asynchronous with respect to the host, so control returns to the host immediately after the call is issued. You can easily associate a copy operation with a non-null stream. However, first you will need to create a non-null stream using:

```
cudaError_t cudaStreamCreate(cudaStream_t* pStream);
```

cudaStreamCreate creates a non-null stream that you manage explicitly. The stream returned in pStream can then be used as the stream argument to cudaMemcpyAsync and other asynchronous CUDA API functions. One common point of confusion when using asynchronous CUDA functions is that they may return error codes from previously launched asynchronous operations. The API call returning an error is not necessarily the call that caused the error.

When performing an asynchronous data transfer, you must use pinned (or non-pageable) host memory. Pinned memory can be allocated using either cudaMallocHost or cudaHostAlloc:

```
cudaError_t cudaMallocHost(void **ptr, size_t size);
cudaError_t cudaHostAlloc(void **pHost, size_t size, unsigned int flags);
```

By pinning allocations in host virtual memory, you force its physical location in CPU memory to remain constant throughout the lifetime of an application. Otherwise, the operating system is free to change the physical location of host virtual memory at any time. If an asynchronous CUDA transfer were performed without pinned host memory, it would be possible for the operating system to physically move an array while the CUDA runtime was transferring it to the device, resulting in undefined behavior.

To launch a kernel in a non-default stream, you must provide a stream identifier as the fourth parameter in the kernel execution configuration:

```
kernel_name<<<grid, block, sharedMemSize, stream>>>(argument list);
```

A non-default stream is declared as follows:

```
cudaStream_t stream;
```

Non-default streams can be created using:

```
cudaStreamCreate(&stream);
```

The resources of a stream can be released using:

```
cudaError_t cudaStreamDestroy(cudaStream_t stream);
```

If there is still pending work in a stream when cudaStreamDestroy is called on that stream, cudaStreamDestroy returns immediately and the resources associated with the stream are released automatically when all work in the stream has completed.

Since all CUDA stream operations are asynchronous, the CUDA API provides two functions that allow you to check if all operations in a stream have completed:

```
cudaError_t cudaStreamSynchronize(cudaStream_t stream);
cudaError_t cudaStreamQuery(cudaStream_t stream);
```

cudaStreamSynchronize forces the host to block until all operations in the provided stream have completed. cudaStreamQuery checks if all operations in a stream have completed, but does not block the host if they have not completed. cudaStreamQuery returns cudaSuccess if all operations are complete or cudaErrorNotReady if one or more operation is still executing or pending execution.

To help illustrate how CUDA streams are used in practice, the following is a common pattern for dispatching CUDA operations to multiple streams.

```
for (int i = 0; i < nStreams; i++) {
   int offset = i * bytesPerStream;
   cudaMemcpyAsync(&d_a[offset], &a[offset], bytePerStream, streams[i]);
   kernel<<grid, block, 0, streams[i]>>(&d_a[offset]);
   cudaMemcpyAsync(&a[offset], &d_a[offset], bytesPerStream, streams[i]);
}

for (int i = 0; i < nStreams; i++) {
    cudaStreamSynchronize(streams[i]);
}
```

Figure 6-1 illustrates a simple timeline of CUDA operations using three streams. Both data transfer and kernel computation are evenly distributed among three concurrent streams.

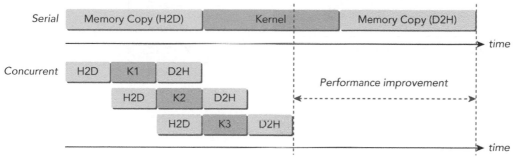

FIGURE 6-1

You might notice that the data transfer operations are not executed concurrently in Figure 6-1, even though they are issued in separate streams. This contention is caused by a shared resource: the PCIe bus. While these operations are independent from the point-of-view of the programming model, because they share a common hardware resource their execution must be serialized. Devices with a duplex PCIe bus can overlap two data transfers, but they must be in different streams and in different directions. In Figure 6-1, observe that data transfer from the host to the device in one stream is overlapped with data transfer from the device to the host in another.

The maximum number of concurrent kernels is device-dependent. Fermi devices support 16-way concurrency, and Kepler devices support 32-way concurrency. The number of concurrent kernels is further limited by available compute resource on devices, such as shared memory and registers. You will explore these limitations through examples later in this chapter.

Stream Scheduling

Conceptually, all streams can run simultaneously. However, this is not always the reality when mapping streams to physical hardware. This section will illustrate how concurrent kernel operations in multiple CUDA streams are scheduled by hardware.

False Dependencies

Although Fermi GPUs support 16-way concurrency — that is, up to 16 grids executing at once — all streams are ultimately multiplexed into a single hardware work queue. When selecting a grid to execute, the task at the front of the queue is scheduled by the CUDA runtime. The runtime checks for task dependencies, and waits for any tasks that this task depends on to complete if they are still executing. Finally, when all dependencies are satisfied the new task is dispatched to available SMs. This single pipeline may result in a *false dependency*. As illustrated in Figure 6-2, only the circled task pairs will eventually be executed concurrently because the runtime will block before launching every other grid. A blocked operation in the queue blocks all subsequent operations in the queue, even when they belong to different streams.

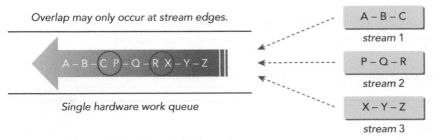

FIGURE 6-2

Hyper-Q

False dependencies are reduced in the Kepler family of GPUs using multiple hardware work queues, a technology called *Hyper-Q*. Hyper-Q allows multiple CPU threads or processes to launch work on a single GPU simultaneously by maintaining multiple hardware-managed connections between the host and the device. Existing applications that were limited by Fermi's false dependencies can see a dramatic performance increase without changing any existing code. Kepler GPUs use 32 hardware work queues and allocate one work queue per stream. If more than 32 streams are created, multiple streams will share a single hardware work queue. The result is full stream-level concurrency with minimal false inter-stream dependencies. Figure 6-3 illustrates a simple case with three streams on three hardware work queues.

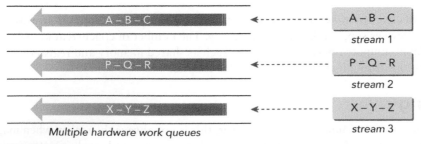

FIGURE 6-3

Stream Priorities

For devices with compute capability 3.5 or higher, streams can be assigned priorities. A stream is created with a specific priority using the following function:

```
cudaError_t cudaStreamCreateWithPriority(cudaStream_t* pStream, unsigned int flags,
    int priority);
```

This function creates a stream with the specified integer priority and returns a handle in pStream. This priority is associated with the work scheduled in pStream. Grids queued to a higher priority stream may preempt work already executing in a low priority stream. *Stream priorities* have no effect on data transfer operations, only on compute kernels. If the specified priority is outside the meaningful range for a device, it will automatically be clamped to the lowest or the highest number in the range. The allowable range of priorities for a given device can be queried using the following function:

```
cudaError_t cudaDeviceGetStreamPriorityRange(int *leastPriority,
    int *greatestPriority);
```

This function returns values in leastPriority and greatestPriority that correspond to the lowest and highest priorities for the current device. By convention, lower integer values indicate a higher stream priority. cudaDeviceGetStreamPriorityRange returns zero in both parameters if the current device does not support stream priorities.

CUDA Events

An *event* in CUDA is essentially a marker in a CUDA stream associated with a certain point in the flow of operations in that stream. You can use events to perform the following two basic tasks:

➤ Synchronize stream execution

➤ Monitor device progress

The CUDA API provides functions that allow you to insert events at any point in a stream as well as query for event completion. An event recorded on a given stream will only be satisfied (that is, complete) when all preceding operations in the same stream have completed. Events specified on the default stream apply to all preceding operations in all CUDA streams.

Creation and Destruction

An event is declared as follows:

```
cudaEvent_t event;
```

Once declared, the event can be created using:

```
cudaError_t cudaEventCreate(cudaEvent_t* event);
```

An event can be destroyed using:

```
cudaError_t cudaEventDestroy(cudaEvent_t event);
```

If the event has not yet been satisfied when `cudaEventDestroy` is called, the call returns immediately and the resources associated with that event are released automatically when the event is marked complete.

Recording Events and Measuring Elapsed Time

Events mark a point in stream execution. They can be used to check if the executing stream operations have reached a given point. You can think of them as operations added to a CUDA stream whose only action when popped from the head of the work queue is to raise a host-side flag to indicate completion. An event is queued to a CUDA stream using the following function:

```
cudaError_t cudaEventRecord(cudaEvent_t event, cudaStream_t stream = 0);
```

The passed event can be used to either wait for, or test for, the completion of all preceding operations in the specified stream. Waiting for an event blocks the calling host thread, and is performed using the following function:

```
cudaError_t cudaEventSynchronize(cudaEvent_t event);
```

`cudaEventSynchronize` is analogous to `cudaStreamSynchronize` for streams, but allows the host to wait for an intermediate point in stream execution.

You can also test if an event has completed without blocking the host application using:

```
cudaError_t cudaEventQuery(cudaEvent_t event);
```

`cudaEventQuery` is similar to `cudaStreamQuery`, but for events.

You can measure the elapsed time of CUDA operations marked by two events using the following function:

```
cudaError_t cudaEventElapsedTime(float* ms, cudaEvent_t start, cudaEvent_t stop);
```

This function returns the time elapsed between the events `start` and `stop` being satisfied, in milliseconds. The events `start` and `stop` do not need to be associated with the same CUDA stream. Take note that if either event was recorded in a non-NULL stream, the returned time might be greater than expected. This happens because `cudaEventRecord` takes place asynchronously, and there is no guarantee that the measured latency is actually just between the two events.

The following code sample illustrates how events are typically used to time device operations:

```
// create two events
cudaEvent_t start, stop;
cudaEventCreate(&start);
cudaEventCreate(&stop);

// record start event on the default stream
cudaEventRecord(start);

// execute kernel
kernel<<<grid, block>>>(arguments);
```

```
// record stop event on the default stream
cudaEventRecord(stop);

// wait until the stop event completes
cudaEventSynchronize(stop);

// calculate the elapsed time between two events
float time;
cudaEventElapsedTime(&time, start, stop);

// clean up the two events
cudaEventDestroy(start);
cudaEventDestroy(stop);
```

Here, the start and stop events are placed into the NULL stream by default. A timestamp is recorded for the start event at the beginning of the NULL stream, and a timestamp for the stop event at the end of the NULL stream. The elapsed time between the two events is then fetched using cudaEventElapsedTime.

Stream Synchronization

Because all operations in non-default streams are non-blocking with respect to the host thread, you will run across situations where you need to synchronize the host with operations running in a stream.

From the host point-of-view, CUDA operations can be classified into two main categories:

➤   Memory-related operations

➤   Kernel launches

Kernel launches are always asynchronous with respect to the host. Many memory operations are inherently synchronous (such as cudaMemcpy), but the CUDA runtime also provides asynchronous functions for performing memory operations.

As you already learned, there are two types of streams:

➤   Asynchronous streams (non-NULL streams)

➤   Synchronous streams (the NULL/default stream)

A non-null stream is an *asynchronous stream* with respect to the host; all operations applied to it do not block host execution. On the other hand, the NULL-stream, declared implicitly, is a *synchronous stream* with respect to the host. Most operations added to the NULL-stream cause the host to block on all preceding operations, the main exception being kernel launches.

Non-NULL streams can be further classified into the following two types:

➤   Blocking streams

➤   Non-blocking streams

Even though non-NULL streams are non-blocking with respect to the host, operations within a non-NULL stream can be blocked by operations in the NULL stream. If a non-NULL stream is a *blocking stream,* the NULL stream can block operations in it. If a non-NULL stream is a *non-blocking stream,* it will not block on operations in the NULL stream. In the following section, you will learn how to work with blocking and non-blocking streams.

Blocking and Non-Blocking Streams

Streams created using `cudaStreamCreate` are blocking streams, meaning the execution of operations in those streams can be blocked waiting for earlier operations in the NULL stream to complete. The NULL stream is an implicit stream, which synchronizes with all other blocking streams in the same CUDA context. In general, when an operation is issued to the NULL stream, the CUDA context waits on all operations previously issued to all blocking streams before starting that operation. Also, any operations issued to blocking streams will wait on preceding operations in the NULL stream to complete before executing.

For example, the following code launches `kernel_1` in `stream_1`, then `kernel_2` in the NULL stream, then `kernel_3` in `stream_2`:

```
kernel_1<<<1, 1, 0, stream_1>>>();
kernel_2<<<1, 1>>>();
kernel_3<<<1, 1, 0, stream_2>>>();
```

The resulting behavior is that `kernel_2` does not start executing on the GPU until `kernel_1` completes, and `kernel_3` does not start until `kernel_2` completes. Note that from the host's perspective, each kernel launch is still asynchronous and non-blocking.

The CUDA runtime provides a function that allows customization of a non-NULL stream's behavior in relation to the NULL stream:

```
cudaError_t cudaStreamCreateWithFlags(cudaStream_t* pStream, unsigned int flags);
```

The `flags` argument determines the behavior of the created stream. Valid values for `flags` are:

```
cudaStreamDefault: default stream creation flag (blocking)
cudaStreamNonBlocking: asynchronous stream creation flag (non-blocking)
```

Specifying `cudaStreamNonBlocking` disables the blocking behavior of non-NULL streams relative to the NULL stream. If `stream_1` and `stream_2` in the previous example were created with `cudaStreamNonBlocking`, none of the kernel executions would be blocked waiting for completion of any of the other kernels.

Implicit Synchronization

CUDA includes two types of host-device synchronization: explicit and implicit. You have already seen many functions that perform explicit synchronization: `cudaDeviceSynchronize`, `cudaStreamSynchronize`, and `cudaEventSynchronize`. These functions are explicitly called by the host to synchronize the execution of tasks on the device with the host thread. You manually insert explicit synchronization calls at logical points in your application.

You have also already seen examples of implicit synchronization. For example, a call to `cudaMemcpy` implicitly synchronizes the device and host because the host application blocks until the data transfer completes. However, as the main purpose of this function is not synchronization, its synchronization side effects are implicit. It is important to be aware of implicit synchronization because inadvertently calling a function that implicitly synchronizes the host and device may lead to unexpected performance degradation.

Implicit synchronization is of special interest in CUDA programming because runtime functions with implicit synchronization behavior may cause unwanted blocking, usually at the device level. Many memory-related operations imply blocking on all previous operations on the current device, such as:

➤ A page-locked host memory allocation

➤ A device memory allocation

➤ A device memset

➤ A memory copy between two addresses on the same device

➤ A modification to the L1/shared memory configuration

Explicit Synchronization

The CUDA runtime supports several ways of explicitly synchronizing a CUDA program at the grid level:

➤ Synchronizing the device

➤ Synchronizing a stream

➤ Synchronizing an event in a stream

➤ Synchronizing across streams using an event

You can block a host thread until the device has completed all preceding tasks with the following function:

```
cudaError_t cudaDeviceSynchronize(void);
```

This function causes the host thread to wait for all computation and communication associated with the current device to finish. As this is a relatively heavyweight synchronization function, it should be used sparingly to avoid stalling the host.

You can block the host thread until all operations in a stream complete using cudaStreamSynchronize, or perform a non-blocking test for completion using cudaStreamQuery:

```
cudaError_t cudaStreamSynchronize(cudaStream_t stream);
cudaError_t cudaStreamQuery(cudaStream_t stream);
```

CUDA events can also be used for fine-grain blocking and synchronization using cudaEventSynchronize and cudaEventQuery:

```
cudaError_t cudaEventSynchronize(cudaEvent_t event);
cudaError_t cudaEventQuery(cudaEvent_t event);
```

Additionally, `cudaStreamWaitEvent` offers a flexible way to introduce inter-stream dependencies using CUDA events:

```
cudaError_t cudaStreamWaitEvent(cudaStream_t stream, cudaEvent_t event);
```

`cudaStreamWaitEvent` causes the specified `stream` to wait on the specified `event` before executing any operations queued in `stream` after the call to `cudaStreamWaitEvent`. The event may be associated with either the same stream, or a different stream. In the latter case, this function performs cross-stream synchronization, as illustrated in Figure 6-4. Here, the wait issued by stream 2 ensures that the event created in stream 1 is satisfied before continuing.

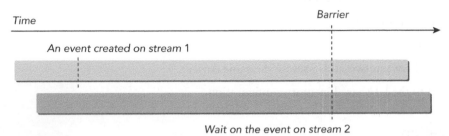

FIGURE 6-4

Configurable Events

The CUDA runtime provides a way to customize the behavior and properties of events:

```
cudaError_t cudaEventCreateWithFlags(cudaEvent_t* event, unsigned int flags);
```

Valid flags include:

```
cudaEventDefault
cudaEventBlockingSync
cudaEventDisableTiming
cudaEventInterprocess
```

The flag `cudaEventBlockingSync` specifies that synchronizing on this event with `cudaEventSynchronize` will block the calling thread. The default behavior of `cudaEventSynchronize` is to spin on the event, using CPU cycles to constantly check the event's status. With `cudaEventBlockingSync` set, the calling thread instead gives up the core it is running on to another thread or process by going to sleep until the event is satisfied. While this can lead to fewer wasted CPU cycles if other useful work can be done, it also can lead to longer latencies between an event being satisfied and the calling thread being activated.

Passing `cudaEventDisableTiming` indicates that the created event is only used for synchronization and does not need to record timing data. Removing the overhead of taking timestamps improves the performance of calls to `cudaStreamWaitEvent` and `cudaEventQuery`.

The flag `cudaEventInterprocess` indicates that the created event may be used as an inter-process event.

CONCURRENT KERNEL EXECUTION

Now that the concepts and APIs for streams, events, and synchronization have been explained, it is time to experiment using several examples. The first example shows how to run multiple kernels concurrently using multiple streams. This simple example will demonstrate several essential issues concerning concurrent kernel execution, including:

➤ Dispatching jobs with the depth-first or breadth-first approach

➤ Adjusting hardware work queues

➤ Avoiding false dependencies on Kepler and Fermi devices

➤ Checking the blocking behavior of the default stream

➤ Adding dependencies between non-default streams

➤ Examining how resource usage affects concurrency

Concurrent Kernels in Non-NULL Streams

In this section, you will use the NVIDIA Visual Profiler (nvvp) to visualize concurrent kernel executions. The kernel used in this example contains dummy computation to simulate useful work being done on the device. This ensures that kernels are resident on the GPU for a long enough period of time so that the overlap is apparent in the Visual Profiler. Note that this example uses multiple identical kernels (named `kernel_1`, `kernel_2`, ...):

```
__global__ void kernel_1() {
   double sum = 0.0;
   for (int i = 0; i < N; i++) {
      sum = sum + tan(0.1) * tan(0.1);
   }
}
```

This is done to make it easier to visualize the execution of different kernels in nvvp.

A set of non-null streams must be created first. Kernel launches issued in each of these streams should run concurrently on the GPU, provided there are no false dependencies due to hardware resource limitations.

```
cudaStream_t *streams = (cudaStream_t *)malloc(n_streams * sizeof(cudaStream_t));
for (int i = 0 ; i < n_streams; i++) {
   cudaStreamCreate(&streams[i]);
}
```

Kernels can then be dispatched in each of these streams using a loop to iterate over streams:

```
dim3 block(1);
dim3 grid(1);
for (int i = 0; i < n_streams; i++) {
   kernel_1<<<grid, block, 0, streams[i]>>>();
   kernel_2<<<grid, block, 0, streams[i]>>>();
```

```
        kernel_3<<<grid, block, 0, streams[i]>>>();
        kernel_4<<<grid, block, 0, streams[i]>>>();
    }
```

The execution configuration for these kernel launches is specified as a single thread in a single thread block in order to ensure sufficient GPU resources to run all kernels concurrently. Because each kernel launch is asynchronous with respect to the host, you can dispatch multiple kernels to different streams using a single host thread at approximately the same time.

To measure elapsed time in this example, two events are also created:

```
    cudaEvent_t start, stop;
    cudaEventCreate(&start);
    cudaEventCreate(&stop);
```

The start event is recorded in the default stream before the loop that launches all kernels. The stop event is recorded in the default stream after all kernels have launched.

```
    cudaEventRecord(start);
    for (int i = 0; i < n_streams; i++) {
        ...
    }
    cudaEventRecord(stop);
```

After synchronizing on the stop event, elapsed time can be calculated:

```
    cudaEventSynchronize(stop);
    cudaEventElapsedTime(&elapsed_time, start, stop);
```

This example can be downloaded in the file simpleHyperqDepth.cu from Wrox.com. It can be compiled using nvcc and when run on a Tesla K40, produces the following output:

```
$ ./simpleHyperq
> Using Device 0: Tesla K40c with num_streams=4
> Compute Capability 3.5 hardware with 15 multi-processors
Measured time for parallel execution = 0.079s
```

The NVIDIA Visual Profiler (nvvp) is included with the CUDA Toolkit. nvvp makes it easy to collect performance metrics (similar to nvprof) but also allows you to visualize the results. For this example, nvvp can be used to display a kernel timeline. The following command will first collect execution data from a sample execution of simpleHyperq, then visualize the concurrent kernel execution:

```
$ nvvp ./simpleHyperq
```

Figure 6-5 shows the timeline generated by nvvp on a Tesla K40. Each color corresponds to the execution of a different kernel and each row corresponds to a different stream, with time increasing to the right. As expected, you can see four concurrent kernels executing on the K40 in the four different streams.

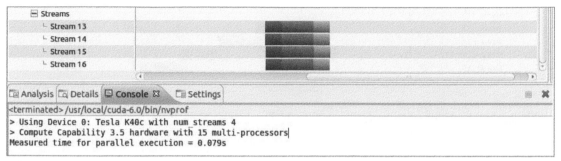

FIGURE 6-5

False Dependencies on Fermi GPUs

To demonstrate false dependencies, you can run the same code on a Fermi device. The output of simpleHyperq on a Tesla M2090 is:

```
$ ./simpleHyperq
> Using Device 0: Tesla M2090 with num_streams=4
> GPU does not support HyperQ
> CUDA kernel runs will have limited concurrency
> Compute Capability 2.0 hardware with 16 multi-processors
Measured time for parallel execution = 0.342s
```

simpleHyperq informs you that the Fermi device does not support Hyper-Q, and that the kernel will run with limited concurrency as a result.

Figure 6-6 shows the timeline for the same application as Figure 6-5, but running on the Fermi GPU. Four streams cannot start simultaneously because there is a false dependency between streams on the Fermi device, which is caused by the shared hardware work queue. Why is stream i+1 able to start its first task at the same time as stream i starts its last task? Since the two tasks are in different streams, there are no dependencies between them. When the last task of stream i is launched, the CUDA runtime schedules the next task from the work queue, which is the first task of stream i+1. Because the first task of each stream is not dependent on any earlier tasks and there are available SMs, it can start immediately. However, the second task of stream i+1 is then scheduled, and its dependency on the first task prevents it from executing, causing task execution to block again.

This false dependency is caused by the order in which kernels are dispatched from the host. This application uses the depth-first approach, launching the full set of operations for a stream before starting on the next stream. The task order in the work queue that results from the depth-first approach is illustrated in Figure 6-7. As all streams are multiplexed into a single hardware work queue, the preceding streams block successive streams.

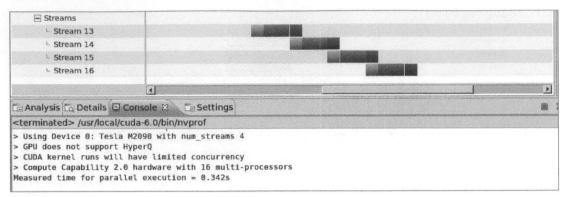

```
▥ Analysis  ▥ Details  ▣ Console ⌧   ▥ Settings
<terminated> /usr/local/cuda-6.0/bin/nvprof
> Using Device 0: Tesla M2090 with num_streams 4
> GPU does not support HyperQ
> CUDA kernel runs will have limited concurrency
> Compute Capability 2.0 hardware with 16 multi-processors
Measured time for parallel execution = 0.342s
```

FIGURE 6-6

To avoid false dependencies on Fermi GPUs, you can dispatch jobs from the host in a breadth-first approach:

```
// dispatch job with breadth first way
for (int i = 0; i < n_streams; i++)
    kernel_1<<<grid, block, 0, streams[i]>>>();
for (int i = 0; i < n_streams; i++)
    kernel_2<<<grid, block, 0, streams[i]>>>();
for (int i = 0; i < n_streams; i++)
    kernel_3<<<grid, block, 0, streams[i]>>>();
for (int i = 0; i < n_streams; i++)
    kernel_4<<<grid, block, 0, streams[i]>>>();
```

Issue order from host: depth-first way

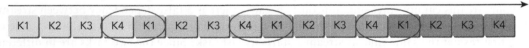

Only the three stream edges are independent.

FIGURE 6-7

Using breadth-first ordering ensures that adjacent tasks in the work queue are from different streams (shown in Figure 6-8). Therefore, there is no false dependency between any adjacent pairs of tasks and concurrent kernel execution is possible.

Issue order from host: breadth-first order

| K1 | K1 | K1 | K1 | K2 | K2 | K2 | K2 | K3 | K3 | K3 | K3 | K4 | K4 | K4 | K4 |

There is no dependence between any adjacent kernels.

FIGURE 6-8

You can download the full code example in the file `simpleHyperqBreadth.cu` from `Wrox.com`. When you compile and run it on a Fermi M2090 GPU, a typical output will be:

```
$ ./simpleHyperqBreadth
> Using Device 0: Tesla M2090 with num_streams 4
> GPU does not support HyperQ
> CUDA kernel runs will have limited concurrency
> Compute Capability 2.0 hardware with 16 multi-processors
Measured time for parallel execution = 0.105s
```

Notice that the execution time has improved three times compared to the depth-first approach. The scheduling of kernel launches can be confirmed with nvvp. Figure 6-9 shows the kernel execution timeline for the breadth-first approach: All streams start simultaneously.

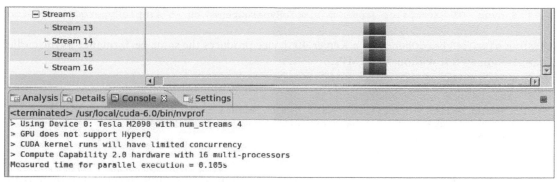

FIGURE 6-9

Dispatching Operations with OpenMP

Previous examples dispatched asynchronous CUDA operations to multiple streams using a single host thread. The example in this section will demonstrate dispatching operations to multiple streams using multiple host threads, using one thread to manage each stream.

OpenMP is a CPU parallel programming model that uses compiler directives to identify parallel regions. Compilers that support OpenMP directives can use them as hints from the programmer as to how to parallelize an application. With very little code, multi-core parallelism on the host can be achieved.

You can also use CUDA while leveraging OpenMP to improve not only portability and productivity, but also performance of the host code. Instead of dispatching operations with a loop as you did in the `simpleHyperQ` example, you can dispatch operations to different streams using OpenMP threads, as follows:

```
omp_set_num_threads(n_streams);
#pragma omp parallel
{
    int i = omp_get_thread_num();
    kernel_1<<<grid, block, 0, streams[i]>>>();
    kernel_2<<<grid, block, 0, streams[i]>>>();
```

```
        kernel_3<<<grid, block, 0, streams[i]>>>();
        kernel_4<<<grid, block, 0, streams[i]>>>();
    }
```

The OpenMP function `omp_set_num_threads` is used to specify the number of CPU cores to be used in OpenMP parallel regions. The compiler directive `#pragma omp parallel` marks the code between the curly braces as a parallel section. When compiled by a compiler with OpenMP support, the marked section will be run by multiple CPU threads. The `omp_get_thread_num` function returns a unique thread ID for each host thread, and is used as an index into the `streams` array to create a one-to-one mapping between OpenMP threads and CUDA streams.

Download the file `simpleHyperqOpenmp.cu` from `Wrox.com`. Compile with `nvcc`, being sure to use the `-Xcompiler` option to pass flags to the host compiler that enable OpenMP support:

```
$ nvcc -O3 -Xcompiler -fopenmp simpleHyperqOpenmp.cu -o simpleHyperqOpenmp -lgomp
```

Testing `simpleHyperqOpenmp` on a Kepler 40 device produces the same performance as the earlier `simpleHyperQ` test without OpenMP:

```
$ ./simpleHyperqOpenmp
CUDA_DEVICE_MAX_CONNECTIONS = 32
> Using Device 0: Tesla K40c with num_streams 4
> Compute Capability 3.5 hardware with 15 multi-processors
> grid 1 block 1
Measured time for parallel execution = 0.079s
```

When is dispatching CUDA operations in parallel from OpenMP useful? In general, if there is additional per-stream work to be completed before, during, or after kernel execution it can be included in the same OpenMP parallel region and overlapped across streams and threads. Doing so makes it apparent that the host work performed in each OpenMP thread and the streamed CUDA operations launched from the same thread are related, and makes the code simpler to write for optimal performance.

More details on using OpenMP with CUDA will be covered in Chapter 10, in the section "A Case Study in Porting C Programs to CUDA C."

Adjusting Stream Behavior Using Environment Variables

GPUs that support Hyper-Q maintain multiple hardware work queues between the host and each GPU to eliminate false dependencies. The maximum number of hardware work queues supported by a Kepler device is 32. However, by default the number of concurrent hardware connections is limited to eight. As each connection requires additional memory and resources, setting the default limit to 8 reduces resource consumption for applications that do not require the full 32 work queues. You can use the `CUDA_DEVICE_MAX_CONNECTIONS` environment variable to adjust the number of concurrent hardware connections, up to 32, for a Kepler device.

There are several ways to set this environment variable. In Linux, it can be set using the following commands depending on your shell. For Bash or Bourne Shell:

```
export CUDA_DEVICE_MAX_CONNECTIONS=32
```

For C-Shell:

```
setenv CUDA_DEVICE_MAX_CONNECTIONS 32
```

This environment variable can also be set directly in the C host program:

```
setenv("CUDA_DEVICE_MAX_CONNECTIONS", "32", 1);
```

Each CUDA stream is mapped to a single CUDA device connection. If the number of streams exceeds the number of hardware connections, multiple streams will share one connection. When multiple streams share the same hardware work queue, false dependencies might occur.

To check the behavior of CUDA streams on a platform that supports Hyper-Q but which has insufficient hardware connections, modify the simpleHyperqDepth example to use eight CUDA streams:

```
#define NSTREAM 8
```

and set the number of CUDA device connections to four:

```
// set up max connectioin
char* iname = "CUDA_DEVICE_MAX_CONNECTIONS";
setenv (iname, "4", 1);
```

Run the modified example on a Kepler GPU with nvvp:

```
$ nvvp ./simpleHyperqDepth
```

Figure 6-10 shows eight streams, but only four-way concurrency. Because there are now only four device connections, two streams share each queue. Dispatching the kernels using the depth-first approach causes false dependencies between the two streams assigned to the same work queue, similar to the results observed when using depth-first order on a Fermi GPU.

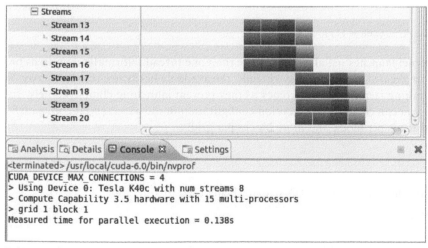

FIGURE 6-10

Next, check the behavior of the breadth-first approach using the same settings. As illustrated in Figure 6-11, all eight streams now run concurrently. Dispatching the kernels in breadth-first order removed the false dependencies.

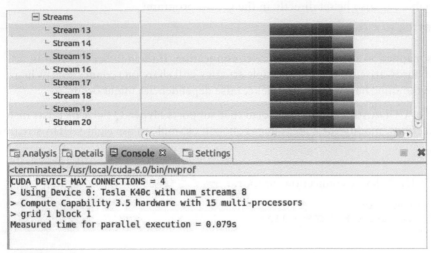

FIGURE 6-11

Concurrency-Limiting GPU Resources

Limited kernel resources can inhibit the amount of kernel concurrency possible in an application. In the previous examples, kernels were launched with only one thread to avoid any hardware restriction on concurrency. As a result, each kernel execution only requires a small amount of device compute resources.

```
kernel_1<<<1, 1, 0, streams[i]>>>();
```

In real applications, kernel launches usually create more than one thread. Normally, hundreds or thousands of threads are created. With so many threads, the available hardware resources may become the primary limiting factor for concurrency as they prevent launching eligible kernels. To observe this in action, you can change the execution configuration in the simpleHyperqBreadth example to use more threads per block and more blocks per grid:

```
dim3 block(128);
dim3 grid (32);
```

You should also increase the number of CUDA streams being used to 16:

```
#define NSTREAM 16
```

After recompiling, check the behavior of simpleHyperqBreadth on a Kepler device using nvvp:

```
$ nvvp ./simpleHyperqBreadth
```

As shown in Figure 6-12, only eight-way concurrency was achieved, even though the number of CUDA device connections is set to 32. Because the GPU is unable to allocate sufficient resources to execute all eligible kernels, concurrency is limited.

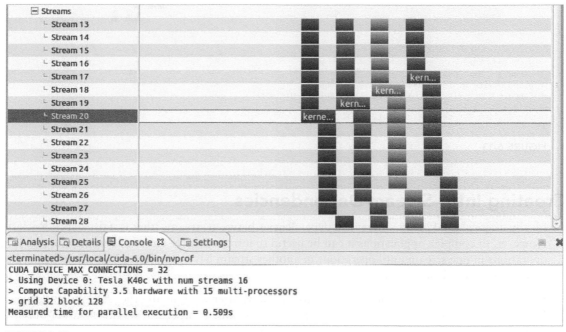

FIGURE 6-12

Blocking Behavior of the Default Stream

To demonstrate how the default stream can block operations in non-null streams, modify the depth-first dispatch loop in simpleHyperqDepth.cu to invoke kernel_3 in the default stream:

```
// dispatch job with depth first ordering
for (int i = 0; i < n_streams; i++) {
    kernel_1<<<grid, block, 0, streams[i]>>>();
    kernel_2<<<grid, block, 0, streams[i]>>>();
    kernel_3<<<grid, block>>>();
    kernel_4<<<grid, block, 0, streams[i]>>>();
}
```

Because the third kernel is launched in the default stream, any later operations on non-null streams will be blocked until the operations in the default stream complete. Figure 6-13 shows the timeline captured using nvvp for this code running on a Tesla K40. The timeline shows how each kernel_3 launch prevents any further execution in all other blocking streams.

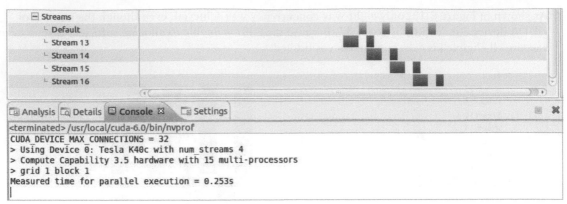

FIGURE 6-13

Creating Inter-Stream Dependencies

Ideally, there should be no unintended dependencies between streams (that is, false dependencies). However, in complex applications it can be useful to introduce inter-stream dependencies that block operations in one stream until operations in another stream have completed. Events can be used to add inter-stream dependencies.

Suppose you want the work in one stream to only start after work in all other streams completes. You can use events to create a dependency between streams. First, create synchronization-only events with the flag cudaEventDisableTiming, as follows:

```
cudaEvent_t *kernelEvent = (cudaEvent_t *)malloc(n_streams * sizeof(cudaEvent_t));
for (int i = 0; i < n_streams; i++) {
    cudaEventCreateWithFlags(&kernelEvent[i], cudaEventDisableTiming);
}
```

Next, record a different event at the completion of each stream using cudaEventRecord. Then, use cudaStreamWaitEvent to force the last stream (that is, streams[n_streams-1]) to wait for all other streams:

```
// dispatch job with depth first way
for (int i=0; i<n_streams; i++) {
    kernel_1<<<grid, block, 0, streams[i]>>>();
    kernel_2<<<grid, block, 0, streams[i]>>>();
    kernel_3<<<grid, block, 0, streams[i]>>>();
    kernel_4<<<grid, block, 0, streams[i]>>>();

    cudaEventRecord(kernelEvent[i], streams[i]);
    cudaStreamWaitEvent(streams[n_streams-1], kernelEvent[i], 0);
}
```

You can download the full code for this example in the file simpleHyperqDependence.cu from Wrox.com. Figure 6-14 shows the nvvp kernel timeline. Note that the fourth stream, streams[n_streams-1], only starts its work once all other streams complete.

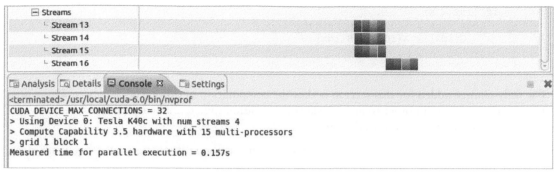

FIGURE 6-14

OVERLAPPING KERNEL EXECUTION AND DATA TRANSFER

In the previous section, you examined how to concurrently run multiple kernels in multiple streams. In this section, you will learn how to run kernels and data transfers concurrently. *Overlapping kernels with data transfers* exhibits different behavior and requires different considerations than concurrent kernel execution.

Fermi and Kepler GPUs have two copy engine queues: one for data transfer to the device, and one for data transfer from the device. Therefore, at most you can overlap two data transfers, but only if their directionalities differ and they are dispatched to different streams. Otherwise, all data transfer will be serialized. It is important to keep this in mind when determining how to best overlap data transfer with kernel computation.

You will also need to examine the relationships between all data transfers and kernel executions in an application to distinguish the following two cases:

➤ If a kernel consumes data A, the data transfer for A must be placed before the kernel launch and in the same stream.

➤ If a kernel does not consume any part of A, the kernel execution and data transfer can be placed in different streams.

In the second case, it is trivial to enable concurrent execution of the kernel and the data transfer: By placing them in separate streams, you have already indicated to the runtime that it is safe to execute them concurrently. However, achieving overlap between data transfer and kernel execution in the first case, where the kernel depends on that data as input, is more complex. You will use the vector addition example to examine how data transfers and kernel execution can be overlapped when a dependency exists between the kernel and the transfer.

Overlap Using Depth-First Scheduling

You are already familiar with the vector addition kernel:

```
__global__ void sumArrays(float *A, float *B, float *C, const int N) {
    int idx = blockIdx.x * blockDim.x + threadIdx.x;
```

```
    if (idx < N)
        for (int i = 0; i < n_repeat; i++) {
            C[idx] = A[idx] + B[idx];
        }
}
```

The only change added for this section is that the computation of this kernel has been augmented by a factor of n_repeat in order to increase kernel execution time to make it easier to visualize computation-communication overlap in nvvp.

The basic structure of a CUDA program implementing vector addition contains three main steps:

➤ Copy the two input vectors from the host to the device.

➤ Perform a vector addition.

➤ Copy a single output vector back to the host from the device.

It may not be obvious from these steps how computation and communication can be overlapped. To enable overlapping in vector addition, you will need to partition the input and output data sets into subsets and overlap communication from one subset with computation from other subsets. Put concretely for vector addition, this will require separating the problem of adding two vectors of length N together into M sub-problems each adding vectors of length N/M together. Because each of these sub-problems is independent, they can each be scheduled in separate CUDA streams and their computation and communication will naturally overlap.

In the vector addition program from Chapter 2, data transfer is implemented using synchronous copy functions. To overlap data transfer with kernel execution, asynchronous copy functions must be used. Because asynchronous copy functions require pinned host memory, the first modification required is the allocation of host arrays in pinned host memory using cudaHostAlloc:

```
cudaHostAlloc((void**)&gpuRef, nBytes, cudaHostAllocDefault);
cudaHostAlloc((void**)&hostRef, nBytes, cudaHostAllocDefault);
```

Next, you need to partition the work in this problem equally among NSTREAM streams. The amount of elements processed by each stream is defined as:

```
int iElem = nElem / NSTREAM;
```

Now, you can use a loop to dispatch communication and computation for iElem elements at a time to several streams:

```
for (int i = 0; i < NSTREAM; ++i) {
    int ioffset = i * iElem;
    cudaMemcpyAsync(&d_A[ioffset], &h_A[ioffset], iBytes,
                cudaMemcpyHostToDevice, stream[i]);
    cudaMemcpyAsync(&d_B[ioffset], &h_B[ioffset], iBytes,
                cudaMemcpyHostToDevice, stream[i]);
    sumArrays<<<grid, block,0,stream[i]>>>(&d_A[ioffset], &d_B[ioffset],
                &d_C[ioffset],iElem);
```

```
        cudaMemcpyAsync(&gpuRef[ioffset],&d_C[ioffset], iBytes,
                    cudaMemcpyDeviceToHost, stream[i]);
}
```

Because these memory copies and kernel launches are asynchronous with respect to the host, the full workload is distributed among streams without any blocking. However, dependencies between input vectors, the kernel computation, and the output vector are maintained by placing data transfer and computation on that data in the same stream.

This example also uses a blocking implementation to calculate a baseline performance for comparison:

```
        sumArrays<<<grid, block>>>(d_A, d_B, d_C, nElem);
```

You can download this full example in the file `simpleMultiAddDepth.cu` from `Wrox.com`. After compiling, use nvvp to display the timeline of copies and kernels:

```
$ nvvp ./simpleMultiAddDepth
```

Figure 6-15 shows a typical timeline from a Tesla K40 device. Eight hardware work queues are used, and four CUDA streams are used to overlap kernel execution with data transfer. Streamed execution achieves nearly a 40 percent performance improvement relative to blocking execution on the default stream. Figure 6-15 shows the following three types of overlap:

➤ Kernels in different streams overlapping with each other

➤ Kernels overlapping with data transfers in other streams

➤ Data transfers in different streams and in different directions overlapping with each other

Figure 6-15 also shows the following two types of blocking behavior:

➤ A kernel blocked by preceding data transfers in the same stream

➤ Data transfers from the host to device blocked by a preceding transfer of the same direction

Though data transfers from the host to the device are executed in four different streams, the timeline shows that they are executed sequentially because they are actually executed through the same copy engine queue.

Next, you can try experimenting with performance by reducing the number of hardware work queues to one and rerunning. Figure 6-16 shows the timeline generated on a Tesla K40 device. Note that there is not a significant difference between Figure 6-16 (with one work queue) and 6-15 (with eight work queues). Because each stream only executes a single kernel, no false dependencies are added by reducing the number of work queues, nor are existing false dependencies (caused by the host-to-device copy queue) removed.

Decreasing the number of work queues in the K40 creates a condition similar to a Fermi GPU: one work queue and two copy queues. If you run the same test on a Fermi GPU, you will find that false dependencies do exist. This is a result of Kepler's work dispatch mechanisms, implemented in the Grid Management Unit (GMU). The GMU is responsible for managing and prioritizing work sent to the GPU. Analysis performed by the GMU helps reduce false dependencies.

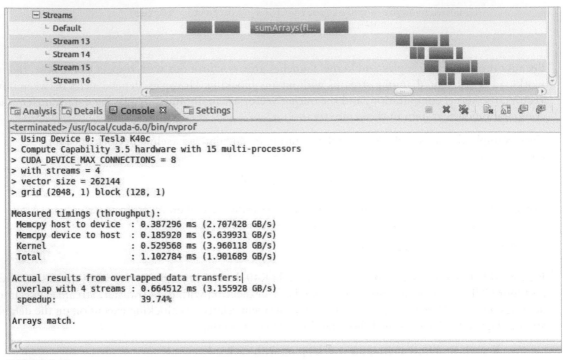

FIGURE 6-15

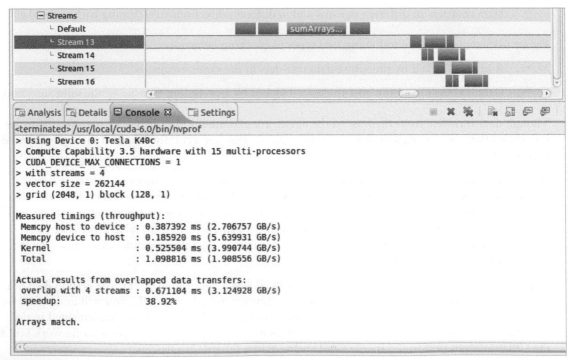

FIGURE 6-16

GRID MANAGEMENT UNIT

Kepler introduces a new grid management and dispatch control system, the Grid Management Unit (GMU). The GMU can pause the dispatch of new grids and queue pending and suspended grids until they are ready to execute, providing the flexibility to enable powerful runtimes, such as Dynamic Parallelism.

In Fermi devices, grids are passed to the CUDA Work Distributor (CWD) directly from the stream queue. In Kepler devices, grids are passed to the GMU, and the GMU manages and prioritizes grids to be executed on the GPU.

The GMU creates multiple hardware work queues to reduce or eliminate false dependencies. With the GMU, streams can be kept as individual pipelines of work. Even when the GMU is restricted to a single hardware work queue, test results above verify that grid-dependency analysis performed by the GMU can help eliminate false dependencies.

Overlap Using Breadth-First Scheduling

Earlier examples demonstrated that Fermi GPUs delivered the best results while dispatching kernels using the breadth-first approach. Now, you will examine the effect of breadth-first ordering in the presence of overlapped data transfers and compute kernels.

The following code segment demonstrates dispatching both computation and communication among streams using a breadth-first approach:

```
// initiate all asynchronous transfers to the device
for (int i = 0; i < NSTREAM; ++i) {
    int ioffset = i * iElem;
    cudaMemcpyAsync(&d_A[ioffset], &h_A[ioffset], iBytes,
            cudaMemcpyHostToDevice, stream[i]);
    cudaMemcpyAsync(&d_B[ioffset], &h_B[ioffset], iBytes,
            cudaMemcpyHostToDevice, stream[i]);
}

// launch a kernel in each stream
for (int i = 0; i < NSTREAM; ++i) {
    int ioffset = i * iElem;
    sumArrays<<<grid, block, 0, stream[i]>>>(&d_A[ioffset], &d_B[ioffset],
            &d_C[ioffset],iElem);
}

// queue asynchronous transfers from the device
for (int i = 0; i < NSTREAM; ++i) {
    int ioffset = i * iElem;
    cudaMemcpyAsync(&gpuRef[ioffset],&d_C[ioffset], iBytes,
            cudaMemcpyDeviceToHost, stream[i]);
}
```

You can download the full example in `simpleMultiAddBreadth.cu` from `Wrox.com`. Figure 6-17 shows the timeline generated on a K40 device using only one hardware work queue. There is no significant difference compared to the depth-first approach because Kepler's bidirectional scheduling mechanism helps in eliminating false dependences. If you run the same test on a Fermi device, you will see that overall performance of the breadth-first approach is worse than the depth-first approach. The false dependencies caused by contention on the host-to-device copy queue prevent any kernels from starting before all host-to-device transfers complete.

Therefore, for Kepler devices you do not need to focus on job dispatch order in most cases. On Fermi devices you need to be more aware of these issues and evaluate different scheduling options to find the best dispatching order for your workload.

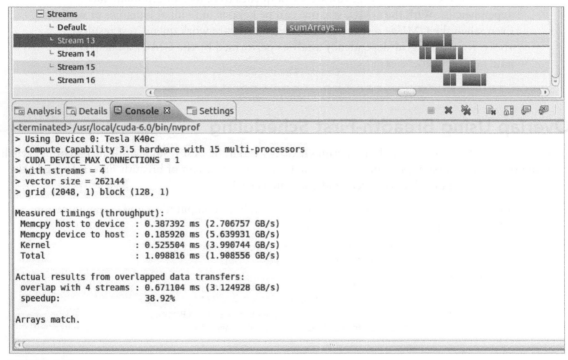

FIGURE 6-17

OVERLAPPING GPU AND CPU EXECUTION

It is relatively straightforward to achieve *GPU and CPU execution overlap* because all kernel launches are asynchronous by default. As a result, simply launching a kernel and immediately doing useful work in the host thread automatically produces overlap of GPU and CPU execution.

The example in this section consists of two main parts:

➤   A kernel is dispatched to the default stream.

➤   Host computation is executed while waiting on the GPU kernel.

The following simple kernel implementing a vector-scalar addition will be used:

```
__global__ void kernel(float *g_data, float value) {
    int idx = blockIdx.x * blockDim.x + threadIdx.x;
    g_data[idx] = g_data[idx] + value;
}
```

In this example, three CUDA operations (two copies and a kernel launch) are issued. A `stop` event is recorded to mark the completion of all CUDA operations.

```
cudaMemcpyAsync(d_a, h_a, nbytes, cudaMemcpyHostToDevice);
kernel<<<grid, block>>>(d_a, value);
cudaMemcpyAsync(h_a, d_a, nbytes, cudaMemcpyDeviceToHost);
cudaEventRecord(stop);
```

All of these operations are asynchronous with respect to the host, and they are all bound to the default stream. As soon as the last `cudaMemcpyAsync` is issued, control is immediately returned to the host. Once control is returned to the host, the host can do any useful computation that does not depend on the output of the kernel. In the following code segment the host simply iterates, waiting for all CUDA operations to complete while incrementing a counter. On each iteration, the host thread queries the `stop` event. Once the event is satisfied, the host thread continues.

```
unsigned long int counter = 0;
while (cudaEventQuery(stop) == cudaErrorNotReady) {
    counter++;
}
```

You can download the code example `asyncAPI.cu` from `Wrox.com`. The following is a typical output from `nvprof` collected on a Tesla K40 device. While waiting for GPU operations to complete, the host thread performed 14,606 iterations.

```
$ nvprof ./asyncAPI
==22813== NVPROF is profiling process 22813, command: ./asyncAPI
> ./asyncAPI running on CUDA device [Tesla K40c]
CPU executed 14606 iterations while waiting for GPU to finish
==22813== Profiling application: ./asyncAPI
==22813== Profiling result:
Time(%)      Time     Calls       Avg       Min       Max  Name
 48.89%  10.661ms         1  10.661ms  10.661ms  10.661ms  [CUDA memcpy HtoD]
 46.04%  10.041ms         1  10.041ms  10.041ms  10.041ms  [CUDA memcpy DtoH]
  3.25%  709.82us         1  709.82us  709.82us  709.82us  kernel(float*, float)
  1.82%  396.13us         1  396.13us  396.13us  396.13us  [CUDA memset]
```

STREAM CALLBACKS

A *stream callback* is another type of operation that can be queued to a CUDA stream. Once all of the operations in a stream preceding a stream callback have completed, a host-side function specified by the stream callback is called by the CUDA runtime. This function is provided by the application. This allows arbitrary host-side logic to be inserted into CUDA streams. Stream callbacks are another CPU-GPU synchronization mechanism. Callbacks are particularly powerful because they are the first example of GPU operations creating work on the host system, the opposite of every CUDA concept described to this point in the book.

The stream callback function is a host function provided by the application and registered in a stream with the following API function:

```
cudaError_t cudaStreamAddCallback(cudaStream_t stream,
    cudaStreamCallback_t callback, void *userData, unsigned int flags);
```

This function adds a callback function to the provided stream. The callback function is executed on the host after all previously queued operations in the stream have completed. A callback is executed only once per `cudaStreamAddCallback`, and will block other work queued after it until the callback function completes. When it is called by the CUDA runtime, the callback function is passed the stream it is being called from, and an error code indicating if a CUDA error has occurred. You can also specify application data to be passed to the callback function using the `userData` argument to `cudaStreamAddCallback`. The `flags` argument is reserved for future use but currently has no meaning; therefore, it must be set to zero. A callback queued to the NULL stream is executed when all preceding work issued in all streams has completed.

There are two restrictions to callback functions:

➤ No CUDA API function can be called from a callback function.

➤ No synchronization can be performed within the callback function.

In general, making any assumptions about the ordering of callbacks relative to each other or other CUDA operations is risky and may result in unstable code.

The following sample code adds the callback function `my_callback` to the end of each of four streams after launching four kernels in each stream. The callback begins to run on the host only after all work in each stream completes.

```
void CUDART_CB my_callback(cudaStream_t stream, cudaError_t status, void *data) {
    printf("callback from stream %d\n", *((int *)data));
}
```

The code for adding the stream callbacks to each stream is the following:

```
for (int i = 0; i < n_streams; i++) {
    stream_ids[i] = i;
    kernel_1<<<grid, block, 0, streams[i]>>>();
    kernel_2<<<grid, block, 0, streams[i]>>>();
    kernel_3<<<grid, block, 0, streams[i]>>>();
    kernel_4<<<grid, block, 0, streams[i]>>>();
    cudaStreamAddCallback(streams[i], my_callback, (void *)(stream_ids + i), 0);
}
```

You can download the file `simpleCallback.cu` from `Wrox.com`. The following is a sample output collected on a Tesla K40 GPU:

```
$ ./callback
> ./callback Starting...
> Using Device 0: Tesla K40c
```

```
> Compute Capability 3.5 hardware with 15 multi-processors
> CUDA_DEVICE_MAX_CONNECTIONS = 8
> with streams = 4
callback from stream 0
callback from stream 1
callback from stream 2
callback from stream 3
Measured time for parallel execution = 0.104s
```

SUMMARY

The concept of streams is a fundamental part of the CUDA programming model. CUDA streams enable *coarse-grained concurrency* by permitting high-level CUDA operations to be queued to independent streams of execution. Because CUDA supports an asynchronous, version of most runtime functions, it is possible to distribute computation and communication among multiple CUDA streams.

Conceptually, if there are dependencies between CUDA operations they must be scheduled in the same stream. For example, to ensure application correctness a kernel must be scheduled in the same stream and after any data transfers it consumes. Otherwise, operations with no dependencies can be scheduled in arbitrary streams. In CUDA, you can typically use three different types of overlap schemes to hide computation or communication latencies:

➤ Overlap of multiple, concurrent kernels on the device

➤ Overlap of CUDA kernels with data transfer to or from the device

➤ Overlap of CPU execution and GPU execution

To fully utilize the device and ensure maximum concurrency, you also need to be mindful of the following issues:

➤ Balance kernel resource requirements and concurrency resource requirements. Launching too many computational tasks on the device at once may result in kernel serialization as work blocks on hardware resources becoming available. However, you also want to ensure that the device is not underutilized and that there is always work queued up for execution.

➤ Avoid using the default stream to execute asynchronous operations if possible. Operations placed in the default stream might block progress of other non-default CUDA streams.

➤ On a Fermi device, consider both depth-first and breadth-first dispatch from the host. This choice can significantly impact performance by eliminating false dependencies in the shared hardware work queue.

➤ Be mindful of implicit synchronization functions, and use them carefully with asynchronous functions to avoid degraded performance.

In addition, this chapter demonstrated the usefulness of the CUDA Visual Profiler (nvvp) in visualizing GPU execution. nvvp allows you to identify opportunities for operation overlap, and makes it easy to visualize the behavior of multiple streams.

CHAPTER 6 EXERCISES

1. Define the term "CUDA stream." What kind of operations can be placed in a CUDA stream? What are the main benefits of using streams in an application?

2. How do events relate to streams? Give an example where a CUDA event would be useful and allow you to implement logic that you could not efficiently implement with streams alone.

3. What can cause false dependencies on GPUs? How do these causes differ between the Fermi and Kepler architectures? How does Hyper-Q help to limit false dependencies?

4. Describe the difference between explicit and implicit synchronization. What are examples of specific CUDA API functions that create implicit host-device synchronization points?

5. How do depth-first and breadth-first ordering differ when executing work from CUDA streams? In particular, how does the Fermi architecture benefit from breadth-first ordering of work?

6. List the different types of CUDA overlapping. Describe the techniques that would be required to implement each.

7. Draw the timeline you would expect to be produced from running `simpleHyperqBreadth` on a Fermi device with `nvvp`, as follows:

   ```
   $ nvvp ./simplehHyperqBreadth
   ```

   Assume that 32 streams are used. Explain the reasoning behind the timeline you drew.

8. Draw the timeline produced by the following command on a Kepler device:

   ```
   $ nvvp ./simpleHyperDepth
   ```

   Assume that 32 streams are used. Explain the reasoning behind the timeline you drew.

9. Refer to `simpleCallback.cu`, and put the callback point after the second kernel launch. Run it with `nvvp` and observe the difference.

7

Tuning Instruction-Level Primitives

WHAT'S IN THIS CHAPTER?

➤ Learning about multiple classes of CUDA instructions and their impact on application behavior

➤ Observing the relative accuracy of single- and double-precision floating-point values

➤ Experimenting with the performance and accuracy of standard and intrinsic functions

➤ Uncovering undefined behavior from unsafe memory accesses

➤ Understanding the significance of arithmetic instructions and the consequences of using them improperly

> **CODE DOWNLOAD** *The wrox.com code downloads for this chapter are found at www.wrox.com/go/procudac on the Download Code tab. The code is in the Chapter 7 download area and individually named according to the Listings and Examples throughout the chapter.*

When making the decision to use CUDA for a particular application, the primary motivator is usually the computational throughput of GPUs. As you learned in previous chapters in this book, in order to achieve high throughput on GPUs you need to understand what factors are limiting peak performance. You have already learned about CUDA tools that can help you determine if your workload is sensitive to latency, bandwidth, or arithmetic operations. Based on this understanding you can generally classify applications into two categories:

➤ I/O-bound

➤ Compute-bound

In this chapter, you will focus on tuning compute-bound workloads. The computational throughput of a processor can be measured by the number of operations it performs in a period of time. Because GPUs have wide SIMT instructions and many computational cores, their peak computational throughput is generally much higher than other processors.

However, not all instructions are created equal. It does not matter how fast your application runs if you do not converge on the correct answer or obtain the expected results. Understanding the strengths and weaknesses of different low-level primitives in terms of performance, numerical accuracy, and thread-safety is important when optimizing your application for throughput and correctness. Knowing when your kernel code is compiled into one primitive or another allows you to tweak the compiler's code generation to suit your requirements.

To demonstrate how low-level instruction tuning can be beneficial, consider the following code snippet:

```
double value = in1 * in2 + in3;
```

This arithmetic pattern of a multiply followed by an add is creatively called a *multiply-add*, or *MAD*, and is very common in a wide range of applications. Any application that manipulates vectors and matrices likely contains many MAD operations as part of executing dot products, matrix multiplications, and other functions in linear algebra. A naive compiler would transform a MAD operation into two arithmetic instructions: a multiply followed by an addition. However, because this pattern is so common, modern architectures (including NVIDIA GPUs) support a MAD instruction that fuses a multiply and an add operation. As a result, the number of cycles to execute the MAD operation is halved. This performance does not come for free. The results of a single MAD instruction are often less numerically accurate than with separate multiply and add instructions. Like the MAD instruction, all of the topics covered in this chapter will feature some tradeoff between one desirable application behavior and another.

In this chapter, you will learn about a variety of relatively low-level CUDA primitives that you can use to tune performance, accuracy, and correctness. You will study exactly how each of these features affects your application at the instruction level. By the end of the chapter, you will understand the advantages and disadvantages of single- and double-precision floating-point values, intrinsic and standard functions, and atomic operations.

INTRODUCING CUDA INSTRUCTIONS

Instructions represent a single unit of logic in processors. While it may be rare for you to directly manipulate instructions while working with CUDA, it is important for you to understand when different instructions are generated from CUDA kernel code, and how the higher-level language features translate to instructions. The choice between two functionally equivalent instructions can affect a variety of application characteristics, including performance, accuracy, and correctness.

These concerns are of particular importance when porting legacy applications to CUDA with strict numerical validation requirements. This section covers three topics that significantly affect the instructions generated for a CUDA kernel: floating-point operations, intrinsic and standard functions, and atomic operations. Floating-point calculations operate on non-integral values and affect both the accuracy and performance of CUDA programs. Intrinsic and standard functions implement overlapping sets of mathematical operations but offer different guarantees of accuracy and performance. Atomic instructions guarantee correctness when concurrently performing operations on a variable from multiple threads. The sections in this chapter will engage you on each of these topics and give you a deeper understanding of their ramifications for compiler-generated instructions.

Floating-Point Instructions

Since the introduction of *IEEE Standard 754* for floating-point arithmetic, all mainstream processor vendors have implemented the standard, including NVIDIA. The standard mandates that binary floating-point data be encoded in three fields: A one-bit sign field, multiple exponent bits, and multiple bits encoding the significand (or fraction), as illustrated in Figure 7-1.

FIGURE 7-1

In order to ensure consistent computation across platforms, IEEE-754 defines 32- and 64-bit floating-point formats, which correspond to the C data types `float` and `double`. Their representations have different bit lengths, as illustrated in Figure 7-2.

float	1	8	23

double	1	11	52

FIGURE 7-2

Given a 32-bit floating point variable with a sign bit s, 8-bit exponent e, and 23-bit significand v the value represented can be calculated as shown in Figure 7-3.

$$(-1)^s \times (1.v_{22}v_{21}...v_0) \times 2^{e-127}$$

FIGURE 7-3

It is important to understand that because of this standard format, floating-point variables can accurately represent values at a finer granularity than integer variables. However, *numerical accuracy* is still limited. The values that can be accurately stored in floating-point format are discrete and finite. For example, consider the following code snippet:

```
float a = 3.1415927f;
float b = 3.1415928f;
if (a == b) {
    printf("a is equal to b\n");
} else {
    printf("a does not equal b\n");
}
```

Because the last digit of a and b differs, you would expect this to print:

    a does not equal b

However, on architectures compatible with the IEEE 754 standard, it will actually print:

    a is equal to b

In this example, neither of the values can actually be stored in the finite number of bits used by the floating-point variables a and b. As a result, these values are rounded to the nearest value that can be stored, which happens to be the same for both.

Floating-point values that cannot be stored correctly are rounded to representable values using a configurable rounding mode. For instance, the previous example used the default behavior, round-to-nearest, which rounds un-representable values to the nearest representable value. Other examples of rounding modes include round-to-zero (always round towards the value with a smaller absolute value), round-up, and round-down.

Another important consideration in floating-point programming is the granularity of represent-able floating-point values. As discussed, floating-point values can represent values at a much finer granularity than integer values. However, they can still only store values at discrete intervals. Additionally, as floating-point values become farther from zero (in both the positive and negative direction), the interval between representable values grows as well (as depicted in Figure 7-4).

Floating-point granularity

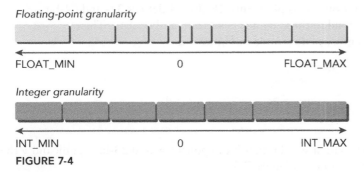

Integer granularity

FIGURE 7-4

You can use the C standard math function nextafterf to find the next highest representable float value from a given value. Table 7-1 shows the differences between a float and the next highest representable float for a few values. Note the drastic loss in precision as the values of *x* increase. These large intervals between floating-point values mean that the choice of rounding mode can have a significant impact on the numerical output of any application in which extreme values can arise.

TABLE 7-1: Representable Floating-Point Values

X	NEXTAFTERF(X) - X
3.14	2.384186e-07
314,159.28	0.03125
314,159,275,180,032.00	3.355443e+07

Instructions that operate on floating-point values are naturally referred to as floating-point instructions. CUDA supports all the usual arithmetic operations for floating-point such as addition, multiplication, division, and subtraction.

As mentioned earlier, CUDA and other programming models that adhere to IEEE 754 support two tiers of accuracy in floating-point: 32-bit and 64-bit. These different formats are also referred to as single-precision and double-precision, respectively. Because double-precision variables use twice as many bits as single-precision variables, double-precision values can correctly represent many more values. This means that the set of double-precision values has both a finer granularity and wider range than single-precision values. For instance, consider a version of the earlier floating-point accuracy example that uses double- instead of single-precision floats:

```
double a = 3.1415927;
double b = 3.1415928;
if (a == b) {
    printf("a is equal to b\n");
} else {
    printf("a does not equal b\n");
}
```

This code produces the expected output:

```
a does not equal b
```

because the nearest representable values for a and b are not the same when stored using double-precision variables.

Note that while all compute-capable NVIDIA GPUs support single-precision floating-point, you will need an NVIDIA GPU of compute capability 1.3 or higher to use double-precision values.

Still, even double-precision values have their limits. A later section in this chapter titled, "Single Precision vs. Double-Precision" will more quantitatively explore the challenges of floating-point programming and the differences between single- and double-precision floating-point.

Intrinsic and Standard Functions

In addition to the separation between single- and double-precision operations, CUDA also categorizes all arithmetic functions as either intrinsic or standard functions. *Standard functions* are used to support operations that are accessible from, and standardized across, the host and device. Standard functions include arithmetic operations from the C standard math library such as sqrt, exp, and sin. Single-instruction operations like multiplication and addition are also included as standard functions.

CUDA *intrinsic functions* can only be accessed from device code. In programming, a function being intrinsic, or built-in, implies that the compiler has special knowledge about its behavior, which enables more aggressive optimization and specialized instruction generation. This is true for CUDA intrinsic functions. In fact, many trigonometric functions are directly implemented in hardware on GPUs because they are used heavily in graphics applications (to perform translations, rotations, and so on for 3D visual applications).

In CUDA, many intrinsic functions are related to a standard function, meaning that a standard function exists that implements the same operation. For example, the standard function for performing a double-precision floating-point square root is sqrt. The intrinsic version implementing the same functionality is __dsqrt_rn. There is even an intrinsic function for single-precision floating-point division, __fdividef.

Intrinsic functions decompose into fewer instructions than their equivalent standard functions. As a result, intrinsic functions are faster than their equivalent standard functions but less numerically precise. This gives you the capability to use standard and intrinsic functions interchangeably, but produce different program behavior in terms of both performance and numerical accuracy.

Standard and intrinsic functions add a significant amount of flexibility to any CUDA application. They serve as fine-grained knobs that you can turn to tweak performance and numerical accuracy on an operation-by-operation basis. In a later section of this chapter titled, "Standard vs. Intrinsic Functions" you will get hands-on experience adjusting these knobs to explore their effects.

Atomic Instructions

An atomic instruction performs a mathematical operation, but does so in a single uninterruptable operation with no interference from other threads. When a thread successfully completes an atomic operation on a variable, it can be certain that the variable's state change has completed no matter how many other threads are accessing that variable. Because atomic instructions prevent multiple threads from interfering with each other, they enable read-modify-write operations for data shared across threads (for example, read the current value, increment it, and write the new value). Guaranteeing the atomicity of read-modify-write operations is especially important in highly concurrent environments, like the GPU. CUDA provides atomic functions that perform read-modify-write atomic operations on 32-bits or 64-bits of global memory or shared memory.

While any device with compute capability 1.1 or higher supports atomic operations, Kepler-based global atomic memory operations are faster than Fermi-based operations, leading to dramatically higher throughput. This may enable performant CUDA-based applications that were previously deemed impractical for GPU execution because of their heavy reliance on atomic operations.

Like standard and intrinsic functions, each atomic function implements a basic mathematical operation such as addition, multiplication, or subtraction. Unlike any other instruction type described so far, atomic instructions have a defined behavior when operating on a memory location shared by two competing threads.

Consider the following simple kernel to help you understand this concept:

```
__global__ void incr(int *ptr) {
    int temp = *ptr;
    temp = temp + 1;
    *ptr = temp;
}
```

This kernel reads from a memory location, adds one to that value, and then writes the calculated value back to the same location. Note that no thread IDs are used to change the memory locations being accessed; every thread in a kernel launch will read and write from the same address. If a single block of 32 threads were launched running this kernel, what output would you expect? You might say 32: Each thread will increment by one. In truth, the resulting value is undefined. The problem here is caused by more than one thread writing to the same memory location. This is called a *data race*, or *unsafe access* to memory. A data race is formally defined as two or more independent threads of execution accessing the same location, where at least one of those accesses is modifying that location. You have no way of knowing which will win the race to write until the program is actually executed. Therefore, the result of this or any application that contains data races is more difficult to determine.

Fortunately, atomic instructions avoid this undesirable behavior. Atomic instructions are accessed through the CUDA API as functions. For example:

```
int atomicAdd(int *M, int V);
```

Most atomic functions are binary functions, performing an operation on two operands. They take as input a memory location *M* and a value *V*. The operation associated with the atomic function is executed on *V* and the value already stored at the memory location, *M*. The result is then written back to the same memory location.

The atomic functions can be split into three groups: arithmetic functions, bitwise functions, and swap functions. The atomic arithmetic functions perform simple arithmetic on the target memory location and include common operations like add, subtract, maximum, minimum, increment, and decrement. The atomic bitwise functions perform a bitwise operation on the target memory location and include bitwise AND, bitwise OR, and bitwise XOR. The atomic swap functions either conditionally or unconditionally swap the value of a memory location with a new value. Atomic swap functions always return the value originally stored at the target location, regardless of whether the swap succeeds. atomicExch unconditionally replaces the value stored. atomicCAS conditionally replaces the value stored if the currently stored value matches an expected value specified by the calling GPU thread.

As an example, recall the earlier increment kernel:

```
__global__ void incr(int *ptr) {
    int temp = *ptr;
    temp = temp + 1;
    *ptr = temp;
}
```

You can re-write the incr kernel using the atomicAdd function. atomicAdd atomically adds a value *V* to the value stored at memory location *M*. The updated incr kernel below uses one statement to increment the value stored at the location ptr and returns the value stored at ptr before the increment.

```
__global__ void incr(__global__ int *ptr) {
    int temp = atomicAdd(ptr, 1);
}
```

With these changes, the behavior of this kernel is now well-defined. If 32 threads were launched, the value stored at *ptr would have to be 32.

On the other hand, what if your application did not require that all threads successfully increment the target? What if you only cared if one or a few threads in a warp succeeded? As an example, consider the kernel below:

```
__global__ void check_threshold(int *arr, int threshold, int *flag) {
    if (arr[blockIdx.x * blockDim.x + threadIdx.x] > threshold) {
        *flag = 1;
    }
}
```

Here every thread is checking its value against a threshold. If that value is above the threshold, a global flag is set. Because all threads are operating on the same global flag, if multiple values are above the threshold then the assignment to flag is unsafe.

It would be possible to remove these unsafe accesses using atomicExch:

```
int atomicExch(int *M, int V);
```

atomicExch unconditionally replaces the value stored at M with V, and returns the old value. Rewriting the check_threshold kernel using atomicExch removes the unsafe accesses to flag:

```
__global__ void check_threshold(int *arr, int threshold, int *flag) {
    if (arr[blockIdx.x * blockDim.x + threadIdx.x] > threshold) {
        atomicExch(flag, 1);
    }
}
```

For this example, is it really necessary to use atomicExch? In this case, if you use unsafe accesses, you are still guaranteed that at least one thread will write to *flag successfully. Using atomicExch does not actually modify the behavior of this kernel. It would be possible to simply use unsafe accesses in check_threshold and still have a functionally correct application. In fact, using atomicExch and other atomic operations may significantly degrade performance. Still, when considering this type of optimization you must be very careful that the operation truly does not rely on the results of every thread being visible. If check_threshold were doing an increment as a way of counting the number of values above threshold, using unsafe accesses would not be valid.

Atomic instructions are powerful in a highly parallel environment like the GPU. They provide a safe way to operate on values shared by hundreds or thousands of threads. While atomic functions do not suffer from additional precision concerns (as intrinsic functions do), their use can severely degrade performance. A later section in this chapter titled "Understanding Atomic Instructions" will explore why.

OPTIMIZING INSTRUCTIONS FOR YOUR APPLICATION

You have seen that there are many choices when it comes to optimizing the instructions your application uses: single-precision or double-precision floating-point values, standard or intrinsic functions, atomic functions or unsafe accesses. In general, each choice has tradeoffs in performance, accuracy, and correctness. There is no single best choice for all applications; the optimal decision depends on your application requirements.

In this section, you will have the chance to look at examples that demonstrate the different advantages and disadvantages of each instruction class.

Single-Precision vs. Double-Precision

As discussed previously, single- and double-precision values differ in the number of bits used to store them. As a result, double-precision variables can represent values at a finer granularity and with a wider range than single-precision variables. To test this, you can download, build, and run the program floating-point-accuracy.cu from Wrox.com. This program stores the value 12.1 into single- and double-precision variables on the host and device and outputs the actual values stored to 20 decimal places. A sample output is provided, as follows:

```
Host single-precision representation of 12.1    = 12.10000038146972656250
Host double-precision representation of 12.1    = 12.09999999999999964473
Device single-precision representation of 12.1 = 12.10000038146972656250
Device double-precision representation of 12.1 = 12.09999999999999964473
Device and host single-precision representation equal? yes
Device and host double-precision representation equal? yes
```

While both the host and device represent the value 12.1 with the same approximation, neither is able to store precisely that value. For this particular example, double-precision values are marginally closer to the true value than single-precision.

The accuracy of double-precision values comes with both space and performance costs. The example floating-point-perf.cu from Wrox.com generates a random floating-point input vector, copies the vector to the GPU, iteratively performs a number of arithmetic operations on it, and then copies the result back. It does this for both single- and double-precision vectors and measures the time required for the transfers and for the kernel. This entire process is run repeatedly to minimize measurement error caused by random variations in execution time. A sample output of this program is provided, as follows:

```
Running 65535 blocks with 256 threads/block over 154990080 elements

Input   Diff Between Single- and Double-Precision
------------
0       1.16110611328622326255e-01
1       1.42341757498797960579e-01
2       1.45135404032771475613e-01
3       1.47929050144739449024e-01
4       1.03847696445882320404e-01
5       1.84766342732473276556e-01
6       1.48497488888096995652e-01
7       1.20041135203791782260e-01
8       1.38459781592246145010e-01
9       1.49065927878837101161e-01

For single-precision floating point, mean times for:
  Copy to device:   129 ms
  Kernel execution: 574 ms
  Copy from device: 201 ms
For double-precision floating point, mean times for:
  Copy to device:   258 ms (2.00x slower than single-precision)
  Kernel execution: 890 ms (1.55x slower than single-precision)
  Copy from device: 401 ms (2.00x slower than single-precision)
```

This example demonstrates two things. First, the performance difference between single- and double-precision floating-point operations in both communication and computation is non-negligible. In this case, using double-precision values nearly doubled total program execution time (though your mileage might vary depending if your application is either computation-bound or I/O-bound). The time to communicate values to and from the device exactly doubled, simply because double-precision values are twice as long as single-precision values. The compute time on the device also increased as both the amount of global memory I/O and the number of bits manipulated by each instruction increased.

This program also demonstrates the large numerical differences between single- and double-precision results that can accumulate in iterative applications as imprecise outputs from one iteration are used as inputs to the next iteration. Iterative applications are therefore more likely to require the use of double-precision variables for numerical accuracy.

It is also important to note that because a double-precision value takes up twice the space of a single-precision value, when you store a `double` in a register (declared locally in a kernel), the total shared register space of a thread block is reduced more than if a `float` were used. You must be extremely careful to properly declare single precision values for `float` values (for example `pi = 3.14159f;`). Any improper declarations that omit the trailing "f" (`pi = 3.14159`) will be automatically promoted by the `nvcc` compiler to double-precision.

Summary

The effects of floating-point operations on application performance and numerical accuracy are not unique to GPUs; you face the same concerns when working with other architectures. However, CUDA and GPUs have these unique qualities:

➤ Added host-device communication with double-precision values

➤ Added global memory I/O with double-precision values

➤ Loss of numerical accuracy due to aggressive floating-point optimizations by the CUDA compiler

In general, if accuracy is paramount for your application then double-precision values are a must. Otherwise, single-precision values can help you reap performance benefits. Table 7-2 summarizes the lessons learned using floating-point operations in CUDA.

TABLE 7-2: Performance, Accuracy, and Correctness of Single- and Double-Precision Floating-Point

	PERFORMANCE	ACCURACY	CORRECTNESS
SINGLE-PRECISION FLOATING-POINT	Better; less communication and slightly improved computational throughput	Good; only uses 32 bits to store values; not only is the range of minimum and maximum values smaller but also the granularity at which values can be represented is larger.	No change; no protection against multi-threaded unsafe accesses
DOUBLE-PRECISION FLOATING-POINT	Good; as a result of twice the bits having to be transferred to the GPU and wider values being operated on	Better; wider range as well as improved accuracy thanks to 64 bits of storage	No change; no protection against multi-threaded unsafe accesses

Standard vs. Intrinsic Functions

Standard and intrinsic functions differ in both numerical accuracy and performance. Standard functions provide full support for a wide range of arithmetic operations. However, many have equivalent intrinsic functions that implement the same functionality but with fewer instructions, improved performance, and lower numerical accuracy.

Visualizing Standard and Intrinsic Functions

One way to visualize the difference between standard and intrinsic functions is to study the instructions generated by the CUDA compiler for each function. Using the --ptx flag with nvcc instructs the compiler to generate an intermediate representation of the program in the *Parallel Thread Execution (PTX)* Instruction Set Architecture (ISA), rather than a final executable. PTX is similar to assembly in x86 programming; it provides an intermediate representation between the kernel code that you write, and the instructions executed by the GPU. As such, it is useful for gaining insight into the low-level execution path of a kernel.

As an example, you can generate the PTX for the following two CUDA functions to visually compare standard and intrinsic functions. To do this, save these kernels to a file named foo.cu:

```
__global__ void intrinsic(float *ptr) {
    *ptr = __powf(*ptr, 2.0f);
}

__global__ void standard(float *ptr) {
    *ptr = powf(*ptr, 2.0f);
}
```

Then generate a PTX file named foo.ptx using the following command:

```
$ nvcc --ptx -o foo.ptx foo.cu
```

The nvcc compiler will generate a file containing the PTX instructions for both of these device functions. You can open foo.ptx with your favorite text editor.

The contents of foo.ptx might be a little confusing if you have not looked at raw instructions before. The first instruction to look for is the special-purpose .entry instruction that marks the beginning of a function definition. Because there were two kernels in foo.cu, there are two .entry instructions in the generated PTX file. With CUDA 5.0, the function signature for the standard function is:

```
.entry _Z8standardPf (
    .param .u64 __cudaparm__Z8standardPf_ptr)
{
    ...
}
```

and for the instrinsic function is:

```
.entry _Z9intrinsicPf (
    .param .u64 __cudaparm__Z9intrinsicPf_ptr)
{
    ...
}
```

Your mangled function names might vary depending on compiler version. What should be familiar are the open bracket immediately after the `.entry` and a matching close bracket later in the file. Just as in C, these brackets enclose the instructions that define each function's logic. For instance, the first function defined in your `foo.ptx` file is the intrinsic version and should look similar to:

```
.entry _Z9intrinsicPf (
        .param .u64 __cudaparm__Z9intrinsicPf_ptr)
    {
    .reg .u64 %rd<3>;
    .reg .f32 %f<7>;
    .loc    14  4   0
$LDWbegin__Z9intrinsicPf:
    .loc    14  5   0
    ld.param.u64    %rd1, [__cudaparm__Z9intrinsicPf_ptr];
    ld.global.f32   %f1, [%rd1+0];
    lg2.approx.f32  %f2, %f1;
    mov.f32     %f3, 0f40000000;         // 2
    mul.f32     %f4, %f2, %f3;
    ex2.approx.f32  %f5, %f4;
    st.global.f32   [%rd1+0], %f5;
    .loc    14  6   0
    exit;
$LDWend__Z9intrinsicPf:
    } // _Z9intrinsicPf
```

It takes 17 lines to implement the intrinsic `__powf` function, and a mere seven instructions to perform a floating-point exponentiation. However, if you take a look at the standard `powf` function defined in your `foo.ptx` file, it is likely much, much longer (344-lines using the CUDA 5.0 Toolkit). While line counts don't translate directly to instructions or cycles, you can imagine the savings in performance are still significant.

However, it is not just performance that separates standard and intrinsic functions; they also differ in precision. To test the differences in both performance and precision, you can download, build, and run the `intrinsic-standard-comp.cu` example from `Wrox.com`. The kernel in this program repeatedly calculates the square of an input value, first using the standard function `powf`, then the intrinsic function `__powf`. This example also uses the C standard math library on the host to perform the same computation and uses the host results as a baseline value. A sample output from `intrinsic-standard-comp.cu` is as follows:

```
Host calculated             66932852.000000
Standard Device calculated  66932848.000000
Intrinsic Device calculated 66932804.000000
Host equals Standard?       No diff=4.000000e+00
Host equals Intrinsic?      No diff=4.800000e+01
Standard equals Intrinsic?  No diff=4.400000e+01

Mean execution time for standard function powf:    47 ms
Mean execution time for intrinsic function __powf: 2 ms
```

As expected, there are huge performance gains using intrinsic functions over standard functions, with nearly 24 times speedup. The numerical results are much more interesting. Not only are the outputs of the CUDA standard and intrinsic functions numerically different, but they also both differ from the result calculated by the host standard math library. However, when comparing the intrinsic result and the standard result, the intrinsic result is an order of magnitude farther from the baseline host result.

PORTING FROM CPU TO GPU

Using CUDA for scientific simulations, financial algorithms, and other applications that demand a high level of accuracy and fidelity generally requires two steps: Porting *legacy applications* from a CPU-only framework to CUDA, followed by verifying the numerical accuracy of the port by comparing results from the legacy implementation and the CUDA version.

Even when using numerically stable CUDA functions, the results of computation from GPU devices can still differ from the legacy CPU-only applications they replace. Because of the inherent inaccuracies of floating-point operations on both the host and device, it can sometimes be difficult to point to one output being more correct than the other. Therefore, porting plans must explicitly prepare for numerical differences and, if necessary, set acceptable tolerances.

Manipulating Instruction Generation

In most cases, the translation of programmer-written kernel code to the GPU instruction set is handled behind the scenes by the CUDA compiler. Rarely will you have the desire to inspect or manually modify the instructions being generated. However, that does not mean you cannot easily direct the compiler to prefer performance or accuracy, or balance both. Two techniques enable tighter control over the types of instruction-level optimizations the CUDA compiler can perform: Compiler flags, and intrinsic or standard function calls.

For example, the __fdividef intrinsic function implements faster but less numerically precise floating-point division, compared to the / operator. Suppose you have the following kernel foo:

```
__global__ void foo(...) {
    float a = ...;
    float b = ...;
    float c = a / b;
}
```

You could simply replace / with the functionally equivalent __fdividef and measure improved performance:

```
__global__ void foo(...) {
    float a = ...;
    float b = ...;
    float c = __fdividef(a, b);
}
```

However, manually tweaking your kernel operation-by-operation is labor-intensive. Compiler flags provide a more automated and global way of manipulating compiler instruction generation. For example, you might want to control generation of the floating-point MAD (FMAD) instruction by the CUDA compiler. Recall that MAD is a simple compiler optimization that fuses a multiply and add into a single instruction, thereby halving the time that operation would take compared to using two instructions. However, this optimization comes at the cost of some numerical accuracy. Therefore, some applications might want to explicitly limit use of the FMAD instruction.

The `--fmad` option to `nvcc` globally enables or disables the FMAD optimization for an entire compilation unit. By default, `nvcc` uses `--fmad=true` to enable FMAD instruction generation as a performance optimization. Passing `--fmad=false` prevents the compiler from fusing any multiplies with additions, hurting performance but likely improving the numerical accuracy of your application.

For example, given the following simple kernel:

```
__global__ void foo(float *ptr) {
    *ptr = (*ptr) * (*ptr) + (*ptr);
}
```

Generating the PTX for `foo` with `--fmad=true` yields a single arithmetic instruction for the kernel body:

```
mad.f32     %f2, %f1, %f1, %f1;
```

Here you can see a single multiply-add MAD instruction applied to three, 32-bit floating-point values, as expected. If this kernel is instead compiled with `--fmad=false`, a different pair of instructions appear in the MAD instruction's place:

```
mul.rn.f32  %f2, %f1, %f1;
add.rn.f32  %f3, %f2, %f1;
```

The compiler flag worked as expected; you can see that `nvcc` did not fuse the multiply and add together into a single MAD instruction.

Note that there are a number of CUDA compiler flags that affect arithmetic instruction generation, besides `--fmad`. A full listing of them is available with the `--help` option to `nvcc`, and is listed in Table 7-3.

TABLE 7-3: Compiler Flags for Guiding Instruction Generation

FLAG	DESCRIPTION	DEFAULT VALUE	EFFECT ON PERFORMANCE	EFFECT ON ACCURACY
`--ftz=[true, false]`	Flushes all single-precision denormal floating-point values to zero. A description of denormal numbers is beyond the scope of this book, but their presence in your application might require all or some arithmetic operations to take less efficient code paths (depending on whether you have a pre-Fermi or post-Fermi GPU).	false	When set to true, this flag might improve performance, depending on the values processed and arithmetic performed in your application.	When set to false, this flag might improve accuracy, depending on the values processed and arithmetic performed in your application.

`--prec-div=[true,false]`	Improves the numerical accuracy of all single-precision divisions and reciprocals	true	When set to true, there might be performance degradation.	When set to true, numerical compatibility with the IEEE standard improves.
`--prec-sqrt=[true,false]`	Forces a more numerically accurate square root function	true	When set to true, there might be performance degradation.	When set to true, numerical compatibility with the IEEE standard improves.
`--fmad=[true,false]`	Controls whether the compiler is permitted to fuse multiply-add operations into a single FMAD instruction	true	Enabling FMAD improves performance, provided there are MAD operations on floating-point variables in your application.	Enabling FMAD might reduce the accuracy of your application.
`--use_fast_math`	Replaces all standard functions in your application with their intrinsic function equivalents. It also sets `--ftz-true`, `--prec-div-false`, and `--prec-sqrt=false`.	false	Enabling `--use_fast_math` implies a number of optimizations being enabled, all of which improve performance.	Enabling `--use_fast_math` might decrease the numerical accuracy of your application.

In addition to the `--fmad` option, CUDA also includes a pair of intrinsic functions that can be used to control FMAD instruction generation: `__fmul` and `__dmul`. These functions implement floating-point multiplication for the `float` and `double` types. While these functions do not affect the performance of the multiplication operation, calling them in the place of a `*` operator prevents `nvcc` from using that multiplication as part of the MAD optimization. For example, in the previous code sample of the kernel `foo`, `--fmad=false` was used to prevent generating a `mad.f32` instruction. The same effect could have been accomplished by inserting a call to `__fmul`:

```
__global__ void foo(float *ptr) {
    ptr = __fmul_rn(*ptr, *ptr) + *ptr;
}
```

Note that `__fmul` and `__dmul` prevent the generation of MAD instructions no matter whether `--fmad=true` or `--fmad=false` is specified. As a result, it is possible to have the MAD compiler optimization enabled globally while improving the numerical robustness of certain computations by selectively calling __fmul or __dmul.

You may have noticed that when __fmul was called in foo, the call was actually to a function __fmul_rn. Many floating-point intrinsic functions (including __fadd, __fsub, __fmul, and so on) explicitly indicate the floating-point rounding mode in the function name using a two-character suffix (summarized in Table 7-4). Recall that because floating-point variables can still only represent discrete albeit fine-grain values, any unrepresentable values must be rounded to representable values. The rounding mode of a floating-point operation determines how unrepresentable values are converted to representable values.

TABLE 7-4: Variants of __fmul with Different Rounding Behavior

SUFFIX	MEANING
rn	Round values that cannot be precisely represented in the current floating-point mode (single or double) to the nearest value that can be represented. This is the default behavior.
rz	Always round values toward zero (i.e., values greater than zero are rounded down and values less than zero are rounded up).
ru	Always round values up toward positive infinity.
rd	Always round values down toward negative infinity.

Now that you have seen the instruction-level changes caused by enabling or disabling the FMAD optimization, you can also observe the effect those changes have on numerical accuracy. You can download, build, and run the fmad.cu example from Wrox.com. This example runs a single MAD operation on the host and a single MAD operation on the device using standard functions. Compiling fmad.cu with different values for the --fmad flag allows you to compare the results of CUDA kernels running with and without the MAD optimization against a baseline value from the host.

First, try compiling fmad.cu with the MAD CUDA optimization enabled. Note that you could also leave the --fmad=true parameter out, as it defaults to true.

```
$ nvcc -arch=sm_20 --fmad=true fmad.cu -o fmad
```

Executing the generated application produces the following sample output:

```
$ ./fmad
The device output a different value than the host, diff=8.881784e-16.
```

As expected, using the MAD optimization led to small numerical errors on the device. fmad.cu can also be compiled with the MAD compiler optimization explicitly disabled:

```
$ nvcc -arch=sm_20 --fmad=false fmad.cu -o fmad
```

Executing the MAD-disabled application produces the following sample output:

```
$ ./fmad
The device output the same value as the host.
```

With FMAD disabled, the values produced by the host and device are identical. However, the device kernel will now require more instructions to perform this computation.

Summary

This section demonstrated the wide-ranging and pervasive impact that standard and intrinsic functions have on program behavior (as summarized in Table 7-5). In many situations, you can control how instructions are generated by the compiler, which is extremely helpful when tuning your application for both performance and numerical accuracy.

TABLE 7-5: Performance, Accuracy, and Correctness of Standard and Intrinsic Functions

	PERFORMANCE	ACCURACY	CORRECTNESS
STANDARD FUNCTIONS	Good; standard functions generally translate to many more instructions.	Better; standard functions are guaranteed to be more numerically accurate than their intrinsic cousins according to the CUDA Programming Guide.	No change; no protection against multi-threaded unsafe accesses
INTRINSIC FUNCTIONS	Better; intrinsic functions make use of native GPU instructions to decrease the number of instructions used.	Good; approximations are generally necessary to enable drastic reduction in instruction count.	No change; no protection against multi-threaded unsafe accesses

Understanding Atomic Instructions

In this section, you will explore how to use atomic operations and learn about implementing correct operations on shared data in a highly concurrent environment. Note that GPUs of different compute capability support different atomic functions. You will need access to a GPU with compute capability 1.0 or above to run the examples in this section.

From the Ground Up

Every atomic function provided by CUDA can be re-implemented using a single atomic function: the atomic *compare-and-swap* (CAS) operator. Atomic CAS is a powerful operation that will not only enable you to define your own atomic functions in CUDA but also aid with a deeper understanding of atomic operations in general.

CAS takes as input three items: A memory location, an expected value at that memory location, and the value you would like to store at that memory location. It then performs the following steps:

1. Read the target location and compare the value stored there to the expected value.

   a. If the stored value equals the expected value, the target memory location is filled with the desired value.

   b. If the stored value does not equal the expected value, then no change is made to the target location.

2. In either case, a CAS operation always returns the value that it found stored at the target location. Note that using the returned value, you can check for a successful swap. If the value returned is equal to the expected value passed, then the CAS operation must have succeeded.

Now, that is just the CAS operation. An atomic CAS implies that the entire CAS process is done without interference from any other threads. Because it is an atomic operator, if the return value of the CAS operation indicates that the write succeeded, then that change must have been made visible to all other threads as well.

To learn more about atomic operations, it will be useful for you to implement an example atomic function from the ground up using CUDA's `atomicCAS` device function. For this example, you will be implementing atomic 32-bit integer addition. The signature for the relevant variant of `atomicCAS` is:

```
int atomicCAS(int *address, int compare, int val);
```

Here `address` is the target memory location, `compare` is the value expected to be at that location, and `val` is the value you wish to write at that location.

So, how might you implement an atomic addition using `atomicCAS`? You will first need to decompose addition into its component parts and define it as a CAS operation. One helpful technique when implementing custom atomic operations is to define the starting and finishing states of the target. With an atomic add, the starting state is the base value that will be incremented. The finishing state is the sum of the starting state and the increment value. This definition translates directly to `atomicCAS`: The expected value is the starting state, and the desired value is the finishing state.

To implement a custom atomic addition function, you will start with a function signature that takes a location to add to and a value to add to it:

```
__device__ int myAtomicAdd(int *address, int incr) {
    ...
}
```

You can calculate an expected value for the target by simply reading the target memory location. The desired value is then defined by the value read plus the `incr` value passed to `myAtomicAdd`. Using these expected and desired values, a call can be made to `atomicCAS` that implements an addition:

```
__device__ int myAtomicAdd(int *address, int incr) {
    // Create an initial guess for the value stored at *address.
    int expected = *address;
    int oldValue = atomicCAS(address, expected, expected + incr);
    ...
}
```

This `myAtomicAdd` function can already perform an atomic add! However, the operation will only succeed if the value read into `expected` is also the value stored at `address` when the `atomicCAS` is performed. Because the target location is shared by multiple threads (otherwise atomic operations would not be necessary), it is possible that another thread will modify the value at `address` between it being read into `expected` and modified by `atomicCAS`. If that happened, the `atomicCAS` would fail because the current value at `address` and the value of `expected` would differ.

Recall that failure is signaled by an `atomicCAS` return value that differs from the expected value. Using that information, `myAtomicAdd` can check for failure and retry the compare-and-swap in a loop until `atomicCAS` is successful:

```
__device__ int myAtomicAdd(int *address, int incr) {
    // Create an initial guess for the value stored at *address.
    int expected = *address;
    int oldValue = atomicCAS(address, expected, expected + incr);

    // Loop while expected is incorrect.
    while (oldValue != expected) {
        expected = oldValue;
        oldValue = atomicCAS(address, expected, expected + incr);
    }
    return oldValue;
}
```

The first three lines of this function are the same as earlier. If the first `atomicCAS` fails, `myAtomicAdd` now loops as long as the last value returned by `atomicCAS` is different from the expected value. Once that condition fails, the swap must have succeeded, and `myAtomicAdd` exits the loop. Otherwise, the expected value is reset to the most recent value read and a retry is made. To match the semantics of other CUDA atomic functions, `myAtomicAdd` also returns the value that was replaced at the target location by returning the most recent value returned by `atomicCAS`.

You can download, build, and run a copy of this code in `my-atomic-add.cu` from `Wrox.com`. Build as follows:

```
$ nvcc -arch=sm_11 my-atomic-add.cu
```

Although the next section covers the atomic functions that CUDA supports natively, it is important to understand that you are not limited to them. With `atomicCAS` you can implement a much wider range of atomic operations as required by your particular application.

Built-In CUDA Atomic Functions

CUDA supports a collection of atomic functions. The subset of those accessible to you depends on the compute capability of your device.

Support for atomic functions starts at compute capability 1.1. At this level, you will have access to functions that manipulate 32-bit values in global memory.

Support for manipulating 32-bit values in shared memory and 64-bit values in global memory starts with compute capability 1.2. Support for 64-bit manipulations in shared memory starts with compute capability 2.0.

Table 7-6 lists the operations for which CUDA supports an atomic function, the associated CUDA device function, and the types supported.

TABLE 7-6: Built-In CUDA Atomic Operations

OPERATION	FUNCTION	SUPPORTED TYPES
Addition	atomicAdd	int, unsigned int, unsigned long long int, float
Subtraction	atomicSub	int, unsigned int
Unconditional Swap	atomicExch	int, unsigned int, unsigned long long int, float
Minimum	atomicMin	int, unsigned int, unsigned long long int
Maximum	atomicMax	int, unsigned int, unsigned long long int
Increment	atomicInc	unsigned int
Decrement	atomicDec	unsigned int
Compare-And-Swap	atomicCAS	int, unsigned int, unsigned long long int
And	atomicAnd	int, unsigned int, unsigned long long int
Or	atomicOr	int, unsigned int, unsigned long long int
Xor	atomicXor	int, unsigned int, unsigned long long int

The Cost of Atomic Operations

While atomic functions are very useful and absolutely necessary in some applications, they may come with a steep performance cost. There are a number of contributing factors to this:

1. When performing an atomic operation in global or shared memory, one of the guarantees made by atomicity is that the change will be immediately visible to all threads. Therefore, at the bare minimum, an atomic instruction is going all the way to global or shared memory to read the current value stored there with no caching allowed. If the atomic instruction is successful, it must also write the desired value to global or shared memory.

2. Conflicting atomic accesses to a shared location might require one or more retries by conflicting threads, analogous to running more than one iteration of myAtomicAdd's loop. Although there is limited visibility on how built-in atomic functions are built, this will certainly be true for any custom atomic operations you implement. If your application loops repeatedly while incurring I/O overheads, performance will degrade.

3. When threads in the same warp must execute different instructions, warp execution is serialized. If multiple threads in a warp issue an atomic operation on the same location in memory, something similar will happen as they conflict with each other. Because only a single thread's atomic operation can succeed, all others must retry. If a single atomic instruction requires n cycles, and t threads in the same warp execute that atomic instruction on the same memory location, then the elapsed time will be $t \times n$, as only one thread is successful on each successive retry. Keep in

mind that the rest of the threads in the warp are also stalled waiting for all atomic operations to complete, and that an atomic operation also implies a global read and write.

To explore atomic instructions, you will be examining some simple examples. First, it is interesting to compare the behavior and performance of atomic operations to unsafe accesses. You can download, build, and run `atomic-ordering.cu` from `Wrox.com`. This small application contains two kernels, named `atomics` and `unsafe`. The `atomics` kernel performs atomic additions from every thread on a single shared variable, saving the old value at the target location:

```
values_read[tid] = atomicAdd(shared_var, 1);
```

The kernel `unsafe` performs the same additions on the same shared variable, but does not use atomic functions:

```
int old = *shared_var;
*shared_var = old + 1;
values_read[tid] = old;
```

That means threads running the `unsafe` kernel are performing global reads and writes without any mechanisms to prevent overwriting each other. Because both kernels also store the old values at the target location, thread conflicts can be visualized as duplicated old values. A sample output is as follows:

```
In total, 30 runs using atomic operations took 3704 ms
  Using atomic operations also produced an output of 6400064
In total, 30 runs using unsafe operations took 11 ms
  Using unsafe operations also produced an output of 100001
Threads performing atomic operations read values 1 3 5 7 17 19 21 23 33 35
Threads performing unsafe operations read values 0 0 0 0 0 0 0 0 0 0
```

The difference in performance is obvious: The version that uses `atomics` took over 300 times longer to run. The final output shows that not all of the additions performed in the `unsafe` version are written to global memory; many are overwritten and never read by other threads. These conflicts are made more obvious by the values listed in the last two lines of the output. While the `atomics` version shows threads with unique increment values, each of the first ten threads in the `unsafe` version incremented from the same value of zero and will therefore all write the same value, one. Note that some additions in the `unsafe` version still complete because the final output was not one, so some threads successfully wrote to global memory and had their values read back.

This example illustrates the steep tradeoff in performance and correctness you will face when deciding where atomic operations are a necessity and where unsafe accesses are an option. You must be very careful when making this evaluation; deciding to use unsafe accesses is not a recommended programming practice, and should only be done if you are certain correctness is maintained.

Limiting the Performance Cost of Atomic Operations

Fortunately, when atomic operations are necessary, there are techniques you can use to reduce the performance loss. You can augment global atomic operations with local steps that generate an intermediate result from threads in the same thread block. This enables the use of local, lower-latency resources such as shuffle instructions or shared memory to produce partial results from each thread block before combining partial results into a final, global result using atomic operations. Of course, for this to be valid, the operation performed must be commutative (that is, the order of operations must not affect the final result). Figure 7-5 illustrates a local reduction to produce a partial result, followed by atomic operations to compute the final output.

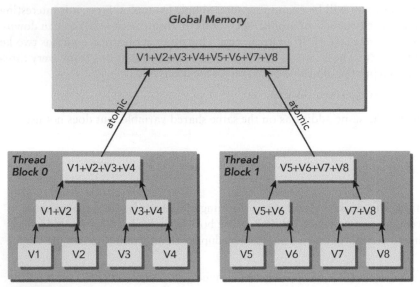

FIGURE 7-5

Atomic Floating-Point Support

One point of note with atomic functions is that they are mostly declared to operate on integer types, such as int, unsigned int, or unsigned long long int. Of all the atomic functions, only atomicExch and atomicAdd have existing support for single-precision floating-point values. None of the atomic functions support double-precision. Fortunately, if your application needs to manage multi-threaded access to shared floating-point variables, there are techniques for implementing your own floating-point atomic operations. At a high level, the idea is to store the raw bits of a floating-point value in a variable of a supported type and issue atomic CAS operations using that supported type.

An example will make this clearer. The following is a version of myAtomicAdd implemented for single-precision floating-point numbers:

```
__device__ float myAtomicAdd(float *address, float incr) {
    // Convert address to point to a supported type of the same size
    unsigned int *typedAddress = (unsigned int *)address;

    // Stored the expected and desired float values as an unsigned int
    float currentVal = *address;
    unsigned int expected = __float2uint_rn(currentVal);
    unsigned int desired = __float2uint_rn(currentVale + incr);

    int oldIntValue = atomicCAS(typedAddress, expected, desired);
    while (oldIntValue != expected) {
        expected = oldIntValue;
```

```
    /*
     * Convert the value read from typedAddress to a float, increment,
     * and then convert back to an unsigned int
     */
    desired = __float2uint_rn(__uint2float_rn(oldIntValue) + incr);
    oldIntValue = atomicCAS(typedAddress, expected, desired);
}
    return __uint2float_rn(oldIntValue);
}
```

Much of this code should be familiar from the previous myAtomicAdd example. The main difference here is the translation of values passed to and returned from atomicCAS using a variety of type-conversion utility functions provided by CUDA. This particular example uses:

1. A cast to change the type of the address pointer from float to unsigned int

2. The use of __float2uint_rn to convert the initial guess, *address, and the desired value, *address + incr, to be unsigned ints containing the same bits

3. The use of __uint2float_rn to retrieve a floating-point number from the unsigned int returned by atomicCAS and calculate what the new desired value is, in case of failure

All of this conversion is necessary because the types required by the application (float) and by the atomicCAS function (unsigned int) differ. CUDA provides a wide range of other type-specific conversion functions including __double_as_longlong, __longlong_as_double, __double-2float_rn, and more. These functions are invaluable for implementing a wide range of custom floating-point atomic functions in CUDA. The full list is available in the CUDA Math API Documentation.

Summary

This section provided an in-depth study on the use of atomic operations in CUDA. It covered background on how atomic operations work in CUDA, the variety of atomic operations available in CUDA, ways to limit the performance impact of atomic operations, and floating-point support in CUDA atomic functions. Table 7-7 summarizes the lessons learned in this section.

TABLE 7-7: Performance, Accuracy, and Correctness of Atomic Operations

	PERFORMANCE	ACCURACY	CORRECTNESS
Atomic Operations	Poor, atomicity imposes a large overhead on simple arithmetic operations.	No effect on accuracy, though few built-in atomic functions support floating-point to begin with.	Guaranteed with conflicting accesses from multiple threads
Unsafe Accesses	Better, unsafe accesses show the same performance as any other global memory access.	No effect	No guarantee of correctness

Bringing It All Together

In this section you will use a simplified but real-world example, NBody, to see how the lessons of this chapter apply to a sample application. The code for `nbody.cu` can be downloaded from `Wrox.com`.

If you are unfamiliar with NBody, it is a common simulation benchmark. It simulates a number of particles and their interactions as each of them exerts forces on every other particle, as depicted in Figure 7-6. NBody is particularly well suited to the GPU, and there is a wide range of literature available on highly optimized versions of NBody on GPUs. The example code provided is not based on those studies, rather it is used here as a straightforward example to improve your understanding. This NBody example iteratively updates velocities for each particle based on the acceleration imparted by forces from all other particles in the simulation. It then updates each particle's position based on the new velocity.

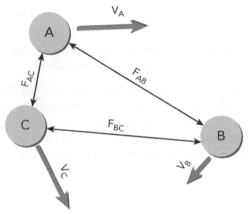

FIGURE 7-6

First, consider `nbody.cu`'s use of atomic operations. This NBody implementation keeps two global statistics: whether any particle has exceeded a certain distance from the origin, and how many particles are moving faster than a certain speed. Because a precise count of particles above the threshold speed is required, the application must make use of atomic operations to ensure complete accuracy of that count. However, because the application requirements only require knowing if any particles have traveled beyond a certain radius from the origin, unsafe accesses can be used to set a boolean flag.

`nbody.cu` is configured to support the use of both single- and double-precision floating-point values for storing particle positions, velocities, and acceleration. The decision to use `float` or `double` is made at compile-time using pre-processor macros. While `nbody.cu` defaults to single-precision, you can explicitly set your choice by adding either -DSINGLE_PREC or -DDOUBLE_PREC on the command-line at compile time. For example, the following is a sample compilation and execution of NBody with single-precision values:

```
$ nvcc -arch=sm_20 -DSINGLE_PREC -DVALIDATE nbody.cu -o nbody
$ ./nbody
Using single-precision floating-point values
Running host simulation. WARNING, this might take a while.
Any points beyond bounds? true, # points exceeded velocity 30262/30720
Total execution time 10569
Error = 5.48078840035512282469e+00
```

Double-precision values can be configured and tested using:

```
$ nvcc -arch=sm_20 -DDOUBLE_PREC -DVALIDATE nbody.cu -o nbody
$ ./nbody
Using double-precision floating-point values
Running host simulation. WARNING, this might take a while.
Any points beyond bounds? true, # points exceeded velocity 30251/30720
Total execution time 60688
Error = 3.66473952850002815396e+00
```

Note the 6 times slow down of overall execution time when using double-precision floating-point! That is a high price to pay for increased accuracy, but a necessity in many applications. Recall from earlier analysis of the `floating-point-perf.cu` example that this slowdown is caused by a combination of:

1. Doubled host-device communication costs due to the `double` primitive type being twice the length of the `float` primitive type

2. Increased I/O costs on the device to load twice as much data from global memory

3. Reduced resources available to each thread in a thread block as fewer `doubles` fit into registers than `floats`, potentially leading to more spills of variables to global memory.

4. Increased computational cost to perform arithmetic operations on twice the number of bits

Note that the compilation above also included a `-DVALIDATE` flag. In NBody, this adds a test for the numerical accuracy of the results by comparing the output from CUDA against the output from a host implementation. The error printed is the mean difference between the particle positions calculated by the host and the device. Using double-precision floating-point values shows a clear improvement in precision, though there is still a significant difference between the values computed by CUDA and by the host with the default flags passed to the CUDA compiler.

Finally, it is also important to study how performance changes when standard or intrinsic functions are enabled using the various compiler flags discussed earlier. Recall from Table 7-3 that `--ftz`, `--prec-div`, `--prec-sqrt`, and `--fmad` each can affect performance and accuracy individually, and that `--use_fast_math` sets all of those options to maximize performance while auto-selecting intrinsic functions in place of their standard function equivalents. Table 7-8 shows a sample of execution times and numerical errors achieved with each flag either set to its most numerically stable or optimized state. These executions were performed with single-precision values.

TABLE 7-8: Changes to NBody Performance and Accuracy with Compiler Flags

DESCRIPTION	`--ftz`	`--prec -div`	`--prec -sqrt`	`--fmad`	`--use_fast _math`	TIME (MS)	ERROR
All flags set to maximize performance	True	False	False	True	True	5336	4.6946
All flags set to maximize numerical accuracy	False	True	True	False	False	12042	0.0000

These results match perfectly with expected results and demonstrate the importance of understanding the compiler flags. With flags set to maximize performance, total execution time improves 2.25 times. With flags set to maximize numerical accuracy, there is no numerical deviation from the host implementation.

SUMMARY

When building a CUDA application you must be aware of the effects on performance and numerical accuracy from: floating-point operations, standard and intrinsic functions, and atomic operations.

In this chapter, you gained a deeper understanding of how to guide compiler instruction generation for your kernels. While the CUDA compiler and libraries normally hide low-level details, that opacity can be a double-edged sword. Automatic compiler optimization removes some of your optimization burden, but can lead to a lack of awareness and visibility into the transformations applied to your kernels. This opacity can lead to difficult-to-debug numerical issues. In addition, lack of awareness of these performance knobs might cause you to miss obvious opportunities when optimizing your application.

With the methodology described in this chapter, you will be better prepared to optimize your applications for performance, accuracy, and correctness. The NBody example illustrates the significant gains associated with:

➤ Single- and double-precision floating-point operations

➤ Intrinsic and standard functions

➤ Atomic and unsafe accesses

This methodology helps you ensure full utilization of GPU computational throughput without sacrificing application correctness. Next, you will learn how to improve your productivity by using GPU-accelerated CUDA libraries and OpenACC directive based compilers.

CHAPTER 7 EXERCISES

1. Translate the following sequence of arithmetic operations into calls to the double-precision intrinsic function __fma_rn. Then, try the same with calls to __dmul_rn and __dmul_rn:

```
a * b + c * d + e * f * g
```

2. Write a program that, given a floating-point value, calculates the next largest and smallest floating-point value that can be correctly represented using the same storage type. Do this for both single-precision and double-precision types and compare the results. Are you able to find any values for which single-precision has a more accurate representation? If not, do you still think they exist?

3. You have seen that unsafe accesses from multiple threads cause unpredictable results. But you have also seen that some guarantees can be extracted from unsafe accesses (that is,

if every thread writes a 1 then the final value can't magically be something else). Consider the following code snippet:

```
int n = 0;
int main(int argc, char **argv) {
    for (i = 0; i < 5; i++) {
        int tmp = n;
        tmp = tmp + 1;
        n = tmp;
    }
    return 0;
}
```

If a single thread ran this application, you would expect the final output to be 5. What if 5 threads ran the same loop in parallel? What are the largest and smallest values n could have? The largest should be self-evident: 25, with 5 increments from 5 threads. However, reasoning about the smallest possible value is more difficult. Hint: n can be less than 5, but it's up to you to figure out why. As a follow-up, how would you use atomic instructions and local reduction to optimize the performance of this code snippet when run in parallel?

4. Based on the `myAtomicAdd` example, implement a custom `myAtomicMin` device function based on `atomicCAS`.

5. Based on the floating-point `myAtomicAdd` example, implement atomic double-precision floating-point addition using `atomicCAS`.

6. The examples in this chapter used atomic operations on global memory locations. CUDA 32-bit atomics are also supported on shared memory for GPUs above compute capability 1.2. Based on what you learned about conflicts in shared memory in Chapter 5, what additional issues do you see arising when using atomic instructions in shared memory?

7. Try compiling the `nbody.cu` example down to PTX with and without the `--use_fast_math` compiler flag. How does the number of instructions generated change?

8. In `nbody.cu`, replace the use of `atomicAdd` with an optimized parallel reduction function based on `reduceSmemShfl` from Chapter 5. Note that you will still need to perform global aggregation of results using an `atomicAdd`. Does this affect performance? Why or why not?

9. Try toggling individual compiler flags when building `nbody.cu`. Are you able to find a combination that performs better than the example provided? Why might performance improve? Can you find a median point with some but not all optimization flags enabled that balances performance and numerical accuracy?

10. Rewrite `nbody.cu` so that it directly calls intrinsic functions, removing the need to specify `--use_fast_math`. Is there any difference between the PTX generated from `nbody.cu` when comparing your version that explicitly calls intrinsic functions to the provided code with `--use_fast_math` set? Keep in mind other optimizations that are implicitly enabled by `--use_fast_math`. Can you manually write an `nbody.cu` that is equivalent to the version generated by `--use_fast_math`? If not, compare the number of PTX instructions to see how close you can come.

8

GPU-Accelerated CUDA Libraries and OpenACC

WHAT'S IN THIS CHAPTER?

➤ Exploring new levels of parallelism with CUDA libraries

➤ Understanding the common workflow shared by many CUDA libraries

➤ Experimenting with CUDA libraries in linear algebra, Fourier transforms, and random number generation

➤ Covering new library features in CUDA 6

➤ Accelerating applications on GPUs with OpenACC directives

> **CODE DOWNLOAD** *The wrox.com code downloads for this chapter are found at* www.wrox.com/go/procudac *on the Download Code tab. The code is in the Chapter 8 download and individually named according to the names throughout the chapter.*

In this book, you have learned a wide range of basic and advanced features in CUDA C. These lessons have enabled you to take advantage of the computational throughput of GPUs when writing new, custom applications or porting existing, legacy applications by hand. However, in many cases the main barrier to building applications in CUDA is development time. It is imperative that you maximize productivity and efficiency when creating or porting applications.

To augment the abilities of CUDA developers, NVIDIA and other institutions provide domain-specific CUDA *libraries* that can be used as building blocks for more complex applications. These libraries have been optimized by CUDA experts and designed to have high-level, highly-usable

APIs with standardized data formats to facilitate their ability to plug in to existing applications (*pluggability*). CUDA libraries sit on top of the CUDA runtime, providing a simple, familiar, and domain-specific interface for both host applications and third-party libraries (depicted in Figure 8-1).

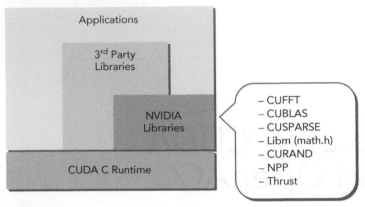

FIGURE 8-1

Another tool that provides a layer of abstraction over CUDA is OpenACC. OpenACC uses compiler directives to annotate regions of code and data for offload from the host to an accelerator device. The compiler arranges for those regions to be executed on the device by auto-generating any necessary memory copies, kernel launches, and other CUDA API calls. OpenACC will look familiar to you: Its usage is similar to that of OpenMP, the directive-based host programming model described in Chapter 6. OpenACC can be integrated with CUDA libraries and hand-coded CUDA kernels. It allows programmers to implement their own kernel code, but dissociates many of the more mundane CUDA programming tasks.

The sections and examples that follow extend your existing knowledge of CUDA, to help you understand these tools and how to integrate them into your applications. You will start by learning about the CUDA libraries listed below, and then explore more details on OpenACC.

➤ *cuSPARSE* includes a range of general-purpose sparse linear algebra routines.

➤ *cuBLAS* includes CUDA ports of all functions in the standard Basic Linear Algebra Subprograms (BLAS) library for Levels 1, 2, and 3.

➤ *cuFFT* includes methods for performing fast Fourier transforms (FFTs) and their inverse.

➤ *cuRAND* includes methods for rapid random number generation using the GPU.

INTRODUCING THE CUDA LIBRARIES

CUDA libraries are no different than system libraries or user-built libraries. They are a collection of function definitions whose signatures are exposed through header files. The CUDA libraries are special in that all computation implemented in the library is accelerated using a GPU, as opposed to a CPU.

There are many advantages to using CUDA libraries, compared to building your own hand-coded CUDA C implementation or using legacy host-only libraries. For many applications, CUDA libraries offer the best balance of usability and performance. The APIs of many CUDA libraries are deliberately made similar to those in a standard library in the same domain. As a result, you can use CUDA libraries in the same fashion as the host-based versions, and realize significant speedup with minimal programming effort. The time required for you to port complex algorithms from CPUs to GPUs can be reduced from months or weeks down to days or hours.

Performance is a key advantage that CUDA libraries have over host-only libraries, and often over hand-coded CUDA implementations as well. The CUDA library developers are leading experts on GPU architecture. CUDA libraries enable you to take advantage of their expertise to rapidly accelerate new and legacy applications.

CUDA libraries also incur low maintenance overheads for software developers. By reusing existing and mature implementations, the burden of testing and managing these complex algorithms in CUDA is delegated. These libraries are rigorously tested and managed by NVIDIA and its partners, removing those tasks from the responsibility of a domain expert or new CUDA programmer.

Still, there are generally some additional steps required to add CUDA libraries to a legacy application, and further optimizations are possible for performance improvement relative to standard host libraries. Please note, there are excellent reference guides freely available online through the NVIDIA Developer Zone. This chapter does not focus on the use of each individual function but rather high-level use and optimization of applications. The examples in this section use CUDA libraries based on case studies of particular libraries.

Supported Domains for CUDA Libraries

As of the writing of this book, there are 19 GPU-accelerated libraries documented and available for download from the NVIDIA Developer Zone. For an up-to-date list, please visit the NVIDIA Developer Zone at `developer.nvidia.com`. A current list and the domain to which they apply are included in Table 8-1.

TABLE 8-1: A Collection of Supported CUDA Library Domains

LIBRARY NAME	DOMAIN
NVIDIA cuFFT	Fast Fourier Transforms
NVIDIA cuBLAS	Linear Algebra (BLAS Library)
CULA Tools	Linear Algebra
MAGMA	Next generation Linear Algebra
IMSL Fortran Numerical Library	Mathematics and Statistics
NVIDIA cuSPARSE	Sparse Linear Algebra
NVIDIA CUSP	Sparse Linear Algebra and Graph Computations

continues

TABLE 8-1 *(continued)*

LIBRARY NAME	DOMAIN
AccelerEyes ArrayFire	Mathematics, Signal and Image Processing, and Statistics
NVIDIA cuRAND	Random Number Generation
NVIDIA NPP	Image and Signal Processing
NVIDIA CUDA Math Library	Mathematics
Thrust	Parallel Algorithms and Data Structures
HiPLAR	Linear Algebra in R
Geometry Performance Primitives	Computational Geometry
Paralution	Sparse Iterative Methods
AmgX	Core Solvers

If your application fits any of these domains, it is strongly recommended that you explore the online documentation for the provided libraries.

A Common Library Workflow

Many CUDA libraries share concepts, features, and a common workflow when being called from a host application. A common workflow while using NVIDIA libraries is as follows:

1. Create a library-specific handle that manages contextual information useful for the library's operation.
2. Allocate device memory for inputs and outputs to the library function.
3. If inputs are not already in a library-supported format, convert them to be accessible by the library.
4. Populate the pre-allocated device memory with inputs in a supported format.
5. Configure the library computation to be executed.
6. Execute a library call that offloads the desired computation to the GPU.
7. Retrieve the results of that computation from device memory, possibly in a library-determined format.
8. If necessary, convert the retrieved data to the application's native format.
9. Release CUDA resources.
10. Continue with the remainder of the application.

Not every library follows this workflow, and even the ones that do might skip certain steps. Still it is important for you to be aware of the behind-the-scenes events at each stage because this understanding may help you with performance tuning or simplify the debugging process. Each of the libraries covered in the subsequent sections of this chapter follow this workflow to some extent. The remainder of this section briefly covers each stage of the workflow, including any new concepts or vocabulary.

Stage 1: Creating a Library Handle

Many CUDA libraries share the concept of a *handle*, which contains contextual library information such as the format of data structures used, the devices used for computation, and other environmental data. For those library methods that accept a handle, you must allocate and initialize the handle before making any library calls. In general, you can think of the handle as an opaque object stored on the host that contains information which each library function may access. For example, you might want all library operations to run in a particular CUDA stream. Although different libraries use different function names, many offer a function that forces all library operations to occur in a certain stream (for example, cuSPARSE uses `cusparseSetStream`, cuBLAS uses `cublasSetStream`, and cuFFT uses `cufftSetStream`). This stream information would be stored in the library handle. The handle provides a way for library information to be stored, but places the responsibility of managing concurrent access to the handle on the programmer.

Stage 2: Allocating Device Memory

For the libraries covered in this section, device memory is either allocated by the programmer using `cudaMalloc` or the library uses `cudaMalloc` internally. Only multi-GPU libraries require the use of an API other than `cudaMalloc` to allocate device memory.

Stage 3: Converting Inputs to a Library-Supported Format

If the format of your application's data is not supported by the CUDA library you are using, it must be re-formatted. For instance, if an application is storing 2D arrays in row-major order, but the CUDA library only accepts arrays in column-major order, you will need to perform some transformations. For optimal performance, every effort should be made to avoid data transformations and to conform to CUDA library data formats.

Stage 4: Populating Device Memory with Inputs

Given the global memory allocated in Stage 2 and the properly formatted data from Stage 3, the next task in Stage 4 simply makes that data available to the library function on the CUDA device by transferring it to device memory. You can think of this as analogous to `cudaMemcpy`, though in many cases a library-specific function is used. For instance, when transferring a vector from the host to the device in a cuBLAS-based application, `cublasSetVector` should be used. Internally, it uses properly ordered and strided calls to `cudaMemcpy` (or some equivalent function) to transfer the input data to device memory.

Stage 5: Configuring the Library

Often, the library function being called must be aware of data formatting, dimensionality, or other configurable parameters. In Stage 5, you manage this configuration process. In some cases, these configurables are simply parameters passed to a computational library function. In other cases, you may need to manipulate the library handle. In still other cases, you may need to manage separate metadata objects.

Stage 6: Executing

Executing the actual library call is the simplest step! You call the desired library function with the properly configured objects from Stages 1 through 5 and reap the performance benefits of a highly-optimized CUDA library function.

Stage 7: Retrieving Results from Device Memory

For this step, you retrieve the output from device memory into host memory in a pre-determined format (likely configured as part of Stage 5 or prescribed by the library). You can think of this as the mirror of Stage 4.

Stage 8: Converting Back to Native Format

In the case that an application's native data format is different from the formats supported by the CUDA library in use, you will need to convert back to the application-specific format. You can think of this step as a mirror of Stage 3.

Stage 9: Releasing CUDA Resources

If the resources allocated by this workflow are no longer necessary, you can release them for use in future computation. Note, there is some overhead in allocating and releasing resources, so it is better to reuse resources across multiple invocations of CUDA library calls when possible. Examples of resources include device memory, library handles, and CUDA streams.

Stage 10: Continuing with the Application

After you retrieve the output from Stage 7 and (optionally) convert to the application's native data representation in Stage 8, you can now continue with any future processing as if the prior computation had not been run on the GPU.

Note, these stages are verbose and might leave the impression that the conceptual and development overhead for CUDA libraries is high. As subsequent sections will demonstrate, this is far from the truth. In many cases, the entire workflow only requires a few lines of code. These details are provided to help you draw analogies from past knowledge to improve your understanding, and to add insight in to the underlying processes.

In the next sections, you will explore in-depth some of the most commonly used CUDA libraries. For each library you will learn related concepts, review an example, and understand the workflow stages.

THE CUSPARSE LIBRARY

The cuSPARSE library implements a wide range of general-purpose sparse linear algebra functions. It supports a collection of dense and sparse data formats on which those functions operate.

Table 8-2 summarizes the set of linear algebra operations supported by cuSPARSE. For more detailed information on any of the following functions, refer to the cuSPARSE User Guide online. Note that cuSPARSE separates functions into levels. All Level 1 functions operate exclusively on dense and sparse vectors. All Level 2 functions operate on sparse matrices and dense vectors. All Level 3 functions operate on sparse matrices and dense matrices.

TABLE 8-2: Sparse Linear Algebra Operations Supported by cuSPARSE

FUNCTION NAME	DESCRIPTION
Level 1 Functions	
axpyi	$y = y + ax$
doti	$z = y^T x$
dotci	$z = y^H x$
gthr	Gathers a set of values from a vector x into a vector x based on indices stored in a third vector z
gthrz	Performs the same operation as gthr, but zeroes the locations read from in y
roti	Applies the Givens rotation to vectors x and y
sctr	Scatters selected elements from a vector x into a vector y based on the indices stored in a third vector z
Level 2 Functions	
mv	At its most basic, mv performs the calculation $y = aAx + by$, though more advanced options provide for additional manipulations.
sv	Solves a sparse triangular linear system
Level 3 Functions	
mm	$C = aAB + bC$
sm	Solves a sparse triangular linear system

In the descriptions of each sparse linear algebra operation, lowercase letters represent vectors, uppercase letters represent matrices, and italicized lowercase letters indicate scalars.

In the next section you will learn about the data formats supported by cuSPARSE, including data format conversion.

cuSPARSE Data Storage Formats

A dense matrix contains primarily non-zero values. When representing dense matrices every value in the matrix is stored in a multi-dimensional array. In contrast, sparse matrices and vectors consist primarily of zero-valued entries and can be more compactly represented by storing only the non-zero values and their coordinates rather than many redundant zero values. There are many ways of representing sparse matrices, eight of which are currently supported by cuSPARSE. This section briefly covers three of the most common storage formats supported for matrices in cuSPARSE.

Dense

The dense matrix format is the one most widely known. This format stores the value for every cell in a matrix regardless of whether it is zero or non-zero. Because these matrices are stored in memory, and memory is inherently one-dimensional, the cells of a dense matrix must be "flattened" and mapped to consecutive, one-dimensional memory addresses. An example mapping from a two-dimensional matrix M to its flattened, dense format T is shown in Figure 8-2.

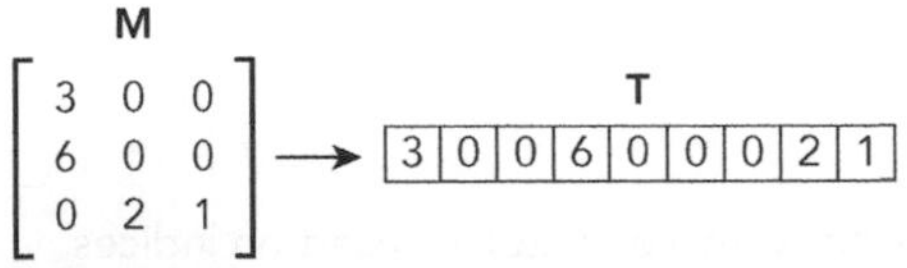

$$M = \begin{bmatrix} 3 & 0 & 0 \\ 6 & 0 & 0 \\ 0 & 2 & 1 \end{bmatrix} \longrightarrow \overset{T}{\boxed{3\,|\,0\,|\,0\,|\,6\,|\,0\,|\,0\,|\,0\,|\,2\,|\,1}}$$

FIGURE 8-2

Coordinate (COO)

For each non-zero value in a sparse matrix, the coordinate (COO) sparse matrix format stores the non-zero value with both its row index and its column index. When referencing a given row and column in a sparse matrix stored in COO format, the value stored is found by matching the target location against stored row and column indices. If no match is found, the value must be zero.

The point at which a coordinate-formatted matrix consumes less space than a dense matrix depends on the sparsity of a matrix, the size of the values, and the size of the type used to store their coordinates. For example, given a sparse matrix storing 32-bit floating-point values and a coordinate format that uses 32-bit integers to represent matrix coordinates, space savings are achieved when less than one third of the cells in the matrix contain non-zero values. This is true because storing a non-zero entry in this particular coordinate format requires triple the space of storing only the value in a dense format. An example mapping from a two-dimensional matrix M to its coordinate representation T is shown in Figure 8-3.

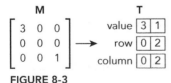

FIGURE 8-3

Compressed Sparse Row (CSR)

Compressed sparse row format (CSR) is similar to coordinate format. The only change is in how the row index for each non-zero value is stored. In coordinate format, an integer was stored for every non-zero value that indicated the row index for that value. Rather than storing the row index for each value explicitly, CSR instead stores an offset to where all of the values belonging to the same row are stored in the value and column arrays.

For example, suppose the non-zero values of a sparse matrix M are stored in array V and the column indices for those values are stored in array C, as shown in Figure 8-4. This formatting is identical to Coordinate but without the row indices.

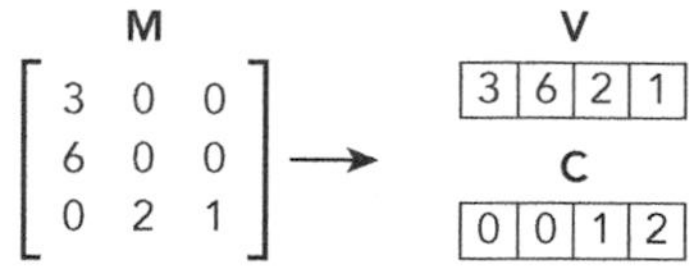

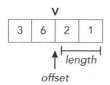

FIGURE 8-4

Since all values in the same row are stored adjacent to each other in V, finding the values of a row simply requires an offset and length in the V array. For example, if you wanted to know only the non-zero values stored in the third row of M, those values could be defined as starting at offset 2 and having length 2 in V, as shown in Figure 8-5. This is how row indices are stored in CSR format.

```
        V
 ┌───┬───┬───┬───┐
 │ 3 │ 6 │ 2 │ 1 │
 └───┴───┴───┴───┘
         ↑├─length─┤
      offset
```

FIGURE 8-5

Using that same offset and length in the C column array would define the column indices that those values are stored at, and therefore it would be possible to fully define each value's location in the original sparse matrix M. When storing large matrices with many elements per row, representing each row with simply an offset and a length is clearly much more efficient than storing a row index for every value.

Now, how should these offsets and lengths be stored for each row? The simplest answer would be to create arrays R_O and R_L each with length nRows, and store the offsets of every row in R_O and the lengths in R_L. However, if a matrix has many rows this requires allocating two large arrays. Instead, it is possible to use a single array R with length nRows+1 where the offset of row i in V and C is stored at index i in R. The length of row i can be derived from the difference between the offset of row i+1 and i. Essentially, the value at R[i+1] is the total number of non-zero values stored in rows 0, 1, ..., and i. R[nRows] is the total number of non-zero values in M. Applying these conventions to the matrix M results in the R shown in Figure 8-6.

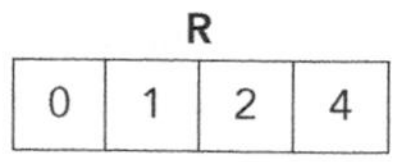

```
        R
 ┌───┬───┬───┬───┐
 │ 0 │ 1 │ 2 │ 4 │
 └───┴───┴───┴───┘
```

FIGURE 8-6

From Figure 8-6, you can therefore find the values and column indices of row 0 in M at offset 0 in V and C and with length 1-0=1. The same process can be applied to row 1 and 2. The total number of non-zero values in M can also be retrieved from the last element of R.

As a result, CSR is able to store sparse matrices with multiple non-zero entries per row in much less space than Coordinate format. The full CSR representation of the example matrix M is shown in Figure 8-7.

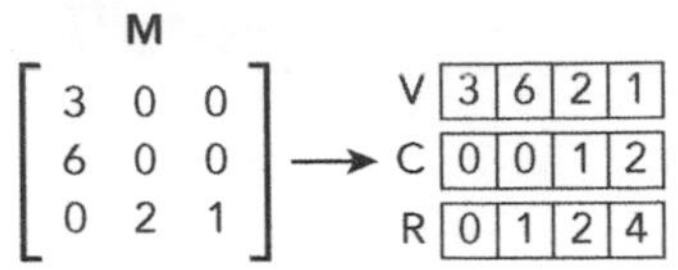

FIGURE 8-7

Transferring a CSR-formatted sparse matrix to the GPU for use by a cuSPARSE function is straightforward. First, assume that you already have a CSR-formatted sparse matrix on the host defined by the following arrays:

```
float *h_csrVals;
int *h_csrCols;
int *h_csrRows;
```

where h_csrVals stores the non-zero values of the sparse matrix, h_csrCols stores the column index for each value, and h_csrRows stores the row offsets into h_csrVals and h_csrCols. Then, you simply need to allocate device memory for each array and transfer it to the GPU:

```
float *d_csrVals;
int *d_csrCols;
int *d_csrRows;

cudaMalloc((void **)&d_csrVals, n_vals * sizeof(float));
cudaMalloc((void **)&d_csrCols, n_vals * sizeof(int));
cudaMalloc((void **)&d_csrRows, (n_rows + 1) * sizeof(int));

cudaMemcpy(d_csrVals, h_csrVals, n_vals * sizeof(float),
    cudaMemcpyHostToDevice);
cudaMemcpy(d_csrCols, h_csrCols, n_vals * sizeof(int),
    cudaMemcpyHostToDevice);
cudaMemcpy(d_csrRows, h_csrRows, (n_rows + 1) * sizeof(int),
    cudaMemcpyHostToDevice);
```

cuSPARSE Storage Formats Summary

Each of the storage formats described in this section is supported by cuSPARSE, and each offers different advantages and disadvantages depending on the characteristics of the data set being processed. A full description of the cuSPARSE data formats is available in Section 3 of the cuSPARSE User Guide. Table 8-3 lists all of the currently supported data formats and the optimal use case for each.

TABLE 8-3: Sparse Matrix Storage Formats

MATRIX DATA FORMAT	OPTIMAL USE CASE
Dense	Dense input data with very few non-zero entries. A dense data format may result in better access locality in the case of dense input data.
Coordinate (COO)	A simple and general sparse matrix format, which will represent sparse matrices more efficiently in terms of space than a dense data format, so long as less than one-third of the input matrix is non-zero.
Compressed Sparse Row (CSR)	Rather than keeping a single integer for every non-zero value to store its row coordinate, CSR keeps a single integer for every row as an offset to that row's value and column data. CSR, therefore, is the space efficient relative to COO when each row contains more than one non-zero entry. However, it does not allow O(1) lookup of a given values row.
Compressed Sparse Column (CSC)	CSC is the same as CSR except in two ways. First, the values of the input matrix are stored in column-major order. Second, the column coordinates are compressed rather than the row coordinates. CSC would be more space-efficient than CSR for input data sets with dense columns.
Ellpack-Itpack (ELL)	ELL works by compacting every row in a matrix down to only its non-zero entries. To retain column information for each value, a separate matrix stores column coordinates for each value. Programmers do not have direct access to ELL formatted matrices, but they are used in storing HYB-formatted matrices.
Hybrid (HYB)	A HYB-formatted matrix stores a regular partition of the matrix in ELL and an irregular partition in COO. This hybrid formatting scheme serves to optimize access patterns on the GPU for matrices that have partitions characterized by different sparsity.
Block Compressed Sparse Row (BSR)	BSR uses the same algorithm as CSR, but rather than storing scalar types as values, it supports storing a two-dimensional block of scalar values. The BSR format (and very similar BSRX format) optimizes the subdivision of a large matrix between multiple CUDA thread blocks.
Extended BSR (BSRX)	BSRX is identical to BSR but uses a slightly different technique for marking the locations of unique two-dimensional blocks in memory.

Formatting Conversion with cuSPARSE

You might recall from the common library workflow that there are two stages related to converting from the application's native data format to a library-supported data format and back. These steps are primarily relevant when the development effort to convert an application to use a cuSPARSE-supported format is too high. For example, many legacy applications might simply use dense matrix and vector formats. However, performing matrix-vector or matrix-matrix operations in cuSPARSE requires that the inputs and outputs are in CSR, BSR, BSRX, or HYB formats.

Note that converting between cuSPARSE data formats implies overhead in both computation to perform the conversion, and space to store the converted copy of what is logically the same data. Therefore, for optimal performance, you should try to avoid frequent conversions.

Still, cuSPARSE provides a variety of format conversion functions to help. Table 8-4 lists the supported format conversion functions. The top row indicates the format for your input (source) data. The left column indicates the format for your output (destination) data. Empty cells indicate unsupported conversions, though if you require an unsupported conversion you might be able to use pipelined conversions to produce the same effect. For instance, dense2bsr is not an explicitly supported conversion but dense2csr and csr2bsr are.

TABLE 8-4: Supported Sparse Matrix Format Conversions

		SOURCE FORMAT					
		DENSE	COO	CSR	CSC	HYB	BSR
DESTINATION FORMAT	**DENSE**			csr2dense	csc2dense	hyb2dense	
	COO			csr2coo			
	CSR	dense2csr	coo2csr			hyb2csr	
	CSC	dense2csc		csr2csc		hyb2csc	bsr2csr
	HYB	dense2hyb		csr2hyb	csc2hyb		
	BSR			csr2bsr			

Demonstrating cuSPARSE

This section will walk through an example cuSPARSE application demonstrating matrix-vector multiplication, format conversion, and other cuSPARSE features. You can follow along by downloading the sample code in cusparse.cu from Wrox.com. A snippet of the core logic is as follows:

```
// Create the cuSPARSE handle
cusparseCreate(&handle);

// Allocate device memory for vectors and the dense form of the matrix A
...

// Construct a descriptor of the matrix A
cusparseCreateMatDescr(&descr);
cusparseSetMatType(descr, CUSPARSE_MATRIX_TYPE_GENERAL);
cusparseSetMatIndexBase(descr, CUSPARSE_INDEX_BASE_ZERO);
```

```
// Transfer the input vectors and dense matrix A to the device
...

// Compute the number of non-zero elements in A
cusparseSnnz(handle, CUSPARSE_DIRECTION_ROW, M, N, descr, dA,
        M, dNnzPerRow, &totalNnz);

// Allocate device memory to store the sparse CSR representation of A
...

// Convert A from a dense formatting to a CSR formatting, using the GPU
cusparseSdense2csr(handle, M, N, descr, dA, M, dNnzPerRow,
        dCsrValA, dCsrRowPtrA, dCsrColIndA);

// Perform matrix-vector multiplication with the CSR-formatted matrix A
cusparseScsrmv(handle, CUSPARSE_OPERATION_NON_TRANSPOSE,
        M, N, totalNnz, &alpha, descr, dCsrValA, dCsrRowPtrA,
        dCsrColIndA, dX, &beta, dY);

// Copy the result vector back to the host
cudaMemcpy(Y, dY, sizeof(float) * M, cudaMemcpyDeviceToHost);
```

cusparse.cu is a miniature example of a legacy application with a native dense matrix data format, ported to use cuSPARSE and the CSR sparse matrix format. It follows a workflow very similar to the common workflow described previously in the chapter:

1. A cuSPARSE library handle is created using cusparseCreate.

2. Device memory used to store the input matrix and vectors in both dense and CSR format is allocated using cudaMalloc.

3. The routines cusparseCreateMatDescr and cusparseSetMatA are used to configure certain matrix properties. cudaMemcpy is then used to transfer all inputs into the pre-allocated device memory. The format conversion routine cusparseSdense2csr is used to generate the CSR version of the dense matrix input with the help of cusparseSnnz, which counts the number of non-zero elements in each row or column of a dense matrix as well as in the entire matrix.

4. cusparseScsrmv is called on the CSR sparse matrix and input vectors to perform the actual matrix-vector multiplication.

5. cudaMemcpy is used to retrieve the final results of the computation in the Y vector from device memory. No transformations are necessary as it is stored and processed in a dense vector format.

6. CUDA and cuSPARSE resources are released using cudaFree, cusparseDestroyMatDescr, and cusparseDestroy.

This example can be built using the following command:

```
$ nvcc -lcusparse cusparse.cu -o cusparse
```

Important Topics in cuSPARSE Development

Although cuSPARSE provides arguably the quickest and easiest route to high-performance linear algebra execution in CUDA, there are certain aspects of cuSPARSE to keep in mind as you explore more and more advanced cuSPARSE functionality.

One of the first challenges you will likely encounter is ensuring proper matrix and vector formatting. cuSPARSE may not be able to detect improperly formatted input data for either computation or conversion functions (for example, passing a CSR-formatted matrix to a function that only accepts COO-formatted inputs). In the event of a mistake, your best diagnostic information will likely be generated by a segmentation fault from within cuSPARSE, or validation errors from your own application.

For cuSPARSE conversion functions, manual validation of matrix and vector format for a small subset of data is manageable. Automated full dataset verification might be possible by performing the inverse format conversion back to the native data format, and verifying that the twice-converted values are equivalent to the original values.

To verify input data format for computational functions, it is recommended that you perform validation against host-only implementations of the same functionality.

Another challenge is the default asynchronous behavior of cuSPARSE methods. This asynchrony should not come as a surprise as it is standard for many CUDA functions, but it might lead to unexpected results when porting from legacy, blocking, host-only math libraries whose results are guaranteed upon return. If you use cudaMemcpy to transfer cuSPARSE results from the device to the host, then the application will automatically block, waiting for results from the device (as in the cusparse.cu example). However, if cuSPARSE is configured to use a CUDA stream and cudaMemcpyAsync, extra care must be taken to ensure proper synchronization is used before accessing the results from a cuSPARSE call.

One additional oddity in cuSPARSE is the convention for scalar parameters, which are always passed by reference. For example, in cusparse.cu the address of the floating-point value beta was passed, rather than simply the value:

```
float beta = 4.0f;
...
// Perform matrix-vector multiplication with the CSR-formatted matrix A
cusparseScsrmv(handle, CUSPARSE_OPERATION_NON_TRANSPOSE,
    M, N, totalNnz, &alpha, descr, dCsrValA, dCsrRowPtrA,
    dCsrColIndA, dX, &beta, dY);
```

If you accidentally pass beta instead of &beta, your application would likely report a SEGFAULT on the host from inside the cuSPARSE library, an error that may be frustrating to debug.

In addition, scalar output parameters may be passed as either host or device pointers. cuSPARSE provides a cusparseSetPointerMode function that adjusts whether cuSPARSE functions expect host or device pointers to be passed for returning scalar results.

cuSPARSE Summary

This section briefly demonstrated the use of the cuSPARSE library, a powerful tool for rapidly taking advantage of GPU computational throughput for sparse linear algebra operations. You learned about the data formats supported by cuSPARSE, some of the operations supported by cuSPARSE, and techniques for converting from native application data formats to cuSPARSE-supported data formats. In the next section, you will learn about a similar CUDA library: cuBLAS.

THE cuBLAS LIBRARY

cuBLAS is a collection of linear algebra routines. Unlike cuSPARSE, cuBLAS is a port of a legacy linear algebra library, the Basic Linear Algebra Subprograms (*BLAS*) library.

Like BLAS, cuBLAS subroutines are split into multiple classes based on the data types on which they operate. cuBLAS Level 1 contains vector-only operations like vector addition. cuBLAS Level 2 contains matrix-vector operations like matrix-vector multiplication. cuBLAS Level 3 contains matrix-matrix operations like matrix-multiplication. Unlike cuSPARSE, cuBLAS does not support multiple sparse data formats; it only supports and is optimized for dense vector and dense matrix manipulation.

Because the original BLAS library was written in FORTRAN, it historically uses column-major array storage and one-based indexing. Column-major refers to how a multi-dimensional matrix is stored in a one-dimensional address space. The section titled "cuSPARSE Data Storage Formats" demonstrated row-major flattening for dense matrices. In column-major flattening, the elements of a column are iterated through and stored in consecutive memory locations before processing the next column. As a result, elements in the same column are located adjacent in memory, whereas elements in the same row are strided. This contrasts with the semantics of C/C++ from which cuBLAS is called, which is row-major, meaning that elements in the same row are stored adjacent to each other. Figure 8-2 shows the result of flattening a two-dimensional matrix into a row-major one-dimensional array. Figure 8-8 shows the same flattening but using column-major ordering.

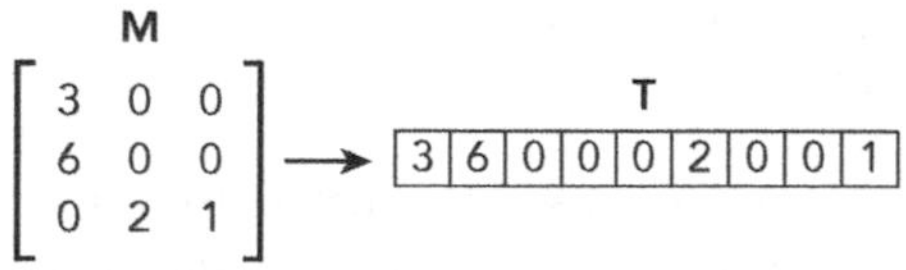

FIGURE 8-8

Put another way, given a two-dimensional matrix to be flattened into a single-dimensional array with M rows and N columns, you can calculate the destination of the element at location (m, n) using the following equations:

$$\text{Row-Major: } f(m, n) = m \times N + n$$

$$\text{Column-Major: } f(m, n) = n \times M + m$$

For compatibility reasons, the cuBLAS library also chooses to use column-major storage. This can be confusing if you are used to the row-major array layout in C/C++.

On the other hand, one-based indexing simply means that the very first element in an array is referenced using the value one rather than the value zero, as it is in C and many other programming languages. As a result, the final element in an N-element array is referenced with the index N rather than N-1, as in zero-based indexing.

However, the cuBLAS library has no control over the semantics of the C/C++ programming language in which it is built, so it must use zero-based indexing. This leads to an odd hybrid situation where the column-major rule of the original FORTRAN BLAS library applies, but not the one-based indexing.

The cuBLAS library comes with two APIs. The cuBLAS Legacy API is the original implementation of cuBLAS that has since been deprecated. The current cuBLAS API (available since CUDA 4.0) should be used for all new development. For the most part, the differences between them are minor, but it is important to be aware that they both exist. All example code in this chapter is from the current cuBLAS API.

In this section, you will find that many concepts from the cuSPARSE common workflow carry directly over to cuBLAS. You must manage handles, streams, and scalar parameters, and the general workflow should look familiar as you work through the example in this section.

Managing cuBLAS Data

Compared to cuSPARSE, the data format and type considerations in cuBLAS are relatively simple. All operations are done on dense cuBLAS vectors or matrices. These vectors and matrices are allocated as contiguous chunks of device memory through `cudaMalloc`, but use custom cuBLAS routines such as `cublasSetVector`/`cublasGetVector` and `cublasSetMatrix`/`cublasGetMatrix` to transfer data between the host and device. Although you can think of these specialized functions as wrappers around `cudaMemcpy`, they are well-optimized to transfer both strided and unstrided data. For example, a call to `cublasSetMatrix` takes the following arguments:

```
cublasStatus_t cublasSetMatrix(int rows, int cols, int elementSize,
    const void *A, int lda, void *B, int ldb);
```

The first four arguments are self-explanatory: They define the dimensions of the matrix to transfer, the size of each element in the matrix, and the memory location of the column-major source matrix A in host memory. The sixth argument B defines the location of the destination matrix in device memory. The use of the fifth and seventh arguments might be less clear. lda and ldb specify the leading dimension of the source matrix A and destination matrix B. The leading dimension is the total number of rows in the respective matrix. This is useful if only a submatrix of a matrix in host memory is being transferred to the GPU. In other words, if the full matrices stored at A and B are being transferred, lda and ldb should both equal M. If only a submatrix in those matrices is being transferred, the values of lda and ldb should be the row length of the full matrix. lda and ldb should also always be greater than or equal to rows.

If you were given a dense two-dimensional column-major matrix A of single-precision floating-point values on the host with M rows and N columns, you could use cublasSetMatrix to transfer the entire matrix using:

```
cublasSetMatrix(M, N, sizeof(float), A, M, dA, M);
```

You could also use cublasSetVector to transfer a single column of matrix A to a vector dV on the device. cublasSetVector takes the following arguments:

```
cublasStatus_t cublasSetVector(int n, int elemSize, const void *x, int incx,
    void *y, int incy)
```

where x is the source location on the host, y is the destination location on the device, n is the number of elements to transfer, elemSize is the size of each element in bytes, and incx/incy is a stride between elements to be transferred. Transferring a single column with length M of a column-major matrix A to a vector dV could be done using:

```
cublasSetVector(M, sizeof(float), A, 1, dV, 1);
```

You could also use cublasSetVector to transfer a single row of that matrix A to a vector dV on the device:

```
cublasSetVector(N, sizeof(float), A, M, dV, 1);
```

This function copies N elements from A to dV, skipping M elements in A at a time. Because A is column-major, this command would copy the first row of A to the device. Copying row i would be implemented as:

```
cublasSetVector(N, sizeof(float), A + i, M, dV, 1);
```

This is a much simpler data model than the one exposed by cuSPARSE. Unless your application significantly benefits from sparse data structures, using cuBLAS will likely improve performance and lead to a simpler development process.

Demonstrating cuBLAS

The cuBLAS example demonstrated here will focus on the uniformity of cuBLAS and its ease-of-use. The performance benefits of GPUs can lead to greater than 15 times speed-up relative to optimized host-only BLAS libraries, and the development effort to use cuBLAS is only marginally greater than that of legacy BLAS implementations.

A Simple cuBLAS Example

This example will perform matrix-vector multiplication on the GPU, a cuBLAS Level 2 operation. You can follow along by downloading the sample code in cublas.cu from Wrox.com or using the following code snippet:

```
// Create the cuBLAS handle
cublasCreate(&handle);
```

```
            // Allocate device memory
            cudaMalloc((void **)&dA, sizeof(float) * M * N);
            cudaMalloc((void **)&dX, sizeof(float) * N);
            cudaMalloc((void **)&dY, sizeof(float) * M);

            // Transfer inputs to the device
            cublasSetVector(N, sizeof(float), X, 1, dX, 1);
            cublasSetVector(M, sizeof(float), Y, 1, dY, 1);
            cublasSetMatrix(M, N, sizeof(float), A, M, dA, M);

            // Execute the matrix-vector multiplication
            cublasSgemv(handle, CUBLAS_OP_N, M, N, &alpha, dA, M, dX, 1,
                        &beta, dY, 1);

            // Retrieve the output vector from the device
            cublasGetVector(M, sizeof(float), dY, 1, Y, 1);
```

Using the cuBLAS library is straightforward. The `cublas.cu` example demonstrates a much smaller subset of the common library workflow compared to the previous cuSPARSE example. It includes the following steps:

1. Create a cuBLAS handle using `cublasCreateHandle`.

2. Allocate device memory for inputs and outputs using `cudaMalloc`.

3. Populate the allocated device memory with inputs using `cublasSetVector` and `cublasSetMatrix`.

4. Execute the `cublasSgemv` library call to offload a matrix-vector multiplication operation to the GPU.

5. Retrieve results from device memory using `cublasGetVector`.

6. Release CUDA and cuBLAS resources using `cudaFree` and `cublasDestroy`.

This example can be built using following command:

```
$ nvcc -lcublas cublas.cu
```

Using the cuBLAS library typically requires less effort than the cuSPARSE library, primarily because cuBLAS is built to be highly compatible with the legacy BLAS library.

Porting from BLAS

Porting a legacy application from a C implementation of the BLAS library to cuBLAS is straightforward. The porting process generally consists of four main steps:

1. Adding device memory allocation calls (`cudaMalloc`) and device memory release calls (`cudaFree`) to the application for any input or output vectors or matrices

2. Add methods to transfer the state of input and output vectors and matrices between the host and device (for example, `cublasSetVector`, `cublasSetMatrix`, `cublasGetVector`, `cublasGetMatrix`).

3. Transform the actual call to the BLAS library to instead call the equivalent cuBLAS routine. This will likely require minor changes to the arguments passed. For instance, the previous example used the cuBLAS function:

```
cublasStatus_t cublasSgemv(cublasHandle_t handle, cublasOperation_t trans,
    int m, int n, const float *alpha, const float *A, int lda, const float *x, int
    incx, const float *beta, float *y, int incy);
```

The equivalent BLAS function from the C BLAS library has a slightly different interface:

```
void cblas_sgemv(const CBLAS_ORDER order, const CBLAS_TRANSPOSE TransA,
    const MKL_INT M, const MKL_INT N, const float alpha, const float *A,
    const MKL_INT lda, const float *X, const MKL_INT incX, const float beta, float *Y,
    const MKL_INT incY);
```

While many of the arguments are the same or similar (trans, M, N, alpha, A, lda, X, incx, beta, Y, incy), BLAS includes the order argument (enabling you to specify inputs in either row-major or column-major order), and cuBLAS adds the cuBLAS handle. Also note that the alpha and beta arguments to BLAS are not passed by reference as they are in cuBLAS. These are minor differences, as they are for all cuBLAS functions, and do not represent a major hindrance to porting BLAS applications to cuBLAS.

4. Finally, you might also choose to optimize your new cuBLAS application after successful implementation. This step can include:

   a. Reusing memory allocations rather than allocating and freeing for every cuBLAS call

   b. Removing redundant device-to-host copies for vectors and matrices that are re-used as inputs for the next cuBLAS call

   c. Adding stream-based execution using cublasSetStream to enable asynchronous transfers. See Chapter 6, "Streams and Concurrency," for more information on how streams can help improve performance

Important Topics in cuBLAS Development

Compared to cuSPARSE, cuBLAS is more familiar and intuitive if you have experience with the legacy BLAS library. As a result, it is easier to understand the processes happening behind the scenes. This simplicity also implies that potential issues that may arise are generally easier to triage than with cuSPARSE.

If you commonly use row-major programming languages, development with cuBLAS can require extra attention to detail. It is easy to use the code patterns with which you are most familiar, for example, flattening an array using row-major indexing. To help, you can define macros to automatically convert zero-based row-major indexing to column-major:

```
#define R2C(r, c, nrows) ((c) * (nrows) + (r))
```

However, even when using macros like this, you must put more thought into the ordering of the surrounding loops. Many C/C++ programmers will be tempted to use:

```
for (int r = 0; r < nrows; r++) {
    for (int c = 0; c < ncols; c++) {
        A[R2C(r, c, nrows)] = ...
    }
}
```

While this code would be correct, it would be suboptimal because it does not linearly scan the memory locations in the array A. For example, if the array A starts at memory location zero, the first three references done by this loop will be to locations 0, nrows, and 2×nrows. Given that nrows might be very large, these widely separated memory accesses would lead to poor cache locality. Therefore, you must take care to invert the order of the loops when using column-major arrays:

```
for (int c = 0; c < ncols; c++) {
    for (int r = 0; r < nrows; r++) {
        A[R2C(r, c, nrows)] = ...
    }
}
```

Be careful when doing so, as you may inadvertently cause poor cache-locality on the right hand side of the assignment instead.

The most alluring aspect of cuBLAS is its ease-of-use when transitioning from the legacy BLAS library. In that case, the only major changes necessary are the additions of device memory management and transfer CUDA calls.

cuBLAS Summary

This section covered the simple and easy-to-use cuBLAS library with a focus on its accessibility and portability for applications that use the legacy BLAS library. The next section focuses on one of the most useful algorithms in scientific computation and signal processing today: the fast Fourier transform.

THE cuFFT LIBRARY

The cuFFT library provides an optimized, CUDA-based implementation of the fast Fourier transform (FFT). An FFT is a transformation in signal processing that converts a signal from the time domain to the frequency domain. An inverse FFT does the opposite. Put another way, an FFT receives as input a sequence of samples taken from a signal at regular time intervals. It then uses those samples to generate a set of component frequencies that are superimposed to create the signal that generated the input samples. Figure 8-9 shows the sum of two signals to form the signal cos(x)+cos(2x) and its decomposition by FFT into frequencies of 1.0 and 2.0. Providing a more detailed understanding of FFTs is beyond the scope of this book.

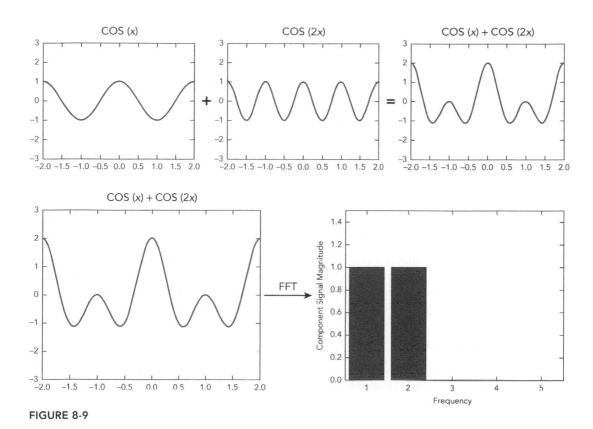

FIGURE 8-9

Using the cuFFT API

cuFFT is often used to refer to two separate libraries: the core, high-performance cuFFT library and the portability library, cuFFTW. The cuFFT library is an implementation of FFTs on CUDA that provides its own API. cuFFTW, on the other hand, is designed with an identical API to the standard FFTW (Fastest Fourier Transform in the West) host FFT library. Similar to how cuBLAS shares much of its API with the legacy BLAS library, cuFFTW is designed to maximize portability from existing code that uses FFTW. A wide range of the functions in the FFTW library are identically supported in cuFFTW. In addition, the cuFFTW library assumes all inputs passed are in host memory and handles all of the allocation (cudaMalloc) and transfers (cudaMemcpy) for the user. Although this might lead to suboptimal performance, it greatly accelerates the porting process. For a full list of supported operations in cuFFTW and cuFFT, refer to the cuFFT User Guide.

Configuration of the cuFFT library is done with *FFT plans*, the terminology that cuFFT uses to refer to its handles. A plan defines a single transform operation to be performed. cuFFT uses plans to derive the internal memory allocations, transfers, and kernel launches that must occur to perform the requested transformation. Different plan creation functions can be used to generate plans of increasing complexity and dimensionality:

```
cufftResult cufftPlan1d(cufftHandle *plan, int nx, cufftType type, int batch);
cufftResult cufftPlan2d(cufftHandle *plan, int nx, int ny, cufftType type);
cufftResult cufftPlan3d(cufftHandle *plan, int nx, int ny, int nz, cufftType type);
```

cuFFT also supports a variety of input and output data types, including:

➤ Complex-to-complex

➤ Real-to-complex

➤ Complex-to-real

For many real-world applications, the most useful type is real-to-complex, enabling you to input real-valued measurements from real-world systems to cuFFT.

Once a cuFFT plan is configured, it is executed using a `cufftExec*` function call (for example, `cufftExecC2C`). In general, function calls take as input the plan, the location where inputs are stored, the location to place outputs, and whether this transform is a forward FFT (time domain to frequency domain) or inverse FFT (frequency domain to time domain).

Demonstrating cuFFT

This section covers a simple example using the cuFFT API to perform a complex-to-complex, 1D FFT. You can download the sample code in `cufft.cu` from `Wrox.com` or follow along in the code snippet that follows.

```
// Setup the cuFFT plan
cufftPlan1d(&plan, N, CUFFT_C2C, 1);

// Allocate device memory
cudaMalloc((void **)&dComplexSamples, sizeof(cufftComplex) * N);

// Transfer inputs into device memory
cudaMemcpy(dComplexSamples, complexSamples,
           sizeof(cufftComplex) * N, cudaMemcpyHostToDevice);

// Execute a complex-to-complex 1D FFT
cufftExecC2C(plan, dComplexSamples, dComplexSamples,
             CUFFT_FORWARD);

// Retrieve the results into host memory
cudaMemcpy(complexFreq, dComplexSamples, sizeof(cufftComplex) * N,
           cudaMemcpyDeviceToHost);
```

The workflow for a cuFFT application varies depending on the complexity of the transform. At its most basic level, the workflow consists of:

1. Create and configure a cuFFT plan.

2. Allocate device memory to store the input samples and output frequencies from cuFFT using `cudaMalloc`. Note that this memory must be typed to support the type of transform you are

performing (for example, complex-to-complex, real-to-complex, complex-to-real). You can perform an in-place transform by using the same device memory for both inputs and outputs.

3. Populate that device memory with the input signal samples using `cudaMemcpy`.

4. Execute the plan using a `cufftExec*` function.

5. Retrieve the result from device memory using `cudaMemcpy`.

6. Release CUDA and cuFFT resources using `cudaFree` and `cufftDestroy`.

This example can be built using the following command:

```
$ nvcc -lcufft cufft.cu -o cufft
```

The example provided in `cufft.cu` generates a sequence of input samples from the function `cos(x)`, converts them to complex numbers, transfers the complex representation to the GPU, and executes a complex-to-complex 1D plan on them before copying the results back. Note that because the same memory location `dComplexSamples` is passed to `cufftExecC2C` for both the input and output argument, this is an in-place FFT operation. A separate output buffer could also be pre-allocated and used to store the output.

cuFFT Summary

This section briefly described the capability of the cuFFT library to accelerate many applications that use FFTs. In the next section, you will look at a CUDA library that generates random numbers and has two APIs: one for creating randomness from the host, and one for creating randomness directly on the device.

THE cuRAND LIBRARY

Random number generation is a critical part of many scientific, cryptographic, and financial applications. A random number generator (RNG) is a function f that takes no arguments but, on each invocation, returns the next value in a random sequence of values. You can visualize it as a pointer traversing through an array filled with random values, as shown in Figure 8-10.

FIGURE 8-10

cuRAND provides a CUDA-based library for rapid quasi- and pseudo-random number generation. The next sections provide some background on random number generation, the configurability of cuRAND, and then two examples of cuRAND's usage.

Choosing Pseudo- or Quasi- Random Numbers

The most important concept to understand about computer-based random number generation is that there is no such thing as true random number generation. Because computers are an ordered system (in order to function properly), there is no inherent source of disorder to draw a random sequence of bits from to form a random number. Certain hardware solutions enable the generation of what are arguably true random numbers, but the RNG algorithms that many libraries use to generate random numbers are well defined and well-structured attempts at producing the illusion of randomness. However, this is not an entirely bad characteristic, and can actually be useful in certain cases.

For example, RNGs start with a seed, a starting value from which to produce a random sequence of values. You can think of this as the very first value in Figure 8-10, on which all other values are based. You can repeatedly provide the same seed to a well-defined RNG algorithm and receive the same random sequence of values every time. This can be useful for testing your application, enabling the reuse of the same random sequence over and over again.

RNGs are divided into two categories: pseudo-random RNGs and quasi-random RNGs. Both have their uses, and both are supported by cuRAND.

A pseudo-random RNG (*PRNG*) uses an RNG algorithm to produce a sequence of random numbers where each value has an equal probability of being anywhere along the range of valid values for the storage type that RNG uses. For example, when retrieving a value from an integer PRNG, the probability of the returned value being 1, `P(1)`, is the same as the probability of it being 2, `P(2)`, or 3, `P(3)`, all the way to `P(INT_MAX)`. This is true for every value returned from the PRNG. This means that just because the last value retrieved was a 2 does not mean that the probability of the next value being a 2 is any lower. In other words, each sampling of a pseudo-random number sequence is a statistically independent event, and does not affect the value observed by any future samplings.

This does not hold true for quasi-random number generators (*QRNGs*). A QRNG makes an effort to fill the range of the output type evenly. Hence, if the last value sampled by a QRNG was 2, then `P(2)` for the next value has actually decreased. The samplings of a QRNG's sequence are not statistically independent.

Both PRNGs and QRNGs are useful in different applications. When true randomness is required, a PRNG is a better choice. For a password-generating application, a PRNG would be a better choice than a QRNG because it would prevent an entity from using information about some of the generated passwords to improve their chances of guessing other passwords in the same sequence.

On the other hand, QRNGs are useful in exploring spaces that are largely not understood. They guarantee a more even sampling of a multi-dimensional space than PRNGs but might also find features that a regular sampling interval will miss. For example, certain applications of Monte Carlo methods benefit from using a QRNG rather than a PRNG.

Overview of the cuRAND Library

The cuRAND library can be used to sample values from both pseudo-random and quasi-random sequences. It is unique among the CUDA libraries discussed here in that it has both a host API and a device API. This means it can be directly called from both host code and kernel code. Many concepts exposed by the cuRAND library are shared between the two APIs, though some options are added when using the device API.

Covering the Concepts

Configuring both the host and device cuRAND APIs requires four options: an RNG algorithm with which to generate a random sequence, a distribution to which the returned values will adhere, a seed from which to start, and an offset into the random number sequence at which to begin sampling. While the device API requires the explicit specification of each of these parameters, the host API will automatically set them to default values if you do not set them yourself.

Both the host and device APIs retain the concept of handles from the other CUDA libraries. In the host API, handles are referred to as *generators*. You can construct a generator with `curandCreateGenerator`. Generators are configured using a collection of utility functions, such as `curandSetStream` or `curandSetGeneratorOffset`. Only a single generator is necessary to access the host API. The device API instead refers to its handle concept as a cuRAND state. There are multiple types of device state objects, one for each type of RNG supported in the device API. However, the role of the state object is still to maintain the configuration and status of a single thread's cuRAND context on the GPU. As a result, you will generally need to allocate a large batch of device state objects, one for each GPU thread.

The first configurable in cuRAND host and device APIs is the RNG algorithm to be used. In the host API, this is configured using the `rng_type` parameter to `curandCreateGenerator`.

```
curandStatus_t curandCreateGenerator(curandGenerator_t *generator,
        curandRngType_t rng_type);
```

In the device API, this is configured by calling an RNG-specific initialization function with an RNG-specific state object, which serves as a cuRAND generator in the device API:

```
__device__ void curand_init(unsigned long long seed,
                            unsigned long long subsequence,
                            unsigned long long offset,
                            curandStateXORWOW_t *state);
__device__ void curand_init(unsigned long long seed,
                            unsigned long long subsequence,
                            unsigned long long offset,
                            curandStateMRG32k3a_t *state);
```

Selecting different RNG algorithms affects the techniques used to generate random values and so might affect both the quality of randomness as well as performance. Both the host and device support a variety of RNG algorithms. For example, to initialize an RNG on the device to use the XORWOW RNG algorithm, you could use the following code:

```
__global__ void kernel(...) {
    curandStateXORWOW_t rand_state;
    curand_init(0, 0, 0, &rand_state);
    ...
}
```

Then, `rand_state` could be used later as a handle for generating random values.

Next, selecting different distributions affects how the values produced by an RNG are distributed across the range of possible values (recall that even floating-point values have a discrete and limited range of values). The relation between an RNG algorithm and the distribution used may not seem obvious. The RNG algorithm can be thought of as a black box that produces a random sequence of bits. These bits have no meaning to the RNG algorithm. Adding a distribution on top of an RNG with a specific return type instructs cuRAND to use those random bits to generate a meaningful value that is characteristic of the selected distribution. The host and device API both support normal, uniform, log normal, and Poisson distributions.

The desired distribution is specified when performing random value generation by calling a distribution-specific function. For example, using a uniform distribution in the host API requires curandGenerateUniform:

```
curandGenerator_t rand_state;
int d_rand_length = ...;
float *d_rand;

curandCreateGenerator(&rand_state, CURAND_RNG_PSEUDO_DEFAULT);
cudaMalloc((void **)&d_rand, sizeof(float) * d_rand_length);
curandGenerateUniform(rand_state, d_rand, d_rand_length);
```

On the device, curand_uniform would be used instead:

```
__global__ void kernel(...) {
    curandStateXORWOW_t rand_state;
    curand_init(0, 0, 0, &rand_state);
    float f = curand_uniform(&rand_state);
    ...
}
```

The third configurable in cuRAND is the seed. The concept of a seed is present for both PRNGs and QRNGs, but each uses different terminology. The seed selected for a cuRAND PRNG is 64 bits of human-provided randomness on which to base the future randomness of the PRNG. Different seeds produce different sequences of random values. The host API enables the optional setting of the seed for PRNGs using curandSetPseudoRandomGeneratorSeed:

```
curandGenerator_t rand_state;
curandCreateGenerator(&rand_state, CURAND_RNG_PSEUDO_DEFAULT);
curandSetPseudoRandomGeneratorSeed(rand_state, 9872349ULL);
```

However a default seed will be selected if it is not specified. The device API, on the other hand, requires explicit setting of the seed for each thread's PRNG. You have already seen the seed being set in calls to the device API's curand_init. The first argument specifies the starting seed for the RNG created:

```
__device__ void curand_init(unsigned long long seed,
                            unsigned long long subsequence,
                            unsigned long long offset,
                            curandStateXORWOW_t *state);
```

The only QRNG supported by the host and device API is based on a Sobol quasi-random sequence (discussion of which is beyond the scope of this book). A Sobol sequence is seeded by direction vectors. Recall that the advantage of a quasi-random generator is that each sampling is not a statistically independent event; a QRNG will deliberately attempt to fill the range of values more evenly than a PRNG. You can think of these direction vectors as a starting direction to begin exploring the n-dimensional space from which random bits are extracted. Hence, they are a seed in the sense that they are a piece of human-provided initial randomness, even though they are called by a different name. In the cuRAND host API, only the number of dimensions to use for QRNGS can be set using curandSetQuasiRandomGeneratorDimensions:

```
curandGenerator_t rand_state;
curandCreateGenerator(&rand_state, CURAND_RNG_QUASI_SOBOL32);
curandSetQuasiRandomGeneratorDimensions(rand_state, 2);
```

However, the device API allows the seed direction vectors to be explicitly set:

```
__global__ void kernel(curandDirectionVectors32_t *direction_vector, ...) {
    curandStateSobol32_t rand_state;
    curand_init(*direction_vector, 0, &rand_state);
    ...
}

curandDirectionVectors32_t *h_vectors;
curandGetDirectionVectors32(&h_vectors, CURAND_DIRECTION_VECTORS_32_JOEKUO6);
cudaMemcpy(d_vectors, h_vectors, sizeof(curandDirectionVectors32_t),
    cudaMemcpyHostToDevice);
kernel<<<blocks, threads>>>(d_vectors, ...);
```

Finally, the fourth configurable in cuRAND is the offset in a sequence of random numbers at which to start. That is, each seed produces a different sequence of random numbers. The offset enables you to jump to the ith random value in that sequence. In the host API, this is set using the function curandSetGeneratorOffset:

```
curandGenerator_t rand_state;
curandCreateGenerator(&rand_state, CURAND_RNG_PSEUDO_DEFAULT);
curandSetGeneratorOffset(rand_state, 0ULL);
```

In the cuRAND device API, the offset is set as a parameter to the curand_init function (similar to seeds):

```
__device__ void curand_init(unsigned long long seed,
                            unsigned long long subsequence,
                            unsigned long long offset,
                            curandStateXORWOW_t *state);
```

Comparing the Host and Device APIs

Deciding whether to use the host or device cuRAND API is an application-specific decision. Both APIs provide similar capabilities in terms of functionality: the same RNGs, the same distributions, and the same configurability of different parameters. However, the methods used to access that capability are very different. This section provides guidelines on the selection process based on your application requirements.

If your only goal is efficient, high-quality random number generation for what is otherwise an entirely host application, then the host API is the best choice. It has been hand-tuned by CUDA experts to produce optimal performance for this use case and is far more usable than writing your own custom kernels to call the device API (as an example under the following section, "Demonstrating cuRAND," will demonstrate). While it is possible to pre-generate random values on the GPU with the host API for later consumption by a GPU kernel, there are no advantages to this. It will likely make the code less readable by separating the producer and consumer of the randomness, it will likely degrade performance with added overhead from the cuRAND host library and kernel launches, and will require that the necessary amount of randomness be known prior to kernel execution.

If you require more control over the generation of randomness, if you are consuming that randomness from a hand-written CUDA kernel, and particularly if your randomness requirements in that kernel change dynamically, then the device API is the right choice. It requires a small amount of development overhead to initialize and manage RNG state on the device but offers much more flexibility when working within a CUDA application.

Demonstrating cuRAND

This section offers two examples of the cuRAND APIs. First, you will look at an example that demonstrates replacing the system `rand` function using the host and device cuRAND APIs. Second, you will look at an example that uses the host and device cuRAND APIs and the system `rand` call to produce randomness for a CUDA kernel.

Replacing rand()

You can follow along with this example by downloading the sample code in `replace-rand.cu` from `Wrox.com`, which uses calls to the host and device cuRAND APIs to generate random numbers for later consumption on the host. This example generates a large batch of random values in one library call and then iterates through them as the host requests new random values. Only when all existing random values are exhausted must it go back to the cuRAND library to generate more randomness.

The workflow for using the host API is the simplest you have looked at in this chapter and includes the following steps:

1. Create a cuRAND generator configured with the desired RNG using `curandCreateGenerator`. Configuration of that generator is possible (for example, using `curandSetStream`), but is optional for the host API.

2. Pre-allocate device memory using `cudaMalloc` for cuRAND to store the output random values in.

3. Generate random values by executing a cuRAND library call, e.g., `curandGenerateUniform`.

4. If destined for consumption on the host, retrieve the generated random values from device memory using `cudaMemcpy`.

The following code snippet demonstrates the cuRAND host API workflow:

```
/*
 * An implementation of rand() that uses the cuRAND host API.
 */
float cuda_host_rand() {
    ...
    if (dRand == NULL) {
```

```
        /*
         * If the cuRAND state hasn't been initialized yet, construct a cuRAND
         * host generator and pre-allocate memory to store the generated random
         * values in.
         */
        curandCreateGenerator(&randGen,
                    CURAND_RNG_PSEUDO_DEFAULT);
        cudaMalloc((void **)&dRand, sizeof(float) * dRand_length);
        hRand = (float *)malloc(sizeof(float) * dRand_length);
    }

    if (dRand_used == dRand_length) {
        /*
         * If all pre-generated random numbers have been consumed, regenerate a
         * new batch using curandGenerateUniform.
         */
        curandGenerateUniform(randGen, dRand, dRand_length);
        cudaMemcpy(hRand, dRand, sizeof(float) * dRand_length,
                    cudaMemcpyDeviceToHost);
        dRand_used = 0;
    }

    // Return the next pre-generated random number
    return hRand[dRand_used++];
}
```

Working with the device API is slightly more involved and includes the following steps:

1. Pre-allocating a set of cuRAND state objects in device memory for each thread to manage its RNG's state.

2. Optionally, pre-allocating device memory to store the random values generated by cuRAND if they are intended to be copied back to the host or must be persisted for later kernels.

3. Initializing the state of all cuRAND state objects in device memory with a CUDA kernel call.

4. Executing a CUDA kernel that calls a cuRAND device function (for example., `curand_uniform`) and generates random values using the pre-allocated cuRAND state objects. This step and the previous step can be merged into a single kernel, but you must be careful that you do not reinitialize the state objects on every kernel call if you want later values in the random sequences.

5. Optionally, transferring random values back to the host if device memory was pre-allocated in step 2 for retrieving random values.

The following code snippet demonstrates the cuRAND device API workflow:

```
/*
 * An implementation of rand() that uses the cuRAND device API.
 */
float cuda_device_rand() {
    ...

    if (dRand == NULL) {
        /*
```

```
         * If the cuRAND state hasn't been initialized yet, pre-allocate memory
         * to store the generated random values in as well as the cuRAND device
         * state objects.
         */
        cudaMalloc((void **)&dRand, sizeof(float) * dRand_length);
        cudaMalloc((void **)&states, sizeof(curandState) *
                   threads_per_block * blocks_per_grid);
        hRand = (float *)malloc(sizeof(float) * dRand_length);
        // Initialize states on the device
        initialize_state<<<blocks_per_grid, threads_per_block>>>(states);
    }

    if (dRand_used == dRand_length) {
        /*
         * If all pre-generated random numbers have been consumed, regenerate a
         * new batch.
         */
        refill_randoms<<<blocks_per_grid, threads_per_block>>>(dRand,
                dRand_length, states);
        cudaMemcpy(hRand, dRand, sizeof(float) * dRand_length,
                   cudaMemcpyDeviceToHost);
        dRand_used = 0;
    }

    // Return the next pre-generated random number
    return hRand[dRand_used++];
}
```

This example can be built using:

```
$ nvcc -lcurand replace-rand.cu -o replace-rand
```

Both of these workflows are illustrated by the replace-rand.cu example. In replace-rand.cu, there are three different functions for retrieving a single, random, single-precision floating-point value between 0.0f and 1.0f. host_rand simply fetches a random value using the host's rand system call. cuda_host_rand uses cuRAND's host API to pre-generate a large batch of random values and then iterates over that batch in successive calls to cuda_host_rand. It keeps track of the number of values that were pre-generated and the number of values already used, and uses that to determine when a new batch must be generated. cuda_device_rand uses the cuRAND device API to perform the same task by pre-allocating a set of cuRAND state objects on the device, using those objects to generate batches of random values and managing the data in the same way that cuda_host_rand does.

One item of note with the cuRAND implementation of rand provided in this example is the jitter created by processing bursts. While the majority of calls to cuda_host_rand and cuda_device_rand will be very fast and consist of only an array reference and a counter increment, every N^th call will need to regenerate a massive batch of random numbers using the GPU and will take much longer. This uneven and unpredictable performance might be undesirable in certain applications. To that end, a slightly modified example is provided in replace-rand-streams.cu on Wrox.com that uses CUDA streams and the cuRAND API's ability to bind to a CUDA stream and asynchronously run random number generation on the GPU while the host application is running. Given sufficient work in the host application to overlap with the random number generation work on the GPU, this enables a new batch of random numbers to be ready before the last batch runs out.

Generating Randomness for CUDA Kernels

You can follow along with this example by downloading the sample code in `rand-kernel.cu` from `Wrox.com`. In contrast to the `replace-rand.cu` and `replace-rand-stream.cu` examples from the previous section, this example uses the cuRAND host and device APIs to generate random values for consumption by a CUDA kernel.

The `use_host_api` function uses the cuRAND host API to pre-generate N random values before calling a simple CUDA kernel that consumes those random values. Note that this requires multiple kernel calls from the host program and cuRAND, as well as device memory exclusively allocated to store the generated random values. The code snippet below shows the generation of random values into dRand using `curandGenerateUniform`, passing those values to `host_api_kernel`, and then transferring the final output of `host_api_kernel` from the device (dOut) to the host (hOut).

```
// Generate N random values from a uniform distribution
curandGenerateUniform(randGen, dRand, N);

// Consume the values generated by curandGenerateUniform
host_api_kernel<<<blocks_per_grid, threads_per_block>>>(dRand, dOut, N);

// Retrieve outputs
cudaMemcpy(hOut, dOut, sizeof(float) * N,
    cudaMemcpyDeviceToHost);
```

The `use_device_api` function uses the cuRAND device API to perform on-demand generation of random values on the GPU. Note that it only requires a single kernel call that includes all cuRAND initialization and execution and also does not require extra CUDA device memory to be allocated to store the random values. The CUDA kernel is able to immediately consume any generated random values. The code snippet below shows the execution of the kernel `device_api_kernel` on the pre-allocated cuRAND device generators in *states* and the transfer of that kernel's final output from the device to the host.

```
// Execute a kernel that generates and consumes its own random numbers
device_api_kernel<<<blocks_per_grid, threads_per_block>>>(states, dOut, N);

// Retrieve the results
cudaMemcpy(hOut, dOut, sizeof(float) * N,
    cudaMemcpyDeviceToHost);
```

This example can be built using the following command:

```
$ nvcc -lcurand rand-kernel.cu -o rand-kernel
```

Important Topics in cuRAND Development

cuRAND is a simple and flexible API to use. The most important part of cuRAND-based projects is to understand your randomness requirements.

For example, selecting different RNGs or different distributions can drastically impact application performance, correctness, and results. Particularly for applications like Monte Carlo simulations for which success is heavily based on the random values used, ensuring that you have properly configured your cuRAND environment to produce the type of random values you expect is important. Given the breadth of applications that rely heavily on randomness, there is no simple guide to the correct choice for your particular application. Please consult your friendly, neighborhood computational scientist.

CUDA LIBRARY FEATURES INTRODUCED IN CUDA 6

CUDA 6 adds two useful features to CUDA libraries: Drop-In Libraries and Multi-GPU Libraries.

Drop-In CUDA Libraries

Drop-In Libraries enable seamless replacement of existing host libraries with certain CUDA libraries. As long as the CUDA library adheres to an identical API to the original host library, you can link your application directly to a Drop-In Library. The goal of Drop-In Libraries is to improve portability from existing legacy applications. In fact, with Drop-In Libraries the application code does not even need to be re-compiled.

Only two CUDA libraries currently support being dropped into an existing application. NVBLAS is a subset of the cuBLAS library that can be dropped in for any Level 3 BLAS function. cuFFTW can be dropped in to replace calls to the FFTW library.

There are two ways to force an application to use a Drop-In Library in place of BLAS or FFTW. First, the application can be recompiled to link to the CUDA library rather than the standard library. For instance, if you have an application app built from a source file app.c that uses the BLAS library, it would normally be built using the command:

```
$ gcc app.c –lblas –o app
```

If you wanted to replace all BLAS 3 library calls in app with their cuBLAS equivalents, app would need to be rebuilt to use the cuBLAS library instead by linking it in place of the BLAS library, as follows:

```
$ gcc app.c –lnvblas –o app
```

A second technique for using CUDA Drop-In Libraries on Linux environments is to force the CUDA library to be loaded before the host library. This can be done using the LD_PRELOAD environment variable, which directs the operating system to look for function definitions in the specified library before checking default locations. This is done using the env shell command, followed by the command you normally use to run the application. For instance, if app from the previous example took no command line arguments and you did not want to recompile it, you could still replace all BLAS 3 routines with their CUDA equivalents using the following command to execute app:

```
$ env LD_PRELOAD=libnvblas.so ./app
```

Consider the `drop-in.c` example available from `Wrox.com` or follow along with the following code snippet. This application makes use of the `sgemm` BLAS routine and is written entirely in C. The following is the core logic:

```
// Generate inputs
srand(9384);
generate_random_dense_matrix(M, N, &A);
generate_random_dense_matrix(N, M, &B);
generate_random_dense_matrix(M, N, &C);

sgemm_("N", "N", &M, &M, &N, &alpha, A, &M, B, &N, &beta, C, &M);
```

`drop-in.c` can be built to run on the host using the following build command. Note that it relies on having the C BLAS library installed and in your library path.

```
$ gcc drop-in.c -lblas -lm -o drop-in
```

To instead run the `sgemm` call on a GPU, simply recompile using:

```
$ gcc drop-in.c -lnvblas -o drop-in
```

or, execute using:

```
$ env LD_PRELOAD=libnvlas.so ./drop-in
```

Drop-In Libraries help remove portability obstacles, and further improve your productivity by making it even easier to take advantage of high-performance CUDA libraries. By simply re-linking or adding an environment setting, you can empower existing applications with massively parallel GPU acceleration.

Multi-GPU Libraries

Some applications contain sufficient parallelism to justify using multiple GPUs to improve performance. Chapter 9, "Multi-GPU Programming," covers more details about how to use native CUDA APIs for multi-GPU acceleration. It is important to discuss the use of multiple GPUs by CUDA libraries here, as it requires less advanced understanding from the programmer and can lead to performance gains and better hardware utilization.

Multi-GPU Libraries (also known as the XT Library Interfaces) were introduced in CUDA 6. They enable a single library call to be automatically executed across multiple GPUs. Because executing across multiple GPUs inherently requires partitioning the work across devices, a multi-GPU library can operate on datasets larger than GPU global memory. As a result, even if your system has only one GPU, you will be able to operate on input data sizes that overfill the amount of global memory available by swapping data partitions in and out of the GPU.

In CUDA 6, multi-GPU execution is supported for some functions in cuFFT and for all Level 3 cuBLAS functions. As a performance optimization, the cuBLAS Level 3 multi-GPU library calls automatically overlap memory transfers with kernel computation.

Using the multi-GPU libraries will require additional development effort. Download the example `cufft-multi.cu` from `Wrox.com` or follow along with the following code snippet. `cufft-multi.cu` runs the same example as `cufft.cu` but uses the cuFFTXT API to spread the work across all GPUs in the system.

```
int nGPUs = getAllGpus(&gpus);
nGPUs = nGPUs > 2 ? 2 : nGPUs;
workSize = (size_t *)malloc(sizeof(size_t) * nGPUs);

// Setup the cuFFT Multi-GPU plan
cufftCreate(&plan);
cufftXtSetGPUs(plan, 2, gpus);
cufftMakePlan1d(plan, N, CUFFT_C2C, 1, workSize);

// Generate inputs
generate_fake_samples(N, &samples);
real_to_complex(samples, &complexSamples, N);
cufftComplex *complexFreq = (cufftComplex *)malloc(
        sizeof(cufftComplex) * N);

// Allocate memory across multiple GPUs and transfer the inputs into it
cufftXtMalloc(plan, &dComplexSamples, CUFFT_XT_FORMAT_INPLACE);
cufftXtMemcpy(plan, dComplexSamples, complexSamples,
        CUFFT_COPY_HOST_TO_DEVICE);

// Execute a complex-to-complex 1D FFT across multiple GPUs
cufftXtExecDescriptorC2C(plan, dComplexSamples, dComplexSamples,
        CUFFT_FORWARD);

// Retrieve the results from multiple GPUs into host memory
cufftXtMemcpy(plan, complexSamples, dComplexSamples,
        CUFFT_COPY_DEVICE_TO_HOST);
```

The primary differences between `cufft.cu` and `cufft-multi.cu` are:

➤ An extra setup step to list all of the GPUs in the current system (using the provided function `getAllGpus`) and configure the cuFFT plan to use those GPUs (`cufftXtSetGPUs`)

➤ The use of `cufftXtMalloc` rather than `cudaMalloc` to allocate device memory across multiple GPUs and associate it with the same cuFFT plan. Note that the resulting allocation information is stored in a `cudaLibXtDesc` object rather than a simple pointer.

➤ The use of `cufftXtMemcpy` rather than `cudaMemcpy` to transfer data from host memory to multiple GPUs and back. Note that `cufftXtMemcpy` supports copying between a host array and a `cudaLibXtDesc` object as well as between two `cudaLibXtDesc` objects. `cufftXtMemcpy` takes directionality just like `cudaMemcpy`, which can be `CUFFT_COPY_HOST_TO_DEVICE`, `CUFFT_COPY_DEVICE_TO_HOST`, or `CUFFT_COPY_DEVICE_TO_DEVICE`. Any device locations used for multi-GPU execution with cuFFTXTT must be expressed as `cudaLibXtDesc` objects.

➤ The use of a `cufftExecDescriptor*` library call rather than `cufftExec*` to perform the actual FFT transformation

This example can be built using:

```
$ nvcc -lcufft cufft-multi.cu -o cufft-multi
```

The cuFFTXT library uses prior knowledge about FFT functions to distribute data between GPUs without breaking the validity of the FFT results (and will do something similar for cuBLAS across multiple GPUs as well).

Adding multi-GPU support requires careful attention during the porting process. If your application exposes sufficient parallelism, then using the multi-GPU CUDA XT interfaces is more straightforward than deploying your own custom multi-GPU implementation. The XT Interface for the cuBLAS and cuFFT libraries is a powerful addition to the CUDA libraries.

A SURVEY OF CUDA LIBRARY PERFORMANCE

Implementing an application in CUDA is always motivated by performance. Therefore, the usability of the CUDA libraries is meaningless if it sacrifices the performance acceleration that you expect from GPU execution. This section briefly covers existing literature on CUDA library performance relative to standard libraries. Keep in mind, as with all performance results, your own experimental results might vary from the ones listed here depending on compilers, hardware, or other environmental factors.

cuSPARSE versus MKL

Arguably, the gold standard for performance in sparse linear algebra is the Math Kernel Library (MKL). MKL is hand-optimized to perform both dense and sparse linear algebra on multi-core CPUs using vector instructions. There is a large amount of literature comparing MKL and cuSPARSE on a variety of computational kernels.

As part of the CUDA 5.0 release, NVIDIA performed a comprehensive performance comparison between cuSPARSE and MKL across multiple computational kernels and multiple datasets. For sparse matrix-dense vector multiplication across 18 different datasets they found that cuSPARSE performance uplift varied from 1.1 times to 3.1 times relative to MKL. Multiplying a sparse matrix by multiple dense vectors yielded even better relative performance, ranging from a little over 3 times speedup to more than 12 times performance improvement. Finally, when comparing tridiagonal solvers between cuSPARSE and MKL, improvements of up to 17 times speedup were reported, depending on dataset size and primitive types (see Figure 8-11).

For the CUDA 6.0 release, NVIDIA performed a similar performance review of the CUDA libraries. Results improved across the board, with sparse matrix-dense vector multiplication achieving 1.8 times to 5.4 times speedup and performance improvements to triangular solvers, Incomplete-LU, and Cholesky pre-conditioners.

Clearly, the cuSPARSE library is highly usable, maintains the performance benefits expected of GPU hardware, and is continually being improved.

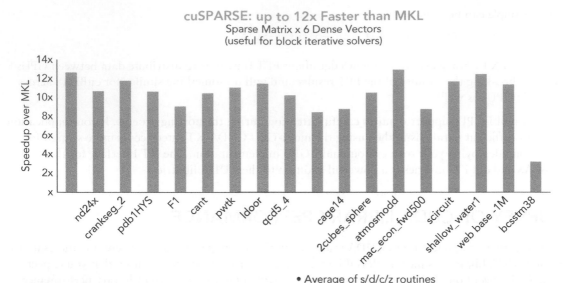

Performance may vary based on system configuration.

FIGURE 8-11

- Average of s/d/c/z routines
- cuSPARSE 5.0 on K20X, input and output data on device
- MKL 10.3.6 on Intel SandyBridge E5-2687W @ 3.10GHz

cuBLAS versus MKL BLAS

Because MKL also includes hand-optimized versions of the BLAS routines, it is a natural comparison point for cuBLAS as well. Like cuSPARSE, cuBLAS has received a large amount of scrutiny in its comparison to MKL.

In the CUDA 5.0 performance report, cuBLAS was evaluated across the full range of BLAS Level 3 routines. Speedup relative to MKL varied from ~2.7 times up to ~8.7 times speedup (shown in Figure 8-12). Deeper investigation into ZGEMM performance demonstrated that cuBLAS maintains a significant performance advantage (> 5 times speedup) over MKL across a wide range of matrix sizes ranging from 512 × 512 to 4,096 × 4,096 cells.

In the CUDA 6.0 performance report, NVIDIA reported 6 to 17 times speedup relative to the latest MKL BLAS. cuBLAS also maintained similar performance improvements relative to MKL for ZGEMM. With the introduction of the multi-GPU cuBLAS-XT library, NVIDIA demonstrated scalability of cuBLAS across multiple GPUs (shown in Figure 8-13).

cuBLAS Level 3: >1 TFLOPS double-precision

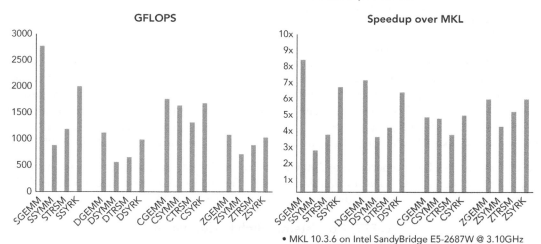

GFLOPS

Speedup over MKL

- MKL 10.3.6 on Intel SandyBridge E5-2687W @ 3.10GHz
- CUBLAS 5.0.30 on K20X, input and output data on device

FIGURE 8-12

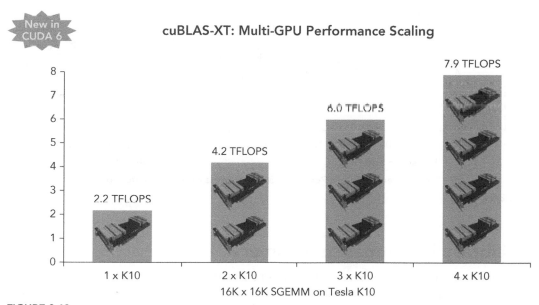

New in CUDA 6

cuBLAS-XT: Multi-GPU Performance Scaling

7.9 TFLOPS

6.0 TFLOPS

4.2 TFLOPS

2.2 TFLOPS

| 1 x K10 | 2 x K10 | 3 x K10 | 4 x K10 |

16K x 16K SGEMM on Tesla K10

FIGURE 8-13

cuFFT versus FFTW versus MKL

The FFTW library boasts excellent performance of single- and multi-dimensional FFTs on multi-core CPUs, claiming performance that is "typically superior to that of other publicly available FFT software, and is even competitive with vendor-tuned codes." Clearly, FFTW targets improved performance as a major goal and, therefore, is a good comparison point for cuFFT. The MKL library also supports FFTs.

NVIDIA's CUDA 5.0 report shows varying performance of FFTs depending on data size, from as low as ~30 GFlop/s up to nearly 250 GFlop/s. Performance evaluation by FFTW on a single core reports anywhere from ~1 GFlop/s up to ~5.5 GFlop/s. Extrapolating from FFTW's highest reported performance of 5.5 GFlop/s and cuFFT's ~100 GFlop/s at the same data size, you would require 20 CPU cores to equal a single GPU running cuFFT. If you compare cuFFT's best performance at ~250 GFlop/s to FFTW's ~5 GFlop/s at the same data size, then the results are much more favorable for cuFFT: It would take 50 CPU cores to equal the computational performance of a single GPU.

With CUDA 6.0, NVIDIA reports up to 700 GFlop/s are achievable on 1D single-precision complex FFTs, and more then 250 GFlop/s for double-precision. The report also emphasizes consistently high performance across a wide range of data set sizes (shown in Figure 8-14).

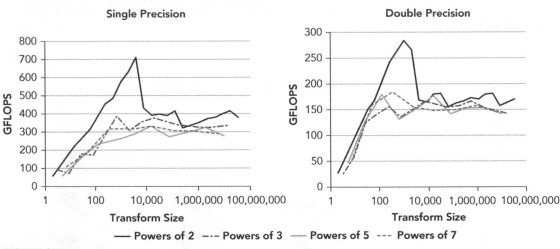

FIGURE 8-14

CUDA Library Performance Summary

In this section, studying performance evaluations of cuSPARSE, cuBLAS, and cuFFT proved that the usability of CUDA libraries does not come at the cost of performance. Having direct access to CUDA implementations of complex computational algorithms delivered by CUDA performance experts is a powerful tool for improving your productivity and accelerating application performance.

USING OPENACC

OpenACC is a complementary programming model to CUDA that uses a compiler directives-based API designed for high performance, programmability, and portability across many platforms. This section will focus on OpenACC concepts and methods, with emphasis on the relationship between CUDA and OpenACC.

OpenACC's threading model is similar to CUDA's, but adds a dimension of parallelism. OpenACC parallelism is split into gangs, workers, and vector elements. At the top level, *gangs* are analogous to CUDA thread blocks. A single gang is scheduled at a time per processor, and a gang can contain one or more threads of execution. Inside each gang, there are one or more *workers*. In CUDA terminology, a worker would be analogous to a warp of threads. Each worker has a *vector width*, consisting of one or more *vector elements* that each execute the same instruction at the same time. Each of these vector elements is analogous to a CUDA thread, in that it is a single stream of execution. The main difference between the OpenACC and CUDA threading models is that OpenACC exposes the concept of workers (that is, warps) directly in the programming model, whereas in CUDA you do not explicitly create warps of threads.

The OpenACC *platform model* is similar to CUDA, but uses different terminology and slightly different abstractions. OpenACC targets a platform with a single-threaded host program that offloads kernels to multiple Processing Units (PUs), where each PU runs one gang at a time. Each of these PUs can execute multiple independent threads of execution concurrently (workers). Each of those threads of execution can perform vector operations with a certain vector width. In OpenACC, *gang parallelism* uses multiple PU's. Parallelism across multiple threads inside a single gang is referred to as *worker parallelism*. Parallelism within a single worker and across a vector operation is called *vector parallelism*. When using OpenACC on GPUs, a PU is analogous to an SM.

OpenACC execution is split into several modes depending on whether work is being parallelized across gangs, workers, vectors, or not at all. For the moment, consider a single parallel region of an OpenACC program for which G gangs are created with W workers in each gang, and a vector width of V for each worker. In total, there could be $G \times W \times V$ total threads of execution processing this parallel region.

When the parallel region starts, execution is performed in *gang-redundant mode*, which is useful for initializing the state of a gang before parallel execution begins. In gang-redundant mode each gang only has a single vector element in a single worker active. All other workers and vector elements are idle. Hence, there are only G active threads of execution. Additionally, every gang is executing identical computation so there is no parallelization of work across gangs at this stage. In CUDA, gang-redundant parallelism would be implemented as a single thread of each thread block executing the same computation:

```
__global__ void kernel(...) {
    if (threadIdx.x == 0) {
        foo();
    }
}
```

At some point in the OpenACC parallel region the application may transition to parallelize work across gangs. In that case, the region enters *gang-partitioned mode*. In gang-partitioned mode, there is still only one active vector element and one active worker in each gang, but each active vector element is executing a different piece of the parallel region. Hence, the work of this computational region is partitioned across gangs. In CUDA, gang-partitioned mode would be implemented as a single thread in each thread block processing a separate data point. For vector addition, a CUDA kernel executing in gang-partitioned mode would look like:

```
__global__ void kernel(int *in1, int *in2, int *out, int N) {
    if (threadIdx.x == 0) {
        int i;
        for (i = blockIdx.x; i < N; i += gridDim.x) {
            out[i] = in1[i] + in2[i];
        }
    }
}
```

What about worker and vector parallelism? Well, when a single worker is active per gang it is called *worker-single mode*. When a single vector element is active per worker it is called *vector-single mode*. Both gang-redundant and gang-partitioned modes are therefore also worker-single and vector-single modes.

In *worker-partitioned mode*, the work of a parallel region is divided both among multiple gangs but also multiple workers. Using all workers in all gangs provides G × W-way parallelism. In CUDA, worker-partitioned mode would be implemented by using the first thread in each warp:

```
__global__ void kernel(int *in1, int *in2, int *out, int N) {
    if (threadIdx.x % warpSize == 0) {
        int warpId = threadIdx.x / warpSize;
        int warpsPerBlock = blockDim.x / warpSize;
        int i;
        for (i = blockIdx.x * warpsPerBlock + warpId; i < N;
                i += gridDim.x * warpsPerBlock) {
            out[i] = in1[i] + in2[i];
        }
    }
}
```

In *vector-partitioned mode*, work is divided among gangs, workers, and vector elements, providing full G × W × V-way parallelism. This is the mode that is most similar to how you have been writing CUDA kernels. As a result of these different OpenACC modes, the parallelism of an application can be adjusted dynamically within a single parallel region of code.

When using OpenACC, *compiler directives* are inserted by the programmer to indicate regions of code that can be, or should be, run in parallel. Compiler directives can also indicate the type of parallelism to use. A compiler directive is a single line of source code that, in C/C++, starts with #pragma. OpenACC directives are uniquely identified with the acc keyword, meaning that all OpenACC directives begin with #pragma acc.

Compiler directives are unique in that, though they are a part of the source code of a program, they may or may not affect the executable generated by a compiler. If a compiler does not recognize or support a certain type of #pragma, it will ignore it and compile the application as if the #pragma was not there. If you run any of the examples in this section, you will need an OpenACC-enabled compiler. Currently, PGI, Cray, and CAPS compilers all support OpenACC directives. The examples in this chapter will use the PGI compiler, but all source code should work across all compilers. Consult your compiler documentation for the flags that need to be added to enable OpenACC.

OpenACC-enabled compilers interpret the OpenACC directives of a program and perform automatic analysis of the source code to auto-generate accelerator source code. As a result, it is possible to automatically execute an application on the GPU by simply adding a few lines of directives. For example, consider the following OpenACC vector add implementation:

```
#pragma acc kernels
for (i = 0; i < N; i++) {
    C[i] = A[i] + B[i];
}
```

The #pragma acc kernels directive marks the following sequential code block as eligible for execution on an OpenACC accelerator (for example, a GPU). If the compiler building this source code is OpenACC-enabled, it analyzes the loop, determines a strategy for parallelizing across gangs, workers, and vectors, and then automatically generates the memory copies, kernel launches, and kernel source code necessary to execute the loop in parallel on a GPU. In contrast, hand-coding (without CUDA unified memory) in CUDA would require 1) converting the body of the loop into a CUDA __global__ kernel, 2) explicitly allocating memory with cudaMalloc, 3) copying data to the device with cudaMemcpy, 4) performing a kernel launch, and 5) copying data back to the host. With OpenACC, all of this is accomplished with a single #pragma.

In addition to compiler directives, OpenACC also offers a number of library functions. These functions may implement identical functionality, complementary functionality, or unique functionality compared to the OpenACC compiler directives.

The remainder of this section will go into more detail about OpenACC directives and their usage. You will start by exploring how compute directives are used to automatically map sequential C code to parallel device execution, and then examine how data directives allow you to manage data movement between the host and device. A brief discussion of the OpenACC runtime API will follow, and this section will wrap up with an example using OpenACC.

Using OpenACC Compute Directives

In OpenACC, compute compiler directives are used to communicate to the compiler how a block of code should be parallelized. There are two compute directives: #pragma acc kernels and #pragma acc parallel.

Using the kernels Directive

#pragma acc kernels takes a more automated and compiler-driven approach than #pragma acc parallel. When the kernels directive is applied to a code block, the compiler automatically analyzes that block for parallelizable loops. When they are found, the compiler can schedule parallel execution using any configuration of gangs, workers, and vector width on each parallel loop. In other words, the compiler automatically determines when to use gang-redundant mode, gang-partitioned mode, worker-partitioned mode, etc. In CUDA terms, the compiler searches the block of code decorated by the `kernels` directive for parallel loops that can be executed in CUDA kernels. Any code within a `kernels` block that cannot be parallelized is still executed, but not in parallel.

As a simple example, consider the code in `simple-kernels.c` available from `Wrox.com`. The core logic is included in the following snippet:

```
#pragma acc kernels
{
    for (i = 0; i < N; i++) {
        C[i] = A[i] + B[i];
    }
    for (i = 0; i < N; i++) {
        D[i] = C[i] * A[i];
    }
}
```

This `kernels` block contains two loops that can be parallelized. If you have a PGI compiler, this example can be compiled with:

```
$ pgcc –acc simple-kernels.c –o simple-kernels
```

Adding the `-acc` flag enables PGI compiler support for OpenACC, allowing it to recognize any `#pragma acc` directives in the provided code. It is also strongly recommended that you add the `-Minfo=accel` flag to the PGI compiler to gain insight into what auto-parallelization is performed. Using `-Minfo=accel` with `simple-kernels.c` produces the following output:

```
$ pgcc –acc –Minfo=accel simple-kernels.c –o simple-kernels
main:
    34, Generating present_or_copyout(C[:1024])
        Generating present_or_copyin(A[:1024])
        Generating present_or_copyin(B[:1024])
        Generating present_or_copyout(D[:1024])
        Generating Tesla code
    36, Loop is parallelizable
        Accelerator kernel generated
        36, #pragma acc loop gang, vector(128) /* blockIdx.x threadIdx.x */
    39, Loop is parallelizable
        Accelerator kernel generated
        39, #pragma acc loop gang, vector(128) /* blockIdx.x threadIdx.x */
```

For now, ignore the statements that mention `present_or_copyout` and `present_or_copyin`. These will be covered in the next section on "Using OpenACC Data Directives." Instead, consider the lines labeled 36 and 39, indicating the source code lines where each loop starts. In both cases, OpenACC automatically finds that the loop is parallelizable. It also prints information on the parallelization strategy used for each loop:

```
#pragma acc loop gang, vector(128) /* blockIdx.x threadIdx.x */
```

This information indicates that both loops are being fully parallelized across gangs and vectors, with a vector width of 128 elements. In CUDA terms, this will map to a thread block size of 128 threads, with as many blocks launched as are necessary to execute the iterations of the loop in parallel.

The `kernels` directive may also be followed by a number of clauses that modify its behavior. For example, using:

```
#pragma acc kernels if(cond)
```

prevents the code block from being executed on an OpenACC accelerator if `cond` is false. This would be useful if you wanted to prevent executing on the GPU if there was insufficient parallelism to make it worthwhile, by doing something similar to:

```
#pragma acc kernels if(N < 128).
```

In OpenACC, there is an implicit wait for all computation to finish at the end of a `kernels` directive. However, if the `async` clause is used then execution will not block:

```
#pragma acc kernels async(id)
```

The `async` clause takes an optional integer argument. This integer is a unique ID given by you to this `kernels` block, allowing the same integer ID to later be used to test for or wait for completion of this `kernels` block. If no integer ID is provided, the `kernels` block still executes asynchronously, but there is no way to wait for that specific `kernels` block. For example, if a `kernels` block was created with:

```
#pragma acc kernels async(3)
```

then the application could later wait for the computation associated with this `kernels` directive by either using the `wait` directive:

```
#pragma acc wait(3)
```

or, by calling the library function `acc_async_wait`:

```
acc_async_wait(3);
```

You can also wait for all asynchronous tasks to complete using an empty `wait` directive:

```
#pragma acc wait
```

or using the library function `acc_async_wait_all`:

```
acc_async_wait_all();
```

In CUDA terms, the `async` directives and functions that use an integer ID are similar to using a `cudaEvent_t` to identify a point in execution you would like to wait for. Then, using a `wait` directive or function to block for that asynchronous task is similar to using a `cudaEventSynchronize` to block on an event. Without an integer ID, the `wait` behavior is similar to a `cudaDeviceSynchronize` call.

You can also add a `wait` clause to `kernels` directives, ensuring that execution of a `kernels` region does not start before either 1) all previous asynchronous tasks have completed, or 2) the task associated with a provided integer ID has completed. Combining `async` and `wait` clauses on `kernels` regions allows chaining of asynchronous accelerated regions:

```
#pragma acc kernels async(0)
{
    ...
}
#pragma acc kernels wait(0) async(1)
{
    ...
}
#pragma acc kernels wait(1) async(2)
{
    ...
}
#pragma acc wait(2)
```

In addition, OpenACC also supports checking if asynchronous computation has completed without blocking. This can only be done using library functions. `acc_async_test(int)` checks if the kernels for a given ID have completed, while `acc_async_test_all` checks that all asynchronous work has completed. If all asynchronous work has completed, a non-zero value is returned. Otherwise, zero is returned.

Note that clauses can be combined. For example, the `#pragma` below would mark a `kernels` region as asynchronous, but only execute it on an accelerator if `N>128`. For this example, the `if` clause applies to the `kernels` directive, not to the asynchrony of the `kernels` directive.

```
#pragma acc kernels if(N > 128) async
```

Using the parallel Directive

While the `kernels` directive and its associated clauses are powerful tools for rapid acceleration of an application, using them might leave you with little control over the actual execution of your application. The OpenACC compiler will automatically analyze your code and choose a parallelization strategy with little input from you. To address this, OpenACC includes another directive similar to `kernels`, but which offers more control over execution: the `#pragma acc parallel` directive. While the `kernels` directive allows the compiler to group the marked code into as many accelerator kernels of whatever parallelism it deems necessary, when using a `parallel` directive all gangs and workers are launched at the very start of the `parallel` region and only cease executing at the end. The compiler is not permitted to adjust the dimensionality of that parallelism in the middle of the `parallel` region, though it can transition between the various execution modes based on your directives. This gives you complete control over exactly how much parallelism is created, just as in CUDA.

The `parallel` directive supports the `if`, `async`, and `wait` clauses, which were explained as part of the `kernels` directive. Additionally, the `parallel` directive also supports clauses that set the number of gangs to create using `num_gangs(int)`, the number of workers with `num_workers(int)`, and the vector width of each worker with `vector_length(int)`. This should be familiar to you from configuring the number of thread blocks and threads per block in CUDA, albeit with an added dimension.

The `parallel` directive also supports the `reduction` clause. The `reduction` clause automatically combines the output of each gang into a single output value, which is available once a `parallel` region completes. The `reduction` clause takes an operation and a variable list to apply that operation to, separated by a colon:

```
#pragma acc parallel reduction(op:var1,var2,...)
```

Each gang in the `parallel` region then has a private copy of each variable `var1`, `var2`,... initialized to a default, operator-specific starting value. When the `parallel` region completes, `op` is applied to the private copies of each gang and output as the final result. For example, if you wanted to sum the variable `result` across gangs the following directive could be used:

```
#pragma acc parallel reduction(+:result)
```

OpenACC supports a variety of reduction operators, including +, *, max, min, &, |, ^, &&, and ||.

In CUDA, the `reduction` clause would be implemented by storing a scalar in `__shared__` memory, updating its value from each thread block, and using atomic operations at the end of a kernel to combine the values written by each thread block. This would take significantly more programming effort than the `reduction` clause but offers more control and customizability (for example, by enabling custom atomic operations).

The `private` and `firstprivate` clauses can also be used with the `parallel` directive. `private` and `firstprivate` clauses apply to a list of variables. When `private` is used, a private copy of each listed variable is created for each gang. Only that gang has access to that copy of the variable, and so changes made to its value are not visible to other gangs or to the host application. For example, in the following code snippet:

```
int a;
#pragma acc parallel private(a)
{
    a = ...;
}
```

every gang in the `parallel` region sets its private copy of a to a different value. Those values are never visible to other gangs or to the host application. Conceptually, you can think of this as similar to a `__shared__` memory variable in CUDA.

The `firstprivate` clause is identical to `private`, but initializes the value of the private variables in each gang to be that variable's current value on the host. In the code snippet below:

```
int a = 5;
#pragma acc parallel firstprivate(a)
{
    ...
}
```

every gang in the `parallel` region would start with a private copy of a with its value set to 5. Any additional changes to a would be private to each gang.

Using the loop Directive

The challenge with the `parallel` directive is that it places more responsibility on you to explicitly mark parallelism for the compiler to accelerate. A `parallel` region always starts in gang-redundant mode. Transitioning to more parallel modes of execution (such as gang-partitioned or work-partitioned) requires explicitly indicating to the compiler that greater levels of parallelism are desired. This is accomplished by marking parallel loops with the `#pragma acc loop` directive, allowing you to directly manipulate the execution mode used for that loop. For example, you could implement the earlier `simple-kernels` example using the `parallel` directive and the `loop` directive to mark the contained loops as parallelizable (shown below). The full code for this example can be found in `simple-parallel.c` on `Wrox.com`.

```
#pragma acc parallel
    {
#pragma acc loop
        for (i = 0; i < N; i++) {
            C[i] = A[i] + B[i];
        }
#pragma acc loop
        for (i = 0; i < N; i++) {
            D[i] = C[i] * A[i];
        }
    }
```

Because no additional clauses are provided to the `loop` directive in this example, the compiler is free to use whatever loop schedule it deems optimal. However, the programmer also has the ability to explicitly control each level of parallelism by adding the `gang`, `worker`, or `vector` clauses to a `loop` directive. When one or more of these clauses are added to a `loop` directive, that loop is parallelized across the respective dimension. For example, consider the following code snippet:

```
#pragma acc parallel
{
    int b = a + c;
#pragma acc loop gang
    for (i = 0; i < N; i++) {
        ...
    }
}
```

Here, the `parallel` region starts in gang-redundant mode. When the `loop` directive is encountered, execution switches to gang-partitioned mode because of the `gang` clause.

However, the `loop` directive is not just valid in a `parallel` region. It can also be used with the `kernels` directive to mark parallel loops for the compiler to turn into accelerator kernels. However, the meaning of its clauses changes depending on the context. Table 8-5 below summarizes the clauses that can be applied to the `loop` directive, as well as how their meaning changes depending on whether they are used inside a `parallel` or `kernels` region.

TABLE 8-5: Loop Clauses

CLAUSE	BEHAVIOR IN A PARALLEL REGION	BEHAVIOR IN A KERNELS REGION
collapse(int)	Marks a loop directive as applying to multiple nested loops. The number of nested loops included is specified with the argument to collapse.	Same as parallel
gang(int)	Indicates that a loop should be distributed in parallel across gangs. The number of gangs is set by the parallel directive.	Indicates that a loop should be distributed across gangs. gang optionally takes a single integer argument: the number of gangs to use when executing the loop.
worker(int)	Indicates that a loop should be distributed in parallel across workers in each gang, transitioning each gang from worker-single to worker-partitioned mode.	Indicates that a loop should be distributed in parallel across workers in a gang. Worker optionally takes a single integer argument: the number of workers to use per gang.
vector(int)	Indicates that a loop should be distributed by vector elements. Causes a worker to transition from vector-single to vector-partitioned mode.	Indicates that a loop should be distributed by vector elements. vector optionally takes a single integer argument: the vector width to use for each worker.
seq	Force the loops marked with seq to be executed sequentially by the accelerator.	Same as parallel
auto	Indicates that the compiler should select gang, worker, or vector parallelism for the associated loop	Same as parallel
tile(int, ...)	Tiles the attached loop(s) by the provided tile size. This converts a loop into two loops: an inner loop of tile_size iterations and an outer loop, which executes sufficient times to match the original code behavior. If attached to multiple tightly nested loops, tile can take multiple tile sizes and automatically place all outer loops outside of all inner loops.	Same as parallel

continues

TABLE 8-5 *(continued)*

CLAUSE	BEHAVIOR IN A PARALLEL REGION	BEHAVIOR IN A KERNELS REGION
device_type(type)	Acts as a demarcator between clause lists for different device types. All clauses following a device_type and until either the end of the directive or the next device_type clause apply only when the loop is being run on the specified device type.	Same as parallel
independent	Asserts that the marked loop is parallelizable, overriding compiler analysis.	Same as parallel
private(var1, ...)	Create gang-private copies of each of the specified variables for the marked loop.	Same as parallel
reduction	See the discussion of reduction earlier in this section.	Same as parallel

You can also combine the `loop` directive with `parallel` or `kernels` in a single `pragma`:

```
#pragma acc parallel loop
for (i = 0; i < N; i++) {
    ...
}

#pragma acc kernels loop
for (i = 0; i < N; i++) {
    ...
}
```

These are simply syntactic shortcuts that expand to `parallel` and `kernels` directives that are immediately followed by a `loop` directive:

```
#pragma acc parallel
{
    #pragma acc loop
    for (i = 0; i < N; i++) {
        ...
    }
}

#pragma acc kernels
{
    #pragma acc loop
    for (i = 0; i < N; i++) {
        ...
    }
}
```

OpenACC Compute Directives Summary

This section covered a variety of OpenACC clauses and directives that can be used to parallelize computational regions of code on an accelerator. While the `kernels` directive is automated and gives the compiler freedom to automatically parallelize a code region without placing that burden on you, the `parallel` directive gives you more control over how code is parallelized. In both cases, the `loop` directive can be used to tell the compiler how to parallelize the attached loop.

While this section provided comprehensive coverage of techniques for mapping computation to the accelerator in OpenACC, you may have noticed that no mention was made of communication between the host application and its accelerator. The `parallel` and `kernels` directives automatically performed all transfers for you. The next section will cover how the OpenACC `data` directive and additional clauses are used to optimize host-accelerator communication in OpenACC.

Using OpenACC Data Directives

It is possible to write OpenACC programs with absolutely no concern for data movement. However, doing so will drastically reduce performance as OpenACC conservatively performs more communication than may be necessary. This section will cover how the `#pragma acc data` directive can be used to explicitly perform communication between the host and an OpenACC accelerator. You will also learn about related data clauses that may be applied to the `parallel` and `kernels` directives.

Using the data Directive

In OpenACC, `#pragma acc data` is used to explicitly transfer data between the host application and accelerator, similar to the different variants of `cudaMemcpy` in CUDA. Like the `kernels` and `parallel` directives, `data` is applied to a region of code. It defines the transfers that must be performed on the boundaries of that region. For instance a variable can be marked as `copyin`, meaning that it should be transferred to the accelerator at the start of the region but not transferred out at the end. Inversely, `copyout` transfers the contents of a variable back to the host at the end of a `data` region, but does not transfer them to the accelerator at the start.

As an example, consider `simple-data.c` available for download from `Wrox.com`. `simple-data.c` is an extension of `simple-parallel.c`. The core logic is included inline below:

```
#pragma acc data copyin(A[0:N], B[0:N]) copyout(C[0:N], D[0:N])
    {
#pragma acc parallel
        {
#pragma acc loop
            for (i = 0; i < N; i++) {
                C[i] = A[i] + B[i];
            }
#pragma acc loop
            for (i = 0; i < N; i++) {
                D[i] = C[i] * A[i];
            }
        }
    }
```

The added #pragma acc data directive informs the compiler that only A and B should be copied to the device, and only C and D should be copied back. This statement also specifies the range of the arrays to transfer, in this case the entire array. In some cases, the compiler may be able to infer the size of the arrays being copied, which would slightly simplify this statement:

```
#pragma acc data copyin(A, B) copyout(C, D)
```

As a result of these simple modifications, the amount of bytes transferred is cut in half relative to the transfers that would be performed without the data directive.

In addition to the data directive, #pragma acc enter data and #pragma acc exit data can also be used to mark arrays for transfer to and from the accelerator at arbitrary points in execution. When an enter data directive is encountered by the compiler, it indicates what data should be copied to the device. That data will remain allocated on the device until either an exit data directive is encountered that transfers it back, or program execution terminates. The enter data and exit data directives are most useful when combined with the async and wait clauses, which they both support. Note that the data directive does not support async and wait clauses.

When an async clause is applied to enter data or exit data it creates an asynchronous transfer of data to or from the accelerator, analogous to a cudaMemcpyAsync. Just as asynchronous copies are useful in CUDA as a way to overlap computation and communication, they can be useful in OpenACC as well. When a wait clause is applied to an enter data or exit data directive, it has the same effect as on kernels or parallel directives: The execution of the communication directive waits for other asynchronous tasks first. Note that communication directives (that is, enter data and exit data) can use async and wait to interact with asynchronous computational tasks (that is, kernels and parallel) and vice versa. Consider the code snippet below:

```
int *A = init_data(N);
int *B = init_more_data(N);

do_some_heavy_work(C);

#pragma acc data copyin(B[0:N]) copyout(A[0:N])
{
    #pragma acc kernels
    {
        for (i = 0; i < N; i++) {
            A[i] = do_work(B[i]);
        }
    }
}

do_lots_more_work(D);
```

Here, the data directive is used to transfer B to the device, then A back. However, because the data directive uses synchronous transfers this application will have to block and wait for potentially massive arrays to be transferred. If the enter data and exit data directives are instead used with the async clause, then communication overhead can be hidden by the computation in do_some_heavy_work and do_lots_more_work:

```
int *A = init_data(N);
int *B = init_more_data(N);
```

```
// copy B to the accelerator asynchronously, with ID 0
#pragma acc enter data copyin(B[0:N]) async(0)

// do work on the host
do_some_heavy_work(C);

// execute this block of code asynchronously on the accelerator.
// use wait(0) to ensure that it waits for the transfer of B to complete first.
#pragma acc kernels async(1) wait(0)
{
    for (i = 0; i < N; i++) {
        A[i] = do_work(B[i]);
    }
}

// copy A back to the host after the kernels region finishes
#pragma acc exit data copyout(A[0:N]) async(2) wait(1)

// do work on the host
do_lots_more_work(D);

// wait for the transfer of A to finish
#pragma wait(2)
```

Here, the `enter data` directive is used to asynchronously transfer B to the device, overlapping with do_some_heavy_work. The `kernels` directive then uses `wait` to ensure that the asynchronous copy of B has completed and launches an asynchronous computational task. Later, the `exit data` directive is used to transfer A back asynchronously, overlapping with do_lots_more_work but waiting for the `kernels` region to complete first. Finally, a `wait` directive must be used to ensure that A has been transferred back to the host.

Like `kernels` and `parallel`, the data directives support and share a variety of clauses. A list of supported clauses and the directives with which they can be used is shown in Table 8-6.

TABLE 8-6: Data Clauses

CLAUSE	BEHAVIOR	SUPPORTED BY?		
		DATA	ENTER DATA	EXIT DATA
`if(cond)`	Only perform the copies if cond is true.	Y	Y	Y
`copy (var1, ...)`	The variables listed should be copied to the accelerator at the start of the data region and back at the end.	Y	N	N
`copyin (var1, ...)`	The variables listed should only be copied to the accelerator.	Y	Y	N

continues

TABLE 8-6 *(continued)*

CLAUSE	BEHAVIOR	SUPPORTED BY?		
		DATA	ENTER DATA	EXIT DATA
`copyout (var1, ...)`	The variables listed should only be copied back from the accelerator.	Y	N	Y
`create (var1, ...)`	Space for the variables listed should be allocated in accelerator memory, but their contents do not need to be transferred to or from the accelerator.	Y	Y	N
`present (var1, ...)`	`present` indicates that the variables listed are already on the accelerator and do not need to be transferred again. At runtime, those locations in memory are found and used in this `data` region.	Y	N	N
`present_ or_copy( var1, ...)`	For variables listed that are already present in device memory, `present_or_copy` behaves the same as `present` by re-using those existing locations in this data region. Variables listed that are not already present are copied to the accelerator at the start of this `data` region and copied back at the end.	Y	N	N
`present_ or_copyin( var1, ...)`	For variables listed that are already present in device memory, re-use those existing locations. Variables listed that are not already present are copied to the accelerator.	Y	Y	N
`present_ or_copyout( var1, ...)`	For variables listed that are already present in device memory, re-use those existing locations and perform no copies. Variables listed that are not already present are copied out of the accelerator at the end of this data region.	Y	N	N
`present_ or_create( var1, ...)`	For variables listed that are already present in device memory, re-use those existing locations. Variables listed that are not already present have space allocated for them on the accelerator but no copies are performed.	Y	Y	N

deviceptr (var1, ...)	deviceptr indicates to the compiler that the listed variables are actually device pointers and so do not need to be allocated or transferred to the accelerator. deviceptr will be discussed further in the section "Combining OpenACC and the CUDA Libraries."	Y	N	N
async(int)	Perform this transfer asynchronously, using the optional integer argument as a unique identifier of this asynchronous copy.	N	Y	Y
wait(int)	Wait for previous asynchronous tasks to complete before starting this transfer.	N	Y	Y
delete (var1, ...)	The delete clause can be used with the exit data directive to explicitly de-allocate accelerator memory.	N	N	Y

Adding Data Clauses to kernels and parallel Directives

Commonly, data directives are closely associated with compute directives as the inputs and outputs are transferred before and after a computational region. While it is possible to use separate directives for each task, OpenACC also supports using data clauses on computational directives to simplify the code.

For example, consider the core logic from the earlier simple-data.c example:

```
#pragma acc data copyin(A[0:N], B[0:N]) copyout(C[0:N], D[0:N])
    {
#pragma acc parallel
        {
            ...
        }
    }
```

Rather than having two separate compiler directives, a single data clause can be added to the parallel directive:

```
#pragma acc parallel copyin(A[0:N], B[0:N]) copyout(C[0:N], D[0:N])
    {
        ...
    }
```

This change simplifies the source and makes it easier see that the `parallel` region and the data transfers are associated.

Both `kernels` and `parallel` support the `copy`, `copyin`, `copyout`, `create`, `present`, `present_or_copy`, `present_or_copyin`, `present_or_copyout`, `present_or_create`, and `deviceptr` data clauses described in Table 8-6.

The OpenACC Runtime API

In addition to compiler directives, OpenACC also provides a library of functions. You saw a few of these when the `async` and `wait` clauses were introduced: The functions `acc_async_wait`, `acc_async_wait_all`, `acc_async_test`, and `acc_async_test_all` are all part of the OpenACC Runtime API. Using functions from the OpenACC Runtime API requires including the header file `openacc.h`.

Many OpenACC programs can operate without ever using the OpenACC Runtime API, as in many cases the compiler directives provide all of the required functionality. However, there are still operations provided by the Runtime API that are not duplicated in the OpenACC compiler directives.

The OpenACC Runtime API can be split into four main areas: device management, asynchronous control, runtime initialization, and memory management. This section will not provide a comprehensive overview of all functions available in the Runtime API, but rather focus on the most useful in each area.

Device management functions provide you with explicit control over which accelerator or which accelerator type is used to execute OpenACC computational regions. Many of the device management functions use the type `acc_device_t`, an enum type that represents the different types of devices supported by an OpenACC implementation. At the bare minimum, all OpenACC implementations must support `acc_device_none`, `acc_device_default`, `acc_device_host`, and `acc_device_not_host`. However, many more may be supported. For example, PGI 14.4 supports the following device types:

```
typedef enum {
    acc_device_none = 0,
    acc_device_default = 1,
    acc_device_host = 2,
    acc_device_not_host = 3,
    acc_device_nvidia = 4,
    acc_device_radeon = 5,
    acc_device_xeonphi = 6,
    acc_device_pgi_opencl = 7,
    acc_device_nvidia_opencl = 8,
    acc_device_opencl = 9
} acc_device_t;
```

A subset of the device management functions is described in Table 8-7.

TABLE 8-7: Device Management Functions in the OpenACC Runtime API

FUNCTION DECLARATION	DESCRIPTION
```int acc_get_num_devices(acc_device_t)```	Get the number of devices available that have the specified type.
```void acc_set_device_type(acc_device_t)```	Run all OpenACC computation on a device with the provided type.
```acc_device_type acc_get_device_type()```	Get the device type of the currently selected device.
```void acc_set_device_num(int, acc_device_t)```	Select a device to use among all devices of the specified type.
```int acc_get_device_num(acc_device_t)```	Get the device number of the device with the specified type that will be used to run the next OpenACC computational region.

Asynchronous control functions allow you to check for or wait on the status of asynchronous tasks. Asynchronous tasks include both asynchronous computation created using `parallel` or `kernels` directives and asynchronous communication created using the OpenACC data directives. A subset of the asynchronous control functions is described in Table 8-8.

TABLE 8-8: Asynchronous Control Functions in the OpenACC Runtime API

FUNCTION DECLARATION	DESCRIPTION
```int acc_async_test(int)```	Test if the specified asynchronous task has completed. If the task has completed, a non-zero value is returned.
```int acc_async_test_all()```	Tests for completion of all previously created asynchronous tasks. If there are no asynchronous tasks running, a non-zero value is returned.
```void acc_wait(int)```	Wait for the specified asynchronous task to complete.
```void acc_wait_async(int, int)```	Forces any tasks following the asynchronous task specified by the second argument to wait for the completion of the asynchronous task specified by the first argument. This does not block the host application.
```void acc_wait_all()```	Waits for all asynchronous tasks to complete.
```void acc_wait_all_async(int)```	Forces any tasks waiting on the asynchronous task specified to wait for all other asynchronous tasks to finish.

Runtime initialization functions are used to either initialize or clean up internal OpenACC state. A subset of the runtime initialization functions is described in Table 8-9. If `acc_init` is not explicitly called by an OpenACC application, runtime initialization is automatically performed as part of the first OpenACC operation of an application.

TABLE 8-9: Runtime Initialization Functions in the OpenACC Runtime API

FUNCTION DECLARATION	DESCRIPTION
`void` `acc_init(acc_device_t)`	Initialize the OpenACC runtime on a device of the provided type.
`void` `acc_shutdown(acc_device_t)`	Disconnect the OpenACC runtime from the currently active device with the specified type.

Memory management functions are used to manage the allocation of accelerator memory and transfer of data between host and accelerator. Hence, in many cases they duplicate functionality of the OpenACC `data` directives and clauses. A subset of the memory management functions is described in Table 8-10.

TABLE 8-10: Memory Management Functions in the OpenACC Runtime API

FUNCTION DECLARATION	DESCRIPTION
`void *` `acc_malloc(size_t)`	Allocates the specified number of bytes on the accelerator, returning the address of the allocated memory
`void acc_free(void *)`	Frees device memory starting at the specified address

`acc_copyin,`
`acc_present_or_copyin,`
`acc_create,`
`acc_present_or_create,`
`acc_copyout, acc_delete`
	Each of these functions takes a `void*` as its first argument and a `size_t` as its second argument. They each implement the same operation as the clause with an identical name, performing that operation using the number of bytes specified as the second argument starting at the host address specified by the first argument

`int`
`acc_is_present(void*,`
` size_t)`
	Checks if the memory region starting at the provided address and with the specified length is copied to the accelerator

Combining OpenACC and the CUDA Libraries

While CUDA and OpenACC are separate programming models, they can be used in the same application. Doing so requires changes to how the application is compiled. The `deviceptr` clause must also be used to share data between CUDA and OpenACC. This section will demonstrate a single application that uses CUDA libraries and OpenACC together in a single source file. The example application can be downloaded from `Wrox.com` in `cuda-openacc.cu`.

cuda-openacc.cu can be split into the following steps:

1. Matrices are allocated on the device using cudaMalloc and handles are created for both the cuRAND and cuBLAS libraries using curandCreateGenerator and cublasCreate.

2. The input matrices in device memory are filled with random data using the cuRAND library's curandGenerateUniform function.

3. Using OpenACC directives, a matrix-matrix multiply is performed in parallel on the GPU.

4. cublasSasum is used to calculate the sum of all elements in the output matrix by summing each row, and then across rows.

5. Device memory is freed using cudaFree.

To build cuda-openacc.cu with the PGI OpenACC compiler, use the following command:

```
$ pgcpp -acc cuda-openacc.cu -o cuda-openacc -Minfo=accel \
    -L${CUDA_HOME}/lib64 -lcurand -lcublas -lcudart
```

Note that here the C++ compiler pgcpp is being used for compatibility with the CUDA libraries. The same -acc argument is retained to enable OpenACC support, and -Minfo=accel is used to display diagnostic information on the parallelization of the OpenACC computational regions. Additionally, the CUDA library path is added to the library path of the compiler so that the definitions of cuRAND, cuBLAS, and CUDA runtime functions can be found. The output of this command is as follows:

```
main:
     70, Accelerator kernel generated
         70, #pragma acc loop gang /* blockIdx.x */
         72, #pragma acc loop vector(32), worker(4) /* threadIdx.x threadIdx.
     70, Generating Tesla code
     72, Loop is parallelizable
     74, Loop is parallelizable
```

Note that a kernel is generated for the loops on line 70 and 72, with the outermost loop using gang parallelism and the innermost loop using worker and vector parallelism.

Most of this code should look familiar to you after a full chapter on CUDA libraries and OpenACC. Only two items may look new.

First, the deviceptr clause is being used with the parallel directive. deviceptr allows an application to explicitly allocate and manage its own device memory, and then pass it directly to OpenACC computational regions. In this case, the cuda-openacc application explicitly allocates its own device memory with cudaMalloc before filling it using cuRAND. deviceptr can then be used to give the OpenACC kernel direct access to that same device memory, rather than having to transfer it back to the host before using copyin. deviceptr is a key component allowing integration between OpenACC and other GPU programming frameworks.

The cuda-openacc.cu example also makes use of cublasSetPointerMode to adjust whether cuBLAS functions expect host or device pointers to be used to return scalar results. In this case, cublasSasum returns a scalar result as its last argument. Initially, cublasSetPointerMode is used to set the mode to `CUBLAS_POINTER_MODE_DEVICE` when summing the rows of the output matrix on the device. When performing the final sum across rows the mode is set to `CUBLAS_POINTER_MODE_HOST` and the return address is set to a variable in the host application's address space. You may recall a brief explanation about the cuSPARSE version of this function, `cusparseSetPointerMode`, in the section in this chapter titled "Important Topics in cuSPARSE Development."

Summary of OpenACC

This section introduced you to the OpenACC execution and programming model. OpenACC is a flexible, easy-to-use, high-performance programming model that complements CUDA and the CUDA libraries in many ways. Compared to the CUDA libraries, OpenACC is more flexible and allows you to write your own computational functions using the C language. Compared to CUDA, OpenACC is more convenient and requires less manual management of communication and computation than CUDA C.

However, OpenACC is not without its downsides. A simple OpenACC implementation that ignores data movement often degrades performance due to unnecessary memory copies. OpenACC by default must be conservative about optimization strategies. Even with the use of the `async`, `copyin`, and `copyout` clauses, OpenACC performance often lags behind hand-coded CUDA versions. Additionally, for many domains, OpenACC simply cannot beat the performance and usability of pre-written, expert-tuned CUDA libraries.

Despite these drawbacks, the balance of OpenACC across performance, usability, and customizability makes it an attractive programming model to complement CUDA for rapid development of high-performance GPU applications.

SUMMARY

This chapter prepared you to make use of cuSPARSE, cuBLAS, cuFFT, cuRAND, and OpenACC to accelerate your application and development process.

The CUDA libraries are powerful in their simplicity, usability, portability, and performance. They were deliberately designed to be familiar to domain experts with past experience in the fields for which they are most useful. Applications that do not require a large amount of customization can make use of these libraries and their component functions as basic building blocks of GPU-accelerated applications.

More importantly, the focus on the general workflow, abstract concepts, and porting process shared among these libraries has prepared you to move beyond the scope of this chapter and explore more advanced concepts in these libraries as well as entirely new CUDA libraries. Although the libraries specifically covered in this chapter were selected because of their applicability to a wide range of use cases and applications, this chapter could only skim the surface of CUDA library functionality.

On the other hand, OpenACC offers you more control over GPU execution than CUDA libraries while eliminating many of the more mundane tasks of GPU programming. In OpenACC, many of the same operations supported by the CUDA API can be performed using simple compiler directives that guide automatic parallelization. In fact, most of the performance lessons taught in this book apply equally to CUDA and OpenACC. Additionally, you can write your own custom GPU kernels in a more intuitive format that is similar to sequential host code. OpenACC reduces complexity relative to CUDA and increases flexibility relative to CUDA libraries.

Overall, this chapter introduced frameworks layered on top of CUDA that offer a more abstract view of hardware and enable you to get more performance from less code. If your application falls inside a domain covered by a CUDA library, the expert-implemented kernels and compatible APIs lead to better performance for less development effort. OpenACC accelerates the development process for custom CUDA kernels by cutting down on hand-written code and automatically performing memory management, work partitioning, and parallelization.

CHAPTER 8 EXERCISES

1. What step is missing from the following cuBLAS workflow:

    1. Read input data from data file in column-major order.

    2. Allocate device memory with cudaMalloc.

    3. Configure a cuBLAS handle with cublasCreate.

    4. Execute matrix-matrix multiplication with cublasSgemm.

    5. Fetch results with cudaGetMatrix.

2. Write a function that takes as input a single dense matrix A, the number of rows M, and the number of columns N and uses a pipeline of cuSPARSE format conversion functions to convert it to the COO format. Assume that this is not a submatrix of a larger matrix. Your function signature should be:

    ```
    void dense2coo(float *M, int M, int N,
        float **values, int **row_indices, int **col_indices);
    ```

3. Use the random matrix generation function generate_random_dense_matrix in cusparse .cu to generate two random dense matrices and perform matrix-matrix multiplication using cuSPARSE.

4. Modify the code you wrote for question 3 to operate on double-precision floating-point values. Note that this will require changes to data initialization, storage, and the cuSPARSE functions used. Use nvprof to measure and explain any performance differences.

5. Take the generate_random_dense_matrix function from cublas.cu. First, reorder the outer loops to iterate over rows and then columns (the opposite of what it is doing right now) without modifying the indices used to reference the array A. Use the seconds function included in the nbody.cu example from Chapter 7 to compare execution time of generate_random_dense_ matrix before and after this change. If there is no significant difference, try increasing the value of M and/or N. What do you observe? What causes this difference in performance? Next, modify the indices used to reference the array A so that the array is now in row-major order. Re-measure performance. How did it change, and why?

6. Using a cuBLAS Level 3 function and the `generate_random_dense_matrix` function from `cublas.cu`, perform a matrix-matrix multiplication.

7. Add CUDA streams to the code you wrote for question 6. You may only use asynchronous functions for transferring data between the host and device (for example, `cublasSetMatrixAsync`, `cublasGetMatrixAsync`). Recall that all executable functions in cuBLAS are already asynchronous by default.

8. cuFFT supports both forward and inverse FFTs. In the `cufft.cu` example from this chapter, `cufftExecC2C` receives `CUFFT_FORWARD` as its last argument to indicate that a forward FFT is desired. What would you need to add to the example to add an inverse operation following the forward operation? After you do so, how do the outputs change? How do these new outputs relate to the original signal samples? Keep in mind, FFTs often require normalization, as they retain information on the frequencies in the signal but not the amplitude.

9. What is the difference between pseudo-random and quasi-random random sequences of numbers?

10. Consider an application you have worked on in the past that used random numbers. How would the behavior of that application differ between using a pseudo-random number generator and a quasi-random number generator?

11. Consider a massive vector addition done across multiple GPUs. Although you have not yet seen the CUDA APIs for multi-device execution, how do you think the multiple, separate address spaces affect tasks like memory allocation and data transfer? How would you partition the work to be done in the vector addition across multiple GPUs? What kind of insight can this give you into the implementation of multi-GPU libraries? How might you design functions like `cufftXtMalloc` and `cufftXtMemcpy` by combining `cudaMalloc` and `cudaMemcpy` with the ability to specify a target device for these CUDA operations?

12. Define the following OpenACC terms: gang-redundant mode, gang-partitioned mode, worker-single mode, worker-partitioned mode.

13. Compare and contrast the `parallel` and `kernels` compiler directives in OpenACC. Be sure to discuss programmability and performance.

14. How is the `loop` compiler directive used in OpenACC? Use it in the example below to achieve maximum parallelism when executing the loop.

```
#pragma acc parallel
{
    for (i = 0; i < N; i++) {
        ...
    }
}
```

Multi-GPU Programming

WHAT'S IN THIS CHAPTER?

> Managing multiple GPUs

> Executing kernels across multiple GPUs

> Overlapping computation and communication between GPUs

> Synchronizing across GPUs

> Exchanging data using CUDA-aware MPI

> Exchanging data using CUDA-aware MPI with GPUDirect RDMA

> Scaling applications across a GPU-accelerated cluster

> Understanding CPU and GPU affinity

> **CODE DOWNLOAD** *The wrox.com code downloads for this chapter are found at* www.wrox.com/go/procudac *on the Download Code tab. The code can be found in the Chapter 9 download section and is individually named according to the names throughout the chapter.*

So far, most of the examples in this book have used a single GPU. In this chapter, you will gain experience in multi-GPU programming: scaling your application across multiple GPUs within a compute node, or across multiple GPU-accelerated nodes. CUDA provides a number of features to facilitate multi-GPU programming, including multi-device management from one or more processes, direct access to other devices' memory using Unified Virtual Addressing (UVA) and GPUDirect, and computation-communication overlap across multiple devices using streams and asynchronous functions. In this chapter, you will learn the necessary skills to:

> Manage and execute kernels on multiple GPUs.

> Overlap computation and communication across multiple GPUs.

➤ Synchronize execution across multiple GPUs using streams and events.

➤ Scale CUDA-aware MPI applications across a GPU-accelerated cluster.

You will see, through several examples, how applications can achieve near linear scalability when executing on multiple devices.

MOVING TO MULTIPLE GPUS

The most common reasons for adding multi-GPU support to an application are:

➤ **Problem domain size:** Existing data sets are too large to fit into the memory of a single GPU.

➤ **Throughput and efficiency:** If a single task fits within a single GPU, you may be able to increase the throughput of an application by processing multiple tasks concurrently using multiple GPUs.

A multi-GPU system allows you to amortize the power consumption of a server node across GPUs by delivering more performance for a given unit of power consumed, while boosting throughput.

When converting your application to take advantage of multiple GPUs, it is important to properly design inter-GPU communication. The efficiency of inter-GPU data transfers depends on how GPUs are connected within a node, and across a cluster. There are two types of connectivity in multi-GPU systems:

➤ Multiple GPUs connected over the PCIe bus in a single node

➤ Multiple GPUs connected over a network switch in a cluster

These connection topologies are not mutually exclusive. Figure 9-1 illustrates a simplified topology for a cluster with two compute nodes. GPU0 and GPU1 are connected via the PCIe bus on node0. Similarly, GPU2 and GPU3 are connected via the PCIe bus on node1. The two nodes (node0 and node1) are connected to each other through *InfiniBand* Switch.

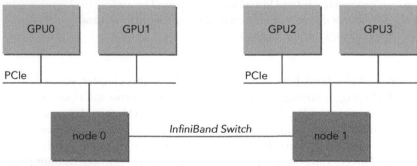

FIGURE 9-1

Each node may have one or more of the following: CPUs connected via CPU sockets and host chipsets, host DRAM, local storage devices, network Host Card Adaptors (HCAs), on-board network and USB ports, and PCIe switches connecting multiple GPUs. Your system may have a root PCIe node with multiple PCIe switches hanging off the root node and connecting the GPUs in a tree structure. Because PCIe links are duplex, it is possible to use CUDA APIs to map a path between PCIe links to avoid bus contention while sharing data among GPUs.

To design a program to take advantage of multiple GPUs, you will need to partition the workload across devices. Depending on the application, this partitioning can result in two common inter-GPU communication patterns:

➤ No data exchange necessary between partitions of a problem, and therefore no data shared across GPUs

➤ Partial data exchange between problem partitions, requiring redundant data storage across GPUs

The first case is the rudimentary case: Each partition of the problem can run independently on a different GPU. To handle these cases, you will only need to learn how to transfer data and invoke kernels across multiple devices. In the second case, data exchange between GPUs is necessary and you must consider how data can optimally be moved between devices. In general, you want to avoid staging data through host memory (that is, copying data to the host only to be able to copy it to another GPU). It is important to pay attention to both how much data is transferred and how many transfers occur.

The second case recalls the concept of a *halo region* from the 1D stencil example in Chapter 5. A halo region refers to the input data which must be accessible to a subset of a problem, but for which that subset does not produce output. Usually, the halo region around a problem partition is relatively small compared to the interior data subset (*inner region*) that does not need to be exchanged. Depending on the communication cost of exchanging the halo regions and the time required to compute the inner region, some overlap of the two may be achieved to reduce overhead in multi-GPU systems. This is similar to the techniques you used to hide data transfer overhead across the PCIe bus between the host and device.

Executing on Multiple GPUs

Features added in CUDA 4.0 made using multiple GPUs straightforward for CUDA programmers. The CUDA runtime API supports several ways of managing devices and executing kernels across multi-GPU systems.

A single host thread can manage multiple devices. In general, the first step is determining the number of CUDA-enabled devices available in a system using the following function:

```
cudaError_t cudaGetDeviceCount(int* count);
```

This function returns the number of devices with compute capability 1.0 or higher. The following code illustrates how to determine the number of CUDA-enabled devices, iterate over them, and query their properties.

```
int ngpus;
cudaGetDeviceCount(&ngpus);

for (int i = 0; i < ngpus; i++) {
    cudaDeviceProp devProp;
```

```
          cudaGetDeviceProperties(&devProp, i);
          printf("Device %d has compute capability %d.%d.\n", i, devProp.major,
             devProp.minor);
    }
```

When implementing a CUDA application that works with multiple GPUs, you must explicitly designate which GPU is the current target for all CUDA operations. You can set the current device with the following function:

```
    cudaError_t cudaSetDevice(int id);
```

This function sets the device with identifier id as the current device. This function will not cause synchronization with other devices, and therefore is a low-overhead call. You can use this function to select any device from any host thread at any time. Valid device identifiers start from zero and span to ngpus-1. If cudaSetDevice is not explicitly called before the first CUDA API call is made, the current device is automatically set to device 0.

Once a current device is selected, all CUDA operations will be applied to that device:

➤ Any device memory allocated from the host thread will be physically resident on that device.

➤ Any host memory allocated with CUDA runtime functions will have its lifetime associated with that device.

➤ Any streams or events created from the host thread will be associated with that device.

➤ Any kernels launched from the host thread will be executed on that device.

Multiple GPUs can be used at once from:

➤ A single CPU thread in one node

➤ Multiple CPU threads in one node

➤ Multiple CPU processes in one node

➤ Multiple CPU processes across multiple nodes

The following code snippet illustrates how to execute kernels and memory copies from a single host thread, using a loop to iterate over devices:

```
    for (int i = 0; i < ngpus; i++) {
        // set the current device
        cudaSetDevice(i);

        // execute kernel on current device
        kernel<<<grid, block>>>(...);

        // asynchronously transfer data between the host and current device
        cudaMemcpyAsync(...);
    }
```

Because the kernel launch and data transfer in the loop are asynchronous, control will return to the host thread soon after each operation is invoked. However, you can safely switch devices even if kernels or transfers issued by the current thread are still executing on the current device, because `cudaSetDevice` does not cause host synchronization.

To recap, fetching the number of GPUs in a single node and the properties of those GPUs is possible using:

```
cudaError_t cudaGetDeviceCount(int *count);
cudaError_t cudaGetDeviceProperties(struct cudaDeviceProp *prop, int device);
```

You can then set the current device using:

```
cudaError_t cudaSetDevice(int device);
```

Once the current device is set, all CUDA operations are issued in the context of that device. The selected device can then be used in the same way as you have been programming GPUs throughout this book.

Peer-to-Peer Communication

Kernels executing in 64-bit applications on devices with compute capability 2.0 and higher can directly access the global memory of any GPU connected to the same PCIe root node. To do so, you must use the CUDA *peer-to-peer (P2P)* API to enable direct inter-device communication. Peer-to-peer communication requires CUDA 4.0 or higher, the corresponding GPU drivers, and a system with two or more Fermi or Kepler GPUs connected to the same PCIe root node. There are two modes supported by the CUDA P2P APIs that allow direct communication between GPUs:

➤ **Peer-to-peer Access:** Directly load and store addresses within a CUDA kernel and across GPUs.

➤ **Peer-to-peer Transfer:** Directly copy data between GPUs.

If two GPUs are connected to different PCIe root nodes within a system, then direct peer-to-peer access is not supported and the CUDA P2P API will inform you of that. You can still use the CUDA P2P API to perform peer-to-peer transfer between these devices, but the driver will transparently transfer data through host memory for those transactions rather than directly across the PCIe bus.

Enabling Peer Access

Peer-to-peer access allows GPUs connected to the same PCIe root node to directly reference data stored in device memory on other GPUs. Transparent to the kernel, the referenced data will be transferred over the PCIe bus to the requesting thread.

Because not all GPUs support peer-to-peer access, you need to explicitly check if a device supports P2P using the following function:

```
cudaError_t cudaDeviceCanAccessPeer(int* canAccessPeer, int device,
    int peerDevice);
```

This function returns an integer value of 1 in the variable `canAccessPeer` if the device `device` is able to directly access the global memory of peer device `peerDevice`; otherwise it returns a value of 0.

Peer-to-peer memory access must be explicitly enabled between two devices with the following function:

```
cudaError_t cudaDeviceEnablePeerAccess(int peerDevice, unsigned int flag);
```

This function enables peer-to-peer access from the current device to peerDevice. The flag argument is reserved for future use and currently must be set to 0. Upon success, the memory of the peer device will immediately be accessible by the current device.

The access granted by this function is unidirectional, meaning that this function enables access from the current device to peerDevice but does not enable access from peerDevice. If you also want to allow the peer device to directly access the memory of the current device, a separate matching call in the other direction is required.

Peer-to-peer access remains enabled until it is explicitly disabled with the following function:

```
cudaError_t cudaDeviceDisablePeerAccess(int peerDevice);
```

Peer-to-peer access is not supported in 32-bit applications.

Peer-to-Peer Memory Copy

After enabling peer access between two devices, you can copy data between those devices asynchronously using the following function:

```
cudaError_t cudaMemcpyPeerAsync(void* dst, int dstDev, void* src, int srcDev,
    size_t nBytes, cudaStream_t stream);
```

This function transfers data from device memory on the device srcDev to device memory on the device dstDev. The function cudaMemcpyPeerAsync is asynchronous with respect to the host and all other devices. If srcDev and dstDev share the same PCIe root node, the transfer is performed along the shortest PCIe path without having to stage through host memory.

Synchronizing across Multi-GPUs

The CUDA API for streams and events introduced in Chapter 6 is applicable to multi-GPU applications. Every stream and event is associated with a single device. You can use the same synchronization functions in a multi-GPU application as you would in a single-GPU application, but you must be sure to specify the proper current device. The typical workflow for using streams and events in a multi-GPU application is:

1. Select the set of GPUs this application will use.
2. Create streams and events for each device.
3. Allocate device resources on each device (for example, device memory).
4. Launch tasks on each GPU through the streams (for example, data transfers or kernel executions).
5. Use the streams and events to query and wait for task completion.
6. Cleanup resources for all devices.

You can launch a kernel in a stream only if the device associated with that stream is the current device. You can record an event in a stream only if the device associated with that stream is the current device.

A memory copy can be issued in any stream at any time, regardless of what device it is associated with or what the current device is. You can also query or synchronize any event or stream, even if they are not associated with the current device.

SUBDIVIDING COMPUTATION ACROSS MULTIPLE GPUS

In this section, you are going to extend the vector addition example from Chapter 2 to take advantage of multiple GPUs. You will learn how to split the input and output vectors across GPUs. Vector addition represents a typical case for multi-GPU programming where there is no need to exchange data between problem partitions.

Allocating Memory on Multiple Devices

Before distributing computation from the host to multiple devices, you first need to determine how many GPUs are available in the current system:

```
int ngpus;
cudaGetDeviceCount(&ngpus);
printf(" CUDA-capable devices: %i\n", ngpus);
```

Once the number of GPUs has been determined, you then declare host memory, device memory, streams, and events for multiple devices. A simple way to maintain these variables is to use an array of data types, declared as follows:

```
float *d_A[NGPUS], *d_B[NGPUS], *d_C[NGPUS];
float *h_A[NGPUS], *h_B[NGPUS], *hostRef[NGPUS], *gpuRef[NGPUS];
cudaStream_t stream[NGPUS];
```

In this vector add example, a total input size of 16M elements is used and evenly divided among all devices, giving each device iSize elements:

```
int size  = 1 << 24;
int iSize = size / ngpus;
```

The size in bytes for one float vector on a device is calculated as follows:

```
size_t iBytes = iSize * sizeof(float);
```

Now, host and device memory can be allocated, and CUDA streams can be created for each device as follows:

```
for (int i = 0; i < ngpus; i++) {
    // set current device
    cudaSetDevice(i);

    // allocate device memory
    cudaMalloc((void **) &d_A[i], iBytes);
```

```
    cudaMalloc((void **) &d_B[i], iBytes);
    cudaMalloc((void **) &d_C[i], iBytes);

    // allocate page locked host memory for asynchronous data transfer
    cudaMallocHost((void **) &h_A[i],     iBytes);
    cudaMallocHost((void **) &h_B[i],     iBytes);
    cudaMallocHost((void **) &hostRef[i], iBytes);
    cudaMallocHost((void **) &gpuRef[i],  iBytes);

    // create streams for timing and synchronizing
    cudaStreamCreate(&stream[i]);
}
```

Note that page-locked (pinned) host memory is allocated in order to perform asynchronous data transfers between the device and host. Also, `cudaSetDevice` is used at the start of every iteration of the loop above to set the current device before allocating any memory or creating any streams.

Distributing Work from a Single Host Thread

Before distributing operations among devices, you need to initialize the state of the host arrays for each device:

```
for (int i = 0; i < ngpus; i++) {
    cudaSetDevice(i);
    initialData(h_A[i], iSize);
    initialData(h_B[i], iSize);
}
```

With all resources allocated and initialized, you are ready to distribute data and computation among multiple devices using a loop:

```
// distributing the workload across multiple devices
for (int i = 0; i < ngpus; i++) {
    cudaSetDevice(i);

    cudaMemcpyAsync(d_A[i], h_A[i], iBytes, cudaMemcpyHostToDevice, stream[i]);
    cudaMemcpyAsync(d_B[i], h_B[i], iBytes, cudaMemcpyHostToDevice, stream[i]);

    iKernel<<<grid, block, 0, stream[i]>>> (d_A[i], d_B[i], d_C[i], iSize);

    cudaMemcpyAsync(gpuRef[i], d_C[i], iBytes, cudaMemcpyDeviceToHost, stream[i]);
}
cudaDeviceSynchronize();
```

This loop iterates over multiple GPUs, asynchronously copying the input arrays for that device. It then launches a kernel in the same stream operating on `iSize` data elements. Finally, an asynchronous copy from the device is issued to transfer the results from the kernel back to the host. Because all functions are asynchronous, control is returned to the host thread immediately. It is then safe to switch to the next device while tasks are still running on the current device.

Compiling and Executing

You can download the file `simpleMultiGPU.cu` containing the full multi-GPU vector addition example from `Wrox.com`. Compile it with the following command:

```
$ nvcc -O3 simpleMultiGPU.cu -o simpleMultiGPU
```

A sample output of `simpleMultiGPU` is:

```
$ ./simpleMultiGPU
> starting ./simpleMultiGPU with 2 CUDA-capable devices
> total array size: 16M, using 2 devices with each device handling 8M
GPU timer elapsed: 35.35ms
```

You can try running it with only one GPU by passing 1 as a command-line option, as follows:

```
$ ./simpleMultiGPU 1
> starting ./simpleMultiGPU with 2 CUDA-capable devices
> total array size: 16M, using 1 devices with each device handling 16M
GPU timer elapsed: 42.25ms
```

While the elapsed time is not reduced by half when you double the number of GPUs being used, a significant amount of performance is still gained.

You can obtain more detail about each device's behavior using `nvprof`:

```
$ nvprof --print-gpu-trace ./simpleMultiGPU
```

An example of the output generated on a system with two M2090 GPUs is summarized below:

Duration	Size	Throughput	Device	Stream	Name
6.5858ms	33.554MB	5.0950GB/s	Tesla M2090 (0)	13	[CUDA memcpy HtoD]
6.5921ms	33.554MB	5.0901GB/s	Tesla M2090 (1)	21	[CUDA memcpy HtoD]
6.6171ms	33.554MB	5.0708GB/s	Tesla M2090 (0)	13	[CUDA memcpy HtoD]
6.6020ms	33.554MB	5.0825GB/s	Tesla M2090 (1)	21	[CUDA memcpy HtoD]
9.8417ms	33.554MB	3.4094GB/s	Tesla M2090 (0)	13	[CUDA memcpy DtoH]
9.8460ms	33.554MB	3.4079GB/s	Tesla M2090 (1)	21	[CUDA memcpy DtoH]
720.49us	-	-	Tesla M2090 (1)	21	iKernel(float*,...)
721.32us	-	-	Tesla M2090 (0)	13	iKernel(float*,...)

Running with only one M2090 GPU produces output similar to that shown below:

Duration	Size	Throughput	Device	Stream	Name
13.171ms	67.109MB	5.0951GB/s	Tesla M2090 (0)	13	[CUDA memcpy HtoD]
13.117ms	67.109MB	5.1161GB/s	Tesla M2090 (0)	13	[CUDA memcpy HtoD]
14.918ms	67.109MB	4.4984GB/s	Tesla M2090 (0)	13	[CUDA memcpy DtoH]
1.4371ms	-	-	Tesla M2090 (0)	13	iKernel(float*,...)

From these results, you can see that operations are perfectly divided between two devices.

PEER-TO-PEER COMMUNICATION ON MULTIPLE GPUS

In this section, you are going to explore transferring data between two GPUs. The following three cases will be tested:

➤ Unidirectional memory copy between two GPUs

➤ Bidirectional memory copy between two GPUs

➤ Peer device memory access in a kernel

Enabling Peer-to-Peer Access

First, you must enable bi-directional peer-to-peer access among all devices, as demonstrated in the following code:

```
/*
 * enable P2P memcopies between GPUs (all GPUs must be compute capability 2.0 or
 * later (Fermi or later)).
 */
inline void enableP2P (int ngpus) {
   for( int i = 0; i < ngpus; i++ ) {
      cudaSetDevice(i);
      for(int j = 0; j < ngpus; j++) {
         if(i == j) continue;

         int peer_access_available = 0;
         cudaDeviceCanAccessPeer(&peer_access_available, i, j);

         if (peer_access_available) {
            cudaDeviceEnablePeerAccess(j, 0);
            printf("> GPU%d enabled direct access to GPU%d\n",i,j);
         } else {
            printf("(%d, %d)\n", i, j);
         }
      }
   }
}
```

The function `enableP2P` iterates over all pairs of devices (i, j) and if peer access is supported, enables it in both directions using `cudaDeviceEnablePeerAccess`.

Peer-to-Peer Memory Copy

After peer-to-peer access has been enabled, you can copy data directly between two devices. If peer access is not supported, this example prints the device IDs for which peer-to-peer access could not be enabled (most likely because they are not connected to the same PCIe root node) and continues without errors. However, recall that if peer-to-peer access is not enabled between two GPUs, a peer-to-peer memory copy between those two devices will be staged through host memory, thereby reducing performance. How that performance reduction affects your application depends on how much time your kernel spends computing and performing peer-to-peer transfers. If enough time is spent computing, you may be able to hide the latency of peer-to-peer copies that pass through host memory by overlapping it with device computation.

With peer-to-peer access enabled, the following code snippet performs a ping-pong synchronous memory copy between two devices one hundred times. If peer-to-peer access was successfully enabled on all devices, the data transfers will pass directly over the PCIe bus without host interaction.

```
// ping pong unidirectional gmem copy
cudaEventRecord(start, 0);
for (int i = 0; i < 100; i++) {
    if (i % 2 == 0) {
        cudaMemcpy(d_src[1], d_src[0], iBytes, cudaMemcpyDeviceToDevice);
    } else {
        cudaMemcpy(d_src[0], d_src[1], iBytes, cudaMemcpyDeviceToDevice);
    }
}
```

Note that there is no device switching before the memory copy because memory copies across devices do not require you to explicitly set a current device. If you do specify a device before a memory copy, it will not affect its behavior.

To measure data transfer performance between devices, `start` and `stop` events are recorded on the same device, wrapping the ping-pong memory copies. Then, `cudaEventElapsedTime` is used to calculate the time elapsed between events.

```
cudaSetDevice(0);
cudaEventRecord(start, 0);
for (int i = 0; i < 100; i++) {
    ...
}
cudaSetDevice(0);
cudaEventRecord(stop, 0);
cudaEventSynchronize(stop);

float elapsed_time_ms;
cudaEventElapsedTime(&elapsed_time_ms, start, stop);
```

Then, the bandwidth achieved by this ping-pong test can be estimated as follows:

```
elapsed_time_ms /= 100.0f;
printf("Ping-pong unidirectional cudaMemcpy:\t\t %8.2f ms", elapsed_time_ms);
printf("performance: %8.2f GB/s\n", (float) iBytes /(elapsed_time_ms * 1e6f));
```

You can download the file `simpleP2P_PingPong.cu` containing this example from `Wrox.com`. Compile and run it as follows:

```
$ nvcc -O3 simpleP2P_PingPong.cu -o simplePingPong
$ ./simplePingPong
```

A sample output of `simpleP2P_PingPong` is below:

```
Allocating buffers (64MB on each GPU and CPU Host)
Ping-pong unidirectional cudaMemcpy: 13.41ms performance: 5.00 GB/s
```

Because the PCIe bus supports full-duplex communication between any two endpoints, you can also perform bidirectional, peer-to-peer memory copies using asynchronous copy functions:

```
// bidirectional asynchronous gmem copy
cudaEventRecord(start, 0);
for (int i = 0; i < 100; i++) {
    cudaMemcpyAsync(d_src[1], d_src[0], iBytes, cudaMemcpyDeviceToDevice,
        stream[0]);
    cudaMemcpyAsync(d_rcv[0], d_rcv[1], iBytes, cudaMemcpyDeviceToDevice,
        stream[1]);
}
```

The test for bidirectional memory copy is implemented in the same file. The following is a sample output:

```
Ping-pong bidirectional cudaMemcpyAsync: 13.39ms performance: 10.02 GB/s
```

Note that the achieved bandwidth has doubled because the PCIe bus is being used in both directions at once. If you disable peer-to-peer access by removing the call to `enableP2P` in `simpleP2P_PingPong.cu`, then both the unidirectional and bidirectional examples still complete without error, but the measured bandwidth will drop as transfers are staged through host memory.

Peer-to-Peer Memory Access with Unified Virtual Addressing

Unified Virtual Addressing (UVA), introduced in Chapter 4, maps CPU system memory and device global memory into a single virtual address space, as illustrated in Figure 9-2. All host memory allocations made via `cudaHostAlloc` and device memory allocations made via `cudaMalloc` reside within this unified address space. The device that a memory address resides on can be determined from the address itself.

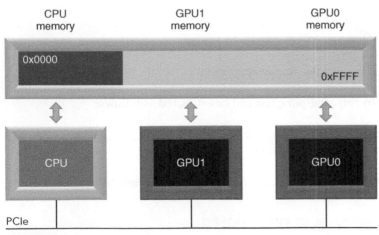

FIGURE 9-2

Combining the peer-to-peer CUDA APIs with UVA enables transparent access to memory on any device. You do not have to manually manage separate memory buffers or make explicit copies from host memory. The underlying system makes it possible to avoid explicitly performing these operations and thus simplifies code. Note that relying too heavily on UVA to perform peer-to-peer accesses can have negative performance implications, as the overhead from many small transfers across the PCIe bus is significant.

The following code demonstrates how to check if a device supports unified addressing:

```
int deviceId = 0;
cudaDeviceProp prop;
cudaGetDeviceProperties(&prop, deviceId));
printf("GPU%d: %s unified addressing\n", deviceId,
       prop.unifiedAddressing ? "supports" : "does not support");
```

To use UVA, applications must be compiled on a 64-bit architecture with devices of compute capability 2.0 or higher, and CUDA 4.0 or later installed. If peer-to-peer access and UVA are both enabled, kernels executing on one device can dereference a pointer to memory on another device.

You can use the following simple kernel (which scales the input array by 2, and stores the results in an output array), to test direct peer-to-peer memory access from the GPU:

```
__global__ void iKernel(float *src, float *dst) {
    const int idx = blockIdx.x * blockDim.x + threadIdx.x;
    dst[idx] = src[idx] * 2.0f;
}
```

The following code sets device 0 as the current device and has the kernel read global memory from device 1 using the pointer d_src[1], writing the result to the current device through the global memory pointer d_rcv[0]:

```
cudaSetDevice(0);
iKernel<<<grid, block>>>(d_rcv[0], d_src[1]);
```

The following code sets device 1 as the current device and has the kernel read global memory from device 0 using the pointer d_src[0], writing the result to the current device through the global memory pointer d_src[1]:

```
cudaSetDevice(1);
iKernel<<<grid, block>>>(d_rcv[1], d_src[0]);
```

These codes are included in the same simpleP2P_PingPong.cu file. The following output indicates that these kernels ran successfully:

```
2. Running kernel on GPU1, taking source data from GPU0 and writing to GPU1...
3. Running kernel on GPU0, taking source data from GPU1 and writing to GPU0...
```

If your GPUs are not connected to the same PCIe root node or peer-to-peer access is disabled, the following error messages will be displayed:

```
> GPU0 disabled direct access to GPU1
> GPU1 disabled direct access to GPU0
```

FINITE DIFFERENCE ON MULTI-GPU

In this section, you will learn how to overlap computation and communication across devices by solving a 2D wave equation using a finite difference scheme. This example extends the concepts from the preceding vector addition and ping-ping examples, as it contains both significant computation and communication operations. Note that while the physical equations and terminology for this example are included in this chapter, understanding the problem mathematically is not required. All concepts will be explained in terms of CUDA programming; the domain-specific information is included for curious readers.

Stencil Calculation for 2D Wave Equation

2D wave propagation is governed by the following wave equation:

$$\frac{\partial^2 u}{\partial x^2} + \frac{\partial^2 u}{\partial y^2} = v^{-2}\frac{\partial^2 u}{\partial t^2}$$

where $u(x, y, t)$ is the wave field, and $v(x, y)$ is the velocity of the medium. This is a second order partial differential equation. A typical approach to solving this kind of partial differential equation is to use a finite difference scheme on a regular Cartesian grid.

Put more simply, the finite difference scheme approximates derivatives using a *stencil* (like the one demonstrated in Chapter 5, albeit a two-dimensional one) to calculate a derivative at a single point on a regular grid by applying a function to multiple local points that surround that single point. Figure 9-3 illustrates the 17-point stencil that will be used as an example in this section. To evaluate the derivative of the central point, the 16 nearest local points to the central point are used.

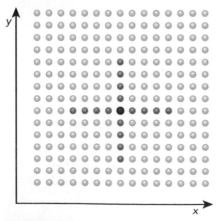

FIGURE 9-3

Computationally, the partial derivatives can be represented by a *Taylor* expansion whose implementation in one dimension is illustrated in the following pseudo code. This pseudo code uses a 1D array der_u to accumulate contributions from the current element u[i], from four elements ahead (u[i+d]), and four elements behind (u[i-d]). The c array stores the derivative coefficients, u[i] is the central point to evaluate, and der_u[i] is the evaluated derivative of the central point.

```
der_u[i] = c[0] * u[i];
for(int d = 1; d <= 4; d++)
    der_u[i] += c[d] * (u[i-d] + u[i+d]);
```

Typical Patterns for Multi-GPU Programs

In order to accurately simulate waves propagating through different media, huge amounts of data are required. This can quickly lead to a single GPU's global memory being insufficient to store the state of the simulation. This requires domain decomposition of the data across multiple GPUs. Suppose the x dimension is the innermost dimension in a 2D array. You can partition the data along the y dimension so that it can be distributed across multiple GPUs. Because the calculation of a given point needs the four nearest points on both sides, you need to add padding to the data stored in each GPU, as illustrated in Figure 9-4. This padding, or halo region, holds the data to be exchanged between neighboring devices on each iteration in the wave propagation calculation.

With the domain decomposition shown in Figure 9-5, solving the wave equation using multiple GPUs uses this general pattern at each time step of the simulation:

1. Compute the halo regions and exchange halo data with neighboring GPUs in one stream.

2. Compute the internal regions in a different stream.

3. Synchronize computation on all devices before proceeding to the next iteration.

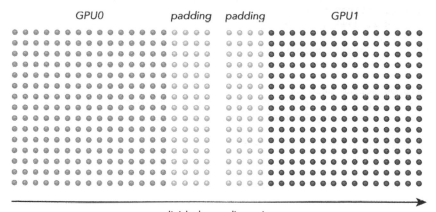

divided on y dimension

FIGURE 9-4

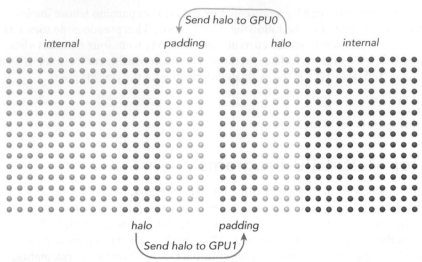

FIGURE 9-5

If you use two different streams, one for halo computation and communication and the other for computation of the inner region, Step 1 can be overlapped with Step 2. If the computation time required for the internal calculations is longer than the time required for the halo operations, you can realize linear speedup using multiple GPUs by hiding the performance impact of halo communication.

The pseudo code for a stencil computation with two GPUs is as follows:

```
for (int istep = 0; istep < nsteps; istep++) {
    // calculate halo in stream_halo
    for (int i = 0; i < 2; i++) {
        cudaSetDevice(i);
        2dfd_kernel<<<..., stream_halo[i]>>>(...);
    }

    // exchange halo on stream halo
    cudaMemcpyAsync(..., cudaMemcpyDeviceToDevice, stream_halo[0]);
    cudaMemcpyAsync(..., cudaMemcpyDeviceToDevice, stream_halo[1]);

    // calculate the internal region in stream_internal
    for (int i = 0; i < 2; i++) {
        cudaSetDevice(i);
        2dfd_kernel<<<..., stream_internal[i]>>>(...);
    }

    // synchronize before next iteration
    for(int i = 0; i < 2; i++) {
        cudaSetDevice(i);
        cudaDeviceSynchronize();
    }
}
```

You do not need to set a current device for the copy operations; however, you must specify a current device before launching a kernel.

2D Stencil Computation with Multiple GPUs

In this section, a simple 2D stencil is implemented using multiple GPUs. Two device arrays are used in the 2D stencil calculation. One holds the current wave field, and the other holds the updated wave field. If you define x as the innermost array dimension and y as the outermost dimension, the computation can be divided evenly across devices along the y dimension.

Because updating one point requires access to the nine nearest points, many of the points will share input data. Hence, shared memory is used to reduce global memory accesses. The amount of shared memory used is equal to the size of the thread block padded with an additional eight points to hold the neighbor data, as illustrated in Figure 9-6 and in the following code snippet.

```
__shared__ float line[4 + BDIMX + 4];
```

The nine `float` values used to store the y-axis stencil values are declared as an array local to the kernel, and as such will be stored in registers. Registers are used here much like shared memory to reduce redundant accesses when loading elements ahead and behind the current element along the y axis.

```
// registers for the y dimension
float yval[9];
```

Figure 9-7 illustrates the shared memory used to store stencil values along the x axis, and the nine registers used to store stencil values along the y axis for a single thread.

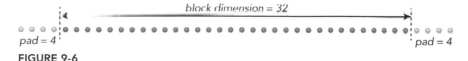

FIGURE 9-6

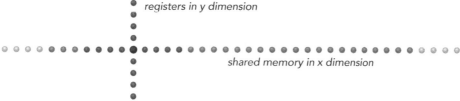

FIGURE 9-7

Once the input data has been allocated and initialized, the stencil computation implementing a Finite Difference (FD) operator in each GPU thread can be written as follows:

```
// central point
float tmp = coef[0] * line[stx] * 2.0f;
```

```
    // stencil computation in the x dimension
    for (int d = 1; d <= 4; d++) {
        tmp += coef[d] * (line[stx-d] + line[stx+d]);
    }

    // stencil computation in the y dimension
    for (int d = 1; d <= 4; d++) {
        tmp += coef[d] * (yval[4-d] + yval[4+d]);
    }

    // update the new value for the central point
    g_u1[idx] = 2.0f * current - g_u1[idx] + alpha * tmp;
```

The full kernel code for the 2D stencil computation is below:

```
    __global__ void kernel_2dfd(float *g_u1, float *g_u2, const int nx,
            const int iStart, const int iEnd) {
        // global thread index to row index
        unsigned int ix  = blockIdx.x * blockDim.x + threadIdx.x;

        // smem idx for current point
        unsigned int stx = threadIdx.x + NPAD;

        // global index with offset to start line
        unsigned int idx  = ix + iStart * nx;

        // declare the shared memory for x dimension
        __shared__ float line[BDIMX+NPAD2];

        // a coefficient related to physical properties
        const float alpha = 0.12f;

        // declare nine registers for y value
        float yval[9];
        for (int i=0;i<8;i++) yval[i] = g_u2[idx+(i-4)*nx];

        // offset from current point to yval[8]
        int iskip = NPAD*nx;

        #pragma unroll 9
        for (int iy = iStart; iy < iEnd; iy++) {
            // set yval[8] here
            yval[8] = g_u2[idx+iskip];

             // read halo part in x dimension: both left and right
            if(threadIdx.x<NPAD) {
                line[threadIdx.x]   = g_u2[idx-NPAD];
                line[stx+BDIMX]     = g_u2[idx+BDIMX];
            }

            // center point
            line[stx]  = yval[4];

            // syn for get data from gmem
```

```
       __syncthreads();

        // fd operator: 8th order in space and 2nd order in time
    if ((ix >= NPAD) && (ix < nx-NPAD)) {
        // update center point
        float tmp = coef[0]*line[stx]*2.0f;

        // 8th order in x dimension
        #pragma unroll
        for(int d=1; d<=4; d++)
            tmp += coef[d]*(line[stx-d] + line[stx+d]);

        // 8th order in y dimension
        #pragma unroll
        for(int d=1; d<=4; d++)
            tmp += coef[d]*(yval[4-d] + yval[4+d]);

        // 2nd order in time dimension
        g_u1[idx] = yval[4] + yval[4] - g_u1[idx] + alpha*tmp;
    }

    // advance on yval[]
    #pragma unroll 8
    for (int i=0; i<8 ; i++) yval[i] = yval[i+1];

    // updata global idx
    idx  += nx;

    // syn for next step
        __syncthreads();
    }
}
```

Overlapping Computation and Communication

The execution configuration for this 2D stencil uses a 1D grid with 1D blocks, declared on the host as follows:

```
dim3 block(BDIMX);
dim3 grid(nx / block.x);
```

The wave propagation over time is controlled on the host by iterating in a time loop with nsteps iterations. During the first time step, a disturbance is introduced to the medium on GPU0 with the kernel kernel_add_wavelet. Further iterations then propagate the disturbance over time. Because the halo region computation and data exchanges are scheduled in stream stream_halo on each device and the internal region calculations are scheduled in stream stream_internal on each device, the computation and communication in this 2D stencil can be overlapped.

```
// add a disturbance onto gpu0 on the first time step
cudaSetDevice(0);
kernel_add_wavelet<<<grid, block>>>(d_u2[0], 20.0, nx, iny, ngpus);

// for each time step
```

```
for (int istep = 0; istep < nsteps; istep++) {
    // add a disturbance onto gpu0 at first step
    if (istep==0) {
        cudaSetDevice(gpuid[0]);
        kernel_add_wavelet <<<grid,block>>>(d_u2[0],20.0,nx,iny,ngpus);
    }

    // update halo and internal asynchronously
    for (int i = 0; i < ngpus; i++) {
        cudaSetDevice(i);

        // compute the halo region values in the halo stream
        kernel_2dfd<<<grid, block, 0, stream_halo[i]>>>
                    (d_u1[i], d_u2[i], nx, haloStart[i], haloEnd[i]);

        // compute the internal region values in the internal stream
        kernel_2dfd<<<grid, block, 0, stream_internal[i]>>>
                    (d_u1[i], d_u2[i], nx, bodyStart[i], bodyEnd[i]);
    }

    // exchange halos in the halo stream
    if (ngpus > 1) {
        cudaMemcpyAsync(d_u1[1] + dst_skip[0], d_u1[0] + src_skip[0],
                        iexchange, cudaMemcpyDeviceToDevice, stream_halo[0]);
        cudaMemcpyAsync(d_u1[0] + dst_skip[1], d_u1[1] + src_skip[1],
                        iexchange, cudaMemcpyDeviceToDevice, stream_halo[1]);
    }

    // synchronize for the next step
    for (int i = 0; i < ngpus; i++) {
        cudaSetDevice(i);
        cudaDeviceSynchronize();

        // swap global memory pointers
        float *tmpu0 = d_u1[i];
        d_u1[i] = d_u2[i];
        d_u2[i] = tmpu0;
    }
}
```

Compiling and Executing

You can download the file simple2DFD.cu containing the full example code from Wrox.com. Compile it with the following:

```
$ nvcc -arch=sm_20 -O3 -use_fast_math simple2DFD.cu -o simple2DFD
```

The following is an example output from a system containing two M2090 devices:

```
$ ./simple2DFD
> CUDA-capable device count: 2
```

```
> GPU0: Tesla M2090 is capable of Peer-to-Peer access
> GPU1: Tesla M2090 is capable of Peer-to-Peer access
> GPU0: Tesla M2090 support unified addressing
> GPU1: Tesla M2090 support unified addressing
> run with device: 2
GPU 0: allocated 2.03 MB gmem
GPU 1: allocated 2.03 MB gmem
gputime:      0.27ms performance:    962.77 MCells/sec
```

The performance metric used is expressed in terms of Mcells/sec. For the 2D case, it can be defined as follows:

$$\frac{nx \times ny \times number\ of\ iterations}{total\ time\ in\ \sec onds \times 10^6}$$

Running with only one device yields the following results:

```
$ ./simple2DFD 1
> CUDA-capable device count: 2
> GPU0: Tesla M2090 is capable of Peer-to-Peer access
> GPU1: Tesla M2090 is capable of Peer-to-Peer access
> GPU0: Tesla M2090 support unified addressing
> GPU1: Tesla M2090 support unified addressing
> run with device: 1
GPU 0: allocated 4.00 MB gmem
gputime:      0.52ms performance:    502.98 MCells/sec
```

simple2DFD demonstrates near linear scaling (96 percent efficiency) when moving from one to two devices. From this, you can conclude that the added communication overhead of transferring halo regions is effectively hidden across multiple GPUs using CUDA streams.

You can also check the concurrency of simple2DFD with nvvp:

```
$ nvvp ./simple2DFD
```

Figure 9-8 illustrates the timeline generated by two devices executing concurrently. Notice that nvvp shows that each GPU is using two streams. You can see how one stream is used for data exchange and computation, while the other stream is used purely for computation.

You can save the state of this application at time step 400 using the following command:

```
$ ./simple2DFD 2 400
```

This command runs the application on two GPUs, and saves the wave field at time step 400 to a data file on disk. The raw data can then be displayed using a plotting tool, as illustrated in Figure 9-9.

It is also interesting to inspect the resource usage of the kernels in simple2DFD. You can add flags to the nvcc compiler to report kernel resource usage:

```
$ nvcc -arch=sm_20 -Xptxas -v simple2DFD.cu -o simple2DFD
```

The following message will be output by the nvcc compiler:

```
ptxas info    : 0 bytes gmem, 20 bytes cmem[2]
ptxas info    : Compiling entry function '_Z18kernel_add_waveletPffii' for 'sm_20'
ptxas info    : Function properties for _Z18kernel_add_waveletPffii
ptxas info    : Used 4 registers, 52 bytes cmem[0]
ptxas info    : Compiling entry function '_Z11kernel_2dfdPfS_iii' for 'sm_20'
ptxas info    : Function properties for _Z11kernel_2dfdPfS_iii
ptxas info    : Used 26 registers, 160 bytes smem, 60 bytes cmem[0], 8 bytes
cmem[16]
```

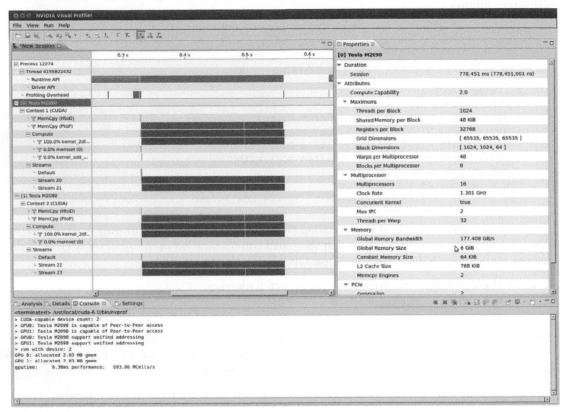

FIGURE 9-8

The last line of output above indicates that the kernel kernel_2dfd uses 26 registers, 160 bytes of shared memory, and some amount of constant memory (for storing parameters to the kernel) per thread.

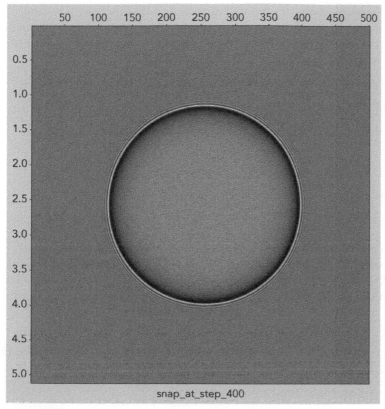

FIGURE 9-9

SCALING APPLICATIONS ACROSS GPU CLUSTERS

GPU-accelerated clusters are widely recognized for providing tremendous performance gains and power savings for compute-intensive applications, relative to architecturally homogeneous systems. When working with very large data sets, you often require more than one compute node to efficiently handle your problem. MPI (*Message Passing Interface*) is a standardized and portable API for communicating data via messages between distributed processes. In most MPI implementations, library routines are called directly from C or other languages.

MPI is fully compatible with CUDA. There are two types of MPI implementations that support moving data between GPUs on different nodes: Traditional MPI and CUDA-aware MPI. With traditional

MPI, only the contents of host memory can be transmitted directly by MPI functions. The contents of GPU memory must first be copied back to host memory using the CUDA API before MPI can be used to communicate that data to another node. With CUDA-aware MPI, you can pass GPU memory directly to MPI functions without staging that data through host memory.

Several commercial and open-source CUDA-aware MPI implementations are available, such as:

➤ MVAPICH2 2.0rc2 (`http://mvapich.cse.ohio-state.edu/download/mvapich2/`)

➤ MVAPICH2-GDR 2.0b (`http://mvapich.cse.ohio-state.edu/download/mvapich2gdr/`)

➤ OpenMPI 1.7 (`http://www.open-mpi.org/software/ompi/v1.7/`)

➤ CRAY MPI (MPT 5.6.2)

➤ IBM Platform MPI (8.3)

MVAPICH2 is an open source MPI implementation designed to exploit *Infiniband* network features to deliver high performance and scalability for MPI-based applications. Two versions exist: MVAPICH2 is a CUDA-aware MPI implementation, while MVAPICH2-GDR is an extension that adds support for GPUDirect RDMA over InfiniBand (more on GPUDirect later in this chapter).

MVAPICH2 is a widely used open-source MPI library for InfiniBand clusters and supports MPI communication directly from one GPU's device memory to another's. The next sections will test the following cases using the MVAPICH platform:

➤ CPU to CPU data transfer over InfiniBand with MVAPICH2

➤ GPU to GPU data transfer over InfiniBand with traditional MPI

➤ GPU to GPU data transfer over InfiniBand with CUDA-aware MPI

➤ GPU to GPU data transfer over InfiniBand with MVAPICH2-GDR and GPUDirect RDMA

CPU-to-CPU Data Transfer

To establish a baseline for comparison, you can test the bandwidth and latency of data transfers over the interconnect between two CPU nodes in a cluster using MVAPICH2. Generally, MPI programs consist of four steps:

1. Initialize the MPI environment.

2. Pass messages between processes in different nodes using blocking or non-blocking MPI functions.

3. Synchronize across nodes.

4. Clean up the MPI environment.

Implementing Inter-Node MPI Communication

The following code segment illustrates the skeleton of a simple MPI program that sends and receives a single message before synchronizing across all nodes and exiting.

```
int main(int argc, char *argv[]) {
    // initialize the MPI environment
    int rank, nprocs;
    MPI_Init(&argc, &argv);
    MPI_Comm_size(MPI_COMM_WORLD, &nprocs);
    MPI_Comm_rank(MPI_COMM_WORLD, &rank);

    // transmit messages with MPI calls
    MPI_Send(sbuf, size, MPI_CHAR, 1, 100, MPI_COMM_WORLD);
    MPI_Recv(rbuf, size, MPI_CHAR, 0, 100, MPI_COMM_WORLD, &reqstat);

    // synchronize across nodes
    MPI_Barrier(MPI_COMM_WORLD);

    // clean up the MPI environment
    MPI_Finalize();

    return EXIT_SUCCESS;
}
```

To test the bandwidth and latency between two nodes, you first need to allocate arrays of size MYBUFSIZE for send/receive buffers, as follows:

```
char *s_buf, *r_buf;
s_buf = (char *)malloc(MYBUFSIZE);
r_buf = (char *)malloc(MYBUFSIZE);
```

Then, bidirectional data transfer between two compute nodes can be performed using non-blocking MPI send and receive functions:

```
// If this is the first MPI process
if(rank == 0) {
    // Repeatedly
    for (int i = 0; i < nRepeat; i++) {
        // Asynchronously receive size bytes from other_proc into rbuf
        MPI_Irecv(rbuf, size, MPI_CHAR, other_proc, 10, MPI_COMM_WORLD,
            &recv_request);
        // Asynchronously send size bytes too other_proc from sbuf
        MPI_Isend(sbuf, size, MPI_CHAR, other_proc, 100, MPI_COMM_WORLD,
            &send_request);
        // Wait for the send to complete
        MPI_Waitall(1, &send_request, &reqstat);
        // Wait for the receive to complete
        MPI_Waitall(1, &recv_request, &reqstat);
```

```
        }
    } else if (rank == 1) {
        for (int i = 0; i < nRepeat; i++) {
            // Asynchronously receive size bytes from other_proc into rbuf
            MPI_Irecv(rbuf, size, MPI_CHAR, other_proc, 100, MPI_COMM_WORLD,
                &recv_request);
            // Asynchronously send size bytes to other_proc from sbuf
            MPI_Isend(sbuf, size, MPI_CHAR, other_proc, 10, MPI_COMM_WORLD,
                &send_request);
            // Wait for the send to complete
            MPI_Waitall(1, &send_request, &reqstat);
            // Wait for the receive to complete
            MPI_Waitall(1, &recv_request, &reqstat);
        }
    }
}
```

In order to obtain an accurate performance measure, the send and receive operations are repeated nRepeat times, and the average of these results is reported. You can download the file simpleC2C.c containing the full example code from Wrox.com. Compile it with the following command:

```
$ mpicc -std=c99 -O3 simpleC2C.c -o simplec2c
```

If you have an MPI-enabled cluster at your disposal, you can run the MPI program on two nodes. Specify the hostnames of two nodes, for example, node01 and node02 (depending on your cluster's configuration), and run the following example:

```
$ mpirun_rsh -np 2 node01 node02 ./simplec2c
```

An example output is as follows:

```
./simplec2c to allocate 4 MB dynamic memory aligned to 64 byte
node=0(node01): other_proc = 1
node=1(node02): other_proc = 0
    size      Elapsed        Performance
    1 KB      3.96 µs     258.27 MB/sec
    4 KB      3.75 µs    1092.17 MB/sec
   16 KB      8.77 µs    1867.12 MB/sec
   64 KB     20.18 µs    3247.61 MB/sec
  256 KB     49.48 µs    5297.96 MB/sec
    1 MB    169.99 µs    6168.63 MB/sec
    4 MB    662.81 µs    6328.06 MB/sec
```

mpirun_rsh is a job startup utility provided by MVAPICH2. You can also run the job using mpirun:

```
$ mpirun -np 2 -host node01,node02 ./simplec2c
```

CPU Affinity

When multiple processes or threads simultaneously require CPU time on a multicore system (for example, in an MPI program), the operating system is responsible for assigning threads and processes to available CPU cores. This means that a process or thread can be paused and moved to a new core at the discretion of the operating system. This behavior negatively affects performance by causing poor data locality. If a process is switched to a new CPU core, none of that process's data is stored locally in the cache of the new core. That process will have to re-fetch it all from system memory. Therefore, binding a process or thread to a single CPU core (or a set of neighboring CPU cores) can help boost host performance.

Limiting process or thread execution to only certain CPU cores is called *CPU affinity*. There are several ways to bind processes and threads to processors. Once the affinity is set, the operating system scheduler must obey the set constraints, and the process runs only on the specified processors.

CPU affinity directly affects the performance of MPI programs. MVAPICH2 provides a way to set CPU affinity at runtime using the MV2_ENABLE_AFFINITY environment variable. You can enable CPU affinity during the invocation of an MPI program as follows:

```
$ mpirun_rsh -np 2 node01 node02 MV2_ENABLE_AFFINITY=1 ./simplec2c
```

You can disable CPU affinity as follows:

```
$ mpirun_rsh -np 2 node01 node02 MV2_ENABLE_AFFINITY=0 ./simplec2c
```

For single-threaded or single-process applications, enabling CPU affinity will provide the same or better performance by preventing the operating system from moving the process or thread from processor to processor. On the other hand, multi-threaded and multi-process applications may experience performance improvement when CPU affinity is disabled.

GPU-to-GPU Data Transfer Using Traditional MPI

This section will examine combining CUDA with traditional MPI to exchange data between GPUs on separate nodes.

Consider a multi-node compute cluster with multiple GPUs per node. Data exchange between GPUs within a node can be implemented using peer-to-peer accesses or transfers, as described in the previous section in this chapter titled "Peer-to-Peer Communication." On the other hand, exchanging data between GPUs in different nodes requires an inter-node communication library, such as MPI. To simplify the exchange of data between GPUs and improve performance, you should bind an MPI process to each GPU in each node.

Affinity in MPI-CUDA Programs

Just as binding an MPI process to a CPU core is called CPU affinity, binding an MPI process to a particular GPU is called *GPU affinity*. Binding an MPI process to a GPU is usually done before the MPI environment is initialized using MPI_Init.

To evenly distribute processes across GPUs in a node, you must first use environment variables provided by the MPI libraries to determine the local ID of a process inside its node. For example, MVAPICH2 guarantees that the environment variable MV2_COMM_WORLD_LOCAL_RANK will be set for each MPI process. MV2_COMM_WORLD_LOCAL_RANK is an integer that uniquely identifies each MPI process in the same node. Other MPI implementations provide similar support. This local ID, or rank, can then be used to pin an MPI process to a CUDA device:

```
int n_devices;
int local_rank = atoi(getenv("MV2_COMM_WORLD_LOCAL_RANK"));
```

```
cudaGetDeviceCount(&n_devices);
int device = local_rank % n_devices;
cudaSetDevice(device);
...
MPI_Init(argc, argv);
```

However, if you first used MV2_ENABLE_AFFINITY to set the CPU affinity of an MPI process, and then used MV2_COMM_WORLD_LOCAL_RANK to set the GPU affinity, you have no guarantee that the CPU an MPI process is running on is optimally co-located with the assigned GPU. If they are not optimally co-located, the latency and bandwidth between the host application and device memory might be degraded. Instead, you can use the Portable Hardware Locality package (hwloc) to analyze the hardware topology of a node and pin an MPI process to a CPU core that is optimally co-located with the GPU assigned to that MPI process.

The following example code uses the MPI local rank of a process to select a GPU. Then, hwloc is used to determine the best CPU core to pin this process to, given that GPU.

```
rank = atoi( getenv( "MV2_COMM_WORLD_RANK" ) );
local_rank = atoi( getenv( "MV2_COMM_WORLD_LOCAL_RANK" ) );

// Load a full hardware topology of all PCI devices in this node.
hwloc_topology_init(&topology);
hwloc_topology_set_flags(topology, HWLOC_TOPOLOGY_FLAG_WHOLE_IO);
hwloc_topology_load(topology);

// choose a GPU based on MPI local rank
cudaSetDevice( local_rank );
cudaGetDevice( &device );

// Iterate through all CPU cores that are physically close to the selected GPU.
// This code evenly distributes processes across cores using local_rank.
cpuset = hwloc_bitmap_alloc();
hwloc_cudart_get_device_cpuset(topology, device, cpuset);
match = 0;
hwloc_bitmap_foreach_begin(i,cpuset)
    if (match == local_rank) {
        cpu = i;
        break;
    }
    ++match;
hwloc_bitmap_foreach_end();

// Bind this process to the selected CPU.
onecpu = hwloc_bitmap_alloc();
hwloc_bitmap_set(onecpu, cpu);
hwloc_set_cpubind(topology, onecpu, 0);

// Cleanup.
hwloc_bitmap_free(onecpu);
hwloc_bitmap_free(cpuset);
hwloc_topology_destroy(topology);

gethostname( hostname, sizeof(hostname) );
cpu = sched_getcpu();
printf("MPI rank %d using GPU %d and CPU %d on host %s\n",
    rank, device, cpu, hostname );
```

```
MPI_Init(&argc, &argv);
MPI_Comm_rank(MPI_COMM_WORLD, &rank);
if (MPI_SUCCESS != MPI_Get_processor_name(procname, &length)) {
    strcpy(procname, "unknown");
}
```

Performing GPU-to-GPU Communication With MPI

Once an MPI process has pinned itself to a GPU with `cudaSetDevice`, device memory and host pinned memory can be allocated for the current device:

```
char *h_src, *h_rcv;
cudaMallocHost((void**)&h_src, MYBUFSIZE);
cudaMallocHost((void**)&h_rcv, MYBUFSIZE);

char *d_src, *d_rcv;
cudaMalloc((void **)&d_src, MYBUFSIZE);
cudaMalloc((void **)&d_rcv, MYBUFSIZE);
```

Bidirectional data transfer between two GPUs using traditional MPI is performed in two steps: First, data is copied from device memory to host memory. Then, data in host memory is exchanged between MPI processes using the MPI communication library:

```
if(rank == 0) {
    for (int i = 0; i < loop; i++) {
        cudaMemcpy(h_src, d_src, size, cudaMemcpyDeviceToHost);

        // bi-directional bandwidth
        MPI_Irecv(h_rcv, size, MPI_CHAR, other_proc, 10, MPI_COMM_WORLD,
            &recv_request);
        MPI_Isend(h_src, size, MPI_CHAR, other_proc, 100, MPI_COMM_WORLD,
            &send_request);

        MPI_Waitall(1, &recv_request, &reqstat);
        MPI_Waitall(1, &send_request, &reqstat);

        cudaMemcpy(d_rcv, h_rcv, size, cudaMemcpyHostToDevice);
    }
} else {
    for (int i = 0; i < loop; i++) {
        cudaMemcpy(h_src, d_src, size, cudaMemcpyDeviceToHost);

        // bi-directional bandwidth
        MPI_Irecv(h_rcv, size, MPI_CHAR, other_proc, 100, MPI_COMM_WORLD,
            &recv_request);
        MPI_Isend(h_src, size, MPI_CHAR, other_proc, 10, MPI_COMM_WORLD,
            &send_request);

        MPI_Waitall(1, &recv_request, &reqstat);
        MPI_Waitall(1, &send_request, &reqstat);

        cudaMemcpy(d_rcv, h_rcv, size, cudaMemcpyHostToDevice);
    }
}
```

You can download the file `simpleP2P.c` containing the full code for this example from `Wrox.com`. Compile it with the following command:

```
$ mpicc -std=c99 -O3 simpleP2P.c -o simplep2p
```

Launch the MPI program with `mpirun_rsh`, as follows:

```
$ mpirun_rsh -np 2 node01 node02 ./simplep2p
```

An example report from a system with two Fermi M2090 GPUs is as follows. Note the sharp decrease in bandwidth and increase in latency compared to the CPU-to-CPU example. This performance loss is caused by the added overhead of transferring data from the GPU before transmitting it using MPI.

```
    ./simplep2p to allocate 4 MB device memory and pinned host memory CUDA + MPI
node=0(node01): using GPU=1 and other_proc = 1
node=1(node02): using GPU=0 and other_proc = 0
        size        Elapsed         Performance
        1 KB        10.24 µs         99.95 MB/sec
        4 KB        11.51 µs        355.88 MB/sec
       16 KB        19.77 µs        828.74 MB/sec
       64 KB        46.34 µs       1414.24 MB/sec
      256 KB       114.31 µs       2293.37 MB/sec
        1 MB       394.07 µs       2660.89 MB/sec
        4 MB      1532.47 µs       2736.96 MB/sec
```

GPU-to-GPU Data Transfer with CUDA-aware MPI

MVAPICH2 is also a CUDA-aware MPI implementation, which supports GPU to GPU communication through the standard MPI API. You can pass device memory pointers directly to MPI functions (and avoid the extra `cudaMemcpy` calls required for traditional MPI):

```
if(rank == 0) {
    for (int i = 0; i < loop; i++) {
        MPI_Irecv(d_rcv, size, MPI_CHAR, other_proc, 10, MPI_COMM_WORLD,
            &recv_request);
        MPI_Isend(d_src, size, MPI_CHAR, other_proc, 100, MPI_COMM_WORLD,
            &send_request);

        MPI_Waitall(1, &recv_request, &reqstat);
        MPI_Waitall(1, &send_request, &reqstat);
    }
} else {
    for (int i = 0; i < loop; i++) {
        MPI_Irecv(d_rcv, size, MPI_CHAR, other_proc, 100, MPI_COMM_WORLD,
            &recv_request);
        MPI_Isend(d_src, size, MPI_CHAR, other_proc, 10, MPI_COMM_WORLD,
            &send_request);

        MPI_Waitall(1, &recv_request, &reqstat);
        MPI_Waitall(1, &send_request, &reqstat);
    }
}
```

You can download the file `simpleP2P_CUDA_Aware.c` containing the full source code for this example from `Wrox.com`. Compile it with the following command:

```
$ mpicc -std=c99 -O3 simpleP2P_CUDA_Aware.c -o simplep2p.aware
```

Before launching the MPI program, you will need to ensure CUDA support is enabled in MVAPICH2 by setting the following environment variable:

```
$ export MV2_USE_CUDA=1
```

You can also set this environment variable during MPI program invocation:

```
$ mpirun_rsh -np 2 node01 node02 MV2_USE_CUDA=1 ./simplep2p.aware
```

An example report from a system with two Fermi M2090 GPUs is included below. Note that for the case using 4MB messages you gain 17 percent performance improvement using CUDA-aware MPI, compared to using traditional MPI with CUDA. Additionally, the code has been greatly simplified without the added step of explicitly transferring data to and from the device.

```
./simplep2p.aware to allocate 4 MB device memory and pinned host memory CUDA + MPI
node=0(node01): using GPU=1 and other_proc = 1
node=1(node02): using GPU=0 and other_proc = 0
    size      Elapsed       Performance
    1  KB     63.78 µs       16.06 MB/sec
    4  KB     14.79 µs      277.03 MB/sec
   16  KB     24.27 µs      675.21 MB/sec
   64  KB     47.65 µs     1375.39 MB/sec
  256  KB    112.43 µs     2331.72 MB/sec
    1  MB    331.16 µs     3166.42 MB/sec
    4  MB   1306.02 µs     3211.50 MB/sec
```

Intra-Node GPU-to-GPU Data Transfer with CUDA-Aware MPI

You can also use a CUDA-aware MPI library to perform a data transfer between two GPUs in the same node. If two GPUs are on the same PCIe bus, peer-to-peer transfers are automatically used. Run the same example from the previous section as follows to perform data transfer between two GPUs on the same node, assuming `node01` has at least two GPUs:

```
$ mpirun_rsh -np 2 node01 node01 MV2_USE_CUDA=1 ./simplep2p.aware
```

The results on two Fermi M2090 GPUs are as follows. As you would expect, transferring data between GPUs in the same node over the PCIe bus yields much better bandwidth and latency than transfers that go across the inter-node interconnect.

```
./simplep2p.aware to allocate 4 MB device memory
node=0(node01): using GPU=1 and other_proc = 1
node=1(node01): using GPU=0 and other_proc = 0
    size      Elapsed       Performance
    1  KB     47.66 µs       21.48 MB/sec
    4  KB     11.33 µs      361.38 MB/sec
   16  KB     26.64 µs      615.02 MB/sec
   64  KB     28.72 µs     2281.90 MB/sec
  256  KB     54.75 µs     4788.40 MB/sec
    1  MB    171.34 µs     6120.00 MB/sec
    4  MB    646.50 µs     6487.75 MB/sec
```

The performance of the previous four examples is plotted in Figure 9-10. These results show that when the data being transferred is more than 1 MB, performance benefits can be gained from CUDA-aware MPI.

Adjusting Message Chunk Size

To minimize communication overhead by overlapping inter-node communication with host-device communication, MVAPICH2 automatically splits large messages from GPU memory into chunks. The chunk size can be adjusted with the `MV2_CUDA_BLOCK_SIZE` environment variable. The default chunk size is 256 KB. It can be set to 512 KB as follows:

```
$ mpirun_rsh -np 2 node01 node02 MV2_USE_CUDA=1 \
    MV2_CUDA_BLOCK_SIZE=524288 ./simplep2p.aware
```

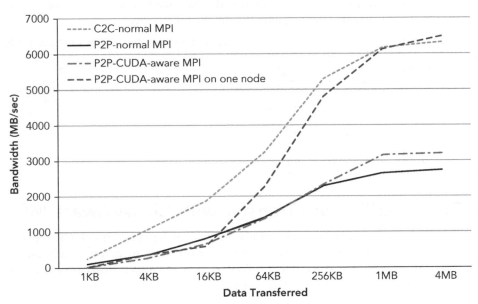

FIGURE 9-10

The effects of changing the chunk size when running on two Fermi M2090 GPUs on two different nodes is as follows:

size	Elapsed	Performance
1 KB	154.06 µs	6.65 MB/sec
4 KB	15.13 µs	270.63 MB/sec
16 KB	24.86 µs	659.05 MB/sec
64 KB	48.08 µs	1363.18 MB/sec
256 KB	111.92 µs	2342.23 MB/sec
1 MB	341.14 µs	3073.70 MB/sec
4 MB	1239.15 µs	3384.82 MB/sec

These results clearly show that for a 4 MB message size, the larger chunk size delivers better performance. The optimal chunk size value depends on several variables, including interconnect bandwidth/latency, GPU adapter characteristics, platform characteristics, and the amount of memory MPI functions are permitted to use. Therefore, it is best if you experiment with different chunk sizes to determine the best performance.

GPU to GPU Data Transfer with GPUDirect RDMA

NVIDIA *GPUDirect* enables low-latency communication between GPUs and other devices on the PCIe bus. Using GPUDirect, third-party network adapters and other devices can directly exchange data via a common host-based pinned memory region that eliminates unnecessary host memory copies, resulting in significant performance improvement in data transfer for applications running on multiple devices. NVIDIA has progressively updated GPUDirect over the years, iteratively improving programmability and reducing latency with each release. The first version of GPUDirect, released with CUDA 3.1, allowed an *InfiniBand* device and GPU device to share the same page-locked buffer in CPU memory. The data being sent from a GPU in one node to a GPU in a different node is copied once from the source GPU to the pinned, shared data buffer in system memory, then copied directly from that shared buffer over the Infiniband interconnect to a matching buffer in the destination node where the other GPU can access it (depicted in Figure 9-11).

The second version of GPUDirect, released with CUDA 4.0, added the peer-to-peer APIs and Unified Virtual Addressing support described earlier in this chapter. These enhancement improved multi-GPU performance within a single node, and improved programmer productivity by eliminating the need to manage multiple pointers between different address spaces.

The third release of GPUDirect, introduced in CUDA 5.0, added *Remote Direct Memory Access (RDMA)* support. RDMA allows a direct path of communication over Infiniband between GPUs in different cluster nodes using standard PCI Express adapters. Figure 9-12 illustrates the direct connectivity of two GPUs over the network. Using GPUDirect RDMA, inter-GPU communication between two nodes can be performed without host processor involvement. This reduces CPU overhead and communication latency.

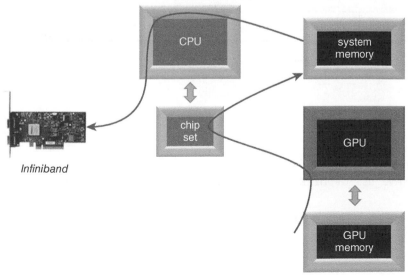

FIGURE 9-11

Because GPUDirect RDMA is transparent to application code, you can use the same simpleP2P_CUDA_Aware.cu example to compare performance between the MVAPICH2 library and the MVAPICH2-GDR library that includes GPUDirect RDMA support. You will need to update your environment with the proper paths to compile the program using a MVAPICH2-GDR installation.

First, collect baseline performance results with the CUDA-aware MVAPICH2 using the mpicc compiler and mpirun_rsh command:

```
$ mpicc -std=c99 -O3 simpleP2P_CUDA_Aware.c -o bibwCudaAware
$ mpirun_rsh -np 2 ivb108 ivb110 MV2_USE_CUDA=1 \
     MV2_CUDA_BLOCK_SIZE=524288 ./bibwCudaAware
```

The following results were reported for two nodes containing Kepler K40 GPUs, connected by a single rail Mellanox Connect-IB network, and using MVAPICH2 v2.0b:

```
node=0(ivb108): my other _proc = 1 and using GPU=1
node=1(ivb110): my other _proc = 0 and using GPU=0
     1 MB     134.40 ms    7801.62 MB/sec
     4 MB     441.00 ms    9501.88 MB/sec
    16 MB    1749.55 ms    9589.42 MB/sec
    64 MB    6553.89 ms   10239.55 MB/sec
```

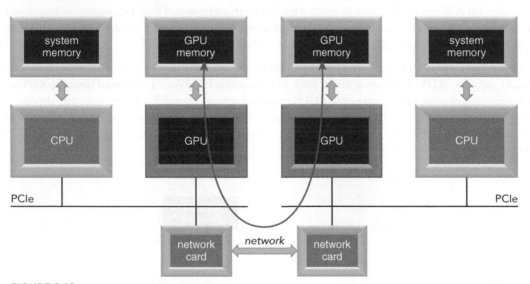

FIGURE 9-12

For comparison, compile the same program with the CUDA-aware MVAPICH2-GDR version of mpicc . Be sure to set the MV2_USE_GPUDIRECT environment variable as part of the mpirun_rsh command, as follows:

```
$ mpicc -std=c99 -O3 simpleP2P_CUDA_Aware.c -o bibwCudaAwareGDR
```

```
$ mpirun_rsh -np 2 ivb108 ivb110 MV2_USE_CUDA=1  MV2_USE_GPUDIRECT=1 \
       MV2_CUDA_BLOCK_SIZE=524288 ./bibwCudaAwareGDR
```

The following results were reported on the same cluster:

```
to test max size 64 MB
node=0(ivb108): my other _proc = 1 and using GPU=1
node=1(ivb110): my other _proc = 0 and using GPU=0
    1 MB      132.50 ms     8242.83 MB/sec
    4 MB      404.15 ms    10401.88MB/sec
   16 MB     1590.29 ms    10801.00 MB/sec
   64 MB     5929.98 ms    11539.94 MB/sec
```

Figure 9-13 visually compares the bi-directional bandwidth for the two test cases below:

➤   CUDA-aware MPI

➤   CUDA-aware MPI with GPUDirect RDMA

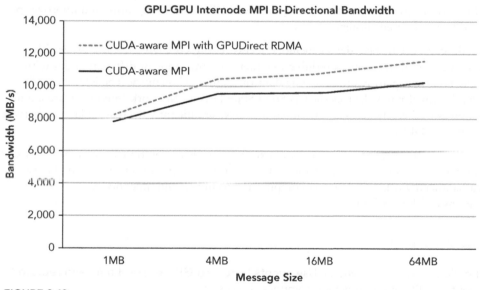

FIGURE 9-13

A notable improvement (up to 13 percent gain) was measured when GPUDirect RDMA was added to CUDA-aware MPI.

Note that as you accelerate the computational portion of your application using CUDA, the I/O of your application will rapidly become a bottleneck for overall performance. GPUDirect offers a straightforward solution to this problem by reducing latency between GPUs.

SUMMARY

Multi-GPU systems are useful for solving real world problems with very large data sets that cannot fit into a single GPU device, or whose throughput and efficiency can be improved by executing multiple GPU tasks concurrently. Typically, there are two configurations for executing multi-GPU applications:

➤ Multiple devices in a single node

➤ Multiple devices in a multi-node GPU-accelerated cluster

This chapter covered techniques and APIs used for multi-GPU programming at both granularities, demonstrating how to manage multiple GPUs and issue commands from the host application.

MVAPICH2 is a popular CUDA-aware MPI implementation that delivers low-latency, high-bandwidth, scalability, and fault tolerance for high-end computing systems using InfiniBand, 10GigE/iWARP, and RoCE networking technologies. Being able to directly pass device memory through MPI functions greatly eases the development of MPI-CUDA programs, and improves performance on GPU-accelerated clusters.

GPUDirect facilitates peer-to-peer device memory access. Using GPUDirect, you can directly exchange data among multiple devices residing in either the same node or different nodes within a cluster. This exchange happens without staging data through CPU memory. The RDMA feature of GPUDirect enables third-party devices such as Solid State Drives, Network Interface Cards, and Infiniband adapters to directly access GPU global memory, significantly decreasing latency between those devices and the GPU.

CUDA provides a variety of ways to manage and execute kernels on multiple devices. You can scale your application across multiple devices in one compute node, or across GPU-accelerated cluster nodes. With a balanced workload that uses computation to hide communication latency, near-linear performance gains can be realized.

CHAPTER 9 EXERCISES

1. Refer to the file `simpleMultiGPU.cu`. Use events to record GPU elapsed time and replace the code segment of CPU timer, and then compare the results.

2. Run the previous executable with `nvprof`, as follows, and identify what is different for two devices versus one device.

    ```
    $ nvprof --print-gpu-trace ./simpleMultiGPUEvents 1
    ```

3. Run the previous executable with `nvvp` as follows:

    ```
    $ nvvp ./simpleMultiGPU
    ```

    Check the results in the *Console Tab* and *Details Tab*. Next, set the arguments to 1 in the *Settings Tab* to run the code on one GPU only. Compare the results with the two GPU case.

4. Put the following at the end of the main loop in `simpleMultiGPU`:

   `cudaStreamSynchronize(stream[i]);`

   Recompile the code and run it with `nvvp` for both cases of one GPU and two GPU, then compare the results with the code in Exercise 9.3 and explain the reason for the difference.

5. In `simpleMultiGPU.cu`, move data initialization (`initialData`) into the main kernel loop. Run it with `nvvp` to see what changes.

6. Refer to the file `simpleP2P_PingPong.cu`. Modify the code section labeled `unidirectional gmem copy` to use asynchronous copies.

7. Refer to the file `simpleP2P_PingPong.cu`. Add code that ping-pongs data between two GPUs based on the bidirectional, asynchronous ping-pong example provided. Use the function:

   ```
   cudaMemcpyPeerAsync(void* dst,int dstDev,const void* src,int srcDev,
                       size_t count, cudaStream_t stream)
   ```

8. Refer to the file `simpleP2P-PingPong.cu`. Use a default stream in the asynchronous memory copy runtime function. Compare the result with a non-default stream.

9. Refer to the file `simpleP2P-PingPong.cu`. Disable P2P access first, and then compare both results of unidirectional versus bidirectional memory copies, and synchronous versus asynchronous functions.

10. Refer to the file `simple2DFD.cu`. Rearrange wave propagation with the following logic: (1) calculate halo on stream halo, (2) exchange halo on stream halo, (3) calculate internal on stream internal, and (4) synchronize each device. Compare the results with the original one and explain the reason for performance changes.

11. Explain how CPU and GPU affinity each impact execution time of an application. Suppose you ran a CUDA-MPI application twice, as follows:

    ```
    $ mpirun_rsh -np 2 node01 MV2_ENABLE_AFFINITY=1 ./simplec2c
    $ mpirun_rsh -np 2 node01 MV2_ENABLE_AFFINITY=0 ./simplec2c
    ```

    The first command enables CPU affinity, while the second does not. Describe the different techniques you would use to establish GPU affinity for each MPI process in both of the scenarios above, and explain why.

12. What is GPUDirect RDMA? How can it improve performance? Describe the three versions of GPUDirect. What are the hardware and software requirements for using GPUDirect RDMA?

13. How could you use MPI functions, `cudaMemcpyAsync`, and stream callbacks to build an asynchronous version of `simpleP2P.c`?

14. Refer to the file `simpleP2P.c`. Change the pinned host memory to pageable host memory to see how the performance will change and explain the reason. If you cannot run it, describe what you would expect.

15. Consider simple `P2P_CUDA_Aware.c`. For platforms without GPUDirect (that is, cannot directly transfer data between PCIe devices) how do you think `MPI_Isend` works when passed a device pointer?

16. MVAPICH's CUDA-Aware MPI allows you to change the chunk size for copying data. Describe how chunk size might affect the internals of CUDA-Aware MPI. Why do larger chunk sizes generally perform better?

10

Implementation Considerations

WHAT'S IN THIS CHAPTER?

- ➤ Understanding the CUDA development process
- ➤ Discovering optimization opportunities using profiling tools
- ➤ Using the right metrics/events to determine most likely performance limiters
- ➤ Integrating NVTX to mark a critical section of code for profiling
- ➤ Using CUDA debugging tools to debug kernel and memory errors in CUDA
- ➤ Porting a real-world application from legacy C to CUDA C

> **CODE DOWNLOAD** *The wrox.com code downloads for this chapter are found at* www.wrox.com/go/procudac *on the Download Code tab. The code is in the Chapter 10 download and individually named according to the names throughout the chapter.*

Modern heterogeneous and parallel systems are not exclusively used for high-performance computing, but also apply to embedded development, mobile development, tablets, notebooks, PCs, and workstations. This ubiquity is causing a paradigm shift in general-purpose software development toward heterogeneous parallel programming as access to these systems becomes more common. Parallel programming has never been more convenient and beneficial, and so understanding how to efficiently and correctly implement parallel and heterogeneous software has never been more important.

This chapter covers the following aspects of CUDA C project development:

➤ The CUDA C development process

➤ Profile-driven optimization

➤ CUDA development tools

A case study is provided at the end of this chapter to demonstrate porting a legacy C application to CUDA C using step-by-step instructions to help solidify your understanding of the methodology, visualize the process, and demonstrate the tools covered in this chapter.

THE CUDA C DEVELOPMENT PROCESS

A software development process imposes structure during product development, aiming to standardize coding and maintenance best practices. There are many software development models, each describing approaches that address special needs for particular situations. The development process for the CUDA platform builds upon existing models and familiar software lifecycle concepts.

Knowledge of GPU memory and execution model abstractions enables you to have more control over the massively parallel GPU environment. It becomes natural to create application subdomains that map to abstract 2D or 3D grids and express your kernel as though it is running sequentially. By focusing on high-level domain decomposition and memory hierarchy management, you are not encumbered by the bookkeeping details of creating and destroying threads. With the CUDA development process, your focus is always:

➤ Performance-oriented

➤ Profile-driven

➤ Guided with insights inspired by abstract models of GPU architecture

Understanding how your application is using the GPU is crucial for identifying performance improvement opportunities. NVIDIA provides many powerful and easy-to-use tools that make the development process both compelling and enjoyable. The following section covers the CUDA development process and CUDA performance optimization strategies.

APOD Development Cycle

APOD is a custom, iterative development process introduced by NVIDIA specifically for CUDA development. APOD is characterized by the four stages in Figure 10-1.

➤ *Assessment*

➤ *Parallelization*

➤ *Optimization*

➤ *Deployment*

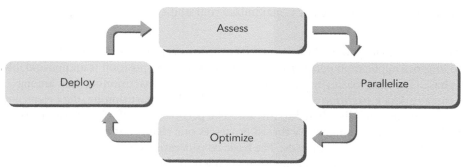

FIGURE 10-1

Assessment

During the first stage, your task is to assess the application to identify performance bottlenecks or critical regions with high computational intensity. Here, you evaluate the possibility of using GPUs to complement the CPU and develop strategies to accelerate those critical regions.

During this stage, data-parallel loop structures containing significant computation should always be given higher priority for assessment. This type of loop is an ideal case for GPU acceleration. To help identify these critical regions, you should use profiling tools to uncover application hot spots. Some codes might have already been converted to use host parallel programming models (such as OpenMP or pthreads). As long as there is sufficient parallelism in existing parallel sections, they also make excellent targets for GPU acceleration opportunities.

Parallelization

Once the bottlenecks of an application are identified, the next stage is to parallelize the code. There are several ways to accelerate host code, including:

➤ Using CUDA parallel libraries

➤ Using parallelizing and vectorizing compilers

➤ Manually developing CUDA kernels to expose parallelism

The most straightforward approach to parallelizing an application is to leverage existing GPU-accelerated libraries. If your application is already using other C mathematical libraries, such as BLAS or FFTW, you can quite easily switch to use CUDA libraries, such as cuBLAS or cuFFT. Another relatively effortless approach to parallelizing host codes is to make use of parallelizing compilers. OpenACC uses open, standard compiler directives explicitly designed for accelerator environments. OpenACC extensions give you sufficient control to ensure data resides close to processing elements and provide a set of compiler directives. These constructs make GPU programming straightforward and portable across parallel and multi-core processors.

For situations in which the functionality or performance required by your application is beyond what existing parallel libraries or parallelizing compilers can provide, writing kernels with CUDA C becomes essential for parallelization. CUDA C maximizes your ability to fully utilize the parallel power of GPUs.

Depending on the original code, you might need to refactor your program to expose inherent parallelism in order to improve application performance. Parallel data decomposition is an unavoidable step during this phase. There are basically two different approaches to partitioning data among massive parallel threads: *block partition* and *cyclic partition*. In block partitioning, data elements to process are chunked together and distributed to threads. The performance of a kernel can be sensitive to block size. In cyclic partitioning, every thread processes one element at a time before jumping ahead by as many elements as there are threads. The basic considerations for data partitioning relate to architecture features and the nature of the algorithm being implemented.

Optimization

After you have organized your code to run in parallel, you then move to the next stage: optimizing the implementation to improve performance. Roughly speaking, CUDA-based optimizations can be applied at the following two levels:

➤ Grid-level

➤ Kernel-level

During grid-level optimization, focus is on overall GPU utilization and efficiency. Techniques to optimize grid-level performance include running multiple kernels simultaneously and overlapping kernel execution with data transfers using CUDA streams and events.

There are three major factors that can limit performance for a kernel:

➤ Memory bandwidth

➤ Compute resources

➤ Instruction and memory latency

During kernel-level optimization, you focus on the efficient use of GPU memory bandwidth and compute resources and the reduction or hiding of instruction and memory latency.

CUDA provides the following useful and powerful tools to help you identify performance opportunities at the grid and kernel level:

➤ Nsight Eclipse Edition (`nsight`)

➤ NVIDIA Visual Profiler (`nvvp`)

➤ NVIDIA Command-line Profiler (`nvprof`)

These profiling tools are effective at guiding you during the optimization processes and offer suggestions for the best course of action to improve performance. `nvprof` and `nvvp` have already been used in many exercises and examples throughout this book.

Deployment

Once you have confirmed that the GPU-accelerated application delivers correct results, the final stage of APOD is to consider how to deploy the system using GPU components. For example, when deploying a CUDA application, it might be necessary to ensure that it continues to function properly even if the target machine does not have a CUDA-capable GPU. The CUDA runtime provides several functions that enable you to detect CUDA-capable GPUs and check the hardware and software configuration. However, your application must manually adapt to the hardware resources detected.

APOD is an iterative process that seeks to convert legacy applications to well-performing and stable CUDA applications. Applications that contain many candidates for GPU acceleration might pass through the APOD pipeline several times: identifying an opportunity for optimization, applying and testing the optimization, verifying the speedup achieved, and repeating the process again.

SPIRAL MODEL

The Spiral Model is a software development approach, which is based on the concept of the continuous refinement of key ingredients using an iterative cycle for:

➤ Analysis

➤ Design

➤ Implementation

It allows for incremental product releases, or incremental refinement, each time around the spiral lifecycle.

The basic approach of the APOD development model is the same as the Spiral Model.

Optimization Opportunities

Once a correct CUDA program has been implemented as part of the APOD Parallelization stage, you can begin to look for optimization opportunities during the Optimization stage. As described in the previous section, optimizations can be applied at various levels, from overlapping data transfers with computations, all the way down to fine-tuning floating-point calculations. To achieve better performance, you should focus on the following aspects of your program, listed in order of importance:

➤ Exposing sufficient parallelism

➤ Optimizing memory access

➤ Optimizing instruction execution

Exposing Sufficient Parallelism

To expose sufficient parallelism, you should arrange concurrent work on the GPU so as to saturate both instruction bandwidth and memory bandwidth.

There are two ways to increase parallelism:

➤ Keep more concurrent warps active within an SM

➤ Assign more independent work to each thread/warp

When tuning for the optimal number of active warps within an SM, you must examine SM resource occupancy limits (such as shared memory, registers, and compute cycles) to find the right balance for best performance. The number of active warps represents the amount of parallelism exposed to an SM. However, a high degree of occupancy does not automatically correspond to higher performance. Depending on the nature of your kernel algorithms, once a certain degree of occupancy is reached further increases will not enhance performance. However, you will still have opportunities to improve performance from other angles.

You can tune for desired parallelism at two different levels:

➤ Kernel level

➤ Grid level

At the kernel level, CUDA adopts a partition approach to allot compute resources: Registers are partitioned among threads, and shared memory is partitioned among blocks. Therefore, resource consumption within a kernel might inhibit the number of active warps.

At the grid level, CUDA organizes thread execution using a grid of thread blocks and gives you the freedom to choose the optimal kernel launch configuration parameters by specifying:

➤ The number of threads per thread block

➤ The number of thread blocks per grid

Through the grid configuration, you can control how threads are arranged into thread blocks to expose adequate parallelism to an SM, and also balance work across the SMs.

Optimizing Memory Access

Many algorithms are memory-bound. For these applications and others, memory access latency and memory access patterns have a significant impact on kernel performance. Therefore, memory optimization is one of the most important areas to focus on when improving performance. The goal of memory access optimization is to maximize memory bandwidth utilization, with the majority of your time focused on the following two prospects:

➤ Memory access patterns (maximize the use of bytes that travel on the bus)

➤ Sufficient concurrent memory accesses (hide memory latency)

Memory requests (loads or stores) from a kernel are issued per warp. Each thread in a warp provides one memory address, and 32 threads together access a chunk of device memory based on the memory addresses provided. The device hardware converts the addresses provided by a warp into memory transactions. The granularity of memory accesses on the device is 32 bytes. Therefore, there are two different metrics that you need to pay attention to while analyzing data movement in a program: the number of bytes requested by the program and the number of bytes moved by hardware. The difference between these two metrics indicates wasted memory bandwidth.

The best access pattern to global memory is aligned and coalesced access. Aligned memory access requires that the first address of device memory requested is a multiple of 32 bytes. Coalesced memory access refers to accessing a consecutive chunk of memory by 32 threads in a warp.

Load and store memory operations have different features and behaviors. Load operations can be classified into three different types:

- ➤ Cached (default, L1 cache enabled)
- ➤ Un-cached (L1 cache disabled)
- ➤ Read-only

The load granularity for a cached load is a 128-byte cache line. For un-cached and read-only loads, the granularity is a 32-byte segment. Typically, a load from global memory on a Fermi GPU will first attempt to hit in L1 cache, then L2 cache, and finally go all the way to device global memory. On a Kepler GPU, L1 cache is skipped for global memory loads. For loads of read-only memory, CUDA first attempts a hit in a separate read-only cache, then L2 cache, and finally device global memory. For irregular access patterns, such as misaligned and/or un-coalesced access patterns, a short load granularity will help improve bandwidth utilization. L1 cache can be enabled or disabled using compiler options on Fermi GPUs. By default, global store operations skip the L1 cache and evict the matching cache line.

As shared memory is on-chip, it has a much higher bandwidth and lower latency than local and device global memory. In many ways, shared memory is a program-managed cache. There are two major reasons for using shared memory:

- ➤ To reduce global memory accesses by explicitly caching data
- ➤ To avoid un-coalesced global memory accesses by rearranging data layout

Physically, shared memory is arranged in a linear fashion and accessed through 32 banks. Fermi and Kepler each have different default bank modes: a 4-byte bank mode and an 8-byte bank mode, respectively. The relationship that maps shared memory address to banks varies with different access modes. When multiple threads in a warp access different words in the same bank, a bank conflict occurs. A many-way bank conflict can be very expensive due to shared memory replay requests. When you use shared memory, a very simple and effective method to resolve or reduce bank conflicts is to pad arrays. Adding a word of padding at the right location can spread accesses across different banks, which results in reduced latency and improved throughput.

Shared memory is partitioned among all resident thread blocks; therefore, it is a critical resource and might limit kernel occupancy.

Optimizing Instruction Execution

There are several ways to optimize kernel execution, including:

➤ Hiding latency by keeping sufficient active warps

➤ Hiding latency by assigning more independent work to a thread

➤ Avoiding divergent execution paths within a warp

Even though a CUDA kernel is expressed in scalar fashion as though it runs on a single CUDA core, the code is always executed in a warp unit in SIMT (single-instruction multiple-thread) fashion. When an instruction is issued for a warp, each thread carries out the same operation with its own data.

Threads can be organized by modifying the kernel execution configuration. The thread block size affects the number of active warps on an SM. GPUs hide latency by having asynchronous work in flight (such as global loads and stores) in order to saturate the warp schedule, pipeline, and memory bus. You can adjust the kernel execution configuration for more active warps or enable each thread to do more independent work that can be pipelined and overlapped. GPU devices with different compute capabilities have different hardware limits; therefore, the grid/block heuristics play a very important role in optimizing kernel performance on different platforms.

Because all threads in a warp execute the same instruction at each step, if there are different control flow paths within a warp due to data-dependent conditional branches, divergence among thread execution might occur. When threads within a warp diverge, the warp must execute each branch path in sequence while disabling threads that did not take that execution path. If large portions of time for your application are spent in divergent code, it will significantly affect kernel performance.

Inter-thread communication and synchronization are very important features in parallel programming and can create obstacles to achieving good performance. CUDA provides several mechanisms that enable you to manage synchronization at different levels. Typically, you have two ways to explicitly synchronize your kernel. You can:

➤ Synchronize at the grid level

➤ Synchronize within a thread block

Synchronizing threads inside potentially divergent code is dangerous and can cause unanticipated errors. You must take care to ensure that all threads converge at each explicit barrier point within a thread block. In general, synchronization adds overhead to a kernel and restricts the flexibility of the CUDA scheduler when deciding which warps in a thread block are eligible for execution.

CUDA Code Compilation

The source code of a CUDA application generally contains two types of source files: conventional C source files and CUDA C source files. Within a device code file, there are usually two types of functions: device functions and host functions that call device functions or manage device resources. The CUDA compiler separates the compilation process into the following two parts, as illustrated in Figure 10-2:

➤ Device function compilation with nvcc

➤ Host function compilation with a general purpose C/C++ compiler

The compiled device objects are embedded in host object files as load images. During the link stage, the CUDA runtime libraries are added to support device functionality.

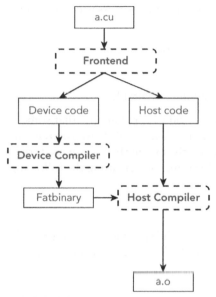

FIGURE 10-2

CUDA provides the following two methods for compiling CUDA functions:

➤ Whole-program compilation

➤ Separate compilation

Prior to CUDA 5.0, the full definition of a kernel function and all device functions it called had to be kept within one file scope; you could not call device functions or access device variables across files. Such compilation is referred to as *whole-program compilation*. Starting with CUDA 5.0, *separate compilation* for device code was introduced (though whole program mode remained the default). With separate compilation, device code defined in one file can reference device code defined in another file. Separate compilation improves CUDA project management with the following benefits:

➤ Eases porting of legacy C code to CUDA

➤ Reduces build time with incremental library recompilation

➤   Facilitates code reuse and reduces compile time

➤   Lets you combine object files into static libraries

➤   Lets you link and call external device code

➤   Lets you create and use third-party libraries

Separate Compilation

CUDA compilation embeds device code in host objects. With whole program compilation, executable device code is embedded in the host object. With separate compilation the process is not as simple. Three steps are involved:

1.   The device compiler embeds re-locatable device code in the host object file.

2.   The device linker combines device objects.

3.   The host linker combines device and host objects into a final executable.

Consider a simple example that contains three files: a.cu, b.cu, and c.cpp. Suppose that some kernel functions in file a.cu refer to some functions or variables in file b.cu. Because you reference across two files, you have to use separate compilation to generate the executable. If you are targeting a Fermi device (compute capability 2.x), you first generate re-locatable objects using the following command:

```
$ nvcc –arch=sm_20 –dc a.cu b.cu
```

The option -dc passed to nvcc instructs the compiler to compile each input file (a.cu and b.cu) into an object file that contains re-locatable device code. Next, you link all device objects together using the following command:

```
$ nvcc –arch=sm_20 –dlink a.o b.o -o link.o
```

The option -dlink passed to nvcc causes all device object files with re-locatable device code (a.o and b.o) to be linked into an object file (link.o) that can be passed to the host linker. Finally, the host linker is used to generate the executable, as follows:

```
$ g++ -c c.cpp -o c.o
$ g++ c.o link.o -o test –L<path> -lcudart
```

Figure 10-3 illustrates the separate compilation process.

Sample Makefile

Listing 10-1 is a sample Makefile that uses separate compilation. You will need to replace the full path names and update the name of the executable file in the sample Makefile to match your working environment. You can extend this sample to compile a typical project that has:

➤   Both C and CUDA C files

➤   Device function or device variable references across CUDA C files

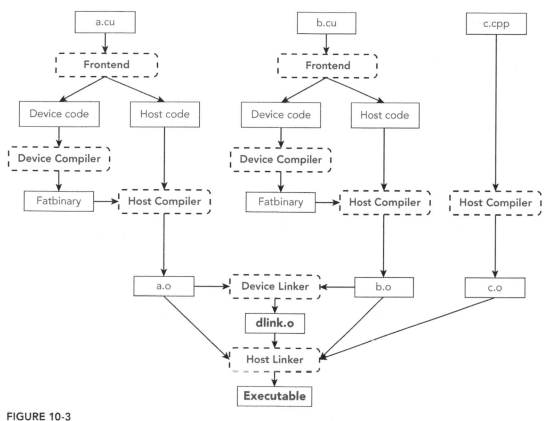

FIGURE 10-3

The file `sample-makefile` can be downloaded from `Wrox.com`.

LISTING 10-1: Sample Makefile (Makefile)

```
SRCS := $(wildcard *.c)
OBJS := $(patsubst %.c, %.o, $(SRCS))

CUDA_SRCS := $(wildcard *.cu)
CUDA_OBJS := $(patsubst %.cu, %.o, $(CUDA_SRCS))

CUDA_PATH := /usr/local/cuda-6.0# specify your CUDA root path
NVCC    := $(CUDA_PATH)/bin/nvcc
CC      := icc
LD      := icc -openmp

CUDA_LIB := -L$(CUDA_PATH)/lib64 -lcublas -lcufft -lcudart
CUDA_INC += -I$(CUDA_PATH)/include
```

continues

LISTING 10-1 *(continued)*

```
CFLAGS    += -std=c99
INCLUDES := # specify include path for host code

GPU_CARD      := -arch=sm_35 # specify your device compute capability
NVCC_FLAGS    += -O3  -dc # separate compilation
NVCC_FLAGS    += -Xcompiler -fopenmp
CUDA_LINK_FLAGS    := -dlink # device linker option

EXEC          := test # specify your executable name
CUDA_LINK_OBJ := cuLink.o

all:  $(EXEC)
$(EXEC): $(OBJS) $(CUDA_OBJS)
        $(NVCC) $(GPU_CARD) $(CUDA_LINK_FLAGS) -o $(CUDA_LINK_OBJ) $(CUDA_OBJS)
        $(LD) -o $@ $(OBJS) $(CUDA_OBJS) $(CUDA_LINK_OBJ) $(CUDA_LIB)

%.o : %.c
        $(CC) -o $@ -c $(CFLAGS)  $(INCLUDES) $<

%.o : %.cu
        $(NVCC) $(GPU_CARD) $(NVCC_FLAGS) -o $@ -c $< $(CUDA_INC)

clean:
        rm -f $(OBJS) $(EXEC) *.o a.out

install:
```

Integrating CUDA Files into a C Project

CUDA provides two sets of runtime API interfaces:

➤ An interface with C++ conventions

➤ An interface with C conventions

When porting from C to CUDA, you might need to prepare device memory and data from C functions by calling CUDA runtime functions. For example, it might be necessary to call `cudaMalloc` from a .c file. To call CUDA runtime functions from C code, you need to include the C runtime header file in your host code, as follows:

```
#include <cuda_runtime_api.h>
```

You can organize your CUDA kernel functions using separate files much like you would with C-based projects. You must then create kernel wrapper functions in the device source files that can be called like a normal C function, but perform a CUDA kernel launch. Because the host functions that are declared in device source files default to C++ conventions, you will also need to use the following declaration to resolve mangled C++ references:

```
extern "C" void wrapper_kernel_launch(...) {
    ...
}
```

The keyword `extern "C"` indicates to the compiler that the host function name should be un-mangled so that it can be linked with your C code. Figure 10-4 illustrates how you can organize a kernel wrapper function using C conventions in separate files.

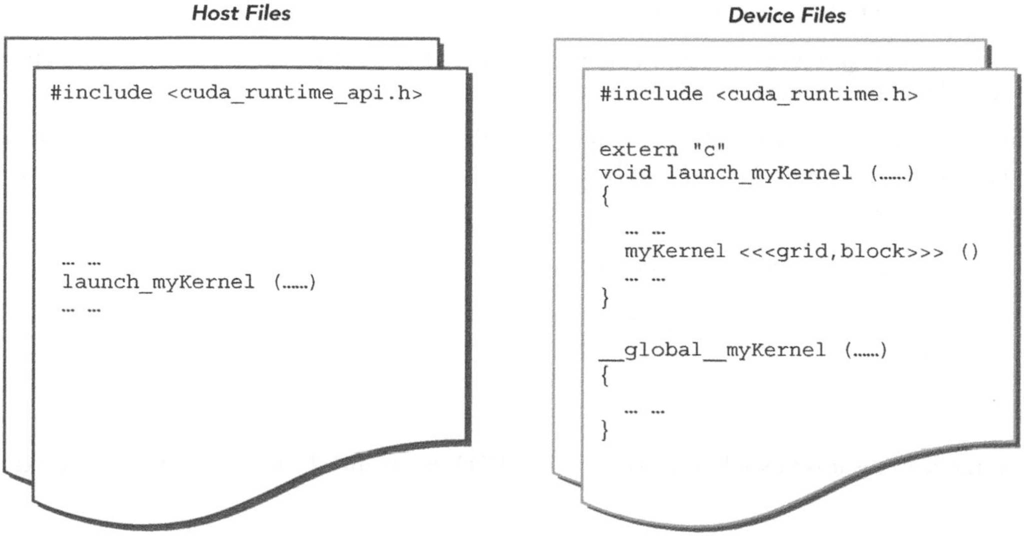

Host Files

```
#include <cuda_runtime_api.h>




... ...
launch_myKernel (......)
... ...
```

Device Files

```
#include <cuda_runtime.h>

extern "c"
void launch_myKernel (......)
{
   ... ...
   myKernel <<<grid,block>>> ()
   ... ...
}


__global__ myKernel (......)
{

   ... ...
}
```

FIGURE 10-4

CUDA Error Handling

Error handling is arguably the least glamorous but most important part of production application development. Building a program that will be able to stand up to the tortures of misuse without undefined behavior is a necessity before deploying any application into a production environment.

Fortunately, CUDA makes it easy to detect errors. Every CUDA API and library call returns an error code indicating either success or details about a failure. These errors codes can be useful in either recovering from the error, or displaying an informative message to the user. Just as in any systems-level software development project, checking these error codes on every function call is a requirement for stability.

One idiosyncrasy of CUDA error checking is its asynchrony. Error codes returned from CUDA function calls may or may not be a result of actions performed by that particular function call. The function may be returning information on an error caused by any previous asynchronous function call which may still be executing. This complicates the process of providing useful error messages to the user or recovering from failure. These problems can be mitigated by defining what operations may run in parallel, and being prepared to handle errors from any function.

CUDA provides three function calls that you can use for error checking. `cudaGetLastError` checks the current state of CUDA for any reported errors. If none have been recorded, it returns `cudaSuccess`. If one has been recorded, it returns that error and clears the internal CUDA state to be `cudaSuccess`. As a result, if multiple calls to `cudaGetLastError` return an error code, the calling application knows that each of those errors is distinct and different from the others (though their cause can still be related).

`cudaPeekLastError` performs the same checks as `cudaGetLastError`, but does not clear the internal error state to be `cudaSuccess`.

`cudaGetErrorString` returns a human-readable string for the CUDA error passed to the function. This is useful for generating user-facing error messages.

You will note that every downloadable example from the website for this book makes use of error handling of some type or another, generally using a `CHECK` or `CALL_CUDA` macro to exit on error:

```
#define CHECK(call) { \
    cudaError_t err; \
    if ( (err = (call)) != cudaSuccess) { \
        fprintf(stderr, "Got error %s at %s:%d\n", cudaGetErrorString(err), \
                __FILE__, __LINE__); \
        exit(1); \
    } \
}
```

In many applications it is possible to recover from CUDA errors, in which case an immediate exit is unnecessary.

PROFILE-DRIVEN OPTIMIZATION

You must be very familiar with the profile-driven approach by now, as you have used this method to optimize kernel functions in every example throughout the book. There are two types of profile tools available for CUDA programming:

➤ NVIDIA profiling tools

➤ Third-party profiling tools

Most developers choose to use NVIDIA profiling tools because they are not only free, but also very powerful. Third-party profiling tools leverage NVIDIA profiling tool interfaces. Both graphical and command-line profiling tools are included in the CUDA toolkit.

Profile-driven optimization is an iterative process to optimize your program based on profile information. Typically, you use the following iterative approach:

1. Apply profiler to an application to gather information.

2. Identify application hotspots.

3. Determine performance inhibitors.

4. Optimize the code.

5. Repeat the previous steps until desired performance is achieved.

The key step is to identify performance inhibitors. CUDA profiling tools will help you to locate inhibitors in your code. The most likely performance inhibitors for a kernel are:

➤ Memory bandwidth

➤ Instruction throughput

➤ Latency

In previous chapters, you used NVIDIA profiling tools to identify these inhibitors. This section briefly summarizes profile-driven optimization using both the Visual Profiler and Command-line Profiler.

Finding Optimization Opportunities Using nvprof

The primary profiling tool for CUDA applications is nvprof. Roughly speaking, there are two types of profiling data you can collect using nvprof:

➤ A timeline of CUDA-related activities on both the CPU and GPU

➤ Events and metrics for kernels

Profiling Modes

nvprof is called from the command line with the following syntax:

```
nvprof [nvprof-options] <application> [application-arguments]
```

You can run nvprof in one of following four modes:

➤ *Summary mode*

➤ *Trace mode*

➤ *Event/Metric summary mode*

➤ *Event/Metric trace mode*

By default, nvprof runs in Summary mode. You can use nvprof-options to switch to other modes. For example, Trace mode can be enabled using the following options:

```
--print-gpu-trace
--print-api-trace
```

GPU-trace and API-trace modes can be enabled individually or at the same time. GPU-trace mode provides a timeline of all activities taking place on the GPU in chronological order. API-trace mode shows a timeline of all CUDA runtime and driver API calls invoked on the host in chronological order.

You can enable event/metric summary mode using the following options:

```
--events <event names>
--metrics <metric names>
```

The event/metric summary mode collects statistics about different events/metrics that occur in applications. Events are hardware counters observed during the execution of an application. Metrics are calculated based on events. For example, number of global memory accesses and number of L1 cache hits are two events supported by nvprof. Using these events, a metric of how well the application is using cache can be derived. While there are built-in metrics, you can also define your own metrics based on hardware counters gathered from the profiler. Using the following options, you can query all built-in events and metrics supported by nvprof:

```
--query-events
--query-metrics
```

You can enable event/metric trace mode using the following option:

```
--aggregate-mode off [events|metrics]
```

In event/metric trace mode, event and metric values are shown for each kernel execution. By default, event and metric values are aggregated across all SMs in the GPU.

Profiling Scope

By default, nvprof profiles all kernels launched on all visible CUDA devices. This profiling scope can be limited by the following option:

```
--devices <device IDs>
```

This option applies to the following modes/options:

```
--events
--metrics
--query-events
--query-metrics
```

When combined with the previous modes/options, the --devices option limits collection of events/metrics to the devices specified by <device IDs>.

Memory Bandwidth

A kernel can operate on a variety of storage types, including:

➤ Shared Memory

➤ L1/L2 Cache

➤ Texture Cache

➤ Device Memory

➤ System Memory (via PCIe)

There are many events/metrics related to memory operations collectable from nvprof. With these events/metrics, you can evaluate the efficiency of a kernel operating on different types of memory. The following subsections summarize which events/metrics you should collect in some typical cases.

Global Memory Access Pattern

Optimally, global memory accesses should be aligned and coalesced. Any access pattern other than aligned and coalesced will result in replay of memory requests. You can use the following metrics to check the efficiency of global memory load and store operations in a kernel:

```
gld_efficiency
gst_efficiency
```

The metric `gld_efficiency` is defined as the ratio of the requested global memory load throughput to the required global memory load throughput. The requested global memory load throughput does not include memory replay operations, while the required global memory load throughput does. The metric `gst_efficiency` is the same as `gld_efficiency`, but for global memory stores.

You can also use the following metrics to check global memory load and store efficiency:

```
gld_transactions_per_request
gst_transactions_per_request
```

The metric `gld_transactions_per_request` is the average number of global memory load transactions performed for each global memory load request. The metric `gst_transactions_per_request` is the average number of global memory store transactions performed for each global memory store request. If many transactions are required for a single global load or store, device memory bandwidth is likely being wasted.

You can check the total number of memory operations using the following metrics:

```
gld_transactions
gst_transactions
```

The metric `gld_transactions` is the number of global memory load transactions per kernel launch, and the metric `gst_transactions` is the number of global memory store transactions per kernel launch.

You can check the throughput of memory operations using the following metrics:

```
gst_throughput
gld_throughput
```

The metric `gst_throughput` is the global memory store throughput, and the metric `gld_throughput` is the global memory load throughput. You can compare these measured throughput values with theoretical peak values to determine if your kernel is close to ideal performance, or if there is still room for improvement.

Shared Memory Bank Conflicts

Bank conflicts are a major performance concern when using shared memory. You can use the following metrics to check if bank conflicts occur in your application:

```
shared_load_transactions_per_request
shared_store_transactions_per_request
```

Bank conflicts cause memory request replays, and the corresponding value for either loads or stores will be greater than one.

You can also check directly for bank conflicts using the following event:

```
l1_shared_bank_conflict
```

This event reports the number of shared bank conflicts due to two or more shared memory requests accessing the same memory bank.

Use the following events to collect the number of instructions executed for shared memory loads/ stores, not including replays:

```
shared_load
shared_store
```

Then, you can calculate the number of replays per instruction as follows:

```
l1_shared_bank_conflict/(shared_load + shared_store)
```

You can also check shared memory efficiency using the following metric:

```
shared_efficiency
```

The `shared_efficiency` metric is defined as the ratio of requested shared memory throughput to the required shared memory throughput. Because the required shared memory throughput includes replay, a lower ratio for `shared_efficiency` implies more bank conflicts.

Register Spilling

When a kernel uses more register variables than the maximum allowed per thread (63 for Fermi and 255 for Kepler), the compiler will spill the excess values to local memory. Spilling to local memory may drastically degrade kernel performance. To evaluate the severity of register spilling, first collect the following events:

```
l1_local_load_hit
l1_local_load_miss
l1_local_store_hit
l1_local_store_miss
```

Then, calculate the following ratios:

```
local_load_hit_ratio = l1_local_load_hit / (l1_local_load_hit + l1_local_load_miss)
local_store_hit_ratio = l1_local_store_hit /
                        (l1_local_store_hit + l1_local_store_miss)
```

A low ratio is indicative of severe register spilling. You can also check the following metric:

```
l1_cache_local_hit_rate
```

This metric reports the hit rate in L1 cache for local loads and stores. If more local loads and stores are being performed, it means more spilling must have occurred.

Instruction Throughput

Instruction throughput is affected primarily by instruction serialization and warp divergence. You can use the following metrics to check for instruction serialization:

```
inst_executed
inst_issued
```

The number of `inst_issued` instructions includes instruction replays. `inst_executed` does not. You can compare these two metrics to determine replay (or serialization) percentage.

Warp divergence also affects instruction throughput by reducing the number of active threads in each warp. You can check for warp divergence using the following metric:

```
branch_efficiency
```

This metric is defined as the ratio of non-divergent branches to total branches. A high `branch_efficiency` indicates that there is little warp divergence. You can also check for warp divergence using the following events:

```
branch
divergent_branch
```

By comparing these two metrics, you can determine the percentage of branches that diverge.

Guiding Optimization Using nvvp

The NVIDIA Visual Profiler is a graphical tool with two features that differentiate it from `nvprof`:

➤ A timeline display of CPU and GPU activity

➤ Automatic performance analysis to aid in identifying optimization opportunities

The NVIDIA Visual Profiler is available as both a standalone application, `nvvp`, and as part of Nsight Eclipse Edition, an all-in-one development environment that enables developing, debugging, and optimizing CUDA applications in an integrated GUI environment. The NVIDIA Visual Profiler is a standalone application that offers cross-platform support for optimizing CUDA C/C++ applications.

The Visual Profiler is organized into the following six views for analyzing and visualizing application performance:

➤ *Timeline view*

➤ *Analysis view*

➤ *Details view*

➤ *Properties view*

➤ *Console view*

➤ *Settings view*

The Timeline view, used in earlier chapters, shows CPU and GPU activity of the application being profiled. Multiple timelines can be analyzed at the same time. Each timeline is represented by a different instance of the view. When multiple timeline views are displayed, status updates are context sensitive to the last operated timeline view. Figure 10-5 shows a timeline view of an application.

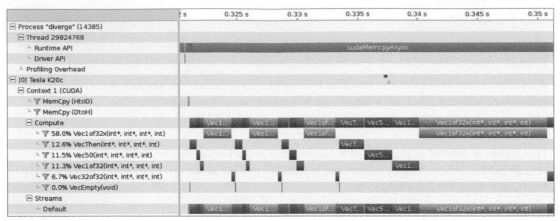

FIGURE 10-5

The Analysis view is used to conduct performance analysis. There are two analysis modes:

➤ *Guided analysis*

➤ *Unguided analysis*

Guided Analysis

In the guided mode, as shown in Figure 10-6, nvvp will guide you step-by-step thorough analysis of the entire application.

In this mode, nvvp will go through multiple stages of analysis to aid your understanding of the likely performance limiters and optimization opportunities, including:

➤ CUDA Application Analysis

➤ Performance-Critical Kernels

➤ Compute, Bandwidth, or Latency Bound

➤ Compute Resources

Unguided Analysis

In nvvp's unguided mode, shown in Figure 10-7, nvvp shows you specific analysis items for your application. Beside each analysis item is a `Run Analysis` button that can be used to generate the analysis results for that item. When the button is clicked, nvvp will execute the application to collect profiling data needed to perform the analysis. Each analysis result contains a brief description of the analysis and a `More. . .` link that directs you to detailed documentation on the analysis.

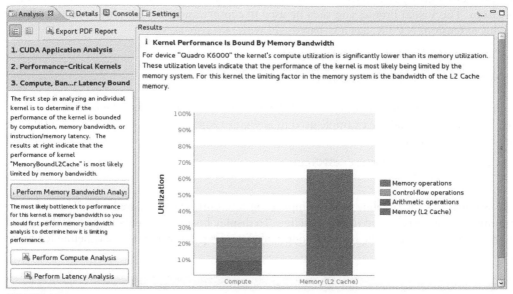

FIGURE 10-6

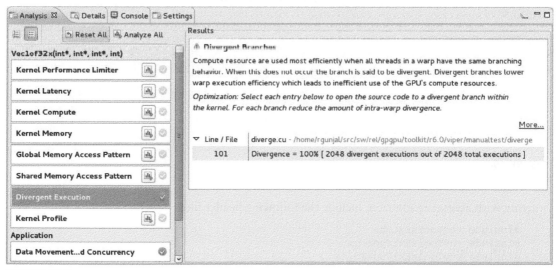

FIGURE 10-7

When a single kernel instance is selected in the timeline, additional kernel-specific analysis items are available. Each kernel-specific analysis item has a `Run Analysis` button that operates in the same manner as the application analysis.

NVIDIA Tools Extension

NVIDIA provides a utility that allows developers to annotate events, code ranges, and resources in an application. The Visual Profiler can then be used to capture and visualize these events and code ranges. This extension, *NVTX*, has a C-based API with two core services:

➤ Tracing of CPU events and code ranges

➤ Naming of OS and CUDA resources

This section demonstrates how to integrate NVTX into an application using the matrix sum example. You can download the example used in `sumMatrixGPU.cu` from `Wrox.com`. Compile it and run it with `nvvp` as follows:

```
$ nvcc -o sumMatrix sumMatrixGPU.cu
$ nvvp ./sumMatrix
```

Figure 10-8 illustrates the timeline of this simple program. Only events related to GPU computation or communication were recorded in this timeline. To display host code events in the timeline, you can use the `nvxt` API to mark the relevant code ranges so `nvvp` can generate the timeline for host events.

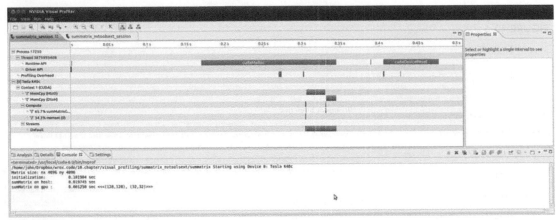

FIGURE 10-8

Starting with `sumMatrixGPU.cu`, include the following header files:

```
#include <nvToolsExt.h>
#include <nvToolsExtCuda.h>
#include <nvToolsExtCudaRt.h>
```

The core NVTX API functions are defined in `nvToolsExt.h`. CUDA-specific extensions to the NVTX interface are defined in `nvToolsExtCuda.h` and `nvToolsExtCudaRt.h`.

Next, define the following new variable in `sumMatrixGPU.cu`. This variable will be used to mark a range of host code.

```
nvtxEventAttributes_t eventAttrib = {0};
eventAttrib.version = NVTX_VERSION;
eventAttrib.size = NVTX_EVENT_ATTRIB_STRUCT_SIZE;
eventAttrib.colorType = NVTX_COLOR_ARGB;
eventAttrib.messageType = NVTX_MESSAGE_TYPE_ASCII;
```

For example, you might want to profile and visualize host memory allocation. First, define the mark name and mark color as follows:

```
eventAttrib.color = RED;
eventAttrib.message.ascii = "HostMalloc";
```

Before allocating the host memory, mark the beginning of the code range with a unique identifier variable `hostMalloc`:

```
nvtxRangeId_t hostMalloc = nvtxRangeStartEx(&eventAttrib);
```

After the host memory is allocated, you then mark the end of the range with the same unique identifier:

```
nvtxRangeEnd(hostMalloc);
```

This technique can be used to mark any range of host code. If you wanted to also mark the last phase of `sumMatrixGPU` that releases memory, simply define the mark name and mark color:

```
eventAttrib.color = AQUA;
eventAttrib.message.ascii = "ReleaseResource";
```

Before releasing all resources, mark the beginning of the range with a unique identifier variable `releaseResource`:

```
nvtxRangeId_t releaseResource = nvtxRangeStartEx(&eventAttrib);
```

After memory allocations are released, mark the end of the range with the same unique identifier as follows:

```
nvtxRangeEnd(releaseResource);
```

A version of `sumMatrixGPU.cu` with these changes is available in `sumMatrixGPU_nvToolExt.cu` from `Wrox.com`. Compile it and link to the extension tool library as follows:

```
$ nvcc -arch=sm_35 sumMatrixGPU_nvToolsExt.cu -o sumMatrixExt -lnvToolsExt
```

A customized timeline with your added events can then be generated with `nvvp`:

```
$ nvvp ./sumMatrixExt
```

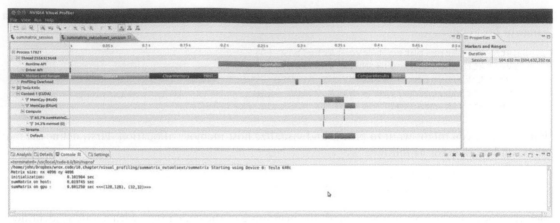

FIGURE 10-9

As illustrated in Figure 10-9, a new row named "Markers and Ranges" was added to the Timeline view. All host side events that were marked are now displayed in that row with the specified colors.

CUDA DEBUGGING

This section covers a variety of debugging tools and techniques specifically designed for use with CUDA applications. The goal of these tools and techniques is to give you the ability to inspect your application code as it runs. In this section, code inspection will be split into two separate, but related, topics: *kernel debugging* and *memory debugging*.

Kernel debugging refers to the ability to inspect the flow and state of kernel execution on the fly. CUDA debugging tools enable you to examine the state of any variable in any thread and at any code location on the GPU. This can be extremely helpful when you are checking the correctness of your application.

Memory debugging focuses on the discovery of odd program behavior, such as invalid memory accesses, conflicting accesses to the same memory location, and other behavior with undefined results. Because memory debugging tools are more automated than kernel debugging tools, they offer a quick way for you to identify errors, or assess the correctness of an application, before delving deeper using kernel debugging tools.

Kernel Debugging

In kernel debugging, you check the correctness of a kernel by inspecting the execution and state of one or more threads. In CUDA, there are three main techniques used for kernel debugging: cuda-gdb, printf, and assert.

Using cuda-gdb

If you are already familiar with the host debugging tool gdb, then you will find cuda-gdb a natural extension. You can leverage your existing gdb knowledge to quickly become proficient at debugging CUDA-based applications.

Before debugging a CUDA application with `cuda-gdb`, you must first compile your program using special flags. This process is nearly identical to compiling host applications for debugging with `gdb` and similar tools. Simply add two flags to `nvcc`: `-g` and `-G`:

```
$ nvcc -g -G foo.cu -o foo
```

These flags embed debugging information for both host and device code, and turn off most optimizations to ensure that your program state can be inspected during execution.

Once the application has been compiled with debug flags, you can launch a CUDA application with `cuda-gdb` just as you would with `gdb`. Given a compiled and linked application `foo`, you pass the executable to `cuda-gdb`, as follows:

```
$ cuda-gdb foo
...
(cuda-gdb)
```

This leaves you at the `(cuda-gdb)` prompt, meaning that `cuda-gdb` has loaded symbols from the executable and is ready to execute. To run the program, simply type the command `run`. Command-line arguments can be included after the `run` command or set using the `set args` command.

In general, `cuda-gdb` fully supports many of the features provided by `gdb` including breakpoints, watch-points, and the ability to inspect program state. However, `cuda-gdb` also provides CUDA-specific debugging functionality. A brief summary of these extensions and an example of their usage is provided in the following subsections.

CUDA Focus

While CUDA applications can contain multiple host threads and many CUDA threads, `cuda-gdb` debugging sessions only focus on a single thread at a time. In order for you to debug multiple device threads in the same application, `cuda-gdb` supports the ability for you to specify the context (that is, the device thread) to be inspected. You can use `cuda-gdb` to report information about the current focus including the current device, current block, current thread, and more.

For example, if the current focus of a `cuda-gdb` debugging session is on a CUDA thread executing on the device, then you can retrieve the full specification of that focus by using:

```
(cuda-gdb) cuda thread lane warp block sm grid device kernel
```

An example output of this command would be:

```
kernel 1026, grid 1027, block (0,0,0), thread (64,0,0), device 0, sm 1, warp 2,
lane 0
```

You can change focus to a different device thread using a similar syntax. In addition to the thread property, you can provide a specific thread, for example, the 128th thread in the current block, using:

```
(cuda-gdb) cuda thread (128)
```

If you do not explicitly set focus properties, `cuda-gdb` will reuse the property values from the current focus.

You can obtain additional information about CUDA focus options using the gdb help command:

```
(cuda-gdb) help cuda
```

Inspecting CUDA Memory

As with gdb, cuda-gdb supports inspecting variables, on the heap (i.e., CUDA global memory) and in registers using the print statement:

```
(cuda-gdb) print scalar
(cuda-gdb) print arr[0]
(cuda-gdb) print (*arr)[3]
```

cuda-gdb can also be used to inspect CUDA shared memory. For example, to access the second word in shared memory the following command can be used:

```
(cuda-gdb) print *(@shared int*)0x4
```

Note that because shared memory is local to each SM, that statement might not evaluate to the same memory cell in every focus:

```
(cuda-gdb) cuda sm
sm 1
(cuda-gdb) print *(@shared int*)0x4
$1 = 0
(cuda-gdb) cuda sm 8
[Switching focus to CUDA kernel 1026, grid 1027, block (18,0,0), thread
(0,0,0), device 0, sm 8, warp 0, lane 0]
27          int tid = blockIdx.x * blockDim.x + threadIdx.x;
(cuda-gdb) print *(@shared int*)0x4
$2 = 4
```

Hence, using cuda-gdb, you can inspect arbitrary shared memory data.

Getting Information about the Environment

You can use the gdb info command to retrieve information about the current CUDA environment and platform. A full list of environmental information can be found using:

```
(cuda-gdb) help info cuda
Print informations about the current CUDA activities. Available options:
            devices : information about all the devices
                sms : information about all the SMs in the current device
              warps : information about all the warps in the current SM
              lanes : information about all the lanes in the current warp
            kernels : information about all the active kernels
           contexts : information about all the contexts
             blocks : information about all the active blocks in the current kernel
            threads : information about all the active threads in the current kernel
       launch trace : information about the parent kernels of the kernel in focus
    launch children : information about the kernels launched by the kernels in focus
            managed : information about global managed variables
```

To report information about all devices in the current system, you can use the `info cuda devices` subcommand. Here is output from a system with two Fermi M2090 GPUs:

```
(cuda-gdb) info cuda devices
Dev Description SM Type SMs Warps/SM Lanes/Warp Max Regs/Lane Active SMs Mask
*   0    GF100GL   sm_20  14    48         32              64 0x00003fff
    1    GF100GL   sm_20  14    48         32              64 0x00000000
```

Note that a number of these subcommands duplicate functionality described earlier in the "CUDA Focus" section of this chapter, and that all of these subcommands operate relative to the current focus of `cuda-gdb`. However, a wider variety of metadata is accessible through the `info cuda` subcommand. Both the `cuda` commands, and the `info cuda` subcommands have their own uses depending on the type and amount of information you are seeking.

CUDA Debugging Tunable Parameters

`cuda-gdb` exposes a number of tunable parameters through the `set` subcommand that are useful for tweaking `cuda-gdb` behavior:

```
(cuda-gdb) help set cuda
Generic command for setting gdb cuda variables

List of set cuda subcommands:

set cuda api_failures -- Set the api_failures to ignore/stop/hide on CUDA driver
API call errors
set cuda break_on_launch -- Automatically set a breakpoint at the entrance of
kernels
...
```

A list of useful tunables provided by `cuda-gdb` is summarized in Table 10-1. You can obtain additional information about each of these parameters by using `help set cuda <tunable-name>`. These parameters can be set using `set cuda < tunable-name> <value>`. The choice for `<value>` for many commands is either `on`/`off`, but others have non-Boolean values.

TABLE 10-1: CUDA-GDB Parameters

TUNABLE	DESCRIPTION	DEFAULT
`api_failures`	Alters how `cuda-gdb` responds to error codes returned from CUDA API functions	ignore
`break_on_launch`	Auto-sets a breakpoint at the start of every __global__ function launched by the user application or by the CUDA runtime	none
`context_events`	Controls informational messages on CUDA context creation and destruction	on

continues

TABLE 10-1 *(continued)*

TUNABLE	DESCRIPTION	DEFAULT
defer_kernel_ launch_ notifications	Controls whether the debugger is notified of kernel launches immediately. Disabling this option can improve debugging session performance	on
kernel_events	Controls how often kernel launch or termination notifications are displayed by the application and/or CUDA runtime	none
launch_blocking	Sets all kernel launches to be synchronous	off
memcheck	Enables the memcheck memory checks as part of this cuda-gdb debugging session	off
ptx_cache	Might enable saving the state of more variables in registers, allowing them to be printed from the debugger	on
single_ stepping_ optimizations	Safely accelerates single-stepping through a kernel	off before CUDA 5.5, on after CUDA 6.0
thread_ selection	Controls selection of CUDA focus. logical selects the thread with the lowest logical coordinates. physical selects the thread with the lowest physical coordinates.	logical
value_ extrapolation	If enabled, cuda-gdb will attempt to guess the value of any variables that are not live but whose values might still be saved in registers.	off

Manipulating these cuda-gdb parameters enables you to get more out of a cuda-gdb debugging session, customizing its behavior to fit your requirements.

Hands-On with CUDA-GDB

To get some hands-on experience with cuda-gdb, download the example debug-segfault.cu from Wrox.com. You will use it to experiment with debugging an invalid memory access in CUDA. First, build debug-segfault.cu using the Makefile provided, which will set the flags –g and –G. Next, load the application into cuda-gdb:

```
$ cuda-gdb ./debug-segfault
...
(cuda-gdb)
```

Use the run command to launch debug-segfault. It does not take any command-line arguments:

```
(cuda-gdb) run
```

You will most likely see a large amount of scrolling text providing information about the CUDA context and kernel events occurring. Eventually, your debugging session will restore control back to the (cuda-gdb) prompt when a memory error occurs in the kernel. The following output indicates an error occurred at line 34 of debug-segfault.cu:

```
Program received signal CUDA_EXCEPTION_10, Device Illegal Address.
[Switching focus to CUDA kernel 1026, grid 1027, block (0,0,0), thread (0,0,0),
device 0, sm 1, warp 0, lane 0]
kernel<<<(1024,1,1),(256,1,1)>>> (arr=0xf00100000) at debug-segfault.cu:34
25                     arr[tid][i] = foo(tid, i);
(cuda-gdb)
```

You can use the list command to inspect the surrounding code for context:

```
(cuda-gdb) list
28      __global__ void kernel(int **arr) {
29          int tid = blockIdx.x * blockDim.x + threadIdx.x;
30          int i;
31
32          for ( ; tid < N; tid++) {
33              for (i = 0; i < M; i++) {
34                  arr[tid][i] = foo(tid, i);
35              }
36          }
37      }
(cuda-gdb)
```

The line where the illegal address access occurred is reported on line 34. That line contains a multi-indirection dereference to the input arr. You can examine the contents of the array being referenced at offset tid by printing the address contained in arr[tid]:

```
(cuda-gdb) print arr[tid]
$1 = (@global int * @global) 0x0
(cuda-gdb)
```

That does not look right. A NULL memory address cannot be dereferenced. You can attempt to dereference that location from inside the cuda-gdb debugging session to double-check the problem:

```
(cuda-gdb) print *arr[tid]
Error: Failed to read global memory at address 0x0 on device 0 sm 1 warp 0 lane 0
(error=7).
(cuda-gdb)
```

Clearly that address is invalid, which means that the contents of arr are either having an invalid value written to them or not being properly initialized. Looking back at the original source code, you should notice that there is no cudaMemcpy that actually fills the device array d_matrix. Adding the following line before the kernel launch fixes this memory error.

```
cudaMemcpy(d_matrix, d_ptrs, N * sizeof(int *), cudaMemcpyHostToDevice);
```

The corrected version can be downloaded from Wrox.com in debug-segfault.fixed.cu. While you are still in that cuda-gdb debugging session, you can also examine the state of other threads on the GPU. Use the cuda command to get the current device, block, and thread, as follows:

```
(cuda-gdb) cuda device block thread
block (0,0,0), thread (0,0,0), device 0
(cuda-gdb)
```

Try switching to other threads on the same device and inspecting the different thread state:

```
(cuda-gdb) cuda block 1 thread 1
[Switching focus to CUDA kernel 1026, grid 1027, block (1,0,0), thread (1,0,0),
device 0, sm 5, warp 0, lane 1]
25                      arr[tid][i] = foo(tid, i);
(cuda-gdb) print tid
$2 = 257
(cuda-gdb) print arr[tid]
$3 = (@global int * @global) 0x0
(cuda-gdb)
```

Clearly a number of threads all had memory errors. Focus was simply placed on the one with the lowest logical thread ID.

You can exit the cuda-gdb session by typing quit and y:

```
(cuda-gdb) quit
A debugging session is active.

        Inferior 1 [process 11330] will be killed.

Quit anyway? (y or n) y
```

CUDA-GDB Summary

This section briefly introduced the use of the cuda-gdb debugging tool for inspecting kernel execution. The usage of cuda-gdb is nearly identical to gdb, so any previous experience you have with the host debugging tool can be leveraged as you gain proficiency debugging CUDA-based applications. For more details on cuda-gdb, you are encouraged to read the CUDA-GDB online documentation that comes with the CUDA Toolkit.

CUDA printf

While host debugging, you might often use printf to print the host's application state. It would be terrific if you could use printf in GPU device code as a simple method of inspecting internal device state. However, collating output from kernels running on the device with thousands of threads presents interesting challenges. Starting with CUDA 4.0, NVIDIA added printf support on the device. The interface to the CUDA-based printf is identical to the one you are accustomed to in C/C++ development on the host (and even requires the same header file, stdio.h), making the transition to the CUDA-based printf straightforward.

There are a few caveats for CUDA-based printf. First, it is only available on GPUs with compute capability of 2.0 or higher. Second, unless you explicitly use CUDA synchronization, there is no print ordering between threads. Third, a fixed size, circular device buffer is used to temporarily store the printf output performed on the kernel before fetching them back to the host for display. As a result, if output is produced faster than it can be displayed the buffer will wrap back around and overwrite older outputs. The size of this buffer can be retrieved using cudaGetDeviceLimit and set using cudaSetDeviceLimit.

There are a few common events that cause the fixed size buffer to be transferred back to the host for displaying:

1. Any CUDA kernel launch

2. Any synchronization using the CUDA host API (e.g. `cudaDeviceSynchronize`, `cudaStreamSynchronize`, `cudaEventSynchronize`, etc.)

3. Any synchronous memory copies, such as `cudaMemcpy`

Otherwise, using `printf` in CUDA kernels is identical to using it in host C/C++ programs:

```
__global__ void kernel() {
    int tid = blockIdx.x * blockDim.x + threadIdx.x;
    printf("Hello from CUDA thread %d\n", tid);
}
```

This makes it a very usable and friendly way for you to quickly debug kernels. However, beware of excessive use of `printf`. You can use thread and block indices to limit the threads that print debug messages so as to prevent thousands of printing threads from overloading the debug message buffer.

CUDA assert

Another common host error-checking tool is `assert`. `assert` enables you to declaratively state certain conditions that must hold true for correct application execution. If an `assert` fails, your application execution either 1) immediately aborts with information about the `assert` that failed, or 2) if you are running in a `cuda-gdb` session, control is passed to `cuda-gdb` so that you can inspect application state at the point where the `assert` failed. Like `printf`, support for `assert` is only provided on GPUs with compute capability of 2.0 or better. It also relies on the same header file as the host, `assert.h`.

The semantics for using `assert` from a GPU are slightly different than from the host. Upon hitting a failing `assert` on the device (that is, any `assert` whose contained expression evaluates to zero), a CUDA thread will immediately exit after storing information about the `assert` that failed. However, this information will only be displayed to `stderr` on the host at the next CUDA synchronization point (e.g., `cudaDeviceSynchronize`, `cudaStreamSynchronize`, etc.). This means that at every synchronization point, information is displayed about any thread with a failing `assert` since the last synchronization point. If you make any CUDA host API calls after the first `assert` failure is detected, your app will return the CUDA error code `cudaErrorAssert`.

Like `printf`, you use `assert` within a kernel much like the host version, as follows:

```
__global__ void kernel(...) {
    int *ptr = NULL;
    ...
    assert(ptr != NULL);
    *ptr = ...
    ...
}
```

Like the host `assert`, evaluation of `assert` can be disabled for release versions of code by compiling with the `NDEBUG` pre-processor macro defined before `assert.h` is included.

Kernel Debugging Summary

This section focused on kernel debugging tools in CUDA. `cuda-gdb`, `printf`, and `assert` are all powerful tools that enable fine-grained debugging and error-checking of running CUDA kernels. Each has its own advantages and disadvantages.

`cuda-gdb` is the most powerful, enabling you to control kernel execution on the GPU, as well as interactive inspection of thread state across the entire kernel. As a result, `cuda-gdb` requires the most manual effort and also has a large impact on the performance of an application.

Even though `printf` is not interactive, it allows you to selectively print debugging messages from CUDA threads to quickly identify bugs in your code.

An assert is great for inspecting application state when known issues or regressions arise while debugging, particularly when used with `cuda-gdb`. However, it is difficult to use effectively if you are debugging a new and unknown problem.

The next section switches focus from directly debugging kernels to using kernel memory access errors to help pinpoint problems.

Memory Debugging

While `cuda-gdb` is useful for performing fine-grain inspection of CUDA kernel execution, and `printf`/`assert` are simple mechanisms for manual error checking, the primary tool used for debugging CUDA memory errors is `cuda-memcheck`. The operation of `cuda-memcheck` is much more automated and coarse-grained in terms of user interaction, but `cuda-memcheck` provides more detailed statistics on memory errors in CUDA kernels. `cuda-memcheck` includes two separate utilities:

➤ The `memcheck` tool

➤ The `racecheck` tool

You use `memcheck` to check for out-of-bounds and misaligned accesses in CUDA kernels. `racecheck` can be used to detect conflicting accesses to shared memory, which could result in undefined behavior. These tools can be useful for debugging erratic kernel behavior caused by threads reading and writing unexpected locations.

Compiling for cuda-memcheck

Compiling applications for `cuda-memcheck` is more complicated than `cuda-gdb`. When you build your application with `-g -G`, these options negatively affect performance. When using the `cuda-memcheck` tools, it is important that your application's performance remain consistent to ensure errors are reproducible. However, some compilation flags are necessary to help you dissect `cuda-memcheck` messages and pinpoint where the problems occur.

There are compilation options that you can use which have a low impact on performance but can drastically improve the readability of cuda-memcheck messages. First, you should always compile with the -lineinfo option. This flag embeds information in the executable that associates file names and line numbers with device instructions. Executables should also always be compiled with symbol information. This allows cuda-memcheck to print host stack traces that pinpoint kernel launch locations. The compilation flags that include symbol information are platform-specific and use the -Xcompiler option from nvcc to pass an argument to the host compiler. For example, on Linux with gcc you would use -Xcompiler -rdynamic. On Windows, you would use -Xcompiler /Zi.

When you use these compilation flags, you will generate an executable that contains sufficient metadata for memcheck and racecheck to display helpful messages, while maintaining performance characteristics that closely resemble the original application.

memcheck

The memcheck tool checks for six different types of errors:

➤ **Memory Access Error:** An out-of-bound or misaligned access to global, local, or shared memory. Misaligned atomic operations can trigger a memory access error, but only when referencing global memory.

➤ **Hardware Exception:** Errors reported by hardware. Refer to Appendix B in the CUDA-MEMCHECK guide (included in the CUDA Toolkit documentation) for details on each possible hardware error.

➤ **malloc/free Errors:** When using CUDA dynamic memory allocation in CUDA kernels, memcheck can find improper use of the malloc and free API calls.

➤ **CUDA API Errors:** Any error code returned by a CUDA API call.

➤ **cudaMalloc Memory Leaks:** Any allocation made by the application using cudaMalloc that was not freed before execution completed.

➤ **Device Heap Memory Leaks:** When using CUDA dynamic memory allocation in CUDA kernels, memcheck finds allocations that were never freed.

Because the debug-segfault application that you debugged with cuda-gdb demonstrated a memory access error, you can compare the diagnostic information from the memcheck tool to that of cuda-gdb.

Suppose you want to check an application named app for memory errors. Once app has been properly compiled to maintain performance but still report stack and line information, memcheck can be invoked using:

```
$ cuda-memcheck [memcheck_options] app [app_options]
```

Running memcheck with the default options on debug-segfault produces the following output:

```
$ nvcc -lineinfo -Xcompiler -rdynamic -o debug-segfault debug-segfault.cu
$ cuda-memcheck ./debug-segfault
========= CUDA-MEMCHECK
```

```
Got error unspecified launch failure at debug-segfault.cu:52
========= Invalid __global__ write of size 4
=========       at 0x00000078 in debug-segfault.cu:25:kernel(int**)
=========       by thread (0,0,0) in block (4,0,0)
=========       Address 0x00000000 is out of bounds
=========       Saved host backtrace up to driver entry point at kernel launch time
=========       Host Frame:/opt/apps/cuda/driver/lib64/libcuda.so (cuLaunchKernel +
     0x3dc) [0xc9edc]
=========       Host Frame:/opt/apps/cuda/5.0.35/lib64/libcudart.so.5.0 [0x11d54]
=========       Host Frame:/opt/apps/cuda/5.0.35/lib64/libcudart.so.5.0 (cudaLaunch +
     0x182) [0x38152]
=========       Host Frame:debug-segfault (_Z10cudaLaunchIcE9cudaErrorPT_ + 0x18)
     [0x138c]
=========       Host Frame:debug-segfault (_Z26__device_stub__Z6kernelPPiPPi + 0x44)
     [0x127c]
=========       Host Frame:debug-segfault (_Z6kernelPPi + 0x18) [0x1299]
=========       Host Frame:debug-segfault (main + 0x277) [0x109a]
=========       Host Frame:/lib64/libc.so.6 (__libc_start_main + 0xfd) [0x1ecdd]
=========       Host Frame:debug-segfault [0xd49]
=========
========= Program hit error 4 on CUDA API call to cudaMemcpy
=========       Saved host backtrace up to driver entry point at error
=========       Host Frame:/opt/apps/cuda/driver/lib64/libcuda.so [0x26a180]
=========       Host Frame:/opt/apps/cuda/5.0.35/lib64/libcudart.so.5.0 (cudaMemcpy +
     0x28c) [0x3305c]
=========       Host Frame:debug-segfault (main + 0x2b8) [0x10db]
=========       Host Frame:/lib64/libc.so.6 (__libc_start_main + 0xfd) [0x1ecdd]
=========       Host Frame:debug-segfault [0xd49]
=========
========= ERROR SUMMARY: 2 errors
```

Not only does memcheck indicate an invalid memory access at line 25 of debug-segfault.cu, but it provides the direction of the invalid access (write), the memory space being written to (__global__), the size of the write (4 bytes), the thread performing the write, and exactly what address caused the invalid dereference. With much less manual effort on your part, memcheck has provided much more detailed and precise information than cuda-gdb regarding the memory error for debug-segfault.

You might note that memcheck also reported a second error, CUDA error 4 returned by a call to cudaMemcpy. Recall that one of the error types that memcheck handles is an error code returned from any CUDA API call. Referring to cuda.h, CUDA error 4 is CUDA_ERROR_DEINITIALIZED, indicating that the CUDA driver is in the process of shutting down. This error is likely caused by the previous memory access error: The driver is recovering from unexpected device behavior.

racecheck

You use racecheck to identify conflicting accesses (commonly referred to as hazards) to data stored in shared memory. Put another way, racecheck looks for multiple threads in the same thread block that are referencing the same location in shared memory without any synchronization, where at least one of those references is a write operation to that location. Debugging of shared memory correctness is particularly important for two reasons:

➤ First, because shared memory is on-chip and shared by a thread block, it is often used as a low-latency communication channel between multiple threads. If you do not take proper care to synchronize those multi-threaded accesses, a conflict might occur. Hence, you need a tool to handle this common use case, because shared memory is more prone to being misused, resulting in conflicting accesses.

➤ Second, shared memory correctness cannot be directly inspected by the host application. Debugging issues in global memory are simplified by the ability to immediately inspect global state from the host. No such direct channel exists for shared memory. Supporting such a capability would require first transferring the state from shared memory to global memory, and then back to the host. `racecheck` does all of the heavy lifting for you.

Consider a simple, single thread block parallel reduction that uses shared memory and local synchronization. To study the effectiveness of `racecheck`, the following example removes that local synchronization, so you can observe the diagnostics generated by `racecheck` in the presence of conflicting accesses. You can follow along in the source code in `debug-hazards.cu`, available from `Wrox.com`.

Start by compiling `debug-hazards.cu` with the compiler options discussed earlier:

```
$ nvcc -arch=sm_20 -lineinfo -Xcompiler -rdynamic -o debug-hazards debug-hazards.cu
```

Before running `debug-hazards`, be aware that `racecheck` generates a large dump file during application execution to be post-processed. `racecheck` also generates verbose reports to the command-line terminal, so it is useful to save terminal output to a file for later analysis. This example sets the location for the dump file using the `--save` CLI argument to a destination that has several hundred MB of free disk space. For larger applications, the dump file will consume even more disk space. This example also redirects terminal output to a log file for later inspection.

Now, `racecheck` can be run to analyze `debug-hazards` using the following command:

```
$ cuda-memcheck --tool racecheck --save racecheck.dump ./debug-hazards > log
```

Examining the log file, you will see many repeated sections similar to:

```
========= WARN:(Warp Level Programming) Potential RAW hazard detected at __shared__
0x7f in block (63, 0, 0) :
=========         Write Thread (31, 0, 0) at 0x000000c8 in debug-hazards.cu:50:simple_
reduction(int*, int*, int, int)
=========         Read Thread (0, 0, 0) at 0x00000128 in debug-hazards.cu:66:simple_
reduction(int*, int*, int, int)
=========         Current Value : 0
=========         Saved host backtrace up to driver entry point at kernel launch time
```

```
=========        Host Frame:/opt/apps/cuda/driver/lib64/libcuda.so (cuLaunchKernel +
0x3dc) [0xc9edc]
=========        Host Frame:/opt/apps/cuda/5.0.35/lib64/libcudart.so.5.0 [0x11d54]
=========        Host Frame:/opt/apps/cuda/5.0.35/lib64/libcudart.so.5.0 (cudaLaunch +
0x182) [0x38152]
=========        Host Frame:./debug-hazards (_Z10cudaLaunchIcE9cudaErrorPT_ + 0x18)
[0x1490]
=========        Host Frame:./debug-hazards
(_Z40__device_stub__Z16simple_reductionPiS_iiPiS_ii + 0xab) [0x135a]
=========        Host Frame:./debug-hazards (_Z16simple_reductionPiS_ii + 0x30)
[0x1398]
=========        Host Frame:./debug-hazards (main + 0x2c2) [0x1142]
=========        Host Frame:/lib64/libc.so.6 (__libc_start_main + 0xfd) [0x1ecdd]
=========        Host Frame:./debug-hazards [0xd99]
```

Start by looking at the first line:

```
========= WARN:(Warp Level Programming) Potential RAW hazard detected at __shared__
0x7f in block (63, 0, 0) :
```

This line indicates three important things. First, a potential hazard was detected! That is a great (or horrible) start, depending on your point of view.

Second, this line reports a Read-After-Write (RAW) hazard. This implies that two threads accessed the same location without any ordering, one doing a read and one doing a write. Because there was no ordering, it is undefined whether the reading thread should load the value before the write or after the write. This undefined behavior is undesirable, and so constitutes a hazard.

Third, this line indicates which block of threads experienced this hazard (recall that hazards on shared memory can only occur within a single block of threads). This information might or might not be particularly useful depending on the application. Because each block in this application is doing identical work, it likely will not be helpful in debugging.

Now, look at the next line:

```
=========        Write Thread (31, 0, 0) at 0x000000c8 in debug-hazards.cu:50:simple_
reduction(int*, int*, int, int)
```

This line provides information on the thread performing the write in the RAW hazard. It indicates the thread ID (31, 0, 0), the address of the instruction being executed (0xc8), as well as the line of source code being executed. The next line provides identical information on the reading thread:

```
=========        Read Thread (0, 0, 0) at 0x00000128 in debug-hazards.cu:66:simple_
reduction(int*, int*, int, int)
```

The following line:

```
=========        Current Value : 0
```

specifies the current value stored at the conflicting location.

The remaining lines show the stack trace from the host location where the kernel was launched that caused this hazard:

```
=========        Saved host backtrace up to driver entry point at kernel launch time
=========        Host Frame:/opt/apps/cuda/driver/lib64/libcuda.so (cuLaunchKernel +
        0x3dc) [0xc9edc]
=========        Host Frame:/opt/apps/cuda/5.0.35/lib64/libcudart.so.5.0 [0x11d54]
=========        Host Frame:/opt/apps/cuda/5.0.35/lib64/libcudart.so.5.0 (cudaLaunch +
        0x182) [0x38152]
=========        Host Frame:./debug-hazards (_Z10cudaLaunchIcE9cudaErrorPT_ + 0x18)
        [0x1490]
=========        Host Frame:./debug-hazards
        (_Z40__device_stub__Z16simple_reductionPiS_iiPiS_ii + 0xab) [0x135a]
=========        Host Frame:./debug-hazards (_Z16simple_reductionPiS_ii + 0x30)
        [0x1398]
=========        Host Frame:./debug-hazards (main + 0x2c2) [0x1142]
=========        Host Frame:/lib64/libc.so.6 (__libc_start_main + 0xfd) [0x1ecdd]
=========        Host Frame:./debug-hazards [0xd99]
```

Now the information provided for the writing and reading thread can be used to analyze the hazard. Recall that the writing thread was at line 50 in the file debug-hazards.cu, executing the function simple_reduction. The reading thread was at line 66 in the same file and function. The relevant lines are highlighted here for convenience:

```
if (tid < N)
{
    local_mem[local_tid] = input_values[tid];
}

// Required for correctness
// __syncthreads();

/*
 * Perform the local reduction across values written to shared memory
 * by threads in this thread block.
 */
if (local_tid == 0)
{
    int sum = 0;

    for (i = 0; i < local_dim; i++)
    {
        sum = sum + local_mem[i];
    }
}
```

The conflict is between a write to local_mem[local_tid] and a read from local_mem[i]. The reading thread is scanning through every entry in shared memory at the same time as the writing thread is filling one of those cells. In the case of this application, the desired behavior is to ensure that all writes complete before the reading thread starts scanning shared memory, and that no additional writes are performed before the scan is complete. Because the error reported was identified as a read-after-write hazard, it must mean that synchronization is missing between the reads being performed as part of the scan and the writes to local memory. So you have a condition where reads are being performed on memory locations before they have been written. As a first attempt at eliminating this race condition, try un-commenting the __syncthreads on line 54, then rebuild and rerun with the same command. This `__syncthreads` will ensure that all writes complete before thread 0 starts scanning, preventing a read-after-write hazard.

Looking at the new output log, a new warning has appeared. Note that this hazard occurs between the same two locations in the code, but is a write-after-read hazard instead. This must mean that now the writes are occurring before the scanning thread can complete. This could only happen if some threads proceed to the next iteration of the outermost loop before the scanning thread completes. The kernel must ensure that before any additional writes are done to a memory location, the scanning thread must finish reading its current value. To prevent this, another synchronization point must be inserted at line 73, forcing all threads to wait for scanning to complete. Rebuild and rerun to see if this prevents the write-after-read hazard.

You should now have a log file that reports:

```
========= CUDA-MEMCHECK
========= RACECHECK SUMMARY: 0 hazards displayed (0 errors, 0 warnings)
```

Great! `racecheck` now finds no hazards in this program. While this does not guarantee that your program is hazard-free, it is a strong indicator that there are no hazards in shared memory.

Debugging Summary

This section briefly covered common use cases for kernel and memory debugging tools in CUDA.

You examined `cuda-gdb`'s ability to inspect running program state on the GPU device, dynamically pausing and resuming threads to check for correctness. An example demonstrated how `cuda-gdb` can be used to debug a memory error.

You also examined the memory debugging features of the `cuda-memcheck` suite and its two tools: `memcheck` and `racecheck`. `memcheck` demonstrated the ability to provide precise information about memory errors, such as out-of-bound accesses, NULL pointer references, device memory leaks, and more. `racecheck` showed similarly precise metrics on potential hazards in shared memory, making debugging of pathologically difficult situations much simpler.

Debugging a CUDA-based application involves inspection of a process running in a separate address space, on physically separated hardware, and outside of any operating system. Although this seems challenging, the tools presented in this chapter make debugging CUDA applications as straightforward as debugging any host application. Using these tools is crucial to being an effective and efficient CUDA developer, particularly as you begin to explore more advanced topics.

A CASE STUDY IN PORTING C PROGRAMS TO CUDA C

Previously, this chapter covered the APOD workflow and described how it could be used to port legacy host applications to CUDA. This section will concretely demonstrate those concepts for you by taking an example legacy application through the full APOD process, ending with an optimized CUDA application.

You can download the legacy application code from Wrox.com in a file named crypt.c. crypt implements IDEA encryption and decryption. The crypt application is made up of three main parts:

1. Application setup is initiated in main. Setup includes reading input, pre-allocating space for output, and reading a secret key: a sequence of bits that must be known to both the sender and receiver of a message to successfully encrypt or decrypt the message.

2. Keys for encrypting or decrypting the input are generated from the shared secret key using generateEncryptKey and generateDecryptKey.

3. The actual encryption and decryption of the input data is done in encrypt_decrypt in 8-byte chunks.

The primary input to crypt is a file to be either encrypted or decrypted. Additionally, crypt takes a key file storing the 64-bit secret key to be used to encrypt or decrypt the input. Utilities to generate example input data (generate_data.c) and a secret key (generate_userkey.c) are provided on Wrox.com. Figure 10-10 outlines the high-level flow of data through the crypt application. Take a moment to familiarize yourself with the implementation in crypt.c.

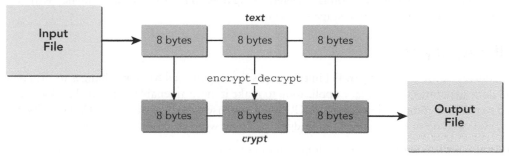

FIGURE 10-10

Assessing crypt

There are many tools available for assessing the performance of host applications. For this example you will use gprof because it is widely available, free, and offers low-overhead profiling.

Before assessing crypt, you need to generate a sample key and 1 GB of sample data, as follows:

```
$ ./generate_userkey key
$ ./generate_data data 1073741824
```

After compiling crypt with the provided Makefile and running it through gprof, the following performance information is generated:

```
  %   cumulative   self              self     total
 time   seconds   seconds    calls  s/call   s/call  name
87.03     49.78     49.78        1   49.78    49.78  encrypt_decrypt
 6.79     53.67      3.89        2    1.94     1.94  cleanupList
 3.59     55.72      2.05        1    2.05     2.05  readInputData
 2.66     57.24      1.52                            main
```

Consider only the leftmost and rightmost columns. On the right are the names of different functions in the `crypt` application. On the left is the percentage of application execution time spent in that function. As you might expect, 87.03% of total execution time was spent inside the `encrypt_decrypt` function that implements the core encryption and decryption logic. From this information, you can conclude that if `crypt` is to be parallelized, that parallelization strategy should be applied to `encrypt_decrypt`.

Discovering performance hotspots is only half of the Assess step. You must also analyze those hotspots for their parallelization eligibility, that is, whether there is a way to parallelize some loop or code section in or around that hotspot, and whether that parallelization strategy has the potential to yield speedup on a GPU.

For the `crypt` example, this step is simple: `encrypt_decrypt` executes the bulk of computation in a loop. On each iteration the function processes a chunk of data from a list of chunks. Because the reads and writes in this loop are all performed on separate chunks, this loop can be parallelized across the input list. There are some complications though. The chunk of data to process on the next iteration is pointed to by the current element. Therefore, there is a dependency between the next iteration (`i+1`) and the current iteration (`i`). Determining how to remove this dependency will be an important part of the Parallelization stage for `crypt`.

Parallelizing crypt

You can convert `crypt` to run in parallel in two stages. First, you need to make changes to the control flow and data structures of the legacy application to make it more amenable to parallelization. Second, you need to port the computation kernels to CUDA C and insert the necessary CUDA API calls (for example, `cudaMalloc` or `cudaMemcpy`,) to bridge the gap between the host and device.

The result of parallelizing `crypt` can be found in `crypt.parallelized.cu` on `Wrox.com`. There are a few transformations that require further explanation to help you understand how the final product is to be prepared for parallelization.

First, the data structures used to store the input and output data were changed from a linked list to an array. This has a number of benefits. First, it eliminates the dependency of iteration `i+1` on iteration `i` that was discovered in the Assessment stage. The data belonging to chunk `i` can now be retrieved using an offset index into an array rather than having to traverse the elements of a linked list. Additionally, an array is a much simpler data structure to transfer to the GPU. Because a linked list relies on pointers, transferring a linked list from the host address space to the device address space implies also updating those pointers to point to the correct element on the correct device. An array can be directly copied using `cudaMemcpy`.

In addition to changing the main data structure of `crypt`, the core computational kernel was extracted to a separate function, `doCrypt`, to make the parallelism more evident. `doCrypt` takes global pointers to input and output, as well as a chunk of data to process. Using this function as an abstraction, the calling kernel can parallelize across chunks of data.

The next step in the Parallelization stage is to insert CUDA API calls at the proper places within `crypt`. The changes for this process can be split into two parts: kernel implementation and memory management.

The changes for the kernel implementation of crypt are straightforward. First, the keyword __device__ is added to doCrypt to indicate it should be executed on the GPU. Second, encrypt_decrypt is declared a __global__ function and the loop it contains is transformed to execute every chunk of data on neighboring device threads based on thread ID. Third, a new function called encrypt_decrypt_driver is added that launches an encrypt_decrypt kernel with a kernel execution configuration determined by the number of input chunks of data.

The encrypt_decrypt_driver kernel also performs memory management for the ported kernel, including:

1. Allocating all memory required for any input and output data
2. Transferring all application data to the device
3. Freeing all allocated device memory

With these simple changes, the crypt application is executing the majority of computation in CUDA. However, you might have noticed a number of ways the performance of this implementation could be improved. The next section will focus on taking the result of this parallelization process and accelerating it to its full potential using profile-driven optimization.

Optimizing crypt

You have been using profile-driven optimization throughout this book. The NVIDIA Visual Profiler nvvp is a graphical tool that offers hints to guide your optimization efforts towards the portions of an application where they can be most effective. In this section, the profile-driven approach will be used alongside an understanding of the crypt application to take the implementation produced by the Parallelization stage and turn it into a well-performing CUDA application.

For the first stage of profile-driven optimization, you use CUDA profiling tools to gain insight into the performance characteristics of your application. With that information, you can then make a decision on where to target optimization efforts. Once you have made changes, you can re-profile your application to help determine next steps, leading to iterative improvements in performance.

To get started, use nvvp in un-guided mode to generate a comprehensive profile including general suggestions for improvement. Setting up crypt in nvvp is as simple as specifying the name of the executable and the location of input and output files in the "Create New Session" popup window, as shown in Figure 10-11.

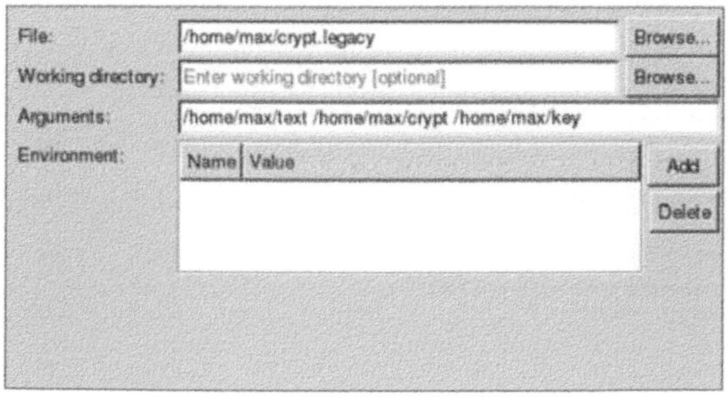

FIGURE 10-11

After collecting profile data by running `crypt` through `nvvp`, a timeline similar to the one in Figure 10-12 will be displayed.

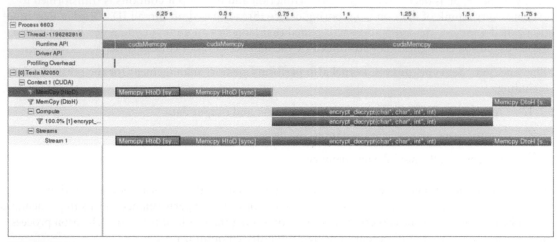

FIGURE 10-12

Note that although the kernel consumes a large percentage of execution time, calls to `cudaMemcpy` also represent a non-trivial portion of this application's execution time. Additionally, because synchronous copies are being used, there is no overlap of communication and computation. You might notice that the transfer from host to device (HtoD) occurs before the kernel is launched, and is split primarily into two `cudaMemcpy` calls: One for the `plain` data and one for the `crypt` data. Based on your knowledge of the application, are both of these transfers necessary? Clearly, the answer is no. The `crypt` data is purely an output array, so transferring its state to the device before launching the kernel has no value. Although being conservative about what to transfer to the device is useful in getting a working implementation as part of the Parallelization stage, during the Optimization stage it is important to be more aggressive. In this case communication can actually be removed.

Hints from the Analysis view's Timeline tab shown in Figure 10-13 are derived from `nvvp` performance statistics. These hints indicate that low copy bandwidth and low compute utilization are significant limiting factors for performance. A number of `nvvp`'s recommendations suggest that you could overlap computation and communication as a way to improve compute and memory performance.

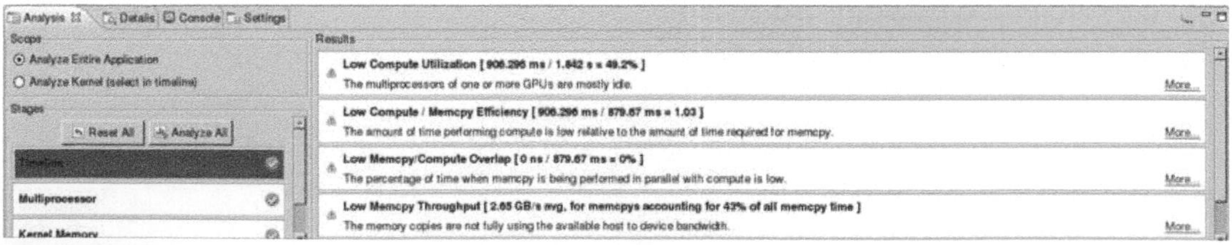

FIGURE 10-13

With these insights, a logical next step is to implement an overlap plan. In the case of crypt, this can be accomplished by dividing the input into smaller blocks and passing one block at a time to the device in separate streams. Then, asynchronous cudaMemcpyAsync calls and kernel launches can be used for each block. Because these operations will be placed in different CUDA streams, the CUDA runtime can execute them in any order, enabling overlap between computation and communication, and better utilization.. The new version of crypt with these changes incorporated is available for download from Wrox.com in crypt.overlap.cu. A snippet of the core code is included here for convenience.

```
CALL_CUDA(cudaEventRecord(start, streams[0]));
CALL_CUDA(cudaMemcpyAsync(dKey, key, KEY_LENGTH * sizeof(int),
          cudaMemcpyHostToDevice, streams[0]));
CALL_CUDA(cudaStreamSynchronize(streams[0]));

for (b = 0; b < nBlocks; b++) {
    int blockOffset = b * BLOCK_SIZE_IN_CHUNKS * CHUNK_SIZE;
    int localChunks = BLOCK_SIZE_IN_CHUNKS;
    if (b * BLOCK_SIZE_IN_CHUNKS + localChunks > nChunks) {
        localChunks = nChunks - b * BLOCK_SIZE_IN_CHUNKS;
    }

    CALL_CUDA(cudaMemcpyAsync(dPlain + blockOffset, plain + blockOffset,
              localChunks * CHUNK_SIZE * sizeof(signed char),
              cudaMemcpyHostToDevice, streams[b]));

    encrypt_decrypt<<<nThreadBlocks, nThreadsPerBlock, 0, streams[b]>>>(
          dPlain + blockOffset, dCrypt + blockOffset, dKey, localChunks);
    CALL_CUDA(cudaMemcpyAsync(crypt + blockOffset, dCrypt + blockOffset,
              localChunks * CHUNK_SIZE * sizeof(signed char),
              cudaMemcpyDeviceToHost, streams[b]));
    CALL_CUDA(cudaEventRecord(finishes[b], streams[b])),
}

CALL_CUDA(cudaDeviceSynchronize());
```

Notice the loop over nBlocks:

```
for (b = 0; b < nBlocks; b++) {
```

The values for block size and offset are calculated as follows:

```
int blockOffset = b * BLOCK_SIZE_IN_CHUNKS * CHUNK_SIZE;
int localChunks = BLOCK_SIZE_IN_CHUNKS;
if (b * BLOCK_SIZE_IN_CHUNKS + localChunks > nChunks) {
    localChunks = nChunks - b * BLOCK_SIZE_IN_CHUNKS;
}
```

This optimization enables streams-based overlap between cudaMemcpyAsync and encrypt_decrypt for blocks defined by blockOffset and localChunks.

The performance improvements from these changes are summarized in Table 10-2.

TABLE 10-2: Crypt Performance Improvement from Computation-Communication Overlap

VERSION	PERFORMANCE
Parallelized Implementation	588.30 KB/ms
Optimized with Overlap	867.58 KB/ms

Now it is time to re-profile and re-target optimization efforts on other sections of code. This process is identical to before but uses the new streams-based executable.

The new results from the Timeline View (Figure 10-14) and Timeline Analysis (Figure 10-15) show that all of the issues from the first run have either been eliminated or reduced. The timeline of program execution clearly shows overlap in communication and computation, rather than massive blocking cudaMemcpy calls.

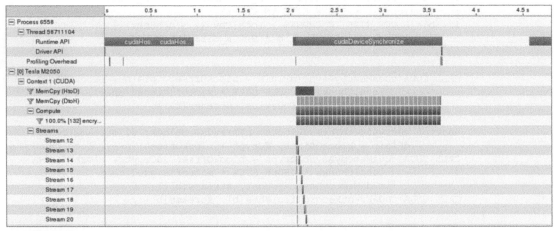

FIGURE 10-14

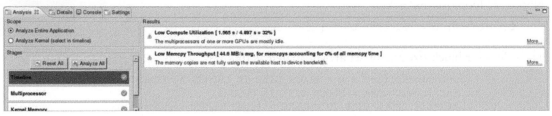

FIGURE 10-15

Deciding on a next step is less obvious than with the previous results. There are a couple of outstanding issues that likely deserve focus in the next stage. First of all, the Timeline Analysis warns of Low Memcpy Throughput. This is a result of doing many small memory copies for each block, rather than a single large copy. However, the overlapping transformation that led to that change clearly had a significant improvement in performance, so the tradeoff in lower memcpy throughput is acceptable.

Selecting the Multiprocessor Analysis view (Figure 10-16) indicates that register pressure might also be a problem. However, this can change wildly with modifications to the kernel code, so performing optimizations targeting register usage this early in the Optimization stage might be a wasted effort.

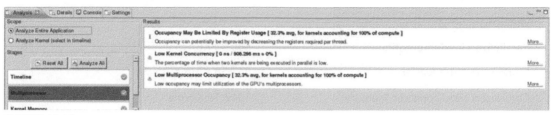

FIGURE 10-16

The Timeline Analysis view indicates that utilization of the SMs is still low. This means that the SMs are likely spending either a lot of time without any eligible thread blocks to schedule, or are waiting for I/O to complete. The Kernel Memory pane also warns of poor global memory store efficiency. From these two indicators, a natural conclusion is that global memory operations in this application might be limiting performance. The next step forward is going to be much more dependent on application-specific knowledge of how global memory is being used.

So, what objects are currently stored in global memory? Currently, the input text, output crypt, and encryption/decryption key are all stored and accessed in global memory. Because chunks of data are being strided by thread ID, each thread is reading and writing neighboring 8-byte chunks in text and crypt. While 4 bytes would be optimal, this still should yield reasonably efficient use of cache and bandwidth because as the accesses are coalesced and aligned.

The access pattern for key is a very different story. Every thread reads from the same location in key at the same time. This would yield much lower global bandwidth utilization, as a full warp of threads will be blocked to read the same 4 bytes from global memory. Because key, text, and crypt are all sharing the global L1 and L2 caches on a GPU multiprocessor, that read might have to be done multiple times if it is evicted from cache by reads or writes of text or crypt. Based on this analysis and the metrics reported by nvvp, it seems that optimizing key's usage is a good next step.

One way to do that is by changing the memory key is stored in. What CUDA memory type supports read-only data structures and is optimized for broadcasting a single element to all threads? That sounds exactly like constant memory! Placing key in constant memory will likely improve both global memory bandwidth and global memory cache efficiency.

A new version of crypt with key stored in constant memory can be downloaded from Wrox.com in crypt.constant.cu. The changes made include:

1. The addition of a __constant__ dkey variable:

   ```
   __constant__ int dkey[KEY_LENGTH];
   ```

2. Changes in the doCrypt kernel to reference the new dkey variable

3. A call to cudaMemcpyToSymbolAsync to transfer the contents of key to the device:

   ```
   CALL_CUDA(cudaMemcpyToSymbolAsync(dkey, key, KEY_LENGTH * sizeof(int), 0,
                      cudaMemcpyHostToDevice, streams[0]));
   ```

The performance improvements gained by this change are summarized in Table 10-3.

TABLE 10-3: Crypt Performance Improvement from Constant Memory

VERSION	PERFORMANCE
Parallelized Implementation	588.30 KB/ms
Optimized with Overlap	867.58 KB/ms
Optimized with Constant Memory	1062.16 KB/ms

Already, performance has nearly doubled from the original CUDA implementation. Time to iterate and retarget additional optimization opportunities!

Following another round of profiling in nvvp, improvements are seen in the metrics from the Timeline and Multiprocessor Analysis views (shown in Figures 10-17 and 10-18, respectively).

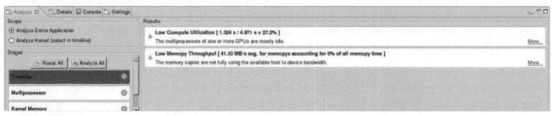

FIGURE 10-17

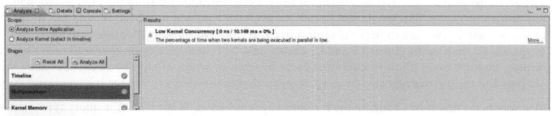

FIGURE 10-18

However, the Kernel Memory pane shown in Figure 10-19 is still reporting low global memory bandwidth utilization.

It seems like this needs more investigation. First, it is important to understand where the value 12.5% is coming from. As an example, consider the first read performed by every thread in doCrypt, an access to a single byte of the plain input:

```
x1   = (((unsigned int)plain[chunk * CHUNK_SIZE]) & 0xff);
```

Because threads are strided by chunk, and each chunk is 8 bytes, the threads in a warp are basically accessing every eighth byte in plain during this load. However, the caching hardware is turning those sparse single-byte loads into two, 128-byte loads from global memory. Hence, from the perspective of the profiling tools, only 1 out of every 8 bytes loaded from global memory is actually being used, and 1/8 = 12.5% utilization.

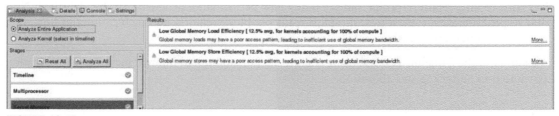

FIGURE 10-19

However, that is not the whole story. As a result of those 128-byte loads each of the later references to plain will likely hit in L1 or L2 cache, depending on your GPU's architecture, and so no global memory references are required. Every byte loaded into cache is used, but may not be a part of that particular load instruction. Hence, this is a case of nvvp reporting suboptimal resource utilization that, with more scrutiny, turns out to *not* be an actual performance problem since the data is cached.

However, the Timeline Analysis still shows a Low Compute Utilization warning. Recall that previous runs also displayed an Occupancy warning in the Multiprocessor Analysis due to register consumption. Both of these warnings indicate that the thread configuration being used for this kernel might not be optimal. As a result, the per-SM registers are being spread thinly across threads in a block, leading to more blocking on I/O as values are spilled from registers, and therefore lowering compute utilization. It is more difficult to verify this conclusion based on analysis of the code. Instead, experimentation with different thread configurations can be used to see if improvement is possible. An updated copy of the crypt application with these changes can be found on Wrox.com in crypt.config.cu. This new revision simply lets you configure the number of threads per block using a command-line argument. Testing the new code across a set of thread configurations produces the results in Table 10-4.

TABLE 10-4: Crypt Performance Improvement as Thread Configuration Changes

THREADS PER BLOCK	PERFORMANCE
32	725.54 KB/ms
64	1165.65 KB/ms
128	1268.07 KB/ms
256	1198.72 KB/ms
512	1062.26 KB/ms
1024	849.59 KB/ms

Although the original default of 512 threads per block performs acceptably, a 19% performance improvement is possible with 128 threads per block. Because reducing the thread block size improved performance, a logical conclusion is that 512 threads per block were causing fewer registers to be assigned to each thread than was optimal.

It is time to once again re-profile and see if any new performance problems can be identified. Note that re-profiling crypt.config with 128 threads per block requires adding a command-line argument to the interactive session configuration in nvvp.

As shown in the Timeline Analysis view (Figure 10-20), additional improvement in SM utilization is attributed to better register allocation.

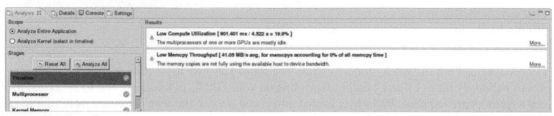

FIGURE 10-20

At this point, nvvp offers no unexplained performance issues. crypt has been successfully transformed through the Optimization stage. As Table 10-5 summarizes, performance has more than doubled from the un-optimized implementation developed in the Parallelization stage. Using profile-driven optimization enables your efforts to be targeted at application characteristics that most affect execution time, leading to productive use of your development time.

TABLE 10-5: Crypt Performance Improvement

VERSION	PERFORMANCE
Parallelized Implementation	588.30 KB/ms
Optimized with Overlap	867.58 KB/ms
Optimized with Constant Memory	1062.16 KB/ms
Optimized Thread Configurations	1198.72 KB/ms

Having developed a highly performing implementation, it is time to move to the next and final APOD stage: Deployment.

Deploying Crypt

crypt is already well prepared for deployment in terms of error handling of both host and device functions. However, you could improve its ability to adapt to new hardware platforms with varying numbers of GPUs, or no GPUs at all.

Multi-GPU Crypt

As cloud providers offer more GPU deployments and organizations increasingly move their production systems into the cloud, the importance of flexibly supporting drastic changes in the execution environment has grown. For `crypt`, this implies adding the ability to split the workload across all available GPUs, as well as falling back on host execution if no GPUs can be detected.

The source code in `crypt.flexible.cu` is an example of a flexible implementation of the `crypt` application that runs on any number of GPUs, including none. `crypt.flexible` selects host or device execution based on the presence or absence of GPUs, indicated by the `cudaErrorNoDevice` error code. Note that `doCrypt` is made into a `__host__` `__device__` function to share code between both implementations, reducing duplicate code and maintenance costs for two copies of the same algorithm.

The core logic for partitioning work across multiple GPUs is included here for convenience:

```
for (d = 0; d < nDevices; d++) {
    CALL_CUDA(cudaSetDevice(d));
    int start = d * chunksPerDevice * CHUNK_SIZE;
    int len = chunksPerDevice * CHUNK_SIZE;
    if (start + len > textLen) {
        len = textLen - start;
    }
    encrypt_decrypt_driver(text + start, crypt + start, key, len,
            nThreadsPerBlock, ctxs + d);
}

CALL_CUDA(cudaEventRecord(finishEvent));

// Wait for each device to finish its work.
for (d = 0; d < nDevices; d++) {
    CALL_CUDA(cudaSetDevice(d));
    CALL_CUDA(cudaDeviceSynchronize());
}
```

In this code, a modified `encrypt_decrypt_driver` is called on each GPU to asynchronously initiate data transfers and a kernel launch. Then, once work has been started on every device, the host pauses and waits for each device to complete.

Hybrid OpenMP-CUDA Crypt

While the previous example in `crypt.flexibile.cu` made use of the CPU if there were no GPUs available for execution, the CPU was left idle if any GPUs were found. While performing all computation on the GPUs of a system may lead to performance improvement, it also leads to underutilization of available hardware. For some applications it is beneficial to support hybrid parallelism: CPU and GPU cooperating in parallel on the same problem.

In general, there are two types of hybrid parallelism:

1. **Data-parallel hybrid parallelism:** The CPU executes the same data-parallel computation as the GPUs but across CPU cores instead of GPU SMs. The CPU essentially becomes another device in the system. In this case, a `__host__` `__device__` function can be used to execute the same logic on both processors.

2. **Task-parallel hybrid parallelism:** The CPU executes different computation than the GPU, computation that is more suited for the host-based architecture. For example, the CPU may execute tasks with more complex control-flow or irregular access patterns.

In both cases, it is necessary to use CUDA streams (and likely events) to overlap CPU and GPU execution (as described in Chapter 6).

`crypt.openmp.cu` contains an example of using OpenMP parallelism on the CPU and CUDA parallelism on the GPU in a single application. OpenMP is a parallel programming model for the host that uses compiler directives to mark parallel regions, similar to OpenACC. The only OpenMP-specific code added is a call to `omp_set_num_threads` to configure the number of CPU cores to use, and the addition of an OpenMP pragma in the host-side computational function `h_encrypt_decrypt`. The compiler hint `#pragma omp parallel for` marks the following loop as parallelizable, and instructs OpenMP to run it across multiple CPU threads.

```
#pragma omp parallel for
for (c = 0; c < nChunks; c++) {
    doCrypt(c, plain, crypt, key);
}
```

`crypt.openmp.cu` also adds logic for partitioning the workload across CPU and GPU with a new command-line argument `cpu-percent` that specifies the percentage of bytes to be encrypted or decrypted on the CPU, with the remainder of the workload offloaded to the GPU.

CPU and GPU computation is performed in parallel by queuing data transfer and kernel execution for each device in separate streams, then launching the CPU threads once the asynchronous CUDA calls return control to the host:

```
CALL_CUDA(cudaEventRecord(startEvent));

for (d = 0; d < nDevices; d++) {
    CALL_CUDA(cudaSetDevice(d));
    int start = d * chunksPerGpu * CHUNK_SIZE;
    int len = chunksPerGpu * CHUNK_SIZE;
    if (start + len > gpuLen) {
        len = gpuLen - start;
    }
    encrypt_decrypt_driver(text + start, crypt + start, key, len,
            nThreadsPerBlock, ctxs + d);
}

int cpuStart = gpuLen;
h_encrypt_decrypt(text + cpuStart, crypt + cpuStart, key,
    textLen - cpuStart);

CALL_CUDA(cudaEventRecord(finishEvent));
```

`crypt.openmp.cu` must be compiled and linked with OpenMP support. If your NVIDIA compiler uses the `gcc` host compiler, this can be done using:

```
$ nvcc -Xcompiler -fopenmp -arch=sm_20 crypt.openmp.cu -o crypt.openmp -lgomp
```

Note that `crypt.openmp` adds two new command-line arguments: the number of CPU cores to use (`ncpus`) and the percentage of the data to process on the CPU (`cpu-percent`). You should specify the `cpu-percent` command-line option using values between 0.0 and 1.0.

You can use the `cpu-percent` command-line argument to study how performance changes as you increase the amount of workload on the CPU. In Table 10-6, example results across a range of workload partitions show that placing work on the CPU is never beneficial for crypt. For this particular application, the overhead of spawning new CPU threads and the slower computational performance of the CPU means that running any amount of work on the CPU leads to lost performance.

TABLE 10-6: Crypt Performance Improvement

WORKLOAD PARTITIONING	PERFORMANCE
0% CPU – 100% GPU	4387.347168 KB/ms
10% CPU – 90% GPU	1533.005859 KB/ms
20% CPU – 80% GPU	861.607239 KB/ms
30% CPU – 70% GPU	716.240417 KB/ms
40% CPU – 60% GPU	479.897491 KB/ms
50% CPU – 50% GPU	367.148468 KB/ms
60% CPU – 40% GPU	299.336578 KB/ms
70% CPU – 30% GPU	270.530457 KB/ms
80% CPU – 20% GPU	222.864182 KB/ms
90% CPU – 10% GPU	198.895294 KB/ms
100% CPU – 0% GPU	189.856232 KB/ms

You will find other applications are able to use CPU and GPU in a way that complements both, and delivers better performance than either processor can achieve alone. For example, the High Performance LINPACK (HPL) benchmark used to classify the Top-500 supercomputers in the world performs best with hybrid execution.

Summary of Porting crypt

In this section, an example application was transformed completely through the APOD process. First, in the Assess stage, gprof was used to profile crypt and determine performance-critical regions, and therefore which sections of code should be optimized for the largest potential performance gain. Then, the Parallelization stage produced a working CUDA implementation of crypt by first transforming the host code to be more amenable to parallelization and then adding CUDA API calls to transfer data and launch kernels. The Optimization stage turned the output from the Parallelization stage into a high-performance CUDA application, using profile-driven optimization to target suboptimal performance characteristics. Throughout the Optimization stage, performance was checked repeatedly to validate that the corresponding changes were improvements, and not regressions. Finally, during the deployment stage crypt was made more adaptable to changes in the execution environment by enabling it to run on any number of GPUs.

In just four straightforward steps, APOD transformed crypt from a legacy, out-of-date, and poorly performing implementation to a modern and high-performance CUDA application that is ready to meet future application requirements.

SUMMARY

This chapter covered a wide variety of topics. However, each topic focused on improving your productivity using CUDA development processes and tools, making you a more efficient CUDA developer while distilling more performance from your application.

You learned about APOD, a four-step iterative process to convert a legacy, sequential C application into a high-performing and durable CUDA application ready for production deployment. APOD is purely an abstract development model, but using the prescribed methodology you can drastically streamline the porting process.

You also learned more about the profile-driven optimization strategy that you have been using throughout this book. You explored how `nvprof`, `nvvp`, and the NVIDIA Tools Extension can help you find performance-limiting characteristics of an application.

The topics of CUDA kernel and memory debugging were also covered. `cuda-gdb`, `cuda-memcheck`, and a variety of constructs built into the CUDA language were demonstrated in the context of debugging CUDA kernels on the GPU.

Finally, you looked at a case study in which the full process of converting a legacy cryptographic application into a high-performance CUDA application was demonstrated. As a result of using profile-driven optimization, performance more than doubled relative to an initial CUDA implementation.

CHAPTER 10 EXERCISES

1. Name the four stages of APOD and the goal of each.

2. An application can be accelerated using CUDA libraries, OpenACC, or hand-coded CUDA kernels. In which APOD stage should the decision be made between the two approaches? What are the main differences you envision being introduced to each stage of APOD depending on the approach chosen?

3. What capabilities are added by separate compilation in CUDA 5? What compiler flags must be added to use separate compilation?

4. Which tool is best used to analyze out-of-bounds accesses in a kernel? Why?

5. What tool is best used to analyze `__shared__` memory usage?

6. What are the three modes of analysis in `nvprof`? What information is each best at gathering?

7. What are the benefits of using `nvvp` versus another profiling tool?

8. Consider your day-to-day development environment. How would `nvprof` and `nvvp` best fit in it? For example, if you regularly work with a remote machine containing GPUs on the same LAN as your local workstation, you might use `nvprof` to gather profiling dumps on the remote machine, transfer them to your local workstation, and analyze them using `nvvp`.

APPENDIX

Suggested Readings

Chapter 1: Heterogeneous Parallel Computing with CUDA

Antonino Tumeo and Politecnicodi Milano. *Massively Parallel Computing with CUDA*.
http://www.ogf.org/OGF25/materials/1605/CUDA_Programming.pdf

David Luebke. *GPU Computing: Past, Present and Future*. GTC 2011. http://on-demand
.gputechconf.com/gtc-express/2011/presentations/GTC_Express_David_Luebke_
June2011.pdf

Mark Ebersole. *Why GPU Computing*. http://developer.download.nvidia.com/compute/
developertrainingmaterials/presentations/general/Why_GPU_Computing.pptx

Will Ramey. *Introduction to CUDA Platform*. http://developer.download.nvidia
.com/compute/developertrainingmaterials/presentations/general/Why_GPU_
Computing.pptx

Chapter 2: CUDA Programming Model

CUDA Programming Model Overview. http://www.sdsc.edu/us/training/assets/docs/
NVIDIA-02-BasicsOfCUDA.pdf

Justin Luitjens. *Introduction to CUDA C*. GTC 2012. http://on-demand.gputechconf
.com/gtc/2012/presentations/S0624-Monday-Introduction-to-CUDA-C.pdf

Ian Buck. *Parallel Programming with CUDA*. http://mc.stanford.edu/cgi-bin/
images/b/ba/M02_2.pdf

Ian Buck. *Programming Environments*. SC 2009. http://www.nvidia.com/content/GTC/
documents/SC09_CUDA_ProgModel_Buck.pdf

Mark Harris. *Introduction to CUDA C*. http://developer.download.nvidia.com/
compute/developertrainingmaterials/presentations/cuda_language/
Introduction_to_CUDA_C.pptx

Chapter 3: CUDA Execution Model

CUDA C Programming Guide, Appendix G. Compute Capabilities. http://docs.nvidia
.com/cuda/cuda-c-programming-guide/index.html#compute-capabilities

CUDA C Programming Guide, Appendix C. CUDA Dynamic Parallelism. http://docs
.nvidia.com/cuda/cuda-c-programming-guide/index
.html#cuda-dynamic-parallelism

Mark Harris. *Optimizing Parallel Reduction in CUDA.* http://developer.download.nvidia
.com/assets/cuda/files/reduction.pdf

David Goodwin. *Performance Optimization Strategies For GPU-Accelerated Applications.* GTC
2013. http://on-demand.gputechconf.com/gtc/2013/presentations/
S3046-Performance-Optimization-Strategies-for-GPU-Accelerated-Apps.pdf

David Goodwin. *Optimizing Application Performance with CUDA Profiling Tools.* GTC 2012.
http://on-demand.gputechconf.com/gtc/2012/presentations/S0419A-Optimizing-
App-Performance-with-CUDA-Profiling-Tools-Part-A.pdf

Profiler User's Guide. http://docs.nvidia.com/cuda/profiler-users-guide/index.html, for
a complete list of events and metrics

Stephen Jones. *Introduction to Dynamic Parallelism.* GTC 2012. http://on-demand.gputechconf
.com/gtc/2012/presentations/S0338-GTC2012-CUDA-Programming-Model.pdf

Timo Stich. *Fermi Hardware & Performance Tips.* http://theinf2.informatik.uni-jena.de/
theinf2_multimedia/Website_downloads/NVIDIA_Fermi_Perf_Jena_2011.pdf

Chapter 4: Global Memory

Andrew V. Adinetz. *CUDA Dynamic Parallelism API and Principles.* http://devblogs.nvidia
.com/parallelforall/cuda-dynamic-parallelism-api-principles/

Justin Luitjens. *Global Memory Usage and Strategy.* 2011. http://on-demand.gputechconf.com/
gtc-express/2011/presentations/cuda_webinars_GlobalMemory.pdf

Greg Ruetsch and Paulius Micikevicius. *Optimizing Matrix Transpose in CUDA.* June 2010.
http://www.cs.colostate.edu/~cs675/MatrixTranspose.pdf

Mark Harris. *Unified Memory in CUDA 6.* http://devblogs.nvidia.com/parallelforall/
unified-memory-in-cuda-6/

Paulius Micikevicius. *Performance Optimization: Programming Guidelines and GPU Architecture
Reasons Behind Them.* GTC 2013. http://on-demand.gputechconf.com/gtc/2013/
presentations/S3466-Programming-Guidelines-GPU-Architecture.pdf

Paulius Micikevicius. *GPU Performance Analysis and Optimization.* GTC 2012. http://
developer.download.nvidia.com/GTC/PDF/GTC2012/PresentationPDF/S0514-GTC2012-
GPU-Performance-Analysis.pdf

Paulius Micikevicius. *Fundamental Performance Optimizations for GPUs.* GTC 2011. http://
on-demand.gputechconf.com/gtc/2010/presentations/S12011-Fundamental-
Performance-Optimization-GPUs.pdf

Chapter 5: Shared Memory and Constant Memory

Cliff Woolley. *GPU Optimization Fundamentals.* 2013. https://www.olcf.ornl.gov/
wp-content/uploads/2013/02/GPU_Opt_Fund-CW1.pdf

Mark Harris. *Using Shared Memory in CUDA C/C++.* http://devblogs.nvidia.com/
parallelforall/using-shared-memory-cuda-cc/

Mark Harris. *Optimizing Parallel Reduction in CUDA.* http://developer.download.nvidia
.com/assets/cuda/files/reduction.pdf

Justin Luitjens. *Faster Parallel Reductions on Kepler.* http://devblogs.nvidia.com/
parallelforall/faster-parallel-reductions-kepler/

Chapter 6: Streams and Concurrency

Justin Luitjens. *CUDA Streams: Best Practices and Common Pitfalls.* GTC 2014. http://
on-demand.gputechconf.com/gtc/2014/presentations/S4158-cuda-streams-best-
practices-common-pitfalls.pdf

Mark Harris. *Concurrency and Multi-GPU.* http://education.ivec.org/training/external/
 NVIDIA/Day2/05-Concurrency-and-MultiGPU.pdf

Thomas Bradley. *Hyper-Q Example.* 2012. http://docs.nvidia.com/cuda/samples/6_
 Advanced/simpleHyperQ/doc/HyperQ.pdf

Steve Rennich. *CUDA C/C++ Streams and Concurrency.* 2011. http://on-demand.gputechconf
 .com/gtc-express/2011/presentations/StreamsAndConcurrencyWebinar.pdf

Chapter 7: Tuning Instruction-Level Primitives

CUDA Best Practices Guide. 2014. http://docs.nvidia.com/cuda/
 cuda-c-best-practices-guide/

Kepler Tuning Guide. 2014. http://docs.nvidia.com/cuda/kepler-tuning-guide/

Maxwell Tuning Guide. 2014. http://http://docs.nvidia.com/cuda/maxwell-tuning-guide/

Lars Nyland, Dale Southard, and Alex Fit-Florea. *GPU Floating Point Accuracy: Theory and
 Practice.* 2014. http://on-demand.gputechconf.com/gtc/2014/video/S4370-gpu-
 floating-point-accuracy-theory-practice.mp4

Lars Nyland and Stephen Jones. *Understanding and Using Atomic Memory Operations.* 2013.
 http://on-demand.gputechconf.com/gtc/2013/presentations/S3101-Atomic-Memory-
 Operations.pdf

Dan Cyca. *Essential CUDA Optimization Techniques.* 2014. http://on-demand.gputechconf
 .com/gtc/2014/video/S4702-essential-cuda-optimization-techniques-acceleware-
 part-4.mp4

Chapter 8: GPU-Accelerated CUDA Libraries and OpenACC

cuSPARSE User Guide. 2014. http://docs.nvidia.com/cuda/cusparse/

cuBLAS User Guide. 2014. http://docs.nvidia.com/cuda/cublas/

cuRAND User Guide. 2014. http://docs.nvidia.com/cuda/curand/

cuFFT User Guide. 2014. http://docs.nvidia.com/cuda/cufft/

CUDA Toolkit 5.0 Performance Report. 2013. http://on-demand.gputechconf.com/
 gtc-express/2013/presentations/cuda--5.0-math-libraries-performance.pdf

OpenACC Standard. 2013. http://www.openacc.org/sites/default/files/
 OpenACC.2.0a_1.pdf

Jeff Larkin. *Introduction to Accelerated Computing Using Compiler Directives.* 2014. http://
 on-demand.gputechconf.com/gtc/2014/presentations/S4167-intro-accelerated-
 computing-directives.pdf

Jeff Larkin. *What's New in OpenACC 2.0 and OpenMP 4.0.* 2014. http://on-demand
 .gputechconf.com/gtc/2014/presentations/S4438-whats-new-in-openacc-2-openmp-4.
 pdf

Michael Wolfe. *Performance Analysis and Optimization with OpenACC.* 2014. http://
 on-demand.gputechconf.com/gtc/2014/presentations/S4472-performance-analysis-
 optimization-openacc-apps.pdf

Chapter 9: Multi-GPU Programming

Axel Koehler. *Scalable Cluster Computing with NVIDIA GPUs.* 2012. http://www
 .hpcadvisorycouncil.com/events/2012/Switzerland-Workshop/Presentations/
 Day_3/3_NVIDIA.pdf

Dhabaleswar K (DK) Panda. *MVAPICH2: A High Performance MPI Library for NVIDIA GPU
 Clusters with InfiniBand.* GTC 2013. http://on-demand.gputechconf.com/gtc/2013/
 presentations/S3316-MVAPICH2-High-Performance-MPI-Library.pdf

Dhabaleswar K (DK) Panda. *Latest Advances in MVAPICH2 MPI Library for NVIDIA GPU Clusters with InfiniBand.* GTC 2014. http://on-demand.gputechconf.com/gtc/2014/presentations/S4517-mvapihc2-mpi-library-gpus-infiniband.pdf

Levi Barnes. *Multi-GPU Programming.* GTC 2013. http://on-demand.gputechconf.com/gtc/2013/presentations/S3465-Multi-GPU-Programming.pdf

Jiri Kraus. *Introduction to CUDA-aware MPI and NVIDIA GPUDirect.* GTC 2013. http://on-demand.gputechconf.com/gtc/2013/presentations/S3047-Intro-CUDA-Aware-MPI-NVIDIA-GPUDirect.pdf

MVAPICH2. http://mvapich.cse.ohio-state.edu/download/mvapich2/

MVAPICH2 2.0 Quick Start Guide. http://mvapich.cse.ohio-state.edu/support/mvapich2-2.0b-quick-start.pdf

NVIDIA GPUDirect. https://developer.nvidia.com/gpudirect

NVIDIA GPUDirect™ Technology And Cluster Computing. 2012. http://www.einfrastructuresouth.ac.uk/cfi/emerald/gpu-programming/numa/nvidia-gpudirect-technology-and-cluster-computing

Paulius Micikevicius. *Multi-GPU Programming.* GTC 2012. http://developer.download.nvidia.com/GTC/PDF/GTC2012/PresentationPDF/S0515-GTC2012-Multi-GPU-Programming.pdf

Paulius Micikevicius. *Implementing 3D Finite Difference Codes on the GPU.* GTC 2009. http://on-demand.gputechconf.com/gtc/2009/presentations/1006-Implementing-3D-Finite-Difference-Codes-GPU.pdf

Tim C. Schroeder. *Peer-to-Peer & Unified Virtual Addressing.* 2011. http://on-demand.gputechconf.com/gtc-express/2011/presentations/cuda_webinars_GPUDirect_uva.pdf

Chapter 10: Implementation Considerations

Adam DeConinck. *Introduction to the CUDA Toolkit as an Application Build Tool.* GTC 2013. http://on-demand.gputechconf.com/gtc/2013/webinar/cuda-toolkit-as-build-tool.pdf

Julien Demouth. *CUDA Optimization with NVIDIA Nsight(TM) Visual Studio Edition: A Case Study.* GTC 2014. http://on-demand.gputechconf.com/gtc/2014/presentations/S4160-cuda-optimization-nvidia-nsight-vse-case-study.pdf

Sandarbh Jain. *CUDA Profiling Tools.* GTC 2014. http://on-demand.gputechconf.com/gtc/2014/presentations/S4587-cuda-profiling-tools.pdf

Thomas Bradley. *GPU Performance Analysis and Optimization.* 2012. http://people.maths.ox.ac.uk/gilesm/cuda/lecs/NV_Profiling_lowres.pdf

Will Ramey. *Languages, Libraries and Development Tools for GPU Computing.* 2014. http://on-demand.gputechconf.com/gtc/2014/presentations/S4874-languages-libraries-development-tools.pdf

NVIDIA CUDA Compiler Driver NVCC, 7. Using Separate Compilation in CUDA. http://docs.nvidia.com/cuda/cuda-compiler-driver-nvcc/index.html#using-separate-compilation-in-cuda

INDEX

C

Q

R

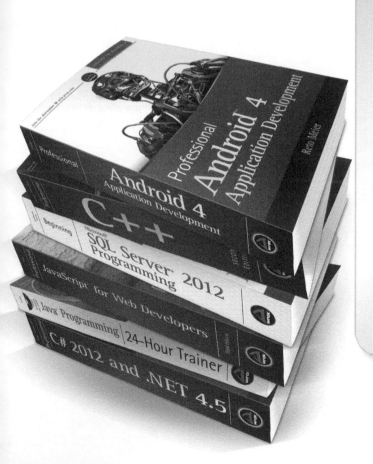

Printed and bound by CPI Group (UK) Ltd, Croydon, CR0 4YY

27/10/2024

14580321-0003